NxLeveL Guide for Business Start-ups

Second Edition

Editor

David P. Wold

Primary Authors

David P. Wold

Dennis Sargent

Martha Sargent

US WEST® FOUNDATION

Western Entrepreneurial Network

University of Colorado at Denver

Dedicated To

Entrepreneurs everywhere striving to reach the next level of success.

Second Edition

Printed in the United States of America

ISBN 1-890730-00-9

Library of Congress Information pending

Table of Contents

Part V: Managing Your Business

Part VI: Marketing Your Business

Part VII: Financing Your Business

Part VIII: Turning Ideas Into Action

Part IX: Conclusion

Part X: Appendix

To NxLeveL Participants, Instructors and Interested Readers

Thank you for choosing NxLeveL. We know there are a wide variety of "off the shelf" entrepreneurial programs from which to choose and we appreciate you selecting NxLeveL.

This is the second edition of *NxLeveL Business Start-up Program.* We need your help to make NxLeveL the very best entrepreneurial training program available.

We want to know what works for you, and where we can improve. Your instructors will be collecting comments and your suggestions are greatly appreciated.

You are very important to us. NxLeveL is a program designed for people like you: Entrepreneurs. Please let us know what you think, and together we will continue to improve the next level in entrepreneurial training programs—NxLeveL.

Bob Horn, Director
Colorado Center for Community Development
Western Entrepreneurial Network
University of Colorado at Denver
Campus Box 128
P.O. Box 173364
Denver, Colorado 80217-3364

NX LEVEL™

Helping entrepreneurs reach the next level of success.

Foreword

Your NxLeveL course was made possible by several parties. Primary funding for developing the NxLeveL training programs has been provided by the U S WEST Foundation. This funding allowed the University of Colorado at Denver to create the Western Entrepreneurial Network (WEN), which is housed at the University.

WEN started with the 14 western states that made up U S WEST's operating territory. Today NxLeveL is used throughout the U.S. and overseas. It began as a partnership between the University and various agencies to provide local training. Local training partners vary from state to state, with the majority being Small Business Development Centers. Other groups include state economic development agencies, community colleges and state universities, public assistance agencies, and a Hispanic Chamber of Commerce. While the University provides oversight and general support for the network, each instructor provides local insight and expertise critical in making this entrepreneurial training a success.

WEN was founded in 1992 on the premise that business training classes were instrumental in developing and strengthening the small business base in the communities it serves. This premise has proven sound in over 200 communities in which WEN facilitated training programs. These programs have trained over 4,500 individuals in 250 classes from January 1996 to July 1997. In these classes, an average of 85% of the participants finished the training, 65% completed a business plan.

The effect of trained participants in the community has been profound. For example, follow-up surveys have indicated that for those participants who own a business, sales increased by 25% within a year of graduation and, each business tends to create, on average, at least one new job in the community. Further, of those graduates not in business, 20% go on to start new businesses.

As impressive as these statistics are, we continued to improve by listening to the comments and concerns of the participants, educators, and state and community sponsors who administer the training. Most felt that the traditional "off the shelf" entrepreneurial books do not contain material specific to their success. They asked for practical material that would cover the issues entrepreneurs face when deciding to either start businesses or grow their existing ones.

NxLeveL is the result of listening to the comments and concerns of thousands of individuals and hundreds of instructors that completed the training. From this input, we set about to improve our curriculum. First we sought out educators, successful entrepreneurs and individuals that truly were experts in their given field. Calling on this group, we developed course materials and curriculum based on that collective expertise, and designed courses and additional materials that were considered vital to a small business owners success. The result was the ***NxLeveL Business Start-ups Program*** and the ***NxLeveL Entrepreneurs Program***. The materials are easy to use, conveniently packaged and reflect the practical applications sought and tested by actual participants.

Another concern was the cost of training materials. ***NxLeveL Business Start-ups Program*** and the ***NxLeveL Entrepreneurs Program*** are designed to be affordable for both the training partner and the participant. Because the U S WEST Foundation agreed to underwrite the cost of these materials and donated NxLeveL copyright profit back into programs, the cost of these materials is substantially lower than that of other national entrepreneurial training programs.

The U S WEST Foundation, University of Colorado at Denver, and the state sponsoring coalitions have teamed to help entrepreneurs start new businesses and reach the next level of success. We understand that a strong base in small business builds a strong community, which furthers our primary goal of developing better, more viable communities.

Letter From the Editor

My fellow contributors and I have conceived, researched and written this course of study for students of all professional and educational backgrounds. The book was prepared for people from urban, suburban and rural communities. In fact, this book is written for would-be entrepreneurs of every age, gender and race, because above all else, entrepreneurship is about diversity. The only requirements for taking this course are curiosity and passion for starting a business.

We hope this text will inspire and inform you as you begin exploring a new business concept. We present the theories and practice of entrepreneurship through real-life examples of many other small businesses. We believe nothing is as inspiring to potential entrepreneurs as the experiences of successful start-ups.

We've designed this text to complement your learning experience in the NxLeveL training program. We have also created it to be a useful reference book for you while you start and grow your business. All of the contributors to this textbook have either started a business or helped others to do so. This text represents a composite of our experiences and is filled with the tools we believe are essential for starting a successful dynamic business. We also direct you to additional sources of valuable information such as local libraries, the internet, small business development centers, government publications, other professionals, friends, mentors and professors.

Entrepreneurship is primarily concerned with innovation and overcoming obstacles. In the businesses I have started I have had a love/hate relationship with the seemingly endless string of challenges I confronted. However, I knew that the day they ended I would be out of business. Challenges were proof that my business was covering new ground and growing. I learned quickly that surprises and obstacles are part and parcel of managing a dynamic business.

In 1989 I went to Eastern Europe on the first of many trips to launch my business, an international trading company specializing in computer equipment. I did business there under the most adverse conditions. For me, no experience more vividly reflects the rewards, challenges and sheer thrill of entrepreneurship.

I have met few people who demonstrate entrepreneurial zeal as did those I met in the communities in Eastern Europe. At the time, everything that region had known was changing or disappearing altogether. Communism was declining. Democracy was being introduced, markets were opening up and the guarantee of lifetime employment was disappearing. Instead of being frightened by uncertainty, many people I met had a remarkable enthusiasm for the possibilities that the future held. Along with the new political and economic liberation came a tremendous surge of personal freedom and entrepreneurial spirit.

Entrepreneurship is about freedom. Few things in life are as empowering as being able to determine for yourself what work you will do, when, where and with whom you will do it. Along with this freedom comes responsibility. As entrepreneurs we do not have direct bosses to answer to, but we do have lenders, investors, family, and the ever present laws of profitability. Most of all, we answer to ourselves. We must be true to our vision and our passion. We should do what we love and design our businesses to reflect the best of what we have to offer.

For myself and the other contributors, entrepreneurship has truly enriched our lives by allowing us to share remarkable experiences with wonderfully unique and talented people. When confronted by new challenges it was the people we worked with, dedication, and a good sense of humor, that kept us moving onward and upward.

It is this pioneering spirit and joy of entrepreneurship that we want to pass along to you. We wish you the best of luck and many good times as you set out on your own entrepreneurial adventures.

David Wold
Mill Valley, California

About the Authors

Preparing the NxLeveL text books was a challenge, and to meet that challenge in the best possible way, we asked several individuals to help us. The authors have a combined 250 years in business, making the sharing of their experiences just that much more beneficial. The authors include professional educators and entrepreneurs that have both educational and practical experience. We'd like to recognize them here.

Primary Authors

David P. Wold is an international entrepreneurship consultant, advising start-up and growing businesses on strategy, management and marketing. He has over 20 years experience growing businesses in the U.S., Latin America, the Middle East, Russia and Eastern Europe. A graduate of the University of Wisconsin, he has a M.I.M. from the American Graduate School of International Management.

Dennis Sargent is Director of the Small Business Development Center at Linn-Benton Community College. He is a CPA and holds an MBA from Oregon State University. Dennis has more than 25 years experience in business consulting, systems design, teaching and management.

Martha Sargent is an Assistant Professor of Accounting and Director of the Small Business Development Center at Western Oregon State College. She holds an MBA from Oregon Sate University and is a CPA. Martha has more than 18 years experience in accounting and teaching.

Contributing Authors

Helen LeBoeuf-Binninger holds BBA, MBA and CPA certificates. She has been involved with small businesses as an entrepreneur and consultant. She currently provides business consulting and training services to small business near her home in Idaho.

Virginia Campbell is the Assistant State Director for the Washington Small Business Development Center. Ms. Campbell has 10 years of Human Resource experience in the private sector working for an electronic manufacturer and has nine years experience as the owner of a small business in the construction industry.

James Deffenbaugh is the Executive Director of a nonprofit community planning and loan organization. He is a past administrator of the California Regional Parks System, and has been an administrative partner for a CPA firm. He has many years counseling and consulting experience with both small and large businesses.

Dawn Gardner is Director of Small Office/Home Office Studies at the Center for the New West and past Director of Small Business Programs for the Colorado Office of Business Development. Dawn, a founding member, serves as Vice President of the Rocky Mountain Home-Based Business Association.

Kris Jon Gorsuch is a graduate of the University of Iowa College of Law. Kris is an attorney specializing in helping entrepreneurs establish successful businesses. He has written and spoken extensively on business development and teaches continuing education classes. He holds Martindale Hubble's highest achievement rating.

Joseph B. Harris is a Business Development Specialist for the Washington Small Business Development Center in Pullman, Washington. He is a former owner of a scientific instrument manufacturing company and recently started a new business venture. He teaches entrepreneurship and business planning at Washington State University.

Robert Horn is the Director of the Colorado Center for Community Development at the University of Colorado at Denver and founder of the Western Entrepreneurial Network. He is an educator and professional planner by training. He holds a masters of Urban and Regional Planning, and has been involved in community economic development for the past eighteen years.

Randy Johnson is Director of the Small Business Development Center for the Community College of Aurora, Colorado. Randy has developed several entrepreneurial training classes and has spoken on such topics as financing, economic development, home-based business and marketing. He is currently President of the Rocky Mountain Home-Based Business Association.

Paul Karofsky started working in his family's business in 1967 and has been involved with small businesses since. He is Director of the Northeastern University Center for Family Business and a lecturer at the University's College of Business Administration, and writes a family business column for several publications.

Yolanda Collazos Kizer is the president of Builder's Book Depot and Casa Feniz Merchandizing, Inc. She has an MBA, and serves on several civic organizations throughout Arizona, including the Governor's Strategic Partnership for Economic Development and the City of Phoenix Commission on the Economy.

Johanna Leestma is a graduate of Vassar College. She has worked in Hong Kong and Thailand. Johanna owned a successful backpack design and manufacturing business before earning her M.I.M. degree from the American Graduate School of International Management. She is a freelance writer and entrepreneurial consultant.

Lorre McKeone of North Platte, Nebraska, has managed three small businesses and spent 7 years as a loan officer before starting her own business, The Executive Extra. She teaches classes, workshops and provides consulting services for small businesses. Ms. McKeone graduated with honors from Hastings College.

William Mullane is employed by the University of Northern Colorado where he works on the U S WEST "Widening Our World" internet technology project. He was a former newspaper publisher and was the communications manager for Schweitzer Mountain Resort. Bill helped create the Royal Saudi Air Force Survival Training Center and curriculum. He has an M.I.M. from the American Graduate School of International Management.

Cameron Wold teaches entrepreneurship classes in California where he is pursuing a graduate degree. Previously with the University of Colorado at Denver he was instrumental in developing the NxLeveL curriculum. A former commercial banker, his expertise includes entrepreneurial training, welfare transition, shared-use commercial kitchens and the specialty food trade. A graduate of Amherst College, he holds an MBA from the University of Southern California.

R. L. Wolverton is a freelance writer and photographer who teaches small business planning. He has owned and published newspapers and magazines, and his writing has appeared in several national magazines. He makes his home in Wyoming.

Editors

David P. Wold is an international management and marketing consultant. He has won awards in advertising in Europe and the United States. Mr. Wold lives in Mill Valley, California.

Production Staff

Western Entrepreneurial Network
University of Colorado at Denver

Project Management
Robert Horn

Cameron Wold

Layout & Design
Curtis Hart

Elizabeth Strammiello

Michele Renée Ledoux

J Fay Design

Part I
Becoming an Entrepreneur

Chapter 1
UNDERSTANDING ENTREPRENEURSHIP

About This Chapter:
- *Entrepreneurs vs. small business*
- *Shattering myths*
- *What makes a good entrepreneur?*
- *Risks, drawbacks and rewards*

Introduction

Every day, thousands of people dream of starting their own businesses. Every day, hundreds of others actually do. What's the difference between "dreaming" and "doing?"

Well, entrepreneurs are usually young. Or Old. They're usually male. Or female. They're usually college-educated—or not. In other words, entrepreneurs come from every imaginable origin and background.

Yet most observers agree that entrepreneurs do have some common characteristics.

First, people who start their own businesses are invariably persistent. Moving a business from start-up to operation means jumping over many hurdles: money, location, "people problems," and many others. To overcome these challenges, entrepreneurs have to be persistent.

Another common characteristic: Passion. Entrepreneurs are passionate about their business idea and about their chances for success. As Anita Roddick, CEO of The Body Shop put it, "Passion persuades—and, by God, I was passionate about what I was selling." These people are doing something they love, and it shows. Entrepreneurship is passion, persistence, and doing what you love.

In the final analysis, none work harder, happier or more productively than people who work for themselves.

Nothing in the world can take the place of persistence. Talent will not; nothing is more common than unsuccessful men with talent. Genius will not; unrewarded genius is almost a proverb. Education will not; the world is full of educated derelicts. Persistence and determination alone are omnipotent. The slogan "Press On" has solved and always will solve the problems of the human race.
—Calvin Coolidge

Entrepreneur vs. Small Business Operator

So, what is an entrepreneur? He or she is a builder—one who sees an opportunity, sizes up its value, and finds the resources to make the most of it. Entrepreneurs are innovators: they have a strong desire to create something new. It may be a new product or a new process, but always a "better idea". The entrepreneur also has a vision of how the business will grow—and the drive to make it happen.

Passion is the cornerstone of the entrepreneurial spirit

Small business operators, on the other hand, are interested in generating an income and a lifestyle for themselves. Their businesses tend to remain relatively small and local, such as the "Mom and Pop" dry cleaner or car wash. Most small businesses have the potential to become entrepreneurial businesses, but their owners choose to keep them small to avoid the problems of growth and the risks of "getting big". Often, the owner does not want to find, train, and manage the employees required by a growing business. Small business operators are generally more concerned with managing what they have, while entrepreneurs are more concerned with developing new ideas, new markets and new challenges.

What is the difference between the manager and the entrepreneur? The manager is the person who organizes the resources. If your goal is to make a path through the jungle, the manager would marshal the personnel, assign the machetes, and design the most effective and efficient means of cutting through the jungle. The entrepreneur, on the other hand, is the person who would shinny up the coconut tree, look over the jungle and find the spot the path needs to reach.

You can be a successful small business operator without being an entrepreneur. But you can't be an entrepreneur without starting as a small business. The difference is that the entrepreneur won't be content to leave the business as it is. They will be out finding new markets, adding to the product line, pursuing other geographic territories or getting involved in horizontal or vertical integration. The entrepreneur will always find new challenges.

Small business operators are really the backbone of this country. You can go anywhere and find hundreds of examples of small businesses that contribute to the local economy, provide jobs, pay taxes, and earn a comfortable living for the owners. Entrepreneurs, on the other hand, are not content with the status quo. They search out new challenges and opportunities.

Importance of Entrepreneurship

The Small Business Administration (SBA) reports that America's small businesses (less than 500 employees):

- Employ 54 percent of the private work force;
- Generate 52 percent of all sales volume; and
- Are responsible for 50 percent of private production.

Small businesses are also providing the majority of new jobs and the jobs they create are more likely to be filled by younger workers, older workers, and women.

Studies show that small firms produce twice as many innovations per employee as large firms. Some would chalk this up to the entrepreneurial spirit of the small business people; others to the ability of a small firm to move more rapidly than large, bureaucratic companies.

Entrepreneurial businesses are job creating machines

Small businesses also help to lead the country out of economic downturns. For instance, during the period from 1980 to 1990, the SBA reports that all of the net new jobs in the economy were created by small firms. During this period, the performance of the nation's smallest firms (those with fewer than 20 employees) created almost 4.1 million new jobs while large firms lost more than 500,000 jobs and firms with 20-499 employees lost 850,000 jobs.

Shattering Entrepreneurial Myths

If that's what entrepreneurs are, then what are they not? There are many common myths that surround entrepreneurship. Let's examine some of them:

- Entrepreneurs are born not made. In fact, almost anyone can learn these skills.
- Entrepreneurs are their own boss. In fact, they work for many people: investors, clients, and employees.
- Entrepreneurs set their own hours. In fact, entrepreneurs work long and hard for their success.
- Entrepreneurs love high-risk ventures. Most successful entrepreneurs do everything in their power to minimize risk.
- Entrepreneurs are all young techies working in Silicon Valley. In fact, entrepreneurship is not governed by age, sex or geography.

As you can see many of our cultural myths are not true at all. Entrepreneurship is mainly defined by persistence, passion, enthusiasm and skills which can be learned.

What Makes a Good Entrepreneur?

Entrepreneurs are a diverse lot. No one gender, age, education level or ethnicity has a particular advantage in entrepreneurship. But certain personalities do. By looking at the profile of successful entrepreneurs, you can assess your strengths against theirs. What characteristics seem to be common? Many entrepreneurs exhibit these:

1. Passion
2. Persistence
3. Good health/energy
4. Creativity/innovation
5. Independence/self-reliance
6. Intuition
7. Self-confidence
8. Lack of need for "status"
9. Willingness to accept challenges
10. Willingness to work hard

Passion

As mentioned before, loving what you are doing seems to be essential to doing it well—whether the doing is ice-skating, cooking, or starting a business.

Another trait often noted in venture creators is sharing that passion with others. Entrepreneurs will often tell more than a listener wants to know about their business because they're passionate about it and feel everyone will be as interested as they are.

Time seems to have very little meaning when we are passionate about what we are doing. The time and effort expended on our "passion" leaves us feeling exhilarated rather than exhausted. Perhaps this is one source of the motivation entrepreneurs need to put in the long hours required to launch their new ventures.

Persistence

Entrepreneurs are determined. They can carry a task to completion and are willing to work longer and harder than others. They will do whatever it takes to "get the job done" which is often critical in overcoming the many daily challenges faced by entrepreneurs.

Part of persistence is discipline. Entrepreneurs often have to do things they don't like to do in order to meet their goals. For example, some entrepreneurs do not enjoy financial record-keeping. Yet most entrepreneurs know this is vital to the success of their business, and make sure financial functions are done properly and on-time.

Good Health, High Energy

Starting a business requires a tremendous amount of energy. Determining feasibility, getting permits, finding a location, and contacting suppliers and distributors are all time and energy consuming. Because of the many demands placed on entrepreneurs, good health and high energy are practically requirements. Without your health and energy, your business would be much more difficult to maintain. In fact, when the owner's health fails, the business is often not far behind. If you wish to be an entrepreneur take care of this valuable asset—good health. You're going to need it.

Creativity/Innovation

New products and services come from new ideas. So do solutions to problems like losing a key supplier or a prime location. Creativity—and flexibility—are valuable qualities in building a business.

Sometimes, being on the outside of a given business or industry seems to make it easier to see a new solution. That's where many entrepreneurs come from. It is important that once you have entered that business, entrepreneurs remember to "step back and take a new look."

Independence and Self-Reliance

When you own your own business, no one else is going to make the decisions for you. Furthermore, you may not have anyone to rely on for the work you're unfamiliar with or don't like. But the many demands of daily business must be met, and the small business owner soon understands the meaning of "the buck stops here."

Tom Kane, an entrepreneur whose background included only experience working in the accounting department of a large business realized he was ill-prepared for start-up realities. He had worked for a large corporation where the human resources

One entrepreneur whose background included only experience working in big business realized he was ill-prepared for start-up realities

department helped in the hiring process, the accounting department did billing and record-keeping, and the janitorial department cleaned the premises. When Tom decided to start his own business, he believed it would be a better plan to go with a franchise company that provided some of the assistance he had come to rely on while working for a major corporation, rather than "go it alone". Advertising copy, human resource policies, and cleaning standards were recommended by the franchiser. Someone described franchising as being in business for yourself, not by yourself—probably an accurate description and one which characterizes a business format that many may find more comfortable.

Whether you choose a franchise, purchase an ongoing business or start your own company, you'll have to rely on yourself to make and carry out your own decisions. By-and-large entrepreneurs enjoy the freedom that comes with this kind of decision-making. They also take on all the responsibilities that come with this freedom. They like to make things happen and the ability to influence and determine outcomes is what draws them to self-employment.

Intuition

Intuition is the ability to see the patterns and possibilities in a set of events—to see beyond the obvious. Some people would call this a gut feeling but whatever you call it, entrepreneurs who have it often have an uncanny ability to predict how a given set of circumstances will affect their business. Entrepreneurs need to trust their intuition to help them make the right business decisions.

Someone who used his intuition or "gut feel" to make a business decision is Dale Alldredge. One day, an inventor walked into Dale's office with something that can only be described as "a chain-saw on a stick." Dale saw an opportunity! He believed this invention could be marketed to parks, transportation departments, and others who maintain trees and shrubs in public areas. This "extension saw" could cut branches up to 15 feet off the ground, avoiding the dangers of climbing trees or the expense and inconvenience of bringing in large machinery. Dale followed his instincts, and they paid off.

Self-Confidence

It obviously takes a great deal of confidence to suddenly "go it alone." New venture owners have to believe in their ability to make their businesses prosper. They are optimistic about the future of their businesses and confident in their ideas, even when others around them aren't.

While entrepreneurs are self-confident about reaching their goals, they are also realistic and open to change. They recognize they can't and don't know everything and therefore ask questions and seek advice from others. Because of their self-confidence, entrepreneurs identify problems and begin working on their solutions quickly. Entrepreneurs are viewed as leaders because they are often the first to identify the problem.

Lack of Need for 'Status'

Entrepreneurs' status needs are satisfied by achieving goals rather than by clothing, automobiles, boats or luxury accommodations. While entrepreneurs may enjoy and partake in some of these luxuries, these aren't the reason for their efforts. Entrepreneurs typically don't judge themselves by external standards, but by whether or not they have achieved their own internal goals and objectives.

New venture owners believe in their ability to make their business prosper

Willingness to Accept Challenges

Much is written about entrepreneurs as risk takers, but in fact they are neither low or high risk takers. Rather, they are willing to accept challenges where they can influence the outcome. Entrepreneurs seldom act until they have assessed the risk. A challenge is highly motivating to entrepreneurs and they enjoy the thrill and excitement of taking on new challenges.

Willingness to Work Hard

Entrepreneurs are inevitably hard-working. One said, "I work only half the time—twelve hours a day." Creating and successfully running a new business takes hard work.

While looking at entrepreneurial aptitudes may be useful, it's important to decide whether the venture is worth doing and whether you want to do it. In the end, it's not by their traits we know the entrepreneur, but by what they do. It is the behaviors of entrepreneurs that distinguish them.

Remember, actions speak louder than words.

Creating and successfully running a new business takes hard work

Entrepreneurship and Timing

Age factors cut both ways in the decision to start a new venture. While people in all stages of life have started successful businesses, it seems that there are times more conducive to taking on a new business venture. For instance, many entrepreneurs start ventures in the middle adult years.

Sometimes, it is just not the right time in an individual's life to start a new business. You may have other things going on in life—a spouse starting a new career, the birth of a child, or significant other events. If a person is entrepreneurial, deciding not to open a business for personal reasons won't result in never opening a business, just delaying it.

Perhaps you have a good job and a reasonably bright and certain future, but you often think about entering the competitive business environment as the leader of your own company. Adversity in the form of a layoff or plant closing may spark entry.

Potential Weaknesses

As human beings we all have strengths and weaknesses. Entrepreneurs have their share. Here are some to watch out for. Look at them as areas that can be improved.

Managers?

Many times, entrepreneurs are not particularly good managers of people. They are often visionary, hard-working, and self-motivated, but are not good at perceiving the "people problems" that are occurring around them. They don't like dealing with personnel issues and have little tolerance for those who aren't equally focused on achieving business goals. Entrepreneurs are a confident lot and believe they can do everything themselves. Because of this, entrepreneurs are sometimes not good team-players and have a difficult time managing teams or fostering teamwork among employees.

Control

Perhaps you believe that no one can make decisions as well as you can. You may be unable to delegate any decision-making authority. If a customer enters a business and finds that no one except the owner can make what appears to be a routine operating decision, it's probably a company where the owner cannot delegate authority and/or is trying to control too much.

Workaholics

There are those who consider their work the only activity in their life. Nothing else is quite as much fun or as exciting as business—so family and outside pursuits don't receive any attention. Needless to say, this can make for unhappy families and, in the end, unhappy entrepreneurs. Even though entrepreneurship demands hard work and long hours, a balanced life with time for family, friends and relaxing pursuits will serve the entrepreneur better than the tunnel vision of a workaholic.

Risks and Drawbacks of Entrepreneurship

It is true that there is a definite risk in going into business for yourself. However, risks can be minimized. Entrepreneurs are not classic gamblers. They are interested in minimizing risks with planning, information gathering, and analysis. Entrepreneurs are willing to take "calculated risks". For the true entrepreneur, however, the rewards of entrepreneurship far outweigh the risks.

Let's look at some of the risks and drawbacks that entrepreneurs face.

- Failure. Entrepreneurs must assume the emotional and financial risks of failure.
- Time. A major drawback to undertaking an entrepreneurial effort is the tremendous amount of time it takes to make the business successful. Most report 60-70 hour per week as normal.
- Family. Because of the strain of operating a business many families suffer.
- Money. Most start-up entrepreneurs have their own money at risk.

Some people regard private enterprise as a predatory tiger to be shot. Others look on it as a cow they can milk. Not enough people see it as a healthy horse pulling a sturdy wagon.
—Winston Churchill

Rewards

Just as there are risks and drawbacks related to entrepreneurship, so too are there rewards. Naturally we are not all motivated by the same things. However, these appear to be the major issues for most entrepreneurs:

- Independence. For many, the freedom to act independently is paramount in their decision to "be their own boss."
- Money. The financial return from your own efforts are not limited to normal work for normal pay.
- Fun. Many entrepreneurs describe what they do as fun—that is, they really enjoy what they do!

Conclusion

Entrepreneurship is a discipline. It requires an ability to spot opportunities and act wisely on them. And just like other occupations, providing a product or service at an attractive price is the basis for getting paid.

Because of the outsourcing, downsizing, and re-engineering at large corporations, entrepreneurial skills may be the key not only to economic independence, but even to survival, in the '90's and beyond. Naturally, there are many risks and rewards in entrepreneurship. But for most entrepreneurs, the joy of running their own business far outweighs the drawbacks.

Don't forget to have fun—that's what it is all about!

Chapter 2
THINKING ENTREPRENEURIALLY

About This Chapter:
- *Why businesses succeed*
- *The nature of profit and business ethics*
- *Bootstrapping and outsourcing*
- *Time management and personal planning*

Introduction

Entrepreneurship is a particular way of thinking and acting. Successful entrepreneurs take opportunities to create new ways to solve old problems. They have perseverance, vision and patience. They are achievement oriented and independent. They are tolerant of ambiguity.

However, entrepreneurship is more than just a bundle of personality traits. It is also a way of thinking and acting from which people can learn and benefit from. How does one think and act as an entrepreneur? By understanding and adhering to the concept of profit. Effectively managing time. Behaving ethically. Leveraging scarce resources. And planning a fulfilling and balanced personal life.

The goal of this chapter is to shed light on these behaviors and inspire start-up business people to learn and practice them. In the end, using these simple practices can dramatically improve the efficiency of your start-up business and the quality of your personal life.

Why Do Businesses Succeed?

There is no shortage of opinions and information about why businesses fail. They ignore their customers, they disregard market conditions, they miscalculate prices. They fail to stick to their plans and budgets. Their businesses lack managerial control.

But more useful to the start-up entrepreneur is information about why businesses succeed. Why not have a target of what to do rather than what not to do? Business success is defined in all sorts of ways: how large or small the business is, market share, profitability, efficiency, or ability to innovate.

Businesses succeed because they:

- Have a clear sense of purpose
- Base their mission statements or goals on realistic expectations of what they can achieve

- Understand their strengths and weaknesses relative to their competitors and focus their operations on these
- Target the right group of customers
- Specialize in solving a specific customer problem
- Experiment with new approaches to customer problems
- Create and stick to strong core values
- Organize their business for maximum flexibility and learning
- Demonstrate powerful responsiveness to their customers, suppliers and partners
- Offer unique value to their customers
- Create strong customer loyalty and repeat business
- Know how to build strong and enduring business relationships
- Develop a new type of product or service that captures a large market share
- Create a reputation for quality, loyalty, and professionalism
- Keep a close eye on costs, pricing and profitability

The Nature of Profit

Businesses exist to make money. Entrepreneurs go into business for themselves hoping to make enough money to give them the lifestyle they want. **Profit** is the result of subtracting your expenses from your sales. It is the difference between what a business earns for selling its products or services and what it pays to produce those products or services. Profit is a return for investing time and money and a reward to the entrepreneur for assuming risks.

One thing entrepreneurs need to be aware of is cash flow. The cash flows only when actual payments are received. Because not all sales bills are paid immediately, a sale is not considered "cash" until you actually receive the money. Sometimes, profitable ventures will fail because of a lack of cash. Using only profit as a measure of your business' success might be deceiving if you don't have sufficient cash flow to run your operations. In addition, a business may have lots of customers lining up to buy its products or services. But if its costs are too high or its prices too low, it will not make a profit. Regularly calculating profitability is an essential reality check for businesses. This keeps them focused on their revenues and expenses. It is the basis for budgets, forecasts and controls. Businesses who understand the specifics of profitability manage their efforts more effectively.

When Barbara Gillies first opened Cook's Kitchen, a gourmet kitchenware store in an upscale neighborhood, sales were brisk and profit margins good. Before Barbara patted herself on the back, she did some future thinking about who her customers were and how she could maintain their loyalty. Because she wanted to insure a constant cash flow stream, Barbara devised a series of cooking classes at the store for which she charged a fee. After seeing the success of the classes, Barbara devised a curriculum of classes to be offered throughout the year to keep her customers coming back for more. Barbara helped to keep up the demand for her products while satisfying her customers' need to expand their culinary horizons.

The lesson? Understand where your profits come from. Create strategies to maximize profitability. Look to both short-term gains and long-term goals of customer loyalty when you implement your business growth strategies.

Bootstrapping

Often times entrepreneurs have little other than their resourcefulness to get their businesses off the ground. For instance, a film student who used her rent money, a modest family loan and credit card debt to finance her first feature film. By using all her available resources, this student practiced bootstrapping. It is a very useful tool for entrepreneurs.

Bootstrapping is the practice of getting by on as few resources as possible. And it is getting the most out of those resources you do have. It is the practice of using one's smarts and creativity to beg, borrow or find the resources needed to start a business. This might include holding down three different jobs to support a new venture. Borrowing money from family and friends. Selling assets, mortgaging a house, or even resorting to credit card financing. Entrepreneurs who bootstrap use all of their wiles to make their business viable.

Top Drawer Publishing is a 4 person team that creates newsletters, company reports and brochures and other graphics for business customers. Last year they signed up one of the largest contracts they had ever undertaken for Medis Corporation.

Mid-year they needed to purchase computer equipment and move to larger office space, but did not have the cash on hand they needed. What they did have was a sizable 60 day account receivable from Medis.

What to do? Top Drawer searched out a factoring company who was interested in buying account receivables. The factoring company knew that Medis was a reliable organization with a solid reputation for paying its bills. Top Drawer struck an agreement in which they sold the Medis' account receivable to the factoring company at face value minus a 10% commission. In exchange Top Drawer received its cash (minus 10%) immediately, and was able to purchase the equipment and sign a new lease. The factoring company made a margin of 10% by taking on the 60 day receivable, and Medis got the stellar services of Top Drawer Publishing.

How does the eager bootstrapping entrepreneur begin to keep expenses down and think and act lean and mean?

- Share or lease office space with a larger business
- Hire as few full-time employees as possible by using independent contractors, temporary employees or services from other businesses
- Use barter arrangements to procure supplies
- Sell wholesale rather than direct to retailers—wholesalers are experts at distribution channel set-up and management
- Collect accounts receivable as soon as possible
- Build strong relationships with suppliers and arrange for longer payment terms
- Use computer technology wisely to create your own promotional pieces, manage sales efforts and keep track of budgets and costs
- Remember to be honest, creative and reliable, never unethical or illegal

Essentially, bootstrapping invites entrepreneurs to use their negotiating and networking skills to help start their business. Bootstrapping is not only about financing your business; it's a way of running a lean company and making the best use of available resources—something to always consider even as your business success takes off. Successful entrepreneurs use aggressive, unconventional ways to minimize costs, generate revenue and maximize profitability.

The Power of Outsourcing

Outsourcing, like bootstrapping is one of the many creative techniques entrepreneurs use to get their businesses up and running. In fact, many established businesses use outsourcing on a regular basis in order to cut costs.

Outsourcing is the practice of hiring independent contractors to help with business operations. **Independent contractors** are individuals who own their own business and hire themselves out to perform specific jobs for their clients. These may include accounting and bookkeeping, sales, product design, promotions or logistics. Independent contractors are usually specialists in their particular area.

Utilize outsourcing and imitate the expertise of big business

Independent contractors cost less to employ than full-time employees. They do not have to have social security tax or income tax withheld, or be paid health insurance in their compensation package. The reason is that contractors provide these things for themselves since they are their own "mini-businesses."

Contractors are specialists in their field, and can be hired on short term or as-needed basis with no commitment for long-term employment. The clever use of independent contractors can allow a start-up business to imitate the professionalism, expertise, and high-quality performance of a much larger business.

When outsourcing, it is important to:

- Use a clear and professionally written legal contract
- Clearly state in the contract that for tax purposes the contractor will not be treated as a full-time employee
- Make sure contractors are covered by their own worker's compensation insurance
- Have appropriate operating licenses

To avoid difficulties, businesses that use contractors make sure to select people with whom they can work and communicate easily. Early on they establish the level of expertise of the contractor, set clear goals, and create clear lines of communication about contract deadlines and performance standards. This way, if problems arise they can be dealt with quickly and professionally.

Use outsourcing to save money, beef up the expertise of your company and remain lean and mean.

Entrepreneurial Ethics

Like everyone else, entrepreneurs are members of their communities. As such they have the responsibility to make positive contributions to their communities and adhere to local, state and federal laws.

Like their larger counterparts, start-ups must operate ethically. **Business ethics** are principles of right and wrong that guide interactions with customers, employees, suppliers, partners, lenders and investors. Some people argue that entrepreneurs face more than their fair share of ethical tests as they struggle to get their businesses off the ground. They understate or "skim" revenues to lower their tax burden, issue inaccurate invoices, or pay employees less than the fair market rate. Unethical marketing behavior may include misleading advertising content or manipulative selling practices.

Although many of these actions are clearly illegal, business ethics go far beyond what is legal or illegal. Ethical dilemmas tempt us to compromise our principles of what is fair or just for the sake of the business or personal advantage. Adherence to ethics speaks to our integrity and sense of responsibility and obligation. It is easy to have strong ethical beliefs. It is more difficult to behave ethically when times are tough and the survival of a business is on the line.

The experiences of a major multimedia company in San Jose, California demonstrate the consequences of unethical and illegal business practices.

Only a few years after its initial public offering, the company began to overstate its sales figures and understate its inventory levels in order to inflate its stock prices. After an investigation by the Securities and Exchange Commission uncovered these illegal practices, the company's stock price plummeted, the business was temporarily shut-down, and the CEO, and other members of management were implicated in criminal charges of fraud.

How do businesses ensure that they behave ethically? By explicitly discussing ethical issues as they arise. Many businesses include in their employee handbook and company manual a statement about their commitment to ethical behavior. Business leaders can set a clear and strong example of ethical behavior. In small businesses the ethical influence of the boss is even more pronounced. Entrepreneurs must back up their beliefs with right minded behavior and create the procedures to ensure that their employees act ethically.

As an entrepreneur, one of your goals is to establish an ongoing relationship with your clients, suppliers and the business community. By acting ethically, you will be establishing your valued reputation for fair dealing within your industry and community. Not only is this good for your conscience, its good for your enterprise!

The lesson? Start-up businesses should reflect in their actions the highest ethical commitment of the entrepreneur.

Effective Time Management

Entrepreneurs have a wider variety of demands on their time than do managers in larger firms. Smaller staffs and budgets combined with the challenges of getting a young business up and running make time one of an entrepreneur's scarcest resources. Many start-up business owners work between 60 and 80 hours a week, and still cannot get all of their tasks completed. Many waste valuable time and resources and fail to perform to the best of their abilities. Why? Because they are not effectively organizing their time.

Delegating responsibility and authority is one of the toughest but most important things an entrepreneur must do

Entrepreneurs who fail to manage their time can fall into a cycle of inefficiency and poor performance. They are too busy to teach employees how to do their jobs effectively. So they end up trying to do too many tasks themselves. They do not have enough time to weed out mistakes and improve practices. They cannot build strong customer and supplier relationships or fully enjoy their leisure time.

Effective time management leads to effective business management. No matter how small a business, entrepreneurs usually cannot do all of the tasks their businesses require themselves. They must delegate duties, and give people the authority to perform the tasks in the most effective ways. After all, you should focus your efforts on what must be done that only you can do: guiding the business by setting goals, and achieving those goals.

How can you begin to practice good time management?

- Record how time is spent over a one week period by listing all of activities and how long is spent on each
- Identify wasted time and "gaps" that can be used better

- List and prioritize tasks and cross them off a master list when they are completed
- Finish tasks in one session
- Create agendas for meeting goals and time frames
- Keep desks clear of clutter
- File papers immediately in hand-labelled files
- Schedule the most important work for first thing in the morning
- "Batch" tasks that can be done together, once or twice a week

Good time management takes discipline and organization, but makes you more efficient and improves the quality of your performance.

Personal Planning

Entrepreneurs have to address personal priorities very early in their venture. Why? Because you have so much flexibility in creating your own work environment and work schedule. Where will the boundaries be drawn between work, family and leisure time?

Issues of family responsibility, community involvement and leisure time take on new meaning when entrepreneurs begin to build their businesses. For many, the traditional boundaries between private and professional time are blurred. It's easy for entrepreneurs to focus too heavily on the rewards that they directly reap from their efforts. But unfortunately, they also shoulder many of the risks: a preoccupation with the business that alienates them from their families and friends. Work that takes them away from their community, athletic and creative outlets. If entrepreneurs aren't careful, they will schedule the all-important "refueling" time out of their lives.

From the outset smart entrepreneurs take the time to evaluate and commit themselves to their personal priorities.

Baked Alaska, a start-up handbag manufacturer demanded at least 80 hours a week from entrepreneur Antonia Bolt. She designed and sewed samples, did the books and sold the finished product. She also spent time meeting with sewing shops and checking on order progress and negotiating bulk supplier contracts. She was very, very busy.

After 4 months in business she realized she hadn't been out on a date in 3 months. She hadn't vacuumed her apartment. And, because she hadn't been taking the time to jog and go to the gym, she had gained 10 pounds. She knew she had an urgent need to create boundaries between work and play.

So, Antonia bought a day planner. She created a weekly schedule not just for business tasks and appointments, but also for social and athletic activities. Everyday at 4 o'clock she would stop working and go for a run or go to the health club. If she didn't feel like working out, then she would go for a walk, go shopping or to her favorite bookstore and read. She also decided that to keep her creativity and enthusiasm up, she needed at least 3 nights out a week with friends, even if it was only to have a cup of tea at a local cafe.

Her final rule of thumb? All work ended at 9 p.m.

"I am looking for something more than money out of work. I expect deep fulfillment and a little fun too."
—Executive of a major U.S. corporation

The best way for entrepreneurs to approach personal planning is to identify what their familial and community responsibilities are. They should also:

- Prioritize activities
- Set working hours and family time
- Allow time for athletic and creative activities
- Take vacations
- Create work time cut-offs
- Create rewards for when major projects are completed

An example of an entrepreneur's weekly plans is illustrated on the following page:

February						
S	M	T	W	T	F	S
						1
2	3	4	5	6	7	8
9	10	11	12	13	14	15
16	17	18	19	20	21	22
23	24	25	26	27	28	

Weekly Planner
February 10-16, 1997

Monday 10	10:30 AM - 12:30 PM Meet with Richard Hersey/Textiles Unlimited - discuss supply agreement and schedule 2:00 PM - 3:00 PM Interview Frances Klein for asst. position 4:00 PM - 5:00 PM Aerobics class
Tuesday 11	9:00 AM - 10:30 PM Women in Business breakfast 11:00 AM - 1:00 PM Review March - June orders 3:00 PM - 4:00 PM Appointment with Flair Boutique
Wednesday 12	8:30 AM - 12:30 PM SBDC Conference - "Financing Sources" 1:00 PM - 3:00 PM Lunch with Robin Grant re: design concepts
Thursday 13	9:00 AM - 10:00 AM Finalize lease with MMC Management Co. 11:00 AM - 12:00 PM Contact Hilton gift shop re: July - Dec. orders 7:30 PM - Class - Marketing/Internet
Friday 14	9:00 AM - 10:30 AM Meet with accountant - review tax returns 1:00 PM - 2:00 PM Present designs to Shelly's Shop 4:00 PM - 5:00 PM Yoga class
Saturday 15	11:30 AM - Golf with Ann 8:00 PM - Movie - Bill
Sunday 16	12:00 PM - Lunch with Mom and Dad

Time Management and Personal Planning

A big part of personal planning for entrepreneurs is also in selecting the type of work they will do. What kind of business will you start? What is your favorite hobby? What particular skills, experience, interests and passions do you have?

"Work needs to fit your personality just as shoes need to fit your feet."
—Marsha Sinetar, organizational psychologist and business consultant

The biggest key to start-up success is commitment. Commitment is easy when entrepreneurs have selected the right type of work. When this happens problems become solvable rather than insurmountable obstacles. Some other key principles of personal planning are:

- Setting goals that are meaningful to you
- Knowing where you are headed and enjoying the ride
- Using your work as a means of self-expression

If you think about it, it simply does not make sense to shut off your personality and your need for challenge and growth while you work. When entrepreneurs build the business that allows them to truly express themselves, they become more confident. They become more responsible. They learn to trust themselves.

The lesson? People are adaptable and multidimensional, but we are not designed to always struggle through life. The key for the entrepreneur is to evaluate their priorities in life, their strengths, interests and goals, and create a business that matches.

Conclusion

What is true entrepreneurial thinking? It is keeping one eye on profit and the other on quality of work and life issues. It is finding clever ways to maximize the resources available to operate the business. It is using time wisely and working within a clear set of values and commitments that guide all your efforts. Entrepreneurs are truly successful when they are able to strike a unique balance between fulfilling work, personal and family responsibilities.

Chapter 3
DEVELOPING A BUSINESS CONCEPT

About This Chapter:
- *Business concept development*
- *Refining the idea*
- *Integrating business and personal goals*

Introduction

Businesses begin with the "birth" of an idea. All businesses start as a concept but many never move beyond the idea stage. Entrepreneurs carry ideas to reality through hard work and focused action. The best idea in the world is of little or no value unless acted upon.

How do I start a new business? What kind of business should I start? Good questions! Often times, start-up entrepreneurs know exactly what they want to do because they are working in the industry in which they want to compete. They know they can do it better, cheaper or faster than the companies they are working for or, they see an unserved market segment and want to fill the gap.

Many would-be business owners don't have a clear-cut business idea and want to know what business or businesses will be successful. You need to explore your interests, experience and personality in order to develop your business concept the right way. Additionally, there are specific methods to help you do a preliminary evaluation of your idea to determine its viability and chances for success.

So What's the Big Idea?

Business makes the world go round. Business is simply people meeting the needs of other people. The ingenuity, creativity, energy, ideas, risk taking and hard work of human beings has produced great material progress for mankind. The pace of change continues to accelerate, offering vast new fields of opportunity to those willing to look at life with an open mind. How do you go about developing a **business concept**? It involves the following steps:

1. Idea/concept creation
2. Defining and refining the concept
3. Researching the viability of the concept
4. Identifying and integrating business and personal goals
5. Identifying and addressing all factors involved in taking the concept from idea to reality

Where do business ideas come from?

Interest and Experience

Have you ever wondered where business people get their ideas for a new start-up? Here is an idea:

Idea Source	Percent
Prior Job	43
Hobby/Personal Interest	18
Chance Event	10
Someone Suggested It	8
Education/Courses	6
Family Business	6
Activities of Friends/Relatives	5
Other	5

Provided by the National Federation of Independent Businesses.

Prior Job

The most common catalyst for new business ideas seems to be work experience. Literally thousands of individuals have worked for everything from quick copy shops to electrical motor repair facilities and decided they could "do it better" than their previous employer. Sometimes employees move to a new geographic area and decide to duplicate their old company there.

Hobby/Personal Interest

Many others take a recreational pursuit or hobby and attempt to turn it into a business. Naturally, turning a hobby into a business involves something the owner has an interest in. Use caution here. While you may enjoy bicycling, will you enjoy running an adventure travel service specializing in bicycling trips?

Chance Event

Some business opportunities just seem to "show up." For instance, one new entrepreneur had a friend with a new baby. This mom wanted to use cloth diapers. Her friend wanted to provide her with a present—diaper service for a month. The friend, however, could not find such a service. She investigated the possibility and started one!

Someone Suggested It

Artists and crafts people often get into business while producing gift items for friends. Then, friends suggest the crafts person go into business and the gift becomes a product.

Education/Courses

Many people pursue business ownership because their education prepares them to become small business operators. Examples include entrepreneurs opening dental practices or veterinary clinics. Graduates of technical schools in such specialties as autobody or small engine repair, are also candidates to open new ventures.

Family Business

If your family has a business, joining the family firm may well be an option. Many entrepreneurs start a business with the idea that it will create opportunities for the next generation, and sometimes it does.

Activities of Friends/Relatives

Contacts in another part of the country may have a successful business that could be copied. Aunt Ellen may have the family recipe for the best brownie ever created, and you can create a business using this unique product. Friends and relatives may have ideas, experiences, and insights that could help develop a business.

As you can see people discover their new ideas in many ways. An idea, however, is not necessarily an opportunity.

A Success Story Born In Hope

Jack Fowler's Ski Resort dream started in Hope: During Easter weekend in April of 1960 Dentist Jack Fowler of Spokane, Washington was returning home with wife Dorothy and the couple's three children from a rained-out ski trip to Montana. While the family took a break at a rest stop in Hope, Idaho on gorgeous Lake Pend Oreille, Jack gazed west at the snow-filled bowls shimmering in the sun 4000 feet above the tiny lakeside community of Sandpoint. An idea was conceived in Jack's mind: "Why drive 6 hours to Montana when I have these gorgeous snow bowls 4 hours closer to home?" Fowler had taken the first step in business creation; he had a new idea!

How to Identify Business Opportunities

While there are ways other than "start-up" to get into business, this chapter is specifically addressing start-up situations like Jack Fowler's. Other chapters in this book address buying an existing business, purchasing a franchise, or joining a family-owned business. However, much of what is written about assessing start-up opportunities can also be used to measure other opportunities for business ownership.

Respond to Un-met or Under-met Needs

Have you ever heard someone say, "I wish there was something for...?" or "Why doesn't someone invent an effective ...?" Each of these situations may offer an opportunity for the entrepreneur. Someone looking for a business opportunity should pay attention to un-met needs identified by acquaintances, friends, relatives and personal experiences.

Keep an Idea File

Jot down ALL of your ideas

As you look for new business opportunities, cut out articles, jot down ideas, and create an idea file. Over the course of a couple of months, virtually scores of ideas may surface. Keeping track of these ideas and assessing them against your personal criteria for business success, may well lead to one worth pursuing.

Networking

Friends, relatives and acquaintances can help you generate ideas. They may describe an un-met need they have noticed. They may be able to pinpoint an opportunity that will be a good fit with your talents and desires. Maybe someone who has traveled to a different part of the country will have noticed a great business idea that they believe may work in your home town.

Research and Study

Do your homework. You should read newspapers, trade journals, business periodicals and trend prediction books. A trend may provide the spark of an idea for a new venture. General business periodicals such as *Entrepreneur Magazine*, *Business Start-Ups*, or *Inc.* may generate some ideas for you. Events happening in the news or the business advertising section in the newspaper may spark a thought.

New Uses for Old Things

Entire businesses have been created from locating old barn wood and turning it into picture frames or bird houses. Glass telephone-line insulators have become candle holders. Old clothes are woven into new rugs. These are just a few of the hundreds of possible new uses for old things.

Old Product, New Market

One enterprising entrepreneur was selling potpourri to the home gift market. As more competition came into that market, the owner repackaged the product for the auto care market. She sold the same product to a new market, and at a higher price! Often times, a superb business idea is not new, but merely a slight twist on something already being done.

Brainstorming

Brainstorming involves being wild and crazy—considering any idea, no matter how unusual or impractical. It might also include taking a business idea or asking for a business idea from a group of people and letting the group develop ideas to make it better. Be sure to analyze the idea's strengths and weaknesses when comparing one business opportunity to another.

Old Idea in New Geographic Area

Are entrepreneurs operating businesses in other parts of the country or world that aren't available locally? This could be a business opportunity.

New Ways to Deliver or Finance an Old Product

Many fortunes have been made on changing where people can buy a product or how they might finance it. Women's hosiery is a good example. Years ago, the only place to purchase nylons was in department stores. A special trip to the store was a big inconvenience for working women who purchase nylons. L'Eggs, a company offering nylon hosiery, convinced grocery stores to offer their product in the sundries section. Grocery story distribution combined with a new packaging scheme changed the entire industry.

Harnessing Trends

According to futurist Faith Popcorn, "**trend bending** is the process of shaping your product or strategy around emerging trends." Harnessing trends means using those changes that are occurring naturally in society to propel your business forward.

Tracking trends is great for new ideas

Unlike advertising, which costs money, trends occur naturally. Getting behind a strong trend can pull your business right along with less effort on your part. You will be able to look around and find others which may have a positive or negative impact on your business idea. Pay attention to trends—they are extremely powerful. Some examples of trends identified with the 1990's are:

- Downsizing
- Corporate outsourcing
- Aging population
- Fitness and health
- Ethical concerns
- Home-based businesses
- Time savers for working families
- Information age
- Return to nostalgia
- Globalization
- Career flexibility
- Environmental concern
- "Edu-tainment"
- Adventure travel

Looking at trends in your marketplace and around the world is important to any business. Just because a business isn't harnessing any of these trends doesn't mean it isn't a viable business. It pays to be aware of trends and their potential influence on your business.

Defining and Refining the Original Concept

Jack Fowler had an idea, a big idea. His concept was "a ski resort"—but what kind, how big, what amenities, a local area or a destination resort? What would it take to bring the idea to fruition? How much money would be needed? What about roads, lifts, lodges, water, sewer? Fowler had many items to address during his early concept development work.

The purpose of concept development is to take the idea or concept for a business and test it against financial, political, and economic reality. This is not so much the creation of a business as the developmental process of determining whether or not efforts should go forward and additional resources be committed to the concept. This involves making "go", "no go", or "change direction" decisions as facts and data are gathered.

Ultimately, a business idea must prove to be economically feasible in order to be successful. Before expending time, energy, and capital on a business idea, the entrepreneur should think long and hard. Success involves finding, developing, and refining a niche or meeting a need that is not being met. Before undertaking formal research it pays to take a "micro" and "macro" look at the business concept and the competitive environment.

Business Concept Development, the Micro View

Taking a "micro view" (looking inside the potential business) of a business concept involves refining a general idea for a business down to specific essentials concentrating on the following:

- Specifically identify the product or service you intend to provide. Can it be done... by you?
- Identify differentiating characteristics that will make your product/service unique and competitive
- Identify your key competitive advantages and disadvantages
- Self Analysis: Are my background and/or skills compatible with the idea? Am I financially secure?
- Identify potential pitfalls and determine whether or not you can overcome them

Overall, do you really have a great idea and can you make it fly?

Business Concept Development, the Macro View

Taking a "macroview" (looking at the big picture) involves taking a broader view of your product or service and the industry into which you're entering by looking for additional opportunities and potential pitfalls:

- Analyze the competitive situation in the industry and in your location
- Is anybody already doing it? If so, can you do it bigger, better, faster?
- If nobody is currently providing your product or service, why not?
- Determine the general tone of the industry into which you'll be entering: Growth industry, stagnant, dying, nonexistent...
- International opportunities
- Fresh opportunities in old industries/markets
- New opportunities in new industries/markets
- Look at general economic trends: Interest rates, inflation, market stability

If, after taking a closer look at your concept, you still feel confident about its potential, you are ready to begin a comprehensive investigation. Concept development is somewhat formal and disciplined, but will better guarantee the value and worth of the exercise and the success of the business.

Researching the Viability of the Concept

An accomplished pilot, Fowler began the next step of his concept development one month after his "Hope" vision by flying over the area known as "Schweitzer Basin" investigating the area's potential for snow skiing. On Memorial Day weekend, barely one month after his vision in Hope, Fowler hiked into the basin with his son and best friend. The trio explored the area and made the first modern day ski turns in Schweitzer Basin. Fowler had begun step three of his inspiration; he researched his idea.

This stage involves research, fact finding and gathering, analytical thinking, and capturing thoughts and ideas on paper. Seek outside advice when analyzing and developing your concept. Friends, family, retired business executives, professors, bankers and SBA officials, can all provide important, unbiased critiques of your idea.

Consider utilizing the following resources when researching your business concept:

- Small Business Development Center (SBDC)
- University and community libraries stock books
- Chamber of Commerce
- SBA sponsored SCORE (Service Corp. of Retired Executives) Chapter
- Banks: business advice, publications, forms, and other services
- The Internet
- SBA sponsored Business Information Center (BIC)

When determining the practicality of your business idea, it's important that you utilize a framework for your decision-making. A step-by-step critical pathway that is logical will enable you to work through your idea in a rational manner. Frequently, we become so excited by our business ideas that we loose track of critical questions we should be asking such as: "Even though I love this idea, will it sell?", "Is this the right time to be introducing this product?"

and "Are my investors willing to wait out another quarter before I start showing a profit?". A critical path seeks to question assumptions we are making in order to come up with the best answer. The simple diagram below illustrates the basic steps involved:

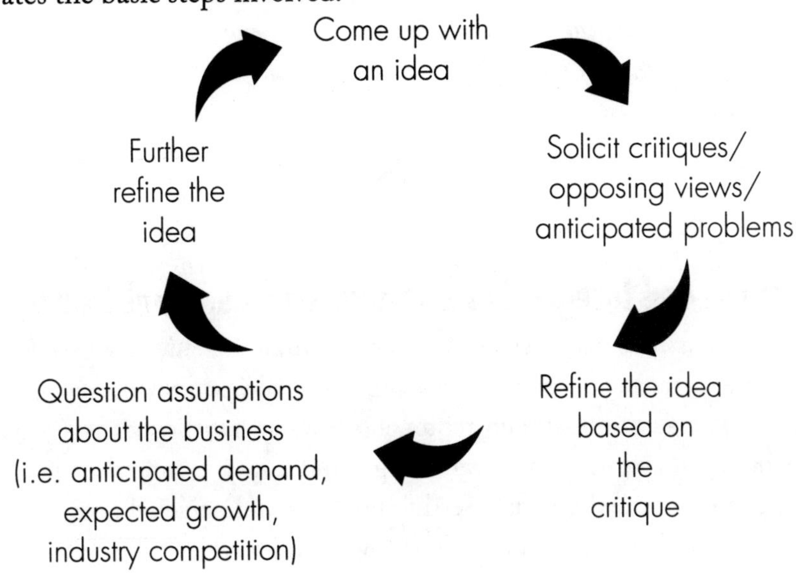

If you implement this process (or something like it) in your decision-making, you can help to insure that the conclusions you reach about your business are clear-sighted and take into account as many parts of your business as possible. While you should not become cynical about your concepts, it is healthy to question your assumptions from time to time to keep your business concept fresh and evolving.

Researching the Concept

Fowler's concept development work revealed that the basin did indeed have great potential as a ski resort. Fowler and his colleagues also determined that the local economy, strong during the summer months thanks to logging and the lake, needed help during winter. In his own words; "As I had it figured, we had the mountain, we had the snow, a lot of local folks wanted a good local ski area, and the economy was crying out for some wintertime action." Fowler continued, "As a kid growing up on a farm I learned... an idea is much like a seed; before planting it, first there has to be fertile ground. In late 1960, all factors seemed to indicate that Sandpoint, Idaho was fertile ground for my idea of a ski area.. I also learned on the farm that there can be any number of unforeseen glitches between planting and harvest time and glitches there were, in vast abundance," explained Fowler. "Thanks to my early experience in the world's riskiest business (farming), I expected them and was prepared to meet them." The concept development undertaken by Fowler and his associates up to this point involved researching areas crucial to the success of his idea; geologic and meteorological data, the political climate, economic factors, financial circumstances... Time and energy had been invested in the idea, but no significant capital resources had been committed.

Identifying and Integrating Business and Personal Goals

Reconciling business and personal goals is essential to achieving true "success" and is an important component of concept development. Success is relative and very personal. Successful entrepreneurs know what they want. If you don't know where you are, where you want to go, and how you intend to get there, you'll probably go nowhere fast. Setting business and personal goals helps keep both the business and the business owner on track.

Creating a goals list during concept development will prove invaluable in keeping both the business and business owner on track. Listing your own business and personal goals in order of importance will help you visualize and prioritize your goals as well as, avoid or minimize conflicts. Below is a list of typical business and personal goals:

Business Goals

- Reach a certain percent profit margin
- Establish a successful business and expand geographically
- Prestige... be the best product/service in the area
- Be the low cost leader of the industry

Personal Goals

- Invest $10,000 per year towards retirement
- Utilize my (writing, artistic, creative) skills
- Build business and retire within 10 years
- Keep business small and do what I love
- Sponsor community events... runs, cycling, concerts
- Minimize risk, even if it means not growing the business

The goals listed above are not mutually exclusive. In other words, striving to grow the business by 30% per year does not rule out spending time with the family. The purpose of listing goals is to set priorities and identify potential conflicts both within and between the two categories. This exercise will help the business and business owner focus and make decisions based on priorities.

From Concept to Reality

Finally, once you have acquired a business idea which seems to fit your personality and talents and meets needs in the market place, how do you evaluate whether it is a business opportunity?

Answering the following questions can help determine if your business idea might work:

Business Owner

- What must be done to turn this idea into a business?
- Do you know how? Can you learn how?

Customers

- Who will be the first customer?
- Why will they buy?
- How many will they buy ?
- Is it possible to reach my potential customer with my sales message?

Product

- Are necessary raw materials, supplies, equipment and production resources available?
- Is there a genuine need for the product?
- Is the need adequate to support a profitable business?
- Is it feasible to produce this product or provide the service?
- Can you acquire the necessary production technology?
- Is the product safe and legal?
- If the product must be serviced or guaranteed, who will do the service and guarantee the work?

Competition

- Who else is in this business?
- How do competitors package, market and price their products?
- How many competitors are there?

- What is my distinctive advantage over them?
- What will make it possible for this business to withstand competition if it comes?
- Who else is in as good or better position to undertake this business?

Business Future

Is there a future in this business?

- Is there room for growth?
- Can the idea be expanded into additional products or services?
- Is the market large enough for expansion?
- Can you expand by taking your product/service to new markets of different industries?
- What kind of a business can this become?
- Why does the opportunity for this business exist?
- Will the opportunity exist long enough to make it profitable?

Financial

- Do I have adequate resources to finance this venture?
- Will this business return adequate profit for my investment in time and money?
- When will break even be achieved?
- When will cash flow become positive?
- How sensitive are your financial projections to variations in key assumptions?
- Is the pay back period fast enough to allow you to stay in business?

Patent or Other Protection

- Can you protect the product with a patent or copyright?
- Does the product infringe on anyone else's patent or copyright?

Risks

- What is the potential downside loss?

Thinking about these questions will give you an advantage in preparing a start-up business plan as discussed in this book.

Eventually, the right combination of people, politics, funding, energy, ideas, and hard work came together in the right place at the right time, and in December of 1962, Schweitzer Basin Ski Resort opened with one chairlift and a day lodge at the base of the bowls where Fowler had first gazed from Hope 2 years earlier. Fowler's concept development lead to the creation of his dream: a challenging ski area close to his Spokane home where he, his family, and friends could indulge in the sport they loved. Fowler's concept development process guided him and his partners through the maze of glitches and challenges encountered while shepherding his idea from conception to reality.

In 1995 Schweitzer Mountain Resort was ranked among the top 20 ski resorts in North America by readers of Ski Magazine and the nearby town of Sandpoint was recognized as one of the prime "next generation ski towns" by Snow Country Magazine. Thirty-three years after Fowler's "vision" in Hope, Schweitzer employed a winter staff of over 500, featured 6 chair lifts, an 82 room hotel, over 200 slope-side residences, over 500 slope-side beds, a fire department, a state of the art water and sewer system, and an assessed property valuation of nearly $50 million.

Conclusion

Every new venture is a unique, individual idea. However, many new ideas as first conceived, are not very valuable. Working with them over time, adding input from knowledgeable sources and investigating them with a critical eye can propel the idea into a real business opportunity.

The hard work that carries dreams to reality is no accident. "Begin with the end in mind" is a saying used by many successful builders of great businesses. Good business concept development work will allow the potential business owner to visualize that "end" and thus, start the new venture on a firm foundation.

Chapter 4
A CUSTOMER-DRIVEN PHILOSOPHY

About This Chapter:
- *Who is number one?*
- *Customer driven companies*
- *Customer service*

Introduction

Whether it's manufacturing, retail or a traditional service business, business is all about customer service. Why? Customers will make a company grow. An entrepreneur has the opportunity to do many things the right way by learning from other businesses. Today, organizations of all types are doing everything they can to simulate the relationship that a small business has with its customer. In a variety of areas, Coca-Cola, General Motors, 3M and even the United States government are striving to "act small." They are creating smaller operating units known as project teams, profit centers, or work groups in order to be more accessible to and communicative with their customers. Successful organizations, large or small, see the customer as the very core of their business. Who is number one? The customer, of course!

"There is no product devoid of an accompanying relationship between buyer and provider."
—Karl Albrecht

In order to truly understand the customer, you must become the customer or at the very least, do everything to experience their world as they do. This includes how a business looks and feels to a customer compared to its competitors. Remember, it is not your customer's job to communicate to you what they value. Their communication occurs automatically in the form of their purchase.

Pitfalls of Product Oriented or Inward Looking Companies

Companies that focus on a particular product or technology instead of on the market are limiting their sales today and their growth (or survival) tomorrow. The same is true for companies whose internal bureaucracies and politics overshadow focusing on the customer. These businesses often subscribe to the "If we build it they will come" school of thought, rather than "What can we build to help our customers get where they want to go?". This is not to say that internal issues are not important. They are critical. But, these should never take precedence over customer issues.

Customers' needs change, and a business must be sure it's watching and listening so it can change, too. Yesterday's product may not serve tomorrow's need.

An outward-focused business cultivates a unique relationship with its customers. This task is not simply out to "make the customer happy." Rather, it involves a company-wide focus on better understanding customers' lives, anticipating changes in their needs, identifying new opportunities to serve them, and generally keeping your business "on its toes." This includes seeing customers' complaints as opportunities to learn and improve.

Customer complaints are opportunities to learn and improve

Why is such an approach so essential to running a profitable, successful business? Because it is increasingly difficult to differentiate a business simply on the basis of the "tangibles": product quality, technology and price. Nor does a business want to limit itself to these factors. Competing on the basis of price alone offers the customer no other way to compare businesses. And if nobody is offering a lower price today, someone may be tomorrow. On what other basis can your company compete?

Winners know that product and service are inseparable. Small companies are in a unique position to adapt to customer needs more quickly and creatively than their larger competitors. This is one of your most essential competitive advantages! Small companies are increasingly doing what the "big guys" do, like engaging in partnerships, strategic alliances, international trade and co-marketing ventures. But those who aren't taking advantage of their smallness to be responsive to their customers are throwing away their most powerful competitive tool.

Carl's Copy Shop, located in the rustic suburb of Chico, CA, already had a steady stream of customers from the local university. However, Carl Thompson realized that in order to keep up with national copy chains, he'd have to diversify the services he offered. So he decided to expand his range of services to include faxing, Internet access and Federal Express mailing services. By creating a one-stop shop for copying and mailing, he was able to compete against the giant down the street. As Carl puts it, "I knew I couldn't compete on a cost basis, so I decided to offer more than copying. I plan on continually innovating my service scheme to keep my customers coming through the door!"

Secrets of Customer-Driven Companies

Winners are businesses that successfully serve and anticipate the needs of their customers. Most successful companies have the following in common:

- Flexibility in leadership's thoughts and actions
- Unique knowledge of customer needs
- Ability to redefine the playing field
- Commitment to changing right along with the customer

Customer Service—a unique and powerful competition tool

Who is Your Customer

Understanding your customer means knowing how they use your product or service, and why they would choose you over your competitor. It means knowing about the customer's life—at work or at home, wherever the product or service is used.

The successful business person can provide a highly accurate profile of their customer(s). And they know when that profile changes.

As noted elsewhere in this book, this knowledge is reflected in the business plan, and in the firm's marketing and operating plans.

Here are some questions to help you demonstrate your knowledge of your customer:

- What my customer wants more than anything in the world is…?
- My customer is in the business of…?
- My customer is in the business because…?
- My customer's three biggest problems are…?
- If they could, my customer would…?
- My customer dreams to be…?
- In the future, my customer wants…?
- My customer is unique because…?

A good business person experiments with being the customer. "What do I want from this business? What do I see? What do I want to know?" You should distill the customer's issues down to two or three main problems.

Create a Customer "Value Profile"

How does your customer define value, and which things does your customer value most? Your customers judge the value you bring to them based on subjective and objective criteria, using the often repeated concept of "quality".

Are your products or services minimal, average, or excellent in quality? Only your customer can determine this. Your job is be the investigator, the listener, and the facilitator who can find out what the customer values, and more importantly, create and sustain the mechanisms to deliver it better than any of your present and future competitors. The way you achieve this will invariably be different than the way any of your competitors do. This uniqueness sets you apart and gives you your competitive edge. Your customer might ask you:

- Why should I be your partner?
- How are you different from your competitors?
- Can I rely on you?
- What is your cost structure?
- What can you do for me that is unique?
- Where do your see your business going in the next 6 months, 1 year, 3 years?

So to begin, you should first identify the business in which you operate. Ask yourself, "What do I offer? What is my product?". Take a moment out to define this as broadly as you can. Think in terms of intangible qualities that you offer such as convenience, creativity, reliability, time, or comfort. An example of this would be the pizzeria which delivers children's birthday pizzas to their customers' homes. This restaurant is in the business of doing much more than delivering tasty pizzas. They are selling convenience, spare time, and fun to their targeted family customers.

Identifying where your customer places value is simply another way of seeking ways to solve your customer's problems. Six basic questions can identify your customer's idea of value:

Walk a mile in their shoes

1. What does our customer want?
2. How does our product/service help our customer solve their problem?
3. What parts of our customer's dealings with us are most important to them?
4. How does our customer view doing business with us or our rivals?
5. What can we do to improve our customer's experience and distinguish ourselves from our competitors?
6. How are our customer's needs likely to change, and how are we preparing for that?

Create the Organization that Helps People Serve People

Your first task in **creating value** for your customer is to be sure your business has the tools it needs to deliver innovative and reliable service. Like many aspects of managing a business, creating a customer oriented business is not a one-time event. It is an ongoing process of building the people, structures and processes that support a strong customer relationship.

Everything that happens within an organization affects customer service

People

The way a business treats its people mirrors the way it treats it customers. It doesn't matter if you have three employees or three hundred, you must create an environment and culture that make your business a place where quality people want to be, and where quality service is delivered. This requires openness, trust and participation at all levels in searching for better ways to serve the customer.

You should:

- **Lay out the goals** of the organization clearly and often.
- **Establish employee training as an ongoing process.** Offer opportunities for people to learn about other functions in the business, market and industry. Create mixed teams to tackle specific problems and brainstorm solutions. Encourage employees to visit customers, sleuth out the competition, and set aside special times to take a fresh look at your business and customers.
- **Ask employees how they contribute to customer value—and how they could do more.**
- **Repeatedly demonstrate that each employee is an "internal customer"** who, without the proper tools, cannot effectively serve the external customer.
- **Create a system of measurement**, recognition and rewards for excellent customer service.

"Our goal as a company is to create customer service that is not just the best, but legendary."
—Paul Hawken

As a small VCR component subcontractor, Randy Regner knows that his business depends on being able to deliver high quality components on time to his client. In an effort to enthuse assembly-line employees, he made it a policy to regularly reward employees with additional vacation days for meeting or exceeding daily production quotas and deadlines. There is a rotating committee of employee leaders who work together to set their monthly production goals and these are proudly displayed around the plant. Employees are expected and encouraged to root out problems on the line and to seek out innovations in production. Because the employees' work is often monotonous, Regner brings in a masseuse every Tuesday and Thursday to give 15 minute stress reducing neck massages to employees. Randy feels it is essential to his business to motivate his employees to handle his customer's demands. By building loyalty with his employees, he is able to deliver the components his client needs.

Strategy

Having a clear strategy to guide your efforts is essential to providing good customer service. It can also stimulate ideas for improving service. Among effective strategies:

- **Get and keep the customer**. Earning the customer's initial business is one thing; keeping it is another. Depending upon the type of business, experts estimate that it costs three to five times more to find a new customer than to keep an old one. Repeat customers represent an ongoing revenue stream that is essential to your business. Consider the woman who buys a bagel that earns the deli $1 for each transaction. If she buys her bagel and does not return again, her business is worth exactly $1. However, if she returns 3 times a week, every week, for a year, that $1 grows to an impressive $156. Each time she comes back she contributes to the long-term revenue stream of the business.

- **Earn customers' loyalty by being loyal to them.** A key to having long-term business relationships with customers lies in repeatedly demonstrating your ability to predict their needs and meet them in creative ways.

- **Continually challenge assumptions.** When the customer shifts priorities, the best businesses see it coming. They also help customers identify new opportunities.

- **Communicate with your customer.** Most important: listen to and observe your customer. Nobody likes bad news, but gathering the bad news is more valuable than collecting pats on the back. Most business owners know what they're good at, but neglect those things that make them less comfortable. Critical feedback from customers can redirect your attention to those things that need improvement. Use every contact with the customer to learn to serve better.

- **Embrace the concept of Total Quality Service (TQS).** This popular management tool can be as important for small businesses as it is to the larger and mid-sized corporations who pioneered it. Much has been written about TQS and **Total Quality Management** (TQM). Your local bookstore will have several publications covering these management tools.

Systems

Systems and processes are the formal tools employees use to realize a strategy. Owners should focus on specific operational tasks that can speed up or enhance service, both internally and externally. To make customer service goals more real, the owner should write them down (see "Sample Customer Service Goals") and post them in a high-visibility spot.

Business owners should create a map of the organization, focusing on where, when and by whom customers are served. At each step, write a description of the tasks and goals involved. As the business grows, the map should be revised.

Manage customer service well and you will have more customers

A Customer Service Plan

Every business should have a **Customer Service Plan** within its marketing plan. This outlines who your customer is and how you deliver service to them. It should include:

- A statement summarizing your service goals to employees
- Your after-sales service practices
- Your return, exchange and customer complaint processing practices
- Your special order or custom service practices
- How different areas of your business deliver service
- Your system of internal training and rewards for customer service
- Your customer service benchmarks

Managing Customer Service

Managing is the process of setting goals, allocating resources and measuring performance. Managing **customer service** within your business requires creating the structures that will support the ongoing service your customers need. Below is a summary of some of the major elements of managing customer service:

- Setting and communicating customer service goals with a written Customer Service Policy
- Periodically reviewing and updating the Customer Service Policy
- Defining customer service Standards of Excellence
- Allocating responsibility and authority for various customer services
- Establishing a refund and exchange policy
- Allocating a "customer expert" who specifically deals with customer needs, trends, complaints; regularly compiles internal Customer Reports
- Creating a formal system by which sales and support people report customer feedback
- Measuring service delivery: set regular intervals for checking service progress
- Identifying how and why service has failed
- Allocating time for brainstorming new service opportunities

Creating these structures and policies early on will ensure that customer service is "built in" to your business. But how can you equip your people to be the best service providers possible?

When Linda Rogers and Gayle Corson decided to open, La Femme, a women's fine lingerie shop in Grosse Pointe, Michigan they knew they would be in competition with other national chains that are devoted to lingerie. However, by researching the lingerie market, they realized that there was an untapped market. Rogers and Corson decided to innovate by reaching out to larger women, petites, and pregnant women — a niche market unserved by the larger stores. Their business supplies fine lingerie to women of all shapes and sizes who have difficulty finding attractive lingerie elsewhere. Utilizing special touches like a complimentary glass of wine for shoppers, personal shopping services, and a frequent shopper card, the proprietors of La Femme recognized that by going the extra yard, they could develop a loyal following. They are now launching their own mail-order catalog and will be opening up a branch in Ann Arbor, Michigan very soon.

Customer Service and Your Employees

Whether you have one or one hundred employees, you and your staff are the first line of direct contact your business has with its customers. Every employee should embody your customer service policy. Let them know what you expect of them. Give them the freedom to innovate new ways to deliver customer service. Let them contribute to and continually improve your Customer Service Policy. Below are some additional suggestions for getting the best service out of your employees:

- Hire inspired, curious and committed people
- Incorporate customer service elements in every job description
- Post your Customer Service Policy prominently in your office
- Teach employees to teach your customers: help employees develop their product expertise and encourage them to share their expertise with customers
- Help your employees to understand all key areas of your business, so that they can quickly answer customer questions and locate appropriate problem solvers
- Teach your employees to find answers to customer questions: It's OK not to know all the answers as long as they know where to get the answers
- Let your employees know how much you value their extra efforts to serve customers; thank them often and publicly for good service

Employees are the most important link to your customers

- Create a system of rewards and incentives for customer service. Tie rewards to things like minimizing customer complaints, product returns, customer wait times, or new customer service ideas
- Identify and reward employees who share knowledge with customers and cooperate with other employees. Peer reviews and customer surveys are a great way to identify your service "stars"
- Educate all of your employees in customer service. Even back office and logistics people should know the important role they play in delivering quality service. Encourage them to view frontline people as their customers

Saturn Motor Company was able to enter the already crowded world of car sales by offering something different—the no pressure car sale. Saturn decided to create a welcoming atmosphere for customers tired of high-pressure, fast-talking salespeople. Saturn has built its softer image around the needs of people looking to buy a car who are unhappy with wheeling and dealing. Salespeople wear non-intimidating khakis and polo shirts. They do not work on commission. They have developed a reputation for customer service—even offering to fly a prospective customer to a showroom 200 miles away from their home. The purchase of a Saturn car is showcased as a celebration where the new car owner is photographed as a pleasant memento of their equally pleasant car-buying experience. The proof of such a customer focused business is in the number of Saturns you see on the highway today.

Sample Customer Service Goals

- Answer all written queries within 2 days
- Answer the phone within 3 rings
- Reduce the number of returned / incorrect orders by 50%
- Increase rate of customer referrals to 2 per customer
- Reduce customer order turnaround time by 50%

Employee policies and practices make your customer service strategy come to life. They provide the goals and the rewards for good service. If you hire people carefully, train them and allow them to be creative, your business will develop a unique and unbeatable service "personality."

Customer Service Practices

The sections above have described what a customer service business looks like on the inside. But what does it sound like and look like on the outside? Here are some of the most important **customer services practices**. These should be a starting point for your own service Strategies. Can you deliver new kinds of service that your customer values?

- When a customer enters your place of business, greet them immediately and pleasantly
- When a mistake occurs, quickly and professionally accept responsibility and fix it

- Always make an extra effort to help the customer find what they need. If customer service is the only thing that sets you apart from your competition, you should go to great lengths to satisfy them
- Follow-up on all customer contacts: always record a customer's name, phone number and order type. After customers call for product information or service assistance, follow up within 2 days to check on their satisfaction
- Make sure employees look professional and tidy when they deal with customers
- Thank your customers every chance you get
- Thank your employees for excellent service every chance you get
- Always answer the phone within 3 rings
- When you or your staff answers the phone, identify yourselves and your business and ask how you may help
- Try calling yourself; call your own business and pretend to be a customer to gauge service levels
- Don't "dump" customers on hold. If you must, ask if you can put them on hold or call them back within 5 minutes
- Periodically survey customer satisfaction with brief questionnaires

Maintaining focus on the customer in the face of the daily challenges of operating a business is one of the toughest parts of being a manager. But keeping your eye on "the big picture" of the business and the customer's problems will always pay off.

Customer Service Tips

- Service is a problem solving passion
- Solving your customer's problems requires persistence
- Good service is contagious
- Listen to the bad and act on it
- All employees are service employees
- Good service is marked by good manners and politeness
- Those who focus on customers grow, those who don't—won't!

Conclusion

The practices and structures outlined above are the beginning of your customer service strategy. This strategy ensures that you are proactive in delivering what your customers need and want.

Your customers are a valuable source of information for your business. If you listen, they will tell you what they want. If you plan your strategy carefully, you can deliver what your customers want faster and better than any of your competitors. After all, this is one of the best competitive advantages there is.

Further, as a customer oriented business you will be able to create long term business relationships, generate enthusiastic referrals, and envision new product and service opportunities. These are the keys to long term profits. Remaining open to exploring new ways to look at your customer will go a long way towards keeping you focused and fresh in your efforts. Businesses that succeed at this have fun watching their profits grow.

Chapter 5
OVERVIEW OF MANUFACTURING, SERVICE AND RETAIL

About This Chapter:
- *Manufacturing businesses*
- *Service businesses*
- *Retail businesses*

Introduction

The three major categories of businesses are manufacturing, retail, and service. Presented here is basic information about the particulars of these businesses so that you can make an informed decision about the type of venture you would like to start.

This chapter is not designed to be is a comprehensive guide on how to begin a manufacturing, service or retail business. There are many books dedicated to each of these subjects, which you can and should use. What this chapter does offer you is an understanding of trends, competition, organizational challenges, and skills needed to excel in these businesses.

As we explore the differences between these businesses keep in mind that these businesses are rapidly changing. For example, look at the icon of fast food—McDonald's. What category of business does it fall into? Is it a manufacturer because it produces or buys ground beef and turns it into hamburgers? Is it a service provider because it sells time savings, convenience, and a safe and clean meeting place for its customers? Or is it a retailer because it sells directly to the public in street front locations? The answer is that McDonald's is all three. This is precisely why it has been so successful. Like many other successful businesses, McDonald's identified where several categories of businesses overlapped and created a truly original business concept.

The World of Manufacturing

Huge conveyor belts chugging along, heavy metal machinery stamping out steel parts and sparks flying. This is what probably springs to mind when most people think of manufacturing. Manufacturing has traditionally been defined as the mass production of components and finished products. Mass production is based on the concept of **economies of scale**. The more that is produced with the same machinery and overhead, the lower the per unit costs and the higher the profitability.

Manufacturing isn't just limited to such large scale operations. It exists in all parts of the world, in every conceivable shape and size. Everyday small bakeries, specialty textile mills, micro-breweries and piece assembly shops manufacture goods for market. They compete fiercely to do so. Manufacturing of one sort or another touches everything you use on a daily basis.

Types of manufacturing operations

There are four basic types of manufacturing operations:

- Make to stock
- Assemble to order
- Make to order
- Engineer to order

Trends in manufacturing

Manufacturing today is very different than it was 20 years ago. Manufacturing is now defined by increased international competition, rising cost of labor, and technological innovations. These have spurred the development of new managerial approaches like **employee work teams, Total Quality Management** and **Just In Time Inventory**. These improvements upon traditional manufacturing models have revolutionized the way the world builds things.

Today manufacturing businesses of nearly every shape and size are influenced by the following major trends:

- Producing innovative and advanced products
- Speed and flexibility of operations
- Teaming of cross-functional employees
- Hiring and training employees to be multi-skilled
- Empowerment–giving more responsibility and authority to employees
- Flattening out traditional organizational hierarchies
- Creating flexible production systems to do smaller production runs
- Environmental issues and regulations

The time element

The name of the game for manufacturers is time. It typically takes 6 months to a year to set up a major manufacturing business.

Time is the most important element of client satisfaction. Why this emphasis on speed? Because in the last 5-7 years business transactions or **cycle times** have compressed by over half. To retain market share manufacturers are redesigning products and creating entirely new models more frequently. They do this because customers are demanding it. Increased competition has added to this trend as has the introduction of more innovative technology capable of speeding transactions.

Time is of the essence in the computer industry where constant innovation is required of all software and hardware manufacturers. In order to meet the changing needs of computer users worldwide, manufacturers are always updating their software programs and computer designs to provide better service. Bill Gates, famous entrepreneur and leader of Microsoft, is a case in point. His recent introduction of Windows '95, an operating system that is faster and easier to use than its predecessor, shows the importance of getting your innovations out to the marketplace as quickly as possible in order to take advantage of consumer demand.

More often than not the customer to whom manufacturers sell are businesses, who in turn assemble a product and must compete with other businesses to meet the demands of customers. With more businesses selling overseas, manufacturers must incorporate into their production schedules enough time to allow for shipping, customs processing, and multiple quality checks. All of these things take time—time that can be minimized by speeding the **front end** processes like sourcing, product development and manufacturing.

The emphasis is on speed—customers demand it

As a result of this emphasis on high speed "lean and mean" production, the definition of manufacturing is being continually reinvented. Today, what used to be considered core to manufacturing (product development, design, assembly, and logistics) is often performed by other businesses through outsourcing agreements, strategic alliances, and partnerships. In fact, a "manufacturer" many not even manufacture any part of their product. They may only assemble it from component parts bought from partners who may not operate in the same state or even the same country. These businesses only manufacture their products in the sense that they control the trademark, patent, design, channels of distribution and after-sales service to the customer.

This represents a shift in manufacturing towards creating a "virtual" organization as opposed to the traditional "vertical" organization. **Virtual** businesses are defined by the number of tasks that they pay other businesses or individuals to perform. The creation of value occurs outside the business.

A well known manufacturer in Maine markets kayaks. In reality, the only function it actually performs is coordinating a network of suppliers and craftsmen who do everything from craft specialty parts to assemble the finished kayak. The virtual manufacturer then markets the finished kayaks to customers via retail sporting goods chains and a mail order catalog.

The virtual model of business spells major opportunity for even the smallest and newest of manufacturers

In contrast **vertical** businesses are defined by the number of core functions (sourcing inputs, shipping and warehousing goods, and distribution) they perform themselves. A **vertical integration** strategy implies that a business controls the supply of all or many of its own inputs, and performs its own value generating activities. Perhaps the most famous example of this comes from the earlier days at Henry Ford's Motor Company. Ford owned and operated its own iron ore mines, steel plants, metal stamping and finishing shops, assembly lines, and sales show rooms. In many ways Ford set the standard for vertical integration.

What does this mean for entrepreneurial businesses? The virtual model of business spells major opportunity for even the smallest and newest of manufacturers. These businesses can step in to perform specific functions for larger manufacturing companies at competitive prices.

Benefits of the Vertical vs. the Virtual Manufacturing Organization

Vertical Benefits

- Cost savings and economies of scale
- Employment security
- Control over strategic information or proprietary technology
- Lower risk: ensured supplies of inputs
- Ability to sell excess capacity for additional revenue
- Faster, shared learning among value creating functions

Benefits of the Vertical vs. the Virtual Manufacturing Organization (cont'd)

Virtual Benefits

- Components are bought at lowest total cost, considering service, quality and impact on lead times
- Lower overhead, quicker break-even
- Greater organizational "stretch": business is able to do more tasks with fewer people
- Suppliers are consolidated to reduce variation in quality, increase control and cooperation, reduce administrative costs

A Look At Vertical Integration:

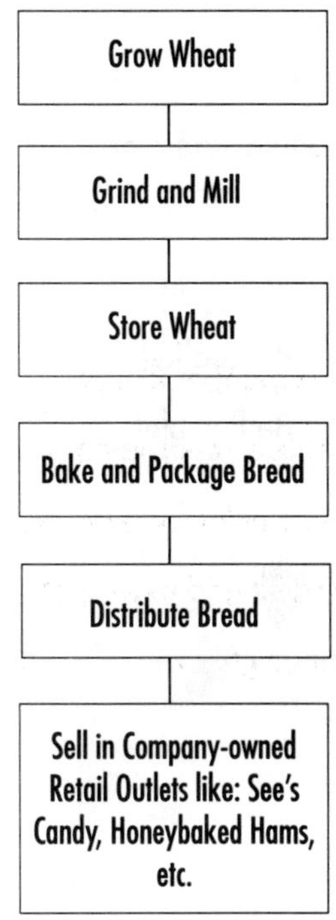

Competitive challenges

For large manufacturers, competition is tougher now than it has ever been. Lower trade barriers, the availability of cheaper overseas labor, innovations in information technology and communications, strategic alliances and partnerships, and shifting consumer demand continually alter the landscape of manufacturing.

The most common practices for competing in manufacturing are:

- Responding to changes in customer needs
- Pricing products competitively
- Delivering high quality and innovative customer service
- Adapting product specifications to global customers
- Striking a balance between customizing and standardizing products
- Cost control while providing high quality products

The manufacturer's business strategy

Like all business people, manufacturers must decide what, where, when and how to produce their goods. Their foremost strategic planning issues are:

- Where to produce the product or components
- The degree to which they will be virtual vs. vertical
- Competitive positioning: Will they lead on price? Quality? Customer service?
- How to incorporate innovative technology into their products or manufacturing process
- Which geographic markets they will serve

- Identifying their target customer segments
- What channels of distribution they will use
- How they will provide after-sales service and technical support

To compete manufacturers of all sizes must:

- Be quick!
- Be quality!
- Be flexible!

The customer

Who are manufacturer's customers? We are manufacturer's final customers because we ultimately drive the cars, eat the bread and type on the computers that are manufactured. However, long before these finished products are sold in the consumer marketplace, they go through several phases of production and assembly.

In manufacturing, supplier and customer relationships more closely resemble partnerships than those in service and retail businesses. Some of the defining characteristics of customer relationships in manufacturing include:

- Anticipating and responding quickly to customer needs
- Varied customer bases, sometimes in other countries
- Designing and producing products tailored to a specific customer
- Quick delivery times
- Close communication links via computer and phone lines
- Extensive technical support and follow up service
- Cooperative sharing of information and production needs
- Service! Service! Service!

Since they often purchase their inputs from a variety of competitors locally, regionally and even internationally, business customers require that manufacturers conform to international standards for quality, performance and size. Customer requirements vary widely depending upon the products they are buying.

A solid relationship with your suppliers is critical

The suppliers

In manufacturing, solid relationships with suppliers can mean the difference between being in business, and being out of business! Some of the most common traits of supplier relationships in manufacturing are:

- Shared turn-around time
- Shared standards of quality
- Close proximity by geography and/or communication
- Flexible and collaborative problem solving
- Joint production scheduling
- Use of backup suppliers
- Tough price competition among suppliers

Operational & Managerial Challenges

A good starting point when analyzing any sort of business is to ask: where and how is value created in the business? Manufacturers (more so than retailers or service businesses) rely on equipment to produce their goods. Also necessary are employees with the expertise to operate the equipment. Let's look at how manufacturers approach their major business functions and issues.

People management

The most successful manufacturers consider their employees to be human assets of greater value than their equipment. Well trained employees are viewed by successful manufacturers as the best defense against competitors who employ lower wage workers. The more skilled an employee, the better able they are to perform multiple functions and identify and correct manufacturing problems. Today manufacturers tend to invest considerable time and money in training and updating the technical skills of their employees and place a great deal of emphasis on reducing employee turnover.

Traditionally, factory worker's hourly pay was based on seniority. Today, many compensation strategies focus on the total output of the business. In businesses with work teams, employees compensation may also be pegged to team performance.

The role of technology

Manufacturers large and small rely on new technologies to:

- Communicate with customers and suppliers
- Control product quality
- Standardize production processes
- Analyze product specifications
- Design products
- Simulate production runs
- Track products from inventory to delivery

What does a manufacturer look like?

In manufacturing businesses all work and processes are tailored to support the core function: manufacturing products. Organizational structures and processes tend to focus on reducing lead times, lowering inventories, speeding machine set-up times, lowering costs, improving quality, and accelerating product delivery times. All add up to competitive advantages in the market place. There is a particular trend among manufacturers today to increase employee involvement. This means using the creative energies of all employees to solve problems with innovative solutions.

Saab is an industry leader in creating employee teams to insure quality control, employee involvement and employee innovations in the manufacturing process. After several years of lagging sales, Saab decided to look within and conducted an extensive study of employee's motivations, work conditions, complaints and ideas for improvements, Saab determined that it would be better to operate its assembly line in a non-traditional way. Rather than utilize the Ford-inspired model of repetitive assembly line work, an entire car is assembled by one work team—from chassis to leather seats. Workers feel they have more of a stake in the finished product and Saab has seen production costs decrease with savings such as lowered employee sick days and decreased production errors!

So, what do manufacturing businesses look like from the inside out? Today, many manufacturers have shifted away from the traditional organizational structure focused on functions (marketing, finance, engineering etc.) towards creating product oriented structures.

Product Focused Organization

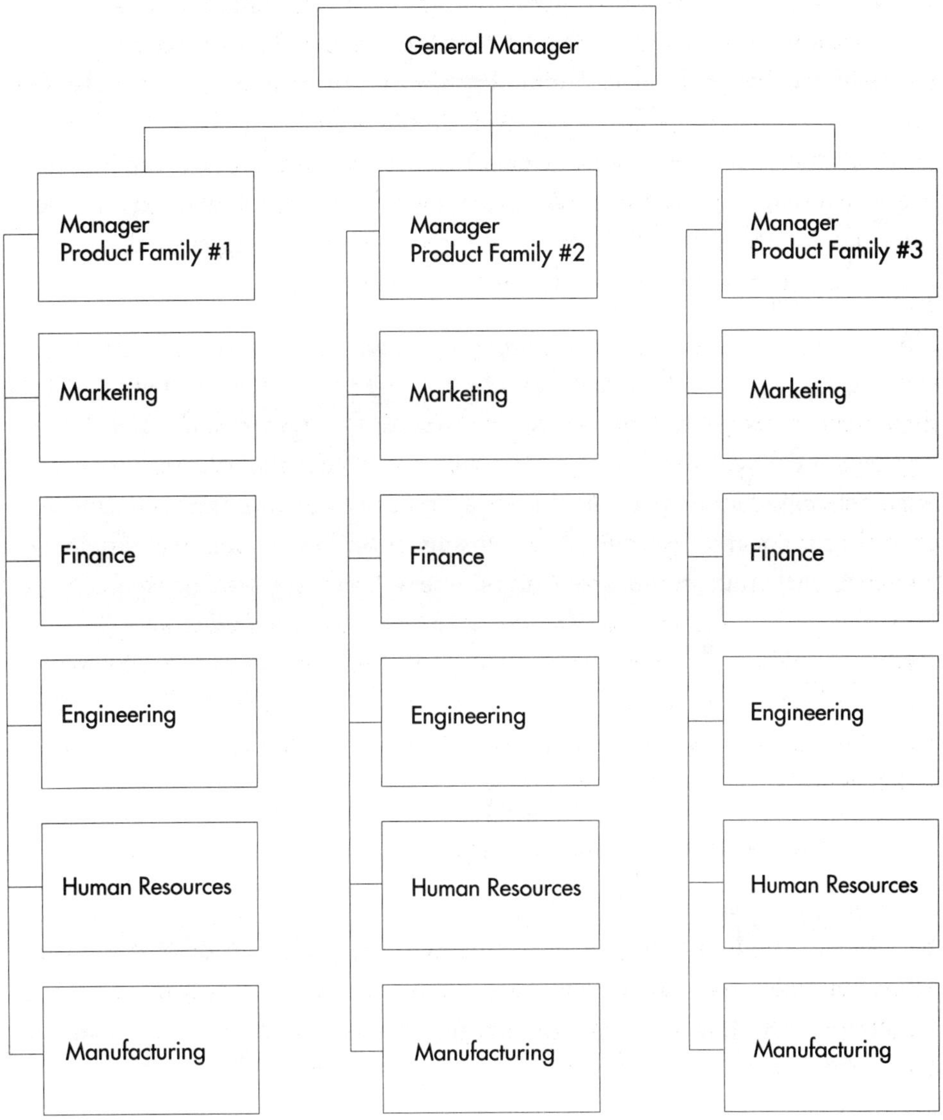

Quality and manufacturing

Manufacturing is consistently reproducing the same process and the same quality product again, and again, and again. Some other elements of manufacturing quality are:

- Satisfying customer needs
- Total control over product and process
- A high performing, multi-skilled employee
- Quality conformance
- Detecting and controlling product and manufacturing defects

Manufacturers maintain quality by inspecting their products at multiple checkpoints and stages in the production process. Ever find a sticker on your new stereo or sweatshirt that says, "Inspected by #9"? This identifies who had the responsibility and the accountability for a particular product's quality. How often and in what degree of detail products are inspected determines their ultimate quality. Manufacturers must continually strike a balance between maximizing the number of quality inspections and minimizing the time and cost of doing so.

Financial issues

Unless you want to build a retail store with gold fixtures and marble floors, starting a manufacturing business requires more financial investment than beginning either a retailing or service business. Plant, machinery, and equipment call for a heavy investment up-front. Once they've set up the business, manufacturer's major financial issues revolve around controlling costs for inputs and materials and counting and valuing inventory. The major elements of manufacturers product and operational cost structure are:

- Worker hours
- Inputs and materials
- Machine time
- Capital overhead
- Product marketing and selling
- Research and development

Are you a manufacturer at heart?

What sort of skill does it take to begin a manufacturing business? What sort of personalities excel in this field? Because manufacturing tends to require more technical expertise than either retailing or service businesses, the most successful manufacturers have educational and professional backgrounds in production or engineering. People who perform well in manufacturing generally:

Are you a talker? A doer? An organizer? A seller? Or, perhaps a little bit of all four?

- Are gifted at identifying and managing new production processes
- Can talk and think like an engineer
- Prefer assembly lines, production schedules and machines
- Have found or invented a unique product or process
- Have long range conceptualization and planning skills

How is manufacturing different?

Manufacturing can require more time, expertise, and financial resources than either retailing or service businesses. Manufacturing relies heavily on capital equipment and the expertise of the owner. Manufacturers are vulnerable to supplier problems, labor costs and union pressures. Manufacturers are often forced to create plans that project well into the future. The time-frame for completing business transactions tends to be longer in manufacturing than in either service or retail businesses. Furthermore, manufacturing businesses tend to be linked to long-term consumer patterns and cycles in the economy.

Transaction trends are longer in the manufacturing business

Start-up opportunities

What opportunities exist for an aspiring start-up manufacturer? There are more opportunities now for the "small guy" than ever before. Given the shift towards the creation of virtual businesses, many opportunities exist for small scale, highly specialized manufacturers to provide inputs to larger manufacturers. Comparatively speaking these limited production operations require less capital investment to begin. Furthermore, given their limited production scope (performing **piece work**) the small manufacturer may need only invest in one or two high quality, hi-tech pieces of manufacturing equipment.

Service Businesses

Hospitals, telecommunications providers, shipping companies, house painters, even baby-sitters all make up the services sector of the economy. The service economy has more small businesses and one-person providers than in either retailing or manufacturing. It is also the fastest growing sector in the U.S economy today.

Service businesses are based on providing expertise and convenience to customers when, where, and how they need it. Many service providers don't work out of their own office. Consider management consultants or computer support experts. During the length of their consulting engagements these service providers may take up residence within the company to whom they are offering service.

Trends in service businesses

The most important trends that are impacting this fast growth business category are:

- **Downsizing of companies:** Large corporations have reduced their numbers of full-time employees and begun relying on a growing number of independent contractors to perform non-core functions.
- **Repairing and re-using existing products:** Consumers are buying more expensive, higher quality durables and they repair and upgrade rather than replace them.
- **The crunch for time:** As more members of households go to work, there are fewer people left at home to do basic household chores. Time is at a premium.
- **Obtaining and processing information:** Because of advances in information technology there is more information available which needs to be organized and processed into usable forms.
- **Bringing order to chaos:** Specialized businesses provide order and create time savings for other businesses and individuals.
- **Targeting niche markets:** Businesses of all types have begun to benefit by dividing larger customers into **niche** markets. The smaller the group, the more targeted a business's marketing efforts can be.
- **Higher expectations for service:** Individuals and businesses expect better service increasing opportunities in this area.

Exceptional service is the key to a great service company

Competitive challenges

Service providers compete on the basis of how well they are able to serve the needs of their targeted customers. In general, the most competitive service businesses are able to:

- Segment their customers
- Provide reliable and consistent service
- Price their services at competitive yet profitable levels
- Provide innovative services
- Deliver their services in innovative ways
- Provide timely or convenient service
- Offer unique expertise

Service businesses are now just beginning to feel the same international competitive pressures that manufacturers have been contending with for over 15 years. For larger service businesses, many customers are already multinational in scope. Providing services to these customers may require a business to perform in a variety of cultural, regulatory, legal, geographic and linguistic environments! Even small service businesses are springing to life to serve international customers.

More so than other businesses, the service business's entire strategy should revolve around the customer

The Service Provider's Business Strategy

More so than other businesses, the service business's entire strategy should revolve around the customer.

The customer

Service businesses sell to other businesses as well as to individuals. In each case customer expectations are as different as the relationship between the buyer and the seller.

A major challenge for businesses offering services is to make real the intangible benefits their service delivers. A tax preparation consultant might point out the tax savings they can offer. Or the employee trainer might focus on the higher worker productivity and long-term cost savings his seminars provide.

Customers of service businesses tend to be interested in the latest and greatest trend. When an idea or process gets "old" a new opportunity exists for an innovative approach. Businesses must be aggressive to keep the customer's interest and loyalty. Service businesses must constantly update their expertise and enhance their service.

Alternative Service Delivery Systems:

- Mail contact
- Computers/Email/Internet
- Telephone contact
- Face-to-face standard delivery
- Face-to-face moderate customization
- Face-to-face total customization

How do companies deliver their services to customers? Either face-to-face as gardeners or doctors do, or indirectly through the mail, telephone or computer. Travel agents often deliver their services entirely through indirect customer contact. They may offer fare quotes over the phone and mail brochures about potential destinations to customers. Unlike manufacturing and retailing businesses, service businesses have a great deal of flexibility as to how, where and when to deliver their service.

Another unique feature of many service businesses is that they can involve their customers in the design and delivery of the their services. Also, customers often make valuable contributions to the organization's structure, policies and performance as well.

Why is this? Because in service businesses more so than in manufacturing and retail businesses, customers have an on-going relationship and multiple points of contact with a service provider. This offers opportunities for feedback, rapport and repeated assessment of customer needs. Truly competitive service businesses maximize this opportunity to increase customer loyalty. Some well known service providers like Southwest Airlines actually ask business customers to be part of teams responsible for hiring customer service agents. A more widespread practice is the use of customer satisfaction surveys. Hotels, car rental companies and even mail order companies use these to gauge their performance and better understand customer preferences.

Operational and Managerial Challenges

Major operational challenges for service businesses include the following:

- Identifying their core service
- Deciding to what degree they will customize or standardize their services
- The professionalism of service employees
- Print, video and voice media that communicate the nature of the service
- Accurately measuring costs and pricing services
- Ensuring consistency and quality in service delivery

Organizational structure

Organizational culture describes a business's values and how people within it interact and perform their duties. Individual employees play a large role in all the elements of the product's creation, design and delivery. Some service organizations operate with a very traditional, layered hierarchy. A **hierarchical management structure** is one in which people are organized in "layers" according to their rank or authority. Vice presidents, area managers, managers, assistants, and hourly employees are examples of different management levels. Examples of hierarchical structures are the U.S Military, traditional accounting firms, and some management consulting firms. Other service businesses have entirely flat management structures. Examples of these would be restaurants, photo processors, roofers and landscapers.

Employee management

Service businesses train and manage their employees differently depending upon the industry in which they operate and the level of service they provide. As more expertise is required of employees, compensation demands rise, as does the need for other types of rewards.

Service businesses know that their employees who interact with customers make or break their business. Employees often have to assess customer needs, tailor the service "package" and control for quality of the service at the same time as they deliver the service. This is a lot to ask. For this reason, service businesses tend to hire people capable of performing multiple tasks, train them to work in teams, and give them greater flexibility in how they perform their specific tasks.

The Walt Disney Company is well-known for its investment in training for its employees who have personal contact with customers at Disney theme parks. Employees are called "cast members" to reinforce the idea that they are providing entertainment for the park visitors, called "guests". Cast members receive intense training on how to approach visitors. For instance, cast members dressed up as a Disney figure are forbidden to talk to guests because Disney does not want to shatter the illusion of the character by a voice that doesn't seem to fit the character. Employees have to enter and leave the parks through specially designed tunnels so that guests do not see them outside of their outfits. Disney goes one step further in its service efforts. Even corporate employees are called "cast members" and must work in a theme park for at least one day, in order to understand the importance of the entire Disney "product". Disney's goal is to create a consistent and reliable image for the company through its cast members: they are courteous, competent, attentive and fun!

What is quality to a service business?
Characteristics of excellence in service business include:

- A quantitative approach to measuring customer needs
- Focus of all the business resources on meeting customer needs
- Continual measurement of performance against competitors
- Focus on service improvement to increase customer satisfaction
- Aggressive efforts to minimize the time to meet customer needs
- Focus on core services that affect cost and customer satisfaction
- Use of technology to enhance contact with customers
- Consistency of performance by delivering the service at the promised time

The service business...

focus or disappear!

Quality in service businesses is often defined as good old fashioned politeness. Courtesy, respect, and downright friendliness can mean the difference between a one time customer and truly loyal fan. Below are listed a summary of these and other elements of service quality.

Service Quality Essentials

- Reliability
- Responsiveness
- Expertise
- Easy access
- Good communication
- Politeness & respect
- Trustworthiness and honesty
- Security and confidentiality
- Knowing the customer's specific needs

Financial issues

Fixed costs generally make up the majority of service providers' costs. For example, a tree trimmer can trim an additional tree using his existing set of tools. Therefore, his cost of pruning one additional tree is minimal. On the other hand, if he wants to trim trees for an entire neighborhood, he will have to hire an assistant and get more equipment. Having done so, the tree trimmer will again be able to trim many more trees, that is, until he hits his new maximum capacity. This is the concept of **incremental capacity gains** for service providers. Service providers have relatively low marginal costs for serving small numbers of additional customers. They must increase capacity in order to meet additional demands.

Are you a service provider at heart?

Service businesses are successful because they know their customer well. They tend to customize the services they provide for each customer. Communication and follow-up with customers are especially important. For these reasons, people who excel in service businesses tend to be:

To be successful–

know your customer!

- Good at interpersonal communication
- Confident
- Creative thinkers
- Self-disciplined and independent
- Flexible
- Able to adapt their knowledge to many different situations
- Expert in a specific field
- Interested in popular culture, and are able to identify and act on major trends

How are services different?

Compared to other types of business, the business of delivering services is flexible and relatively low-cost to enter. Service businesses tend to have:

- Closer relationships with customers
- Lower overhead
- Easier entry and exit into business
- Less emphasis on geographic location of the business
- A smaller management team, often just one person
- More uncertain demands on employees

Opportunities

Given the explosive demand for services, there are many opportunities for start-up businesses. Trends in the service sector suggest that many niche markets are opening up. Corporate downsizing, outsourcing, and the globalization of business have combined to create many new service sector jobs. Small service businesses are stepping in to provide speedy, niche services to businesses of all types as well as to individuals.

Retail Businesses

The crowds are streaming in, the registers are ringing, and somewhere over an intercom a voice is saying, "Attention K-Mart shoppers!" This is the sound of retailing in action. Perhaps no other type of business is as familiar to Americans. Wal-Mart, Safeway, Nordstrom, True Value and Ben and Jerry's have become part of our national consciousness. They provide us with the products we need, at the prices we want, and the social interaction we enjoy. They offer us the latest in fashions, food and fun.

Trends in retailing

Retailing has been going through a profound shift in the past 15 years. More large-scale retailers have emerged and more shopping malls have cropped up to house scores of national chains. In many towns, malls have replaced downtown areas by offering safe, clean, convenient and stylish environments where people can buy everything from sleeping bags to sushi.

Nearly 30% of all new businesses are retail. Retail stores buy merchandise from wholesalers or manufacturers and resell these goods directly to consumers. The value they provide customers is in conveniently assembling and displaying products, and creating a unique and compelling environment in which to buy.

Many people compare retailing to theater. Restaurants are one of the largest categories of businesses that fall under the mantle of retailing. They know better than anyone the value of attracting and retaining customers. Retailers create a distinct environment that influences consumers, and inspires them to buy. How do they do this? By understanding the customer they are targeting, and creating environments that appeal to them.

Swedish homeware and furniture retailing giant IKEA has been hugely successful at doing this. It offers supermarket style shopping areas and sample rooms that maximize and play upon the youthful, cost consciousness of targeted customers. IKEA even has elaborate play areas for kids, in-store restaurants offering Swedish food, and huge grocery style carts for customers. The experience of shopping in an IKEA is fun, distinctly Swedish and very entertaining.

There are many different types of retailers. Consider a few:

- Store retailers
- Mail order
- Automatic merchandising
- Direct, door-to-door selling

The trend toward large scale, "chain" retailers notwithstanding; many are still run by the owner, who began the business because they have expertise and an interest in a particular type of product. These retailers often lack sophisticated purchasing, planning, cost control, and merchandising expertise. They are simply in the business because they love their products and the customers they serve.

Small scale retailers have been remarkably resilient in the face of heavy competition from the retailing giants. Why? They offer consumers personal service, low stress buying experiences and a down home atmosphere.

Mass retailers simply don't provide this type of service. Ever try getting some technical information about a CD player from a salesperson at a huge department store? Large retailers may not attempt to provide high quality service. Instead they have focused on offering a wide selection of products at competitive prices.

The retailer's business strategy

Like other businesses, successful retailers segment their customer base and focus on meeting their needs.

Target! Target! Target!

Best Buy sells electronic goods to middle income families. Their customers want to browse and buy in one visit. They don't need extensive information or technical support. Best Buy has focused on delivering a wide selection of products, creating an open and light environment, and offering low prices.

The other end of the spectrum is a provider of high cost products accompanied by "luxury" service. Patagonia, a sports clothing store, is a great example. Some of their high performance, all weather coats retail for over $400, and are nearly indestructible. And what if your dog finds a way to chew a hole in your new Patagonia foul weather sailing jacket? The company will replace it immediately, no questions asked. Salespeople at Patagonia match the profile of their target customer: they are well educated, serious outdoor types. They are experts on the clothing and the conditions in which they can be used. Unlike Best Buy, Patagonia spends money on hiring and training employees who will inspire customers to buy their gear. Both businesses are successful because they create their business strategies around their customers.

Location, location, location!

Perhaps the single most important element that determines success in retailing is location. Customers will shop where it is convenient. Identifying the right location for a retail store is a very tricky task. Large, national retailers like Home Depot and Wal-mart spend millions of dollars paying experts to perform market research to identify the spot where their business will have the best chances of succeeding.

How do retailers decide on location? First and foremost they target their customer. Where their customer lives, works and shops are key indicators of good locations.

Secondly, retailers consider the type of merchandise they sell. If they carry specialty products, they might not be as choosy about a central location, since customers will be willing to travel further to find their product. If a retailer carries convenience goods (coffee, fast food, photo copying services) then they will locate themselves in convenient spots for their customers. When choosing a location, retailers consider:

- Corners of blocks (they have higher visibility and more traffic)
- Who their retailing neighbors are
- The cost of renting space
- The image or feel of the block or neighborhood
- The image of the building and retail space
- Parking availability for customers
- The location and number of competitors
- Zoning regulations
- Traffic flows
- Nearby landmarks, industries and tourist attractions
- Opportunity for expansion
- Demographic characteristics of the area

Great locations: where the customer lives, works and shops

A word on shopping centers

The popularity of homogenous suburban shopping centers shows no signs of subsiding. Therefore, you may have to consider these venues as viable locations for your business. Locating in a mall however can have some downsides. Tenants are required to join tenant's associations and pay dues and maintenance costs. They are also required to abide by the rules and regulations of the management of the mall regarding store hours, holidays, and window displays.

In the long term, many retailers feel that shopping malls, with a proven record of success, are the surest bet. Many consumers feel that shopping malls are safer, cleaner, and more attractive than other shopping locations. Malls do offer some clear advantages: they have security, high traffic, well organized promotional events, lots of parking, and long business hours. Of course, the choice to locate a business within a mall depends on the customer a retailer is hoping to attract. The rule of thumb: if your customer is there, you should be too.

For a more detailed presentation of shopping malls, see Chapter 22 *Becoming a Retailer*.

Retail is like a theatrical performance

Creating and managing an image

In retailing image is everything. The newer, cleaner, more innovative and colorful products look, the better they sell. The look of the retail space itself is also of critical importance. If retailing is like a theatrical performance, then the retail space is the stage, and the sales people are the actors. This comparison is not as silly as it sounds. When customers buy a product they are "buying into" the store and the person who sells to them. They are buying because there are traits in the store that they want to emulate: style, class, organization, friendliness, attractiveness or professionalism. Successful retailers know that every element of their retail package must consistently and effectively communicate the message of the business.

Is your business's image hip and trendy? Young and Sporty? Seasoned and Subtle? Natural and Healthy?
PROJECT IT!

Take for example the new masters of retail clothing, The Gap. Can you guess what type of image they are trying to create and who their target customer is? Listen to the hip, top 40 music in the background. Salespeople are young and are usually wearing GAP clothing. Become inspired by the neatly folded, brightly colored stacks of clothing. Smile at the reasonable prices. All of these elements add up to create a unique and compelling buying environment for their customer, the 16 to 35 year old, stylish, creative and cost conscious consumer.

The customer

Who are retail customers? Well—everyone! The relationship between customer and retail businesses tends to be informal, habitual and convenience-based. Selling occurs at specific and limited points in time, rather than as part of an on-going sales and service relationship. Among franchises and mass retailers, very little customization of products occurs for the customer. For the most part, standard products at standard prices are purchased. There is usually no negotiation.

Supplier relationships

Most small retailers buy their merchandise from local wholesalers. However, a major trend in supplier arrangements is for major retailers to bypass wholesalers entirely (and their markups) and push for direct purchase from manufacturers. This allows them to buy in large volumes and charge lower prices to their consumers. Retailers who order large quantities can do what is called **specification buying**. They ask the manufacturer to change the packaging or characteristics of the merchandise to fit their merchandising needs.

On the other end of the spectrum is another trend among smaller, boutique segment of retailing. Here, the number of specialized sales representatives is growing. These people act as liaisons between retailer and manufacturer, and tend to carry a whole line of varied but complementary products. One example of this is clothing and jewelry representatives.

In general, retailers enjoy a very different sort of relationship with their suppliers than do manufacturers. Rather than a close, collaborative partnership, retailers and suppliers tend to have more limited, traditionally structured relationships. One notable exception is the relationship franchisees share with their parent organization, the franchisor. Here, the franchisor is the retailer's supplier and sales partner. They offer bulk discounts and special deals on merchandise, promotional and sales support, managerial guidelines and performance standards.

Operational and Managerial Challenges

The basic managerial issues that retailers must deal with are very similar to service businesses. This is because retailers are fundamentally service providers. After all, retailers were the first businesses to develop what today is known as customer service.

Organizational structure

Focus on your customer

Regardless of whether a retail business is run by a single owner or a team of employees, the same core functions must be performed: buying and selling merchandise, providing customer service, and managing finances. Unlike manufacturing businesses, only the largest of retail businesses organize themselves into product departments. Most smaller retailers simply have a salesperson or two who sell all of the store's merchandise and assist all of the customers. An employee or the owner may also perform the essential back-room functions of ordering and pricing merchandise.

Following is a chart depicting typical managerial and organizational functions:

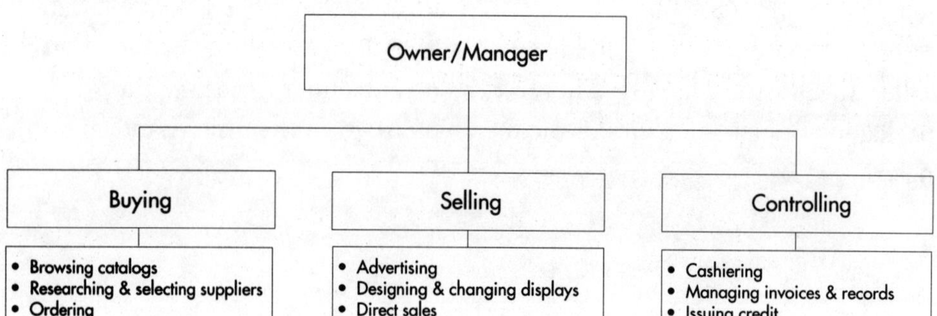

Employee management
In the past, many retailers tended to overlook the importance of their employees. Today, to their detriment, many still do. Retailers tend to focus their energies on merchandising, display store layouts and pricing rather than on their employees. Many small retailers simply don't have experience with hiring, training and rewarding employees.

Employees are a powerful contributor to retailer's profitability. They can project the image of the business and communicate the features and benefits of products.

Retailers typically compensate their employees with hourly wages and enhance their earnings with discounts on store merchandise, bonuses during peak sales periods, and commissions on sales. By encouraging employees to purchase store merchandise at discounted rates, retailers can create enthusiastic, real-life advertisers for their products. The Gap has been very successful at doing this. Their employees embody the look and image of the retailing giant, and provide a handsome source of annual revenue for the business.

Like manufacturers, successful retailers know that well trained employees are one of their best assets. A few training strategies commonly used in retail businesses are:

- Assigned readings
- College courses
- Job rotation
- Management training
- Customer profile training
- Successful selling practices
- Product specification and performance training

Train and reward your employees

Quality and retailing
Quality for retailers is defined by two major elements, the quality of the merchandise and the quality of the service. Careful selection of suppliers and manufacturers is the first step in ensuring quality in a retail venture. The next step is ensuring that service is of the highest quality. What is the mark of a truly high quality retail service?

- Knowledge about the product
- Knowledge about care and performance of the product
- After sales service and assistance
- Return policy

- Willingness to special order products
- Home delivery
- Customization products or services for clients
- Availability of restrooms
- Gift certificates, credit and check policies

Financial issues

The amount of investment it takes to begin a retailing venture can vary widely depending on your target market. Retailing start up costs also vary depending on:

- Whether you rent, buy or build your retail space
- The type of merchandise you will be selling
- The decor and image you want
- The size of the space you want

One of the major cost elements of retailing is inventory. Managing inventory includes all planning and stocking activities. Effective managers project their sales figures and plan for their inventory needs so as to ensure the fastest possible **turn-over**, or sale, of merchandise. By limiting the amount of inventory held, they can reduce storage, stocking and maintenance costs. Having the right inventory of products on hand allows businesses to reliably meet customer needs.

Knowing which items are "hot-sellers" and which items are "slow-movers" and pricing accordingly, is a key element of good inventory management. A word of warning: Too many small retailers simply buy what they like without considering who their customer is. The science of ordering appropriate merchandise, pricing and displaying it to sell is called **merchandising**.

Use of technology

Explore using affordable technology

Today even owners of the smallest stores can keep their own accounting records, create budgets and reports, process supplier invoices, manage payroll and inventory and perform pricing calculations with computers. There are hundreds of affordable, specialty software programs that are created specifically for small businesses.

Are you a retailer at heart?

Are you people oriented? Service oriented? These are the two most important traits for retailers. Generally speaking, retailers are community or neighborhood oriented, and have a knack for selling. Successful retailers have the ability to create a unique and seamless image for their store, in which all elements complement each other: the store sign, display windows, layout and design, and the appearance and service of employees. Successful retailers have an eye for detail, a flare for color and design, and an understanding of human temperament. Sometimes managing a small retail store can be a pleasurable, informal hobby. But the truly competitive retailer must use careful strategies to target their customer, practice good merchandising skills and keep a close eye on their costs and prices.

Retail opportunities for entrepreneurs
There's always an opportunity in retailing for a well researched, well located, carefully realized retail concept. If you feel you have the ability to seize upon or begin the next big trend, retailing might be for you.

Fashions, changing lifestyles, innovative technology, and increasing discretionary income mean new opportunities for new variations on old themes. The key to success for the small entrepreneur interested in retailing is targeting a particular customer segment and going after it.

Conclusion

Manufacturing, service, and retail operations all have unique challenges and rewards. In each industry, start-up costs, the competitive environment, relationships with suppliers and customers, timeliness, and innovation all play key roles in determining the success of your venture. Manufacturing tends to attract individuals who are intrigued by engineering processes, are interested in producing something of value and who are not intimidated by production schedules, machines and large capital investments. Business people who start-up service ventures commonly are good at interpersonal communication, have expertise in a particular field, like to be flexible and can adapt to trends quickly and seamlessly. If retail attracts you, you generally love to help people and are very service oriented. Let your interests be your guide in determining what type of business captures your imaginative passion and matches your entrepreneurial vision. Once you have finalized your choice, take a deep breath and step to it!

Chapter 6
ASSESSING YOUR PERSONAL AND BUSINESS APTITUDE

About This Chapter:
- *Personal assessment*
- *Business skills assessment*
- *Lifestyle assessment*
- *Mission statement*

Introduction

When most people think about starting a business, they tend to focus on the competitive and cultural climate of the industry in which they want to start that business. First and foremost, starting a new business requires paying attention to you. Before you can decide what type of business to begin, or whether or not to even start a business, you need to assess your personal and business skills. Successful entrepreneurs continually review these issues and gauge their skill set to identify those areas in which they need improvement. The key is to routinely assess your performance and solicit feedback from family, co-workers and friends. If you are willing to go through this exercise, you can develop a truly effective entrepreneurial skill base.

Knowing what you know... starting point for real learning

This chapter is composed of three different questionnaires designed to broadly assess your **personal** and **business skills.**

The best way to approach this chapter is by taking a step back and looking at yourself and your achievements from an objective perspective. Again, friends and co-workers can help. Ask them to answer these same questions with you in mind, then review with them how and why they answered the way they did.

After completing the assessments, and doing some old fashioned soul searching, you will draw together your insights and values into a personal mission statement that can guide your efforts in starting your business.

The point of this exercise is not to get the highest score, or to identify the true entrepreneurs and screen out the rest. This assessment chapter is simply a tool for you to gauge your personal and business skills, make the best decisions about whether to go into business, and identify the skills that you need to improve. Your scores do not guarantee success or failure. Entrepreneurs are made not born, and habits that define them can be acquired. The purpose of this chapter is to clarify your starting point and inspire you to develop your portfolio of skills. So find a quiet place to work, get a sharp pencil, and begin getting to know a new entrepreneur!

Your Personal Assessment

People are defined by the way they act: how they interact with people, how they make decisions, what their natural talents are and how they get things done. In large measure, a person's personality and performance is revealed by the unique composite of their habits. A persons daily habits reflect skills, motivation and past learning. Habits are learned and modified everyday, and impact how people view themselves and are viewed by others. The purpose of a personal assessment is to help you see more clearly the habits you possess and to compare these to the core traits of entrepreneurs. Remember, this is a starting point for you to identify the skills you might need to improve upon as you begin your entrepreneurial venture.

Excellence is a habit

Read each statement and enter a score in the right hand column based on your feelings. Use a scale of 1 to 4, 1 being "I strongly disagree" and 4 being "I strongly agree". For example, if you consider yourself highly organized, you would strongly agree with the statement, "I am highly organized in the way I conduct myself and my work" and give yourself a score of 4 points. If you consider yourself somewhat less than highly organized, you might score this a 3 or a 2. When you are finished scoring, calculate your total by adding all points in the score column.

1 = strongly disagree
2 = disagree
3 = agree
4 = strongly agree

Personal Assessment

Statement	Score
I enjoy competition in both work and play.	
I often set goals for myself.	
I often meet the goals I set for myself.	
I set limits for myself and follow them (with money, time, projects).	
I am happiest when I am responsible for myself and my own decisions.	
If given a choice, I prefer to work with other people on a project.	
In group situations I usually take a leadership role (setting the agenda, organizing duties, recording decisions, establishing criteria, etc.).	
I do things on my own. Nobody has to get me going.	
I work best when there are no precedents for what I am doing.	
I enjoy putting myself "on the line."	
When I start something, I am able to generate enthusiasm and commitment among other people.	
I believe that "luck favors the prepared mind."	
I do not perform well when other people set goals and define tasks I am to do.	
I am an on-time kind of person.	
I enjoy seeking out new challenges.	
I thrive on inventing new ideas, products, concepts.	
I find it exciting and exhilerating when circumstances change and I must adapt or expand my abilitics.	
I enjoy speaking in front of groups of people.	
I have strong intuition, and I listen to it.	
I have many natural talents.	
I often identify new skills I need and work at acquiring them.	
I prefer to be very busy.	
I enjoy the task of juggling several tasks at once.	
I can make up my mind in a hurry if I have to. These decisions usually turn out to be good ones.	
I get excited about new opportunities, ideas or projects just about every day.	
Personal Total Points	

Scoring between 25 and 62 points in this exercise represents a mid to low range score. This could mean that starting a business may not be for you. Becoming an entrepreneur can be a stressful and challenging experience, and if focusing your energy wholeheartedly in a project are not among your strengths, you may want to consider different alternatives to starting your own business. A mid to low range score may also mean you lack confidence in certain areas and with training and experience, you could develop these skills and abilities.

Partnering with other people or going to work in a small, entrepreneurial business to identify and learn about the areas in which you need to improve may be for you! Perhaps your self-confidence is lower than you'd like, you feel you're not as creative as you need to be, or you feel you lack "natural" leadership abilities. Chances are, if you go back and look closely at your past achievements, you will find that you possess more good qualities than you think you do. This book will help you to develop many of the key personal skills needed for successful entrepreneurship: being a good leader, enhancing creativity, and innovative capacity for problem solving, to name a few.

If you scored in the mid or upper level of this range, you already possess many of the key habits needed to dive into entrepreneurship. A score between 63 and 100 points indicates you are well on your way to having the right mix of personal skills to weather the challenges of entrepreneurship. You enjoy setting your own goals and achieving them, and you are comfortable with taking some risks. On those statements you scored yourself below a 3, consider ways to enhance these skills. Your ability to identify your weak areas and seek out ways to improve upon them speaks to how successful you will ultimately be in your entrepreneurial venture.

Your Business Skills Assessment

Entrepreneurs have limited time and resources and must continually make choices about how to maximize their resources to be most effective. This requires focus on what they do best and understanding what they don't do well in order to direct others to do it. Making these types of decisions requires a basic knowledge of business: financial management, marketing, sales, analyzing trends, personnel and use of computers. You will have to be a jack-of-all-trades. It is particularly important to know early on which skills you have and those you will have to learn or delegate to others.

The skills revealed in this exercise can be acquired if you work at it. Chances are you possess far more business skills than you think you do, and can learn those skills you don't have more easily than you think you can.

Work through the following statements, scoring yourself with a scale of 1 to 4, 1 being "I strongly disagree" and 4 being "I strongly agree." To rate yourself with these statements, consider past and present activities, including community, religious or professional organizations, work, family, or hobbies. Chances are, you routinely use many business skills without knowing it!

1 = strongly disagree
2 = disagree
3 = agree
4 = strongly agree

Business Assessment

Statement	Score
I keep track of my personal finances and balance my checkbook every week.	
I create monthly and yearly budgets for myself and follow them.	
For any given period of time, I know what I spend on medical costs and living expenses.	
I know within $100 how much it cost me to operate my car last year.	
Even if I don't prepare my tax return myself, I understand the concepts regarding taxation.	
I know how to borrow money from a bank.	
I have an excellent credit rating.	
I enjoy getting "out there" and selling an idea or product to people I have never met.	
Give me five minutes, an audience, and a great product, and I can make a sale.	
I understand how to calculate profitability and perform break-even analysis.	
I understand the difference between fixed and variable costs.	
I regularly read business books to improve my skills.	
I am able to utilize a computer to efficiently manage my work and personal finances.	
I have an e-mail address — and use it.	
I regularly read *Inc.* and other weekly business magazines.	
I would press customers for full payment up front, or if they refused, negotiate with them for a 50% deposit or unconventional payment terms.	
I have work experience in the industry or field in which I am interested in starting a business.	
I have successfully managed people by: setting goals, delegating responsibility, and addressing performance.	
When negotiating a decision with a friend, co-worker or salesperson, I am confident in identifying and communicating my interests and succeed at maximizing my outcome.	
I understand the basics of how different products and services are distributed and why.	
I have hired and fired people.	
I know how to effectively interview and assess potential employees.	
I understand how the concept of "cash flow" impacts business decisions.	
I am comfortable giving presentations and know how to create professional, effective presentations.	
I know how to use computer software to create effective presentations.	
I know how to prepare an invoice.	
Business Total Points	

If you scored between 25 and 62 points on this assessment, take some time to narrow the specific areas of business in which you need to develop skills. This book addresses all of the major skills needed to start and manage a growing business. In addition, there are countless community college and adult continuing education courses that focus specifically on basic accounting, finance and marketing skills. Read everything you can get your hands on that will improve your business skills. Talking with experienced business people is also a great way to get real life knowledge about business skills. Seek out people who are working in your targeted field and ask them which business skills have been crucial to their success. Learning new business skills is a continual process in today's marketplace.

If you scored above 63 points, you may already possess basic business knowledge. However, this same advice applies to you. Identify business skills you need to learn and focus on these!

Your Lifestyle Assessment

Assessing lifestyle preference entails what you value as a human being. It speaks to who you are, the priorities in your life that guide all of your decisions and what motivates you. You will need to study these personal issues in order to create a compatible work and personal life fit.

Work through the following statements, answering and scoring yourself in the same way you did for the previous assessments.

1 = strongly disagree
2 = disagree
3 = agree
4 = strongly agree

Lifestyle Assessment

Statement	Score
My friends would describe me as a high energy person.	
My health is generally good.	
I can support myself without taking money out of my business for 1 year.	
If I needed to, I could keep my full-time job and run my new business on the side.	
I have no problem working 10-12 hours a day, 6 days a week, including holidays.	
I am willing to work 60 hours or more a week.	
My family will tolerate my working 60 hours or more a week.	
I consider myself a high performer.	
I know I can work productively for long hours and meet deadlines, no matter what it takes.	
I have very good physical stamina.	
My family obligations rank number one on my list of priorities.	
At the expense of professional stability and perhaps higher income, it is important to me to be able to determine when and where I work.	
Foremost among my personal goals is the freedom to pursue my own ideas.	
I am prepared to lose my savings.	
Beginning my own business is all about making money.	
I am prepared to sacrifice the amount of money and/or time that I am able to commit to community, religious, or charity obligations during the first five years of my business.	
I can go a year without a vacation.	
I have the enthusiastic support of my family to pursue an entrepreneurial venture.	
I am comfortable setting, evaluating and achieving my own 1, 3 and 5 year plans.	
I understand that part of my job description in my new business would include sweeping the floor, typing letters and taking out the trash.	
When I think about the future, I envision positive, new growth opportunities.	
It is important to me to create my own space in which to work.	
I am comfortable working in a "gray area" where the boundaries between my work and personal life are sometimes hidden.	
I don't get sick very often.	
Lifestyle Total Points	

Your score reveals if you are flexible enough to take on the challenges and uncertainties of beginning a new business. If you scored below 62 points, financial, family, community, or other personal responsibilities may be a considerable source of conflict to you. Look at the statements where you indicated either a 1 or a 2 and you may be able to draw some conclusions about how time, money, family, health and other considerations factor into your ideal lifestyle. This does not automatically disqualify you from pursuing your own venture! This simply reveals some of the realities of your life and gives you the parameters within which you must make business decisions. Likewise if you scored in the upper ranges between 63 and 100 points. This is your starting point for understanding what type of business opportunity is best for you to pursue, and how you can make it fit with your lifestyle.

Personal Mission Statement

With these insights in mind, now is a great time to write your personal mission statement. The statement represents the values and principles on which you base your life. To most of us, these are not crystal clear because we don't often take the time to examine how or why we do what we do. However, this is precisely what you should do on the eve of beginning your own business. Your personal mission statement is unique to you, and can look and sound any way you want it to. Consider the following sample as a starting point to compose your one-page mission statement written in bullet points or sentence form. This statement can serve as a guide for the creation of your new business's mission statement. Be creative, true to yourself, and let inspiration guide you!

A personal mission statement is a reflection of who you are and what you believe in!

Sample Personal Mission Statement:

- *My family comes first.*
- *I strive to be honest in everything.*
- *I will finish everything I start.*
- *I want to set standards among my peers for commitment and dedication.*
- *I will take time to day dream.*
- *I need to laugh at myself when appropriate.*
- *I will ask other's opinions and learn from them.*
- *I want to listen more than I speak.*
- *I will always make time for others.*

After making a list for your personal mission statement, it's a good time to synthesize these into your business's mission statement.

Sample Business Mission Statement:

- *I believe the future of the U.S. economy lies in Americans' ability to increase their rate of savings.*
- *My business will help people to accomplish this through low-cost investment advisement.*
- *I will limit our client base to those people who have between $100 and $10,000 to invest because these people are in need of financial advice, but are never solicited by financial advisors because they aren't considered "worth the effort".*
- *I will call my business "Net Worth."*

Conclusion

What motivates you? Independence? Money? Fun? Creativity? Recognition? Security?

Understanding personal issues, skills and talents is the first step in creating the business opportunity that is best for you. Having done these assessments prepares you to acquire the skills you need, allows you to clarify your goals, and inspires you to create the life work you want. So, regardless of what you scored, give yourself an A+! This chapter was designed to inspire you to continue learning. After all, you are a work in progress!

Part II
Planning Your Business

Chapter 7
WHAT IS BUSINESS PLANNING?

About This Chapter:
- *What is planning?*
- *Importance of planning*
- *Defining the business concept*
- *Keys for success*

Introduction

Entrepreneurs pride themselves on being individuals full of action. They invent a new product, manufacture and sell it. Planning may sound like an academic exercise better suited for large corporations, the classroom, or consultants. But planning plays an extremely important part in the success of a small business.

Small businesses are always impacted more by changes in the economy and markets than their larger competitors. The very fragility of a small business makes planning so important. This chapter takes a look at the basics of planning.

What is Planning?

Process

Planning is the dynamic process of preparing your business for the future. Focusing on the planning process is the purpose of this chapter; subsequent chapters will focus on the results of this process.

Planning is a dynamic process

Software Solutions, Inc.

Joe Murrow, owner of Southern Software Solutions Inc., wanted to promote his software products at the annual Comdex show in Las Vegas. He had read about the show in various industry publications but knew very little of the details, so he decided to do some research.

Joe gathered information about the number and types of people that usually attend Comdex and the estimated costs to his company should they attend. Joe and Marketing Manager Barbara Fabric then made a list of the advantages and disadvantages of participating. As part of their research, they looked into alternative ways of spending their marketing dollars. Finally, after three months of research, they decided to budget marketing dollars for the Comdex show the next year.

The research Joe and Barbara did indicated that attending the show would accomplish several objectives that other marketing approaches would not: (1) their potential customers attended this show and based buying decisions upon contacts and information obtained at the show, (2) attending the show would allow them to actually demonstrate the benefits of their products, and (3) greater sales would be generated by attending the show.

Once the decision was made, they began to develop a written plan for themselves and their employees. Since attending a major trade show requires a serious investment in terms of time and money, the plan would keep them focused and organized.

The process used by Joe and Barbara is an example of planning. Notice that the process did not begin with the written plan. They began by doing research, an important part of any planning process. The writing phase is usually the last phase of the planning process. Joe started with a goal in mind and then went through a process to decide if the goal was a good one and then, worked on how to best accomplish the goal.

Key Management Function

Managers have five major functions in a business. They plan, organize, staff, direct, and control the operations of the business. All five are important for success. These functions need to happen in the order listed. Note that planning is first. The four remaining functions assume that sound planning has already happened.

Major management functions

- Planning
- Organizing
- Staffing
- Directing
- Controlling

Types of Planning

There are three common types of planning processes:

Strategic Planning

Strategic planning is the systematic process of evaluating the impact of your business environment and the major decisions you face. The goal is to ensure long-term success. Focus your attention five years into the future when considering strategic planning.

Operational Planning

This process focuses on the actions that must be taken in the short term, usually one year. When operational planning is not based on a strategic plan, your business runs the risk of making decisions that seem good today but could have a negative long-term impact. Ideally, operational planning should occur after strategic planning has been completed. However, small businesses are usually short-term oriented and, thus emphasize operational planning.

Financial Planning

Financial planning includes the process of preparing budgets and projected financial statements. These "numbers" must be updated whenever any planning activity is undertaken. The "numbers" are merely a numerical representation of the strategic and operational planning processes.

Financial planning: the process of preparing budgets and projected financial statement

Results

The above mentioned processes result in the following:

- **Business Plan**: The document resulting from a planning process is usually referred to as a business plan. A complete business plan contains three major components: strategies, actions, and projected financial statements. A fourth area, policies and procedures, is also important to the planning process but is not included in the business plan.

- **Marketing Plan**: A plan that focuses solely on the marketing function of your business. Portions of the marketing plan appear in the business plan.

- **Strategic Plan**: Strategic plans are the result of the strategic planning process. The strategic plan is contained, often in its entirety, in the business plan.

- **Annual Work Plan**: Annual work plans are the result of operational planning. An annual work plan is very detailed and only the highlights appear in the business plan.

- **Financing Proposal**: A financing proposal is not really a planning document. Financing proposals are developed for the purpose of securing financing and not for the purpose of managing the business. The majority of the financing proposal is usually taken from the business plan, although it is really a by-product of the planning process.

- **Feasibility Study**: An entrepreneur investigating starting a new business may engage in an abbreviated planning process to determine whether to proceed with the new venture. The result is called a feasibility plan. This is an important tool for anyone contemplating a start-up business.

Importance of Planning

Why should small business owners devote a portion of their valuable time to the process of planning for the future? Let's take a look at a variety of benefits associated with the planning process.

Planning:

- helps to pinpoint underlying reasons for any recurring daily problems
- guides daily actions for employer and all employees
- effectively communicates the owner's plan and goals to others
- helps the owner to focus on customer service and cost effectiveness
- provides a systematic way to identify new opportunities
- greatly increases chances of business success

A Look at the Whole Business

The planning processes described in this chapter require the business owner to evaluate the entire business. Daily decision making often focuses on solving a series of individual problems that may not seem connected at the time. Planning helps discover the underlying reasons for the recurring daily problems. The process also results in the identification of business opportunities that are currently being overlooked.

Framework for Daily Decision Making

Small business owners are often frustrated that their employees don't make the right decisions when solving daily problems. Your employees have an interest in the success of your business—continued employment! Thus, they want to work in a manner that benefits your business. A business plan is a document which guides daily actions. This assumes that the employees are involved in the planning process or, at the very least, receive training about the parts of the plan that impact them!

Useful Communication Tools

The business plan puts useful information in writing that can then be communicated to employees, investors, creditors, and other interested parties. The major problem with keeping your business plan "in your head" is the difficulty of communicating your plan to others.

Increase Chance of Success

The business world is becoming increasingly competitive and small businesses must find a well-defined market niche. Furthermore, they must service their market in a manner that is customer-oriented and cost-effective. The planning process forces you to address these issues. Thus, the well-planned business has a better chance of being successful.

Future Business Opportunities

The products, services, and delivery systems offered by small businesses are in a constant state of change. Change always presents new opportunities to the prepared business owner. The planning process provides a systematic way to identify new opportunities.

Feedback Results in Improvement

The written plan is not the end of the planning process. In fact, the process is continuous. Constantly evaluating how the business is actually doing versus what was planned is invaluable. This ongoing comparison of planned results to actual results provides a terrific opportunity to continuously improve the business operation.

Act Not React

Small business owners often talk about suffering from "burnout" or feeling like a fire fighter responding to the latest emergency. A business plan is analogous to a good fire prevention plan. There will still be some daily fires but the number will be fewer and how to best respond will have been determined. The business plan also allows employees to handle problems.

Key Questions

The process helps you sort through hundreds of questions and concerns about your business and focus on the handful that are causing the majority of your problems. This is called the **80/20 rule**:

> "In any organization 80% of the problems can be solved by focusing on 20% of the underlying causes (customers/suppliers/employees/policies). Similarly, 80% of the opportunities result from 20% of your customers/suppliers/employees/policies."

When to do Planning

Planning is often begun as a reaction to some key event such as seeking financing or buying a business. This is not sufficient to successfully start and grow a business. Planning needs to be integrated into the ongoing management of your business.

Continual Process

Planning should be done on a continuing basis. It is a key part of managing your business and needs constant attention, just like marketing and bookkeeping. It makes sense to concentrate your planning activities during an annual process but you should be **working the plan** constantly.

Planning Cycle

Planning is a seven-step process. All seven of these steps are taking place on a daily basis in a well-managed business. The seven steps are:

A successful business completes all seven steps in the planning cycle!

- **Step 1** is the planning process which prepares the business for the future.
- **Step 2** is taking action by making decisions that implement the plan. Every business owner makes decisions either with or without a plan. A plan provides you with a guide for taking the right actions.
- **Step 3** is what results from the action. Something happens as a result of every decision. This occurs regardless of a plan.
- **Step 4** is to measure the results and record this measurement in records of the business.
- **Step 5** is to compare the actual results to your planned results. This can't be done unless you have done the planning in Step 1.
- **Step 6** is to explain why the actual results vary from the planned results. This is done whether the variance is positive or negative. You will learn a great deal about how your business really functions as a result of this step.
- **Step 7** is to integrate the changes you want to make in the plans as a result of what you learned in step 6.

Who Does the Planning?

Owners Take the Lead

You must be actively involved in the planning process. Don't delegate all the responsibility to an employee, a team, or a consultant. It is great to have others organize and participate in the process, but you must be seen as a strong advocate of the process.

The business owner must be actively involved

Assemble a Planning Team

Now that you are committed to being actively involved in the process, it is time to identify the other members of your planning team. Why should you use a team approach? Can't the owner just write the plan and then tell the employees what to do? No, not successfully. You must involve key employees to make them feel a sense of ownership in the plan. This greatly improves the chances of successful implementation. Besides key employees, you may want to involve professional advisors in your planning process. It is common for a business to hire an outside facilitator to keep the planning process running smoothly. His or her role is to facilitate the planning process, not control or participate in it.

Now that you have assembled your team, it is time for your first meeting. At the initial meeting, you should define a time line for future meetings and for completing the planning process. Make sure that everyone on the team understands their responsibilities, both at the meetings and in the work done between meetings.

Defining the Business Concept

Every business is unique. The business issues important to a personal services business are different than those of a manufacturer or a retailer. For example, your business faces challenges different than your competitors or other types of businesses in your community. Planning provides you the opportunity to define what factors make your business unique.

To define your business concept, you have to answer some hard questions

Although you may be anxious to start planning for a successful future, there are some questions to answer first. As you work on the questions in this section, keep a list of difficulties you encounter; they will be helpful in the next section.

- What business am I in?
- What is being offered to the customer?
- Who wants to buy what is being offered?
- Why does the customer want to buy from my business?
- When do customers buy what I am offering?
- How will customers find my business?
- How much will my customers pay?

Review your answers to the above questions and write a one-page definition of your business. Now you have answered, "What business am I in?"

Let's take a look at how Simply Shoes, a retail shoe store, used these questions to define their business concept. The following is the result of their efforts.

Simply Shoes: Business Concept

Simply Shoes is a partnership of Sara and Bob Abbott and Dave and Maria Brookes. Simply Shoes is a retail shoe store located at the corner of 5th and Main and sells medium-to high-quality dress and casual shoes at discount prices to adult and young adult customers. The current owners purchased the business this year and plan to increase style and size selection, double sales, develop a loyal customer base, and emphasize good customer service.

Simply Shoes fills a void in the local retail shoe industry by offering high quality shoes at discounted prices. This is made possible by careful attention to purchasing, which is done by the partners through direct contact with brokers and manufacturers. The marketing strategy calls for targeted marketing to identified customer groups and projected sales to reach over $350,000 for the coming year. To accommodate a desired increase in selection, the partners propose to remodel existing space, providing more visibility of merchandise and room for displaying more styles.

As you can probably tell by reading their description, the partners have already done some planning but decided it was incomplete and are starting a complete planning process before finalizing their decision to remodel.

Keys for Success

A well-executed planning process can have a tremendous positive impact on a business. Conversely, the frustration of a process that does not result in agreement on the future of the business can be devastating. Here are some ideas for making your planning process a success.

- Owner assumes the lead role
- Plan involves everyone in the business
- Planning is a process
- Plan in definable steps
- Plans reflect reality
- Have a contingency plan for the worst case
- Plans should be flexible
- Identify how specific goals and objectives will be achieved
- A plan is built on the skills of staff who will implement the plan
- Assumptions are documented
- Revise the plan when needed

The Perils of Operating Without a Plan

In 1994, Sandra Workman started Affairs of the Heart. In two years, this catering business was successful beyond Sandra's wildest dreams. She had moved twice to larger quarters, hired 10 additional full-time and 15 part-time employees, and had a well-deserved reputation as "the caterer to the 'movers and shakers' of Elktown". The future for Sandra and her business looked bright.

In 1996, things started to go awry. Sandra was facing yet another move to accommodate increased business, she had increased her staff to 15 full-time and 30 part-time employees, and cash flow was becoming an on-going crisis. She couldn't figure it out—she was generating more revenue than ever, still enjoyed her stellar reputation, and her business was growing—why couldn't she pay her bills? How would she ever find the time to locate and renovate another space?

Sandra was determined to make Affairs of the Heart a long-term, successful business, so she hired a business consultant. After several months of studying every facet of the business (and running up a significant bill), the consultant came back to Sandra with her analysis. Every problem Sandra was trying to deal with was a result of the lack of planning. Sandra had never developed a business plan. She thought she didn't need one! The consultant helped Sandra develop and write a business plan, including critical sections on future growth, marketing, and budgets.

At the end of 1996, Affairs of the Heart closed out its books with a profit, had not moved to a larger space (that was in the plan for late 1997), and still was the premier caterer in Elktown.

Conclusion

The planning process described in this chapter will help your business prepare for a competitive business environment. You will be ready to compete today but, more importantly, you will be positioned to be successful in the long term.

Is the planning process really the same for all types of businesses? Yes, the steps in the process are the same but the results are different for every business. You wouldn't expect a manufacturing company that specializes in high-quality custom orders to have a plan similar to a fast-food restaurant.

Nor would you expect a wholesaler of farm implements to have a plan with much in common with a consulting company that specializes in customer service training. You must customize your plan for your business.

Planning is the key to success for guiding your business through difficult times and terrific times. Take the first step, begin today to utilize the planning process.

Chapter 8
THE START-UP BUSINESS PLAN

About This Chapter:
- *Why do a business plan?*
- *Who uses a business plan?*
- *How to prepare a business plan*
- *How to present your plan*

Introduction

People often say, "Eureka! I've got the perfect business idea!" or "Someone should make a business out of that!". The truth of the matter is that many of the best business ideas are never realized because people don't put them to the test. The Start-up Business Plan does just that. It defines the specific requirements for your new business.

The Start-up Business Plan is the first step in making your vision a reality

The Start-up Business Plan outlines the basics of a business concept: the business' mission, objectives, products or services, management, and the basic marketing and financial plan. It is the document designed to reveal whether or not a business idea is workable. Many businesses use the business plan as an exercise to test their ideas and stimulate thinking. Compiling the information that goes into the plan helps to clarify goals and focus attention on critical issues.

Creating a business plan is a process composed of many tasks. At each step you will learn more about whether yours is a viable business idea. You will also fine tune the business concept making it all the more likely that your start-up business will succeed.

The Start-up Business Plan demonstrates a business's commitment to its mission. It shows that you are undertaking your business with sincerity, professionalism, and foresight.

The Start-up Business Plan is the culmination of all of your market research, analysis and strategy formulation. It defines: who your customers are; what your product or service is; how much it will cost to start your business; and the specific actions to meet your targets, minimize risk, and serve your customers. This plan is designed for start-up entrepreneurs who are at the beginning stages of "testing the waters" of a new business idea. Of course you can expand this plan with more elaborate financial data, cash flow and market projections.

The Start-up Business Plan informs and inspires

If a business plan compiles all of your planning efforts together, then why are we presenting it here, before we have introduced basic marketing and financial concepts? Because this chapter gives you a vision of where you are headed. It highlights the work you will need to do and the concepts you will need to understand to get a business up and running. The Start-up Business Plan is the capstone of your efforts. Each chapter in this textbook introduces elements that are in some way contained in the business plan.

Who Uses a Start-up Business Plan?

The start-up business plan has three primary audiences:

- The internal management team
- Potential lenders, investors and trade creditors
- Potential partners, advisors, and employees

The Start-up Business Plan examines the elements that will affect the success of your business

Whether you're starting a new business, expanding an old one, or just wondering how to improve your current business, a business plan is an excellent operating tool for the business. It helps you assess your strengths and weaknesses. It is a map for the business that can be referred to and updated. If there are changes in the market, among your customers or competitors, you can revisit the plan and revise it to keep you on track.

In the beginning you may be the internal management team, but as your venture grows and key employees are added, the business plan is the common language for all departments and functions within the business. The business plan is one critical way members of the internal management team communicate with one another.

The Start-up Business Plan is also a potential fund-raising tool. Banks, investors, Community Development Financial Institutions (CDFI's), and other lending institutions use a business plan to evaluate the wisdom of lending to an entrepreneur. They look at the document to get insight into the abilities of the business owner and the potential profitability of the business. The start-up business plan may make the difference in establishing trade credit with your vendors. Without an established trade line, most start-up ventures are required by their vendors to either prepay or provide cash on delivery (C.O.D.) for their order.

Another audience for the business plan is potential employees, mentors, and partners. It presents information that is essential for anyone seriously considering participating in your venture. The Start-up Business Plan should be clear, to the point, and catch and hold people's attention. It should ignite in others the same enthusiasm that you feel about your business idea. It paints a picture of who you are, what direction you are headed in, and what your approach is for achieving your goals.

What do Critical Readers Look for in a Business Plan?

Potential lenders, employees, partners, or advisors—just about everyone who reads a business plan—looks for the same information about the business:

- Is the business idea viable?
- Are its products or services new, unique, or in some way better than current offerings?
- Does the business create or cater to a new market?
- Is it a growth market?
- Are the cash flow and sales projections realistic?
- Can the business be profitable and service its debt?
- Does the business truly understand and place priority on customer needs?
- Is the business concept clear, focused, and intelligently presented?
- Is the business concept based on sound research and analysis?

Every year one graphic design firm in Eugene, Oregon, rewrites their basic business plan. In it they identify their new goals and work to determine if those goals are attainable. Before they write their plan they review their market and prepare customer and competitor profiles. They challenge their positioning strategy and their choice of target customers. Are they offering the right services to the right types of customers? Is their pricing on target? Is the right message being communicated in their promotions? Are they staying within their budgets and generating their expected profits?

The business plan: a road map highlighting routes amongst road blocks and detours

Management and employees all agree that the approximate 160 hours spent developing the plan every year is well worth it. The end result? A working document that outlines goals, strategies, and tactics with target dates attached to each. The company has a terrific track record of consistently meeting its goals. Is this a coincidence? We think not—planning works!

Components of a Start-up Business Plan

The major components of the plan are:

- Cover Page
- Table of Contents
- Executive Summary
- Background Information
- Description of Products/Services
- Management Structure and Organization
- The Marketing Plan
- The Financial Plan
- Conclusion

A good plan tests ideas and focuses goals

Getting Started

The Start-up Business Plan is the summary of all your market research and analysis. Before you start drafting your actual plan, revisit your original business concept. Review your assumptions. Before you can communicate these clearly to anyone else, you should be perfectly clear and confident about the general direction in which you want to take your idea.

Businesses often list and prioritize the different ingredients they will need in order to pursue their business idea. Imagine you want to open a cafe/ laundromat. Although there are two other laundromats in your town, they are poorly lit and maintained and completely lacking in appeal. Your vision is to create a place people will want to come to do their laundry. While they wait for their laundry they can have a good cup of coffee and a fresh sandwich. They can socialize or they can sit at a table to read or write postcards.

Next, list some of the things you are going to need: knowledge of maintaining laundry machines and running a cafe, laundry equipment, restaurant supplies, utensils, a logo, licenses and permits. Because you may eventually be seeking outside investors or lenders, start to think like one. Ask yourself, "What is so great about my laundromat? What makes it unique? What resources do I have available to get started? How long before I will make a profit? What is my competition like? What are my long-term and medium-term plans as I grow?".

Once you've done this, it's time to start drafting your plan. You will write each element of the Start-up Business Plan in your NxLeveL workbook.

The Executive Summary

The Executive Summary is the "opening argument" of the business plan. It's your chance to take the floor and convince your audience that your business is worth a go. It is the most important section of the plan because it is the first thing readers see. It must capture and hold their attention. Potential investors will scan it to determine whether or not the rest of the business plan is worth reading.

The Three C's:

- Clear
- Concise
- Convincing

The executive summary contains condensed versions of all the major sections of the business plan. For this reason, you should write this section last. You need a full understanding of all the proceeding sections and how they relate to each other in order to present a more effective summary.

Keep in mind the "Three C's" to creating an effective executive summary: be clear, concise, and convincing. Clarity enables those unfamiliar with the industry to understand the general scope and feasibility of your business. If you use terms common only to people in your industry, someone from the outside the industry may stop reading it altogether. The summary should be short and to the point; all of your supporting data will be contained elsewhere. The summary is your chance to convince others that your idea is a viable one.

Background Information

This section briefly outlines the personal skills and experience of the entrepreneur as they relate to the proposed business: "Have you worked in the industry before?", "Do you have specialized expertise that gives you a unique advantage?" and "What new skills do you need and how will you acquire them?".

The business concept is a workable idea that fuels your start-up

This section also presents the personal financial resources of the entrepreneur. What assets do you have? What other sources of income are available to you? What can you invest in the business yourself?

Start-ups often use this section to present their **business concept.** This is a brief but compelling description of why the business should exist. It is a raw idea restated in one sentence as a business opportunity. It presents the business' offering and the need it fills.

Products and Services Description

Any business plan should describe in some detail the products or services that you will offer. What value will be delivered to customers? What is the company's mission, how fully developed is the product or service idea? This is your opportunity to demonstrate the focus and scope of the business. A business's **mission statement** states, in the broadest terms possible, what the business hopes to be and do. For example, "To help people work more efficiently and comfortably" or "To provide healthy, energizing juices" or "To take the anxiety out of tax preparation".

You should spend a fair amount of time developing a mission statement for your company. All subsequent strategies and tactics should be directed towards achieving this mission.

One good example of a mission statement was developed in a business plan by a publishing company that started a monthly outdoor magazine. The publication, called TRiPS, was circulated in Santa Cruz, California. The mission statement was pretty straightforward and simple: "The purpose of TRiPS is to promote outdoor adventure and travel so people see, feel and know how good it is to be outside."

Finally, businesses should explore growth and product expansion potential. For example, if you've decided to start a graphic design service, this could eventually lead into providing Web-site design and editing services to small businesses in your community. Demonstrating forethought in the early stages of planning carries weight with those interested in participating in a business.

Management Structure and Organization

This section usually begins by describing the legal form of ownership of the business. Will it be a limited partnership? A sole proprietorship? A corporation?

This section presents the people and structures that will make the business run smoothly and successfully. At what point do you estimate you will need additional personnel? What are the responsibilities and qualifications of your team? Businesses often attach resumes to this section to highlight the strengths of the team.

In the management section you should describe how different parts of the business work together. Who will report to whom? Which area of the business will be responsible for which functions? Businesses often illustrate this with an organizational chart. An **organizational chart** is a blueprint of the management hierarchy. It details reporting relationships and where different parts of the business exist in relation to one another.

Your management team may consist of only you, or a combination of you and external contractors that you hire on a short-term basis. What tasks will you be responsible for and what tasks you will rely on outside services, consultants, mentors, and helpers to perform? Will you do accounting and payroll yourself, in-house or hire an accountant or bookkeeper? Will you use outside sales representatives? What functions will you rely on distributors or agents to perform?

The management section of the business plan is a good place to present possible weaknesses within the business and obstacles you anticipate. Businesses often list potential challenges along with contingency plans for trouble-shooting and solving these problems.

The Marketing Plan

The marketing plan identifies the markets the business intends to serve. It outlines the business's unique strengths relative to its competitors. It describes how the business will be positioned in its market. The marketing plan contains the following sections:

- **Industry Description**
  Which industry will the business compete in? What are the industry trends that will impact the business? Where is the industry headed in the next 1, 3 and 5 years? What are your key qualifications for competing in this industry?

- **The Target Market**
  Who will the business be targeting with its products or services? How large is the business's market? How fast is it growing? What is the target customer profile? What is their purchasing behavior? What do customers value? How often do they buy?

Demographic and psychographic data are used to help describe the target market. **Demographic data** gives quantitative information like people's address, age, income level, spending patterns, and family composition. **Psychographic data** gives qualitative information about people's life-styles. What are their hobbies? Beliefs? Attitudes? This information determines all marketing strategies including those regarding product, price, promotion, and placement.

- **Competition, Competitive Advantage and Product or Service Differentiation**
  Who will the business be competing against? Is the market already saturated with other companies? What does the business offer that's better than the competition? What are its unique strengths? Weaknesses?

  A major aspect of the market analysis is a list of possible barriers to entry. What are the initial start-up costs of going into business? What special skills or expertise are required to compete? How long will it take to set up the business's operations? What government regulations apply to the business? This section introduces the marketing strategy to address how the business will overcome obstacles to achieve its objectives.

- **Market Strategy**
  What does the business hope to achieve in its markets? What strategies and tactics will it use to achieve these objectives? This section outlines what mix of product, pricing, placement, and promotion strategies the business will use to compete and serve its target customers. What promotional strategies will it use? Newspaper or periodical ads? Radio? Direct mail? Will the business create its own Web site and register with several search engines or link to other related Web pages? What sort of customer service will the business provide? How will products or services be packaged? Will products be widely or selectively distributed? How much will marketing efforts cost and how long will each tactic be used?

This section presents how the business will provide products or services. Where will your supplies come from? How will products be produced? Distributed? Sold? How will you maintain production levels to meet customer orders?

General pricing information is also included in the plan. What will you charge for your product or service? How have you calculated your costs and your profitability? How will your price position you in the market? Will you offer any special discounts to entice new business?

The Financial Plan

A solid financial section is crucial for an effective business plan. This is where the business lists the financial requirements for launching the business. What sources does the business have for start-up financing? What equipment does the business require and how much will it cost? What other "fixed and variable costs" will the business have?

In the financial plan businesses estimate their sales, revenues, and expenses for the first year of business. They also present assumptions upon which these estimates are based.

Entrepreneurs have a tendency to be over optimistic in developing the financial plan. The truth is many business ventures fail because of faulty predictions in the financial planning section.

Give room for error. Be wary of numbers that seem too good to be true. Doing so will allow you to adjust the prices of your product or services if necessary. If there's no way to make a profit, you will want to reconsider your business concept.

You need to present enough information to determine whether there is a potential for profit. You should make sure you are not undercapitalized. **Capital** is the cash or material assets, tools, property, or equipment the business requires to operate.

Be wary of numbers that seem too good to be true

The financial plan contains several items that give a quantitative profile of how the business will operate. An **income statement** details the revenues and expenses that you anticipate and shows whether the business will generate a profit or a loss. A **cash-flow analysis** starts with the income statement and then makes adjustments for "non-cash" items to determine your companies cash position. For a given period of time will the business have cash to pay its loans and other debts? Cash-flow analysis is needed to determine if sufficient cash will be on hand to meet your schedule of financial obligations.

The **balance sheet** lists all of a business's assets and liabilities. It reveals the company's overall worth at any given point in time.

Details of each of these sections of the financial plan are given below.

Income Statement

An income statement is a financial report showing revenues earned, expenses incurred, and the resulting **net income** or **net loss.** In this section, start-up businesses predict their monthly Income Statement for the first year of business and quarterly for the two years that follow.

Once businesses have settled on the prices they will charge, they estimate how many units they will sell or how much service income they will generate. This income, without any consideration for expenses, is called **gross sales.** Then they subtract their **cost of goods sold.** This is what they paid for their supplies and other inputs to produce the product or service. The cost of goods sold is then subtracted from their gross sales to determine their **gross profit margin.**

Next businesses calculate how much they will have to expend each month to operate. How much will they pay for salaries, wages, rent, utilities, and insurance? The sum of these expenses equals **total operating costs.** Included in this is the **depreciation** of any equipment. For example, if your brand new Power PC computer is worth $6,000 today, in a year it may be only worth $4,000. The depreciation is an expense of $2,000, which is part of your operating costs.

Businesses subtract their operating costs from their gross profit margin to determine their predicted **net profit before taxes.**

"In business, you can't be in control if you aren't on top of your cash flow."
–Norm Brodsky
in *Inc.* magazine,
October 1996

Cash Flow analysis

Cash flow analysis is perhaps the most critical financial tool. Here you calculate how much actual cash is coming in and out of your business. It is a tool particularly useful for determining when and how much money a business will need to borrow during an annual cycle. Or, when and how much cash is available to pay bills each month.

This section is important, especially when businesses have large **accounts receivable.** This is the unpaid balance of money owed to the business by customers. Consider the example of the business that manufactures T-shirts and ships 500 along with an invoice due to be paid in 30 days. If the T-shirt business has an outstanding bill due in two weeks, it won't be able to count on the income generated by this sale to pay current expenses. It carries the risk that its accounts receivable will not be paid in time for it to meet its own obligations for the cost of cloth and labor.

How do businesses calculate cash flow? They start by calculating how much cash they have on hand. Then they add **cash receipts.** This is cash generated from "cash sales" and collection of accounts receivable. Any loans received from banks or other lenders is also included as an addition to the cash position.

After all cash coming into the business is calculated, the next step is to determine all cash going out from the business over that same period. **Cash disbursements** is the total of these outgoing cash expenses. Cash disbursements include the cash paid out for inventory or payments made to reduce accounts payable, and all other expenses associated with operating the business, such as: salaries, rent, utilities, office supplies, etc. The key word here is cash. Remember our depreciation example. Depreciation is a non-cash expense and *would not* be included in our list of cash disbursements. Cash disbursements also include the cash the business needs to repay its loans. Businesses must also factor in any cash the business owner withdraws for personal compensation. The sum of these figures is the **total cash disbursements.**

Subtracting total cash disbursements from cash receipts results in the business's ending cash position. The tracking of incoming and outgoing cash is referred to as **cash flow**. It is sometimes hard for the start-up entrepreneur to imagine, but businesses can show a profit, but have negative cash flow. Likewise, some businesses, at the end of their cycle, post a loss, yet have a positive cash flow.

When there is more cash coming in than being paid out, of course, businesses have a **positive cash flow**. While it is possible for businesses to operate profitably with a negative cash flow, this is not an advisable way for start-up businesses to operate. Maintaining and planning for a positive cash flow at all times allows the business to safely meet its operating expenses and debts.

The Reality of Cash Flow

Alpha Beta Computing had been in business for almost 15 years. It had ticked along nicely over the years and supported its two partners, Sue Albright and Nils Ericson, as well as provided jobs for 8 employees. The company, located in a suburb of Los Angeles, was a distributor for other company's software packages.

Last year, the opportunity of a lifetime came along. Alpha Beta had the chance to become the exclusive distributor for one of the hottest software companies in the country. If the deal came to fruition, their customer base would double almost overnight and sales would increase dramatically. Sue and Nils flew to Seattle and made an oral presentation to the software company. Two weeks later, they received the contract.

Six months elapsed since the contract was signed, and sales for Alpha Beta almost doubled. But Sue and Nils had a serious cash flow problem, and they couldn't pay their bills. The increased sales resulted in dramatically increased costs and many of the new accounts were much slower in paying their bills than the company's old accounts. Sue and Nils sat down with their accountant and developed a cash flow analysis for their business. By cutting expenses and factoring in the increased amount of time for some accounts receivables to be paid, they are back on track. In December of 1996, they had a positive cash flow and their realistic projections for 1997 look good.

Balance Sheet

A balance sheet is a profile of a business's assets and liabilities. It is an itemized report of the net worth of a business at a given point in time. **Assets** are any items of value owned by the business. These include cash, accounts receivable, inventory on-hand, any prepaid expenses (current assets) and land, buildings and equipment (non-current assets). **Depreciation** is the decrease in value of assets from wear and tear and the passage of time. **Accumulated depreciation** represents the total of all the non-cash expenses associated with an asset and is subtracted from the asset to give its net value. This net value may or may not have any actual relationship to the true market or sale value of that asset.

Liabilities are debts owed in the long and short term. These include accruals, accounts payable, bank mortgages and other bank debts.

By subtracting total liabilities from total assets businesses calculate their overall **net worth**.

Assumption sheet

An assumption sheet shows investors that the figures on which the financial plan is based are reasonable and carefully chosen. An assumption sheet shows your justification for including projected income or expense items in your financial plan. It demonstrates that you carefully considered your market and made financial assumptions based on solid knowledge of the business. This section is also beneficial later, as you review your plan and test your initial assumptions and see whether they have changed.

All this section needs to contain is a brief sentence describing each assumption about:

- The target customer
- The industry
- The economy
- The competition
- Potential employees
- Potential suppliers

The Closing Section of the Start-up Business Plan

The final section of the Start-up Business Plan is a summary of your exploratory efforts. It contains a feasibility statement and an action plan. Given your research, calculations, and projections, is yours a viable business idea? Can you profitably operate your business? This is the time for you to make a judgment call about whether or not this is a business worth pursuing and if you are the right person for the job. If so, what do you expect to achieve and when do you expect to achieve it? What is your long-term vision for the business?

If you decide the business is worth pursuing, the action plan clearly spells out the action steps for start-up. It prioritizes and schedules your tasks and tactics and outlines what you will achieve in the next 1, 3, and 6 months.

The Start-up Business Plan Checklist

- ❑ Prepare background information
- ❑ Skills and experience
- ❑ Financial capability
- ❑ Business concept
- ❑ Business objectives
- ❑ General description of business

Describe Product or Service

- ❑ Create mission statement
- ❑ Describe customer benefits

- ❑ Decide on business location
- ❑ Estimate product development stage
- ❑ Project future products or services

Design Management Structure

- ❑ Prepare organizational chart
- ❑ Discuss responsibilities of key employees
- ❑ Discuss employee qualifications
- ❑ Explore contractors or outside support
- ❑ Identify start-up mentor

Evaluate the Market

- ❑ Define current and future industry trends
- ❑ Create target customer profile
- ❑ Estimate market size
- ❑ Identify competition and market advantage
- ❑ Review possible barriers to market entry
- ❑ Explain market strategy
    - Price
    - Placement
    - Product
    - Promotion

Compile the Financial Plan

- ❑ Determine start-up costs
- ❑ Prepare basic income statement
- ❑ Project cash flow for one year
- ❑ Project sales levels
- ❑ Prepare a balance sheet
- ❑ Prepare an assumption sheet

Determine Your Long-Term Goals

- ❑ Predict potential risks
- ❑ Create risk-prevention strategies

Write Executive Summary

- ❑ Consolidate and summarize all accumulated data
- ❑ Adjust original business concept as needed
- ❑ Determine target reading investors/lenders and write accordingly

Finishing Touches

- ❑ Proofread document
- ❑ Create/collect graphs, charts, and photographs
- ❑ Reread entire business plan
- ❑ Determine overall feasibility of plan
- ❑ Give plan to friends, advisors, or family for review
- ❑ Determine if follow-up on full-fledged business plan is necessary

Is Your Business Venture Feasible?

You've drafted your plan. You've completed your Start-up Business Plan checklist. Look at all the information you've accumulated. Does your business plan make sense? Will it meet your financial requirements? Is there a real demand for the product or service you wish to provide? See if the results of your business plan indicate true market potential. Determine whether you'll seek investors and establish who they would be.

Ask yourself if you need to continue to develop your business concept into a full-fledged business plan. If you plan to get financial assistance from family or friends, the information contained in the Start-up Business Plan will probably suffice. But you will likely need to present a more detailed business plan if you are seeking funding from other investors or banks.

When you are satisfied with your results, you can start putting together your executive summary.

The Start-up Business Plan may be for your eyes only, so you can get a good idea of the overall feasibility of your business idea. However, it is wise get the input of friends, family, employees, and advisors before you commit to a plan.

A weak plan can be fatal for your business

A weak plan can be fatal, not only because it may turn away potential lenders and investors, but because it won't properly direct you towards success. Do yourself a favor and be honest when you are creating your plan. It is so easy to paint a glorified picture of your idea, your qualified staff, or your ability to create a business that will take off. Do a reality check. Look at your assumptions. Are they likely to be accurate? Have you addressed all the questions lenders or investors will ask? Do you have the skills and resources to be successful?

A realistic business plan helps you to clearly see the realities of business ownership. It helps to identify your weaknesses and strengths so you can budget the time, energy, and money to improve those areas that need it.

Don't beat yourself over the head if you find major problems with your plan. This is typical. Rome wasn't built in a day and neither are successful businesses. You can always revise and improve your plan.

Finally, don't be a slave to your plan. If new opportunities arise that were not considered in the original plan, don't avoid them simply because they weren't discussed as options in your plan. There's more than one way to get to your final destination.

Above all, the Start-up Business Plan is a working document. It should evolve over time as you learn more about the market and about yourself.

A Polished Presentation

Remember that the Start-up Business Plan is a tool for you to attract investors, advisors, and employees. You may at some point be called on to present it to someone who has "the power" to make your business a reality. For this reason, you should think about how you will present the plan, both in writing and in person.

A business plan separates "doers" from "talkers"

The presentation of a business plan can boil down to a few important minutes. All your painstaking research, planning, and documentation means nothing if you cannot present your ideas clearly and convincingly, in a few minutes. Initially, that's about all the time most lenders or investors will take to look at your plan. So you have to pique their interests with an organized plan that utilizes visual cues. The goal is to provide instant information with impact.

The written Start-up Business Plan should be:

- Typed and printed on quality paper
- Absolutely free of spelling and grammatical errors
- Presented in a hard folder or binder
- Contain charts and graphs that are consistent in style
- Be clear, to the point, and easy to read
- Give brief definitions of industry specific terminology

Once you've cleaned up your document formatting and proofreading, it is then ready to be passed along to a trusted friend or relative for review. Keep an open mind as to their input.

When you present your Start-up Business Plan in person, you should:

- Dress cleanly and professionally
- Speak slowly and clearly
- Look directly and confidently at your audience
- Prepare and budget your time in advance
- Present a compelling executive summary in the first 30 seconds
- Use the next 2-3 minutes to provide details and supporting information
- Finish with a clear conclusion and detail of what you want from the listener
- Use simple charts or tables to clarify ideas and focus attention
- Practice! Practice! Practice!

Conclusion

The Start-up Business Plan is an operating plan for the entrepreneur, a financing proposal for lenders, and an inspirational information vehicle for potential partners and employees. It is the product of all of your market analysis and financial calculations. It is also the capstone of your participation in the NxLeveL training program for start-up businesses. When you have completed the soul searching and the actual work that go into the plan, you should be proud. You will have done what few other people have: You have taken the first step in making your entrepreneurial dream a reality!

Remember, the Start-up Business Plan is the most useful tool for any business concept. It tests the viability of the business idea. All new ventures begin with hopes and fears. This document will aid you in confirming your hopes and confronting your concerns about your business.

Chapter 9
CONTINGENCY PLANNING

About This Chapter:
- *Setting your limits*
- *Why you would want to get out*
- *Which way out?*
- *Dealing with bankruptcy*

Introduction

It may sound odd, but the same day you begin your business you should begin preparing your **exit strategy** out of the business. This involves setting the limits by which you will consider leaving the business and investigating your various possibilities. Why do this? Because having limits for your business and your personal involvement in it can give you a concrete benchmark against which you can judge your business's progress or lack thereof. Revisiting these parameters when you are in the thick of running your business can provide you with a much needed reality check. The reasons you may choose or be forced to end your business can include boredom, the pursuit of a better opportunity, a terrific buy-out offer, or bankruptcy.

Welcome aboard!

Got your return ticket?

This chapter covers the situations in which you might exit your business. In all of them, your understanding of the basic considerations and personal issues involved in each will make the process a lot easier. So, as you plan the start of your business, take a moment to do a little contingency planning.

Why Would You Want Out?

It's sad but true: in many cases young businesses go belly up financially and have no choice but to call it quits. But there are also brighter scenarios in which you might choose to exit your business. For example, someone wants to give you a fabulous amount money for your business. If and when this day comes, some of your motives might be:

- You've identified a better opportunity elsewhere
- You're bored and want a new challenge
- You think that your business has achieved all the growth it can
- You lack the skills or interest in taking your business to the next level
- You are no longer working 70 hours a week (only 60!)
- You want to diversify your assets
- Your interests and/or those of your founding team have changed
- You are ready for retirement

Knowing When To Say When: Your Quantitative Limits

Your preset exit limits represent a safety net against personal and professional loss for the entrepreneur. These exit limits might look something like this:

"If my business experiences the following, I will seriously consider calling it quits":

- The business has overdue bills exceeding $25,000
- The business has fallen below $500,000 in sales
- The business has accumulated over $100,000 in long-term debt
- Profit margins have fallen below 12% over 2 consecutive quarters

"If my business experiences the following, I WILL call it quits":

- The business has overdue bills exceeding $35,000
- The business has fallen below $200,000 in sales
- The business has accumulated over $150,000 in long-term debt
- The business has experienced 3 consecutive quarters of declining profits
- Profit margins have fallen below 10% over 3 consecutive quarters

On the upside, you might also create limits to your involvement in the business once it becomes too large or too successful. This might be measured by a certain level of sales, customers, or employees. Your motivation for setting this sort of limit might be your interest in a given quality of life or your recognition that you simply lack the expertise or interest in managing a large enterprise. Once these limits have been reached it will be your signal to either hire a full-time manager to take over for you or to remove yourself in order to start your next business.

Your limits are your personal safety net

Remember, these limits need not be etched in stone, but they do need to be well-thought out and written down. Keep them handy and revisit them often as your business grows.

Knowing When to Say When: Your Personal Limits

The above list presents some common reasons that motivate entrepreneurs to get out of their businesses. However, only you can know why you want out. Having set the financial limits for your involvement in the business, your next step is to identify your own personal limits.

Knowing when to say when is a lot easier if you begin your business having outlined your personal and professional goals. This distinguishes *your* goals from the goals of your business, and, as you invest more and more of yourself in your business, can help you make appropriate decisions regarding your life.

You'll be more prepared to answer this question if every so often (maybe 2 times a year) you sit down and update your personal 1, 5, and 10 year plan. Consider your personal ambitions as well as your commitments to your family and friends. Set concrete goals for yourself just as you do for your business. Consider some examples:

- By age ___ I want to have a personal net worth of $___
- By age ___ I want to be earning $___ a year
- I want to retire at age ___
- I want to own a house by age ___
- I want to spend at least ___ hours a day with my children/family
- I want to take a ___ month trip to South America by age ___

Your business is fun, challenging, and exciting, BUT it's not the whole story!

Your goals should be concrete, measurable, time-bound, and attainable. Without these characteristics you don't have a goal on your hands, you have a wish. These goals might broadly include:

- Personal investment targets
- Your spouse's occupation
- Acquisition of personal assets
- Developing new skills
- Switching careers
- Travel and adventure
- Additional education or degrees
- Financially supporting your parents
- Moving to a different city, region, or country
- Community service or volunteer work

Setting Your Exit Goals

You now know when and why you might want to exit your business. What do you want to get out of the process? Even in the most difficult financial times, entrepreneurs still have some power to decide if the venture will continue, in what form, and what they will walk away with at the end of the day. Considering how fast you want out, how much on-going participation you want in the business, and how much of your ownership you want to liquidate are all decisions that will all influence your choice of exit strategies.

The Couch Potato

Consider for a moment the experiences of one inspired entrepreneur in Santa Cruz, California. Having grown a successful investment consulting business, she found that she was spending more time with her computer and her telephone than with her young children. Working with a good attorney and banker, she sold off her interest in the business, and using her profits, began a new venture in couch retailing. In structuring this business, she was guided by insights she gained in her investment business. Her priority? Having time to spend with her family and working in a more relaxed environment, with people who were part of her community. Her new business, Couch Potato Couches, was open for business 4 days a week. In these 4 days, she was able to do the administrative work for the business and sell enough couches to support herself and sustain the kind of lifestyle she valued: she was able to spend a big chunk of her time at home being a mom!

How Do I Get Out of Here?

Entrepreneurs have several avenues by which they can exit their businesses. Each depends upon how profitable and successful the business has been and what their personal goals are. Some common exit scenarios include:

A genie can make "wishes" come true but only you can achieve your "goals"!

- Selling out to an individual
- Selling out to another company
- Selling your stock within the company
- Selling your stock in a public offering

Also, consider these less happy scenarios for your exit:

- Business failure and bankruptcy
- Being shown the door by your investors or directors

The Nitty Gritty of Selling Your Business

For one reason or another you've decided to sell your business, but just how do you do it? This may seem like a confusing process, but remember that at each step of the deal there is whole cast of experts who work exclusively with the buying and selling of businesses. Attorneys, accountants, brokers, investors, bankers, and consultants all come in different shapes and sizes to help even the smallest of firms. For further discussion on this topic, see the Chapter 11 *Valuing and Buying a Business.*

There are two general approaches small business owners use when selling their businesses. Perhaps the most common, low cost, and informal way that entrepreneurs use is word of mouth. By talking to your partners, your investors, your friends, members of your community, and "working" your professional network you might be surprised how quickly you will find a potential buyer!

Spread the word... and suitors will come calling!

However, if you want to approach the sale of your business more methodically, the other course of action is employing the help of a professional business broker

Small Business Brokers

Business brokers are used primarily when one individual is selling their own business to another individual. Most business brokers work with small businesses. Regardless of whom they work with, business brokers operate in the same way: they evaluate companies, post listings in various journals, newsletters and newspapers, and advertise and promote the businesses they're brokering in much the same way as realtors do. Business brokers might help someone to find a business who want to get out of big business and migrate to a smaller environment

Business brokers can operate locally, regionally, or nationally, and can specialize by industry or geographic location. Just open up a copy of *The Wall Street Journal* or your local newspaper and you will see scores of listings

Valuing Your Business

No matter how unique your product or how knowledgeable your employees, the truth of the matter is that your business is valued by buyers simply on the basis of cash flow and asset evaluation. This can be a simple listing of the valuables of a business: assets, real estate, etc. There can be exceptions to this rule, as in the case of a business possessing a key piece of real estate. If your shoe retailing business is located on a strategically placed corner in your neighborhood, and Starbuck's Coffee wants to come to town, you might find that your business is worth a lot more than just the revenues it can generate by selling shoes! However, most businesses must rely on their cash flow and/or significant tangible assets as measures of their market value. Some other indicators of your business's worth are its:

- sales growth
- historical profitability
- industry market conditions

If you enlist the services of a business broker, one of the first things they do is assess the value of your business. In this way, you will be able to stay focused on the day-to-day task of actually running your business.

Evaluating Buyers

How do you put a price tag on your business?

Should you choose not to work with a business broker, a key task for you will be evaluating potential buyers. You should first develop a list of the criteria that will guide this evaluation process. You should also consider the advice and consent of a good accountant who can assist you in the valuation process. These criteria should include:

- Financial strength
- Type of industry
- Size of the company
- Reputation
- Their experience in acquisitions
- Knowledge of your industry and market
- Geographic location
- Ownership of the company (privately or publicly held)
- Degree of synergy between both business's core competencies

Once you've listed your criteria for selecting a buyer, rank them according to their importance to you.

Given these criteria, the one that will probably be most important to you will be the financial health of the individual or company who is attempting to buy your business. Entrepreneurs often strike a deal whereby buyers will pay them a small portion of the sale price of their business in cash, and then pay the remaining amounts in installments over time. Generally, these are paid out of earnings taken from the business itself. For this reason, it is very important for you to assess the buyer's ability to profitably manage your business. Many times, potential buyers will ask the seller to stay on and "teach them the business". This is often beneficial to both parties. The buyer benefits from the seller's years of experience and management of the business. The seller can stay behind and "guard the value of the business", especially important when the purchase is being financed in installments out of the business' cash flow.

Legal and Tax Implications

The tax implications for the sale of your business can be huge and can seriously affect the profitability of the undertaking. Likewise, there are many legal guidelines that vary from state to state that govern the transfer of ownership in a business. Therefore, before you sell all or a part of your share in the business, you should seek the assistance of an experienced tax attorney and securities lawyer. In addition, a small business broker can help you navigate through both the tax and legal issues of the sale of your business.

Maximize your gains by minimizing your taxes

Selling Your Stock to the Public

In the past decade, many start-up companies, such as software or other technology-oriented companies, have made headlines by going public at very early stages of their growth and with very minimal levels of sales. In the process, they have made millionaires for their founders. How do you explain this phenomenon? High-tech companies of all sorts often possess unique technical knowledge or intellectual property that makes them particularly attractive to larger companies wanting to acquire that know-how. This explains the rush by large companies like Microsoft, Novell, and IBM to snap up small companies with even smaller earnings, and pay handsomely to do it.

This, however, is much less common in other industries in which the value of a company is judged on the basis of its earnings and cash flow. What does this mean for you and your small business? It means that unless you have developed a unique and innovative technological process or product, you will probably not be participating in a public offering of your venture. However, if you grow your business to significant profitable levels (this could occur anywhere between $5 to 20 million in sales) you might be in a position to consider offering your stock to the public. High-growth businesses in select industries do this everyday to raise additional capital or to liquidate their ownership in the business.

To sell your stock to the public, your first essential step is selecting a quality investment banker. Chances are you've never participated in an **IPO** (an **initial public offering**) of stock before, but there are many experts out there to help you. Your key investors, lawyer, accountant, consultants, and banker will all be essential to the process and can help you select a good investment banker.

Dreaming of millions?

think:

- high tech
- high growth
- high profits

When structuring an IPO, you should identify the following:

- The percent of ownership to be sold
- The pricing of the shares of stock
- The timing of the offering
- The compensation to the investment banker

There are many legal and regulatory guidelines to public offerings of stock. Most of these focus on having the business audited by outside accountants to verify the accuracy of its valuation and projections and the release of timely and accurate information to potential investors. Your lawyer will be indispensable to your business as it works to meet disclosure deadlines, file documents, and prepare contracts governing the transfer stock. In short, your lawyer will make sure that the whole transaction is on the up and up!

Being Shown the Door

This scenario usually occurs when the business has outgrown the ability of the entrepreneur to manage the enterprise. It can also occur when the entrepreneur's interest in operating the particular business is exhausted. In these cases, a group of major investors or the directors of the company might ask the founder to relinquish day-to-day control over management.

The Business Failure

Unfortunately, for many businesses the exit path leads directly to bankruptcy court. What is **bankruptcy**? It is simply the inability by a business to pay its debts. This can be the result of under capitalization, poor cash management, or over expansion. Sometimes a business's bankruptcy is the result of a single, major occurrence, like the failure of a large customer to pay off its account, a major lawsuit, a loss of inventory or equipment due to fire, or the call of a large debt by a lender.

Bankruptcy in the United States is regulated by The Bankruptcy Reform Act of 1978. This act regulates all sorts of bankruptcies. Presented below are the major sub-chapters which cover different types of bankruptcies:

Chapter 11—Voluntary

When an entrepreneur is unable to pay debts in a timely manner, he may voluntarily petition for the protection of the U.S. District Court. If approved, this protection allows the business to continue operations under a set of legal guidelines designed to protect the interests of the business's creditors. In this case, the business seeking protection is given 120 days in which to submit a plan of reorganization, which will guide the business for the duration of the bankruptcy. This plan includes provisions for paying off different classifications of creditors, the preference order, timing and so forth. In some cases, the court may appoint a trustee to take possession of all assets of the company and oversee operations. The bankrupt entrepreneur may also raise new funds by selling shares in the business, borrowing money, or selling assets.

Chapter 10—Involuntary

Under this chapter, the creditors of a business have the right to petition the court to demand a company's reorganization. This petition may be submitted when a creditor's (or group of creditors) claims exceed $5,000. A debtor (the entrepreneur) may contest this petition, and if successful, may seek reimbursement for all legal costs from its creditors. If it is unsuccessful, the procedure here is similar to that under Chapter 11 Bankruptcy proceedings.

Chapter 7—Liquidation

This is the legal chapter that covers the most extreme cases of business bankruptcy: the situation in which the business must liquidate or sell off all of its non exempt assets to cover the business's debts. If the entrepreneur submits a voluntary bankruptcy petition under Chapter 7, it is a voluntary recognition that the business is bankrupt. Along with this statement, a businessperson must usually submit an up-to-date statement of income and expenses. An involuntary bankruptcy under this act is very similar to those under Chapters 10 and 11, with the exception that the business's assets are liquidated to pay off its creditors.

Is the glass half empty or half full?
Half of all businesses fail in their first four years
—OR—
Half of all businesses succeed beyond 4 years.

Personal

And what about the effect that bankruptcy might have on you personally and professionally? No doubt you are worn out, dispirited, and embarrassed. However, in truth, bankruptcy doesn't have to mean the end for you, the entrepreneur. It is historically proven that most successful entrepreneurs have endured and learned from multiple failures before finally achieving success. This is why it is critical for you to identify how and why your business has failed and learn from your mistakes. What caused your business to fail? Was it bad luck or was it a weakness you have in one area or another? Is it a skill or talent that you can acquire in order to improve the chances of success of your next venture? What lessons have you taken away from the experience?

Some of the many valuable lessons to be learned from bankruptcy include:

- In starting their business, few entrepreneurs review their exit strategy
- Entrepreneurs stray from their core competencies
- Entrepreneurs undertake expansion too quickly
- Many entrepreneurs are undercapitalized
- It's difficult to separate the entrepreneur's ego from the business
- Entrepreneurs invest too much time in seeking additional customers and too little time serving the ones they have
- Entrepreneurs tend to file for bankruptcy protection too late

Chances are, having failed once, you will better understand the dynamics of a market and the correct mix needed to run a successful business: market research, capitalization, cash management, and people management. Your negotiating skills will almost certainly have improved.

It's Really Happening! What Do I Do Now?

How do you know when you're going bankrupt? If you know the warning signs you might be able to avoid trouble or at least minimize it when it hits. These signs often are linked together, once one happens, the others may not be far behind. At the outset, every entrepreneur should have a general understanding of the protections available under U.S. bankruptcy law and begin establishing a relationship with a capable and trustworthy attorney in the event that you should *really* need one.

Here's the scenario: Your creditors are calling on the phone in a panic, your two largest customers just failed for the fourth time to pay off their accounts, your banker is getting antsy. What should you do?

The first thing you should do is contact your lawyer. If your lawyer recommends filing for bankruptcy, do it fast. Your goal is to file for bankruptcy before your creditors join together into a group and file first to force you into bankruptcy. Your voluntary bankruptcy declaration will buy you a 120-day holding period in which you submit a plan of reorganization and another 60 days while the court and your creditors evaluate it. During this period your business is not required to pay off any of its debts. After this period of time, you have two courses of action: ensure that your plan to make your business profitable again works or begin planning the liquidation of your business.

Bankruptcy's Red Flags

- Lack of management control and accountability over finances and spending
- Lack of inventory or supply to meet orders
- Lack of planning and paper documentation of major transactions
- Key people leave the company
- Business offers large discounts to customers who pay cash
- Bank requires subordination of its loans
- Payroll taxes are not paid
- Employee benefits are not funded
- Suppliers require cash payments
- Increase in customer complaints

During this process of trying to stay afloat, your key task will be to keep in contact with customers to inspire their confidence and continued loyalty to your business. You'll want to keep creditors up to date on all developments and stay in touch with stockholders. Your investors are probably more concerned than anyone about your business and their investment in it. You might keep them appraised of details via a newsletter and for larger investors, a personal phone call from you. Last, but not least, you must communicate with your employees, who more than anyone else feel the uncertainty of the business on daily basis. You should share with them the details of the business's reorganization and keep them focused on the key tasks at hand. After all, in the most basic sense, the very future of your business depends on them!

You've Sold Your Business, Now What?

Experienced entrepreneurs agree: learn all the lessons you can and move on

You were working 70 hours a week and now you are sitting in your garden reading travel magazines. The thrill of the day-to-day operations of your business are behind you, and a lot of professional uncertainty lies ahead. What is your next step? As mentioned at the start of this chapter, looking at the "big picture" of your personal and professional life before you exit your business will help you immeasurably after you exit your business.

Having done this, your transition into the next phase of your life will be a lot easier. The key to this will be taking time to think about the business you left and the lessons you've taken with you. Then you can celebrate your victories and do some of the things you've always dreamed of doing!

A great actor gives a great performance but always knows when to exit stage left

Exiting Doesn't Mean You Have To Say You're Sorry

Anderson and Associates, a public relations firm located in a suburb of Washington, D.C., opened its doors for business in 1990. Dylan Anderson, the owner, had always planned to give it up. One of her priorities when she started the company, in fact, was establishing a contingency plan for the future: she wanted to sell the business at some point in time as she and her husband, who would retire in 1996, planned to relocate to the Maryland coast and build their dream house on the beach.

By late 1995, Anderson and Associates had evolved into a very successful company. Clients included several national associations located in the Washington area as well as some major corporations. Dylan had worked hard to establish her business and made sure all the key elements were there: attention to financial details, an energetic and creative staff, customer service, and the company was very profitable. By mid-1996, Dylan had not one but three bidders seriously interested in buying her business.

Dylan and her husband ushered in the new year of 1997 in their new house overlooking the Atlantic Ocean. The new owner of Anderson and Associates (another entrepreneur) celebrated the new year and his new venture in the company's office.

Conclusion

As you exit your business, remember that the things made you an entrepreneur—drive, wit, fearlessness, and charm—will not disappear the day you cash out of your business. You might take some well-deserved time off, but before long, no doubt, the wheels of your imagination will be churning out new ideas and opportunities for professional growth.

Chances are you have experienced some priceless learning by starting your own business. You've learned more about a particular industry, serving customers, hiring and managing people, and keeping track of a business's finances. You might even have learned a few new things about yourself. As you exit the business with these insights in hand, you will be uniquely equipped to set new goals and create the personal and professional life you desire. Now that you know these things, dive in and start a new business today!

PART III
BUSINESS START-UP OPTIONS

Chapter 10
OVERVIEW OF START-UP OPPORTUNITIES

About This Chapter:
- *Starting a business*
- *Purchasing a business*
- *Purchasing a franchise*
- *Other alternatives*

Introduction

You may have decided to start your own business after an event triggered your entrepreneurial desires and abilities. Sometimes inheriting a family business or having people ask for your opinion on how to develop a product or service can lead to your self-employed business success. At other times the loss of your job or an accident that limits your physical abilities will get you to think about your work in a different way and inspire you to start your own business. The point is, there are many reasons why people go into business for themselves. And there are many options for entering into business.

Not all opportunities are based on starting a business from the ground up. Countless alternatives are waiting to be developed or discovered by an inspired, creative mind. This chapter presents common and alternative entry strategies to help you get started on your quest.

Common Entry Strategies

A basic road map of options for those who want to own and operate their own business follows:

1. Start a business
2. Buy an existing business
3. Purchase a franchise business

Starting a Business

Starting a new business can be the most exciting method of getting into business, as it permits you the most freedom. You get to develop the strategies, marketing approaches, employment requirements—everything. You won't be constrained by someone else's way of doing business. If successful, you will have the satisfaction of knowing you did it all yourself.

A new invention

One popular belief is that a new invention is the best way to guarantee success. Although it is true that new businesses can be started on the basis of an invention, this road to success may be long and arduous. Although an invention is exciting to the inventor, the device may prove to have little commercial value. Perhaps no one wants the product or the market is too small to be viable. Careful market research is the key to determining potential demand for the product.

Inventors: how are your business skills?

Another reality is that the inventor may be a genius at developing a new device but does not possess the aptitude or skill for running a business. Most inventors do not realize the time and money it takes to bring a new product to market.

If you intend to start a business based on an invention, it is best to face the reality of the marketplace. You must see if there is a viable market, determine how you will finance your endeavor, understand the limitations on a business built on one product, and be prepared to spend a lot of time and energy getting your product in front of your potential customers.

Spin-off of an existing product or service

Suppose you are working for a landscaping contractor as a buyer. In the course of your work you realize no one has a good stock of seedless cherry or plum fruit trees. With a little research you located a supply of seedlings, found an area where you can grow them, and discovered a source for the capital needed to start your venture. This is an example of a simple spin-off business grounded in your personal knowledge and experience.

There are many opportunities in developing spin-off options and they are often successful. Equipped with a good plan, current business skills, and real-world information about all aspects of operating this business, the prospective owner has the chance to put in place the best aspects of developing a new business.

Turning a hobby into a business

Here is an idea—do what you enjoy! If you start a business, why not do something you love? You will have a much better chance of making a success of your venture if you develop a business from a hobby you enjoy.

Two things stand out when developing a business out of a hobby. First, though you may view your business as an opportunity to work at your hobby, you must recognize that the product or service has an economic value. You will need to run the business for profit. Second, remember that you are running a business and not pursuing a hobby. As the business develops, you may not have time to enjoy your hobby the same way as you did in the past. Let's say you love fly-fishing and have scoped out some of the best spots for fly fishing in your state. If you decide to start a business acting as a fly-fishing guide, be prepared to give up those leisurely fishing trips.

Have a hobby? Start a business!

Awareness of a given customer

Entering into business for yourself is a risk. The greatest risk is that there will be no customers to buy your product or service. Therefore, there is great advantage in starting a company if you have a customer ready to purchase your product. In fact, there are cases where the customer is so willing to purchase your product they will help in the development of your company. They may be willing to provide financing or place an order large enough to provide you with the financial resources to establish your business.

However, there are some potential problems to consider. First, you need to insure that your customer is financially capable of meeting their commitments. Second, even though they claim they need your product, it doesn't mean they have the capability of marketing it. Third, if you rely on only one customer, you are subject to their economic cycles and they can dictate your price, production runs, and potential profitability.

John Vail's River

John Vail lives near the Tallahatchie River in Mississippi. He had always loved spending peaceful Sunday afternoons fishing on the river. One day, his boat struck a large plank of wood submerged beneath the water's surface. The following Saturday, he and a friend rented scuba gear and dove near the site. They pulled several of the 12-foot planks that were resting in the ooze. The planks had been cut over 100 years ago and had been floated down the river as part of a raft on their way to a finishing mill 20 miles down river. In this process, many planks did not reach the final destination, getting caught in the underbrush on the river's edge and had gradually sunk to the river's bottom.

John had an idea. He had recently been laid off from his job as an adjuster at an insurance company. He felt he needed to get out of the office environment and his first true love was the river. He contacted a local mill that provided lumber to a furniture manufacturer in North Carolina. Because the furniture company prided itself on its use of recycled lumber, John set up an arrangement with the mill owner to provide him with the historic planks. The mill would then dry the wood and prepare it for supply to the manufacturer. John needed equipment to start his lumber reclamation business, so the mill owner, who was eager to obtain such high-quality wood, agreed to help John finance the cost of a boat and mechanical winch for wood excavation. John now runs a thriving business on the river, where his heart had always been.

The number of major companies needing new products, services or parts is almost unlimited. If you can find a fully qualified buyer, you may be able to establish your company with limited risk. Consider this customer only the starting point for your enterprise.

Unfulfilled market need

Knowing and understanding your customer's needs is one of the most important factors affecting the success or failure of a business. Many businesses are started with the recognition of an unfulfilled need. Establishing a business in this manner also means doing all the things necessary to deliver the service or product that fills this need.

Many times people are deceived into believing such a need exits. Friends may agree that your idea is great and should sell like "hot cakes" when in reality their opinion is clouded by friendship. Or, the market for specialty products or services may be too small to sustain a business on a long-term basis. Spend the time necessary to determine how large the market for your product is and what percentage of the market will provide you with sufficient sales to grow your business.

Expansion of a part-time activity

One way to develop a full-time business is to expand on a part-time activity in which you're involved.

Grow part-time work to a full-time business

Specialty Pottery

Jane Dillard had always been engaged in making art in one form or another. She studied painting and on the side she dabbled in pottery. While exhibiting her paintings at various art shows, she began to bring along some of her pottery. Although her training had been in painting and she enjoyed the art form, she found that her pottery created more consistent sales than her art. Soon Jane began to concentrate on making pottery full time. She produces a specialty line that she sells to wholesalers. Because it was expensive to get started, Jane set up her production facility gradually and brought on skilled labor as her business expanded. Today she has customers throughout the western United States and Canada.

There are definite advantages to starting a business in this manner: you have the opportunity to observe market demand; to grow with your interest and capabilities; and to develop your client base to the point where it can sustain a full-time business.

Chance

Many entrepreneurs are in business for themselves due to chance. Opportunities come to all of us at some point in our lives. The real skill is recognizing the opportunity and having the energy to pursue it.

Chance and Initiative

Jon Sullivan and Tim Tucker were working for a large TV cable company installing updated equipment. The equipment they replaced was in good working order but was designed for a smaller operation; as the cable company grew, they were constantly replacing the lower capacity equipment. When Jon and Tim returned to the shop and asked what to do with the old equipment, their boss told them to dispose of it.

Jon thought that there must be a market for used equipment and he knew where many small systems were located nationwide. Jon and Tim got together and placed a small advertisement in an industry magazine offering to sell the used equipment. They were amazed by the number of calls they received. Within a week they sold all the used equipment they had. Next, they made a deal with their boss: they would buy all the used equipment from their employer at a predetermined price. They also called other large cable companies and found that they were also disposing of their equipment. For the first six months they only bought parts of systems from large communities.

The business was doing so well after the first six months, they realized that they could quit their jobs and begin selling full time. Jon and Tim came upon an opportunity by chance, but they took the initiative to capitalize on a market they knew already existed!

Professional or technical expertise
Many people have a specific technical education or have acquired various skills through prior business experience. These skills can be used in building a business. The time and energy spent acquiring a specific skill will aid greatly in developing your business. If you are a nurse and want to move from hospital-based work to consulting for an HMO on healthcare costs and hospital stays, your schooling and work experience will obviously be major factors in your business's success.

While it is true that some technical skills are required for all businesses, it's also important to remember that your skills may need to be augmented by the expertise of others. Seek advice from those professionals who can fill your skills gap.

Desperation
Although desperation is not the preferred method to discover your entrepreneurial creativity, it does provide an avenue for some. You may be the victim of downsizing, right-sizing, reduction in force, merge and purge, or any of the various methods corporate America has found to reduce their work force. Once you lose your job, you may find that no one in your area needs your skills. Or your situation may be caused by the death of a spouse which makes it necessary for you to find a better way to earn a living. Any number of reasons can cause you to recognize that your best option for earning a living is to work for yourself.

Buying an Existing Business

Many businesses will buy an existing business to round out the services they can offer. For instance, a local marketing firm might be interested in purchasing a direct-mail fulfillment house in order to better develop its business. Likewise, if you've always wanted to own your own gift shop and your favorite local store is for sale, you might consider buying the store in order to jump-start your dream.

Start up by purchasing a going concern

By buying an existing business, you can:

- Avoid lead time required to launch the business
- Understand expected income, expenses
- Acquire an existing customer base
- Take hold of an established image

Although buying a business may not offer the same opportunity for creativity found in starting a business, there will be many ways to express your ideas by improving the image, expanding the customer base, and streamlining operations. On the other hand, if the business is thriving, you can avoid much of the uncertainty of a start-up operation.

Most successful acquisitions are accomplished by knowledgeable, adequately-financed business people. When acquiring a company, it's important to understand the numerous tax and financial maneuverings available for acquiring and financially restructuring an existing company.

Purchasing a Franchise Business

Franchises are independently-owned businesses that provide the business owner with much of the entrepreneur's independence, while presenting less risk than other types of entry strategies.

Franchising is a method of business expansion whereby a business owner or manager allows others to market products or services under his or her name and trademark and in strict adherence to a prescribed system. In return, the franchisee pays a fee and, usually, an ongoing royalty. Moreover, the franchisee pays all of the costs of getting into the franchise.

In effect, a franchisee is able to launch a new business with fewer growing pains. Someone else has already developed an operating system that works. It is like a cook using a recipe created and tested by a master chef; he or she can be pretty sure of getting good results on the first attempt. It is comforting to have ongoing support services from the franchise. It also means being able to draw from the collective strength in buying, advertising, product development, and market research that the franchise offers.

Not every franchise is a guarantee of success. Many small, less expensive franchises are under-funded, lack a good training program, and fail to provide necessary support. Many of the large, well-known franchises are too costly for many beginning entrepreneurs. Although this may be true, the support and proven business successes of many franchises make them an attractive starting point for the entrepreneur.

Alternative Entry Strategies

In this section we will explore some of the non-traditional ways that people have used to enter the world of self-employment.

Technology Transfer

Technology transfer is an uncommon yet viable business entry method. Certain procedures and products developed by state and federal agencies are made public and available for commercial use. The objective is to turn a product developed in governmental labs into a commercial product.

Separating Potatoes

The specific gravity weight separator developed at the National Energy Laboratory in Idaho is a good example of technology transfer. The process was a means to separate nuclear waste by its specific gravity, regardless of the size of the sample.

Turning technology into a business

In southern Idaho, where many of the nation's finest potatoes are grown, a common problem in digging up the potatoes is separating them from the field rocks. A farmer in Twin Falls, Idaho, became aware of the process used to separate nuclear waste and wondered if the same process could be adapted to separate potatoes from dirt and rock.

After just a year of development, the farmer was able to adapt the separator to farm use. He felt that he could manufacture the machine and sell enough of them to establish the product name before the major farm equipment companies started developing and manufacturing their own separating equipment. Today his machine is considered the premier potato separator.

There are many other technology transfer options available. In several universities and colleges, products are developed and offered for commercial development. NASA and other governmental scientific agencies are also good sources for technology transfer ideas.

Purchasing a Business in a Different Locale

Most people who consider purchasing a business limit their search to available businesses in their immediate geographic area. If you limit your search to your immediate area, you could miss many excellent opportunities. Consider looking at communities where small manufacturing, publishing, catalog, or food processing companies might be available for sale. The key elements to consider in your search are:

Is the business. . .

- Simple to learn
- In line with your goals
- Transferable to your community

If you buy a business in another town, you get all the advantages of buying an existing business but are not dependent on your local market to support your venture.

Licensing Your Idea

Licensing is an option you might consider if you have developed a product or product idea that you want marketed. Under a **licensing agreement**, you give another party the right to produce and/or market the product. In exchange for granting this right, you would receive a percentage of income from the sale of the licensed product.

Licensing is also beneficial if you want to manufacture and/or distribute a product that is trademarked or copyrighted by someone else. You might manufacture toys based on a popular children's film through a license with the film company. Or produce software for a small, independent software development company. In both instances, you are using your manufacturing expertise and creating a highly-recognizable product.

Licensing arrangements are common in industries such as electronics, apparel, and software. Obviously, some products are more suitable for licensing than others. Licensing is not risk-free as many people are in the business of producing "knock-off" products. If you license another party to produce and distribute your product, you should first take every precaution to protect the intellectual property rights associated with your product, such as trademarks, copyright, or a patent and make sure that your licensee takes steps to protect your trademark as well.

Another risk you may face is selecting a party that is unsuccessful in marketing or manufacturing your product. Try to avoid getting stuck with a poor performer by making sure your license agreement contains measurable performance standards or the right to license others to produce and market your product or idea.

Colonial License

Colonial Williamsburg, Virginia, is a lovely restored 17th century village where the life of early colonists is recreated for thousands of visitors yearly. However, the price of admittance to Williamsburg covers only a portion of the operating expenses of the village. The trustees of Williamsburg needed additional funds to help cover maintenance of the historic property. They entered into a licensing agreement with a large home furnishings company to allow the company to produce linens based on historic designs found at Williamsburg. Not only is Williamsburg bringing in income from its licensing deal, but it is getting publicity from tags included in the linen's packaging that explains the design period represented by the style of linens the consumer is purchasing.

Buying a Good Idea

Buy a good idea!

Sometimes it can be just as creative to find someone with a good idea, product or business which you can purchase. Someone might be willing to sell their idea because they don't have the desire, time or the money to start a business of their own. As with any start-up business, you must take time to research the market and determine if there is enough demand to support the business you have in mind.

Copy an Idea From Somewhere Else

The basic concept of fast-food hamburger restaurants is not exclusively a McDonald's idea. In fact long before there was McDonald's, there were Tasty Freeze and Dairy Queen restaurants. Burger King was not an original idea. Many fast-food restaurants have patterned their operations similar to the successful chain operations that went before them. The point is, if you are going to pattern an operation after some successful business, use the essence of the approach to operations. Don't copy names, duplicate products, or infringe on the protected rights of businesses.

If you choose to copy someone, do it within the framework of the law. In fact, you may find that in talking with the owner of the business you wish to emulate, if you don't plan to infringe on their market, they may be willing to be a mentor to you.

Joint Venture

A new business idea is only as good as the resources marshalled to make it a business reality. If you have an idea you believe in, but lack the capital or knowledge to manufacture it, consider a partner who possesses the skills or resources you lack. Typically a situation like this occurs among family members or friends. Concentrate on looking for someone who possesses the skills or resources you need to develop your business. Find a partner you respect and whose skills complement your own. It is best to set out in a joint venture agreement the rights and responsibilities of each partner. Many times large companies will consider a joint venture with you if you can add value to the venture. The corporation may be able to provide funding and guidance to make your idea a success!

Buy into an Existing Operation

Buying into an existing business can be a sound strategy for business ownership. This option enables you to focus your energy on further developing the company, rather than dealing with many of the start-up problems. The major opportunities are found with:

- Companies in the developmental stage
- Small manufacturing companies
- Specialty or niche-oriented companies

In pursuing this option you should exercise caution to be sure the company is financially sound and that you can work with the current owners. Because it is an ongoing concern, you will have a chance to take the business one, or even ten steps, further along in market share and profitability.

Conclusion

There are many ways to pursue self-employment. Use your creative talents as you study various entry strategies. Common methods of entrepreneurship include starting a business from the ground up, buying an existing business, or purchasing a franchise. Don't forget to explore the less common entry strategies such as technology transfer, licensing, and joint ventures.

Selecting whether to start or acquire a business is rarely easy or clear cut. However, the process can be greatly simplified by establishing desired criteria for evaluating the options to starting or purchasing a business. Exploring many options simultaneously is a time-consuming process, but one that is well worth your effort.

Chapter 11
VALUING AND BUYING A BUSINESS

About This Chapter:
- *Buying a business*
- *Valuing a business*
- *Cash flow methods*

Introduction

Many times entrepreneurs are described as those who start their businesses from scratch. However, just as often, entrepreneurs purchase an existing business.

This chapter is designed to help you:
- Understand the advantages of buying a business rather than starting from scratch
- Establish your own criteria for buying a business
- Know where to look to find candidates to buy
- Know how to analyze a business to determine whether or not you should buy it
- Submit the offer
- Negotiate the deal to finalize the purchase

Advantages and Disadvantages of Buying an Existing Business

It's difficult to say that one method of getting into business is better than another. Each person has his or her own personality, criteria, and set of circumstances. However, there are pros and cons to each venue and by exploring some of the advantages and disadvantages of purchasing a business, you may find it easier to decide which method is best for you.

Buying a business is the quickest way to be your own boss

Advantages to Purchasing an Existing Business

- **The Hardest Part Is Done:** Probably the biggest advantage to buying an existing business is that someone has already gone through the difficult process of getting things started. You can walk into a going concern. This lowers the risk of failure somewhat, since you can evaluate what has already been done.
- **Hurry Up!:** If you have the "entrepreneurial fever" and are anxious to get into business fast, if you want to be your own boss right now, buying a business is the quickest way.

- **How Much?:** It may be less expensive to buy a business than to start the same thing. Of course, be careful when talking about price. Read further in this chapter on how to value a business. Although there are bargains available, if the price looks too good to be true, it probably is.
- **Expanded Market Share:** By purchasing a going concern, you already have an established market share. This means you have a presence in the market that you won't have to create.
- **Initial Capital:** Although the cost of buying may or may not be less than starting from scratch, at least the dollar amount is known and there will be fewer surprises than trying to estimate start-up costs.
- **Location:** If your business depends on a good location, buying a business with an existing good location can be a real advantage, especially if all the other good locations are taken.
- **Personnel:** The new buyer won't have to search for employees with the right skills and training. Of course, once you become boss, you will have to determine if you have the best people in the right spots.
- **Inventory:** The present business owner should already have inventory on hand and be aware of what customers want. This reduces the risk of a new business ordering types and quantities that may be unwanted.
- **Customers:** An existing business will have an established customer base. The buyer doesn't have to go through the process of creating product awareness. The customer list can be a valuable asset to the new owner.
- **Contracts and Licenses:** The established business should already have all the licenses required to operate in the city and state where it is located. It may also have contracts with vendors, landlords, etc., that allow it to operate effectively and efficiently.
- **Control Systems:** An established business should already have control systems in place, such as accounting, inventory, and personnel systems. The new owner doesn't have to create these, merely fine tune what's already there.
- **Image:** One of the biggest jobs of a business is to create the right image in the minds of its customers. If the business has already created such an image, it can be a huge advantage to the purchaser.
- **Credit:** A going concern will already have relationships established with vendors and suppliers.

Disadvantages To Purchasing an Existing Business

Each of the above advantages could also be a disadvantage. For example, customers may have a negative image of the business, the location may be bad, or the business may have bad relations with creditors. Other possible disadvantages:

- **Did They Tell the Truth?:** Although you don't want to assume a person is dishonest, sellers of businesses are notorious for misrepresenting the actual condition of their businesses when they are for sale. Sometimes these problems are difficult to spot until after the purchase.
- **Yesterday, Today, Tomorrow?:** Remember, the more things stay the same, the more they change. Has a major change or shift occurred that will affect the business? Has a new competitor moved into the area? Is the market shifting away from these types of products? Has a new government regulation been enacted? If you are unfamiliar with the industry in general, you may not find out about these problems until it's too late.

Finding a Business To Buy—Where and How

This section assumes you have made the decision to purchase an existing business and you are now beginning your search for the perfect candidate.

Analyze Your Personal Criteria, Skills, and Abilities

The first step is to decide what kind of business you want to be in. You must examine yourself and decide what it is you want from a business. This will dictate where you begin your search. The following criteria will help you analyze yourself:

Look within FIRST!

- What do you want to get out of the business?
- How much capital can you put into the business?
- Do you have the right business skills and experience?
- What skills do you lack?
- Do you enjoy this type of business activity?
- How much risk are you willing to take?
- Is this the size of company you want to buy?

Use the above questions to screen potential purchases. Once you have done this, it will be easier to look at only those companies that you would be happy owning.

Armed with your personal criteria list, you can start the search for an acceptable business to purchase

Where to Find Prospective Businesses for Sale

Armed with your personal criteria list, you can start the search for an acceptable business to purchase. Sources of businesses for sale generally fall into two categories: publicly available information and private information.

Public Sources:

- Small Business Administration
- Newspaper advertisements
- Landlords
- Trade journals
- Chamber of Commerce
- Real Estate brokers
- Business brokers
- Business counselors
- Shopping centers

Private Sources:

- Personal referrals
- Acquaintances
- Attorneys
- Accountants
- Bankers
- Suppliers
- Stockholders
- Former employers
- Venture capitalists

The best strategy in locating a good quality prospect is to begin by networking among the private sources listed above. Let your banker, attorney, and accountant know that you are interested in purchasing a business and ask them to keep their eyes open for such an opportunity. Don't expect instant results. Be patient and wait for the right opportunity.

Analyzing a Business Before You Buy

Once you have found businesses that seem to fit your criteria, you will need to do a complete, in-depth analysis to decide whether or not they are worthy of further consideration. This can be a daunting task and having a team of experts help with your analysis will make a difference.

Checklist for Analyzing a Business

The last section asked broad questions designed to make you think about the vital parts of a business. Below are specific questions that you should ask to help you assess the health of the company. Of course, not every question applies to every business, but most questions will apply to most businesses. The answers are necessary for you to make a good judgment about whether or not you should be interested in buying.

Prepare a checklist prior to purchasing a business

- Why does the owner want to sell?
- What is the physical condition of the business?
    - Equipment
    - Inventory
    - Building
- What is the financial condition of the business?
- What is the potential for the products and services?
- Who are the existing and potential customers?
- What is the competitive environment?
- What legal aspects should be considered?
- What is the overall history of the business?
- Who owns the company and is it publicly or privately held?
- Who is in top management?
- What are the company's current strategic plans?
- How is the company structurally organized?
- How many employees does the company have? How long have they worked there?
- How is the human resources function managed?
- What kind of accounting system is in place?
- What budgeting and expense controls are in place?
- What do the company's balance sheets, income statements, and cash flow statements reveal over a period of five years?
- How does the company manage its short-term and long-term cash and investments? How much debt does the company have?
- Does the company have any unpaid taxes and/or lawsuits pending?
- What type and how much insurance coverage does the company have?
- How solid are the company's supplier and vendor relationships?
- What kind of marketing and sales promotion activities is the company currently engaged in? What are the plans for future market innovations/promotions?

- How tight is the market for the company's products and how much market share does the company control?
- How does the company's current pricing structure match against its competitors? Does the company offer deep discounts to large-scale customers?
- What is the company's sales history during the past five years?
- Does the company have an established distribution network and sales force?
- Where is the business located? Near transportation and shipping lines (if manufacturing)? In a busy suburban mall (if retail)?
- How strong is the company's manufacturing base? How old is its manufacturing equipment? Does the company own or lease its equipment?
- What condition are the company's physical facilities in? Does the company own or lease its facilities?

Narrowing Your Choices

No one can make the final decision about which business to buy but you. Answering the appropriate questions above should give you a good view of the business you are considering. Now it's time to use that information to narrow the alternatives to your top choice of an acceptable business. The following questionnaire will help make the process easier.

Circle the number that best corresponds to your understanding of the prospective business. Be honest with yourself in answering these questions.

	Strongly Agree				Strongly Disagree
1. I could never start a company this good from scratch.	5	4	3	2	1
2. This business gives me exactly the kind of lifestyle I want.	5	4	3	2	1
3. Success in this business requires skills and strengths I currently possess.	5	4	3	2	1
4. This is the right part of the world, country, state, city for me to live in. I will be happy living here.	5	4	3	2	1
5. I have a good relationship with a banker or other lender who would be willing to help finance this business.	5	4	3	2	1
6. The present owner thinks I will fit in well with their business.	5	4	3	2	1
7. I have been very thorough in gathering information about the business. I have investigated all the questions in the previous section.	5	4	3	2	1

8.	The current owner has been completely honest and has provided answers to all my questions.	5 4 3 2 1
9.	I have done a thorough job of gathering information to make an accurate cash flow projection.	5 4 3 2 1
10.	I have been able to accurately calculate a price ceiling and apply my required rate of return (see next section).	5 4 3 2 1
11.	I have been objective in my evaluation. I have also looked for reasons "not" to buy the business.	5 4 3 2 1
12.	I have done a good job of assessing the present employees, their strengths and weaknesses.	5 4 3 2 1

Add up your score for each business you have been considering. The highest score indicates a business that you should give the most consideration to. Although this is not a fail-safe method, it gives you a tool to use in finding a business that will allow you a good chance for success.

Valuing a Business

How Much is the Business Worth?

Once you have made the decision to purchase a business, the most difficult question to be answered is, "How much is this business worth?" The answer to this question is always the same: "The business is worth whatever the buyer and seller agree it is worth."

While this may seem like a simple answer, it illustrates the basic principle of **valuing a business.** Even though there may be a science to deciding what a business is worth, there is also a lot of art to the process. Never let anybody tell you that the price they have established was done "the right way" and that there can be no further discussion.

The buyer and seller have different incentives for placing a price on a business, and this results in an endless variety of methods and prices. Let's look at what motivates both the buyer and seller:

Seller—The seller probably sees the business as "my baby." They may have started the business from scratch, or seen it grow due to their efforts. They will have an inflated estimate of what the business is worth because of this "creation factor."

Once the first offer has been made, the negotiations begin

Buyer—The buyer probably has limited resources, which will be used not only for the purchase price, but also to make any changes needed to make the business more successful. The buyer wants to pay the lowest possible price.

There is always a middle ground between these two positions.

Valuation Methods

There are numerous methods for valuing a company, and, to make it even more complicated, different terms are often used to describe the same method. The box on this page lists some of the methods and terms. The last three, however, are the most common, and they are discussed in detail below.

Valuation Methods

- Projected Discounted Future Earnings
- Market-Based
- Percentage of Gross Annual Revenues
- Multiple of Earnings
- Asset
- Stream of Earnings
- Estimates

You should be familiar with the pros and cons of using each of these three methods. This knowledge will make you a stronger negotiator when the time comes to discuss price. And, as with almost every entity of business, there are specialists who concentrate on valuing a business. For a fee, a valuation firm will take on this task for you.

Asset Valuation

This method places a value on the assets of the company (building, property, machinery, inventory, etc.) and uses this value to price the business. Since this method tends to give lower values, it is commonly used by buyers. Common methods are as follows:

- Book value (known as balance sheet method)
  - Tangible book value
  - Adjusted tangible book value
- Replacement value
- Liquidation value
- Excess earnings

Stream of Earnings

This method derives the company's value from its profits, earnings, or cash flow (or their multiples or present values). This method usually gives a higher value, and so is typically used by the seller. Common methods are as follows:

- Multiple of earnings
- Price/earnings ratio (P/E)
- Discounted future earnings (discounted cash flow)
- Return on investment (ROI)

Estimates

Estimates are based on what the business owner thinks the price should be, using the selling price of other businesses or a "hunch" of what they would like the price to be. This method is usually arbitrary and should be avoided if at all possible. Common methods are as follows:

- Fixed price
- Market value

You are probably asking yourself, "Which of the various methods should I use to establish a beginning price for negotiations? What do I really need to know to make an informed decision? How do I go about the mechanics of establishing what the company should be worth to me?"

This next section will offer some practical tools to use in answering these questions. Examples will be given that you can use to actually do your own calculations.

Consider Buying a Business as You Would Any Other Investment

As you search for a business to buy, you should also be looking at other possible places to put your money. Other places will include investing in the stock market, a money market fund, T-bills, a savings account, or a variety of other investment instruments. All have the potential to give you a return on

Once you have made the decision to purchase a business, the most important, and most difficult question to be answered is, "How much is this business worth?"

your money. By regarding the purchase of a business as an investment, you can evaluate all investment possibilities on the same terms. You will then be able to answer the question, "Which investment will give me the best return on my money?"

Your investment choices fall into two basic categories: passive and active. A passive investment is one in which you are not actively involved in generating the money. Examples are a savings account or the stock market. An active investment is one where you are actively involved in the day-to-day project generating money. Owning and working in your own business is a good example of an active investment.

If you can make a 10% return on a passive investment (with little or no time required on your part), does it make sense to buy a business that gives you anything less than a 10% return, but requires your full-time attention? Your job, then, is to determine if the business you want to buy is a better investment than all of the other investment alternatives open to you.

A Business's Greatest Worth Is Its Ability to Generate Cash

A company's assets, both tangible and intangible, are good for only two things: (1) they can be sold for cash or (2) they can be used by the business to generate cash.

The buyer and seller have different incentives for placing a price on a business, and this results in an endless variety of methods and prices

Sold for Cash

A company's **tangible assets**, such as equipment, inventory, buildings, etc., can be sold for cash (liquidated). Even though they may be more difficult to value, the **intangible assets**, such as good will, customer lists, or the value of a patent, can also be sold.

Generate Cash

The most important function of the company's assets is to generate cash. To illustrate this point, lets look at Better Plastics, Inc., a manufacturer of auto parts. Their assets, including special machinery, were valued at $100,000. The company is currently up for sale.

> Scenario 1: Their records showed that they had a negative cash flow of $1,000 for each of the past 3 years. How much would you pay for the company?
> Scenario 2: Their records show that they had a positive cash flow of $50,000 for each of the past 3 years. How much would you pay for the company?

In Scenario 1, you should ask yourself the question, "Why should I pay $100,000 for the privilege of losing $1,000 a year?" Yes, you could sell the equipment for $100,000, but you haven't really gained anything. However, if this same equipment could generate $50,000 in positive cash flow each year, you would be far better off to keep the equipment and use it as a cash machine.

It should be obvious that the real value of a company's assets is in its ability to generate cash. The emphasis on the valuation, then, should not be on how much the assets themselves are worth, but on how much cash they can generate.

How To Value a Company

Why the big emphasis on the ability of the company to generate cash? There are two reasons: (1) it is the best way to evaluate the company as an investment, and (2) it is the best way to place a dollar value on the business. If cash flow is so important, what is cash flow, and how do you measure it?

Definition

Cash flow is simply the movement of money through the business. Cash comes in through sales, cash goes out by paying the bills. **Net cash flow** is the difference between what comes in and what goes out. A **positive cash flow** means that, at the end of any given time period, more cash has come in than has gone out of the business.

How can cash flow be used to evaluate the business as an investment? How can cash flow be used to place a value on the business?

In order to answer these questions, it is necessary to perform two critical steps: (1) identify a company's past cash flow and (2) estimate potential future cash flow. Your reason for performing these steps is to determine a range of prices you are willing to pay for the new business.

Many times, business owners will estimate what they think the price should be based on such things as selling price of other businesses or a "gut hunch" of what they would like the price to be

Step 1: Historical Cash Flows

Historical cash flows should be obtained for as many previous years as possible. A good rule of thumb is that it is obligatory to get at least the past 3 years' records. If the company is not 3 years old, get as much of the company's financial information as possible.

A few companies will generate a periodic cash flow statement, but the vast majority of small businesses will not have cash flow statements available for your inspection. Most businesses do prepare two financial statements. The first, **a balance sheet,** shows the company's assets and liabilities. The second, **an income statement**, shows the company's profit (or loss) after expenses are subtracted from revenue.

If no cash flow statement is available, you can make one by looking at the income statement. If the company is on a cash basis accounting method, cash flow can be deduced from the income statement by subtracting from the expenses any amount deducted for depreciation, since depreciation is not an actual cash expenditure. If the business is on an accrual basis, adjust the income statement by receivables, payables, and any loan principle, principal points, owner withdrawals, and income tax they may be paying. An accountant's help in this area is vital.

In order to get a true picture of cash flow, it is also necessary to make further modifications to the income statement. Modifications are necessary for two reasons. The first because most business owners try to make their income statement show as little profit as possible. The reason is that the smaller the profit, the less taxes the business has to pay. The second reason is that when business owners have decided to sell their business, many will try to make the company look more profitable than it really is by not recording (or understating) expenses. They do this to justify a higher price.

An important area where profits and losses can be juggled is in **cost of goods** sold. By overstating or understating inventory, you can increase/decrease the profit/loss significantly. To check this, you can require that an independent inventory count be conducted to verify the owner's estimate of inventory valuation.

As the potential new owner, you need to know how profitable the company has really been. Many accountants use a technique called "recasting" or "reconstructing" to get a true picture of the business's profitability. This means that they will modify the cash flow to reflect the probable profitability of the business had it been run as a profit center of a large corporation. In the case of an owner who tries to minimize profits, deductions for such items as company cars used personally by the owner and first-class travel are backed out. The cost of professional management is substituted for the owner's sometimes inflated salary. In the case of an owner who tries to inflate profits, make sure they have reasonable amounts listed for such expenses as wages, taxes, legal and accounting fees, supplies, insurance, and all other operating expenses. If there is little or no amount in these areas, adjustments must be made.

You should now have a good idea of what the actual historical cash flow has been for this business. Your reason for looking at past cash flows is to establish the highest price you are willing to pay for the business. This will become clear as you complete Step 2: projecting future cash flows.

Step 2: Projecting Future Cash Flows

Step two is to forecast or project what the business' cash flows will be in the future. First a word about forecasting or projecting. In the business world, these are words that mean "educated guessing." Admittedly, a guess is just that, a guess. But the emphasis must be placed on the "educated" part of this term. This is where doing your homework can pay off in finding businesses that are selling for bargain prices or in finding businesses that truly hold upward profit potential.

Once you have done your homework, the next step is to project the cash flows that will result from your ownership. The information in Table 1 is an example of how to prepare a cash flow forecast. You could use a blank form to enter the information you gather about future cash flows of a business you are evaluating.

The most important function of the company's assets is to generate cash

The projecting of future cash flows allows you to see the future potential for this business. It also allows you to determine an upper amount you would be willing to pay.

Step 3: Use Historical and Projected Cash Flows to Place a Value on the Business

Now that cash flows have been established, they can be used to place a value on the business by calculating the **net present value** of the cash flows. Net present value can be described as follows:

Dollars earned by the business in the future are worth less than dollars earned today (due to the loss of purchasing power). However, **future cash flows** can be "discounted" to today's dollar value. Using a **discount rate** (interest rate adjusted for risk) a net present value is calculated to show what future dollars are worth today.

The calculation of a net present value allows us to determine the dollar value of the business today, even though we are looking at annual cash flows for as much as 5 years into the future.

There are 4 steps to calculating net present value:

1. Estimate cash flows for the future.
The process of estimating cash flow has already been discussed. But part of our negotiating technique requires us to calculate two different sets of cash flow:

a. Historical cash flow–Use the historical cash flow to calculate the business's present growth rate. Use this growth rate to project future cash flow. If past cash flow has grown at 10% per year, then your estimate is that future cash flow will grow 10% per year. If the company has not grown in the past 3 years, or has been erratic, this becomes a negotiating tool for lowering the price. This estimate will give you the minimum value you will be willing to pay.

b. Your confidential cash flow–You should calculate your own cash flow, but for your information only. Keep this confidential. You want to estimate what effect your own changes will make on the cash flow. This will give you an idea of the upside potential for the business and the maximum you will be willing to pay.

Step 2. Determine an appropriate discount rate.
The discount rate is a risk-adjusted interest rate you would expect from a comparable investment. The risk adjustment is to compensate you for taking the risk of buying this business, since it's impossible to buy a "sure thing."

Cash flow is simply the movement of money through the business

For example, if you could invest in a government guaranteed security, such as T-bills, and earn 7% interest, and a relatively low-risk business opportunity seems to justify a small 2% premium, then the discount rate for valuing that business would be 9%. If the business seems to be risky, a large risk premium of 10% could be assigned, resulting in a 17% discount rate. Most small businesses are assigned risk premiums between 5% and 10%. As a result, discount rates for most small business valuations range between 12% and 22%, but its not uncommon to find discount rates as high as 35%.

In the negotiation process, its important to understand the procedure of setting the discount rate. If you feel the business is high risk, you will assign a higher discount rate. The higher discount rate results in a lower price for the business. Since you and the present business owner may disagree on the riskiness of the business, you can use this as a negotiating point to bargain for a lower price.

Step 3. Determine a reasonable life expectancy for the business.
Most experts agree that future cash flows should be estimated for the next 5 years. Any estimates beyond 5 years cannot be based on reliable information.

Step 4. Determine the net present value of the cash flows.
The value of the business is determined by calculating the net present value of the projected cash flows, using the discount rate you have decided on. Using the data from the example in Table 1, a value can be calculated for the ABC Company. A growth rate of 10% per year is assumed for the data in the table.

Table 1: ABC Company Cash Flow Projections

	1997	1998	1999	2000	2001
Revenue					
Product 1	100,000	110,000	121,000	133,100	146,410
Product 2	100,000	110,000	121,000	133,100	146,410
Total Revenue	200,000	220,000	242,000	266,200	292,820
Expenses					
Cost of Product 1	50,000	55,000	60,500	66,550	73,205
Cost of Product 2	50,000	55,000	60,500	66,550	73,205
Wages	25,000	27,500	30,250	33,275	36,603
Outside Services	250	275	303	333	366
Supplies—office & operating	500	550	605	666	732
Repairs & Maintenance	500	550	605	666	732
Advertising	5,000	5,500	6,050	6,655	7,321
Car, Delivery, and Travel	500	550	605	666	732
Accounting and Legal	1,000	1,100	1,210	1,331	1,464
Rent	6,000	6,000	6,000	6,000	6,000
Telephone	2,000	2,000	2,000	2,000	2,000
Utilities	1,200	1,200	1,200	1,200	1,200
Insurance	1,000	1,000	1,000	1,000	1,000
Taxes	1,000	1,100	1,210	1,331	1,464
Loan Repayment	12,000	12,000	12,000	12,000	12,000
Miscellaneous Expenses	1,000	1,000	1,000	1,000	1,000
Owner's Withdrawal	35,000	40,000	45,000	50,000	55,000
Total Expenses	191,150	210,325	230,038	251,221	274,023
Net Cash Flow	**8,050**	**9,675**	**11,962**	**14,979**	**18,797**

Where your homework can pay off: finding businesses that are selling for bargain prices or finding businesses that truly hold future profit potential.

Projecting cash flows allows you to see the future potential for a business

Example: Using the information in Table 1, calculate the value of the ABC Company.

Step 1. Estimate cash flows for the future. You have determined that the revenues and expenses for the next 5 years will be those in Table 1. Your evaluation of ABC Company's historical cash flows shows that they have been growing by 10% per year. The cash flows in Table 1 show an increase in revenues of 10% per year. These are the cash flows to be used:

Year 1 - $ 8,050
Year 2 - $ 9,675
Year 3 - $11,963
Year 4 - $14,979
Year 5 - $18,797

Step 2. Determine an appropriate discount rate. Let's assume that you could invest in the stock market and make a return of 10%. This is your best alternate investment. It is also assumed that you feel that the ABC Company is not very risky, so you assign a risk premium of 5%. The total discount rate will be the total of the best alternate investment rate plus the risk premium, or 15%. This means that you want a 15% return on your investment in this company.

Step 3. Determine a reasonable life expectancy for the business. In this case we will assume the business will be a going concern 5 years from now, so we will use 5 years of projected cash flows.

Step 4. Determine the net present value of the cash flows. Using present value tables from a financial handbook, a financial calculator, or computer spreadsheet, use the present value factors for 15% (the discount rate). Multiply the present value factor by the cash flows for each year. The total of the discounted cash flows is the value of the business.

	A	B	C	D
1	**Year**	**Net Cash Flow**	**Present Value Factor**	**Today's Value**
2	1	$8,050	0.8695	$6,999
3	2	$9,675	0.7561	$7,315
4	3	$11,963	0.6575	$7,866
5	4	$14,979	0.5717	$8,563
6	5	$18,797	0.4972	$9,346
7	**Totals**	**$63,464**		**$40,089**

Since most people have access to a computer spreadsheet, that is probably the easiest method to use to calculate net present value. The following example shows how to calculate net present value using Excel, a popular spreadsheet offered by Microsoft.

	A	B
1	Year	Cash Flow
2	1	$8,050
3	2	$9,675
4	3	$11,963
5	4	$14,979
6	5	$18,797
7	NPV	$40,089

In Excel:

Enter the cash flows for years 1-5 in cells B2 through B6.

Type the following formula in cell B7: =NPV(15,B2:B6)

The discount rate, here at 15%, is entered in the formula in cell B7. Change the discount rate and cash flows to fit your situation.

The calculated value of ABC Company is $40,089. This means that if you purchase the ABC Company today for $40,089, and the projected cash flow for the 5 years were generated, you would realize a 15% percent annual rate of return on your $40,089 investment over the 5-year period.

In the negotiation process, its important to understand the procedure of setting the discount rate

You must remember one principle in price negotiations. The higher the price paid, the lower your rate of return. For example, if the price for ABC Company was $46,204, the rate of return would only be 10%. In order to set a price ceiling above which you will not go in negotiations, decide on your lowest acceptable rate of return. Recalculate the net present values at that rate, and that is your highest acceptable price. You should be prepared to walk away from negotiations if the present owner will not accept at least this **price ceiling** amount.

As stated earlier, in addition to this valuation, you should also prepare a cash flow that you keep confidential. These amounts reflect improvements you will be able to make to the company to increase cash flows. Using the net present value of the higher cash flows, recalculate the value of the company. This will give a higher value to the company, meaning you may be willing to pay a higher price for the company than the historical cash flows justify. However, since the possibility of this happening is much more risky, you should weigh the evidence carefully before using this method.

Earlier in this chapter, it was stated that this method of calculating a business's value would allow you to answer two questions. Lets look at the answers to those questions.

1. How can I compare this investment with other investments that are available to me? The answer is that at a price of $40,089, and given all the assumptions made, the return on your investment in this business will give you a 15% return. You can now compare that return with all the other alternative investments.
2. How can I tell how much a business is worth? You have calculated that the business is worth $40,089. You now have a starting place in price negotiations.

Professional Appraisers

Should you hire a professional appraiser to establish the value of the business you want to buy? There are pros and cons to this question.

The advantage of hiring an appraiser is that they know how to go through the process of gathering the necessary information to value a company

The advantage of hiring an appraiser is that they know how to go through the process of gathering the necessary information to value a company. They could be used to document, for tax purposes, the process of arriving at the agreed upon price. The disadvantage of using an appraiser is that, as you have seen, there are an infinite number of ways to arrive at a price.

Perhaps the best approach is to work with an accountant or CPA that you trust. The accountant can help you gather the information, which you will then use to calculate your own price and return on your investment.

Let's Make a Deal—Negotiations

Now that you have made your top choice from all the acceptable alternatives, it's time to make an offer. It is absolutely essential for you to have established your own **price ceiling**—a price above which you are no longer willing to consider negotiating. By knowing your limits, you gain power in the negotiations.

The Offer

Once armed with the highest price you are willing to pay, you are ready to make an offer. The following items are some of the important elements of the offer:

- Price
- Method of payment
- Lease and leasehold agreements
- Contracts
- Seller assistance
- Personnel
- Operating documents
- Intangible assets
- Assumption of liabilities
- Non-compete agreement

Negotiations

The end objective of the negotiation process should be for both sides to walk away reasonably satisfied. A win/win situation will create goodwill on both sides. Without the goodwill of a win/win deal, situations may develop that could be detrimental to your business's success (such as the previous owner telling all his old customers you are unreasonable to deal with). If it's not possible to make both sides happy during the negotiations, perhaps you should look for another business to buy.

Price

It seems to be a general rule that whenever a seller's first asking price is accepted, the seller always wonders if they could have gotten more out of the deal. On the other hand, if the buyer's first counter offer is accepted, the buyer always wonders if they could have gotten the business for an even lower price. To help avoid "buyer and seller's remorse," as a general rule you should not offer the full asking price.

The higher the price paid, the lower your rate of return

What if the asking price is significantly below the price ceiling you have established? You should still counter offer, but by a smaller amount.

How much below the asking price should your offer be? Any counter offer you make should be justifiable. If your assessment of the company shows the cash flows will not support a certain price, this is ample justification for a lower price. In addition, your investigations of the company should have made you aware of other areas that would justify a lower price, such as old inventory, an unproductive family member on the payroll, or repairs that need to be made to the building or equipment. Be on the lookout for these negotiating chips. They all can be used to justify a lower price.

If the asking price is significantly above your price ceiling, what should you do? The first step is to counter with a price that can be supported by the cash flow, which is your price ceiling or lower. If that does not leave you with negotiating room below your price ceiling, you must decide whether to walk away or accept a higher price but with more favorable terms.

Terms

What's more important, price or terms of the agreement? There are no hard and fast rules in this area. You must assess which is most important to your particular deal. If the seller is firm in price, you should dictate the terms to your advantage. If terms are most important to the seller, you should dictate price. Above all else, you should evaluate each offer according to the return you will receive on your investment in the company. The reason you have established a ceiling price is so that you will be able to calculate your return based on any changes in terms.

Should you pay a higher price if you can dictate the terms? You should always evaluate the deal in terms of the rate of return on your investment. For example, you've established that your ceiling price for the plastics company is $100,000, which will give you the 15% return you require. The seller insists that the price can not go lower than $150,000. However, the seller is willing to carry the contract for 25 years, with payments of $6,000 per year. Your original offer assumed you would need a $100,000 loan for 5 years at 10% interest, with payments of $25,488 per year. These new terms mean an increase in cash flows of more than $19,000 per year, which more than gives you your 15% return. Should you pay more than your ceiling price? In this case, the obvious answer is YES!

Conclusion

As you have seen, many of the valuing and buying decisions you make depend on you and what you want. By establishing a list of criteria and remaining true to yourself and your criteria, you will greatly improve your chances of success. There are no hard and fast rules about placing a value on a business. The business is worth what the buyer and seller mutually decide it is worth. The various methods presented here will serve as a starting place for negotiations. However, it is important for you to know what rate of return you require. This knowledge allows you to place an upper price limit or "walk away" price. The involvement of your team of professionals will insure your objective evaluation, so always include your accountant, attorney and business advisors in the decision.

Chapter 12
FRANCHISING

About This Chapter:
- *Opportunities in franchise businesses*
- *Is a franchise right for you?*
- *What you can expect in a franchise contract*

Introduction

In a franchise, the **franchisor** allows another person called the **franchisee** the right to sell or distribute a service or product under the franchisor's system in a certain area. In return, the franchisee pays a fee called a **royalty** to the franchisor. A tremendous growth in the number of franchises has occurred during the last 40 years. Today there are over 600,000 franchises in operation in the United States. Worldwide, there are many thousands more. The economic impact of franchising is staggering. A few years ago it was estimated that one-third of all retail sales occurred in franchises, and this number is increasing annually.

Franchising is a growing method of doing business

The growth of franchising can be traced to three primary reasons. The consumer public has become much more mobile and subject to national advertising than in the past, and there is comfort in knowing the goods and services will be of uniform quality whether they are bought in North Dakota or New Mexico. Secondly, the small business person can begin a franchise without many of the problems of starting from scratch. Finally, the franchisor saves on capital and personnel from having the franchisee start its stores throughout the service area. In this chapter, we will explore what franchises are, how they work, and whether one is right for you.

Common Franchise Formats

Franchises can be structured in any number of ways, but generally they are categorized as:

- Business-format franchises
- Brand-name franchises
- Product-distribution franchises
- Affiliate franchises

The brand-name franchise allows the franchisee to market products or services under a brand-name to take advantage of the name familiarity of that product or service. Affiliate franchises are groups of similar businesses which join for the purpose of marketing their services in a general way. Product-distribution franchises usually operate under a license from the franchisor to allow marketing of the franchisor's products and services in specific areas. The business-format franchise is probably the type of franchise most of you would be involved with and is the fastest-growing type of franchise. Because it is so comprehensive in scope, it will be the model we will work from, but the issues we address in this chapter can also be applied to the other types of franchises.

Regulation

State and federal franchise regulation

In a franchise, a person is often given the exclusive right to sell a company's product within a defined region. These agreements are not considered restraint of free trade because they do not monopolize an entire market, such as all hamburgers, but only that franchisor's (Speedy's Burgers) products.

To illustrate the incredible growth in franchising over the past 20 years: It wasn't until 1978 that the Federal Trade Commission (FTC) adopted regulations covering franchises. California was the first state to regulate the sale of franchises and it still requires that you register a franchise operation with the Department of Commerce. About 25 states have adopted some type of franchise regulations. Generally, these rules require registration by the franchisor prior to selling franchises. They also address the parties' relationship under the franchise agreement, particularly regarding renewal and extension of the term. Most regulations also require that certain disclosures be made by the franchisor to the franchisee. But these laws are primarily disclosure laws which rarely focus on the specific details of your deal. You should review your franchise agreement carefully, and it is highly recommended that you retain legal counsel experienced in franchises to assist you from the very beginning.

Other laws affecting franchises include state securities laws and unlawful trade practices acts. In addition, the brokers who sell new franchises are often regulated under business transactions statutes which require disclosure of certain information to the franchise purchaser, establishment of escrow accounts, and providing other financial protection. If you are considering franchising your operation for sale to others or serving as a broker yourself, you must consult with your attorney before you start. The penalties for violating federal or state law in the sale of franchises can be extreme.

A Turnkey Operation

The primary advantage of franchising is that the small business owner is immediately able to compete with larger companies by utilizing the goodwill, quality standards, and experience of the franchisor that would take years to acquire if the owner operated an independent shop. More advantages include:

- Access to experts
- Increased purchasing power
- Aid in lender negotiations
- Sample business and operating plans

A franchise has many advantages

Jeff Martin wanted a change of pace in his life. He had worked as a salesperson for a computer company for 15 years and wanted to strike out on his own. He investigated various business opportunities and decided to purchase an ice-cream store franchise. He received two months training as part of his purchase because the franchisor wanted to insure that its brand name and quality were consistent. Jeff found it exhilarating to own his own business while at the same time receiving support from the franchisor.

The Downside

Operating under a franchise is not for everyone. Some franchisors are control-oriented and monitor and regulate virtually every aspect of your business. It is in the franchisor's best interest to see the franchisee succeed, because in virtually every franchise their royalty check is based upon the amount of your sales. The more you sell, the more they make. Some disadvantages are:

- Too much franchisor control
- Royalty payment problems
- Inflexibility on the part of the franchisor
- Insensitivity to local markets

There are some problems in operating a franchise

Scams

You should be aware that there are numerous franchising opportunities that lure the uninformed entrepreneur into an investment scheme where the franchisor literally takes the franchisee's money and runs.

Ada Briscoll signed a franchise agreement with AV Computing, Inc., to open a local branch of AV Computing and to sell its newly created anti-virus software program. A section of the franchise agreement required Ada to purchase a large inventory of software from the franchisor. Because she wanted to get her franchise up and running, she agreed to this provision, although she questioned it while negotiating the franchise agreement. Ada felt that the extra inventory would sell quickly due to the huge demand she had read about in business trade journals.

Ada quickly sold the software to several local government agencies who started frantically calling her when the software did nothing to protect their data from the viruses that were plaguing them. After more careful inspection of the software, Ada determined that it was seriously flawed. When she called AV Computing for assistance, she got a standard message saying that the number had been disconnected.

Franchise trade shows are a quick way to gather a lot of information

One way to avoid a scam is to investigate the franchise meticulously before you invest in it. Face-to-face contact with the franchisor can reveal a strong sense of the success of the organization. It's also a good idea to contact some of the franchisees directly to determine their successes and to identify any problems that they have encountered with the franchisor.

The Preliminaries

How to Find out About Franchise Opportunities

How do you even get started? Go to the library and read what you can find. The Internet will have some useful information as well. Talk with people who currently own franchises and see what they say. Check the business section of financial and business newspapers and periodicals. Many franchisors and owners of franchises who are looking to sell will advertise in these publications.

Franchise trade shows now are held in several large cities. You can see products and services which you may not have even considered. There will be booths explaining how to select and operate franchises. You may even have the opportunity to obtain information on franchise fees, royalties, and related issues from a large number of possible franchisors. This may allow you to quickly see if one franchisor's terms are in line with the market. A word of warning—many of the franchisors at these trade shows are small, ill-organized operations. Caution is the byword.

Investigating the Franchise Opportunity

Before making application for a franchise do your homework! Are the products and the systems proven? Is the franchise new to your area and is it new to the region as a whole? Is this product on the upswing of a new idea, or the downside of consumer desires? Have you seen an operation in place? Can you visualize one in your area? Would the demographics and economy of your area support this type of business? It may not be a good idea for a "mechanical idiot" to try to buy a muffler shop franchise. A low-income retirement community may not be the best place for a trendy, expensive neck tie franchise. Could you realistically learn this business and would you like it? Would you be proud of this franchise's products and service?

The Application

At this stage, the franchisor will want to know some things about you as well, including your financial status, experience, and capability to perform. These applications are often very detailed and you may not like giving a stranger all this personal information. However, if the franchisor doesn't ask for much detail about yourself, this may indicate they are not careful enough about their business and you may not want to continue with your franchise application with this company.

Deposit Agreement

After your application has been accepted, you are typically requested to make a good faith deposit. This will usually be required before the franchisor will disclose to you many details of the operation. Deposits usually run between $2,000 and $10,000. Before you make a deposit, be sure you review the deposit agreement and insist that it be refundable if you cannot strike a deal. Further, see to it that the deposit is in escrow and not co mingled with the franchisor's operating funds. You will also want your deposit to serve as a reservation of your franchise.

Laura Phipps was not careful enough in her drive to own an interior design franchise. She deposited $7,000 with Designs on Wheels, a regional window treatment franchise that provides in-home design consulting and development. Because Laura didn't review the franchise deposit agreement carefully enough, when she was rejected by the franchise as a potential franchisee, she lost half her deposit, $3,500, to franchisor "investigation fees."

Examining the Franchisor

By now you have made application to the franchisor and have qualified. You still have two difficult tasks ahead. The first is a detailed examination of the franchisor which you now can do, because at this point the franchisor should be willing to disclose to you its financial and operational details. Expect to sign a non-disclosure agreement. If you negotiated your deposit agreement properly, you will be entitled to a refund if you do not like what you see in this very important step in your due diligence. Remember, if the franchisor appears reluctant to provide you with information, or is in a big hurry to sign you up, you should take these as warning signs to stop and not go forward with this company.

The following are some questions to ask:

- Can the franchisor deliver all that has been promised?
- Is the assistance to your business operations worth the interference?
- Does the franchisor have a good track record?
- Have you checked a credit rating service like Dunn & Bradstreet, called the Better Business Bureau in the franchisor's home town, the state's attorney general's office, and the FTC?
- Is most of the franchisor's income from franchise fees (immature business) or from royalty payments (shows ongoing successful franchises)?
- Do you understand what you will be getting and what you will be expected to do?
- Are you permitted to interview any franchisees you choose, or are you given an exclusive list?
- Is there any market research in your area for this type of product and at what price?
- Has the location of your shop been carefully evaluated?
- How are you going to construct the type of store they require?
- How does the franchisor administer the franchise and what kind of help is it willing to supply to a new or struggling franchise?
- Are the training commitments more or less than you reasonably need?
- Do you have sufficient funds to make the purchase payments without severely affecting your capital needs in the short term?
- Does the franchisor have valid trademarks or patents on the products you will be selling?
- How many franchises have been sold this year and over the last 5 years?

Is the location a good pick for your kind of business?

- How many have failed?
- Do the franchisees collectively have a voice in management or a seat on the board?

These are a number of the issues you need to consider before you get to the details of the franchise agreement.

Buying an Ongoing Franchised Business

There are many unique issues you should be aware of when you are considering the purchase of an on-going franchise. You must make sure that the franchisee has the right to sell it to you. Most likely you will need the consent of the franchisor. Is your seller considering this a sub-franchise, where he or she will take royalty payments in addition to the purchase price and those royalties which you are obligated to pay directly to the franchisor? Does your seller operate other stores within the same franchise in the area to compete with you? If so, are they successful, and would you want to become part of a team or a competitor with your seller?

Because you will be buying into a complex business relationship, it is important that you also investigate the business as if you were buying the franchise directly from the franchisor and study the terms of the underlying franchise agreement accordingly. It is highly recommended that you have a feasibility study prepared by an expert to determine whether you are buying into a booming or declining enterprise. In retailing, this is often referred to as the **product life cycle** analysis. One thing which makes investigation difficult is that the franchisor often has restrictions against the distribution of information in its operations manual to third parties. But it is essential that you review these operations documents carefully before you purchase an ongoing franchise.

Understanding the Franchise Agreement

You are now at the last step before you begin business as a franchisee. Every franchise agreement is different, but most of them address the following issues in one form or another. Remember, all your careful analysis is wasted if you agree to a contract that is unfair to you or is one which you cannot perform. Do not be afraid to ask the franchisor to explain why they think a particular term is fair or necessary. The agreement is negotiable even though it comes on a "standard form." Every location and franchisee presents different issues and opportunities, and these must be included in your particular agreement. You can rely on experienced legal counsel to help you negotiate a fair deal, or you can always walk away if you cannot reach an agreement with the franchisor.

Contract Term and Extensions

Is the initial term long enough and can the franchisor restrict renewal in some way? Alternatively, you may want a short initial term in case things don't work out, but you may want the automatic right to renew without additional fees. Many states regulate how extensions are granted by the franchisor so they cannot be cut off too soon and injure the franchisees. Also, the type and length of notice required prior to renewal is very important because if you miss that date you could find yourself unable to renew.

Franchise Fee and Royalties

Usually, the initial franchise fee does not include the inventory, fixtures, or supplies which you will be required to purchase. The royalty you must pay can be based upon net or gross sales. Issues to consider are: When is the royalty due? Is there a cap or a declining percentage in your favor as your sales go up? How often and at whose cost will an audit of your books take place? If your books are in error, the agreement will typically provide that you pay the expense of audit, which can be substantial. You should understand the extent and the nature of your reporting requirements and the required accounting methods.

Supplies

Will you be required to purchase all your supplies from the franchisor? Do you get a discount based on economy of scale or do you pay a premium for name familiarity? Are the initial stock-up requirements merely a disguise for a clever pyramid scheme?

Territory

Territory can be the key to your success in franchising

One of the critical elements in a franchise agreement is the extent of the territory over which you have been granted the franchise. You must determine whether it is exclusive or non-exclusive (i.e., other franchises can be granted in the area by the same franchisor). A franchise is not always an exclusive right. On the other hand, will you have the obligation to open additional stores in the area or lose your exclusivity or even your franchise? Is the exclusive market area too large so as to overextend your resources, or too small so that you will find yourself competing with another franchisee in your area?

Physical Plant

Identify the extent to which the franchisor controls or assists you in locating a site, constructing the improvements, and furnishing the interior. Many retail franchises are promoted not only by the product they sell but by the physical appearance of the store. Will the franchisor own the building and lease it to you, or will you be expected to construct the improvements? Determine what rights the franchisor has to inspect your premises and operations so you can be prepared for franchisor visits.

A franchise often requires a special building and fixtures

Training

Many franchisees receive the equivalent of a masters degree in small business administration in one month. In others franchises, you are thrown a manual and told to get to it. Your agreement should clearly identify what training is to be provided, when and where, and at whose expense. Will your employees receive training from the franchisor, or is that your obligation?

Management Assistance

One of the common elements of a franchise is that the business practices throughout the franchise system are uniform. This can be a great benefit to the small business owner who does not have the experience, education, or desire to work up the management procedures for the business and then maintain them. Your contract should spell out what ongoing management assistance the franchisor will provide.

Marvin Johnson of New Orleans was surprised and happy to learn of the extent of franchisor support behind his newly-purchased Italian Cafe franchise. Not only was he trained for 3 months on site at another Italian Cafe, but his training was on-going. The franchisor provided seasonal promotional materials such as table tents and T-shirts for wait staff as well as advertising in local papers for his franchise. Johnson knew he couldn't provide this type of marketing so soon into his business start-up phase, and he appreciated the franchisor's guidance and involvement in helping to make his Italian Cafe a success.

Your shop is judged by what other franchises do

Marketing

One of the major advantages to a franchisee is the value of the existing marketing program of the franchisor. Name and product recognition are crucial to most retail franchises. Will you be required to spend a certain percentage of your gross sales on additional advertising? What percentage of your royalty payment will go to area, regional, and national marketing by the franchisor? Do you have the right to audit the franchisor's books to see that they are performing their continuing obligations?

Quality Control

It is important for both the franchisor and the franchisee to see that uniform standards of quality are maintained throughout all franchises. A bad product or sleazy business practice in one location will hurt all franchisees, because your trade name is theirs, too. The franchisor should insist that you and all others franchisees follow the procedures and maintain the established standard of quality. You will want to insist that the franchisor keep the other franchisees on the same path and give you remedies if they fail to do so.

Trade Secrets

Most franchisors sell the franchise in large part based upon the franchisor's "trade secrets" which includes the product, the operations manual, and the management system. The agreement will often provide that every aspect of the business is a "trade secret" and you may be required to keep that information confidential. You may also be prohibited from competing against the franchisor when the franchise is terminated or from opening non-franchised outlets while the agreement is in place. Without these protections, the franchisor is subject to unfair competition. However, you should review these provisions carefully to avoid undue restrictions on your right to operate other businesses or to earn a living once the franchise is terminated.

Transferability

Can you sell the franchise to someone else?

The franchise may be the most substantial asset in your estate. At some time, you may wish to sell the business or pass it on to your children. For these reasons, the transferability provisions of the agreement must be reviewed carefully. The franchisor, on the other hand, has sold the right to use his or her name, product, and operational methods in part based upon your financial position, experience, and reputation. Therefore, the franchisor will want the ability to review the qualifications of your buyer, just as they did yours when they sold you the franchise. In addition, the franchisor may want to reacquire the franchise, and it is quite common to see options or rights of first refusal granted back to the franchisor.

Jim Thompson had it all figured out. He had owned a successful convenience store franchise for 15 years and planned to retire to Key West, FL. Because he always dreamed of fishing off the Keys, when Thompson signed his initial agreement with the franchisor, he checked to make sure that the transferability provisions provided for the eventual sale of his business. Due to his long-range planning, Thompson enjoyed 15 years of business ownership and was able to sail off into the Florida sunset!

Termination

Careful consideration must be given to the termination provisions in any contract, but these are very critical in a franchise agreement. The franchisor will want to be able to terminate the agreement if the franchisee is not committed to the team and fails to follow the program, is unsuccessful or goes into bankruptcy, is dishonest and takes the process to another location or provides it to a third party, or is delinquent and fails to pay royalty payments timely. For these reasons, the termination provisions in a franchise agreement are often very strong in favor of the franchisor.

Can you get out?

Alternatively, you need to protect your investment in the franchise, and you also want the ability to terminate or get damages if the franchisor is not delivering all that has been promised. You may also want to include a buyout provision in the event you wish to voluntarily terminate the franchise. Buyouts often have complex formulas because the franchisor may want the continuing royalty payment, but cannot quickly get a new franchisee in place. In a buyout, the franchisor wants you to pay damages based upon the expected return for the remainder of the contract term, less the franchisor's costs of performance of its duties to you, the franchisee.

Alternatively, if the franchisor defaults and the agreement is terminated, does the contract provide for your recovering some portion of your initial franchise fee? Does the contract provide for liquidated damages? What items are to be returned to the franchisor? You will want a clear delineation of these things so you are not subjected to claims after termination.

Conclusion

Franchises are a popular way of doing business. They offer the small business person incredible advantages in leveraging of purchasing power, name and product recognition, tested physical plant layout, operations manuals, training, and business management assistance. However, they can also be burdensome in terms of paperwork and expense. Use caution when considering a franchise. If successful, the franchise will benefit both parties and provide you with much of the support necessary to reach your franchising goals!

Chapter 13
BUSINESS OWNERSHIP DURING RETIREMENT

About This Chapter:
- *Retirement trends*
- *Entrepreneurship in retirement*
- *The promise and pitfalls of retirement business options*
- *Success strategies for businesses started in retirement*

Introduction

In 1991, life expectancy in the United States reached 79 years for women and 72 years for men. By the year 2000, life expectancy is projected to reach 80 years for men and 84.5 years for women. Today, 1 of every 10 Americans is over 65 and by the year 2040 that number is expected to be 1 out of 4. People are living longer, have greater retirement savings, and have a need to feel a part of a productive, advancing world.

People are living longer, healthier lives

Paradoxically, as life expectancy has climbed, retirement age has tumbled. The Social Security Act gave powerful sanction to a "normal" retirement age of 65 and private pension plans developed thereafter overwhelmingly adopted this same retirement age. In spite of powerful institutional rules which set retirement age at 65, a steady erosion of that norm has taken place. Today the average worker stops work at age 61. Several factors are responsible for this move to retirement at a younger age than in the past:

- Early Social Security benefits
- More companies offer early retirement options
- Higher earnings and accumulated net worth

Many retirees are seeking ways to make their retirement fun, challenging, and enriching, and are finding satisfaction through their entrepreneurial ventures.

Work After Retirement

Many of today's "young elders," aged 55 to 75, are unsatisfied with a retirement revolving around leisure activities and have expressed a desire to continue working until 70 or beyond. Some seniors continue to work out of economic necessity, others want to remain active while supplementing their retirement income. Still others look to the improved physical and mental health they experience when working. Consequently, studies have found that for many early retirees, retirement is not a once-and-for-all decision. A sizable proportion of older workers indicated that they have had significant and sustained work experience after their retirement from the corporation that had employed them most of their life.

Americans are opting to rejoin the work force after retirement

The American Association of Retired Persons (AARP) estimates that in 1993, about 3.5 million older Americans were actively working or seeking work. Others have estimated this number may be as high as 5 million. A recent U.S. News and World Report poll found that 45% of new retirees surveyed either already are or expect to be working after age 65 and this trend is expected to accelerate.

In the past, continuing work in old age was difficult due to the physically demanding nature of work. Today, the economic shift into service-related work and jobs in information industries provides a wealth of opportunities for older workers seeking flexible schedules and tolerable work loads.

Entrepreneurship in Retirement

Is self-employment a viable alternative for seniors?

Increasingly, retirees who want to stay in the labor market are considering self-employment. In 1993, about 834,000 or 24% of older workers were self-employed. Also, corporate downsizing continues to free up talent which is increasingly finding its way into business start-ups. A survey of dismissed workers in the second quarter of 1994 revealed that approximately 15% had formed their own business.

Others see self-employment as an act of liberation. Tired of working in organizations with little prospect of advancement and job security, these workers are striking out on their own. As massive changes continue to hit the corporate world, self-employment is viewed as a way to gain control of one's life, career, and future. For those with the necessary skills, drive, and ideas, entrepreneurship is increasingly attractive.

Other retirees have embraced self-employment as an opportunity to pursue a new career or occupation. This group sees retirement as an opportunity to begin again, a chance to use talents and energies not fully explored in previous work. Perhaps the new business allows for wider contacts with more people than a previous job, or the chance to become involved in skilled craft work that had previously been just a hobby.

Retirement Businesses

The scope of retirement businesses is broad. Among retiree businesses you will find traditional Main Street firms, specialized consultants, high-tech innovators, mom-and-pop retail stores, craftsmen, and strategic alliances. Retiree business opportunities generally fall into 3 primary categories: micro-businesses, traditional businesses and consultants.

Promises and Pitfalls of Retirement Business Options

Micro-Business—The Promise

For many retirees, the satisfaction of self-employment comes not from the potential to make lots of money or create a giant business. Instead, these people seek a business that allows them to pursue a cherished dream, to work on activities they value, to take the pressure out of work and discover the pleasure of creating their own enterprise. The key compensation in a micro-business is not monetary. The reward of these tiny businesses is intangible and a highly personal **psychic income**. Psychic income cannot be measured in dollars but it is a more important and powerful motivational tool than any monetary rewards. It encompasses such things as control of action, personal challenge, family focus, and the ability to determine and direct an alternative way of life.

The rewards of the very small business are very personal

Small businesses often afford the owners a more relaxed and flexible work schedule. Others find they are putting in many, perhaps more hours than they did when they worked for others. Self-employment for these retirees translates into the ability to make choices based solely on their own desires, rather than the needs of children and the constraints of a job. It is a liberating feeling.

Micro-Business—The Pitfalls

The micro-business option is only possible if the retiree is assured of reasonable retirement income from other sources. If retirement income is insufficient to cover all the retiree's expenses, it is unlikely that these tiny businesses can fill the void.

On the other hand, micro-business owners must be careful to monitor their earnings so that their business income does not significantly jeopardize retirement earnings. This is a particularly important consideration for retirees earning slightly more than the allowed amount under the Social Security earnings test guidelines. It is conceivable that retirees may lose 90 cents on the dollar—or more—of their earnings to a combination of lost Social Security benefits and increased taxes. In some extreme cases, it may actually cost money to go to work. Under current (1995) regulations, you could lose as much as $1 in Social Security benefits for every $2 earned and also have to pay taxes on 85% of your Social Security benefits if your income exceeds a certain level. (This level changes annually. For the latest information about earnings limits, contact your Social Security office.) This is not a serious disincentive for those earning substantially more than the limit or those age

70 or older (when the benefit reduction no longer applies). But it can be quite punitive for those making slightly more than the earnings limit. The formula is complex and it would be wise to consult with an accountant to find out if it pays to work. In some cases it may prove wise to delay your initial filing for Social Security benefits.

The Watchmaker's Dream

Monitor the impact of business earnings on other retirement income

Throughout his forty years as a metalworker at a large industrial concern, Frank Lozano had always cherished a dream. He wanted to be a watchmaker but lacked the skill and the time to do so. After his grown children moved away from home, he spent his free evenings and weekends apprenticing himself to a local watchmaker to learn the intricacies of watch design and repair. After retiring from his metal-working position, he knew that he could make his dream come true.

A small, local drive-through photo development shop had been closed for several years and the landlord had given up trying to rent the property. Frank contacted the landlord who was only too happy to rent the space to Frank for a fraction of what he was originally asking. Now Frank runs a part-time shop where he repairs watches for people on the go. Although Frank doesn't look to his business as his sole source of retirement income, it satisfies his psychic needs. His dream has become a reality.

Traditional Business—The Promise

A traditional business offers the potential for both monetary and psychic rewards. Success may mean substantial earnings, the fulfillment of a lifelong dream of business ownership, and the satisfaction of creating an enterprise of value in the community. The shift to a service economy and new technologies such as fax and computers makes it easier to set up small businesses.

Retirees often bring cash, experience, and credibility to business ownership

In launching a new, traditional business, the retiree often has an edge over younger entrepreneurs. Many retirees have two very valuable assets in their business arsenal—an established credit history and extensive contacts. Since traditional businesses generally require capital investment and operating funds, their contacts and past experience will be instrumental in establishing working agreements with suppliers and lenders.

Older entrepreneurs may also have a stronger financial base from which to launch their business. They may not have the fixed expense commitments of their younger counterparts—mortgage payments and the expense of raising children. When the business is doing well, they may be in a better position to invest more of their own money. If they have been productive in previous work and have provided well for their retirement, they may not even take a salary, preferring to plow their earnings back into the business.

Traditional Business—The Pitfalls

Retirees who leave big companies to start their own business often find out it is a lot harder than they expected. Many encounter problems in managing their new small business with their old big-company mind-set. They miss their executive secretary, business lunches, and strategic planning impacting thousands of people. It may take some time for them to realize how many people provided them with data and handled the details. Now, they will have to do all this themselves or pay dearly for it. They are not always prepared for the intricate, hands-on management required in a small business. This may not be the "retirement" many had envisioned.

Building a successful business is likely to require a significant investment of time and money

In the early stages of the traditional business, a large portion of the earnings must be plowed back into the business, particularly if it is growing rapidly. Consequently, earnings of self-employed business people are generally lower than what they used to receive and initially may be non-existent. If you want to open your own retail store, you'll need enough initial capital to buy inventory, refurbish the store, and pay rent for up to two years before it starts paying for itself. Retirees must be very honest with themselves as to what their earnings requirements are and whether a traditional business can meet these needs.

Some retirees jump at the chance to buy an existing business which has established customers and reputation, a viable location and store inventory. But look before you leap. Find out why the owner is selling. Is he really just retiring or moving on? The market may be changing, perhaps a major competitor has stolen much of the business or the business may have a bad reputation. To avoid these pitfalls, have an accountant review the business's past financial records and visit with the suppliers for the business, other area companies, and the local chamber of commerce.

Other retirees quickly invest in a franchise. Be aware that any franchise is likely to require capital beyond the initial investment and many don't live up to their promises. Even a franchise business is likely to demand more time, more patience, and more round-the-clock responsibility than anticipated.

However, don't let these cautionary tales deter you from researching a franchise opportunity. Many valuable franchises are started by retirees every year!

A Franchise for the Grandkids

When Margaret Gaynor retired from her nursing career at the age of 62, she wanted to go into business for herself and also to provide employment for her numerous grandchildren. As Margaret puts it, "I wanted my grandkids to understand the value of work and the value of family." She purchased an ice-cream shop franchise to fulfill both needs. While Margaret is busy running the business, she is training her oldest granddaughter to eventually take over. The shop provides decent wages for her grandchildren who are saving for cars and college, and it provides them with exposure to running a thriving community-based business.

Building a successful business does not happen overnight. Retirees in their early '50's statistically have more time to reach success in their endeavors than those that are 70 years old. While age bias is technically prohibited, age cannot help but be a factor in decisions made by lenders and investors. An extremely common and costly mistake made by entrepreneurs is to seriously underestimate the capital required to fund the business and the amount of time it will take to get the enterprise into a profitable position. New ventures nearly always take more time and cost more than expected. So, with careful planning and a detailed analysis of your venture's capital needs, you will be well on your way to entrepreneurial success.

Consultants—The Promise

Consulting is by far the most popular form of post-retirement entrepreneurship. Answering to a variety of names—consultants, free-lance professionals, independent brokers, manufacturer's reps—these entrepreneurs are in the business of selling their knowledge, contacts, and experience. Except in rare fields where you can apprentice as you free-lance, you must acquire the necessary skills and background before you start. For most people this means years rather than months of working for someone else.

Long-term experience and in-depth knowledge can give seniors an edge

Consequently, retirees are naturals to the consulting industry and generally have an edge over newcomers to the business.

Labor Department statistics indicate that consultants now account for more than one-third of self-employed people in the U.S. Demand for their services is coming from downsized companies and struggling small firms who need expertise to solve specific problems but can't afford hiring this type of high-priced talent on a permanent basis. Increasingly, we are seeing a trend toward "outsourcing"—farming out jobs formerly done in-house to independent professionals in areas like advertising, sales, writing, and graphic design. Companies particularly value the expertise and seasoned judgment self-employed senior workers bring to projects, without the heavy salary and benefits they would otherwise pay them as full-time employees.

Retirees are likely to have extensive contacts with old bosses, former colleagues, past employees, peers, suppliers, contractors, advisors, and customers. These contacts not only provide valuable information, they tend to become a virtual marketing and sales force for the competent and valued free-lancer.

Construction Consultant

Henry Penkul, a thirty-year veteran controller of a major international architectural and construction company retired at the age of sixty-five. Not content to spend his retirement playing golf, he first started working as a consultant to his former employer, offering his expertise on construction project costing. He later expanded to include consulting for local and state government on large-scale construction projects. His work week is less busy than when he worked full time for his former firm, and now he has the luxury of saying "No" to a project whenever he wants to take a vacation or pursue other interests. By drawing upon his expertise in his field and through the use of industry contacts and his reputation as a "straight shooter," he was able to set up his own shop and to enjoy a fulfilling semi-retirement.

As free-lancers, retirees have an opportunity for independence where no one is dependent on them for a salary, overhead is generally low, and they are not faced with automatic retirement. Seniors can advance as far as their talents and energy allow. While they may end up working longer hours than ever before, they will be working for themselves. A consultant who left an executive position at a major computer company to start her own business said, "I know I'm not moving up a ladder anywhere. I know I'm not building equity in a fantastic start-up that I can sell and retire on next year. That's OK. I'm getting to be a whole person. I don't have a job. I don't have a company. I have a life."

Consultants—The Pitfalls

While some consultants can finance their initial start-up from severance pay and rely on a spouse's income for living expenses in the early years, many still start out undercapitalized and have difficulty obtaining financing from traditional lenders. Lenders view these soloists as either too small to bother with or much too risky. With little in the way of hard collateral to back a loan and uncertain prospects for sales, they often encounter more difficulty than traditional small business owners when it comes to raising capital. Cash flow can become problematic as consulting is often a case of feast or famine. When working on a project, marketing the business usually suffers. When a project is completed there may be a lag in income while the free-lancer lines up more work.

Business can be feast or famine

Even for successful start-ups, the financial rewards may be meager. David Evans, president of NFRA, an economic consulting firm, reports that workers who lose their jobs and start a new business can expect to take a pay cut of at least a third in the first year. IRS figures are even bleaker. The average income of a business owned by one person is less than $14,000 a year.

Another common difficulty that many people discover is that they aren't cut out to go it alone. They resist working on areas of their business they dislike (typically bookkeeping and marketing). They miss the camaraderie of an office full of co-workers. Think carefully about your business personality before you "go solo." If, however, you want to fly like an eagle, consulting may be the path for you!

Success Strategies for Businesses Started in Retirement

Regardless of the type of retirement business chosen, there are four key steps to success:

Protect Retirement Funds

While there is no single prescription for success, it is important to avoid putting assets needed for later years at such risk that the owner could not survive a failure. For millions of people who have lost their jobs in the corporate world, there is a great temptation to use retirement funds and severance pay received from their previous employer to fund their new businesses. Retirees, with a lump sum pension payment in their pocket, are

Don't put your retirement nest egg at risk

often prime targets for business opportunity scams. (See Chapter 14 *Operating A Part-Time Business* for tips on evaluating business opportunities and identifying fraudulent offers.) If these fledgling businesses fail, the retirees are forced to seek nearly any kind of employment to survive and face the daunting task of rebuilding their retirement cushion late in life.

To avoid these unhappy consequences, determine the minimum amount you must keep in your retirement accounts to assure a reasonable standard of living and then build a fire wall between you and these retirement funds. Keep the money in long-term investments and conduct your business as if these funds were not accessible to you. Decide up front that under no circumstances will you allow these funds to be jeopardized. This may mean that the start-up phase for your business will be a bit rougher and will take a little longer, but you can be confident that no matter what happens to your business, your retirement income is assured.

Seek Out Low-Risk Business Options

Choose a business with low capital investment requirements:
Whenever possible, seniors should avoid spending heavily for capital items. Younger people establishing a full-time business may need to spend thousands of dollars for a facility, equipment, and merchandise. If they should lose all or part of their investment they still have many years to rebuild their savings or repay loans. Seniors don't have this luxury. Start out small. You can't afford to risk your nest egg, because you don't have time to recoup it if things go wrong.

Sell your knowledge and experience rather than costly inventory:
One way to minimize risk is to provide a service rather than selling products. Service businesses offer several advantages to the entrepreneur. Often, they can be started at home on a small scale with limited investment in capital equipment and low overhead. Service firms can be built around expertise or technical knowledge the entrepreneur already has. Expenditures for personnel, facilities, and equipment can often be kept to a minimum.

Capitalize on experience over inventory

Do Your Homework

Far too many businesses are established by retirees with strong technical background in an industry but little managerial experience. In fact, the skills needed to run a business are quite different from those required for success as a specialist in a large firm. People who like a chain of command, clearly defined job descriptions, and carrying out specific orders may not be suited for self-employment. Entrepreneurs must be generalists, with at least a basic understanding of all aspects of their business.

To prepare for business ownership, you can start by attending classes and seminars on small business management and entrepreneurship. Sometimes the best time to go back to school is while your own children are in college. (Applications for student financial aid ask how many members of the family are attending college.) Develop a business plan. By putting your ideas down on paper you will be forced to think realistically about your venture. You will have to make your assumptions explicit and challenge them. A plan is also a critical element in securing credit and attracting investors. A study by AT&T revealed that a small business with a plan was far more likely to make it than one without this tool. Many chapters in this book deal with planning issues. Use them.

If possible, get some hands-on experience in the field. Visit with others who are self-employed and ask them about the skills and abilities they think are most important for success. Work on a part-time basis on weekends or during vacations in a similar, established firm to see what the business looks like from the inside. If paying employment is unavailable, volunteer your services.

Start work before you retire

- prepare mentally
- prepare financially
- get a head start on operations
- test drive your business concept
- prepare a business plan

Conclusion

Business ownership in retirement can be an immensely satisfying and worthwhile activity. Too often older workers fail to recognize the tremendous untapped potential inherent in their years of accumulated knowledge and experience. Seniors possess not only technical knowledge and expertise, but also life knowledge. Retirees can make significant contributions and can discover much fulfillment in their own businesses. With careful planning and attention to managing risk, self-employment may very well open the door to some of the best years of your life.

Chapter 14
OPERATING A PART-TIME BUSINESS

About This Chapter:
- *Are part-time businesses "real"?*
- *Benefits of part-time businesses*
- *Challenges for moonlighting business owners*
- *Growth and transition issues*
- *Success strategies for part-time businesses*

Introduction

While "official" sources peg part-time business ownership at 2 million people, other sources suggest that the number of sideline ventures may be much higher. John Case, in *The State of Small Business, 1995,* bases his estimations on the number of Schedule C Tax Returns filed in 1992. Of the 21 million filed, approximately 6 million were filed by corporations and partnerships. The remaining 15 million were filed by sole proprietors. Of these, three-fifths were full-time businesses leaving approximately 6 million part-time ventures.

In an age when individuals can be linked electronically to form a variety of new and unique business arrangements, the term **virtual company** was coined to describe sole proprietors who are technically in business alone, yet through strategic alliances with others throughout the world are actually directing the work of many other people.

Many part-time businesses operate as a part of the "informal" or "underground" economy. People participating in "off-the-books" activity typically use cash only and don't pay taxes on their transactions. Researchers at the University of Michigan discovered that in one year, 4 of 5 consumers purchased something from the informal sector. They hired a neighborhood teenager to baby sit their kids, paid cash to a carpenter, bought items from sidewalk vendors, or firewood from a rural homeowner.

There are many different venues for part-time work and entrepreneurs have been increasing their involvement in part-time businesses over the past several years.

Benefits of Part-Time Businesses

Owners of part-time businesses often conduct these ventures after a full day's work in a traditional job. These moonlighting activities fill up the evenings and weekends of these entrepreneurs, requiring that they expend high levels of energy and commitment to these enterprises. What would motivate people to take on this kind of responsibility? Part-time businesses offer unique benefits to the entrepreneurs who start them:

The time has come to take charge of our own employability

- Job security
- Income patching
- Feasibility testing of a business concept
- Personal satisfaction

Job Security

The working environment all over the world is undergoing massive, radical changes. To remain competitive in a global economy companies have moved rapidly to replace workers with technology and to streamline top-heavy companies through layoffs, restructuring moves, and downsizing. Human resources consultant and author Colin Campbell describes this incredible change in the work place as follows: "Half of all jobs that will exist 10 years from now don't exist at the moment. And half of the people currently employed will be downsized out of a job. There is a sea change under way. People are having to prepare for a world they can't quite see yet."

While most business experts suggest that acting like an entrepreneur on the job will improve your job prospects, many workers today are taking this thinking a step further and actually starting their own companies. These individuals are seeking to gain control of their lives, careers, and economic destiny by launching part-time businesses while at the same time keeping their current employment for as long as they can.

Experts are predicting that by the end of the decade fewer than half of all jobs will be permanent, full-time positions. Hiring will be dominated by a "just-in-time" or "as-needed" mentality and will revolve around short-term contract or project-based work. Given this economic climate, self-employment looks increasingly attractive to many who view it as a means of assuring job security.

Income Patching

In many households income from traditional jobs is insufficient to pay all the bills. In certain regions of the country, job opportunities are limited or nonexistent. Many individuals and families trying to insure self-sufficiency have resorted to creating their income-producing jobs through part-time businesses. A ranching family in Wyoming, located 50 miles from the nearest town, has great difficulty finding part-time work for family members. But with modern advances in electronic communications and universally available overnight shipping options, they have an opportunity to produce and market products all around the world. Tagged **micro-businesses,** these small enterprises are primarily involved in wholesale, trade, or service businesses. In a survey of micro-entrepreneurs conducted by the Aspen Institute's Self-Learning Project, 56% rely on these little businesses as their primary source of earnings while 49% are **patchers**—patching their living from two or more income sources.

Tiny businesses are helping to pay the bills

Here are some facts about micro-enterprise:

- 90% are sole proprietorships—66% employ the owner-operator only
- 46% earn a profit in a normal month, 7% break even in a normal month
- 47% have gross sales of less than $1,000 per month
- 21% have gross sales of $1,000 to $2,499 per month
- 25% have gross sales of $2,500 or more per month

Part-time Ad Executive

Chandra Lewis was working as a copywriter for a national advertising firm. The firm's clients were major international companies. She wanted to branch out and eventually have her own advertising firm that specialized in advertising for non-profit organizations. She started out slowly by offering to do low-cost advertising for a local food bank. Her successful campaign enabled her to test her skills, gain some prominence in the local non-profit market, and through referrals, she was able to ultimately pursue her goal. She eventually left the large firm and started her own agency on a full-time basis.

Feasibility Testing of a Business Concept

Part-time ventures allow budding entrepreneurs the opportunity to test the waters of self-employment before plunging in on a full-time basis. Working for others for a wage can never fully prepare someone for the level of responsibility they will face as a business owner. One of the best ways to gain insight into the risks and rewards of entrepreneurship is to launch a part-time business. This is a lower risk opportunity to test your level of commitment in making your own business enterprise succeed. If you have what it takes to make a part-time venture profitable, the odds favor the likelihood of succeeding in a full-time business.

Part-time ventures act as trial runs for full-time enterprises

Personal Satisfaction

For some entrepreneurs the reasons for starting their own part-time business are non-monetary. Perhaps you seek personal fulfillment through the pursuit of some special interest area. You may be exploring personal talents or developing unique product concepts. The opportunity to express your ideas and do things exactly as you want is one of the primary advantages of self-employment. Entrepreneurs relish the excitement and challenge of running their own show.

Accounting Whiz

As a new junior accountant at a regional accounting firm, Mark Howzer had many student loans that he wanted to pay off as quickly as possible. During the busy tax season leading up to April 15, Mark worked weekends on individual tax returns to supplement his income. This was his way of filling the gap between his salary and his educational debts.

Business ownership is a "quality of life" option

Challenges for Moonlighting Business Owners

By definition, part-time businesses share top billing with other important career or personal responsibilities. The challenge of part-time self-employment is to effectively juggle the demands of the business with all the other aspects of the owner's life. The key issues for part-timers are:

Work Conflicts

An employer's attitude toward moonlighting activities can range from support to outright prohibition. Unless you are operating under a formal employment contract which specifically states or implies that employees cannot moonlight, your employer cannot rightfully prohibit you from doing so. However, if the business interferes with your work performance there may be grounds for dismissal. The safest approach is to systematically identify potential situations that could cause difficulties for you on the job such as:

Avoid doing anything on the job that you wouldn't want your own employees to do

- Conflict of interest issues
- Interference with work obligations
- Business ethics

Some business owners have found it helpful to openly discuss their business activities with their employer and assure them that this new enterprise will not interfere with work responsibilities. Others say this type of discussion is like waving a red flag before a bull and should be avoided. Use your best judgment on which tactic to use with your own employer.

Family Commitments

Taking on a part-time business in addition to regular work and household obligations can put a tremendous strain on family relations. Operating a successful business, even a part-time enterprise, requires constant and diligent effort. It is bound to change family dynamics. It may take a while before other family members take the business seriously. They may resent the time commitments required and clamor for your attention. Conflicting emotions may lead to self-doubt about the business. You may have to negotiate with your family to get chores done that you previously handled or you may have to let some chores go entirely. Make sure you begin your business with your family's buy-in. Because your time constraints will be great, be up-front with family members about the time commitments your business will require.

Preserve family time

Time Constraints

Even though you plan to operate your business on a part-time basis, customers will expect top-level service from you. Therefore, time management and organizational skills will be of utmost importance. It may well be worth the time and investment to attend time management training sessions, invest in planning and organizing systems, or even hire a planning expert to assist you with setting up efficient business systems.

Credibility Issues

Since so many part-time businesses and service firms operate from the home, they may not be taken seriously. The fact that the business itself is conducted at odd hours (before and after work and on weekends) may make it difficult for customers to reach you during "normal" business hours.

Invest in organization and planning skills and project a professional image

To make your business more credible, increase the professionalism at every level. Dress appropriately for the work that you do. Answer all calls professionally using your business name. Hire an answering service or invest in a good quality answering machine and return all calls as soon as possible. Insure that all business correspondence, business cards, labels, and packaging are in line with the image you seek to convey. If you need to have family members get involved in helping to handle customer calls, make sure you train them on how you'd like your business calls to be handled.

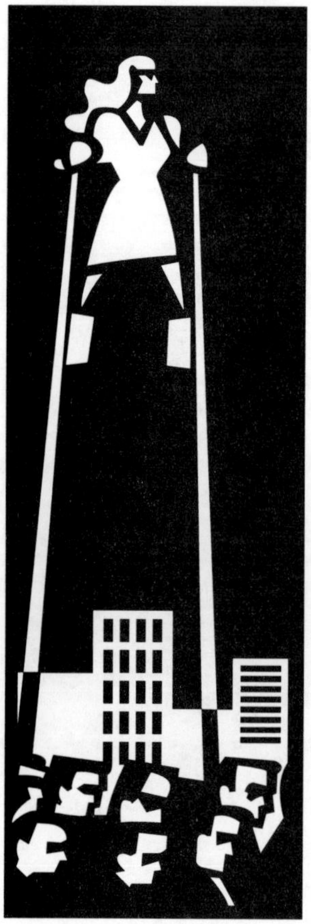

Financial Concerns

Venture Economics, a market-research firm, estimates that an entrepreneur will spend an average of $8,000 (for office supplies and equipment) to start a home-based business. The same business located in prime office space would require start-up capital of $50,000. A retail establishment like a bakery or video store could cost as much as $200,000 to launch and a manufacturing plant could run into more than one million dollars in initial investment.

Because of the inherent limits on available capital, most part-time businesses are service-oriented. They generally require a lower initial investment. For example, self-employed carpenters, mechanics, and plumbers often start out with their own box of tools and add to their equipment as the need and cash flow dictates. In service businesses one of the highest costs may be the initial and continuing education that service-providers must engage in to remain competent in their field.

Growth and Transition Issues

Every successful business owner inevitably faces the question of growth. To survive, a business must continuously evolve to meet changing market demands. Many very small businesses resist growth and the complications it can bring. This may be a mistake. In studies of the government's Small Business Data Base, Bruce Phillips and Bruce Kirchhoff discovered that the tiniest companies and those that never added even one employee were more likely to fail than all other new companies studied. On the other hand, growth that is too rapid or which moves in too many unrelated directions may deplete business resources and lead to its eventual demise.

To grow or not to grow? That is the question!

Successful part-time business owners develop a clear concept of their business direction and actively work to manage growth. When faced with the potential for expansion, a business owner can opt for one of three strategies:

- Limit growth and keep the business small
- Continue in your full-time job and hire employees
- Quit your full-time job and take over the full-time management of your business

Option 1: Limit Growth and Keep the Business Small

In manufacturing, growth may be valuable due to the costs of capital equipment and the economies of scale. But in knowledge-based service firms there are no economies of scale. A successful one-person business owner expressed this rationale for limiting growth: "There is a subtle tendency in our society to belittle the very small business person, to champion growth at the expense of other issues. In my view, there are people for whom growing bigger is a disaster, a promotion to incompetence." Expansion in businesses built solely around the expertise, wisdom, and personal service of one key person may be disastrous.

Tom Fuegner, a personal consultant in San Francisco, earning $100,000 on his own, wrestled with whether to grow or not. Tom decided against growth when he calculated that he would have to hire 7 more people and increase revenues to $800,000 a year before he would make any more money.

If limited growth is the right strategy for you, you need to become very clear about business direction and priorities. Three critical areas are: (1) clarity of purpose, (2) ability to rank work by order of importance and (3) turn away work that does not build the business.

Option 2: Continue in Your Full-Time Job and Hire Employees

In the early stages of a new venture, the founder does whatever it takes to get the business launched, from making sales calls to sweeping the floors. But with success comes more work than one individual can handle, particularly if he or she is trying to run the business while holding down a full-time job. To avoid total burnout and increase the chances of continued success it becomes imperative that additional help be hired. Business owners today have the advantage of a wealth of management talent at their disposal as a result of corporate downswing. There are immensely talented and experienced people who would join the management team of a growing business.

Delegate both responsibilities and authority

If you adopt a strategy for high growth, it will be important to delegate. Many who have painstakingly built their business find it very tough to surrender any of the authority to managers. As the business grows, the founder simply won't be able to do it all, even if he or she works 24 hours a day. Until you recognize this and truly delegate, the business will not prosper. Further, your job will suffer as you stew about what is happening in the business while you are at work.

Option 3: Quit Your Full-Time Job and Take Over the Full-Time Management of Your Business

For many part-time business owners it is a dream come true when their business grows to a point where they can justify quitting their regular job. Begun as a sideline, these owners had always hoped and planned for the day when it became a full-time endeavor. But they quickly discover that managing a grown-up company is very different from running a small, part-time venture.

Develop systems and management teams

Success will require you to become more organized and systematic. In the early days, quick response to changing situations is more important than discipline and systems. As the company grows, the situation changes. Your approach to handling each problem as it came up must now be streamlined. Systems for solving these problems must be implemented. As the business grows the owner will face increasingly complex issues. It would be wise to build a management team to assist with these issues and bring the company to a new level of sophistication.

Success Strategies for Part-Time Businesses

Here are some successful strategies that are time tested and may prove useful as your consider the future for your part-time business:

- Beware of "business-opportunity" scams
- Run the business like a business
- Be clear about goals and priorities
- Choose a business you love

Beware of 'Business Opportunity' Scams

Self-employment has steadily increased since the 1970's, increasing numbers of people are looking for ways to start their own businesses. There has been a corresponding increase in the number and variety of business opportunity scams. Fraudulent offers, which can be found in ads on TV, radio, and in reputable newspapers and magazines, promise hefty incomes for a few hours of easy work. With business opportunity scams reaching epidemic proportions, the Federal Trade Commission (FTC) is stepping up efforts to crack down on these fraudulent activities.

Prospective entrepreneurs can take the following steps to protect themselves from scams:

- Ask for a copy of the Disclosure Document required by the FTC
- Send for a copy of the consumer bulletin "Business Opportunity Fraud"
- Check with the Better Business Bureau
- Contact your State Attorney General's office
- Call the National Fraud Information Center at (800-876-7060)
- Call trade associations
- Have a business lawyer or accountant review the deal

If it looks too good to be true, it probably is

Business opportunities, even legitimate ones, can be very risky. It is difficult to sort out the bad from the good. Warning signs that the deal is too good to be true are when:

- Promo ads promise exceptional earnings for part-time work
- You don't need any experience to succeed
- High-pressure sales tactics urge quick action
- Products sound too good to be true
- Sellers won't put promises in writing or provide references
- Large, up-front payments or start-up inventory is required

Run the Business Like a Business

If you are seriously committed to your business your chances of success are very good. In a study of small businesses, Douglas Handler, an economist with Dun and Bradstreet, discovered that 80% of the businesses surveyed were still in business 3 years later. Those small businesses which appear on the statistical radar only to fade away are usually part-time diversions.

Prepare a Business Plan

Every successful business undertaking begins with a solidly conceived business plan. Confidence, passion, and determination will take an entrepreneur a long way, but ultimately, more entrepreneurs would succeed if they would take the time to complete a business plan. By systematically reviewing the industry, the customers, the competition, the costs and profit potential of the business, the business owner is able to evaluate and make adjustments as needed on paper first and identify deficiencies that need to be addressed.

Run a Professional Operation

Even a part-time business out of your home can be a first-class act. Find a corner of your house that can be devoted exclusively to the business and set up an organized office there. Install a separate business line with an answering machine. Get business cards and stationery printed. Return customer phone calls promptly. Insure a quick turnaround on bids and correspondence. Honor the commitments you make. Meet with an accountant and set up an effective bookkeeping system.

Be Clear About Goals and Priorities

The part-time business owner juggles a multitude of conflicting demands from his job, his business, and his personal life. Business success at the expense of losing your family is no success at all. Balance and clear objectives are key ingredients in the part-time entrepreneur's success formula.

Choose a Business You Love

Be passionate about your business

Some people start part-time businesses out of fear. They have watched friends and relatives lose jobs and fear the same could happen to them. They decide to start a part-time business as a precaution against being laid off. The problem here is that businesses based on fear or a negative attitude don't work.

Marsha Sinetar, in her book *Do What You Love, The Money Will Follow*, makes the point that successful entrepreneurs have what it takes to see the task through when the chips are down. And part of what drives them is a love of what they do. Passionate business people are natural marketers, their enthusiasm is infectious, they exude excitement—even joy—in their work. When you enjoy your business, success is bound to follow.

Conclusion

Part-time business ownership requires a person with the energy level and commitment to work long hours and balance a variety of conflicting commitments. For the right person it can be a dream come true! It has often been said that the person who is happiest is the one who is doing a job that he would do even if he didn't get paid to do it. For many people, part-time business ownership is an opportunity to do just that—a chance to use the free hours after work to pursue a dream, a business idea which is intriguing and compelling. The fact that it also can be a money-making proposition is icing on the cake and, ultimately, the reward for the owner's enthusiastic investment of time and energy.

Chapter 15
HOME-BASED BUSINESS

About This Chapter:

- *Advantages and disadvantages*
- *Setting up the business: issues and ideas*
- *Managing the home-based business*

Introduction

What is the economic impact of home-based businesses?

Home-based business is one of the fastest growing forms of entrepreneurship in the United States. Corporate restructuring and rapid growth of telecommunications and information technologies have created an explosion of full and part-time home-based businesses. According to the latest statistics, a new home business starts every 11 seconds, creating 8,219 jobs each day. These businesses generate over $401 billion in revenues each year.

Dramatic changes in our society have forced many people to rethink traditional ways of earning a living. Today's home-based business owners could be as capable of running million dollar high-tech companies as they are of running cottage crafts businesses from home. As a result, home-based entrepreneurs are becoming a major force in the business world.

This phenomenon is being fueled by several factors, including:

- Corporate layoffs
- Military downsizing
- Advanced technology
- Growing family responsibilities
- Company outsourcing
- Quality of life

Successful home businesses include everything from desktop publishing to dog-walking to public relations. But home workers, increasingly, are professionals and white collar workers who serve new markets and provide needed services and products to fast-growing firms and corporations.

LINK Resources, Inc., a New York marketing research firm, shares basic facts about the current home-based business owners:

- 80.1% are married
- 51.9% have children under 18
- 24.4% have children under 6
- 55.4% have a college degree
- $49,000 is the average income
- 38.5 years is the average age

Rural areas, particularly, tend to have a large percentage of home-based businesses for several reasons: (1) many small farm, ranch, and other agriculture-based operations are in fact home-based businesses; (2) in areas where jobs are often scarce and/or low paying, many rural residents create their own jobs by running a part- or full-time business from their homes; (3) rural areas generally do not have the zoning and other restrictions that discourage home businesses in metropolitan areas; (4) corporate restructuring and changing lifestyle preferences are sending increasing numbers of "Lone Eagles," "Country Hawks," and other former city dwellers to rural areas of the country because advances in technology have made it possible to "telework" or run small businesses from their homes.

Telecommuters are commonly referred to as "Lone Eagles"

Work-at-Home Opportunity Scams

Home-based business frauds and scams have been springing up all across the country. Your best weapon as a consumer is information. If you suspect fraud in a home-based business opportunity investigate the company through the Better Business Bureau, your state's Attorney General's Office, a Consumer Affairs Agency, your local Small Business Development Center (SBDC), Service Core of Retired Executives (SCORE), the Small Business Administration (SBA) or the U.S. Government's Postal Inspection Service (if fraud is conducted through the mail).

Be aware of home-based business scams

Some business opportunities to avoid include:

- Chain letters
- Multilevel marketing
- Fake employment opportunities
- Get paid for reading books
- Vacation and free gift scams
- Free seminar scams
- Envelope stuffing
- Make money at home ads
- Distributorship fraud
- Developing mailing lists
- Home assembly programs

Advantages and Disadvantages

Is your home the best place to locate your business? There are potential advantages and disadvantages of operating your business from the home.

Potential Advantages

- A home office allows flexibility in scheduling personal and work obligations
- Independence to work on your own
- Lower start-up costs, less overhead, money saved on parking, lunches
- Tax advantages of operating a business from home
- Home-based businesses can have a positive effect on the community

Potential Disadvantages

- Feelings of isolation are common for home-based business owners
- Operating a home-based business can cause loss of privacy for family members
- The home-based business may have an uphill battle in gaining credibility
- Zoning restrictions may be a problem in some communities
- Business may have personal interruptions from family, friends, and neighbors
- Space may be limited when setting up a home office

Types of Home-Based Businesses

According to recent information, there are over 200 different types of home-based businesses. *Entrepreneurial Magazine* notes that currently the following 10 businesses are the fastest growing:

- Bill auditing services
- Computer tutor and trainer
- Real estate appraiser
- Management consultant
- Public relations specialist
- Business plan writer
- Desktop publishing
- Export agent
- Janitorial and cleaning services
- Bookkeeping service

As your look forward, here are some areas where there may be future growth:

- Cleaning services
- Computer consultant/programmer
- Executive search
- Management consultant
- Medical transcription service
- Paralegal
- Public relations specialist
- Temporary help service

Look into franchised home-based business opportunities

Setting Up a Functional Office

Understandably, home business working environments differ in relation to the type of business you are working in. Depending on your needs, a home office can be furnished with a simple folding table and chair, or impressive office furniture and personal computers. However, it is important to set aside a specific work area. Consider the following questions:

- Where in the home will the business be located?
- What adjustments to living arrangement will be required?
- What are the start-up costs?
- How will your family react?
- Will customers ever come to your home office?
- Will household noise or activity pose problems?
- How convenient is the space for delivery of materials, or for a customer to enter and leave?

Home-based office equipment

- A separate business telephone line
- Answering machine or voice mail service
- Fax machine
- Personal computer and printer
- Computer modem
- Applicable computer software packages
- Photocopier or access to one
- Filing cabinets
- Miscellaneous supplies

Projecting a Professional Business Image

A professional image is important

Developing a professional image is an important part of building credibility with your customers. What business image do you project? Key factors to consider are:

- Your address—you may want a p.o. box instead of a rural address
- Business graphics—logo design, business card, letterhead, signs, etc.
- Telephone answering service, e-mail, fax
- Separate place of work and business entry
- Establish regular hours of work
- Prompt response to mail and phone messages
- Business-like communications

Dealing with Laws and Regulations: Zoning

When considering a home business, you need to know what the zoning laws are in your neighborhood. **Zoning laws** vary from community to community and can usually be checked by contacting your local city hall and requesting the zoning ordinances for your area. The most common restrictions are:

- No on-site sales
- Space limitations/parking
- No deliveries
- No storage of inventory
- Restrictions on pollution from noise, hazardous waste, and odors
- No business signs
- Potential fire hazard
- No employees other than family members

In addition to local zoning you must be aware of state and federal legislation on labor laws.

Employee vs. Independent Contractor

People who offer their services to the general public are usually considered **independent contractors.** The single most important characteristic of independent contractors is freedom from control and financial risks. If you plan to use independent contractors rather than employees, be sure to take the IRS test.

The IRS uses a list of 20 factors to determine whether a worker is a common law employee or an independent contractor. The state's Unemployment Insurance Liability Unit and the Division of Worker's Compensation use similar guidelines.

Check with the IRS on the 20-factor test

The general rule is that an individual is an independent contractor if the employer has the right to control or direct only the result of the work and not the means and methods of accomplishing that result. Independent contractors are hired to accomplish a particular job. The relationship between the hiring party and the independent contractor is contractual.

Taxes and Home-Based Business

The IRS is very exacting in its requirements for home businesses. Records of the business must be meticulously kept.

What tax advantages are associated with a home business? In order to qualify for home business tax deductions, you must meet certain tests or requirements outlined by the IRS. Basically, the part of your home for which you are claiming deductions must be used both exclusively and regularly as one or more of the following: 1) the principal place of business for any trade or business in which you engage; 2) a place to meet or deal with your patients, clients, or customers in the normal course of your trade or business; and/ or 3) a structure that is not attached to your house or residence and that is used in connection with your trade or business.

In any given year, deductions which are indirectly related to your business cannot exceed the gross earnings of the business. Indirect expenses are those expenses including real estate taxes, mortgage interest, rent, utilities and services, insurance, repairs, and depreciation. The business portions of these expenses are deductible. You can only deduct a percentage of the home expenses equivalent to the square foot percentage of your home occupied by your business. Direct expenses that benefit only the business part of your home, which might include painting and repairs to your work area, are fully deductible.

See IRS publication 587 on business use of your home

The IRS publishes special guidelines and tax packages to assist the home-based business person in figuring his or her tax deductions. If you need an accountant to help you with your taxes, use one.

Home-Based Business Insurance Needs

Every type of business, whether in-home or not, requires insurance protection. Yet many people starting home businesses fail to consider their insurance needs. A carefully planned insurance program is vital to the protection of your business and personal assets.

There are several types of insurance coverage which the home business owner should consider. Your particular business may not require all of the following forms of insurance, but you will probably require a few: Product Liability and Worker's Compensation; Burglary, Theft, and Robbery; Fire; Business Life; Credit; Fidelity Bonds and Security Bonds; and business use of home computers.

When organizing your business insurance program, the following steps should be taken:

- Define the different perils your business may face and rank them according to those which present the greatest loss risk
- Cover your largest risk first
- Shop around for the best, most cost-effective coverage
- Avoid duplicate coverage
- Periodically review your insurance program; coverage needs may change

Since insurance coverage is an important and complex matter, you are well advised to work closely with an insurance broker. See Chapter 25 *Managing Risk* for more information.

Home-based businesses need to check with an insurance agent or broker for pricing; shop around for services and price

Managing a Home-Based Business

It is important for the home-based business owner to not only have knowledge in business but also to possess good management skills. To run a successful business you need to manage time, money, and people. The more efficiently you run your business, the greater its chances for success.

The following are some tips to create a more professional home-based business:

- Establish and follow regular work hours
- Make business calls during normal work hours
- Treat interruptions as if you were working at a job outside the home
- Educate family, friends, and neighbors regarding your business
- Get out of the house at least once a day
- Keep up your contacts with trade and professional associations

Does starting a home-based business mean leading a life of loneliness and isolation? Not necessarily, if you follow a few basic tips:

- Have lots of work; loneliness is rarely a problem when you're busy with clients
- Don't procrastinate; force yourself to begin whatever task you're avoiding
- Become active in your related professional organization; stay abreast of changes in your profession; become better known among your peers

Home businesses must network like other small businesses

- Join a formal networking group; your local chamber of commerce or similar networking groups that offer regular networking sessions and business seminars
- Start an informal support group; meet with other home-based business owners to discuss common business issues
- Take a course; learn a word processing program or become certified in your industry
- Find a telephone buddy; connect with somebody who cares about you and who will welcome your calls to chat, complain or brag
- Use the Internet to connect electronically with people
- Schedule regular social activities; plan a weekly breakfast with a friend or an exercise class at the gym
- Get to know your service providers by chatting with your suppliers, delivery person, or bank teller
- Volunteer; give back to your community

Use the Internet and a telephone buddy to stay in touch

Creating contacts outside your home office will not only increase your business associates but the networking opportunities may increase your bottom line. **Networking** business-to-business is one of the most important and successful ways of marketing your home business. A network is a system of supportive people who are interested in one another and willing to help each other succeed. Your involvement in even one established home-based business network could make the difference between success or failure in your business.

Conclusion

Successful home-based business owners learn by their own experiences and those of others. As a home-based business person, you can overcome feelings of isolation and give and receive valuable information by joining networks and being active in professional and trade associations. This will also build a marketing network for your service or product. Then continually evaluate which organizations and resources best serve your business information and networking needs. Home-based businesses have led many entrepreneurs to a new freedom and prosperity.

Chapter 16
FAMILY-OWNED BUSINESS

About This Chapter:
- *Family business today*
- *Family and business systems*
- *Managing by communicating in the family business*
- *Preparing for succession*
- *Seven steps to passing the baton*

Introduction

Explaining what's involved with a family business is a little like peeling back an onion. Just as one discovers a very complex structure in an onion while peeling away the skin, a family business that appears uncomplicated on the surface can have considerable complexity underneath. The complexity arises from the blend of family issues with business issues and the multiple relationships among family members and non-family employees working in the business.

More than 50% of the U.S. gross domestic product (GDP) comes from family-owned businesses

In the sections to follow, we will explore the issues family-owned businesses face. Included among the topics covered are:

1) How family businesses differ from other companies, and why they need to professionalize their management practice.
2) The distinction between family as a unique entity and its business as a separate system.
3) The importance of managing by communicating (MBC) in family businesses.
4) The steps that owners, usually members of the senior generation, as well as the younger generation of family members, can take to ensure financial survival and continuity of family control into the next generation.

Family Business Today

The definition of a family business is any business in which two or more family members have a substantial ownership interest and, in most cases, also participate in senior management. In most, though not all family enterprises, ownership is closely held and concentrated within the family.

A third of all companies listed on the New York Stock Exchange are family businesses

Family businesses now employ more than half of the nation's work force, and they are growing at a time when most of the large publicly held corporations have been reducing their workforce through "downsizing" and "restructuring." Although large corporations are well known to the public, 80% to 90% of all commercial enterprises in the U.S. are family businesses. They account for

One-third of family businesses survive through a second generation

One-tenth of family businesses survive through a third generation

more than 50% of U.S. Gross Domestic Product (GDP), and they also constitute a third of all companies listed on the New York Stock Exchange. Some family-owned enterprises are not only quite large, but are well known to the public, for example, Coors, and Anheuser-Busch.

Professionalization: The Key to Family Business Survival

In today's increasingly competitive climate, success and survival require a more professional management culture. Historically, fewer than one third of family businesses have survived through the second generation and fewer than one in ten through the third generation. The average life-span for a family business is just 24 years. True, bad economic conditions and poor business judgment explain some of these failures. However, a major reason for the low survival rate is the family's failure to adequately prepare and train younger family members, along with a failure to develop a competent business succession plan. There appear to be four major reasons for this failure:

- It's tough for senior family members to address their own aging and mortality.
- Many seniors worry that their children won't run the business the way they did, and don't believe the younger generation's way of running things will be as good as their way.
- Many seniors are concerned about their own long-term financial security, which sometimes causes them to postpone transferring control until it is too late.
- Many are too personally tied to the business and lack other interests that would satisfy their needs for fulfillment after retirement.

The Family and Business Systems

What is unique about family business is the merger of two distinct systems: the family system and the business system. This often leads to overlapping and confused roles. For example, if the boss is the mother, she isn't just "Mom" but also the "Chief Executive Officer." Family members in a business have a dual relationship as members of the family (as sisters, parents, cousins, children, etc.), and then as employees in the business. And management of the business relationship can easily become entangled with and confused by the family relationship.

Family Owned Clothing Business

Consider the case of the following family business, owned by a family that built a successful retail clothing company in Texas:

Two brothers worked in a business with their mother. Although mom held the position of president, she often found herself saddled with the added role of "Chief Emotional Officer" when called upon to referee fights between the two brothers. Their sibling rivalry, which began in childhood, wasn't confined to the family but spilled over into the business. The brothers' continuing childhood rivalry and their mother's need to intervene was inappropriate for the business.

Is the boss "Mom" or is she the "CEO"?

In a family-owned business, decisions can be guided not only by the goals of the business but by the expectations of the family. Sometimes this makes very good sense. A parent may naturally want his or her child to manage the business, even though a better trained non-family member might be available. So, business needs must be respected and business criteria applied. Unfortunately, integrating the demands of both systems in ways that lead to satisfactory outcomes for both the family and its business can become a stressful exercise. The intersected area in the diagram below shows the zone of potential conflict. Family business owners need to walk a fine line in balancing the demands of the two systems.

Family and Business Systems

The owner's offspring also have to grapple with the ambiguity of overlapping roles.

Dad feels that his newly married daughter has done a good job on a research assignment for the business and decides to reward her with a bonus. He tells his daughter not just that she did a good job but that she probably can use some extra cash having just started a family of her own. The daughter may wonder whether she got a gift from her Dad or a bonus from her boss.

Why do overlapping roles pose a problem? In the family system, the criteria for deciding what's fair and right usually differ sharply from the criteria appropriate for business relationships. In the family, fairness may require equal treatment of children without regard for performance. In the business, reward is assumed to be based on skill and performance alone. The family is characterized by strong emotional feelings, often having a long history. In the business, rationality and objective judgment are applauded. The family is based on love, while relations in the business are based on respect which in turn depends on an individual's work performance.

All family members in the business, both the senior and the younger generation, share responsibility for creating a professional business environment necessary to ensure survival over the long term. This requires getting the right fit between the expectations appropriate for family relationships and the criteria appropriate for business decisions. Success in this collaboration between seniors and the next generation will determine whether the current owners will be able to pass the baton on to the next generation, and also whether the younger members will be prepared to accept the baton and run with it.

Integrating the expectations of the two systems and knowing how to draw the boundary lines is one of the most difficult tasks the family business leader must perform. It requires competence in managing relationships and then properly communicating expectations about those relationships to all family members, especially where family and business roles overlap. Although all family members share responsibility in this task, it is up to the leader to take the initiative in managing the boundaries between the two systems because the leader has ultimate authority and control over the business.

Establishing the Boundaries

Members of a family business are likely to disagree on the extent to which family interests should be allowed to intrude into the business.

Mom feels that all her children, whether they have worked actively in the business or not, should have equal ownership. Dad recognized that only some of his offspring have invested their careers in the business and feels very differently. A way must be found to reconcile the two contrasting views of fairness. Perhaps the children active in the business can be given more ownership while the other children receive help with their educations or the capital needed to launch businesses of their own. Or, the active children might receive voting stock while the inactive children get non-voting stock. There are many ways to solve these kinds of problems, if communication between family members is open and frank to start with.

Family members must also work hard to prevent well-entrenched family expectations from entering the workplace. For example, if the family has a history of dismissing "junior's" ideas around the kitchen table—just because age and experience are all that really count when ideas are debated at home, how will "junior" feel when he has good ideas for the business but sees them dismissed out of hand around the conference table at work? He is apt to question his value to the business and may decide to leave.

Two siblings, John and Mike Moore, work together in their family textile business. They have a history of rivalry going back to childhood. Because of that history, it is probably best to have them placed in jobs where neither reports to the other. Having the siblings work in different departments can help insulate the business chain of command from conflicts that developed much earlier in the family setting. Of course, much depends on the individual family situation. Above all, it is important that family members candidly discuss their concerns and decide on how the boundary between the two systems is to be drawn. If the family neglects to do this at an early stage, it risks real trouble later when a business succession plan for transferring ownership and control is under consideration.

A family business won't help family relationships improve

Expectations for Performance

In well-functioning family businesses, family members are not just held to the same standards as non-family workers but are actually held to higher standards.

Family members answer to a higher standard

Family members, either as current or future owners, are expected to work harder in the business because of the stewardship obligation that comes with ownership. Although this is usually an unspoken principle, it is intuitively understood by family and non-family employees alike. It demonstrates to employees, suppliers, and customers the family's commitment to the business. For this reason it is always good for business and is one of the unique strengths of a family-owned business.

Employee morale can suffer if children are hired and promoted without having to meet or exceed the same skill and education criteria required for non-family employees applying for similar positions. Problems can be created for a child who is given favored treatment because non-family employees are less likely to take the son or daughter seriously. An increasing number of family businesses are dealing with this problem by encouraging younger family members to work elsewhere before entering the family business. After they have built a solid track record working for somebody else, they are able to enter their own family's business with more credibility. They have proven to family and non-family colleagues alike that they can earn their own way.

Sometimes this becomes a formal policy, called a "rule of entry" for family members, and represents another way that family business owners can professionalize their management practice. Rules of entry and advancement help to keep the boundary line between family and business clearer.

Managing by Communicating

Because relationships are such a key element in a family-owned business and to a smooth passing of the baton when the senior generation decides to transfer control and ownership to the next generation—a process called "succession planning" has become a useful tool for family business. What is required is the ability to be flexible and to listen to what others are saying in order to understand other family members' differing perspectives in the search for common ground when transfer is being considered.

It all boils down to "MBC"—Managing By Communicating. The key to successful management has everything to do with how the younger and older members manage their communications, first within the family, and then with one another in the business and also with non-family employees. Precisely because the leader of the business exercises ultimate authority, he or she must be a good listener so that all perspectives get a hearing when important issues are being addressed. In fact, MBC works best when the leader does more listening than talking. As a wise entrepreneur once said, "After all, we do have two ears, but just one mouth."

MBC

- To try to understand the complexity that arises from the overlay of family role relationships. Mom may be mom, but if she's the president at work, she's the boss. A daughter may be dad's "favorite" but at work she's just one of the employees.
- To understand that while love is appropriate in the family, what counts in the business is respect, which only work performance and merit can deliver. Family members get only the respect they earn in the business, just like any non-family employee.
- To create and then communicate rules of entry and exit as early as possible so family members know the rules are being fairly applied and that they exist to ensure the well-being of the business. For example, if family members who leave the business know they will be required to sell back their stock, or that a college degree is a prerequisite for entering management, then everyone knows the score in advance, reducing the likelihood of conflict.
- To communicate a training plan, so that younger generation members who prove their value receive ever increasing amounts of responsibility. Allowing them to make mistakes is good for the business because it's the only way they can grow in business judgment.
- To develop a succession plan in consultation with the family so that all interests are fairly represented. Key non-family managers should also be consulted along with respected outside advisors and other professionals. The plan should be communicated in a way that preserves goodwill within the family and also among non-family employees.

The competent practice of MBC in the family business absolutely requires that those who are part of both systems feel free to express their disagreements

Conflict Must Be Confronted, Not Avoided

The expression of conflict is healthy. Avoidance of conflict can harm both the family and the business. What good MBC practice requires is candid and open discussion of disagreements. If dad fails to tell his son about his negative assessment of his work performance based on an objective evaluation because he doesn't want to hurt his "child's feelings," then his son won't be able to grow in the business. Or, when a daughter in the company fails to discuss her anger over dad's reluctance to hold a poorly performing family member accountable, just because dad doesn't want to disturb the family peace, she, too, is failing to practice good MBC. Younger generation members have an equal responsibility to confront conflict to help keep the boundaries between family and business clearly drawn.

Planning for Succession

Manage conflict, don't avoid it

When the time comes to work out a formal succession plan for transferring ownership and control, it will go smoothly only if family relationships have been managed properly during the early years, long before the attorneys and financial planners have been called in to hammer out the details. If you are a senior family member, and have ownership, you have a duty to initiate this planning. Make sure that family members participate and that the next generation being groomed for senior management has been adequately prepared. If you are a member of the younger generation active in the business, you have a right to expect the necessary training. All family members and key non-family employees should be told the rationale for the choice of the successor.

Many seniors don't want to let go

The founder and other members of the senior generation in the business need to understand that they have to pass the baton of leadership at some point, even though they may be reluctant to retire and let go of their "baby." Because so many owners have spent most of their lives building their businesses, letting go isn't always easy—especially if they really enjoy their work. Plus most know that their kids won't run the business the same way they did. And for many, that "not the same way" means "not as well."

As stated earlier, no one wants to address issues of his or her own aging and mortality. This "planning process" is contrary to the quick decision-making style typical of entrepreneurs. But in order to effect the succession transition of a family business from one generation to the next, planning is essential.

Planning for Financial Security

Members of the senior generation must plan for their financial security and estate planning as a part of the succession planning process. Family business owners need to be sure their estate plans are compatible with their plans for transferring ownership and control of the business.

Above all, seniors who will continue to depend on the success of the business for their post-retirement livelihood need a plan that can provide the necessary safeguards for themselves while at the same time giving the younger generation sufficient operational control over the business. Some retiring owners do this by maintaining control at the board level, transferring their voting shares to children in the business over a period of years. In other cases, the seniors may receive preferred stock with fixed dividends or retain company real estate with a long-term lease to the company.

Planning for Life Outside the Business

In addition to the business succession plan, retiring seniors must have a good personal plan. For some who may not wish to exit the company completely, this may mean carving out a new niche for themselves in the business—as advisor-consultant to their children—or perhaps launching a new career altogether. If the family has created a charitable foundation, involvement in philanthropy is an option.

Senior family members must prepare for a new chapter in their lives

Planning for the post-management years should be just as important to retiring seniors as their financial planning. However, that's something they have to build for themselves, just like the successful business that is finally being passed down to the next generation. The succession is more apt to go smoothly when seniors have something useful to occupy themselves with after leaving the business. They can cultivate outside interests. Before retirement, plan ahead, and devote some time to experiment with different hobbies and activities.

Whose job is it to plan the management succession?

A succession plan is not something that owners can simply turn over to their attorneys, accountants, and financial planners. Although these specialists are certainly needed, the plan deserves the owner's serious attention. Other family members and key non-family employees should be included. Increasingly, owners draw on the experience of outside advisors and consultants. They are sometimes invited to sit on an advisory board. The owner relies on the board for strategic business planning assistance. These advisors can help with succession planning because they provide an objective judgment regarding the skills and experience successors will need, given the company's future outlook and direction. Family members in business, by contrast, may have vested interests to protect which may conflict when it comes to determining the successor.

Another advantage of involving outside advisors and consultants is that parents are spared the painful dilemma of having to choose the successor from among several children. Having an objective judgment from non-family advisors helps to soften the disappointment, and blunt the pain of those who will not be receiving the baton when it is passed. As a result, family relationships may be less apt to suffer damage.

Often times, the children themselves are consulted about the plan. Hopefully, their interests and desires are fully considered. When the owner neglects to include members of the younger generation in this planning, he or she risks having the business controlled "from the grave." Successors then have very little choice but to accept the business as it was left to them. Indeed, the parents may find that they left the business in the hands of a child who even in his or her own eyes was neither the most motivated or capable candidate for leadership.

By incorporating the younger generation's ideas into the final plan, the owner can rest more easily because the responsibility for the future of the business has been shared and will result in greater acceptance.

How outside advisors can help.

Outside advisors can be especially helpful in this process of involving other family members—just as they can help with the design of the succession plan itself. Because outsider advisors and experts stand apart from both the business and family systems, they are not entangled in the emotional tugging and pulling that often goes on within the family. They are less apt to "play favorites" and for that reason can help ensure that divergent interests have been adequately represented.

If you decide to establish a board of advisors made up of experienced individuals who provide occasional advice but who lack the authority and legal responsibilities they would have as directors, you want to be certain you receive unbiased, objective opinions. As regards succession planning, advisors should have no stake in the outcome. Vendors, customers, professional service providers, consultants, employees, members of the board of directors, and relatives (unless they are key principals) should not be included on a board of advisors.

Outside advisors can lend an objective view

Above all, your advisory group should focus on the long-term interests of the company. In the event you decide that compelling family needs come first, which could mean having to make sacrifices in the business, you at least will have had the independent views of unbiased outsiders to aid in this decision.

Prepare the younger generation.

Not all members of the younger generation are instantly qualified. For most, preparation for a new leadership role requires the acquisition of more knowledge, skills, and experience. As noted earlier, younger generation members need to be given the opportunity to learn, which also means learning from their mistakes. Owners can give their children increasing amounts of authority in the business, but they should do this over a period of time rather than all at once. With each demonstrated accomplishment, more authority should be granted.

There is an important difference between giving members of the younger generation more authority and responsibility simply because they insist on it, and giving it based on demonstrated achievement. Still, when in doubt, it is better to err in the direction of giving too much control rather than too little. The owner's children cannot grow in the business unless they have the opportunity to fail. That means the senior generation must feel comfortable about relinquishing a reasonable amount of control before the succession occurs.

The younger generation must acquire knowledge, skills, and experience

Younger members of the family need not stand idly by, waiting for new responsibilities to be thrust upon them. They should actively seek new responsibilities whenever possible. This does not mean getting involved in a power struggle or an internal revolt. Rather, younger members should make their case for taking charge, by bringing forth a well-thought-out plan for change, backed up by innovative ideas and compelling arguments.

Develop new designs for succession.
In addition to boards of outside advisors, formal rules of entry, advancement and exit and training programs for grooming family members, owners are coming to understand the advantages of innovative new designs for succession.

For example, choosing the eldest child, which had been the prevailing succession pattern, is no longer an "automatic" choice. One solution that has worked for a number of companies is to hire an interim CEO, an experienced non-family outsider, both to run the company and to mentor younger family members until they are ready to take control.

The "president for life" pattern of tenure that characterized most family businesses in the past is also changing. Some owners decide that they are ready for a change well before the "normal" retirement age. In most organizations today, the average tenure in a managerial job is four to seven years. While this is not true of every family business owner, it is becoming an increasingly popular option. Of course, that means that the senior generation should be working on their business succession plan and preparing the next generation sooner rather than later.

Finally, among the innovative designs for succession, are co-successor strategies, sometimes called "co-presidencies." Although the rule against having a divided leadership is standard wisdom in mainline organizational practice, there are the inevitable exceptions. What happens, for example, if the evaluation of two or more children active in management turns out to be a toss-up—just too close to call? Both may be equally eager to run the business and both may be equally qualified.

Presidency of a family business isn't a life sentence

There are co-presidencies that have worked out well. One of the successors gets the title and responsibilities of chief executive officer (CEO) while the other assumes the duties of president. In other cases, several family members will be found to constitute the "Office of the President"—all sharing in the exercise of control equally. While authority can be successfully shared in this manner, it is still advisable that each family member be given clearly defined duties and responsibilities. Although power may be shared, their roles in the business should be differentiated. Of course, how well this works out will depend on how well they have gotten along before. Sibling rivalries may preclude this type of arrangement. Yet there are also many cases where sisters, brothers, and cousins have developed good work relationships based on love, trust, and mutual respect and can work together as co-successors in the business. This is more likely to be true for family businesses where the boundary between the family and business systems was carefully drawn to relate to one another in the business environment as colleagues with reward and recognition being determined by work performance, rather than one's status in the family.

Communicate the succession plan.

When the time for passing the baton finally arrives, it is important that you as owner communicate the succession decision in the right way to your children, other relatives, and non-family managers. No matter how rational the plan, no matter how objective the candidate assessment process was, some relatives and employees are apt to be disappointed. Here, too, good MBC—managing by communicating—can be helpful. Announcing the decision in a respectful manner can be the difference between success and failure. Even though you have put the company in the right hands and have used the right estate planning tools, you must still communicate the decision in a way that will preserve good will among family members and non-family employees alike. Without that good will, even a soundly run company will eventually find itself running into trouble.

If the best plan is communicated poorly, it will fail

Pass the baton.

Passing the baton from the older to the younger generation involves more than just the drafting of a formal succession plan. It begins much earlier and involves both generations in a process of communication and learning as preparation for the eventual transfer of control.

7 Steps to Success

For members of the younger generation:

1) *Learn the stories about the business; spend time with your parents and other senior relatives to demonstrate your knowledge and interest in the business.*
2) *Don't short change your education. This is the era of life-long-learning. Focus on training for leadership; interact with challenging minds; use your imagination to better equip you to compete for excellence.*
3) *Work full-time for somebody else first. Experience another boss and another company. Make your mistakes elsewhere. Broaden your exposure working outside the family business .*
4) *Get paid fairly. Resist the "golden handcuffs" that would tie you to your parent's business too early; take no more nor less than you are truly worth to the business. Develop good financial judgment, in both business and personal finances.*
5) *Try to avoid reporting to your parents in their business until you've worked at lower levels, reporting to non-family managers who will evaluate you objectively. Your parents may not be able to provide objective appraisals of your work.*

For members of the older generation:

6) *Set a strategic direction for the future of the business and match future leadership to it. Plan for the transfer of management and ownership. Accept that you have to pass on the baton. Secure your own financial future. Think about a new role and the challenge that new pursuits can provide. It's a time of stress and uncertainty, but it can be done well if planned for in advance.*
7) *Run with your children for a while as the baton is passed, then let the next generation move ahead. They own the track now. It's time to watch the race, and root for the new family team.*

As tough as it is, as hard as it seems, the successful perpetuation of a family business may just well be the closest you will ever come to immortality.

Conclusion

Family-owned businesses face unique problems arising from the overlap between family roles and work relationships. However, more family business owners have begun to look at ways to professionalize their management practices, including policies that will help maintain clear boundaries between the family, and its expectations, on the one hand, and the business systems on the other. These include formal plans for training and mentoring the younger generation, rules of entry, advancement, and exit that apply to all family members equally, improved communication and the willingness on the senior member's part to discuss company policies and their succession plans candidly with family members and key non-family employees alike. In addition, business owners are beginning to consider the advantages of bringing outside advisors into the picture, to provide an independent, objective assessment of both business strategy and succession plans.

To build the strongest possible foundation for this new professionalism in family-owned businesses, owners and other key employees need to learn the basic principles of MBC—of managing by communicating. That's because the most important issues pertaining to family businesses arise from the complexities involved in managing the relationships of family and non-family employees within the business.

Chapter 17
WOMEN IN BUSINESS

About This Chapter:
- *Advantages of business ownership for women*
- *Challenges of women-owned businesses*
- *Success strategies*

Introduction

Women are moving into the ranks of the self-employed in increasingly large numbers. In the early 1970's less than 5% of all businesses were owned by women. By 1994, this number had risen to 37% and experts predict that by the year 2000, half of all businesses will be owned by women. Women who entered the ranks of corporate businesses in the 1960's and 1970's have gained work experience and confidence. For many women, entrepreneurship is the logical next step.

Advantages of Business Ownership for Women

Historically, women entrepreneurs were divorced or widowed women who started small service or retail operations out of financial necessity. These establishments generally remained small and labor-intensive. Today women are choosing self-employment for a variety of reasons:

- Control and Flexibility
- Opportunity
- Independence

Control and Flexibility

By far the most common reason women cite for striking out on their own is control of their time, their finances, and their futures. Women today are most often the primary, if not only, caregiver for their children, their elderly parents—or both. They need flexibility to manage all their varied responsibilities—something traditionally not available in a typical job. During the 1970's and 1980's many women put off having a family in order to pursue their careers. In the 1990's many are seeking a new lifestyle that will allow them to have a family yet not give up the careers they have worked to create. Women know they will probably work harder in their own business than in a job, but they control when and how they get that work done.

Opportunity

The Industrial Age has given way to the Information Age and the nature of work in America has changed

Self-employment is seen by many women as an opportunity to escape low-pay, dead-end jobs. Women today comprise more than 95% of the "helping professions" like secretaries, nurses, child care workers, bank tellers, and dental assistants. Such jobs are traditionally the lowest paid in our society with limited opportunities for advancement. Despite gains in recent years, women still earn, on average, about 60 cents for every dollar earned by men in the same occupation. Women who find themselves in low-paid work see self-employment as an opportunity to do something that interests them and has the potential for unlimited income if they are successful. While current statistics indicate that self-employed women are, in fact, not earning as much as their wage-and-salary counterparts, this could be due to the fact that these businesses are still quite new and many of these new entrepreneurs are working less than full-time while their children are young. As these firms mature and owners devote more time to them, the potential for increased income and opportunity should also grow.

Snapshot of women-owned businesses

Surveys completed by the National Foundation for Women Business Owners and Dun and Bradstreet Information Services in 1994 and 1995 revealed the following facts about women-owned businesses:

- Own 7.7 million companies—37% of all U.S. businesses
- Generate nearly $1.4 trillion in sales each year
- Provide jobs for 15.5 million people
- Employ 35% more people in the U.S. than 1994 Fortune 500 companies do worldwide
- Are well established—over 28% have been in business 12 years or more

For other women, self-employment is an opportunity to create work in areas where jobs are non-existent. In rural America, the family farm is in jeopardy. It is becoming increasingly difficult for small agricultural enterprises to succeed. The answer for many rural families has been to seek work off the farm to supplement their dwindling farm profits. These second income sources have allowed many families to keep their farms and a lifestyle they cherish. But in some cases, there are no jobs available or the farm location is so remote it is not economical to work in town. In situations like these, women are finding ways to start their own businesses and supplement the family income.

One woman uses her creative talents and the modern technology of a computer to design stationery and recipe cards which are marketed in gift stores across the Midwest. A farm wife with experience working for the economic development department in her state now offers marketing assistance to other small businesses. Another woman designs fabrics and craft patterns which are sold nationwide in a major chain of discount stores. A rancher's wife makes jellies from the wild fruit in the sandhills of Nebraska. Some of these businesses are very small and just bring in a little extra spending money. Others have grown to substantial companies making significant contributions to the state or region's economy.

With modern advances in technology and transportation, it is possible for a woman to transact business via fax and computer and ship products directly from her location to anywhere in the world. These are women who would otherwise be unemployed because their location prohibits them from finding traditional jobs. And in many cases they are not only supplementing their own incomes, they are creating job opportunities for others in their communities as their businesses grow and expand.

Many women-owned businesses create job opportunities in their communities

Independence

In today's economy, downsizing and restructuring are common. Large corporations are systematically reducing the number of full-time workers they employ and are utilizing more temporary and contract workers. Job security has become a thing of the past. Many women are responding to this trend by turning to self-employment. This may seem a peculiar way to gain security since success is never assured and the entire business could be lost at any moment. Yet self-employment does offer a woman the independence to run things the way she sees fit and to have some control over the course the business will follow. Rather than feeling like a pawn which is picked up or discarded at the pleasure of a large company, self-employed women feel they are more firmly in control of their own destinies.

In addition, the "glass ceiling" effect has motivated many women to become entrepreneurs. Talented women who have been challenged throughout their careers while moving up the corporate ladder reach a point where there is no longer opportunity for growth. They are barred from moving further up in corporations because of entrenched "old boy" networks that refuse to leave. These women decide to channel their frustrations productively—by going into business for themselves.

Other women are finding that corporate structures do not allow them to fully explore their talents due to glass ceiling limitations. Instead, they are taking charge of their careers by becoming their own bosses. However, not all women starting their own businesses have had years of experience. Some women are choosing to branch out on their own directly out of college or business school. These women are part of the entrepreneurial fever of the 1990's and are finding satisfaction and freedom in what they do.

The Woman-Owned Business

In 1992, the Small Business Administration reported that 85% of women-owned firms were in retail trade, finance, insurance, real estate, and services. However, new female businesses in more non-traditional fields such as wholesale trade, agriculture, mining, manufacturing, and engineering have been opening at a faster rate than that of men.

Nearly all of the women entrepreneurs surveyed had a strong, positive role mode—often their own mother

A large proportion of women-owned enterprises are service-oriented. Service firms are attractive to women because they generally require a much smaller investment to get started and can often be run from the home. It is estimated that 80% of women start their companies in the home. However, between 1975 and 1990, there was a dramatic shift in female ventures away from personal services (like beauty salons or dressmaking shops) and into business industries.

The top businesses for women are:

Retail Sales	7.6%	Personal Services	3.7%
Consulting	7.6%	Word Processing	3.5%
Educational Services	4.1%	Real Estate	3.5%
Public Relations	3.9%	Advertising	3.2%
Career Counseling	3.9%		

Most female-owned companies are fairly small—the average business employs fewer than 5 people. Service firms are generally smaller as they are less labor intensive than other types of businesses. For many women, remaining small is a choice. Many remain one-person operations. They are not necessarily interested in the trappings of the business—a big office and lots of staff. Their focus is on having an enterprise that they can control and that fits well with their other responsibilities. The smaller size of women-owned concerns is also partly due to the fact that most of these businesses are not very old. As of 1986 only about a third of all women-owned businesses had been operating for more than 5 years. Continuing research by the National Foundation of Women Business Owners and Dun and Bradstreet suggest that change is underway. The number of women-owned companies with 100 or more employees grew by 18.3% from 1991 to 1994.

Female businesses tend to employ higher percentages of women. It is common for two-thirds of the employees in these companies to be female. Since 75% of the nation's poor are women and children, and women are starting businesses at twice the rate of men, the benefits of these hiring practices are enormous. Women-owned firms are also introducing new products and concepts designed to meet the specific needs of women.

As one woman entrepreneur explained, "Growing is more than growing in size; it's growing in knowledge and ability to do what you do better—it's growing in a lot of ways"

"Drive-Em"

One example of this trend is a Texas-based company called "Drive-Em." A mother who found herself constantly chauffeuring her children to their various activities decided to open a business to help other working parents like herself. Parents purchase a book of 5 tickets for $15. Each ticket is good for a ride anywhere in the small town. Children need not worry about carrying cash or computing a tip for the taxi driver. Parents are assured that the driver will act just like a parent. If the child is nowhere in sight when she goes to school to pick him up, she will go into the school and find him. If she takes the child to soccer practice she will not leave until he has located his coach. This novel idea and others like it are being pioneered by women to help other women with the multitude of roles and responsibilities they must juggle each day.

An in-depth study of women-owned businesses based on U.S. Census data over 11 survey years (from 1967 to 1984) revealed some interesting facts about these companies. This nationally representative sample of over 5,000 women, aged 30-44, reported the following:

1) Roughly two-thirds of the women who enter self-employment leave it after about 3 years.
2) Individuals who continuously stay self-employed for a few years are likely to do so in the future.
3) Individuals who exit self-employment are likely to re-enter self-employment in the future.
4) The likelihood of entering and surviving in self-employment increases with increased levels of education.

The results of this study indicate that self-employment, like careers, may be interrupted for women, but that women with self-employment experience are likely to become business owners again, and those with higher levels of education are likely to have a higher survival rate.

Women and Family-Owned Businesses

In the 1940's a woman's involvement in family-owned businesses was largely unrecognized and uncompensated. Her many roles may have included that of mom, spouse, sounding board, negotiator, and bookkeeper but she was neither employee nor stockholder. While she definitely had a part in the risk and the effort devoted to the business, the enterprise was clearly sustained and directed by the husband. Many agricultural operations continue to operate in this way today.

For women, entrepreneurship is a life strategy—a way to integrate both their family and their career needs

Sometimes a woman becomes a reluctant business owner through succession. Her self-employed husband dies or divorces her and she inherits the company. With children to raise and obligations to honor, these women are thrust into the role of an entrepreneur whether they want it or not. Some choose to sell the business immediately. Others take on the challenge of managing it themselves. Women who have found themselves in this position advise other women to take an active interest in the business early on.

Increasingly, couples are opting to start ventures together as equal partners. These co-entrepreneurs are creating new models for business ownership and marriage. Responsibilities are divided between the two based on their individual talents and skills. Personal and professional life merges with both the husband and wife equally involved in home and work responsibilities.

Women in this role can move more easily between their work and family life and children are often raised to participate in the business early in life.

Little Caesars

Marian Ilitch formed her company, Little Caesars pizza shops, in 1959 with her husband Michael. Since then, the Ilitches have accomplished a great deal together. Marian, who worked the register in their first store, now oversees the finances of 4,700 Little Caesars stores, a quarter of them company-owned, generating systemwide sales of $2 billion!

An increasing number of daughters in family businesses are moving into positions of ownership through inheritance and succession. Another evolving model finds women in ownership positions with brothers or sisters. These enterprises are either the result of a start-up venture by the siblings themselves or a business acquired through an inter-generational transition.

Challenges for Women-Owned Businesses

In addition to all of the obstacles the typical entrepreneur must overcome in starting up a business, the woman entrepreneur faces some unique challenges of her own:

- Financing the business
- Establishing credibility
- Family issues

Financing the Business

The National Women's Business Council, created by Congress in 1988 to review the status of women business owners nationwide, found that the most significant barrier to the success of women-owned firms is the lack of capital. They also concluded that women in business generally take fewer risks in terms of expansion, usually because of under-capitalization.

For some women, self-employment is an opportunity to create work in areas where jobs are non-existent

Another study of nearly 700,000 women-owned companies found that over two-thirds of this group had experienced difficulty in getting bank credit and had turned to private sources or business earnings for both short-term and long-term capital needs. Three-fourths of this group had used personal capital for start-up costs. As a result, women frequently start their ventures with half the amount used by male businesses owners (an average of $11,000 versus $22,000). Commercial credit cards—one of the most expensive sources of credit—serve as a primary source of financing for about 52% of establishments owned by women. Only 18% of all other ventures rely so heavily on commercial credit cards for capital.

Women owners continue to be largely underserved by banks. There are 3 factors which appear to be primarily responsible for the difficulties women have in securing credit for their business:

1. **Nature of women-owned businesses:** Women in service firms have little to offer the bank as collateral for their loans. Collateral preferred by banks are hard assets like land, equipment, or inventory which can be readily sold in the event that the entrepreneur defaults on his/her loan. It may be difficult for a service business to meet the stiff collateral requirements of most lending institutions when its primary assets are the entrepreneur's talent, knowledge, and employees. Retail stores have the advantage of being able to offer inventory as collateral, but banks will only provide credit for a portion of the inventory to minimize their risk in case the shop fails and the goods must be sold at auction for a fraction of their actual value. Banks will rarely consider funding 100% of the cost of business start-up or inventory purchase. They are more likely to require that the entrepreneur invest at least one-third of the funds needed out of his/her own resources. And for most women these resources are fairly limited.
2. **Limited credit history:** Many women entrepreneurs have never obtained credit in their name only and do not have a credit card of their own. Even if they have been instrumental in repaying debt incurred in their marriage, this progress will be reported on their husband's credit record unless they have taken steps to establish their own credit separate from their spouse. With no history of successful debt repayment, financial institutions are unlikely to extend much new credit in a new and untested venture. As these businesses mature and develop track records of performance, banks will be more willing to negotiate loans.
3. **Weak financial skills:** Traditionally, women were not brought up expecting to be their own source of financial support. Many lack formal education or relevant job experience in finance. They may also have had limited experience dealing with lenders and lack the confidence to aggressively seek the funding they need to finance their operation. Finally, they often seek financing before they have

The Small Business Administration, in 1992, reported that 85% of women-owned firms were in retail trade, finance, insurance, real estate, and services

prepared a complete and well-documented loan package. This only further weakens their credibility with the lenders they approach.

To improve the odds of successfully securing financing, women entrepreneurs can:

- **Establish a track record and gain experience in dealing with money:** Experience in bookkeeping and money management can be acquired by handling the family finances and helping with the bookkeeping tasks at a church, trade association, or other organizations. You can establish your own credit record by securing credit cards, charge accounts, checking accounts and insurance policies in your name only. If these companies require a spouse to sign the credit application, you should seek another company. A personal loan to buy a car or equipment can be taken out in your name only and repaid in full in a timely fashion. Even if you do not need the money, this is an opportunity to learn how the loan process works and establish credit before approaching the bank for a commercial loan.
- **Understand your credit rights:** The Equal Credit Opportunity Act of 1974 states that "It shall be unlawful for any creditor to discriminate against any applicant on the basis of sex or marital status with respect to any aspect of a credit transaction." This law applies to all credit-granting institutions including banks, retail businesses, and credit card companies. While interpretations of this law make it more applicable to the protection of consumer credit rights rather than business credit, it still guarantees all women the right to a written refusal from the lender so she can understand the basis for the credit denial.
- **Find the right bank:** Banks have a wide variety of lending philosophies. A bank in Colorado has a $25 million loan pool for Colorado women-owned companies. A bank in Chicago sponsors seminars to help women develop business plans and obtain financing. The only way to find a bank that is receptive to a female enterprise is to interview them as you would a prospective employee and keep searching until the right bank is located. This means seeking out a banker before the company is in desperate need of funds to determine interest rates, procedures, and requirements prior to actually applying for a loan. You will want to find a banker who is familiar with businesses like yours and has financed other women-owned firms the size of your own. It will be important to find a loan officer you feel you can trust and communicate with easily.

Female businesses tend to employ higher percentages of women

Racing Strollers

Only when Mary Baechler was turned down for a bank loan did she figure that it was probably time to learn more about how financial statements work and what they should be telling her about her business. Baechler co-founded Racing Strollers, Inc., with her then-husband in 1983. The company manufactures strollers that are specially designed for parents who want to bring their babies on walks or jogs. Fortunately, the banker who turned Baechler down was sympathetic. The banker recommended the Baechler hire a local consultant to assist in setting up financial systems as well as reexamining pricing and customer-services policies. The consultant set up informal meetings with bankers, lawyers, and other professionals who might provide advice. The banker got Baechler a better accountant who determined that Racing Strollers' costs were too high. Only after Baechler understood more about her monthly profit-and-loss statements, etc., and what she could do to cut costs and boost profits, did her company really start to take off.

- **Provide the necessary collateral.** Before approaching any lender you must determine what assets or other security you can offer to back your loan request. Banks will generally limit the amount they loan to a given percentage of the assets offered as collateral. In a company with few hard assets to back the loan, women must come up with alternative sources of collateral.
- **Offer personal assets as collateral for a commercial loan.** This might include a second mortgage on your home, bonds that were received as a gift, stocks that were inherited, and/or cash value in a personal life insurance policy.
- **Sublease** part of the building to another business and assign the lease payments to the bank.
- **Find someone to co-sign or guarantee the loan.** This last suggestion is controversial. Many women, intent on succeeding on their own, resist asking others to co-sign their note. Others see it as the only way to get any meaningful sum of money. In cases of inadequate collateral, a co-signature may be a requirement of financing. Banks may also ask you to carry life insurance and secure an assignment on the proceeds of these policies in order to protect the lending institution if you should die.

- **Provide the lender with everything needed to approve the loan.** When initially seeking loan funds it is wise to first ask the bank for a loan application packet and complete all necessary information before approaching the lender again. A carefully prepared business plan which shows that the applicant understands her venture and has a feasible concept is of primary importance. Lenders will also want to see income tax returns, current and past financial statements, a written loan request stating amount requested, use of the loan funds, and proposed repayment plan. The more complete the loan package, the faster the loan decision can be made. If you are weak in finance you may be wise to contact an accountant or financial advisor to help you prepare the loan application. In a survey of small business lending practices it was found that the usual reasons for denial of a loan application were (in order): poor credit rating, lack of competence, poor cash flow or working capital, poor market for a product, poor collateral, and low owner's equity. A carefully prepared business plan and loan application will address each of these areas and assure lenders that you can handle each of these challenges.

The federal government's Small Business Administration (SBA) has an Office of Women's Business Ownership (OWBO) which has a $4 million training program and a Women's Pre-Qualification Loan Program which in fiscal year 1995 prepared 413 loans totaling $37.7 million. Check with your state chamber of commerce to investigate economic incentives your state can offer to your enterprise by way of loans or training.

Success Strategies for Women Business Owners

Success for any entrepreneur, male or female, is dependent on many factors. These include knowledge, sound business practices, drive and ambition, common sense, imagination, financial and communication skills, the ability to organize and take risks, persistence, flexibility, a goal orientation, and the willingness to work hard. For women there are other areas of focus that can help.

As an entrepreneur, a woman must exercise a certain level of independence, persistence, and the self-confidence to succeed on her own

Balance

Gladys Edmunds heads Edmunds Travel Consultants in Pittsburgh which employs 17 employees and had gross annual sales of $5 million. This winner of Avon's Woman of Enterprise Award advises women entrepreneurs to "knock off the superwoman stuff." Many female entrepreneurs have felt pressured to not only "do it all" but to do it perfectly. Not wanting their business to interfere with what they feel is expected of them as a wife and mother, these women attempt to have successful businesses, cook gourmet meals, nurse their babies, entertain their friends, and remain dynamic partners for their husbands. Perhaps you feel entrepreneurship is allowed only if you don't neglect your other duties. Women must learn that men and children are quite capable of taking on more responsibility in the home. They must be ready to hire specialists whenever and wherever they need them, whether it's a financial planner or a housekeeper. A successful entrepreneur accepts the trade-offs that her life demands. Long-term success is only possible when a woman has learned to balance her life in all ways—allowing time for work and time for play, time with family, and time alone.

Support Network

A strong support system is important at all stages of a venture but especially during the start-up phase when the entrepreneur and those around her are most likely to have doubts about the viability of the enterprise. Women need both moral support and professional support.

- **Moral support**: Women typically see their husband as their biggest source of support. A woman is fortunate when this key person in her life sees the business idea as feasible and works to help the woman succeed. In addition, many women have developed a circle of friends who support their efforts and give them encouragement. These may be other entrepreneurs who face the same challenges or close personal friends who cheer the women on as they pursue their ideas. These vital supporters act as a sounding board, provide a different perspective, give continuous encouragement and at times help out with the actual work of the company.
- **Professional support:** Entrepreneurs also need support with the technical aspects of running a business. Over 30% of women entrepreneurs report that they have a mentor who provides moral support as well as professional guidance. This could be a professional colleague, a valued teacher, a former boss, or anyone else who can answer questions and guide development as business owners.

Physique for Her

Susan Stuart, the owner of Physique for Her, a maker of women's sports apparel, found a mentor in Tom Hardt, an executive at K-Swiss sneaker company and an esteemed sporting-goods marketer. She called him for some international marketing advice: She was checking the reference of a distributor in the Netherlands who had worked with K-Swiss and Tom also cleared up a discussion that she had been having about whether or not to drop prices when she decided to export. Hardt explained that it was a big mistake to try to have the same margins internationally. Seeing that she could learn a lot about international sales from Hardt, Stuart asked if Hardt would teach her about international marketing. It was the beginning of a long mentorship. That kind of free training has helped Physique for Her to grow to $9 million in annual sales.

Other sources of professional support include:

- **Customers** who can offer advice about the product or service and create interest in and support for the company.

Conceptual Works

Sharon Mendez graduated from college with a degree in aerospace engineering and dreamed of starting her own software business, but she did considerable research on the potential market before leaving here job in a Texas engineering firm. Six years ago, Conceptual Works, Inc. was born. The first few months in business weren't glamorous at all. Working out of her home with the help of some experts, she wrote proposals for prospective government customers and made cold sales calls. After she gave several failed sales pitches, Mendez said one prospective client told her bluntly that it was the worst presentation she had ever heard. But the woman offered advice on how she might improve her pitch. "From that, I learned an important lesson," says Mendez. "Always solicit feedback. Know your customers."

Keys to success:

- Get advice
- Solicit feedback
- Know your customer
- Set up support network
- Learn finance and accounting
- Focus on service

- **Suppliers** who can offer advice on how the industry works, what the competition is doing, and trends which can impact the business. A solid foundation with suppliers can help establish credibility with lenders and with customers. This can be a particularly powerful alliance if a reciprocal arrangement can develop that benefits both your company's and your supplier's businesses.
- **Experts** such as lawyers, accountants, insurance agents, manufacturing representatives, market research firms, management consultants, and advertising agencies offer objective sounding boards and have specific knowledge important to entrepreneurs dealing with issues involving risk.
- **Trade associations** offer highly specific industry information and contacts with others in similar businesses who understand the challenges the entrepreneur faces. Relationships established through these associations often end up being an extension of the moral and emotional support of friends and family.
- **Community organizations** like the Chamber of Commerce and various civic and service groups afford the opportunity for an entrepreneur to become acquainted with other successful people in the community where she operates. These contacts provide information about the business environment where the company is located and often open the doors for surprising alliances that benefit both parties.

Entrepreneurs need support with the technical aspects of running a business

Continuous Learning

The world is constantly changing. The business person who fails to keep up with the latest trends will be left behind. The successful entrepreneur makes it her business to read and study not only what is happening in her industry and the economy but also to look at what other successful business people have done and emulate their methods. For women, this is of particular importance since many come to entrepreneurship with less formal training than men in the financial and technical aspects of their business.

A variety of opportunities are available to entrepreneurs:

- **Conventions and trade conferences** provide the opportunity to gather pertinent industry information in a short period of time. These events offer short, special sessions designed to give participants the most current and relevant information about topics of particular interest to people in the industry. There are also opportunities to meet with experts, suppliers, and other competitors. Displays and booths give entrepreneurs ideas for their own companies.

- **Adult education classes:** Universities and community colleges offer business courses on a continuing basis. In addition to the traditional classes which meet on college campuses, many institutions now offer distance learning options where people in remote locations can attend classes via interactive television technology or can complete course work through home-study programs.
- **Workshops and seminars:** Private and governmental agencies offer a wide variety of seminars geared toward providing business training in a more concentrated, information-specific format which is generally shorter and less expensive than formal college courses. Many private trainers will customize the training for individual communities or businesses if desired.
- **Business periodicals** provide an excellent avenue for continuous learning. Several business periodicals, both industry-specific and general, should be part of an entrepreneur's regular reading.
- **The Internet** is the latest tool for gathering information. This new technology links computers world-wide through phone modems and gives a business person access to up-to-the-minute information on an infinite number of topics. New search tools and on-line services are making it increasingly easy for novice computer users to tap into highly specific information or link up with others with similar interests anywhere in the country or the world. This is an especially intriguing option for women in home-based businesses who have had difficulty forming effective networking contacts.

More help: join networks of like-minded women

Networking

Meet, talk, join, lead. Up-and-coming entrepreneurs can learn as much from peers as they can from those who are more experienced. Many company builders get into peer groups—either by joining existing ones or starting their own. Discussions may include everything from hassles with government regulators and larger competitors to ways to test price points and protect trademarks. The National Association of Women Business Owners (NAWBO) offers CEO roundtables, conferences, and workshops. CEO roundtables are usually put together by people in the same industry or in the same geographic area. Such roundtables are cited by increasing numbers of people as the most powerful and consistent way to hear new ideas, receive feedback, and get emotional support.

Cara's Carats

Jane Mason, a NAWBO member and founder of Cara's Carats, a jewelry business, is a seasoned networker. Through her networking efforts as a board member of three organizations she has developed a database with over 1,000 people. She has launched several new product lines, or made product modifications, as a result of informal suggestions from people she has met through networking. She also met another jewelry designer who gave her invaluable advice on manufacturing and retail distribution.

Being able to balance multiple tasks, both at work and at home, is a key element in the success of any business

Conclusion

The number of women entrepreneurs has increased dramatically over the past few years and continues to grow. Citing independence, flexibility, and the ability to control their destinies, these women are changing the face of U.S. businesses. Women entrepreneurs face the same challenges that all entrepreneurs face, but through careful investigation of funding sources, establishing credit histories, developing their own support networks, and continued learning, women business owners are taking charge of their ventures and flourishing in unprecedented numbers. These women are navigating a steady course and are the role models for women entrepreneurs of the future!

Chapter 18
MINORITY BUSINESS DEVELOPMENT

About This Chapter:
- *Opportunities for minority entrepreneurs*
- *Government initiatives for minority businesses*
- *Strategies for success*
- *Challenges for minority-owned businesses*

Introduction

In the U.S., minority-owned businesses range from small start-up ventures to large conglomerates. While the circumstances that have led minorities to self-employment are often very different, overall there has been a continuing growth within minority-owned and operated businesses as illustrated below:

Minority Business Growth Within the Three Main Ethnic Groups Is As Follows:

	1982	1987	1992
Black-owned firms	308,000	424,165	620,912
Hispanic-owned firms	233,975	489,973	862,605
Asian-owned firms	187,691	439,271	705,672

Minority businesses have traditionally succeeded by finding niche markets under-served or ignored by the dominant businesses

In today's business environment that includes affirmative action and minority set-aside programs being challenged, an increasingly tight-fisted market on business loans and pressure from all sides to cut back, minority-owned firms must be more innovative than ever. Despite the challenges, today's minority-owned businesses use their flexibility and savvy to do more than just stay float in the turbulent marketplace. They are swimming—full steam ahead!

Opportunities for Minority Entrepreneurs

Following the civil unrest of the 1960's a number of public and private programs were initiated to encourage and promote minority businesses.

In 1969, President Nixon signed an executive order creating an Office of Minority Business Enterprise—later renamed the Minority Business Development Agency (MBDA)—in the Department of Commerce, to be responsible for coordinating programs geared at promoting minority business enterprise in the public and private sector.

MBDA programs specifically target socially or economically disadvantaged entrepreneurs. Socially disadvantaged individuals are those who have been subject to racial or ethnic prejudice or cultural bias. Economically disadvantaged individuals are socially disadvantaged people whose ability to compete in the free enterprise system has been impaired due to diminished capital and credit opportunities.

Equity Capital

Government assistance is available

Specialized Small Business Investment Companies (SSBICs) and Minority Small Business Investment Companies (MESBICs) are privately owned venture capital firms whose private capital is supplemented (leveraged) by debt or preferred equity which is provided through open market financing guaranteed by SBA. SSBICs provide equity capital and long-term loans exclusively to minority firms. Currently there are 94 of these venture capital firms located in 21 states.

Federal Procurements

Section 8(a) of the Small Business Act established the basis for minorities to receive federal contracts on a sole-source or limited competition basis. Eligible firms must be at least 51% owned and managed by a citizen of the United States who is determined by SBA to be socially and economically disadvantaged. Each federal department designates a portion of that agency's purchases that are held out of general procurement competition and earmarked strictly for small and minority businesses. This sheltered market access is coordinated by the MBDA and operated by the SBA. In addition, both FAR (a compilation of regulations called the Federal Acquisition Regulations) and Public Law 950-407 require prime contractors to set aside certain percentages of large contracts for minority firms.

Encouraging signs for black entrepreneurs have been in the growth of a small sector of "big" black-owned businesses

Managerial and Technical Support

Minority and Indian Business Development Centers (MBDC and IBDC) have been established to increase the number of minority-owned businesses, help existing firms expand and minimize business failures. Centers are generally located in areas with large concentrations of minority populations and minority-owned businesses.

Corporate Procurement

In 1972, Corporate America's purchases from minority owned firms totaled less than $100 million. Today, annual purchases from minorities exceed $25 billion. America's largest companies are leading the way to stronger alliances with minority businesses. Nearly three-fourths of Fortune 500 companies have minority vendor programs.

What lies behind this growing commitment to minority businesses? Executives point to several key benefits of increasing the level of business they conduct with minority firms:

- **Better Suppliers:** For corporations which are downsizing and searching for ways to streamline and cut costs, having a broader base of suppliers to choose from allows them to identify those enterprises with the best quality at the most reasonable price. Minority businesses are traditionally smaller, with fewer layers of management. Their lower overhead frequently translates into lower prices.

- **Open New Markets:** As ethnic markets continue to expand in America, businesses are seeking out ways to tap into these groups. Together, Blacks, Hispanics, Asians and Native Americans represent more than one-fourth of the population of the United States and have tremendous buying power. Buying from minority suppliers helps return money to minority communities through the business and its employment of other co-ethnics which increases their ability to buy the products these corporations sell.

- **The Power of Diversity:** The success of America is in no small part founded on its diversity. Any time large and growing sectors of the population are not participating fairly in the opportunities for success, this equates to a loss in the productivity, creativity and potential of our nation as a whole.

Challenges for Minority-Owned Businesses

While it is evident that a great many minority-owned businesses are positioned to contribute to both job growth and the overall economic health of minority communities, some daunting problems remain:

- Limited access to capital
- Business size may restrict ability to compete
- Affirmative action programs are being challenged

Limited Access to Capital

According to a recent national survey conducted by Yankelovich Partners for the National Minority Supplier Development Council and *Fortune Magazine*, the chief concern of minority entrepreneurs is lack of access to capital. A majority of those polled who had tried to get new capital ended up with far less than they asked for and a third of the entrepreneurs reported finding no credit at all. The reasons given by banks for denying credit were not enough collateral and weak financial statements.

Marcus Cooke and Paul Wilkinson, both students of economics and black history at DePaul University longed to start their own business after graduating in the late 1980's. One day Cooke, a basketball fan, had a brainstorm: Why not try to develop a line of athletic wear with a basketball theme? But the partners needed start-up funds to buy merchandise, hire artists to create designs and screen-printers to imprint those designs on the clothing. A successful heart surgeon who had know Cooke since he was a teen agreed to loan the start-up money after Cooke gave him a 20-page business plan. The result was Hoops, Inc., a sportswear company that generated $650,000 in sales in 1995. The company produces clothing depicting youths in action poses on the basketball court and the clothing line is now carried by major retailing chains.

One of the keys to financing your business idea is ingenuity. Research all available funding sources, both traditional and non-traditional. It helps to have an effective business plan that you can sell to potential investors. The plan should show the strength of your idea and the seriousness of your intent. Capital can be found—be patient and persistent!

Business Size

Minority businesses start small and often have difficulty securing the financial and human resources to expand. This is an area of concern for many corporate buyers who would like to utilize minority businesses more fully. It is your task to convince corporate buyers that your small company can provide them with what they need. Your size is your company's greatest asset—flexibility and customer service are your keys to success.

Affirmative Action Programs are Being Challenged

There is growing apprehension in minority communities about the possible dismantling of affirmative action programs and the detrimental impact this could have on minority businesses.

While many in the minority business community fear that opportunities will vanish and gains will be lost if affirmative action programs are ended, others see this trend as a call to action. Bobby Bramlett who started his company, Aire Sheet Metal in 1971 makes this observation: "I think the attempts to eliminate affirmative action are the first major wake-up call. Unless we empower ourselves as business owners, we will continually be burdened with the decisions of others as to how, and to what degree, they will empower us."

Success Strategies for Minority Business Owners

Now, more than ever, minority business owners need to sharpen their business skills to succeed. It will not be enough to just master the basics of business planning, organization, funding and marketing. They must also understand how their ethnic status impacts their opportunities for success. Three strategies for success as a minority business owner are:

- Strive for excellence and keep your skills current
- Build on relationships and contacts
- Seek partnerships with larger companies

Strive for Excellence and Keep Your Skills Current

Frank Martinez, co-founder of a Latino-owned California packaging company advises that "Nothing is going to help you if you don't have the basic fundamentals for your business or if you really aren't good at your business, because you're going to have to be competitive." Ultimately, success will go to those businesses with a proven ability to meet the needs of their clients in a competitive environment.

Now, more than ever, minority business owners need to sharpen their business skills to succeed

A key to remaining competitive will be an understanding of and access to information technology. Small businesses who know how to effectively utilize these new technologies can compete on an even footing with large companies.

Clarence Wooten, Jr. and Andre Forde left their consulting jobs with a sizable software development contract in hand. That contract helped the two start Baltimore-based Metamorphosis Studios. They launched their full-service interactive multimedia design firm in 1993. The company provide interactive marketing and consulting services as well as CD-ROM products. So far, Metamorphosis has developed multicultural edutainment CD-ROM titles based on books for Bingwa, a black-owned Atlanta-based software publisher. Forde acknowledges that access to capital is probably the biggest obstacle for black firms in the industry. Metamorphosis kept its costs down by creating a "virtual corporation" by hiring freelancers from different parts of the country who communicate by phone, fax and computer.

According to a recent national survey conducted by Yankelovich Partners for the National Minority Supplier Development Council and Fortune Magazine, the chief concern of minority entrepreneurs is lack of access to capital

By hooking into available technology, minority-owned businesses can grow their businesses from regional or local enterprises into one more national in scope, exposure and contacts.

Build on Relationships and Contacts

Much of the success of minority enterprises is founded in the support networks available to them through their ethnic communities. They have traditionally had access to "social capital"—a mix of both financial and non-financial assets (community patronage, investment, labor, etc.) which the entrepreneur's community is willing to invest in the minority business. Community trusts, churches and other ethnic associations may be instrumental in accumulating capital which new businesses can draw upon to get started. Patronage of the minority business and promotion outside the group are other ways a strong ethnic community can be an asset to a new venture.

Minority business organizations are groups like the National Association of Black Women Entrepreneurs or the Hispanic Organization of Professionals and Executives. These types of organizations offer a wide variety of services including training, annual conventions or trade fairs, publications, mailing lists, and in some cases financing options.

As you increase your contacts with others in similar positions, you can open up the possibilities for cooperative ventures together. In some cases you can join or create a purchasing network to increase your buying power in the marketplace. Or you may be able to form strategic alliances, where you offer a more valuable product or service by working together than you could by marketing yourselves separately. Many minorities aggressively try to do business with other minority businesses which lends strength to the entire minority community.

In 1972, corporate America's purchases from minority owned firms totaled less than $100 million. Today, annual purchases from minorities exceed $25 billion.

Today minority suppliers have started forming strategic alliances just the way many giant companies did in the 1980's. One good example is the success of Blair Temporaries & Staffing, a consortium of minority-owned firms that provide nationwide temporary staffing services to Bell Atlantic and its associated companies. Another is the Premier Network Services Group, a nationwide network of minority-owned insurance companies. An additional consortium is Intergy, Inc. consisting of three companies in related oil and chemical fields that service Polaroid through this alliance.

Use creativity when looking for new clients. One Hispanic businessman makes it a point to read *Hispanic Business* magazine to learn about Hispanics who have been promoted to executive positions. He then contacts them as his first point of entry into a company he is trying to win over as a client.

Become involved in the bigger community outside your ethnic groups. Increase your visibility so that potential customers will know about you. One way to do this is to join boards or to become involved in civic activities. The contacts you forge as you work on broader community issues can be worth a great deal when you later have an opportunity to market your products or services to these same people.

Seek Partnerships with Larger Companies

As big companies continue to downsize and streamline their operations, they increasingly look for outside companies that can take over functions previously done internally. Small, aggressive, minority companies are often well-suited to help out.

Richard Cozart, manager of supplier diversity and minority opportunities at K-Mart in Michigan helped to launch a K-Mart private label line of African-American hair care products in 1996. He identified Thomco, Inc., a minority-owned company in Michigan as the potential supplier of these products. At the time, Thomco was manufacturing a very small, inexpensive line of hair care products. Cozart helped Thomco develop the new line and advertise it. Within 18 months, the line was being introduced in K-Mart, as a quality line at a reasonable price.

Some guidelines for increasing your chances of partnering with a larger company:

- Learn all you can about your prospective partner
- Identify how you can help
- Exceed expectations
- Provide top-level service

A prime example of how minority entrepreneurs can benefit from forging joint ventures is Quincy Jones, legendary arranger, composer, producer and publisher. Jones has consistently partnered with other major media companies to form new businesses where he could have access to distribution in major markets. Jones is able to turn a profit from repackaging his properties for distribution in other formats, cross-promotions or by creating new businesses. Today his core holdings generate more than $100 million in annual sales revenues!

Conclusion

While minority businesses face challenges, entrepreneurship still offers great promise for those who are willing to persevere. Columnist Edward Wills is a black businessman who sees entrepreneurship as America's best hope for creating a society that does more than mouth the word equality. As he sees it, "one entrepreneur opens a business. He employs others, some of whom may be his next-door neighbors or relatives. This entrepreneur's ability to pay salaries means his employees can maintain or improve their standard of living, eventually putting more resources back into the neighborhood. This is economic self-help. It is following the American dream. With the creation of these businesses goes the formation of character, pride and business skills that are used to build new businesses, create stronger families and reduce the tax burden for all."

Chapter 19
EXPORT AND IMPORT

About This Chapter:
- *Going global*
- *Exporting*
- *Importing*

Introduction

We are now living in the age of the global village. What does this mean for you? Opportunities! It means there are people just like you, in other countries, looking for opportunities to import and export goods and services. Today, money and materials move at a rate faster than ever before. Many Americans have travelled overseas and seen products and services which they think would sell quite well in the U.S. Likewise, they have seen opportunities for the sale of U.S. products and services in other countries. Is the time right for you to explore opportunities around the globe? This chapter will help you decide if you are ready to take on the challenges involved in international trade.

A Word About International Trade

International trade is the commerce between businesses from different nations. The first highly-organized trade can be traced back to the Silk Road between Europe and China, and in the salt trade in the Middle East. International trade involves importing and exporting. **Importing** is the business of purchasing goods or services from a party outside your own political borders. **Exporting** is the business of selling goods or services outside of your political borders.

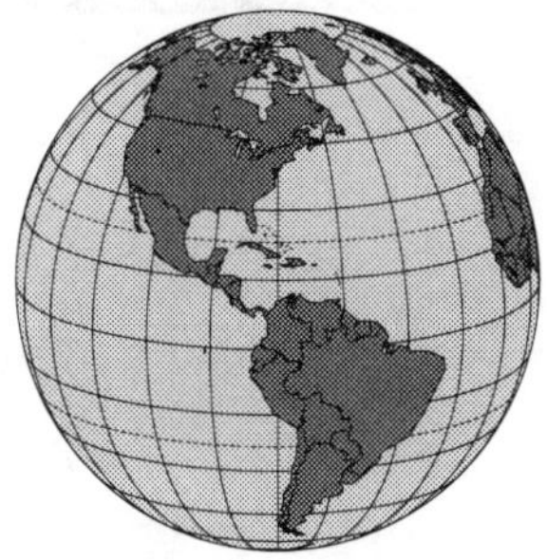

Millions move from Miami to Milan in a millisecond

The U.S. market has become a fertile ground for international commerce. We have a physical and financial infrastructure which makes it easy to transport goods and obtain payment for goods and services. In addition, English has become the accepted language of international business. Does this mean that you will not have any problems in doing business overseas? Well, not exactly. There are many obstacles to be overcome in dealing with people of other cultural backgrounds. This requires that you do extensive research on the country, the industry, and the companies with which you plan to trade. You might consider another necessary tool of the trade: patience. Because of the cultural barriers and varying levels of language proficiency that you will encounter, it will take more time to execute a deal. By being patient with those with whom you do business, you will be more likely to develop lasting personal relationships, thus facilitating better business relationships.

Cross-Border Payment

You might be thinking: "How do I know that I will get paid once the deal is done?" International finance has progressed right along with the movement of goods across borders. Investors seek out investment opportunities that are the best bets, based on a country's political and economic stability. As an example, both European and Asian companies own interests in high-tech companies here in the U.S. Part of the reason they invest here is because we have a politically and economically stable environment. They balance investments in their own geographic area with investments here to take advantage of our high-tech prominence, and to receive a good return on their investment. How does that money get here? Huge amounts of capital move into and out of the United States with the push of a button. Cross-border payment—while complex—can be safely done by a competent financial institution. A banking partner can assist you in the financial processes of buying or selling goods and services. This involves payment, insurance, and transportation—each of which is executed in a specific order.

What About Tariffs?

One of the first issues that you might encounter as you search for markets around the world is **tariff barriers** (taxes on imported or exported goods). Through the General Agreement on Tariffs and Trade (GATT), an international agreement to lower tariffs and trade barriers, international commerce has become easier as tariffs have come down. Although the majority of the world's countries subscribe to GATT, each GATT conference has been a hotbed for complaints and accusations that a given country has been victimized by other countries' unfair trading practices. As such, it has been difficult to get everyone involved in the treaty to agree on everything. This has led to an outcropping of trading blocks. These are regional agreements which allow for unrestricted trade between certain groups of countries, usually contiguous to each other, or, at the very least, geographically close.

Examples of trading blocks include the North American Free Trade Agreement (NAFTA), the European Community (EC), the Association of South East Asian Nations (ASEAN), and the Asia-Pacific Economic Conference (APEC)—the last of which is planned for the year 2010. Within each of these of these trading blocks, tariffs—and sometimes border checks—have been reduced or altogether eliminated. The result is a more favorable trading environment, and fewer concerns for a trading block member when trading with a business located in a country within the trading block.

Opportunities and Challenges

How can you gain from the lowering of trade barriers as an export or import company? The opportunities depend on your product or service and whether it is marketable in a given country. With the tearing down of trade barriers and the formation of trading blocks, you can look into ways to market your product to a group of countries by using one country as a hub.

Countries differ in the way they value time, practice business, and treat their employees. For example, in many South American countries, businesses close during the heat of the day, and work in the morning and the late afternoon and evening when it is not as hot. In other countries, such as Japan, certain formal rules of etiquette are essential to understanding business dealings. You will want to pay close attention to the way in which business is conducted in other countries. This can be best examined by visiting the companies which you are considering as partners. In doing so, you will get a taste of what a given country is like, how they do business, and what special considerations you will have to take into account.

Overseas?

Why would you want to seek out business overseas when you have opportunities to do business right here at home? International business is more challenging and difficult, but those who are involved in it will likely admit that there is a certain degree of excitement in overcoming the challenges of operating in an unfamiliar environment. By virtue of your doing business in a certain country or region, you will become an expert at overseas trading in your industry. Other companies who want to do the same may seek you out for advice or as a partner to promote their goods along with your own.

One of the factors involved in doing business with a different country—especially those which are located across the Atlantic or Pacific—is the difference in time zones. A common problem that employees working overseas for, or with, American firms experience is the lack of concern for a good night's rest. For example, if you get out of a meeting in your Denver office at 10 a.m., what time is it in Singapore? What do you do if you need to

I'm sorry. Did I wake you?

solve a problem right away? Sometimes, a situation just can not wait. However, there are probably cases in which a few extra hours will not do any harm on your (U.S.) side, and will mean much appreciated sleep for your employee or business partner in Singapore.

When "yes" means "no"

Although English has become the language of choice in international communication, this does not necessarily mean that you can rely on your mother tongue to carry you through an international business deal from beginning to end. Current thinking on this issue encourages those doing business abroad to at least obtain a basic understanding of common expressions in a given language, such as "thank you," "yes," "no," "please" etc. In addition, you might consider familiarizing yourself with the meaning of gestures and body language in the country with which you trade. Common physical gestures in the U.S. can have little or no meaning in other countries. You will more quickly pick up the nuances of gestures which your business partners make when they speak, and your conversation will go all the more smoothly. Your counterpart in the foreign business with which you deal will appreciate your efforts to understand the basics of his or her language, culture, and history. Professional translators are available if you require in-depth negotiations.

Marge Piercy did the right thing before she started importing Thai spices and food products. Marge was running a specialty foods catalog company since 1977 and in 1989, with increased requests from her customers for Thai food ingredients, she decided to expand her offerings to include these products. Before embarking on her venture, she asked several contacts who owned Thai restaurants who their suppliers were in the U.S. and Thailand. She investigated the etiquette and "rules of the game" of doing business with Thailand by attending a weekend seminar sponsored by her local university's MBA executive education department. Once Marge felt confident in her knowledge of both the business and culture of Thailand, she embarked on her mission. The addition of Thai spices and foods to her catalog was such a success that she is now looking to add Senegalese foodstuffs!

Every country has its regulations. In addition to tariffs there are other non-tariff barriers (NTB's). NTB's can come in many forms, including language differences, excessive regulations, and quotas. Your ability to deal with these issues will depend on how much you know about the market in which you plan to operate. Some inexperienced companies take one look at the language and regulatory differences in a foreign country and decide that it is not worth the effort to sell there. Other, more experienced companies can look at the same set of circumstances and think that it is the same or a little more difficult to do business there than in the other countries in which they operate. The point here is to have patience and persevere. If you go one step further than the next guy, you may find that the extra step was all that it took for your product to gain acceptance in the market.

Evaluating Potential Export Markets

One of the first steps that you might consider when you form an export organization is to evaluate your market opportunities. There are a few different routes you can take in performing this step. If you plan to conduct your business on your own, you will have to think about the following factors:

- Which markets are large enough to justify a marketing effort?
- In which markets will your product most likely be accepted?
- What is your competition, both foreign and domestic?
- What political and cultural factors could affect the success of your product?
- Are there any tariff or non-tariff trade barriers which you need to take into account?
- How will you price your product?
- What will your expected sales volume be?
- What additional costs will you occur?
- What would you expect your profit to be?

This process usually requires extensive market research on the target countries and industries in each country in which you will be competing.

Other alternatives include seeking the assistance of an export management company or going through an export company. **Export management companies** do not take title to your goods: they seek out buyers for your product or service. They can be very expensive, and may not be worth the cost in the long run because your margins would continue to deteriorate. However, they might be worth it in the short-term as a market-entry strategy. **Export companies** take title to your goods, which means that you have less control over what happens after your product leaves your factory.

No matter which avenue you take, you will want to know as much about the country and its markets as possible. This will involve researching the countries through information resources such as the National Trade Data Bank (NTDB), local and state international trade agencies, and international banks. Your local International Trade Administration (ITA) can offer valuable assistance, frequently at little or no cost.

Measuring Competitiveness of Products and Services

How will you find out whether there is demand for your product in a particular country, and how it measures up to the competition? Again, the ITA can provide you with valuable information in this area. They have access to statistics by product and service category, and lists of manufacturers with whom you will compete or to whom you might sell your product.

In conducting your research, you should consider the following methods:

- **Historical Information:** You should determine trends and seasonality.
- **Current Environment:** By observing what has happened or is expected to happen in the near future—such as tariff reductions or changes in regulations in a given country, you can ferret out niche opportunities for your products.
- **Market Testing:** There are services available in other countries to evaluate your product against similar products in a given country's market. Many firms use this method to find out exactly where and when they should initiate their marketing efforts.
- **Personal Visits:** Before trading, it is imperative to visit your trading partners more than once. The personal insights you gain will be invaluable.

It is important to remember that, since you will be operating in an unfamiliar environment, market evaluation is a critical step in preparing to sell abroad. It will validate or alter any ideas that you have, and may even steer you in a direction that you had not originally anticipated.

Product Modifications for Export

One of the major difference of doing business in foreign markets is the need to modify products for individual markets. You will have to take into account the changes necessary to make your product comply with regulations, adapt to customer tastes, and thus increase the likelihood that your product will succeed.

Some of the factors which you might consider include:

- Language changes to labelling and packaging
- Adjustments to product size
- Replacing the U.S. system of measurement with the metric system
- Taking into account different electrical standards
- Special transport requirements
- Local preference issues such as color and texture

The Coca-Cola Company has been very successful at exporting its product overseas, while retaining its strong brand and logo identity. In some countries, additional sugar is put into Coke's product mix, while in others, it is made less sweet and more carbonated. The point here is that Coca-Cola was one of the first beverage companies to truly attack the world market and to capture the enormous potential that the overseas consumers offer.

Will you need to change or add to the language which appears on your product? You bet! Regulations in many countries require that you describe the contents of your product—frequently in excruciating detail in the local language. While some products sell well abroad primarily because of their trendy American lettering, in most cases a product with labeling and packaging printed in the local language can be marketed more easily than those which are not altered. Regarding transportation, most other countries do not possess the capability you are used to in the U.S. Loads will have to be broken down into smaller quantities to be distributed by light rail, pickup truck, or hand cart. You might want to check on the capabilities of the freight carriers in the country to which you plan to ship as you plan the size of your loads.

Are Countries Ready for Your Product?

There are a number of issues that you have to consider regarding your product's fit in a given country market. Will your product be used in a similar manner to the way it is used in the United States? Considerations here include:

- **Familiarity:** Are you selling into an existing market, or will you have to promote a novel item or service which has never been seen before?

- **Capacity:** Does the country to which you are selling have the infrastructure to support your product in terms of transportation, industrial need, or average home size?
- **Alternative Uses:** How will the people of the country to which you are selling use your product? Bicycles and satellite dishes are used in other countries in different ways. The former can be used as the primary means of transportation, and the latter can be used primarily for telephone communications rather than television reception.
- **Specifications:** Does your product meet safety codes?

By researching these factors, you can tailor your product and market in a way that will maximize product receptiveness.

Becoming an Exporter: Logical Steps

The steps that you take in preparing to export a product can be standardized. All companies interested in export should follow these to sell their product outside of the U.S. The basic steps include:

Steps to success

- Do market research
- Prepare a marketing plan
- Explore sales and distribution options
- Make sales
- Prepare your product for shipping
- Comply with documentation requirements
- Ship your product
- Manage risk
- Obtain payment

These items are explained in the sections which follow.

The International Marketing Plan

Although many of the steps in preparing a U.S. marketing plan are included in the international plan, there are significant differences. The international marketing plan steps are listed here:

- **Evaluate your export market alternatives:** In which country are you most likely to succeed? What are the population demographics of that country?

- **Distribution options:** How will you ship the product? Who will you use to market and distribute your product once it gets there? What are the advantages and disadvantages of direct marketing, or of going through an importer?
- **Competition:** Who are they? How will they react to your efforts? Might you be able to work with them to sell your product? Is there room for you in the market?
- **Pricing:** How will you price your product? How will the price of your product be affected by duties and non-tariff trade barriers (such as regulations affecting customs clearance)? Will your product still be price-competitive once it gets through all of the layers of distribution?
- **Promotion:** How will you promote your product in a given market? Is the channel that you are using the most efficient to get the job done? What about advertising? How can you assist your sales representatives, through incentives, to promote your product most effectively?

An international marketing plan Is ESSENTIAL!

Your international marketing plan will serve as your road map to success. Just as you build relationships in your home market, you will have to build relationships in your foreign markets. Familiarity and trust are keys to your success. Each of the components of your plan is not fixed in stone; however, it is recommended that you work with your representative to explore your options in each area and weigh the benefits against the costs involved. If you do this, you can establish the degree of flexibility which is required to adapt to the unique challenges that you will encounter.

International Sales and Distribution Options

How do you get your product to your foreign customers? There are three basic alternatives you might consider in solving this problem:

Direct marketing

Direct marketing can range from selling directly to the consumer—through a foreign office or catalogue sales, to establishing a relationship with an import company in a given country. The advantages to direct marketing include retaining control of the product and a higher share of the profits. However, this is the most expensive option, since you must support a full-time direct marketing staff and assume all of the marketing costs.

Know your trading partner FAMILIARITY & TRUST the keys to success

Distributors and agents
An export distribution alternative involves the use of distributors and agents. These two differ in one important way: a distributor takes title to your goods, but an agent does not. Using an export distributor means that you will lose control of the product and gain the least in terms of profits. The advantage of this method, however, is that the distributor is building business for you that you otherwise would not be able to create yourself.

When Simon Timmons began his software development company, one of his products was an accounting software package. After careful investigation, he decided to try to sell his product to newly privatized companies in Mexico. He initially worked with an export distributor that had been recommended to him because this particular distributor had already developed many contacts with purchasing agents at the companies Simon wanted to target. This worked as a great initial entree into the Mexican market for Simon. Later Simon and his agent formed a joint venture in Mexico to develop software applications specific to that market.

Export agents promote your goods or services and receive a fee for their work—usually on a commission basis. This allows you to retain control over your goods and avoid paying for in-house export staff. However, it does cut into your profits because there is a commission involved.

Partners and strategic alliances
There are many overseas companies who are looking for quality product lines and services which will compliment their current offerings. This is particularly important for service businesses. Two examples of strategic alliances are high-tech foreign companies investing in large and small high-tech firms in the Silicon Valley, and American consulting companies forging relationships with firms abroad. You can also approach other companies in your industry either in the United States or in other countries to explore export alternatives.

Other export organizations
There are two other types of export companies which deserve mention: **export management companies** (EMC's) and firms which buy and then repackage goods for export. An export management company is a hybrid between an agent and an in-house export staff. They work for you on a salary

or commission basis to promote your product through their own office. EMCs are used when maximum control over your product is desired, but you do not want to support an in-house staff. Re-packagers buy your products, which are usually not ready for export, and repackage them to meet the requirements of the country in which they will be sold. This type of company uses its expertise in exporting to find markets for and sell domestically produced goods in other countries. EMCs and re-packagers are usually listed in the yellow pages or local trade directories in port cities.

A Word About Making It Legal

When you develop a relationship with an individual or a company of any kind to export your goods, you will want to make sure that the agreement is in writing. This will protect you from infringement on intellectual property rights and other problems that can occur from cross-border trading. It is also recommended that you patent your goods in the countries to which you plan to sell. This will give you the most security possible against somebody else stealing your idea!

Shipping and Documentation

The first time that you export your goods, you might be amazed at the shipping documentation which is required to see your goods through to a foreign market. Do not be alarmed! These procedures apply to all parties involved in export. Rest assured—this process does get easier as time goes by.

Use the services of a freight forwarder to handle your export shipping and documentation. **Freight forwarders** are experts in handling export documentation and shipping needs, and using them will allow you to focus on what you do best—instead of tending to unfamiliar paperwork. These companies can be found in the yellow pages of most major cities.

Bill of Lading

A **bill of lading** is the shipping contract which outlines the terms of the shipping agreement and the means by which the goods are shipped. The time at which you receive a copy of the bill of lading depends on whether the freight is paid in advance or not. In the latter case, you receive a copy after the goods have been delivered to their point of destination.

Customs and Duties

The customs process and the duties that you might have to incur are two very important factors involved in the export of goods. **Duties** are the import taxes which are paid, based on a preset tariff rate. As these two issues are interrelated (duties depend on the declared value of your goods and, in some cases the freight and insurance costs), an explanation of the customs process will offer insight on what to expect in terms of duties to be paid.

Clearing customs requires you to be very careful not to make any mistakes in the documentation which accompanies your goods. A mistake in the date, port of origin, port of entry, or any other part of the forms can mean delays in shipment and unnecessary expenses. You will want to make sure that your customer has access to the following documentation—free of errors—upon the arrival of your goods:

- Entry documents
- Letter of Credit
- Commercial or proforma invoices
- Bill of Lading
- Packing lists
- Evidence of the (insurance) bond

One entrepreneur in California mistakenly dated his shipment to arrive one year after the actual date. He was dismayed to find out that customs in Japan wouldn't clear his container load of chicory for an entire year! He had to fly to Tokyo to personally take care of the customs problem. This cost him all the profit he expected to make on the transaction.

In addition, duties may be assessed on a number of different charges that are incurred through the trade. You will want to provide information on any fees that have accrued between you, the seller, and your buyer. Some examples include:

- Packing costs
- Sales commissions
- Licensing or related fees
- Amount of sale

By anticipating all of these requirements, you can provide your buyer with all of the documents and information related to the trade so customs will not hold up the transaction.

Managing Risk

When you conduct business outside of the borders of the United States, there are risks involved that are not present when doing business inside the U.S. The first issue that you might consider is whether your trading partner will follow through on the deal from start to finish. You can alleviate some of this type of risk by going to see your customers, and by inviting them to visit you in the U.S. This "trust-building" stage is very helpful in establishing the foundation for a lasting relationship.

Also, you might take into account transportation and insurance. There are a very large number of transportation alternatives available to move your product to a foreign port. A competent insurance company can offer comprehensive coverage on your goods so that you can eliminate the risk of loss if the goods are damaged, stolen, or simply "disappear."

Another consideration is **currency fluctuation**. Unique to international trade, this problem can be hedged through investment in currencies equal to the amount of your order. Large corporations engage in this type of transaction every day, and use it to ensure the stability of their business outcomes. If you have the financial resources available, this is an effective way to balance out the risk involved in an investment in goods which are headed to a foreign port. Another way to eliminate risk is to demand payment in U.S. dollars. This is common practice for many companies who do not wish to or cannot afford to hedge, and is an effective way to eliminate the risk involved.

Political risk is yet another factor which you might take into account. Some countries are known for their unfavorable business environment—due to political instability or unfriendliness toward American interests. "War risk" can be insured against through a blanket insurance policy via your freight forwarder. The U.S. Department of State can provide you with information on the country with which you plan to do business.

One unlucky entrepreneur exporting hand tools to Nigeria got caught in the middle of a civil uprising! His shipments were stolen by thieves posing as custom officials. He was unable to trace the "disappearing" shipments due to the breakdown in governmental control over the country. If he had only read the U.S. State Department's report prior to entering into the Nigerian market, he could have been warned that civil strife was imminent!

Getting Paid!

Financial organizations around the world have established a means to facilitate payment for goods or services which are traded between countries. The safest way for you to conduct business with a foreign buyer is to build a relationship with a local bank in the foreign country which is capable of serving your export financing needs. They provide a valuable link in the trading process by dealing with your customer's bank and arranging for payment upon receipt of the goods or services. The following list is provided to introduce you to the terms with which you will need to be familiar when arranging for international payment:

- **Irrevocable Letter of Credit (L/C):** This is a contract for payment which is arranged by your bank and your foreign customer's bank to assure payment to you. Always make sure that your letter of credit is irrevocable.
- **Bill of Exchange:** This is a financial instrument which is used to pay you through your bank from a foreign bank.
- **Bill of Exchange—Bankers Acceptance:** This is a demand for payment from your bank to your foreign client's bank based on the L/C.
- **Documents against payment:** These are the documents which are required to obtain payment on an international trade.
- **Cash against documents:** The payment, based on the letter of credit, which your customer makes through their bank to your bank.
- **Documents against Acceptance:** The process of checking the original letter of credit against the documentation which your client provides after they have received the goods.

Your bank or freight forwarder will know a great deal about the meaning of these documents. You might consider tapping their expertise so that you do not miss a step in setting up a letter of credit or obtaining any other form of payment.

Methods of Payment

Methods of payment are described below, along with the advantages and disadvantages for you and your customers.

- **Cash in advance:** This is the most favorable means of payment for you. Payment is made in advance of shipment, and there is no risk to you. This is not a standard means of payment in international trade, and is usually used only when circumstances make any other form of payment impossible or very risky (such as for a foreign client with an open account who has neglected to pay his previous bills). Your customer is completely dependent upon you to ship the goods in the manner in which you have agreed.

- **Sight Letter of Credit (L/C):** This type of payment is made when the goods are shipped. The only risk involved for you with this type of payment stems from the possibility of the order's cancellation. Your customer can be assured that they will receive the goods, but they are still dependent upon you to ship the goods in the manner upon which you agreed.
- **Time Letter of Credit (L/C):** Under this mode, payment is made after the goods have been received, but payment must be made, regardless of the condition of the goods. There is little risk involved for you when you use this mode of payment. Your customer does not have the security that damage to the goods can be reconciled with you.
- **Sight Draft for Collection:** In this case, your customer does not pay for the goods until they are seen, and can refuse to pay if the goods are not to their satisfaction. You incur the risk that they might not pay, and your client still relies on you to ship the goods as originally agreed.
- **Time Draft for Collection:** This type of payment is made after your customer has received the goods. Your risk comes from the fact that your customer may choose not to pay. In addition, your customer has possession of the goods before they actually need to make payment.
- **Open Account:** This is similar to the method which is used for domestic payment. There is no risk to your client. This method might be used when your customer has a very stable relationship and long track record with you.

Evaluating Products and Services for Import

In an export transaction there is always an exporter involved. Likewise, in an import transaction there is always an importer involved. This means that many of the things which were discussed in the section on export can be applied in the context of import, simply by thinking of export in reverse.

In finding products or services for import, you will need to examine your alternatives based on the following criteria:

- **Quality:** Does the product or service meet your minimum requirements?

- **Price:** Is it low enough to justify sourcing a foreign firm?
- **Quantity:** Do they have the manufacturing or labor capacity to fill your order on a continuous basis?
- **Familiarity:** Do you know about your vendor's culture, and do you feel comfortable operating in that environment?
- **Language:** Do they have a competent English-speaking staff?
- **Terms:** Will they agree to shipping and payment terms which are preferable to your company?
- **U.S. Tariffs:** Are there U.S. tariffs on the products which you are importing, and, if so, do they apply only to certain countries?
- **Political Stability:** Will changes in the local government affect your business dealings?
- **Distribution:** How many hands will the goods pass through before they leave the country? Can your price be lowered by importing more directly?
- **Dependability:** How dependable are your trading partners? Will they fulfill their commitments?

By considering these issues in your search for a foreign provider of goods or services, you will be better able to choose the right vendor for your needs. It is no coincidence that quality is listed first. The most common problem with foreign products or services is with quality. It is also the most difficult to solve. Visit your potential overseas vendor more than once! Check on their capabilities and background.

Becoming an Importer: Logical Steps

You have decided to expand your horizons and look out across your borders for sources of materials and services. The following steps are recommended before you decide on a foreign supplier:

- Perform a vendor search
- Evaluate effects on quality and delivery
- Do market research on potential domestic buyers, or benefits associated with materials substitution
- Prepare a marketing plan

- Make sales
- Manage risk
- Anticipate payment requirements to your foreign vendor

These issues are discussed in the sections which follow.

The International Marketing Plan

In the same way that you consider the marketing factors in your target country if you plan to export a product or service, you will need to consider your opportunities within the United States when you are establishing your import marketing plan. These considerations include:

- **Market demand:** Is there a demand for the product or service which you plan to import into the U.S.? What kind of product or service is your competition providing at this time that you can provide at a higher quality or a lower cost?

- **Market location:** Where is your market? How will it be distributed? Is the U.S. port of entry strategically located so that in-country transport is minimized? Will you be able to ship the goods directly from the port-of-entry?

- **Price:** How does the price of your imported good or service compare to its domestic counterparts? Is the price savings large enough to justify sourcing a foreign vendor over a domestic supplier?

- **Promotional considerations:** How will you market your imported goods or services? What particular markets will you target? Does the product or service deserve broad-based advertising, specific promotion, etc.?

Your international marketing plan for import will serve as your guide to success. You might consider developing a plan which takes into account the challenges that you will encounter in promoting your imported product or service, and which is flexible enough to allow you to adapt to unexpected obstacles—such as competitors' price-cutting. By developing this plan, you will be better able to take advantage of opportunities and manage your risks.

International Sales and Distribution Options

What form will your import business take? There are many possible roles that you can serve in buying or representing goods or services from overseas vendors.

Direct

With regard to import, direct marketing means that you are the first source to which a foreign supplier is selling their product or service, and that you will resell directly to the end user. The advantage to this method is that you retain the highest share of the profits from your domestic marketing efforts. The disadvantage is that your marketing costs can be much higher, since you are responsible for marketing the imported product or service to the end user.

Being a distributor and agent

Perhaps you are debating whether you should become an import agent or an import distributor for an overseas company. As an example, you might consider importing hot chili peppers from Mexico as an import agent. In this case, your role is to seek out customers for the Mexican hot chili peppers here in the U.S. What will you do to research the U.S. market, make sales, and arrange the deal? How will you get paid? In most cases, agents receive a commission on the sales which they produce.

With respect to being a distributor, your responsibilities would extend beyond the marketing role. If you were importing sardines from Norway as a distributor, you would arrange for the purchase of the sardines—including all customs, insurance, and freight requirements. You actually take title to the goods, so the business risk transfers to you sometime after the goods have left your foreign vendor's facility (the exact time depends on the terms of sale). Acting as an import distributor involves more risk than acting as an agent, but the rewards can be greater. Once you take title to the goods, you can set the sale price.

Partnering and strategic alliances

There are many foreign companies who are interested in expanding their business to the U.S. market through an American company.

An Australian training firm recently developed a program to teach accountants how to better market their services to individual clients. Their market research led them to the U.S. The Australians partnered with a series of American professional training organizations, which had American CPA firms as their clients. The advantage to partnering for the Australians was the ability to quickly establish their sales training program in the U.S. The advantage for the American professional training organizations was the commission received from the Australian training firm.

Other import considerations

Issues of shipping, documentation, customs, duties, and managing risk are all very similar to the case of the exporter. A customs broker can assist you with these concerns to ensure that your business deal goes smoothly. Your primary concern as an importer is to develop your market here at home. This means that, provided you achieve sales targets, your overseas partner will likely be satisfied with your performance.

Getting Paid!

You will need to be concerned with the payment of your vendor through proper international banking channels. This will mean keeping track of all of the necessary documentation. If you become an import agent or work on any other kind of commission basis, you will want to keep tabs on all of the transactions that take place between the overseas company which you represent and the companies that actually purchase the goods

Conclusion

Going global is big news today. To succeed in an import or export business, you need an effective marketing plan. If you are planning to export goods or services, you need to pay attention to the special cultural needs of your foreign markets. If you are planning to import, you will want to closely examine your market here in the United States to increase the chance that your product or service will be a success. International trade is an exciting and rewarding field. So get ready and go global!

Chapter 20
STARTING A CONSULTING BUSINESS

About This Chapter:
- *Why businesses hire consultants*
- *Your skills set*
- *Determining your costs*
- *Managing the client*

Introduction

If you think that consulting is only for the large, high-powered corporate players, think again. Consulting is one of the fastest growing self-employment sectors in the U.S. economy. In fact, the vast majority of consulting businesses are made up of less than three people. Who are these show 'em-how-to-do-it types? They are people who consult on such things as personnel management, animal care at zoos, art acquisitions for big companies, software installation, irrigation engineering, and personal financial planning. These people see opportunities to sell their expertise to businesses, nonprofit organizations, and individuals. They recognize that consulting offers them a unique opportunity to create value for their clients, realize their professional ambitions, and control their own work schedule. For these reasons, consulting can be an ideal choice for entrepreneurs.

Businesses in nearly every industry are facing strong competition. In order to compete effectively, businesses need employees with better skills and more expertise. Because of this, many businesses hire consultants to update their workers' skills, improve their managerial techniques, infuse their businesses with new perspective, and deliver innovative solutions to old problems.

In addition, businesses are downsizing and laying off many of their employees. This places more demands on the people that they do retain. Therefore, businesses are spending money on training and enhancing the performance of those employees they do keep.

Starting and managing a consulting business shares many of the same challenges as starting any other type of business: identifying the customer, marketing the product, and controlling costs. But there are some unique issues and challenges associated with consulting. Fundamental to a consultant's success is the ability to manage the customer, control costs, and deliver what he or she contracted to deliver.

The goal of this chapter is to highlight the specifics of consulting businesses and help the first-time entrepreneur better understand how consultants work. We will also look at a personality profile of the successful consultant and identify where opportunities lie for consulting businesses.

Consulting ABC's

Consulting is more labor intensive than nearly any other kind of business. The resources a consultant needs are fairly limited: a computer, a desk, a telephone, some enthusiasm, and a great sense of humor. The real value created by consultants comes from their expertise, experience, and innovative approach to attacking problems. Consulting also requires a person to communicate the value of their expertise to the right people at the right time. Understanding a potential client's needs, being able to sell your services, manage your time, collect payment, and keep ahead of competition by constantly updating your "product" are the necessary ingredients required to make you a successful consultant. For these reasons, to be a successful consultant, it is simply not enough to be an expert in a given field. This is truly a job for a juggler!

Why Do Businesses Hire Consultants?

Before you can sell your services, you need to understand why businesses and individuals hire consultants. Consider these reasons:

- A "breath of fresh air" for issues, challenges, and opportunities
- Technical assistance
- Time-crunch project
- Good contacts
- Accelerate their learning curve
- Enter a new business
- Meet seasonal requirements
- Mediate a situation
- Specialized skills
- New solutions for specific functions like marketing or finance
- Employee training
- Re-engineering processes
- Need for unbiased, objective opinion

Often businesses can hire outside consultants for these needs more cheaply and easily than they can use their internal resources. In other cases, they simply do not have the skills or resources to fill their own needs. Even the most nimble and creative of businesses can use a fresh perspective. Consultants can provide a comparatively low-cost, low-risk, low-obligation source of up-to-date expertise. In fact, in some larger businesses today, it is not at all uncommon to have multiple teams of consultants from different companies working to find a solution for the same problem. Once they've done their work and have been paid, the company then has a whole menu of choices for action from which it can choose.

The Business Strategy

Your Personal Plan

So, you still think you may want to be a consultant? You believe you possess an area of expertise and you like working with people. Perhaps you are even eager to branch out on your own. But where do you begin? The first step is to take a look at your personal and professional goals: In what kind of environment do you want to spend your time? What kind of people do you enjoy being around? What lifestyle do you want? What professional ambitions do you have?

This is the logical time for you to consider other things such as:

- Which fields or functions do you want to specialize in?
- Where you want to locate (a city, suburban area, or countryside?)
- What is your time frame for starting this business?
- How much money do you want to earn in your first, third, and fifth year?
- What help will you need from friends, spouse, or professional contacts?

Self-confidence is the name of the game!

With these things in mind, consider for a moment some of the most important personality traits of a successful consultant. Do you have many of these?

- Excellent communication skills
- Highly organized
- Innovative thinker
- Independent
- Enjoy challenges
- Practical
- Self-confident
- Disciplined
- Imaginative
- Self-starter
- Good negotiator
- Energetic

Remember, talents are abilities you are born with, skills are abilities you have acquired through experience

Your skill set

The next step for you is to consider your skill set. As a consultant your most valuable asset will be the skills and experience you have to offer. Right along with these is the confidence to communicate them to clients. This is how your skills generate revenue for you. Take a moment now to review your skill sets and unique expertise.

Think of this activity as taking inventory of all of your past achievements and abilities that you will bring to a consulting practice. Keep an eye out for unique combinations of skills: perhaps you know how to research medical issues and you know a lot about animal care. By thinking creatively about how these skills intersect, you might find a lucrative opportunity for yourself in researching and writing grant proposals for veterinary medical businesses. Think in the broadest possible terms about your abilities, and don't be shy to write down even the silliest of skills (like being able to balance a spoon on your nose!). Often times people's most unique and marketable skills are those that they've forgotten they have.

Try the following exercise to ignite your thinking:

- Make a list of all of your past achievements in work, church, school, hobbies, and community activities. What are some of the major problems you have been able to solve?
- List the skills that you used that were instrumental in these achievements. How did you use these skills to solve a given problem?
- What were the "people" issues in the problem? What skills did you use?
- What natural talents do you have that allowed you to solve problems?
- What skills are you missing that you will need to learn?
- What skills or talents will you need to hire?

Other questions to ask yourself are: Do any of my bundles of skills have something in common? What unique spin do I put on my problem solving? Which of my skills did people really value? Which skills do I particularly enjoy using?

Having done this skill and talent assessment, take a moment to consider some of the major activities that consultants are paid to do. Do you see any overlap with your personal skill sets?

What consultants do

- **Research:**
  Identifying suppliers, target markets, experts, customer tastes and trends, product information, shortcuts, or new strategies.

- **Invent:**
  New training, managing, or cost-control techniques, designing events, processes, or schedules, adapting new ideas to old problems.

- **Communicate:**
  Negotiating contracts, arbitrating disputes, translating and interpreting, interviewing, writing summaries or analysis, assisting others to clarify goals and views, managing difficult people.

- **Motivate:**
  Selling a new idea, product, or process, manage creative talent, focus people's energy and induce collaboration, recruit and train leadership, raise capital for business or nonprofit ventures.

- **Analyze and Predict:**
  Classify and define relationships between data, identify trends, plan and predict financial, operational, time, or human resource needs.

- **Evaluate and Recommend:**
  Assess financial value, effectiveness of strategies or processes or communication techniques; recommend solutions, approaches, suppliers, experts, information sources.

Consultants sell these skills in every type of business and nonbusiness setting: design, farming, engineering, logistics, finance, administration, human resources, plant operation, purchasing, ranching, and selling. They sell them to individuals to help them manage time, finances, school, events, and home life.

What skills and talents do you have?

Now think about the skills and talents you outlined above. Do you see opportunities to connect several of them together to solve common problems? Chances are, as you browse your list and think creatively, you will find many opportunities to explore.

The last part of your personal skills inventory is to assess your business skills. These are the practical skills to sell, organize, and control finances you need to run your consulting business. These skills will, in large part, determine the success or failure of your business. To understand your abilities in each key area and which areas are in need of improvement, take a moment to review the list you created. Which business skills did you use in each case? How did you use them? What were the results? How could you improve the outcome? After you've taken this inventory, you might consider the following areas which are key to managing a consulting business:

- General knowledge of business
- Marketing
- People management
- Planning and forecasting
- Sales
- Financial management
- Computer skills
- Business communication/ correspondence

Keep in mind that you maybe a little rusty in some of these areas. There are many ways for you to update your skills quickly and easily. This book covers many of these areas, as do a myriad of specialty books and community college courses. But the real point of this exercise is to help you identify the skills you will need and discover those which you already have.

Process consulting develops consistent, long-term business relationships

Process vs. Event Consulting

Consultants are generally divided into two general categories. One type focuses on doing a specific, event-oriented job, like performing a one-time computer system upgrade. More successful consultants focus on selling an on-going process to clients. This type of consultant would train clients as they upgrade to new computer systems. See the difference?

Process consultants have more flexibility in where and to whom they can market their services. They are able to leverage their specific skills into creating a general expertise that they can adapt to different problems. They can negotiate, identify variables, analyze situations, and construct a longer-range solution. In the process, they often work more closely with clients, develop repeat business, and acquire new skills. Consider the following examples:

- Fixing a broken sink/being able to coordinate the installation of new plumbing systems
- Baking a wedding cake/planning the wedding event
- Helping a farmer plant a single crop/offering a year-round soil testing and erosion program

- Installing new hardware/selecting the appropriate hardware and software and training employees to use it

Being a process-oriented consultant will help to smooth out the peaks and valleys of your business: those times when you are busy delivering your services and those times in between engagements. Process-oriented engagements deliver more value to your client and better income for you.

Your Customer

What you have just done is begin the process of selecting and defining the "product" for your consulting business. Having identified your skills and talents, let's take a look at your market and potential customer base.

Small consulting businesses tend to specialize in a particular subgroup of expertise: tax preparation for agricultural businesses, personnel payroll for performing arts organizations, or promotional strategies for nonprofit ventures. In many cases, the more specialized or "niche oriented" your consulting expertise, the higher the rates you can charge, the more demand there is for your services, and the wider the geographic area you will have to serve. However, the downside for many people is the need to travel more and work long hours.

You know what you are good at, and what you enjoy. Now let's have a look at the market. Consider:

- Current trends in the economy
- Current issues in your community
- Current consumer trends
- Needs in your community
- Your own needs and those of your friends
- The time necessary for solving a given problem
- The frequency with which a given problem or issue presents itself
- How costly a given problem or issue is to solve for individuals or businesses

Determining Your Costs

Before you can bid for a single client or close a single sale, you must know what your operating costs are. One of the most common mistakes made by consultants is underestimating their overhead and overestimating their billable time. Many first-time consultants learn this the hard way.

To avoid this, start by carefully and systematically calculating your total overhead expenses. Consider every cost that will allow you to serve clients. This will include, but may not be limited to:

- Rent
- Computer supplies
- Phone/Fax/E-mail/postage
- Specialty equipment
- Equipment rental
- Retirement
- Advertising
- Taxes
- Books and reports
- Insurance
- Travel
- Miscellaneous office supplies
- Printing
- Express packages
- Gas and automobile insurance
- Interest payments
- Licensees
- Utilities
- Salary

As you review all of the expenses that make up your overhead, prepare a comprehensive table of what you have budgeted. Be aware of these costs as they are a fundamental element in understanding your overhead, controlling your costs, and ensuring the profitability of your consulting business.

One of your tasks is to decide what to pay yourself. To begin, you need to take a look at the market for the services you are selling. What are the going rates? Some consultants charge their clients by the day (generally when they are spending entire days on the project), while others charge their clients by the hour (when their time is divided among other projects or clients).

A true recipe for disaster... doing more and earning less!

Finally, with these two figures in mind, the next step is to decide what percent of profit you want to be making. This is the percentage margin that you will add on to all of your fees. Having done this, you'll need to calculate your **overhead rate**. This is the percentage rate that you will charge clients on each billable hour to cover your overhead. This may sound confusing, but it's not as tricky as it sounds.

Calculation of Overhead Rate for Vic's Veterinary Consulting Group

The cost of overhead is generally expressed as a percentage of labor rate. To calculate the daily dollar amount of overhead to charge to clients, Vic would divide his ***total overhead costs*** *for the month (rent, electricity, medical equipment, assistants, etc.) by the number of days that he expects to be billing clients. This daily amount is added to the labor rate that he charges his clients.*

For example:

Vic's monthly overhead = $1,000.00
His estimated amount of client billing days : 15
Vic divides $1,000 by 15 to calculate his ***daily overhead*** *= $66.60*
Then, he divides $66.60 by his daily labor rate of $75 (or his hourly rate if he chooses)
to get the ***overhead rate*** *= .88 (or 88%)*
To charge for daily overhead, Vic simply multiplies his daily labor rate by .88 and adds on his profit margin:

Vic's Daily Labor Rate =	*$ 75.00*
Overhead Rate (88%) =	*$ 66.00*
	$141.00
Profit (20%)	*$ 28.20*
Total Daily Billing Rate =	*$169.20*

You've just learned one of the basic, yet most important skills for any consultant. Now the trick is to make sure the numbers you plug into this equation are accurate and up-to-date. This requires that you frequently review your costs, adding increases or new costs.

Selling Your Expertise

Know your client

In the consulting game, selling and bidding for contracts is the essence of the business. All careful cost analysis, personal and business planning, and unique expertise won't do you a bit of good if you can't communicate your benefit to potential clients and successfully bid for contracts. This is the part of business that is often the most intimidating to many first-time consultants: explaining that your services are unique and why a client should pay for them.

What clients want more than anything else is results. Regardless of how many degrees you have, how impressive your resume, or how charismatic your personality, at the end of the day, people pay for results. There are a few general steps that consultants follow to sell their services:

- Know your client
- Educate your client
- Pick your opportunities

Produce better results by knowing and educating your client

There are in fact, some situations in which you might want to walk away from a prospective client, despite the fact that they fall in your target market. Why? Consider a few:

- There is serious direct competition
- You have questions about the client's ability to pay you
- You have questions about the clients' true understanding of their need, your specialty, and what you can and cannot achieve for them
- You have questions about your ability to achieve results for the client
- Your personality does not match the client

Making presentations

Being able to communicate the benefits you provide to a prospective client requires that you have the ability to confidently and clearly communicate your ideas. For this reason, good presentation skills are crucial to consultants. The presentation is an opportunity to spotlight your talents, demonstrate your confidence, and aid the client in clarifying the particular problem. A good presentation sells the client on your solutions for their problems. For a more detailed discussion of selling and presentation skills, see Chapter 39 *The Art of Selling*.

Selling is no longer about pulling "a quick one," or fast-talking a client into buying something they don't need or want. Today, what is known as **strategic selling** emphasizes a client-focused approach, in which the needs and issues of the client come first. This serves the interests of the consultant as well, who, having clearly identified the clients' need, will best be able to give the client what they pay for. Selling today is about building long-term relationships and becoming a partner committed to the growth and success of your client. This philosophical approach should be clear to your prospect as you present your consulting services.

So, how does one make an effective professional presentation? Even the shyest of individuals can follow some basic steps that will ensure a clear and positive presentation. Your presentation should:

- Review your professional credentials
- State your client's problem areas
- Outline how you plan to solve the problems
- Highlight the features of your service
- Forecast the benefits of your service, in dollar terms
- Identify the cost and time frame for delivering results

- Define what you are going to deliver
- Close and ask for the business

Aside from the content of your presentation, there are some general approaches to giving effective presentations that you should keep in mind:

- Exercise authority and confidence
- Always outline what you intend to present
- Make strong, clear, positive statements
- Dress to match your audience
- Be energetic
- Be true to yourself
- Have a positive mental attitude
- Use a logical, well-organized style
- Use humor
- Keep it short and to the point
- Always ask for the business

Effective presentations attract new clients

Bidding for Contracts

The bidding game is a very common practice among businesses looking to hire consultants. Very often consultants are asked to submit a **bid** which reflects their best ideas on the scope of the work, the cost to do the work, the different expertise required, and the time frame involved to complete the project.

Bids are almost always required, except in the unusual case in which a business opts for a **sole-source** contract. A sole-source contract uses only one provider, and there is no competition for the job. As sole sourcing is rare, consultants must be prepared to submit bids. And why not? It is in the best interest of the buyer: the bidding process uncovers the best service provider at the most competitive rates.

Just how do you go about preparing a cost estimate for a bid? The process can be broken down into the following tasks:

- Map out the entire project and identify its components
- Assign detailed cost estimates to each component
- Total the costs for all components
- Calculate your overhead, and apply your overhead rate and profit margin to total costs

As you prepare your bid, the most important task is to assign costs to the various components of the contract. For example, a professional trainer might break a prospective contract into some of the following components:

- Determine training requirements
- Measure existing skills of employees
- Develop training objectives
- Design training progress measures
- Write training outlines
- Formulate training schedules

Vic's Veterinary Consulting Group

<u>Bid Estimate Worksheet</u>

1. ***Consultant's Time***	
4 weeks x 5 days/wk. x $200 /day =	*$4,000*
2. ***Assistant's Time***	
8 days x 8 hours/day x $10 /hour =	*$ 640*
3. ***Materials***	
$100	*$ 100*
4. ***Travel***	
2,000 miles x $.20 /mile =	*$ 400*
5. ***Total Cost***	***$5,140***
6. ***Contingency Calculation*** *+ 10%*	***$ 514***
7. ***Final Bid***	***$5,654***

To assign costs to each component, you will want to calculate the following:

- **Direct Labor:** This is an estimate in hours or days of the amount of time that you and/or your personnel will spend on each component of the contract. Multiply this estimate by the labor rate for each employee to get your total direct labor costs.

- **Direct Expenses:** This is an estimate of the expenses you will incur to complete each component of the project. These direct expenses may include additional materials, equipment, printing and photocopying, or transportation.

It is good practice to create a standard pricing sheet for your consulting practice. Create a format in which all of your standard expenses are listed as well as spaces for unusual or one-time expenses. This is where a good software package will come in handy for you.

Bidding is the name of the game!

Brian Langford began his career in the hotel business right after he graduated from college with a degree in Hotel/Motel Management. His climb—from manager trainee to vice president of sales in one of the nation's best-known hotel chains—was meteoric. But that didn't come as a shock to the people who knew Brian. He had all the requisite skills: he was very self-confident, he had more energy than most, he communicated with others extremely well, he was incredibly organized, and he was very creative in his approach to problem solving.

Although Brian enjoyed (actually relished) his work, he began to feel that something was missing. In 1993, he took some time off to think about what he really wanted to do. It didn't take long for him to reach a conclusion. He loved his job, but what he really wanted was to be his own boss. He used the rest of his vacation to make lists of his skills and talents, and to review businesses that would utilize those skills and talents.

In 1994, Brian Langford started his own consulting company out of his townhouse in New York City targeted specifically at the hotel business. His first clients were smaller chains that didn't have sales and marketing experts on staff. By 1997, Brian's company occupied very nice office space on Park Avenue, had 5 employees plus support staff, and counted cities researching the feasibility of adding/renovating city-owned convention space among its clients. The work can be exhausting and the travel brutal, but Brian has never regretted his decision. He's still in the business he loves and he calls the shots!

Signing a Contract

The starting point for a successful relationship with your client is a solid contract. A good contract is a clear contract. This document offers you and your client more than just legal protection in the event that things go wrong; it is an opportunity to clearly spell out deliverables and time frames. The more clearly these are defined, the better your client will be able to judge your performance. Also, by defining what you can and cannot do in the contract, you will reduce the "wiggle" room for your client and their ability to avoid paying for your services.

Client problems to beware of:

- Client lies
- Client pays but doesn't participate
- Client doesn't pay
- Client acts unethically
- Client expects miracles

Contracts can take many shapes and sizes, but ultimately they are the tool that initiates cooperation between consultant and client. They can be a basic letter of agreement, or they can be formal documents with clauses and sub-clauses. Contracts generally contain the following essential information:

- The parties and the nature of the contractual relationship
- The scope of work
- Various deadlines and checkpoints
- Performance expectations and deliverables
- A payment schedule
- Support the consultant will receive from the client
- Contingency plans for unexpected problems

There are many different types of consultant-client contracts. Here is a summary of some of the most common:

Fixed-Price Contract

These are contracts that state a flat dollar amount which you will be paid for performing specific services. If your costs end up being higher than you expected, you lose money. On the other hand, if you are able to perform the contract more quickly or under your estimate, then you keep the additional profit. Your payment is contingent upon the completion of the contract. You may structure the contract to include interval payments as the contract is incrementally completed. A common example of this would be earning 25% of the fee upon signing the contract, 50% somewhere at the midpoint, and the remaining balance within 10 days of completing the contract.

Fixed Fee Plus Expenses Contract

In cases when direct expenses are difficult to predict or calculate, a consultant might prepare a fixed fee contract and then bill separately for expenses. In this case, direct labor and overhead would be included in the fixed fee.

Daily Rate Contract

One of the simplest and least risky ways to contract for service is with a daily rate. In cases in which a contract is highly unpredictable, a client's personality difficult to work with, or you just want to ensure the easiest possible billing scenario, the daily rate contract can be ideal. Under this type of contract the client usually assumes all risk for overruns.

Time and Materials Contract

This contract is very similar to a daily labor contract, except that the consultant pays for all expenses, including handling charges. Here, the client does not pay the expenses directly. They do however pay labor and overhead rates as they would for a fixed price contract.

Cost Reimbursement Contract

In these types of contract, consultants are repaid for costs that they incur in the course of the contract. These are used in cases when the consultant cannot accurately predict costs. In order for a client to accept this type of contract, they will require that they have the ability to monitor the consultant's costs. Consultants perform more of a cost-management role than as principle deliverers of value: they run less risk of not being paid and do not earn the profit usually associated with fixed-price contracts. Key to these types of contracts is clearly defining reasonable costs that both the client and consultant agree upon.

Retainer Contract

In this type of contract the consultant is paid a fixed monthly or yearly fee to operate on an open-ended basis for the client. Here, the consultant is on-call to the client for a set period of time or project. Both sides agree on a billing rate for additional work, usually an hourly or daily rate. This type of contract makes sense for consultants when they can accurately predict the amount of time and expenses a given project will require. Clients enjoy this type of contract because it gives them easy and reliable access to you.

Performance Contract

These are contracts in which pay is contingent upon the performance of the consultant. Therefore, agreement on what "performance" or "deliverables" mean is crucial! Performance should be measurable in monetary or other quantitative terms. This can be a valuable approach when a consultant is working with a hesitant or highly risk-averse client: the performance standards are clear and the results tangible.

Consulting Operations: Managing the Client

So you've made a smooth and professional presentation, prepared and delivered a competitive bid, and finally, won the contract. Congratulations! You're in business.

Key to any successful business relationship is listening and communicating. This is particularly true of client-consultant relationships. Knowing what your deliverables are at the outset, and conversely, helping your client to understand what is expected of them, will make your relationship a successful one. This will also protect you from possible legal difficulties in the unfortunate event that things don't go as you planned.

Listening and communicating are the keys to excellent client-consultant relationships

For different consultants a deliverable means different things. It can be a systematic analysis of a situation ending in a written report. It can be a hands-on job such as reengineering and rebuilding an irrigation system. It can mean training the client to do something themselves, and then overseeing their performance.

There is in fact a fairly standard process that consultants tend to follow when working for clients. Here are some of the major steps that you can use and adapt as you work with your clients:

Diagnose

As almost everyone knows, diagnosing a problem is the first step in solving it. Often the objective point of view that a consultant can bring a problem is their most valuable contribution. Ask questions, review practices, look at the track record, and talk to people who are relevant in the client's organization.

Design

Designing a solution starts with creating as many solutions as possible. Look at the problem from every possible angle and imagine even the most outlandish scenarios for solving it. Again, work with your client closely on this one: they know better than you what their needs are. Remember, do not be limited to what they suggest. This is the whole reason they have hired you, to think "out of the box."

Implement

Create a plan that includes: who will do which tasks, what your objective will be, time line, why things are being done, and how you will coordinate all the activities.

Measure

One key to success is setting specific points at which you will check your performance and gauge your progress. This allows you to make corrections and refocus on your targets. It is essential to get feedback from your client.

Managing the expectations of your clients is critical to your success. Good people skills are essential: listen carefully, pay attention to body language, and read between the lines. Work with your client to form realistic expectations. Then fulfill them.

Protecting Against Competition

Your best defense against competitors is your ability to stay current and constantly update your expertise. Consultants are often expected to be "cutting edge" authorities in their given area of expertise. You should view continually enhancing your skills as investing in your competitiveness.

Keep current:

- Review progress
- Update skills
- Work towards goals

Your ability to compete also arises out of your unique insight into your clients' needs. By demonstrating a particular authority over your clients' challenges and drawing a clear and understandable link between these and your services, you enhance your professional relationships.

After each contract, ask yourself what unique challenges you confronted, what you learned, what you did well, and what you want to improve for next time. Your motto should be: "Review progress, update skills, and work towards goals."

Taking some of these measures to protect yourself against competition can also help ensure that you will have add-on or repeat business with the same client. It is far easier and cheaper to expand an existing business relationship than it is to go out and cultivate a new one.

Tips for the start-up consultant

- Minimize cost by sharing office space
- Create a private and organized home office
- Use small business and word processing software
- Sell results, not theory
- Have fun: people like people who can laugh and keep perspective
- Focus on selling a process vs. a specific job
- Look for unusual customers or opportunities to use your expertise
- Speak in public and give lectures (this is free publicity!)
- Create a newsletter for clients and potential clients
- Balance time by serving existing customers and prospecting for new ones

Conclusion

Today there are more opportunities than ever for first-time consultants. Remember that it takes more than the right temperament and a particular specialization to become a successful consultant. You must manage clients, control costs, and deliver what you promised to be successful.

In order to remain up-to-date, successful consultants take additional coursework, work at different companies in different industries, and most importantly, keep an open mind to new ideas. It is this change mentality that makes consulting such an exciting and fulfilling business. In the end, imagination and a willingness to look at a situation from a new perspective are your best assets in fulfilling your clients' needs. If the information contained in this chapter excites you, consulting just may be the game for you!

Chapter 21
CONSTRUCTION CONTRACTING

About This Chapter:
- *Types of contracting businesses*
- *Planning and scheduling*
- *Running a job*

Introduction

Becoming a construction contractor can be one of the most challenging of careers. Construction is a high risk industry and requires a builder to be a contractor. A **builder** has the skills to complete a project—pouring concrete, framing walls, installing windows. A **contractor** manages the contract, provides project management, financial management, construction expertise and logistics management.

Statistics indicate that the people who start and operate successful construction companies have prior experience in the industry. If you are thinking of becoming a contractor, you should consider the following:

- Work with a construction company before starting your own business
- Get experience in managing people and finances
- Develop a business plan
- Hire a good accountant and attorney

In this chapter we will explore the various types of contracting work and the steps you can take to start your own contracting business.

State Rules and Regulations

Entry into the construction industry is different in every state — some require training and testing before you are given your contractor's license, while in others you simply apply for the license. In all cases, you must provide the contractor's board with verification of liability insurance and a surety bond before your license will be issued. If you register in multiple states, you must meet each state's requirements before your license is issued.

Williamson Construction is a contractor whose main business is in Washington. He has a contractors license for Washington. If Williamson decides to work in Oregon he must complete 16 hours of approved instruction before a license is issued. If he decides to work in Colorado each trade requires knowledge of the Uniform Building Code sections pertaining to that particular craft.

Types of Contracting Businesses

Construction contracting businesses may work on residential, commercial or industrial projects as either a general or specialty contractor. The category that you select is very important because it has an effect on the type of work that you may do as well as the amount of bonding and insurance you will be required to carry. If you work outside of your registered category, you may be penalized and/or run the risk of losing your contractors license.

The following definitions can aid you in deciding the type of construction work you will be doing:

Residential

Residential construction includes single-family houses, multifamily structures of four units or less including condominiums and mobile homes. It also includes non-residential buildings that have a ground area of 4,000 square feet or less and are not more than 20 feet in height from the top surface of the lowest floor to the highest interior overhead finish.

Commercial

Commercial construction encompasses a great variety of project types and sizes. They include but are not limited to: schools, medical clinics, shopping centers, restaurants, office buildings, warehouses, and light manufacturing plants.

Industrial construction: large complex projects

Industrial

Industrial construction involves very large scale projects that have a high degree of technological complexity and include facilities such as oil refineries, steel mills and nuclear power plants.

Heavy and Highway

Heavy and highway contracting is a specialized type that comprises work building highways and interstates, including overpasses, tunnels, bridges and sometimes temporary rechanneling of streams and/or small dams to accommodate completion of the bridgework. The use of heavy equipment requires care in hiring of qualified heavy equipment operators.

Specialty Trades

Specialty Trades include the following:

- Plumbing, heating, a/c
- Electrical
- Plaster, drywall, insulation
- Flooring
- Concrete
- Glass and glazing
- Wrecking, demolition
- Tree services
- Chimney, structural cleaning
- Farm work
- Painting, paper hanging
- Masonry, stone work
- Tile, marble, mosaic
- Roofing, siding, sheet metal
- Structural steel erection
- Excavation work
- Equipment installation
- Pest control
- Inspection services
- Cabinetry and interior finish work

In addition to determining the type of construction work that you will be doing, you must decide whether you will be a general or specialty contractor. Typically a **general contractor** coordinates all tasks in a construction project **Specialty contractors** (see list above) usually serve as subcontractors to the general contractor of a project.

Register with the state before starting your business

While enjoying woodworking as a hobby, John Hansen decided to pursue this as a post-retirement business. With his wife, Pam, taking care of the bookkeeping, John was able to start his own kitchen cabinet making business. He started by re-doing several friends' kitchens and built his business through referrals and advertising in local newspapers. John succeeded by limiting his work to specialty contracting in cabinetry work.

Five different registration categories have been established for construction contracting. When you apply for a contractor's license, you will need to register in one of the following categories.

General Contractor—All Structure

Businesses who register in this category will be able to work on commercial, industrial, public works, and/or residential construction projects. They are also permitted to do specialty contractor work.

General Contractor—Residential Only

Businesses registering in this category construct new homes, do home remodeling or work on small nonresidential structures. General contractors in this category may also do specialty contractor work.

Specialty Contractor—All Structures

This category, as in the General Contractor-All Structures, may work on commercial, industrial, public works and residential construction projects. Contractors in this category may specialize in two unrelated trades or crafts.

Specialty Contractor—Residential Only

This category is for residential contractors who may specialize in unrelated building trades or crafts. This category includes tree service and manufactured housing.

Limited Contractor

This category is for contractors who gross less than $30,000/year in all construction activities, including labor and materials. A limited contractor may work on any kind of property and supervise and/or perform any number of specialties.

To be eligible you must meet all of the following requirements:

- You expect to gross less than $30,000/year from your business
- You agree that if your gross construction business volume exceeds $30,000 during the year, you will immediately notify the contractors board, increase your bond and insurance coverage
- There are no open or unsatisfied claims against previous registrations

Subcontractors

Subcontractors are typically experts in their field of work. For an individual or business to be considered an independent (sub) contractor rather than an employee, they must meet certain tests regarding freedom to perform, independence and work location.

Licensing and Bonding Requirements

When you apply for your construction contractor's license, you must provide proof that you are carrying Liability Insurance and a Surety Bond. Each state and each construction category require different values on the insurance and bonds. For example, in the state of Oregon, a General Contractor - All Structures must carry a $10,000 bond and $500,000 in liability insurance coverage. A Specialty Contractor - All Structures, must carry a $5,000 bond and $100,000 in liability insurance. The state application form will provide you with the amounts that are required.

Liability Insurance

Liability Insurance provides protection to you the contractor due to a loss that you may cause to people and/or property as a result of your contracting work.

A painting contractor who refinishing woodwork on a remodel project inadvertently left rags that had been used to clean the stripping agent off the wood in the upstairs hall. The unoccupied house became very warm over a hot summer weekend and the rags ignited. The painter's liability insurance reimbursed the owner for damages to the home caused by the fire.

Surety Bonds

Surety Bonds are security from claims filed against your business. If for any reason you are unable to complete a contract, the project owner can request payment from you and/or file a claim against your bond. A claim can be filed if you do not satisfactorily complete the job according to specifications.

Claims can be filed against your business within one year after the date the structure/project was occupied or two years after the structure/project was completed, whichever comes first. Claims can be filed by the owner of the project or the general contractor who is dissatisfied with the work of a subcontractor. Subcontractors can file claims against general contractors for nonpayment as agreed to in the contract.

Each state requires that a contractor carry bond and liability insurance. The amount of coverage required will depend on the category in which you register. Liability insurance and surety bonds must be carried during the entire time you are registered as a contractor. If you do not comply, you are subject to termination of your registration and a civil penalty.

Performance Bonds

Bonds protect project owners against incompletion

Performance Bonds are similar to surety bonds in that they will provide a project owner with funds to compete a project if you are unable to perform. These bonds are usually required for large projects, however, there are no set rules for requiring a performance bond. The owner of a project or the general contractor can require that you carry a performance bond or the general contractor may cover you under their bond.

Insurance bonding companies are reluctant to provide bonds for new contractors, making it difficult to bid on larger projects. Bonding companies require that you fill out a questionnaire about the project. You will be required to answer questions about your personal and business assets, type of job you are bidding, duration of the contract, your ability to do the job, and penalties for non-completion. They will also look at what other work you have on hand and if you bid the job appropriately. The first time you apply for a performance bond, you may be required to compete the application process prior to your submitting a bid. Check with your insurance agent.

The Small Business Administration (SBA) has a program to help smaller business obtain performance bonds. The SBA is authorized to guarantee up to 90 percent of losses incurred under bid, payment or performance bonds on contracts up to $500,000.

Planning

The Business Plan

People very seldom go through life without making plans or setting goals for themselves. Every time you think about going on vacation, you develop a plan, think about where you will go, what you will do when you get there, and how you are going to pay for the trip. The success of your construction business will certainly be more dependent on good planning than your vacation.

You need to set goals and develop a mission statement for your business. This will be easier to accomplish if your marketing plan is developed first. In writing your marketing plan, you will need to ask yourself the following questions:

- Who are my customers?
- What are the economic trends in my area?
- What area of construction will I focus on?
- Why does the customer need my services?
- Why is my service better than my competitors?

After working for ten years doing plumbing for a large construction company, Mary Rivoli decided to open her own shop. A series of state mandated low-income townhouses were proposed for her town. So, Mary contacted all the general contractors bidding on the project and was able to secure a potential subcontract for plumbing with all but three of the bidders. Fortunately for Mary, one of her contractors won the bid and her plumbing business, Mary R's Plumbing, was launched.

Marketing your services is profitable only when you consider what the market's needs are and if your business is capable of answering those needs profitably. Before you go any further in your planning process take some time to look at the economic trends.

Business plans for construction companies

- What is the prime rate?
- What are the current interest rates for construction projects (new homes, remodeling work, commercial projects)?
- What are the occupancy rates for apartments, office buildings?
- Is the community experiencing inflation or a recession?
- What is the unemployment rate?
- What types of projects are being built and/or planned for the near future?

If you are planning on building homes, you may want to consider other types of projects if your community is experiencing a high unemployment rate, if interest rates are high or the area is in a recession. There may be a need for new homes, but people will not be able to buy them. Additionally, you need to determine how many new homes are under construction—you will be competing to sell your homes along with everyone else.

Once you have answered these questions, you need to become more specific about your customer. Before you start writing your marketing plan, you need to answer a few more questions:

- Do I want to do residential work or commercial projects?
- What size of projects do I want to do?
- Where do I want to work?

You have written down your answers to all the questions above, you know about the economy, you have determined who your customers are and the types of projects you want to work on. Now you need to identify how you are going to reach your customers and how you are going to market your services.

Advertising your services:

- Place an ad in your local newspaper
- Purchase an ad in the yellow pages
- Post flyers in your neighborhood
- Develop printed material which describes your services

Marketing your service:

- Develop a portfolio with written and pictorial examples of past projects
- Make sales calls with prospective customers
- Volunteer to do work for free
- Build relationships. Ask for referrals from satisfied customers

Use professional marketing tools in your contracting business to increase sales

In any case, you want to tell your customer who you are and why your services are better. Always include your contractor's license number. Your marketing efforts will take time so don't give up. As a construction contractor you will find that the quality of your work will serve as your best marketing tool but it can't be your only tool. Use the suggestions in the marketing chapters of this book and the workbook to develop an up-to-date marketing plan for your business.

Start-up Costs

Planning the financial aspects of your business has to be constructed as carefully as the projects you build. Putting together a financial plan is only half the job—financial stability is tied to productivity and financial management. Your bid must cover your indirect and direct costs plus profit.

You need to plan and spend cautiously. Unlike many other businesses, in construction contracting customers don't immediately pay for service. The following is a list of some of the things you need to consider as you are starting your business—many will be dependent on the type of construction work you will be doing and the beginning size of your operation.

- **Office:** Many new contractors work out of their homes, trucks and garages. As the company grows, many move into offices.
- **Telephone:** A business phone number is critical. A fax machine, pager, and a cellular phone are very useful as well.
- **Office Equipment:** Unless you are bidding relatively large projects and using software to help you bid and schedule projects, you will have very little need for office equipment. A good bookkeeping system and typewriter will get you through the start-up phase.
- **Office Supplies:** Plan on purchasing business cards, stationery, forms for estimating, contracts, bid and scheduling forms. You will also need to purchase invoice forms, envelopes and stamps.
- **Field Equipment:** This is one of the largest expenses for new construction companies. You will need to plan carefully, giving consideration to the type of equipment needed to complete the projects for which you are bidding.
- **Insurance:** Give strong consideration to purchasing an insurance policy for your equipment, including hand tools.
- **Materials and Labor:** At the start of each new project, you will need money to buy materials, pay wages, taxes, and overhead until the job is completed.
- **Money to Live on:** Until cash starts coming in, you will need money for your personal expenses.
- **Licenses:** Apply for and secure all appropriate licenses

To evaluate the financial position of your business, the following table shows expense ratios that have been compiled and published by the Internal Revenue Service, U.S. Treasury Department and major lending institutions. They apply to small contracting operations with sales less than $1 million per year. Expense ratios are always taken as a percentage of total revenue (sales). Compare your percentages with these and note the items that are out-of-balance:

	General Contractors	Sub-Contractors
Sales (contract revenues)	100%	100%
Materials and subcontracted work	44	44
On site wages (excluding owner)	19	23
Gross Profit	37	33
Controllable expenses		
Off site labor	2	1
Operating supplies	3	2
Repairs and maintenance	1	1
Advertising	1	1
Auto and truck	less than 0.5	less than 0.5
Bad debts	0.5	0.5
Administrative and legal	0.5	0.5
Miscellaneous expense	2	1
Total controllable expenses	13	9
Fixed expenses		
Rent	1	1
Utilities	1	1.5
Insurance	1	1
Taxes and licenses	0.5	0.5
Interest	less than 0.5	less than 0.5
Depreciation	2	2
Total fixed expenses	6	7
Total expenses	**19**	**16**
Net Profit	**18**	**17**

Employees

As an employer, in addition to paying wages, you are responsible for withholding and paying taxes. Job site safety and workers compensation insurance will be required. All of this generates additional expense and record keeping, including the following:

- Wages
- Worker's compensation insurance
- Taxes
- Unemployment insurance

Construction Estimating and Bidding

Decision to Bid

The most important thing that you can do prior to bidding a job is to determine if the project is right for your business. Deciding to bid a job that is larger than any others you have done, outside your area of expertise, or a large financial commitment could lead to failure. These are the criteria you should consider when deciding whether or not to bid a job:

- Job size
- Complexity
- Location
- Labor/Equipment
- Owner/Architect
- Owner's financial integrity
- Competition
- Compatibility (with other projects in progress)

Estimating

Once the decision to bid has been made, you must prepare your estimate. The success of your business depends on bidding and estimating projects correctly.

Review the plans and specifications carefully, visit the site, work on one estimate at a time and have someone check your figures. The most common errors in estimating projects are:

- **Copying errors**—mistakes in copying items from one paper to another
- **Math errors**—making errors in addition, subtraction, multiplication, division
- **Labor estimates**—errors in estimating the actual labor costs (taxes, benefits) and time to complete specific parts of the project
- **Omissions**—leaving out materials, labor, overhead or equipment

Here is a list of the most common types of bids:

- **Fixed Price Bids:** This is the most common form of bidding a job. You will estimate all of the cost to complete a project, including materials, labor, equipment, overhead and profit. When you have completed your estimate and turned it in to the project owner, you have committed to completing the job for that price.

- **Time and Materials (cost plus):** One of the more desirable forms of bidding a job. The project owner agrees to pay you for all reasonable time that it takes you to complete a project and all costs of the materials plus a fee for mark-up. The fee that you negotiate with the project owner should include overhead expenses, labor, equipment costs and profit.
- **Material Costs:** During the estimating process, you will need prices on materials. The price you pay for materials will be your wholesale price. The price to the customer will be the retail price.
- **Labor Costs:** It is important to know how much you will pay each employee to perform specific tasks. In addition, you will need to add taxes and benefits. Another major component of the estimate is to determine the length of time it will take an employee, under normal conditions, to complete a task.

TYPICAL BID FORMULA		
Material	x	Material Price per Unit
	PLUS	
Labor Hours	x	Labor Cost per Hour
	PLUS	
Contractor Burden (FICA, FUTA, S.U.I., Ins.)		
Equipment Cost per Job		
Sub-contracted Items		
Direct Overhead (Supervision, Fees, Utilities, Permits)		
Indirect Overhead (Office Expense, Accounting, Legal)		
	=	**Subtotal**
	PLUS	
Escalation (Annual Rate, approx. 10%)		
	=	**Subtotal (Job Cost)**
	PLUS	
Contingency (2% of Job Cost)		
	PLUS	
Profit (5% to 8% of Job Cost)		
	=	**CONTRACT PRICE**

Contracts

An agreement or promise between two or more parties to complete a specific task is considered a **contract**. A contract must contain the following four elements in order to be considered a good or valid contract.

- **Offer and acceptance.** You make an offer to a client to do a specific task and they accept.
- **Consideration.** This is the other party's promise to pay you to construct a project.
- **Competent parties.** You and your client are both of sound mind, and able to make clear decisions.
- **Legal purpose.** The project or task proposed in the agreement is legal.

Contracts protect both parties to an agreement

When two parties agree to do specific tasks on a handshake, you have entered into a **verbal contract**. For example, you agree to build a deck for your neighbor for $800. It would be better for you to put this in writing to avoid any misunderstandings that might arise. While working on a project, you must keep complete records of your expenses and time involved in completing the project. **Job Cost Accounting** is essential for both general and specialty contractors. It is wise to establish spreadsheets on which actual job costs can be entered against each bid item, including a final column for deviations from the original bid.

Having kept accurate job costs accomplishes several things:

- Aids in making better bids on the next proposal
- Establishes good information for billing for additional work outside the scope of the original contract due to:
  1. Field Change Orders
  2. Change Orders from owners or architects
  3. Additional work due to previously unknown conditions
  4. Support for alleviation of Penalty Clause charges for additional time spent making the above changes

Remember, having an agreement in writing provides protection to both parties in the agreement.

Construction Contracts

In some states, there is a legal requirement that any construction project that exceed $2,500 must have a written agreement. When the original price of the contract is under $2,500 but increases during the course of completing, a contract must be drawn.

In addition to the elements listed above, your contract must clearly state, in the Terms and Agreements section, the following items:

- Liens
- Fire insurance
- Clean-up detail
- Penalty clause (if any, for late completions)
- Permits
- Worker's compensation
- Changes to contract
- Union or non-union considerations or requirements

You might want to consult with an attorney who has a strong background in construction law to help you draft the contract and to assist with ensuring you are in compliance with state and local regulations.

Job Start-up and Completion

Financing the Project

Cash flow problems?

Many new construction companies start their businesses using their personal assets. Problems occur when the payment for one job hasn't been received and the business needs cash to start another project. If you find yourself in this situation you need to begin investigating alternate sources of financing:

- Obtain a home owner's equity loan on your home
- Sell or rent your home
- Sell your accounts receivables. Banks or factoring companies will purchase receivables at a discounted rate
- Borrow money against your accounts receivable
- Offer discounts to clients if they agree to pay in advance
- Obtain cash discounts or credit terms from suppliers

Typically, construction loans are terminated at the time the construction project is completed. Alternative sources of financing then become effective. Residential housing loans are usually obtained through a local bank. Commercial building or institution construction loans are obtained through a commercial lender.

Scheduling

Experienced contractors know that the two most important steps in making a profit on a project are planning the work and keeping on schedule. Regardless of whether you are the general contractor of a project or a specialty subcontractor, you will need to plan and schedule your work.

As a general contractor, you will need to prepare tentative plans by putting together all the elements of the job; determine the approximate number of days to compete each one and the approximate dates when each element should start. Be realistic, plan a schedule that is workable. Initial steps in scheduling are:

- Break the project down into tasks
- Determine how long each task will take to complete
- Determine the sequence for each task

After listing all of the elements, assign time-frames for each element and list them in the order they need to be completed. Next, determine what equipment you need and list the labor that it will take to complete each element of the project. When the project contract has been signed, you will need to notify your subcontractors. They will need to schedule their time and labor for your project, as well as order materials. Develop a time and work schedule for your subcontractors.

There are many formal ways to develop scheduling activities using systems such as *Critical Path Method* (CPM), Bar Charts or calendar scheduling. Sophisticated computer programs have been developed and are great for very large projects. You need to pick the process that is right for your business, be as accurate as possible, stay on target, and remain flexible enough to accommodate changes in the scope of work.

Progress Reports

Progress reports are requested by the client when working on large projects. They provide the general contractor and owner with information on how well the project is progressing. If you are working as a specialty contractor, you should have your employees turn in progress reports so that you can schedule your own projects. A progress report will provide three vital pieces of information:

- Compare actual progress against the schedule
- Identify where there are problems
- Specify action you will take to correct the delay or reschedule other elements

Building Codes and Inspections

Building codes originated as a part of the building regulatory process for the safety of the public. Examples of building codes are: fire escapes or exits, maximum rise per steps on a stairway, handicapped access, etc. As a contractor, you will be held responsible for conforming to building codes for your project. Building codes have been developed on a national, state and local level. In additional to the general building codes, there are specialty codes for plumbing, electrical and mechanical construction.

Inspections

You can expect various organizations to inspect the project you are building to ensure that you are complying with state and local building regulations and for other, varied reasons. You will need to schedule inspections by:

Plan time for inspections

- Building inspectors from the local government
- Architect and/or the owner of the project
- Loan officer

When you develop your project schedule, include inspections as they will take time and may delay other elements of the project. Your primary concern is to make sure that the work to be inspected is ready. Inspection delays can cause other problems such as:

- Rescheduling other elements of the project
- Reschedule other projects
- Time spent changing problems to satisfy the inspector
- Money to make changes
- Money to workers who are waiting to proceed

Job Site Safety

Safety; job one!

The very nature of construction work makes it dangerous. You need to protect yourself and your employees as much as possible from factors that can lead to injury. Having a job site safety program can save you money in claims, maintain work progress, and decrease insurance premiums. At least 80 percent of all injuries in the construction industry are caused by:

- Slips and falls
- Trenching and excavation
- Incorrect lifting
- Electrical operations

Billing

Payment for your work should be agreed upon between you and your client and in all contracts. In some cases, you may be able to obtain payment in advance for work, especially if you are ordering special materials.

- **Draws:** Generally, you will be paid for your work on a regular basis throughout the project with payment contingent on work completed minus any retainage. Smaller projects may be paid when the entire project is completed. Delays in payment can and should be expected. If you are working as a subcontractor, you may not receive payment for up to 60 days after you have submitted an invoice. The same with small jobs—once you have completed the job and invoiced the owner, you may not be paid for several weeks. Always obtain a written, signed, payment schedule.
- **Retainages:** Larger construction projects can withhold payment of up to 10 percent of your entire contract for one year. This is done as insurance against unsatisfactory work or against problems that you would need to correct. In some cases, you can negotiate for the retainage to be reduced or not withheld.

For many subcontractors, cash shortfalls can occur because the retainage may have been more than your profit margin. If you find yourself in need of the money, check with your bank—they may give you a loan using the retainage as collateral, or buy the retainage at a discounted rate.

Conclusion

The construction business sometimes affords the new entrepreneur an opportunity to start a business with less capital than many other types of businesses. There are five basic types of contracting: residential, commercial, industrial, specialty trades, and heavy and highway. Planning and scheduling are the two most critical elements in successfully managing a construction business. Many experienced contractors suggest working for successful companies involved in the field that interests you prior to opening your own business. The construction business can be fun, exciting, and financially rewarding for those who revel in the challenges of building great things!

Chapter 22
BECOMING A RETAILER

About This Chapter:
- *Types of retail opportunities*
- *Finding a good fit*
- *Planning a retail store*
- *Retailing in shopping malls*

Introduction

At one time or another most of us have sold goods or services. As a young child you may have set up a lemonade stand or done yard work for a neighbor. Maybe you sold some of your "slightly used" clothes and housewares at a weekend garage sale. You were selling products or services to the final consumer—you were retailing.

Retailing is defined as "all the activities that result in the offering for sale of merchandise or services to consumers for their use. Retailing is the final step in bringing goods to the consumer."

Retail businesses are among the most popular forms of entrepreneurial ventures. As illustrated in the following chart, retail stores account for 25% of the total number of small business firms with less than 20 employees. Many of these retail establishments are owner operated, and have fewer than five employees.

Small Business Establishments by Industry

Services	34.5%	**Mining**	0.5%
Finance & Insurance	9.0%	**Construction**	9.0%
Retail	25.0%	**Manufacturing**	9.5%
Wholesale	7.0%	**Agricultural Services**	1.5%
Transportation	4.0%		

Source: U.S. Bureau of the Census, County Business Patterns, 1992

Retail small business ventures are characterized by ease of entry when compared to manufacturing. This is primarily due to the relative ease of securing retail rental space and low capital requirements. Unfortunately, small retail businesses have a very high failure rate.

Peet's Coffees and Teas

In 1966, when Peet's Coffees and Teas opened for business in Berkeley, California, it was the only player in town. Other specialty coffee businesses flourished in the 1920's and '30's but most went out of business after the depression. By the time 1966 rolled around, the founders of Peet's saw an opportunity to sell a product they loved in a neighborhood they liked: North Berkeley.

The corner store opened to sell the highest quality coffee, teas and accessories (mugs, teapots, and tea strainers). Peet's bought only the best beans and roasted them to perfection. It sold in bulk to restaurants, hotels, and in smaller quantities to its retail customers. Peet's enticed customers to buy 1 pound bags of beans by offering them samples of brewed Peet's coffee. Eventually, over time, this practice evolved into selling cups of coffee, tea, scones, muffins, and other treats in the store.

Types of Retail Opportunities

Retail opportunities are limitless. The key is to determine what the consumer wants, what price they will pay and how to sell at a profit. Most people assume that it is necessary to open a store but there are many "non-store" retail opportunities, including:

- Mail order through catalog
- Sales on the Internet (setting up a commercial web site)
- Direct selling or door to door
- Self-service or vending machine

Finding a Good Fit

Finding the right fit

Just as customers are interested in purchasing a well fitting pair of shoes, so too should the prospective retail business owner be concerned with a good fit. In determining your compatibility and adaptability to retail business ownership, consider the following:

Customers

Do you like dealing with people? Retailing is a business that is totally dependent on customers. You must enjoy people contact to be a successful retailer. You must continuously be looking for ways to keep your existing customers and find new ones.

Can you deal with constant change? Customer buying habits frequently change and so must you to be successful.

Products
Are you familiar with the product or products you will be selling? If not, how much are you willing to learn? Product knowledge is critical in a small retail environment.

Suppliers
Are you a firm, assertive negotiator? You will need to negotiate the best price and ensure that deliveries are timely.

Long hours
The best times for customers to shop are when they are not working. Expect to work late hours and weekends. Is this schedule for you? Even if you have staff to run the operation, you are ultimately responsible for any major problems or emergencies that occur. Is your family life compatible with long hours?

The name of the game in retail is customer service

Landlords
Unless you own your retailing space, you will have a landlord. Be prepared to negotiate the best lease you can get. In most locations your landlord, or their managing company, may limit some of your choices. Your lease may dictate the size of your exterior signs, what products are exclusive, and operating hours. You may also be expected to help pay for the maintenance of common areas.

Employees
Unless you own a very small establishment, you will need to hire employees. They will look to you for leadership, motivation and technical knowledge. Can you give clear directions, delegate responsibility and evaluate performance? These are responsibilities that directly impact the success or failure of a retail venture.

Record keeping
Retailing is a transaction intense business and largely cash based. Are you able to develop and maintain excellent record keeping systems and controls? If not, are you willing to learn? In most states you will pay sales taxes based on sales. You are also subject to unannounced audits of your sales transactions.

Security
Shoplifting, employee theft and potential robberies are inherent risks of the retail business. Creating controls and safeguards are essential to running a profitable retail business. Are you the vigilant, well-organized type?

Peet's Thirty Years Later....

In 1966 Peet's Coffee was a completely novel concept. The little store had a small customer base, but also had no competition. It was the best, and only coffee roaster and retailer around.

Things have changed. In the 1990's the market for gourmet coffees exploded and chains of coffee retailers began cropping up in major cities all over America. They charge premium prices and offer espresso drinks in every size, shape, and color. They compete by being everywhere their customers are, serving coffee drinks fast, and just the way customers want them. And what of Peet's? Doing better than ever, thank you.

Peet's continues to succeed as a coffee retailer (which is really just one arm of its business—it also sells products wholesale and by mail-order) by focusing on its most important success factor: the best coffee beans.

Peet's has and always will compete on the basis of taste. And, it makes no bones about its philosophy, "Pay for the best or go back to the rest." This may sound extreme to some, but in a crowded field of coffee retailers, Peet's succeeded by establishing and fiercely defending its position as the premier coffee bean roaster. Peet's doesn't target the average supermarket shopper. Their target customer is the discerning coffee enthusiast, who knows what good coffee tastes like and is willing to pay more to enjoy it.

Where do Retail Business Ideas Come From?

Retail business generally grow out of an entrepreneur's past experience with a particular product, service or industry. Often times people begin retailing businesses based on a particular hobby, interest or expertise.

Retail operations arise when entrepreneurs identify a product or a service that they believe will sell. For example, if you love music and are a skilled guitarist you might decide to open a guitar store.

Entrepreneurs also might identify a new market or an opportunity to fill an un-met need in an existing market. For example, take the entrepreneur who realized that there was no healthy food available in airport terminals. He decided to open a juice bar in his local airport. In this case the market was already clearly defined: health conscious, time-pressed airline passengers. This entrepreneur's task was to identify what customers wanted, what they were willing to pay and what it would cost him to operate his retail operation.

Often times entrepreneurs enter retail by buying an existing retail operation from someone who wants to get out of the businesses. They calculate that they can operate more cost effectively, offer better service, and generate higher profits than the previous owner.

Market Strategy

Market research is an important part of your initial retail business plan and should heavily influence your site selection, pricing strategy, and product mix. Here are some marketing questions which relate directly to retail:

- Who is your customer? (age, income, sex etc.)
- Do they live in the area?
- Do they work in the area?
- How far will they have to travel to come to your store?
- Which routes do they most commonly drive?
- When do your customers shop? (lunch hour, after work, weekends)
- How do they get to your store?
- What payment options do they prefer? (credit card, check, cash, layaway)
- What motivates them to buy? (price value, visual appeal, impulse)
- Who is your competition?
- How are customers' existing needs being met?
- What is most important to your customers when they shop?
- How satisfied are your customers with existing offerings?
- How important are prices? Service? Store cleanliness? Signage? Lighting? Hours? Payment options?

For other ideas see the section of this book on marketing and selling.

Planning forces you to prepare for difficult contingencies

Product Planning

The process of planning the types of products a retail business will offer is called **merchandising.** Retailers create a merchandising strategy to maximize profits. They try to offer the right mix of products and services at the right prices to achieve their retail objectives. Merchandising includes the following tasks:

- Identifying and describing your target customers
- Determining the needs and wants of your target customer using your market research and analysis
- Forecasting sales for a given period
- Planning the assortment of merchandise you will offer
- Receiving and checking your products for quality
- Tracking sales to identify what sells and what doesn't

Next, businesses determine what the **shelf life** is for their products. This can vary from a few days (food products), months (tobacco, film, over the counter medicine), or an entire season (fashion apparel).

In addition to shelf life, products have a **product life cycle** that includes four stages: introduction, growth, maturity and decline. Each stage of the product cycle offers both opportunities and risks.

During the **introduction stage,** a product or service is introduced to the consumer. Your customers may have little knowledge about this product. Test these items by buying in smaller quantities before displacing other items in the store.

In the **growth stage,** product sales are expanding and enjoy more customer interest. You are likely to face business competition during this stage. Be creative and work with your supplier and offer variations of the product or better pricing.

During the **maturity stage** the product has saturated the market. The retailer can choose from a number of competing suppliers and negotiate a better price.

By the **decline stage,** consumer demand for the product diminishes. Ordering at this stage should slow. You may even need to mark down the remaining inventory.

How do these phases of the product life cycle impact start-up businesses? Where your products are in their life cycle will determine the way you order, display, price and promote your products.

Width of product assortment

A key part of merchandising strategy is determining the product assortment you will offer. The **width** of a product line describes how many different types of products are offered. If you have a bookstore, will you sell a variety of categories of books or will you limit yourself to business titles or children's books? If you are selling sports apparel, will you sell tennis, golf, running and camping apparel? Or will you focus just on offering aerobics clothing? Remember, you cannot carry everything as you have limited cash and limited display space.

Depth of product assortment

Assortment **depth** refers to the number of each item or style that a store offers. Again, if you are selling sports apparel, will you offer your tennis skirts in 3 colors or 10? How many of each size will you carry? How many different labels or styles will you offer?

What merchandise will you carry? Why?

Keep in mind that many suppliers have a minimum purchase requirement or will sell in fixed, bulk quantities.

Suppliers

Once the product mix has been determined, retailers identify where they will source their products. They develop a **supplier list.** Smart retailers take time to cultivate strong relationships with their suppliers so that they can rely on getting the products they need, at the best possible prices.

Supplier Tips

When selecting which suppliers to source your products from, you should consider the following:

- Do they carry the type and quality of products your customers want to buy?
- Are their prices fair?
- Can they offer you attractive payment terms and conditions?
- Are they honest and professional in their dealings?
- Do they deliver reliably what you ordered when you need it?
- Do you work well together? Are they eager to help you?

Some sources of potential suppliers include Business-to-Business Yellow Pages, trade publications, trade associations, libraries, merchants that carry the same product line, and trade shows.

Retailers often create a standard form to use when dealing with suppliers. Many computer programs are available for assembling databases for this purpose. Here is an example:

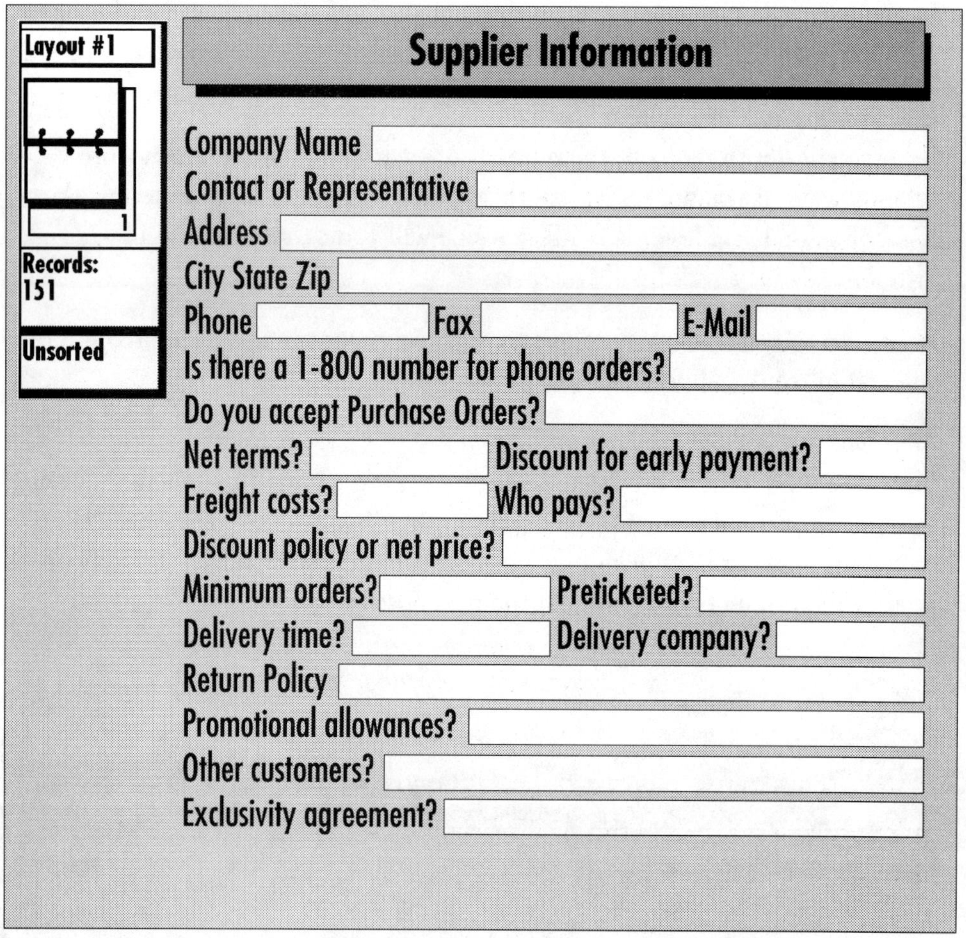
Layout #1

Records: 151

Unsorted

Supplier Information

Company Name

Contact or Representative

Address

City State Zip

Phone | Fax | E-Mail

Is there a 1-800 number for phone orders?

Do you accept Purchase Orders?

Net terms? | Discount for early payment?

Freight costs? | Who pays?

Discount policy or net price?

Minimum orders? | Preticketed?

Delivery time? | Delivery company?

Return Policy

Promotional allowances?

Other customers?

Exclusivity agreement?

Create a supplier database to streamline ordering and billing

Pricing

Price is one of the most important variables that retailers can control to make their businesses profitable. Prices must fit with your costs, customers, competitors, and your market. The way you set your prices will also be impacted by the type of product you sell, its seasonality, perishability, style, and how quickly it sells.

In order to operate a profitable retail store, your price must:

- Cover the cost of the product, plus overhead expenses and profits
- Be in a price range that your customers are willing to pay

Oddly enough, businesses often undercharge for their products by only focusing on covering the expenses and making a set margin of profit. They fail to take into account what the market will bear, which may be considerably higher than what their cost structure is.

In the retail business, the **costs of goods** (the cost of acquiring a product) includes the price paid for the merchandise, handling, freight charges, and import duties. **Overhead expenses** include rent, wages, advertising, utilities, and supplies.

Retailers use **markup** or **mark-on** is the difference between the price you pay for the product and your final selling price. The markup is established as a percentage of the cost or as a percentage of the retail price.

A price based on **markup percentage on cost** is determined by adding a percentage of the cost of an item to the total cost of goods:

Cost of shirt	$5.00
X Markup %	50%
= Markup amount	$2.50

Cost of shirt	$5.00
+ Markup amount	$2.50
= Selling price	$7.50

Pricing your merchandise

A more common markup strategy in retail is to base the markup on the retail price. Retailers often do this by dividing the cost of the product by the markup percentage:

$$\frac{\text{Cost of shirt} \quad \$5.00}{\text{Markup Percentage } .50 \ (50\%)} = \text{Retail Price } \$10.00$$

You may decide to use a standard markup percentage for all the merchandise, or you may have different markups for different products. The key is to make sure the average markup or gross margin is enough to cover the operating expenses and still meet your target profit margins.

Another pricing practice among retailers is to price merchandise according to the **suggested retail price** recommended by the manufacturer. This is the easiest way to determine prices but can get into trouble if the margin between the cost of goods and the suggested retail price is not enough to cover operating expenses.

Another pricing strategy includes basing your prices on those of the competition. You may set prices at the same level, or at a higher or lower level than your competitors. All three of these strategies create problems if you do not monitor your gross margins and sales volume to insure that you cover costs and operating expenses.

The simplest retail pricing technique of all is called **keystoning.** Keystoning involves simply doubling all of your costs to arrive at your final selling price. For the sports apparel retailer who calculates their total cost for one leotard at $20, would set their selling price at $40. Pretty easy, huh?

Peet's Supply Link

Peet's controls its product every step of the way. It begins by buying the best green coffee beans from the best suppliers, all over the world. Peet's has a leg up on its competitors, since it has developed some very strong relationships with its suppliers over thirty years ago. Peet's roasts, packages, and brews its own beans into perfect cafe lattes, espressos, cappuccinos and mochas in 30 Peet's retail stores.

Peet's also sells some the most unique, high quality coffee and tea accessories available. Ceramic mugs and tea pots are often hand-made, and sold only in limited quantities. The selection of supplies is sourced carefully and updated frequently.

Inventory control

Inventory:

Too little?

Too much?

Many small business owners do not manage inventory until it is too late and the business is in a real crisis. What is an inventory crisis? Having too few products on hand to fill customer orders. Or, having too many products on hand that are cluttering shelves and tying up precious capital. It is important to have enough inventory to keep your store visually appealing and to avoid missed sales. Lack of inventory control results in increased costs associated with merchandise storage, taxes and insurance.

The best inventory systems are those that quickly and accurately enable the retailer to determine what needs to be ordered based on:

- What merchandise is on hand
- What merchandise has been ordered, but not delivered
- What has been sold during a given period

Manual inventory systems have been around a long time. Unfortunately, too many small retailers rely on visual control and "gut" analysis. New technology has made the use of computers to control inventory easy and affordable. These include **point-of-sale cash registers** and **bar code readers.**

Many retailers, large and small, think that by purchasing a computer system, their inventory problems are over. An automated inventory system will produce better management reports and assist in controlling inventory. However, it will accomplish little unless you are prepared to accurately and regularly log the data on products sold, products received and products on order.

Stockturn

One of the ways to measure your business's health is to monitor the stockturn. **Stockturn** is the number of times the average inventory **turns over**, or is sold in a given period. Many retail businesses will calculate the stockturn rate for each category of products they sell. Are running shoes selling more quickly than golf shoes? Are mystery novels selling more quickly than children's picture books?

Stockturn analysis by department or category type allows retailers to have a more detailed understanding of their customers' buying patterns. This also helps them to take action to correct a problem in a specific product category or department.

Don't wait until you are in trouble to get control of your inventory!

If stockturn is too fast, you may be expending too much time and money reordering and paying extra freight costs by ordering too small quantities. You might also be losing sales due to lack of product. If stockturn is too slow, you may be trying to sell the wrong products to the wrong customers. You may also be charging the wrong prices.

Calculating stockturn can vary by industry. Guidelines for calculating stockturn can be found in industry publications.

Markdown, discount and return policies
Markdowns or sales are important tools for the retailer. Markdowns should be utilized to:

- Clear out slow moving or dormant stock
- Dispose of broken or unpackaged items
- Meet a competitor's price
- Make room for seasonal or promotional items or new product line
- Provide dollars needed to purchase better selling items

A **discount** is a reduction in the sale price of merchandise. Some common discount practices include:

- Employee discounts (extra benefit for employees)
- Quantity discounts (discount dependent on number or dollar amount)
- Professional or trade discounts
- Seasonal discounts

Location, Location, Location

Location alone can make the difference between the success or the failure of a retail business. Whether you are looking for a free standing location or a store location within a shopping center, location is critical and believed by many to be the most critical component of your retail strategy. If you are not located where your customers can conveniently find you and shop, your store will have a difficult time being profitable. Unfortunately, many prospective retailers make location decisions based on impulse or emotion. How should they make their selection? By considering who their customers are and where they shop.

Retailers also need to balance the cost of different locations with the different levels of sales they might generate. Which of these sites would you select?

Location is the most critical element in retail strategy

- A downtown storefront with $10,000 in monthly rent, capable of generating $20,000 in sales a month

Or:

- A store front location on a neighborhood shopping street costing $2,000 a month in rent, where you can also generate $20,000 a month in sales?

Many small retailers save money on rent by choosing to locate themselves outside of central business districts. Depending on their products or services, they often choose sites in secondary business areas and neighborhood shopping areas. Listed below are some guidelines.

Careful evaluation of location is critical

When evaluating the city in which your business may be located, consider the following:

- Concentration of targeted customers
- Growth or decline in population
- Income and spending patterns
- Competition
- Governmental incentives provided for business relocation or start-up
- Health of the local economy

When evaluating an area within a potential city, consider the following:

- Types of customers and business in downtown, suburban and residential areas
- Access routes and traffic patterns in potential locations
- Public transportation routes
- Zoning restrictions
- New construction or development
- Appearance of the area
- Local bankruptcies or closures

When narrowing the selection to a specific site, consider the following:

- Existing anchor tenant or other tenants (look at their lease terms)
- Retail compatibility
- Parking availability
- Completing retail establishments
- Costs, lease, rent and tenant improvements
- Pedestrian traffic patterns
- Security for customers and employees
- Past tenant's type of business and reason for closure

Shopping Centers

Shopping centers aren't necessarily just for large, national retail chains. Because there are so many types of shopping centers, no start-up retailer should ignore the possibilities that such a location offers.

Thousands of shopping centers in all shapes and sizes dot North America. There are malls in urban, suburban and rural areas. There are small neighborhood strip malls and super sized regional malls. Many malls actively look for small, local, specialty retailers to complement and add color to their mix of larger retail tenants. The basket of different goods and services that a mall creates to serve its target customers is known as its **merchandising units.**

Anyone who has ever shopped in a mall knows that they are located to be convenient and easily accessible for a specific group of shoppers. Just as individual retailers do, mall planners look at data about their target customer's work and leisure activities before they select a site.

Is a shopping mall location right for your retail concept? To guide you, consider the following types of shopping malls:

Location, Location, Location!

- **Neighborhood shopping centers.** This is the smallest type of mall, offering on average of 50,000 square feet of selling space on a four acre site. These can be configured in a strip pattern creating a "strip mall." They cater to the needs of as 1,000 to 40,000 people who live within six to ten miles of the area. The major tenant is usually a national or regional drug store.
- **Community shopping centers.** These are usually situated on approximately ten acres of land and offer approximately 140,000 square feet of selling space. They serve between 25,000 and 150,000 customers who live within a five to eight mile radius of the mall. The **anchor store**, or major tenant is usually a mass merchandise retailer like Target, Kmart or a large supermarket.
- **Regional shopping centers.** Regional shopping centers can cover thirty acres of land and offer up to 300,000 square feet of retail selling space. They often serve as many as 300,000 people who can might come from as far away as forty miles to shop. There are usually two anchor stores, one at each end. Tenants also include many national and regional retailers, as well as a motel, movie theaters, and restaurants. **Super-regional shopping centers** even larger versions of the regional center model. They offer as much as four million square feet of retail space.

Before making any location decisions, start-up retailers should consider the benefits and costs of locating their business in a mall:

Benefits of shopping centers:

- Open for business 5 or 6 nights a week
- Good security
- Mall wide promotional activities: sales, concerts and seasonal events
- Clean, good maintenance
- Good customer draw
- Convenient customer parking

Downsides of shopping centers:

- Monthly maintenance dues
- Other tenant's fees
- Management restrictions on hours of operation, window displays, holiday operations

Peet's Customers: Up Close and Personal

When Peet's opened in 1966 the owner served customers from behind the counter. He got to know them personally and shared his enthusiasm and expertise of coffee. He knew that the way Peet's beans were brewed was critical to the quality of the coffee they produced. Thus he began brewing coffee in his store, and selling the best quality brewing equipment and accessories to his customers.

Today, Peet's continues this level of customer service, because it has to. In the late 1980's they began to notice changes in the market. New cafes were opening in response to a growing taste for high-end coffee. Peet's realized that it had at most 4 years to prepare itself for a major onslaught from new competitors. They decided that if their competitors were to steal Peet's customers, they would have to steal them one customer at a time.

Peet's best defense? Customer service.

Store Design

The store's fundamental purpose is to sell merchandise. Successful retailers configure their stores for customer convenience, and to use selling and display space in the most effective ways. All of the elements of your store design should be developed with this purpose in mind. The environment you create in your store will impact your customers both physically and psychologically, so do not miss the opportunity to create an environment that encourages your customers to come in, buy, and return in the future.

Design a store that brings customers in and excites them to buy

Store design should appeal to all five senses: sight, sound, smell, touch and taste.

Store front

Store fronts are the first communication point with a customer. Your store's exterior will communicate attitude, price, value, and market.

The primary components of the store front include:

- The overhead or exterior sign: This should be clean, well maintained, easy to see, and be designed to reflect the look and feel of your business concept.
- The show window(s): Think of this as a stage where you can present the most compelling reasons for customers to come in and buy. Window displays should be kept clean and current. Get help from a professional designer or creative friend to create up to date, colorful and enticing displays.
- The store entrance: Make sure your doorway is wide enough so that customers can easily enter and leave the store. Your doorway should be clean and inviting. Retailers often use unique door handles, trim, window panes or curtains to make their store entrance more appealing. It is important to keep the area immediately in front of your store well swept and clear of debris, ice and snow.

Clever, Low-cost Promotion Tips:

- Play appealing music
- Make your store smell good so that customers will linger: scents like coffee, citrus, leather, and floral can create a positive lasting impression
- Use quality, high intensity, well directed lights to direct customers' attention where you want it
- Invite customers to touch and sample products
- Offer free coffee and snacks
- Create "street appeal" by setting up outside racks to display your goods, putting balloons or flowers on outside railings
- Post articles, good reviews and other information about your store, products or services in prominent places in the store
- Offer in-store customer social/informational events: seminars, speakers, champagne brunches, product introduction parties or birthday events

Store interior

The store's interior should maximize your sales activities, create customer satisfaction and produce operating efficiencies. Every square foot of space costs you money, so make sure that you plan carefully and use it well.

Many retailers calculate exactly their **costs per square foot**. They do this by dividing their monthly total rent by their total square foot area of selling space.

Store layout consists of allocating space for two basic store activities:

- **Selling Area.** A selling area is dedicated to merchandise displays and the area in which the interaction between the customers and the store employees takes place. Try to anticipate customer traffic flow. Keep in mind that customers usually shop from right to left. Remember, your selling area should be designed for maximum convenience, speed and natural flow. Your task is to create the ideal environment in which your employees can sell and people can buy.

Great store interiors sell merchandise

- **Non-Selling Area.** The store's non-selling area includes checkout, dressing rooms, return desk, storage area, promotions, back office, and ticketing. These areas should be kept clean, well organized and secure. Make them easy to survey and access, so that you can quickly serve customers and restock shelves. Remember that employees need at least 28-30 inches of clearance space for easy movement behind counters.
- **Flooring.** Flooring should be composed of durable materials that are safe, can handle heavy traffic and are aesthetically appealing.
- **Ceilings.** By lowering or raising the ceiling, the store can be more intimate and cozy or more formal.
- **Lighting.** Lighting is a critical component of merchandising. Lighting showcases merchandise and helps create a desired mood and atmosphere.
- **Decor or theme.** Decor or theme can create an atmosphere that enhances, neutralizes or detracts from the merchandise. Paint, wall paper, photos, pictures, and murals can all be used to create the selling environment that is right for your customers and your products or

services. You should select your materials based on their cost, durability, ease of maintenance, and fit with the overall concept of your store. If at all possible, work with an interior designer to help select colors, textures and develop a theme.

- **Fixtures.** Fixtures are used for displaying, selling, and stocking activities. They include carts, shelves, countertops, display cases, floor stands, peg boards, racks, stocking bins, desks, and islands. You may have noticed that some stores are utilizing fewer floor fixtures and trying to merchandise heavily on the walls. A store cluttered with fixtures is often a deterrent to shopping. Start-up retailers can offer purchase fixtures at discounted prices from other businesses or retail equipment dealers.

The Best Defense: Customer Service

Peet's predictions were right on: within a few years Starbuck's and other coffee chains began opening on every corner, directly challenging Peet's business. But did they? Peet's made sure they couldn't.

Peet's ensures that every customer receives the best cup of coffee every time they come into a Peet's store. Each cup is prepared to perfection by counter staff who are careful, quick and friendly coffee experts. Peet's employees are interviewed carefully, trained extensively and paid more than average. And they earn it. Customers come back again and again because they know they will get exactly what they want, expertly prepared every visit.

Peet's also aggressively seeks out and pays for the best retail locations. One of the keys to customer service is being where your customers are. If that means paying more for a prime location, then so be it.

At Peet's, the numbers speak for themselves: on a sales per store basis, Peet's consistently outperforms its largest competitor, Starbuck's.

Customer Service: The Real Competitive Advantage

With the advent of superstores and discount stores such as Wal-mart and Price Club, it is becoming a real challenge for small retailers to compete and retain customers. Small retailers simply cannot compete with the low prices, volume supplier agreements, high cost-high traffic locations, and huge promotional budgets of national and regional retailers.

So what can a start-up retailer do? Compete on the basis of customer service. Customer service is everything you do to make your customer's experience easier, more convenient, cost-effective, and even fun. Start-up retailers can leverage their small size to really get to know their customers and deliver what they need when and where they want it. Smart businesses offer customer service that is a mix of basic, expected services and "extras" that make a lasting positive impression on the customer.

For small businesses, some small effort to deliver unique customer service can cost very little and create long term customer loyalty. When conceived of and used creatively, customer service can truly differentiate you from your competitors. By helping to generate positive word-of-mouth, good customer service is one of your best promotional tools.

At minimum, shoppers expect the following services:

- Courteous, professional attention
- Convenient store hours
- Easy access parking
- A clean, enjoyable shopping environment
- Prompt service
- Bagging of purchases
- Speedy and sincere resolution of complaints

Use your knowledge of your customers to deliver truly excellent customer service

You may also want to offer:

- Free delivery
- Free estimates
- Customization of products or services
- A generous return policy
- Expert guidance on use and maintenance of products
- Follow up service
- Special discounts and promotions
- A store newsletter
- Holiday events
- Birthday specials
- Customer bulletin board for community announcements
- Check acceptance
- Gift certificates

Create a "Customer Service Statement" and post it in your store

- Creative gift wrapping
- Refreshments
- Play area and toys for children
- Bathrooms
- Shopping baskets
- Public telephone

Niche retailing
Niche marketing, or uniquely positioning your business, is another way to enjoy retail success. Large retail chains will not carry product lines that have slow stockturn, are difficult to procure from suppliers or appeal to a very limited market. While large firms profess to have excellent, personalized customer service, it is often difficult to deliver due to high staff turnover. This is where the small retailer can be very competitive. Do your homework. Find out what products and/or services you can provide that large competitors can not or will not.

The Peet's Information Flow

Another key to Peet's success is staying on top of what is selling in each of its stores. In 1982 Peet's installed a computer system that has evolved into a central computer that "interrogates" the cash register in each and every store. The system records daily sales logs, bank deposits and other cash flow information. Sales and financial data can be tracked in "real time" at the Peet's headquarters, so managers know, at any given moment, what is selling and what is not.

Likewise, the business can track sales patterns for different products and different locations. Using this data, Peet's makes critical decisions about new product offerings and store placements.

Using Technology

Another area where small retail businesses can remain competitive is with the utilization of technology. Large retailers must convert huge divisions or the entire operation when converting to a new accounting system or **point-of-sale** (POS) system.

The proliferation and affordability of personal computers, business software and other technological enhancements are changing the way small retailers do business. Some of the most common technological enhancements are presented below.

Point of sale inventory systems
These systems allow inventory tracking by adjustments made at the point of sale. Every time an item is sold, it adjusts the inventory. Of course it is necessary to habitually input merchandise received, returned, and eliminated from the inventory due to theft or damage. These systems may include bar code tickets which are scanned by a bar code reader to get the price and product identification number, or you may manually enter the product by entering a product identification number or name.

Point of sale systems help analyze stockturn by item, alert you when it is time to reorder, keep track of gross margins and maintain a customer mailing list.

Accounting and payroll programs
Some programs may include accounts receivable, accounts payable, general ledgers and payroll. Others may include only one of these accounting components.

Many retailers use technology to aid efficiency

It is preferable to set up a point-of-sale inventory system that interfaces directly with your accounting system.

When searching for a software program to operate an inventory control system, or automated accounting or payroll in your store, you may want to:

- Comparison shop several systems/software programs
- Get referrals from similar retail business owners or trade associations
- Get a demonstration from the distributor
- Check with your accountant for compatibility with their system
- Ask for a list of other stores using the hardware or software; contact them and ask how the system is working for them
- Contract for training assistance and trouble-shooting

On-line services via modem
These afford easy access to market research and current trends on your specific retail trade. On-line catalogs, electronic ordering and payments, and electronic mail are but a few of the technological offerings available as we move toward the "paperless" purchasing of merchandise.

Little Details—Big Success

At the end of the day, what makes Peet's Coffees and Teas so successful? An uncanny attention to detail. They pay close attention to their core product—coffee beans—at every stage in the business. Peet's continually looks for better ways to serve its customers. They keep their retail stores clean, inviting, and stocked with the highest quality, most unique products. Peet's employees are trained to appreciate the details as well. Milk is consistently heated to an optimal temperature for every cafe latte, scones are purchased from the best local bakery, cups are filled to the rim every time, and every employee can answer any question about Peet's coffees at any time.

Peet's is successful because it has placed itself where even its fiercest competitors cannot get to: the hearts of its customers.

Conclusion

Many people perceive retail to be an easy business in which to operate and succeed. The business of retailing requires careful and on-going planning, a love of serving people, a keen sense of the consumer trends, and solid system for operations and controls. Successful retailers also have a knack for presentation. They know how to create unique environments where people want to buy and work.

If you decide that retailing is a great fit for you, muster your creativity, do your homework and planning, and enjoy the retail trade's many rewards.

Part IV
Things to Consider Before You Start

Chapter 23
GOVERNMENT REGULATIONS AND TAXES

About This Chapter:
- *Where laws affecting your business come from*
- *Business tax structure*
- *Specific areas of business regulation*

Introduction

How does the legal system affect your business? How can you use it to protect your business interests and plan for your retirement? We will answer these and other questions you may have concerning the law by beginning with a discussion of the legal system itself and some of the major areas of business regulation.

American Legal System

The structure of the American legal system consists of statutory laws, judicial interpretations, and administrative rules originating from the executive, legislative, and judicial branches of government. All of these can affect your business.

Statutory Law

The U.S. Congress is made up of the Senate and the House of Representatives. In order for a bill to become law, it must be enacted by both chambers. Once enacted, it becomes part of the United States Code. A similar procedure takes place in each of the 50 states. The federal code is subject only to the U.S. Constitution. The state statutes are subject to their own state constitutional limitations, but also must conform to federal law and the U.S. Constitution. States can regulate activities which take place within their respective borders; for instance, how businesses incorporate or the requirements for obtaining a driver's license.

Since different statutes govern different aspects of business practice, it's a good idea to always insist that your contracts with other parties include a representation by the other party that they are in compliance with all federal, state, and local laws and regulations. For example, if you are working with a toy manufacturer, you should ask the manufacturer to represent to you that they are in compliance with federal laws regarding child safety standards.

Judicial Interpretation and Common Law

Common law is made by the courts applying prior decisions

The federal court system consists of:

- United States Supreme Court
- Eleven appellate circuit courts
- Federal district courts
- Federal magistrates

In addition, there are federal courts established for:

- Bankruptcy
- Court of claims
- Tax court
- Customs court
- Court of patent appeals

The federal courts hear cases of federal law or which involve issues crossing state lines or waterways. Each of the states has a supreme court and most have an intermediary level of appeal as well. The states also use local trial courts which are usually based upon county lines.

The courts hold trials, hear appeals from lower courts, and probate estates. They also review the decisions of administrative agencies and the actions of both state and federal legislatures for conformity with federal law and constitutional requirements. In reviewing the actions of the other two branches of government, the courts establish law through their interpretations. This is called the **common law**. The courts use decisions from previous cases that are similar to the one they are hearing as a basis for their judgments.

Administrative Rulemaking

Agencies make law through rules

Under executive branches of both the federal and state governments, various administrative agencies have been established to implement **federal codes** and **state statutes**. These agencies can create law by way of administrative regulation. Many laws affecting business originate from administrative rulemaking. An example of agency rulemaking are the worker safety regulations of Occupational Safety and Health Administration (OSHA). It is interesting to note that in many states, the agencies have established a court within the state to handle the enforcement of their specific regulations.

Civil and Criminal Systems

There are two further divisions of the law, namely civil and criminal law. A **tort** is a **civil law** action where the plaintiff (the person bringing the action) sues the defendant (the person being sued) in order to be "made whole" after being injured by the defendant. Remedies are generally either money damages or injunctions where the court orders a party to cease doing something that is damaging to another party. Punitive damages may be awarded by the court or jury in outrageous circumstances to make an example of a wrongdoer. Punitive damages levied against a company for an accident caused by its known drunken truck driver puts other companies on notice that they cannot allow such acts to take place. These damages are meant to punish the wrongdoer and are not calculated to restore the injured party to its normal condition prior to the accident.

A common example of a tort is an automobile accident cause by the negligence of one person. The court may make the defendant pay money damages to the plaintiff which may include compensation for the "pain and suffering" endured by the plaintiff. **Criminal law**, on the other hand, concerns the rights of society as a whole versus the actions of one person. Criminal justice is enforced by the state or federal government and its purpose is to maintain the public peace and safety. Criminal penalties range from fines to jail terms.

Sometimes the lines become blurred and one event can trigger very different responses from the legal system.

Al's Asbestos, your next door neighbor, knowingly allowed toxic materials to leak onto and contaminate your property and one of your employees was killed as a result. You have a statutory civil law remedy for the injury to your property and you may be able to get an injunction against Al's to prohibit further dumping. Your employee's family would have a common law tort action for personal injury or wrongful death. In that case, punitive damages may be in order because Al had prior knowledge of his dumping. The state may have a criminal complaint of homicide, and finally, the state environmental regulating agency would have an administrative action against Al's for violating environmental laws and regulations!

Local Government

In addition to the state and federal legal systems described above, you should also be aware of local regulations, often called ordinances. These can cover a wide variety of circumstances, such as zoning and building codes, requirements for business licenses, signage regulation, and so on.

International Regulations

International Law: you must comply with "local" laws when doing business overseas

If your company has offices in or does business with other countries, it is highly recommended that you comply with that country's laws and regulations. An attorney whose focus is international business can help in advising you on this matter. Even if the country's laws may seem strange to you at first, it's important to remember that persistence, diplomacy, and complying with the law will always help your reputation abroad.

Arbitration and Mediation

Some states have begun to recognize that the traditional method of resolving legal disputes (the civil lawsuit) is too expensive and time consuming. One response has been **arbitration** administered under the court system. A person called an arbitrator is appointed to decide the conflict and is vested with the authority of the court. Informal proceedings take place under a fast-track time schedule. Many contracts now provide for this procedure in lieu of litigation. You may want to spell out in your contracts that the arbitration is binding and nonappealable, since in some states those issues are left to the parties.

Mick Laughton, an organic farmer in Gilroy, CA, was having problems getting his distributor, Sun Products, to comply with their contract for distributing his farm's produce. Under their arrangement, Sun was required to distribute Mike's organically grown fruits and vegetables to chain stores throughout California. Over the course of one year, Mike saw his customer base slide from 10 chain stores to 3. He asked around and discovered that Sun Products was marketing other growers' produce in the same area. Mike was furious, and telephoned Sun Products immediately to complain. Sun Products claimed that their agreement with Mike was not exclusive. Because there was an arbitration clause in the contract, Mike called in an arbitrator to settle the dispute. The arbitrator ruled that Sun should pay Mike $100,000 for lost business and agreed that the two could terminate their already *damaged working relationship. Despite the problems with Sun, Mike was happy because he was compensated for the damage that Sun Products did and he was now free to find another exclusive distributor. If Mike had tried to sue Sun Products in court, the costs and lawyers' fees would have been prohibitive. Arbitration was a great solution.*

A similar, but wholly voluntary, and even less formal process is **mediation.** The primary difference between arbitration and mediation is that the mediation process is non-binding. The mediator is usually selected to assist the parties in communication, to deliver an unbiased point of view, and to help the parties reach a settlement. Mediation often preserves business relationships because the process is far less adversarial than a lawsuit or even arbitration. Of course, the participants must have a desire to resolve the dispute or the process is ineffective. Again, the savings to the parties in time and cost are often significant.

Areas of Governmental Regulation Affecting Businesses

No one could hope to list or explain all the laws and regulations which may affect your business. Each state and city has its unique set of rules. What follows is a sample of some of the regulations you may encounter.

Taxation

Federal and state income tax

Federal, state, and local governments all have the power to collect taxes. Income taxes are assessed on personal and corporate income. One of the primary objections to operating a business in the "corporate" form is the potential for double taxation. Your company's profits are taxed, and any income paid to the company's owners as dividends is taxed for each individual as well. The legal structure of a business will be discussed in greater detail in a later chapter. Most states have an income tax structure parallel to the federal system.

Sales tax laws may require registration of your business

Sales tax

All but three states have enacted sales taxes, which affect business by taxing transactions. There are many different methods of sale taxation. Some states tax nearly all transactions, including professional services, such as doctors and attorneys, as well as transactions at your local retailer. Other states exempt "necessity" items, like food and clothing purchases, from sales taxation. Others attempt to pass this level of taxation on to transient visitors through motel and occupancy taxes, gas taxes, and similar taxes. Most states that use sales taxes also require that you register your business with the state taxing authority. Some even require a bond in order for you to receive a tax reporting identification number. In a few states, the counties and even some cities have local taxing authority. Check with your accountant or state department of commerce to make sure you know how your business will be taxed.

The Brewmeister

Tom Davenport, maker of a specialty micro-brew, called "Brew-You Brew," was astonished to discover just how much he'd have to pay in taxes once his business was operational. Not only was he responsible for federal and state income taxes on his profits, but he also had to pay the Bureau of Alcohol, Tobacco, and Firearms (BATF) bi-monthly sales taxes on all shipments of beer out of his brewery going to wholesale distributors. He was also responsible for state alcohol beverage control agency taxes in forty states, along with sales and use taxes in each of the states where he had to have a permit to do business. The fines for missed or late payments to the BATF were enormous. After 4 years of dutifully paying all of his required taxes, Tom got so frustrated that he decided to name his latest flavored ale "Tax-You Brew" and to introduce the beer to the public on April 15!

Property tax

Most states also assess taxes against real estate as a means of funding state government. The property tax structure can take on interesting twists, such as your equipment being taxed as real estate or personal property. The nature of your business may have unique tax benefits or unusual burdens, depending on its location. Another issue to consider when locating your business is that many states have adopted enterprise zones or similar devices where businesses are given tax breaks for locating in certain areas. Urban renewal districts can also result in favorable real property taxation assessments. Your state's tax structure should be addressed with your accountant and lawyer before starting a business.

Business license fees

Many local jurisdictions can tax your business under a system of business license fees. You should consult with the city finance department before locating your business to determine what, if any, local business fees are assessed. Some states also assess special fees for regulated professions and industries, such as beer, wine, and spirits manufacturers, so check with your state department of commerce.

Employees

Payroll/withholding

The federal government has a standard system for requiring employers to deduct and pay various payroll taxes on their employees. These include the Federal Insurance Contributions Act (FICA), which is the social security tax, and the Federal Unemployment Tax Act (FUTA). The employer is also required to withhold sums from their employees for state unemployment compensation, injured worker compensation, and consumer protection escrow. In large metropolitan areas, city taxes are often withheld. As an employer, you must make quarterly (sometimes monthly) payments of income tax withholdings to the government. Incorrect or late payments can result in severe penalties against your business! Anyone who has observed an IRS lock-out has seen the devastating effect of the failure to pay withholdings.

Some employers will attempt to avoid federal withholding requirements by calling their workers "independent contractors." In most states, persons or businesses performing labor or services for others (called the owner in this example) will be considered to be independent contractors if they:

Don't forget to make timely withholdings

- Are free from the direction and control of the owner, except that the owner can always specify the desired results
- Are responsible for obtaining all their own licenses and business regulations
- Provide their own tools or equipment to assist them
- Have authority to hire employees to assist them
- Payment is received upon completion of specific portions of the project
- File tax returns as a business and not as a W-2 wage earner from the owner's business
- Hold themselves out to the public as an independent business through business cards, advertisements, telephone listings, etc.
- Perform work for more than 2 owners in a year
- Have a place of business outside that of the owner

You should carefully review the IRS qualifications and your state's laws regarding independent contractors.

Many businesses use independent contractors during their start-up phase. Frank Lang began his kitchen remodeling business by hiring independent contractors to help him with cabinetmaking. As his business grew, Frank eventually hired a cabinetmaker as a full-time employee. In this way, he was able to first grow his business without having to worry about complying with federal payroll taxes.

Responsibility for the acts of employees

Under civil law, the general rule is that the employer is responsible for acts of the employees which injure another person and which occur within the scope of their employment. If your delivery person hits a child in a crosswalk while the employee is on a business errand, your business is probably liable. Liability means money! This is the primary reason why many businesses buy liability insurance and incorporate to avoid personal liability.

Wage and hour regulation

The federal government has established a minimum wage under the Fair Labor Standards Act. Most states have also adopted such requirements. Also included are state and federal requirements regulating "child labor," overtime, provision for periodic breaks, consecutive hours worked, and other such provisions. You should familiarize yourself with the laws and keep updated on the most recent increases to the minimum wage.

OSHA

Worker safety is critical to your business

The Occupational Safety and Health Administration (OSHA) sets guidelines for worker safety. Governing the guidelines are a complex series of regulations by both federal and state agencies. There are severe financial penalties for failure to comply with these regulations. Because it makes good business sense to provide a safe and healthy workplace for your employees, compliance with OSHA regulations is a must.

The hiring process

Under Title VII of the Civil Rights Act of 1964, your business is prohibited from discriminating against someone on the basis of their race, color, sex, national origin, and age. Consequently, there are a number of federal and state codes and regulations affecting your hiring process. You may not inquire about a person's age, religion, or sexual practices. It is a good rule of thumb not to ask any questions in the interview which are not job-related. It is also strongly recommended that you establish a standard set of questions to be used as a checklist in your interview process. These matters will be discussed again in more detail in Chapter 30 *Managing Human Resources.*

Harassment

Anti-discrimination concepts have also been utilized by the government to discourage harassment in the workplace. Harassment can take many forms, such as in job placement and promotion or in permitting sexual harassment to occur in the office. Your best guide for avoiding those problems is to adopt and enforce an employee policy manual which specifies what conduct will not be tolerated by the company.

Your business cannot tolerate harassment

Americans with Disabilities Act

An employer cannot discriminate against the disabled, either in the work force or in facilities which are open to the public. The regulations have been formulated so broadly that they include the size of rest room doors, the height of keyboards, the type of door handles used, etc. You should be aware that these regulations exist and try to familiarize yourself with the sections that apply to your business.

Organized labor laws

The National Labor Relations Board has adopted a number of significant statutes and administrative regulations relating to unfair labor practices and collective bargaining with labor organizations. Some states require union employment or its equivalent in public projects. If you are going to have a manual labor force or bid on public projects, you may want to consult with the state department of labor for the applicable regulations.

Family leave

Many states have adopted legislation providing for parental leave for pregnancy, family illness, and elder care. These standards are often phased in based upon the number of employees. Again, your state department of labor will be able to assist you with these guidelines.

Consumer Protection

There are a number of federal and state consumer protection regulations affecting everything from consumer credit to warranties. Your local chamber of commerce can direct you to the appropriate resource in your county to assist you in complying with consumer protection regulations. These requirements fall primarily within three categories:

Consumers are protected in most states from unethical business practices

Unlawful trade practices
Most states have established statutes which define minimum standards of fair dealing in consumer transactions.

Warranties
The federal government has an "anti-lemon" law which provides for minimal requirements for written warranties in consumer transactions. This is in the nature of a disclosure requirement and is not a requirement that you actually provide a warranty. The most common example of this is a used car. The owner is required to disclose any defects in the car to a potential buyer, but the seller doesn't have to provide any type of warranty that the car will be working next month.

Uniform Consumer Credit Code
The Uniform Consumer Credit Code has been adopted in a number of states. It establishes a uniform system of regulations for consumer credit contracts and government usury, which is the legal rate of interest.

Department of Commerce

Professional licenses
Most states have a department of commerce or similar state agency which regulates specific businesses. For example, the state's real estate division will regulate licenses for sales, property management, and escrow. The insurance division usually regulates the types of policies which can be sold and who can sell them. There are a number of other divisions which establish regulations and requirements for persons engaged in specific business activities. A call to the department of commerce or it's equivalent can often save you a great deal of frustration later.

Business registry
A state's department of commerce often maintains the state's business registry. Its duties include the registration of assumed business names and trademarks, annual corporate and partnership filings, and administration of state securities laws.

Banking and finance
Most states also have a department of banking and finance which issues regulations concerning mortgage lending, money brokers, consumer credit, formation and merger of banks, and bank holding companies.

Uniform Commercial Code

The Uniform Commercial Code (UCC) was drafted in response to the need for uniform regulation in all states for such business contracts as bills of lading, warehouse receipts, and letters of credit. The UCC also regulates bank interactions such as checks passing through the interstate stream of commerce. The UCC was intended to remain uniform throughout the states (except Louisiana, which did not adopt it). The scope of the UCC is staggering. There are literally thousands of pages of commentary written about the UCC and each of its nine articles. Because of its breadth, most businesses directly or indirectly encounter the UCC every day.

The UCC affects almost everything your business does

The UCC is broken down into chapters dealing with checks and promissory notes, contracts between businesses, security interests and liens on personal property, and maintenance of security investment accounts. The UCC also requires manufacturers to protect the users of their products through product liability standards. Some states' commercial codes also regulate bulk sales, which is the sale of substantially all of a business's assets.

Article 9 of the UCC is very important in establishing rights to collateral. It provides for **liens** (comparable to mortgages on real estate) on personal property, such as inventory, equipment, or accounts receivable. A uniform system for filing these liens is established and priorities are defined. This is important when you borrow money and the bank wants your assets as collateral. You can also use the provisions of Article 9 when you place goods with another business on consignment or deliver products and accept a note in lieu of a cash payment. Your lawyer can help you weave through these laws.

Environmental Laws

Hazardous materials

In the 1960's a number of environmental laws were passed, such as the Clean Air Act and the Clean Water Act. Later the Environmental Response Compensation and Liability Act (CERCLA or "Superfund") and the Resource Conservation and Recovery Act (RCRA) were adopted, and together, these affect virtually every business and real estate transaction. Most states have laws and regulations parallel to RCRA and CERCLA. Under RCRA, the handling of hazardous materials is regulated from their creation to disposal. Virtually any business which deals with compounds that could be dangerous to its employees or the public is regulated. Your state's department of environmental quality will often have a complex permitting system for tracking hazardous material from "cradle to grave." If your business handles any chemicals, you should check to see if they are regulated.

Make sure your business complies with environmental laws

CERCLA, and its equivalent state laws, create a method for cleaning up hazardous substances which were previously released into the environment. Under CERCLA, there is a series of potentially responsible parties identified in any cleanup activity, and those parties are then allocated the responsibility of paying the costs of the cleanup. Most of us have heard of the "Love Canal" cleanup, but many of us do not realize that Superfund legislation can reach down to your own dry cleaning or welding shop. Under CERCLA, a new owner of land or even a long-term tenant can be held liable to clean up an environmental dump caused by a prior owner or tenant. The one exception is if you tried to investigate the land's condition before you leased or bought the property. Therefore, it is very important that you review the prior history of a property before you buy or lease it. There are environmental consultants who are very capable of providing these "Phase 1" audits for you.

When Roger Zwicki bought the Morris Paint Company through a bankruptcy sale, he thought he was getting a bargain. Zwicki wanted to open his own specialty paint factory after having worked for a major paint company for over 20 years. However, in Roger's eagerness to buy, he neglected to do some important investigation of the property on which the factory was located. Three months into production of his specialty paint line, Roger was visited by federal officials who informed him that he was standing on a Superfund targeted site. Four years later, Zwicki had to declare bankruptcy himself, due to the high cost of cleanup.

Petroleum storage tanks

Many businesses will use petroleum products in the operation of vehicles and machinery or heating oil for furnaces and boilers. Most states now regulate the storage tanks themselves as well as the cleanup of any petroleum products which may have leaked from tanks in the past. This seems to be the area of greatest impact of environmental laws on small businesses. These cleanups can often exceed several hundred thousand dollars.

Be cautious of any property which has had fuel tanks

Wetlands

Under the authority of the Clean Water Act, the Army Corps of Engineers and the various state environmental agencies have adopted regulations identifying and protecting wetlands. Primarily, these rules involve the filling or other disruption of wetlands and mitigation of any impacts in wetland areas. The regulations go far beyond those "riparian" areas which lay along streams and lakes. They also extend to areas which are seasonally inundated with ground water. Before you start a cut or fill project, you should consult local regulations.

Zoning

The basic concept of zoning is the exercise of government to legally regulate the use of land and the structures thereon to protect the health, safety, and general welfare of the public. Zoning divides the community into districts or zones and regulates each district regarding the use of the land. Check with your local building or zoning department.

Bankruptcy

General

The Constitution establishes a bankruptcy court and requires the federal government to provide for relief from excessive debt through the Bankruptcy Code. Bankruptcy laws affect many businesses and unquestionably add to the paperwork you must deal with when you request a loan. The best strategy for dealing with bankruptcy is to know your customers. Do not let accounts become too stale. Know the reputation and financial status of the parties with whom you enter into contracts. Consider retaining a lien on property under Article 9 of the UCC. The worst strategy is to wait until you receive a notice of the filing from the bankruptcy court. If you do receive notice of a vendor's bankruptcy, you must stop your collection efforts. The best thing to do is gather your paperwork and go see your lawyer. There are basically four types of bankruptcies with which you should be familiar:

Your customer's bankruptcy can bankrupt you if you aren't careful

Chapter 11—Business reorganization

The Bankruptcy Code under Chapter 11 provides an opportunity for businesses which find themselves unable to meet current cash flow but which have assets to come up with a plan to reorganize and pay off some of their debt. The debtor remains in possession of its property and proposes a plan to the bankruptcy court for restructuring its debts. Usually creditors without liens get nothing. Until a plan is approved by the court or the case is dismissed, the creditors are prohibited from foreclosing against the insolvent party. A creditor's committee consisting of the ten largest unsecured creditors is established to assist the court in formalizing the plan of reorganization. Even though the court supervises the plan, it is up to you to see that your rights as a creditor are protected.

Chapters 11, 12, and 13 involve a restructuring of the business and its debts

Chapter 12—Farm bankruptcies
Typically, the land-rich, cash-poor farming enterprise which cannot make current loan payments is faced with cash flow problems arising either from a single season crop which had a bad yield or falling market prices. Under Chapter 12 of the Bankruptcy Code, farm enterprises are permitted to reorganize in much the same way as businesses can under Chapter 11.

Chapter 13—Reorganization for individuals with regular income
Individuals who have regular income can adjust their debts under Chapter 13. This chapter is also available for restructuring the debts of a sole proprietorship. The debtor continues in possession of assets and proposes a plan for payment of debts and reducing appears on long-term debt over time. A trustee collects the payments and distributes the funds to the creditors. When the plan is fully performed, the debtor receives a discharge from all debts except those long-term secured debts, such as home mortgages, whose maturity dates extend beyond the term of the plan.

Chapter 7—Liquidation
This is often referred to as "straight bankruptcy." All states have adopted "exemption" laws which allow debtors to keep an interest in certain assets such as $25,000 equity in their home, a motor vehicle, tools of the trade, and clothing. The Bankruptcy Code adopted these exemptions to help the debtor make a fresh start after the bankruptcy proceedings conclude. At the beginning of the case, the debtor's non-exempt assets are collected by the trustee, creditors' claims are scheduled, and priorities are established. The non-exempt assets are liquidated and the claims are paid pro rata, according to their priority. The creditors with liens on property under Article 9 of the UCC will obviously fare better in bankruptcy than "unsecured" creditors without liens. The debtor then receives a discharge of its financial obligations in order to start over. Many Chapter 11, 12, and 13 cases ultimately end up in liquidation because the plans are not properly performed.

Conclusion

Virtually every aspect of modern business faces regulation to some extent. It is a fact of life. It is a good idea to educate yourself about regulations that apply to your business. Although laws and regulations may seem to be a maze, you can prosper through careful compliance with them. In the chapters that follow, some of these ideas and strategies will be discussed in greater detail to assist you in your start-up business.

Chapter 24
LEGAL STRUCTURE OF YOUR BUSINESS

About This Chapter:

- *What type of business entity will work best for you?*
- *How do you operate as a corporation?*
- *Generating capital through a business structure*

Introduction

What type of business entity do you want to own? There are several forms of business entities for you to consider. Selecting the one which is right for you involves tax, estate planning, and financial considerations. The most common types of business ownership are discussed in this chapter along with the advantages and disadvantages of each. A note of clarification: when a "closely held" business is referred to, it means one which is owned by a few people whose stock isn't publicly traded. Normally, closely held businesses have 25 or fewer owners, and most closely held businesses are owned by one or two individuals.

Selection of the Business Entity

Sole Proprietorship

The most common form of closely held business is the sole proprietorship, which is run by an individual, often under a trade name. In a sole proprietorship, the individual operates the business and there are no outside shareholders. It is the simplest way of doing business and avoids the potential for double taxation assessed on corporations. But, you can be exposed to personal liability for every act and debt of the business and there will be no room for expanding through new owners and their capital. Also, many of the tax deductions available to other forms of business organizations, such as expenses for health benefits and defined benefit pension plans, are unavailable to the proprietor. A sole proprietorship terminates at the proprietor's death, so it is difficult to work into an effective estate plan.

Sole proprietorship is the most common form of business ownership in the U.S.

When Mary Ligori opened her travel agency in 1971, she decided to do so as a sole proprietorship. She wanted to avoid corporate taxation and felt her risk of exposure for personal liability would be minimal. Her successful agency now has three offices and continues to grow. Sole proprietorship has worked well for Mary Ligori.

General Partnership

A general partnership is formed when two or more persons jointly create a business. Their partnership is based upon an agreement (either written or oral) to operate a business together. The partnership files an "informational" tax return, and the partners must also report their portion of the partnership's income or loss on their individual tax returns with what accountants call a "K-1" statement. The Uniform Partnership Act has been adopted by most states and it sets forth the rights and duties of the partners to each other and to third parties who deal with the partnership. It also provides uniform procedures for dissolution and winding up the business. You can customize your partnership agreement's terms to deal with management issues, distribution of profits, and the authority to conduct business on behalf of the partnership. You will also need to file to protect your partnership's trade name.

Partners are jointly and severally liable for all the obligations of the partnership. This means that you can be held liable to a third party for the entire debt of and the torts of the partnership even though you may only have a partial interest! This is the primary disadvantage of doing business as a partnership. Another disadvantage is that many partnerships terminate upon the partner's death, so it is hard to use them in estate planning.

Joining an ongoing partnership to invest in oil well exploration in the South China Sea was an investment opportunity that Jim Carruthers did not want to pass up. The China Sea partnership needed more funding and was opening up to new partners for infusions of cash to expand its operations. Jim's total investment of $200,000 bought him a 1/16th interest in the exploration company. Unfortunately, several months after joining, a China Sea partnership tanker carrying tons of oil was overturned. The environmental clean up required was too expensive for the partnership to bear, and because he was jointly liable, Jim's personal assets were used as collateral for a portion of the clean up. Jim vowed he would never form a partnership again unless he read, with a lawyer, the partnership agreement more carefully.

Limited Partnership

A limited partnership is a special form of partnership in which certain individuals or corporations operate as the **general partners**. They are in charge of managing the day-to-day activities of the business. **Limited**

partners are **silent investors** and do not participate in day-to-day management. Limited partners may, however, vote to dissolve and wind up the affairs of the limited partnership. The limited partners are only liable for partnership debts to the extent of their investment. So, if you invested $15,000 as a limited partner, regardless of the activities of that partnership or the extent of its obligations, you would be exposed to only $15,000 of losses.

Strict formalities must be observed by the limited partners to avoid the joint and several liability of the general partners. The Uniform Limited Partnership Act, which is adopted by most states, addresses the partners' duties, liabilities, and rights in windup and dissolution. A certificate of limited partnership must be filed with your department of commerce and you'll need to file to protect your trade name. Some states also require the use of "Ltd." to accompany the trade name of a limited partnership.

Corporations

A corporation is a separate legal "person" wholly apart from the individual shareholders who own it. All states have laws which describe how corporations may operate within that state. How a corporation works will be discussed in greater detail later. For now, the different types of corporations that will be discussed are:

Most large businesses are C-Corporations

C-Corporation

Most large businesses in the United States operate as "C-Corporations." The letter "C" refers to a subchapter of the Internal Revenue Code for corporate tax purposes. Generally, these are large, publicly held companies, but they also include small and even single owner companies. If you start a C-Corporation you can be the only shareholder, be the board of directors, hold all the corporate offices, and are the only employee! The distinguishing characteristics of a C-Corporation are that it may have more than one class of stock (such as common stock and preferred stock), may have an unlimited number of shareholders, and taxes on its profits are paid by the corporation as a separate tax paying entity. This can result in the double taxation previously discussed. However, this can often be avoided by careful year-end planning.

S-Corporation

These corporations are distinguished from C-Corporations because their profits and losses are not reported at the corporate level, but are passed on to the individual, and reported on the owner's personal tax returns in much the same way as partnerships. S-Corporations are limited to one class of stock and must file their tax returns on a calendar year. They are restricted to 35 shareholders. In order for your company to become an S-Corporation, you must file a special election with the Internal Revenue Service within certain deadlines depending on when you file your articles of incorporation with your state's department of commerce. The S-Corporation provides a substantial tax benefit for the entrepreneur in that it may allow you to pass the losses of your business through to your personal tax return. For many individuals, this has a significant benefit in the early years of their business, because your business may generate "paper losses" (being able continue to run your business even if you don't turn a profit for the first few years) but still make enough money to pay you a salary.

You should be aware that you can switch from being an S-Corporation to a C-Corporation (and vice-versa) only once during the existence of your company. So, if you are going to make this election, carefully consider the change!

Export corporations

If your business is organized for import/export, then you may want to consider formation as a Foreign Sales Corporation, or an Interest Charge Domestic International Sales Corporation. These two highly-specialized types of corporations provide the import or export business with significant tax advantages. You may want to set up a subsidiary export corporation run under your regular manufacturing company. You should talk to your accountant and lawyer about this.

Professional corporation

Most entrepreneurs will not be able to operate as a professional corporation because most states only permit that type of corporation to be used by doctors, lawyers, accountants, and other persons who are regulated and licensed by the state as professionals. The concept of limitation on liability will be discussed later in this chapter, but you should be aware that in most states professional corporations do not provide the shareholders any freedom from personal liability.

Non-Profit corporations

You will probably not want to consider operating as a non-profit corporation because you are an entrepreneur. In most states, that form of business entity is restricted to those corporations which operate as charitable, religious, or educational enterprises which do not have the purpose of making a profit. Any profits which are earned by the business cannot be passed through to the individuals. Non-profit corporations do not have shareholders because the assets of the corporation do not belong to any individuals and most states require that when the corporation is dissolved, the assets must be delivered to another non-profit corporation which operates with the same general public purpose. A non-profit corporation is run by a board of trustees and it generally hires an executive director to manage its activities. That person, and the other employees, can be paid salaries. Typically, you will find your local animal shelters, churches, youth organizations, senior citizen services, and similar types of public service enterprises formed as non-profit corporations. The state will often review and monitor the activities of non-profit corporations to insure their compliance with the state's non-profit corporation laws.

Cooperatives

A common method of doing business in the early 20th century was the employee-owned cooperative. Cooperatives do not provide the owners the tax benefits of a corporation, but they do have the unique feature of passing all profits through to the owners. Typically, the owners are the employees of the business. Occasionally, members of a "community" may feel more in touch with the concepts of a cooperative. A communally run natural food store may be the type of business to choose this form of operating entity. If you elect to do business as a cooperative, then you will need a written contract establishing the cooperative enterprise which describes how it will be managed on a day-to-day basis.

Business Trusts

Business trusts were popular late in the last century, before many states recognized the existence of the corporation. Two or more persons combine their resources and operate their business under a business trust. It is formed by the adoption of a Declaration of Trust and the business is managed by trustees for the benefit of the holders of "certificates of beneficial interest." **Bylaws** are often adopted. Bylaws are a set of guidelines by which a business is governed. Business trusts should not be confused with ordinary trusts, because their purpose is to make money and not to conserve and protect an estate. Business trusts are used infrequently today because some courts have held that they are not distinct legal entities and because modern corporate laws are much more flexible than previously. The primary disadvantage in using the business trust is that the certificate holders may be personally liable, as partners, for the debts of the trust if they retain any control over the trustees. The IRS taxes the business trust as it would an association, so there is the possibility of double taxation.

L.L.C.—new kid on the block

Limited Liability Companies

The **limited liability company**, or "LLC" is a new form of ownership. It is established by an operating agreement which is similar to the bylaws of a corporation. Most states also require that you file limited liability articles and annual reports with the department of commerce. You should have your lawyer assist you in this process. This form of entity combines the best attributes of partnerships and S-Corporations. The LLC is taxed like a partnership, but liability is limited like a corporation. One of the distinguishing features of an LLC is that the parties may allocate in their operating agreement their shares of gain or loss, which does not have to be equal to the percent of their investment. Therefore, if one party can utilize losses better than another due to their personal tax situation, operation as an LLC allows beneficial allocation of that tax benefit. In addition, you may have two or more members of an LLC and you may establish classifications of owners through the operating agreement, unlike the restrictions on an S-Corporation. Transferability of ownership is addressed in the buy/sell provisions of the operating agreement. LLC's can also be used effectively in estate planning. The tax advantages and freedom from personal liability make the LLC an ideal business entity for the ownership and operation of real estate, where there is more than one owner. They are also being used by many other closely held businesses as well.

Operating Within the Corporate Structure

How a Closely Held Corporation Works

Many of you will operate your business as a closely held corporation. It is the form of entity which is most familiar to accountants and lawyers and because corporations have been around for such a long time, the rules which apply to them and the applicable tax code provisions are well established. Shares in corporations are also easy to transfer for business and estate planning purposes. The following discusses in greater detail how corporations work and what will be required if you desire to operate your business as a corporation.

Corporate Formation

A corporation is formed by filing **Articles of Incorporation** with your state's department of commerce or equivalent. This document sets forth the basic statement of why the corporation is formed and what type of business it will be, the incorporators, the principal place of business, and the duration of the corporation's existence. Corporations may have an unlimited life, extending far beyond the death of the initial shareholders. The articles also serve to register the corporate name. Bylaws are the operating guidelines for the company. They set out all the details on how the corporation is to function, the rights and duties of the shareholders, the board of directors and the officers, and how the corporation winds up its business. Once the articles have been filed, the corporation must have its organizational meeting. At that meeting, the bylaws are approved, stock is issued, the first board of directors is elected and the corporation officially begins conducting its business. A corporation is not completely formed until all of these steps have been taken. In addition, your first organizational meeting is a good time to formally adopt the **buy/sell agreement** and **employment agreements**.

Board of Directors

The activities of the corporation are managed by its board of directors. In the case of a single-owner, closely held corporation, the board often consists of the shareholder, one or two family members, and one or two other trusted advisors. When there are several owners, they usually each have a seat on the board, at least initially. Typically a board is five or fewer persons. The board elects its chairperson at the annual meeting of the corporation and the chairperson runs the board meetings until replaced or voted against at the next annual meeting. The board sets the policies of the company. The board will also elect certain officers to be in charge of the affairs of the corporation.

Officers

Typically, a corporation's officers include a president, treasurer, and secretary. Most states allow for a closely held corporation to elect one person to one or more officers. The officers actually run the company. They hire and fire the employees and work to grow the business. Again, in many closely held companies, you may be the chairman of the board, the president, treasurer and CEO all at once!

Shareholders

The shareholders of the company are those persons who own its stock. Ultimately, all power in the corporation rests with a majority of the shareholders, for they elect the board of directors. If the shareholders are dissatisfied with the management of the company they may hold a special meeting and either elect a new board of directors, or require that the board replace the officers or other employees. Their rights and duties are set out in the bylaws. Individual shareholders are liable for the debts of the company only to the extent of their investment in the shares. This will be discussed later.

Shareholders own part of a company by owning "stock"

Annual Meeting

The board of directors and shareholders must each have an annual meeting. However, most states allow for these meetings to be held jointly. The bylaws of the corporation will establish when the meetings are to be held, what type of notice must be given, and what activities may take place at that meeting. The bylaws should also address the number of persons on the board of directors to be elected each year.

Books and Records

Keep good records!

Most states require that certain records be kept by the corporation. The shareholders of the corporation have the legal right to review its books and records, such as annual minutes and financial statements. To ensure that your business remains classified as a corporation, you must observe certain corporate formalities. As stated above, one of these is to hold an annual meeting. Another is to document the major activities of the corporation by way of the corporation's annual meeting minutes. Your corporation should maintain a minute book which contains a number of very important documents, including the registry of shareholders, a copy of the articles of incorporation, the bylaws, organizational minutes and each of your company's annual meeting minutes. The annual minutes should describe salaries paid to the principals, loans to and from the corporation, major purchases or sales of equipment and real estate, leases, and major policy decisions. In addition, the minutes should describe the adoption of employment agreements with key persons, pension or medical plans, reimbursement for vehicle expenses, authorizations for major travel expenditures, education and similar actions. The annual minutes will assist your accountant in the preparation of the annual tax return, and also serve as evidence to support that tax return in the event you are audited by the IRS.

Annual Reporting

Most states require that your corporation file an annual report with the department of commerce. This report may be a simple pre-printed form that indicates that your corporation is still in business, the location of your corporate office, and the principal person in charge. Other states have a more complicated form for annual reporting. In any event, it is important that you file the annual report to avoid the department of commerce classifying your corporation as delinquent in filing and then terminating its corporate charter. While the formalities of operating in a corporate form may sound complicated, in fact, they are not. Your lawyer and accountant are there to help you and they should handle much of the paperwork for you.

Liability—The Corporate Shield

One of the main reasons why people operate their businesses as a corporation is the "corporate shield" doctrine or limitation from personal liability. As mentioned previously, the liability of shareholders of a corporation generally extends only to the amount of their investment.

Limited liability: the corporate shield against personal liability

If you invested $50,000 in ABC, Inc., generally, your potential liability would not exceed your investment of $50,000. For example, if ABC owed $1 million to its landlord and trade creditors, and if you did not personally guarantee any of that debt, then you would not owe any of its personally, even if you were the only shareholder.

It is very important that the corporation strictly adhere to the rules governing corporations so that the corporate shield will not be "pierced" by the creditors of the corporation. The most common reason for "piercing" is because the corporation did not have annual meeting minutes or did not file its annual report. This can have extreme consequences to the investors. Another reason the courts allow the shield to be pierced is when the corporation is a sham and the owners have depleted its assets for their own benefit and to the injury of its creditors.

The major exception to the rule of the limited liability is the Doctrine of Primary Actor Responsibility. This applies to all grants of limited liability to limited partners, LLC members, and corporate shareholders. A person is always responsible for their own actions regardless of whether they occur in the context of a corporation or sole proprietorship.

Let's say you are a $20,000 investor in a corporation, but are also an employee. You will be personally liable for any damages that you cause to other persons even though you are employed by the company. For example, if you are a shareholder of Welders, Inc. and are also the only welder for this company and there is some negligence in a welding project which injured the client, you may be liable personally for any damages caused by faulty welding. In addition, your investment of $20,000 may be at risk if the company is found liable for your negligence.

The principles of insurance as a means of allocating risk will be discussed in a later chapter. You should remember that operating as a limited partner, LLC member, or shareholder in a corporation may not, under all circumstances, shield you from personal liability from torts. The best way to allocate that risk may be through insurance against losses.

A final thought on this topic: operating in a limited liability corporate form may not absolve you from personal liability to the government for unpaid taxes if you are in a position of authority in your business. The government will hold you personally liable to make the payment!

Mechanisms for Generating Capital

Equity Financing

In all states there is a requirement that your business have some amount of equity capital. In other words, the owners must give some value to the company to give it life and to support the company's giving them limited partnership shares, LLC memberships or corporate stock. Corporations, limited partnerships, and LLC's share a common benefit in that they allow the organizers to finance the operations of the business through their own investment, as well as by seeking capital from outside investors. One of the consequences of financing your business through the investment of third parties is the loss of control. These consequences will be discussed in greater detail in a later chapter.

Some corporations use a device called "preferred stock" to raise capital from outside investors. This class of stock is often non-voting and it is "preferred" to the common stock when it comes to payment of dividends to the shareholders. It often has a set dividend payable to those shareholders before any dividends are payable to "common" shareholders. Remember that taxes must be paid on dividends received by preferred shareholders.

Bob's Wise Web Page started out by offering preferred stock to its initial investors at $5 per share. Once Bob's business took off, he decided to offer common stock to later investors at $3 per share. When his company profits rose by more than 150% in his third year of operation, he was able to offer a dividend to those first fearless investors who purchased Bob's preferred stock.

You should also be aware that the federal government and all of the states have adopted securities regulations which regulate the way you can sell investment opportunities, called securities. The federal regulations generally apply if you publicly offer a security for sale across state lines, more than $5 million is involved, or more than 35 investors are solicited. In that case, your security sales will be regulated not only by federal law, but also by the federal Securities and Exchange Commission (SEC) with whom you will have to register your securities.

Many states have similar **"blue sky" (registration)** provisions, but their regulatory thresholds are lower to cover smaller businesses. Typically, states require registration if the solicitation is made to 25 or more persons and over $1 million in investment is sought. Even if your sale of securities is not subject to state registration, the disclosure laws are applicable, and are generally aimed at preventing fraud. Disclosure laws require that the company offering its securities for sale disclose specific detailed information about the company to insure that the public has enough knowledge on which to base their investment decisions. Be sure to consult with your lawyer before making a public or private offering of a security to make sure you comply with registration and disclosure requirements. If you are considering a public offering which requires registration, you can expect a complicated, time-consuming and expensive process. Financing your business is discussed in much greater detail in a later chapter.

Debt Financing

Another method of financing the business is through debt. This often takes place through the traditional relationship of a business and its bank. Generally, the bank will require a personal guaranty of the obligations of the corporation by the principal shareholders of the company, and will most often require collateral to secure the debt. Therefore, in order to get a loan of $50,000 to purchase new equipment, you will probably have to personally sign on the loan and grant a lien on the title to that equipment in favor of the bank. You may have to put up your personal assets as collateral as well. As a side note, you may want to insist on the personal guaranty of the principal of a corporation to which you sell goods on credit. That way, you will have a guarantee on the debt owed to your business by a corporation which could be just an empty shell with no real assets.

A second method of debt financing for closely held businesses is for the principal shareholder to loan additional funds to the company for its operation. You should document these loan transactions in your annual minutes, and prepare a promissory note payable to the principals by the business. The principal may also want to consider taking some collateral for the loan so if the business becomes insolvent, there is something of value remaining for the principals. This is important because if the business fails, a third party to whom the business owes money may attempt to attach the business's interest in that asset if it has not been previously pledged as collateral to the principals.

Venture capitalists finance dynamic, growing businesses

Bonds

A type of capital raising device which is a cross between a stock and a loan is called a bond. This instrument is a security too. The corporation sells the bond to a third party for a fixed price and agrees to pay interest on that amount. The face amount of the bond is to be repaid from future profits on a certain date and the bond holder is given no collateral.

Venture Capital

Many start-up businesses are unable to acquire capital by borrowing money from the local bank. A common secondary method is to look to venture capitalists. These lenders will often finance new businesses but under onerous terms. They typically require the personal guaranty of the principals, together with a lien on all the assets of the business, and in addition, they often require a majority interest in the company through shares of its stock. Therefore, you may find your lender is also your majority shareholder. Many owners get squeezed out of their businesses this way. You should review these circumstances very carefully with your lawyer and accountant before you agree to any such terms.

Government Financing Programs

Many states have adopted grants, loan programs, and other financing devices to assist small businesses. These programs are constantly changing in response to the political and economic climate of the various states. The most commonly recognized program is the Small Business Administration which cooperates with local lending institutions to make loans which might exceed the risk tolerance of that local bank. Basically, a bank will provide the loan funds and the SBA guarantees up to 80% of the amount loaned. There are also many other programs unique to each state. You should consult with your local economic development organization to determine those resources which might be available to your business.

Forms of Ownership	Advantages	Disadvantages
Sole Proprietorship	Low start-up costs Owner in direct control Minimal working capital requirements Tax advantage to owner	Unlimited personal liability Lack of continuity Difficulty in raising capital Ownership limited to one person
General Partnership	Ease of formation Low start-up costs Broader management base Direct sharing of profits	Unlimited personal liability Lack of continuity Difficulty in raising additional capital Bound by acts of partner
C-Corporation	Limited liability Separate legal entity Transferable ownership Ease of raising capital	Activities limited by the charter and regulations Most expensive form to organize Double taxation
S-Corporation	Limited liability Taxed as ordinary income to shareholders Transferable ownership Ease of raising capital	Must have calendar year Limited to 35 shareholders Expensive form to organize Only one class of stock is permitted
Limited Liability Company	Freedom to choose options Tax attributes of a partnership Flexible management Transferable ownership	No case laws Expensive form to organize Relatively new legal entity Limited transfer of interest

Conclusion

There are a number of different forms of business entities, but the most common form is still the closely held corporation. This may change in the future as most states have adopted laws allowing the formation of LLC's. The choice of the form of your business entity can affect how easy the business may be to transfer to your family, employees or a third party purchaser, the amount of liability you assume personally, and how both you and the business are taxed. Before you select an entity, and look for ways to finance it, you should consult with your lawyer and accountant in order to put in place the best business and tax planning strategy. Remember to follow all the rules governing your particular type of entity to ensure that the business is able to continue in that form and that you retain all rights and benefits you intended to have as a business owner. It is highly recommended that you seek advice from your lawyer and accountant when considering the legal structure of your business.

Chapter 25
MANAGING RISK

About This Chapter:
- *What to expect from your advisors*
- *Techniques you can use to protect your interest*
- *The squeeze and how to avoid it*
- *Insurance*

Introduction

You have worked hard to establish your business and you want to protect against risks of any kind. Internal risk might be your fellow investors forcing you out of your position because you no longer agree on the direction in which the company is headed. An example of external risk would be a customer who sues you for damages if your product injures them in any way. It is important that you take precautions to protect your business from potential risk from the very start. In order to do so, this chapter examines how to choose your business's advisors and how to identify and help to prevent disruptions in your business due to risk.

Seek the Help of Qualified Advisors

When you start your business, you may soon find that you don't have all the answers and you will need to seek the help of outside advisors. In this section, the focus is on advisors who help in the legal aspects of protecting your business. You should interview your professional advisors to find a fit in personality, objectives, and business philosophy. Someone who has experience, but who will remain in their career during your business's foreseeable future can be a valuable asset to your business. The hourly rate your advisor charges is one consideration in the overall cost of professional services. Experience and efficiency are extremely important. Lastly, trust your gut feelings. You have not become successful in your business by missing the cues and signals coming your way by verbal and nonverbal communication. Find someone you like who will help you grow your business.

Find advisors you can really rely on

Accountant

Probably the most important advisor you can enlist for your team is a qualified accountant. An accountant can help you organize your books and help you in business management, tax reporting, and strategic planning. One problem start-up businesses have is that they do not take this first step in their business organization. Later, they find that their accounting system is not set up properly, their tax reporting has not been done accurately or in a timely fashion, and that there is no room to grow within the system which they have established. Start-up businesses can perform the day-to-day bookkeeping either in-house or through a bookkeeping service in order to save money. Your accountant can then be used for the more complex planning and organizational issues.

Insurance Agent

It is highly recommended that you establish a good relationship with a qualified **business insurance agent**. Throughout this text we have referred to the need to insure various risks as a means of avoiding disastrous consequences. This topic is discussed in more depth in the later part of this chapter.

Banker

Plan for financial needs before they occur

It is inevitable that during the course of your business you will need outside capital either for major improvements, such as buying a new computer system or a new building, or for cash flow management and operating funds. It is much easier to obtain funding in a timely manner if you have already established a relationship with a banker. It is difficult for a banker to immediately respond to a loan request without having had the opportunity to review your business plan and tax returns, and conduct an on-site visit of your facilities. A periodic lunch meeting with your accountant and banker is a very good way of protecting your business.

Lawyer

How to find a business lawyer

You will undoubtedly need a lawyer for advice in organizing your business and complying with all the laws and regulations covering your business. The most practical way of selecting a business lawyer is by referral from your accountant. They are familiar with the law firms in your area that provide specific business services. Another person to ask is your banker. You might also place a call to the president of the local county bar association or the director of your Chamber of Commerce. The world of **business law** is quite complex and it is recommended that you find a lawyer or firm which specializes in business work. If your lawyer or accountant is not familiar with the types of things discussed in the previous chapters, they may not have the experience necessary to help you protect your business.

Important Business Protection Techniques

Now that you have your professional advisors on board, it is time think through difficult situations which you may confront in the future. You will need to determine ways to protect your business against internal and external attacks. The rest of this chapter assumes that you will be in business with someone else.

Participate Prior to Purchase

If you are buying an ongoing business, you can learn more from the former owner than you could ever learn from a textbook or from talking to dozens of professional advisors. You can observe firsthand what works and what doesn't. It is best to keep your eyes and ears open and your mouth closed.

Retain the Prior Owner in Advisory Capacity

If you are buying an ongoing business, and you have not had the opportunity to work directly with the former owner prior to purchase, you should consider retaining that person as a consultant. The business contacts and practical experience of the former owner are truly invaluable assets in almost any business acquisition.

Keep your eyes open

Participate in Management

If you are one of several owners in a business, you should not overlook your role in management. Because you are in charge of one department does not mean you should ignore the big picture. Take the opportunity to review all management reports and talk with other executive staff to make sure that all the functions of the business are flowing smoothly.

Maintain a Majority Position

When you are doing business with other co-owners, it is easy to lose sight of the fact that the majority owners will ultimately control the business. If you must take a minority position, try to have all other owners have equal minority interests (i.e. all of you hold one-third interest).

Importance of Bylaws/Operating Agreement

One of the first methods of protecting your business interests from internal threats is by carefully drafting the **corporate bylaws** or **operating agreement**. Remember that bylaws are adopted by a corporation, and an operating agreement refers to the contract between partners or limited liability corporation members. Some things you should consider in your by-laws are:

Take time to carefully consider your bylaws or operating agreement

- Location and timing of meetings
- What percentage of ownership is required to call a meeting?
- What business can be conducted by what percentage of the ownership interests?
- How are the officers or board of directors elected?
- Who has the authority to enter into contracts, sign checks, and bind the business to other obligations?
- How is employment handled?
- What method is in place for terminating the employment of those with an ownership interest?

Buy-Sell Agreements

A properly drafted buy-sell agreement is important to the future success of your business, no matter what type of entity you operate under, and regardless of whether there are two or twenty owners. It is one of your most important business protection devices. The types of issues which should be addressed are:

- How can an owner be expelled from employment or ownership?
- How do you voluntarily terminate the business relationship and get your money out?
- What happens upon divorce or death?
- Do you fund the buy-out upon death or disability with some type of insurance policy?
- How do you feel about future generations inheriting the interest of a deceased or retiring owner?

You should consult with all your business advisors to arrive at strategies to resolve these questions.

How to Deal with the Vocal Minority

Regardless of their percentage interest, it seems there are some owners who want to control the affairs of everyone they come in contact with. They will try to dominate your business operations. It is important to recognize these individuals early on. You may have to rely on the terms of your buy-sell agreement in order to buy out the disruptive minority owner.

Avoid Problems from Inactive Shareholders

In some business organizations certain owners will always remain inactive. Many other owners will simply be content in their role as a "silent investor," until things go bad, and then they will take the opportunity to second-guess everything you have ever done. The most effective strategy in dealing with these types of inactive owners is to keep them advised of the business operations by providing regular reports and inviting their participation at annual meetings.

A totally different approach has to be taken with an inactive owner who is expected to be an active participant. For example, if the three partners all agree to contribute equally to the duties of the business, and one is not pulling his or her weight, then appropriate action must be taken. Maybe there is a personal problem and counseling may be effective. It may be necessary to terminate the inactive owner's interest. Working with your professional advisors can be a great assistance in dealing with problems relating to inactive owners.

Squeeze-Outs

The business **squeeze-out** typically takes place for one of three reasons. The company is merged into or taken over by another business, the owners have a divergence of business interests, or one of the owners has wrongfully taken the business opportunities for their private benefit.

A **merger** is a blending of two businesses. Mergers most often happen because two businesses have compatible opportunities. The result can be very positive. Negative consequences can be the loss of opportunity for former owners and the dilution of their percentage ownership interests.

Sally's Sodas, a New-Age beverage company, merged with Just Juice Company, a subsidiary of a major food and beverage manufacturer. At first, Sally's shareholders were enticed by the increase in their share price due to the merger. After some months they were dismayed to find that, instead of having a 10% share of the small start-up, they now owned less than one-tenth of one percent of a major corporation! Their ability to exercise control over corporate decision making was severely limited.

Merger/take-over can result in loss of position

Divergence of business interest or policies often takes place when two or more of the owners view the business going in one direction and one or more of the other owners view it going elsewhere.

Of the three most common reasons for squeeze-out, misappropriation of the business's opportunities is the most difficult. Sometimes an individual will take advantage of the business' opportunities for themselves because they do not feel that the company is qualified to handle those opportunities. For instance, a partner in a construction company might refer a project to his cousin's construction company for a commission if he determines that his own company cannot handle the assignment. Most often it is the result of one owner attempting to better his or her position at the expense of the others. Your buy-sell agreement should address whether all potential opportunities belong to the business or whether each owner can seek to gather and retain these opportunities for themselves.

Squeeze out warning signs include:

- deteriorating relationships
- removal from the board or termination as an employee
- stock dilution
- disappearing assets
- withholding dividends

Warning Signs of a Squeeze Out

The warning signs are not always apparent, but an owner who actively participates in management will most often be able to detect a squeeze-out well in advance of it actually taking place.

How to Protect Yourself

The best way to protect yourself against squeeze-out is to have provided for a fair way of treating each other in your bylaws or operating agreement in the first place. If the rules for termination are well defined in your buy-sell agreement, and if the method for valuing the business interests is clearly set forth, the disputes may not go away, but they certainly will be less adversarial.

Dissolution

There are three phases to the dissolution of a business:

Windup

Windup occurs once the owners decide that the business should stop functioning rather than having one owner's interest bought out by the other owners or by a third party.

Liquidation

After the affairs of the business have been wound up, the outstanding contracts performed, the obligations paid, and the various entanglements separated, you still have to liquidate the assets of the company and distribute the funds or the assets themselves to the owners based upon their percentage interest.

Reorganization

Once the old company has been dissolved, many owners find that this is a new opportunity for rebirth, and reorganization.

Insurance

When business owners get together for coffee at the local cafe, one of the things they often complain about is insurance. They feel overwhelmed and overcharged. They talk about horror stories of local businesses that were wiped out because they thought they had adequate coverage, but discovered after a disaster that they were under-insured. Part of their frustration stems from not understanding insurance and, in some cases, their reliance on insurance agents that were not properly qualified to serve the needs of business.

In the case of operating a business from home, your household insurance will probably not cover your business venture. A separate policy or upgrading the present house insurance to cover the business is a necessary cost of doing business.

Insurance is a complicated issue. Lawsuits abound in our society and uncertainty hurts all businesses. Remember, you may be legally liable for damages even in cases where you exercised reasonable care. Similarly, you may be liable for the acts of others under contract with you. You may also be held liable for property of others placed in your care. All are insurable with the right policy. "Better safe than sorry," is an old adage that should apply to insurance coverage and your business.

Choosing an Agent

People buy insurance in two ways: through an agent or through a broker. Agents work for one or more insurance companies and are paid a commission for each policy they sell. Brokers are hired by the customers and they receive a fee for their services. Brokers generally do business with large companies that want customized insurance packages for specialized needs. Agents generally provide more standardized coverage.

The industry has two types of insurance agents: **direct writer** and **independent agents**. Direct writers represent only one insurance company, while independent agents represents multiple insurance companies. Direct writers tend to be more familiar with the product they offer because they only represent one company. An independent agent offers an array of products from a variety of companies which often means they offer more competitive prices.

Choose an agent the same way you would choose any other business associate or supplier. A good insurance agent should ask you enough questions and spend sufficient time with you to thoroughly understand your business. By asking "what if" questions, the agent can gather enough information to determine all potential areas of loss for your business. For your part, you need to be honest with your insurance agent. Agents can only give good advice on complete information.

Personal referrals are the best method for choosing an agent. Ask your banker, accountant, or other businesses for a recommendation. You may need several agents for the various types of insurance you need. Selecting an insurance agent should be based on the following:

- Personal referral about reputation
- Services offered
- Agent's communication skills
- Cost

Getting three bids and checking references is recommended. You should understand exactly how your premium is calculated and make sure the agent's estimate is correct.

A good agent becomes the interpreter of your insurance needs. They should pick the policy that is in your best interest and is competitively priced. The agent is your contact with the insurance company. You will need to have confidence in your agent should a claim arise.

What Do I Need?

Perhaps you already have some insurance. What type of coverage do you need? There is no specific answer to this question because not all businesses are alike. Insurance is a necessity in most businesses. The standard advice is to only insure against what you can't afford to lose. If you cannot afford to pay 100 percent of a business loss, you need insurance.

In most cases, insurance is required as a condition for a bank loan. In a sole proprietorship, adequate insurance is critical because you are personally liable for all debts. Having adequate insurance is one way to manage this possible risk of being personally liable for your business's default on loans.

Do you need insurance for your business?

Many business owners naively believe their business doesn't need insurance. Even in the case of home-based businesses, thinking your homeowner's policy will cover any business loss is a huge mistake. Even if you have a home office, you are not likely to be insured if your office equipment is stolen or if a client slips on your sidewalk and injures his or her back.

Insurance can contribute to your success by reducing the risks under which you operate your business. As a business owner, it is your responsibility to find out what coverage you need before you are faced with a claim. Don't be fooled that coverage should be kept at a minimum due to the cost of the insurance. The basic steps to begin developing your insurance program are:

1. Go over the coverage you already have
2. Develop a plan to determine what further insurance is needed, and how to buy it economically
3. Obtain professional advice

Ask your agent to look at your present coverage to analyze what additional areas of risk your business exposes you to, and recommend the types and amounts of insurance your business requires. The four kinds of insurance most businesses should have includes:

- Fire insurance
- Liability insurance
- Automobile insurance
- Workers' compensation insurance

Types of Insurance

The insurance industry generally divides it coverage into two main categories: **property and liability** and **life and health.** Property and liability are the most important types of insurance for business. A property policy provides insurance on your building and other physical assets. Liability protects you against claims of injury or property loss resulting from negligence on your part. Life and health coverage is primarily seen as part of your employee benefit package. It may also insure the owner and/or partners.

Most property and liability coverage is offered as a package policy covering a number of risks at once. Many business policies include both property and liability coverage and protect against many hazards. You should be careful with package plans. Do not assume that a package policy covers all of your insurance needs.

Do not assume one business policy covers all your insurance needs!

Gus Rizzo felt that, even though low cost, his package insurance policy would handle any risks that his restaurant, La Dolce, might encounter. Unfortunately, a fire caused by cooking oil swept through his restaurant, resulting in much smoke-related damage. Although Gus's policy covered the cost of restoring his restaurant, he was not covered for the loss of income due to his restaurant's closure. Because he was unable to serve lunch or dinner for four weeks, Gus's losses mounted up, even as his restaurant was being refurbished. Gus made a point of insisting that his next insurance policy included coverage for business interruption.

Property losses must be reported within 60 days, unless an extension is granted. Liability policies generally require immediate notification. There must be proof of loss. If you have a loss, insurance companies compensate your losses in four ways:

1. Pay cash for the actual cash value of the loss
2. Repair the insured item
3. Replace the insured item with like materials
4. In liability cases, pays court costs, legal fees and interest on judgments in addition to the liability judgments themselves

There are other specialized types of property and liability insurance your firm may need. Insurance companies have developed coverage for almost everything. In most cases, all are written as separate policies. Examples include:

- Credit insurance
- Title insurance
- Aviation insurance
- Crop insurance
- Errors and omissions insurance

If you need specialized insurance, your agent can tell you about coverage available. The coverage most businesses should consider is as follows:

Liability Insurance

Liability insurance protects your business if, for example, someone suffers a bodily injury while on your site and sues you for damages. Your insurance policy should cover your costs for these damages. Many policies will also cover injuries like libel and slander (if you are in the publishing business, for instance). The cost of liability insurance is generally related to the risk of your industry. Thus, if your company deals with toxic waste disposal, the cost of your liability insurance will probably be much greater than that found in a non-hazardous industry.

Product Liability

Product liability insurance protects you against injury or property loss due to a product defect or design flaw. The frequency of these types of lawsuits has grown over recent years. An example of this is the senior citizen in New Mexico who sued McDonald's after spilling hot coffee on her lap while driving.

Professional Liability

Professional insurance protects people whose business involves services or consulting. People who are self-employed in fields such as law, engineering and accounting, need professional liability insurance to protect both their personal and business interests. Generally, these professions will be sued for malpractice by their clients for giving allegedly faulty advice.

Completed Operations Insurance

CPAs or other licensed professionals need this type of insurance to protect themselves against any errors or omissions in the products they provide to their clients. For example, you ask an accounting firm to value a company that you're thinking of investing in. After you rely on their valuation and purchase the company, you find out that the valuation was highly overinflated. You can sue the accounting firm for failing to report three straight years of no growth. The accounting firm's completed operations insurance would help them to cover any damages they may have to pay to you as a result of your lawsuit.

Business Property Insurance

Most businesses need business property insurance to protect company equipment or assets that are stolen or damaged by fire, flood, vandalism or other unfortunate incidents. Other hazards, such as windstorm, hail, smoke, and explosion can also be insured. The coverage is written for a specific value such as the cost of replacing a building or its market value. Premiums are based on the insurable value.

Business Interruption Insurance

This type of insurance protects a business against the loss of business due to some disaster. Common reasons are fire or weather damage. It is particularly important to some industries, especially those with a high risk of fire damage, like restaurants.

Commercial Auto Insurance

Commercial auto insurance is not much different from the automobile insurance most of us have on our personal cars. Most commercial auto policies include property coverage for the vehicle itself, as well as liability coverage for damage caused by the driver of the vehicle to other vehicles and persons. Also covered is the cost of injuries to the driver and passengers of the vehicle. If your company has more than five vehicles, you can buy **fleet insurance** to cover them all on one policy. If you are transporting people for a fee, you will need a special type of endorsement or policy.

Surety or Fidelity Bonds

Bonds are similar to insurance. You can buy a bond as insurance for a customer or other third party to guarantee that you will perform some specific action for a customer. Bonding is very important in the construction industry where the bond guarantees the you have the financial capacity to perform. If you fail to perform as agreed, the client can get a settlement to cover their losses. You can also buy fidelity bonds for employees to protect the business against employee dishonesty and theft. Fidelity bonds should be used to cover both cash and merchandise losses.

What about key man insurance?

Key-Man Insurance

One of the problems faced by many small firms is the loss of a key employee or partner. **Key-man insurance** protects the company against financial loss caused by the death or disability of a valuable employee or partner. The key person is insured with life and disability insurance. The business is usually the policy owner and beneficiary.

Life and Health

Employee benefits, such as group life, health coverage and pension plans, are commonly offered as additional compensation in lieu of salaries or wages. Not surprisingly, health care is the fastest growing component of employee benefits. Many small businesses offer benefits to attract and hold good employees. Benefits vary greatly among industries. Manufacturing firms tend to pay more in benefits in term of dollars per employee than the non-manufacturing sector.

Employee benefits are a major decision for most small companies because of the cost involved. It becomes a trade off between retaining good employees and the cost of doing so. The reason most companies provide employee benefits include:

- Recruitment and retention of employees
- Improve morale and worker satisfaction
- Help employees stay healthy and productive

In some instances, benefits are required by state or federal statues. Social Security and Workers' Compensation are two examples. Some key benefits you might consider for your employees are as follows:

Workers' Compensation Insurance

Worker's Compensation insurance covers employees when they are injured on the job and is required by law in every state. Requirements in each state vary. Most require that businesses have some type of benefits that cover medical and rehabilitation cost and lost wages for employees hurt on the job. It consists of two components. The first part covers medical bills and lost wages for the injured employee. The second encompasses employers' liability, which covers the business owner should the spouse or children of a worker permanently disabled or killed decide to sue. In some states, a third optional element has been added to protect the business against employment practices liability, such as claims from sexual harassment, discrimination, and the like.

Workers' compensation is required by law in every state

Life Insurance

Life insurance often comes as part of a health insurance package. If not, term life insurance can be purchased for your employees at a reasonable cost.

Group Health/Medical Insurance

Choosing the most economical and effective health insurance plan can be difficult. There are many providers and policies, including HMOs, private providers, and Managed Care Programs. Your agent can be invaluable in finding the best coverage. Health care is designed to cover the cost of care associated with a serious illness or accident. Many plans now include the issue of "wellness," such as the screening for breast or colon cancer, or high blood pressure. Most plans are either comprehensive or scheduled. Comprehensive plans provide universal coverage to an employee after a deductible amount has been paid by the employee. In other words, they pay health care expenses up to a certain amount. Scheduled plans specify the amount they will pay for each health care item. The cost of any health care plan is determined by the "work" done by the business. The riskier the occupation, the higher the cost of coverage.

Pension Plans

Health care—the riskier the occupation, the higher the cost

Providing retirement savings is one of the most effective measures a business can offer to recruit and retain good employees. Most small business do not offer a pension plan. Only 20 percent of companies with less that 20 employees have an employee-based pension plan. The primary reason is cost. Generally, there are two types of plans: a defined plan that pays a set amount and a contribution plan that promises, but does not guarantee a set amount.

An example of a contribution plan is profit sharing. A company makes a undefined contribution based on a profitability formula. As you know , profitability changes every year. A defined plan guarantees a certain level of income at retirement. The best example is public employee retirement plans where retirees are guaranteed a set amount based on length of service and wage level.

Self-Insurance

Many small firms are looking at self-insurance as a way to cover the medical needs of their employees. Consider self-insurance carefully! Self-insurance is a practice of choosing not to purchase health coverage, but paying claims of a specific type and cost as they occur. The business only purchases what is called "stop-loss" insurance to protect the business against major catastrophic illness/accidents and expenses.

Your Insurance Checklist

This checklist is an excellent means to evaluate your insurance needs:

Types of Insurance	Required	Type/Coverage	Annual Cost
Protecting Your Business			
General Liability			
Product Liability			
Completed Operations			
(Errors/Omissions)			
Professional Liability			
Automobile Liability			
Fire and Theft			
Business Interruption			
Fidelity Bonds			
Surety Bonds			
Protecting Yourself			
Personal Disability			
Key-Person			
Life Insurance			
Medical			
Protecting Your Employees			
Group Health			
Life			
Pension Plan			
Workers' Compensation			

Conclusion

Risks abound in our world. Entrepreneurial businesses in particular should address these risks at the onset of business operations. You will work hard to establish your new business. It only stands to reason that you would want to protect your interests by taking precautions from the beginning. Seeking out the advice of professionals in accounting, insurance, banking and law will enable you to make informed decisions regarding protection techniques. Developing lasting relationships with your advisors will help you with the management of business risk such as partnership or shareholder problems, squeeze-outs and insurance coverage. Take the time now to set in motion a program to protect your business. You'll be glad you did!

Chapter 26
INTELLECTUAL PROPERTY RIGHTS

About This Chapter:
- *What is intellectual property?*
- *How and why you should protect these rights*
- *Contracts you can use to protect your intellectual property rights*

Introduction

When you start your business, your ideas and know-how, otherwise known as "intellectual property," are some of your greatest assets. **Intellectual property law** consists of laws and regulations that help you protect your ideas from unlawful use or infringement by others. There are basically two reasons why you should legally protect your ideas: (1) to prevent other businesses or former employees from unlawfully using your ideas to compete against you, and (2) to clarify who owns the right to intellectual property developed by your business and employees.

Why Protect Your Ideas

If you don't protect your intellectual property, you can lose these to your employer, dishonest employees, or your competitors. Under the Doctrine of **Work Done for Hire**, those ideas you create while employed or commissioned by someone else are owned by your employer. For this reason, you may wish to have a clause in your employment or engagement agreement which addresses the ownership of your ideas. An interesting problem can arise if you are employed by your own corporation. If your ideas are created while you are in the employment of the corporation, and if those ideas have not been reserved by you individually, then the corporation may own those ideas. If the corporation then sells its assets to a third party, or its assets are seized by the court or creditors in order to satisfy the corporations obligations, you may find that the copyrights, patents, trade secrets, and other intellectual property of your business may belong to a third party. This is a further reason to identify the ownership of the intellectual property in your employment agreement, even if you are a single shareholder corporation.

Your ideas may belong to your employers unless you agree otherwise

How to Protect Your Ideas

File the proper form to protect your business name

Business Names

Most businesses operate under an assumed business name. A substantial amount of your marketing efforts will go toward customer recognition of that name and the goodwill that is associated with that name. Therefore, you will want to protect it against misuse by other parties.

Most states provide for the registration of **assumed business names.** This is most often accomplished by filing a simple form with the state department of commerce. Most states provide for either statewide registration or by each county. If your car repair business is named "Action Automotive" and you reserved this name in one county, it may be available for use by another person in another part of the state unless you reserve it statewide. Most states require that the assumed business name be filed at the time you begin using that name in order to offer full protection.

Your business name will be valuable to your business. In the event a third party uses your business name, or one which is deceptively similar, you may have the ability to seek a court injunction to prevent them from using that name. Most often, courts rule that the first business to use or register the name has the right to continue using it. It is important that you register your business name as soon as possible. Even if you register your name statewide, it is possible the court will allow another business to use it if it is located in a different area and does not cause you any harm.

How to register your trademark

Trademarks

A **trademark** is a word or symbol used to identify a company or its services and products. The Nike® trademark swoosh is a symbol of that company's products. A trademark is different from your business name in that your name identifies your business, while the trademark is your insignia or brand name.

The federal trademark office provides nationwide registration of trademarks. Once you have created a trademark you can conduct a trademark search at the federal trademark office to determine if your mark is unique enough to register nationwide. Federal registration takes about a year and is good for 20 years. The mark must be unique and cannot be recognized by the marketplace as belonging to another company.

Trademark

If the Posh Pita Company has been baking pita bread for 10 years and using a smiling pita bread as its symbol, you wouldn't be able to trademark a smiling pita bread as your new company's logo. Even if the Posh Pita Company didn't register its smiling pita with the federal trademark office the smiling pita is still instantly recognizable as the logo for the Posh Pita Company.

A state trade name search will not substitute for a federal trademark search. There are firms in Washington, D.C., which will conduct searches for a fee or you can retain a "patent" lawyer to help you. Some states also register trademarks. Check with your state department of commerce. For most closely held businesses, state registration may be sufficient. Either way, registering your trademark is fairly easy, inexpensive, and very valuable. Register your trademarks as soon as possible to avoid losing your rights to another party!

How to protect your trademark

You can enforce **infringement** of your trademark by suing the infringer. Normally, you would want to get a court injunction to stop their use of your trademark and most state's statutes provide for triple damages to the winner. Merely registering your trademark will not insure against infringement. If a person can show that they were using the mark before you registered it, then they have a valid defense. Also, if their use is not causing you injury or confusing your customers, then the court may not protect you. So, a federal registration for the logo of a local coffee shop probably will have little practical value unless you plan to go nationwide. There are companies which, for a fee, maintain nationwide surveillance of trademarks and can assist you in protecting your mark.

Virtually every retail business trademarks its name. Think of Starbucks Coffee, The Gap, or the Pottery Barn. When these companies were started, they might have been local or regional concerns but they soon caught on and became national chains. If you are contemplating your business growing to a national enterprise, it pays to trademark your name early on.

Copyright

Another way of protecting your ideas is through a copyright. Any original work which can be printed can be copyrighted. Magazine and newspaper articles, songs, pictures, novels, computer software programs, and similar ideas which can be printed are subject to **copyright protection.** Your copyright can be protected by registering it with the Register of Copyrights in Washington, D.C., or by noting on the document itself that it is subject to copyright by using the term "copyrighted" or the symbol ©, giving your name, and showing the year of first publication. However, you can lose copyright protection if you allow publication of your work without the copyright notice. Copyright notices and registration are very inexpensive and remain good for up to 50 years after your death.

Many recording artists and composers have been financially hurt over the years because they signed away copyrights on their recordings to large record companies. Every time a song plays on the radio or on a jukebox, the copyright holder of that song is due a royalty. If the songwriter did not copyright his or her song, he or she misses out on thousands of dollars in royalty fees.

How to stop infringement on your copyright

Enforcement against copyright infringement is similar to the process used to protect trademarks. You can sue to prevent someone from using your copyrighted work or for monetary damages, or both. If the work is federally registered, you may also get statutory damages and attorney fees. Many companies are having difficulty operating in the international marketplace because some foreign countries may not protect intellectual property to the same level that we do in the United States. This has been a reoccurring problem, for example, in China. Bootlegged computer software, CDs, and other printed material have cost American businesses millions of dollars overseas. You should note that the law of protecting intellectual property is rapidly evolving. Many Asian countries are considering stronger laws. In Europe the Community Trademark law will allow one-step international registration in the European Union. In the U.S., there is much discussion about insuring that copyrighted material remains protected as it is transmitted over the Internet.

Patents

Hire a patent lawyer to search records at the U.S. Patent Office

Let's say you just invented a great new way to remove wine stains from fabrics. You want to make sure once you start to market your product that your competitor won't copy your product's ingredients. How do you do this? By obtaining patent protection. A **patent** is the protection of a unique invention or process by registration with the United States Patent Office in Washington, D.C. In order to apply for a patent, you must conduct a patent search. Unless you are extremely familiar with the operations of the Patent Office, you should engage an attorney who specializes in intellectual property to apply for your patent. The cost depends on the complexity of the invention and will often cost more than a trademark search.

Once your search is complete and you determine that your invention is, in fact, one which is unique enough for patent protection, then it's time to file an application for obtaining a patent. The application must describe the invention and include drawings. The process is complicated and most applications are examined very carefully by the patent office. You must file the application within one year of when you start using the invention. Generally, patents are good for 17 years.

Patents are good for 17 years

Once you obtain your patent, you have the right to exclude others from using, selling, or manufacturing your wine stain remover. Once your patent is granted, be sure to mark the product showing the patent or you lose your protection. With a patent, you can license your patent to someone else who will produce and market your product. Typically, you do this through license for a fee or a royalty based upon the frequency of use of the product. Even without a patent you can allow others to use your product for a fee under a well-drafted **license agreement.**

Just a word about using the term **Patent Pending** on your product. If you are not intending to apply for a patent, then using that term may be illegal. Secondly, it gains you nothing. You either have a patent or you don't.

Enforcement against patent infringement is much the same as enforcing copyrights and trademarks. As a practical matter, it is often difficult to protect a patent because of the complexity and the expense. You may want to carefully consider whether a patent application is really the best thing for your business. The application requires that you disclose a great deal about the steps taken in the process and the diagrams of your invention. You may simply be providing a blueprint for your competitors to take advantage of your products without having to put all their money into the research and development of such a product. You may be better off keeping your invention or process to yourself and protecting it as a trade secret.

Trade Secrets/Customer Lists

Trade secrets are the confidential business information, methods, and processes used in your business which are not of common knowledge but which have not been protected by patent registration. For example, customer lists and related statistics are trade secrets. For most small businesses, trade secrets are their primary intellectual property. Without them, the business

Your trade secrets are your most valuable intellectual property

You can use a contract to protect your trade secrets

would have a very difficult time succeeding, and they are often what separates a successful business from another which may not be so successful.

In many states, trade secrets and customer lists are given statutory protection against theft or misuse under the Uniform Trade Secrets Act as long as you take reasonable steps to maintain their secrecy. Even if an invention or process is not so unique as to allow you to protect it by patent registration, it may still be a protected trade secret under state law.

You should also consider protecting your trade secrets through contractual agreements. One such contract would be with your employees. You may make it a condition of employment that all trade secrets and customer lists remain the property of the business and that they cannot be used or distributed to third parties by your employees. You should also consider requiring the employee to assign to the business all inventions and discoveries made during employment. A second type of contract you may need is a **non-disclosure agreement** where you ask another company you're dealing with which may come into contact with your trade secrets or customer lists to keep these confidential.

Typically, misuse of trade secrets arises when an employee has left your employment and attempts to use these secrets to compete against you. The remedies against such acts are often injunctions, where the court requires the offending party to stop using that information and to return it to the owner. Money damages can also be awarded against the offending party, since in many instances, you cannot stop the harm that's been done to your business. Finally, if trade secrets and customer lists are protected by statute, it may be a crime to steal those items.

Non-Disclosure

When Mike Johnson fired his assistant, Shirley Frasier, for non-performance, he never dreamed of all the trouble she would cause after she left the company. As a start-up business, Johnson's Marketing Works provided strategic marketing services to several beverage companies. When Shirley Frasier left the company, she took with her several crucial files on competitive industry analysis after deleting them from Johnson's computer. Because Johnson did not have the foresight to have Shirley Frasier sign a non-disclosure agreement when she started working at Marketing Works, Johnson had a difficult time trying to right the wrongs that Shirley did after she left the company with the files.

Agreements to Protect Your Secrets

Non-Competition Agreements

Non-competition agreements are intended to restrain a person from competing with your business. They are typically used when an employer does not want its employees to take unique knowledge developed by the company when an employee leaves and tries to compete with that employer. Non-competitive agreements are also used when a business is acquired by a new owner and that new owner does not want the former owner to simply start another business in the area, contact all his or her old customers, and compete against the very business he or she just sold.

Most states regulate non-competition agreements, and some also address the content of trade secret agreements. You should have your lawyer check into this and help you draft these agreements so they will be enforceable. Generally, one of the requirements will be that the agreement be entered into at the beginning of the employment. Another common requirement is that the non-competition agreement be limited in time and distance. This is to avoid anti-trust (monopoly) law violations and to allow for future employment by that former employee or former owner.

Most competition agreements must be narrow in scope and duration

Non-Competition

If Sally's Hair Salon were to employ Betty as a stylist, it would more than likely be a violation of these legal requirements if Sally insisted upon a non-competition agreement that prohibited Betty's competition statewide, for 10 years. These prohibitions would not be reasonably limited in either time or distance because it is unlikely that Sally's customers come to her from all over the state. It is also unlikely that even if Betty were competing within the same town it would hurt Sally's business if Betty began competing with Sally more than a year after the termination of her employment with Sally.

Non-Disclosure Agreements

A non-disclosure agreement typically requires that the party receiving information about your business cannot disclose it to any third party or use it for themselves. They are often used when you allow another company to acquire non-public information about your business, such as a company reviewing your operations, books, and records for purposes of a potential acquisition or merger, or where you have retained a consultant to assist you in the management of your enterprise. It is highly recommended that before you allow an outsider or another company to have access to any of your books or records, trade secrets, customer lists, or even inspect your physical plant, that you have such an agreement in place. A well-drafted agreement will also provide for injunctive remedies as well as damages in the event of a breach of that agreement.

Another area that you should think about protecting are your computer files. Make sure that you have password protection for files that should only be seen by you if you are on a network system. Disgruntled employees have been known to erase crucial files before they leave. A tape backup system will help avoid this problem. In addition, more and more companies are focusing their efforts on trying to maintain the confidentially of e-mail correspondence. If you are thinking of starting a web-site on the World Wide Web, it is a good idea to install controls that don't allow the material on your site to be changed or destroyed by a hacker.

Conclusion

Even if you do not think your business has "intellectual property," such property is probably your greatest capital asset. You do not have to be in the business of bio-tech or computer research to have methods or processes which are not commonly known and which you should seek to protect. Who your customers are, and what and how often they order, is vital information. There are various methods of protecting your intellectual property under both state and federal registration and state safeguard statutes. Our best advice to you is to see your lawyer early and use these protections to your full advantage. Now, that's a good idea!

Chapter 27
CONTRACTS AND LEASES

About This Chapter:
- *The elements of a legal contract*
- *How the Uniform Commercial Code affects your contracts*
- *Some frequent contract issues*
- *Leases and some common terms*

Introduction

Contracts are the center of business activity. Without them, there would be no agreement on the terms of purchases or sales of goods or services, and therefore, there would be no reason for your business to exist. In transactions involving the sale of goods, the **Uniform Commercial Code (UCC)** has significantly impacted the common law of contracts. Article 2 of the UCC applies primarily to the "sale of goods" and most of its provisions are limited to transactions between businesses. The following focuses on some of the UCC's most important provisions and identify the differences between the UCC and the common law of contracts and how these affect your business.

Elements of a Contract

A contract can be as simple as walking into the corner grocery store, picking up a bottle of milk, showing it to the owner with whom you have done business for 15 years, nodding, and the owner's entry of the price on your account. All the elements of a contract are present. The owner offered the goods for sale, you agreed to purchase them at a price, and value was exchanged when you got the milk and the owner recorded an account receivable. Now, let's discuss the more formal requirements of contracts and how they may affect your business transactions.

Formation

In order to determine whether you have a deal, the first question is, have you both agreed to the same thing? Under the common law, there must be a valid offer for goods or services and an acceptance of those goods and services at an agreed upon price. If the buyer proposes any alternative term or any variation, this changes the original deal and becomes a counteroffer from the buyer to the seller. The **counteroffer** is then subject to the seller's acceptance or rejection. The counteroffer terminates the original offer and substitutes the counteroffer in its place. At this point, the seller isn't required to accept the counteroffer or even live by the original offer. In other words, the counteroffer terminated the offer and only the counteroffer is then on the table.

A simple example of this would be if you went to a fruit vendor and he said, "Three oranges for one dollar," and you responded, "How about four for seventy-five cents?"

This common law rule caused problems in the modern business world because so much of our business dealings are done by a preprinted form. The fine print of my proposal may be different than your purchase order, which may be different than our shipment statement, and so on. In response to this exchange of paper with conflicting terms, the UCC has a "battle of the forms" provision. The effect of this, in most instances, is that the terms of the forms which are the same are deemed the contract terms, and those which are different, so long as they are not material to the transaction, are thrown out and replaced by the standard "gap filler" terms of the UCC. However, if the terms in the competing paperwork are so different that the parties in effect don't have an agreement, then the UCC provides that no contract was ever formed. The UCC also recognizes contracts established by conduct like the milk buying example, even though a written document between the parties may not otherwise form a contract.

Under the common law, an offer of contract is only open for a reasonable amount of time or until the seller withdrew it prior to acceptance

Under the common law, an offer of contract is only open for a reasonable amount of time or until the seller withdraws it prior to acceptance. Under the concept of **firm offers**, the UCC allows the parties to agree to leave the offer open for a stated period of time and that agreement in itself is a contract.

Consideration

In order for the contract to be enforceable, there must be some value or **consideration** passing between the two parties. In the corner grocery store example, you received the milk as consideration and the grocer received your implied promise to pay at the end of the month. Consideration can consist of many different kinds of value. Forbearance, or the giving up of a right, can be consideration. So, if you had the right to purchase some shares of stock under an option (as discussed in a later chapter), you could agree to give up that right as consideration for the company performing some other duty, such as agreeing to ship you two boxes of parts you wanted. Contracts can also be supported by mutual promises. You can promise to design specialized computer software for a company with delivery six months from now and they can promise to ship you a new laptop two months thereafter. You have a contract. The court does not usually concern itself with the fairness of the consideration unless one party has acted with fraud or under undue influence (with a threat of physical harm, for example).

Capacity

In order to enter into a contract, the parties must have the mental capability to do so. For that reason, most states contracts with minors for unessential goods or services are unenforceable against the minor. Likewise, you cannot contract with a person who does not have the mental capacity to understand the nature of the transaction regardless of their age, i.e., someone with Alzheimer's. Another example of lack of capacity is when the person with whom you are dealing is too intoxicated or under the influence of drugs, prescribed or otherwise, to form the necessary understanding of the deal. The serious consequence of dealing with a party who does not have capacity to enter into the contract is that the transaction is void.

If you sell your new Corvette to a minor, and he wrecks the car that night, you might have to sue the minor to void the transaction and you could be forced to return the money to him, even though all he returns to you is the broken steering wheel!

Legality

For a contract to be **enforceable**, the terms of the transaction must be legal. In most states, for example, one could not enforce a contract based upon a gambling transaction or one for prostitution, or child labor, or any number of other transactions which are deemed to be void for public policy reasons.

For a contract to be enforceable, the terms of the transaction must be legal

The Statute of Frauds—Written Agreements

The "Statute of Frauds" provides that contracts exceeding $500, or which cannot be performed within one year, must be in writing. Most states also require that any type of transaction involving real estate be in writing, regardless of the value or time frame. The writing does not have to be fancy, you just need to outline the essential elements. A contract was once enforced for the sale of a subdivision lot which was written on the back of a cedar shingle. The parties were identified by their initials, the price was "10K cash," and the property was described as "lot 16." Like every general rule of law, the Statute of Frauds is different in every state and there are many exceptions to it. The UCC expands this concept and allows the contract to be any type of written memorandum between the parties, such as a series of letters which collectively could be construed to represent the contract terms. The UCC specifically excludes specially manufactured goods from the Statute of Frauds.

The existence of the goods made under the unique specifications of the buyer is evidence enough that the parties had an agreement to manufacture those goods under those specifications.

Common Contract Issues and Terms

Most business contracts will include many of the following terms. When you receive a contract you should make sure that you understand all the conditions of the deal.

Performance

Performance means the actions you are to complete under the contract. For instance, you might be required to deliver ten desks to an office by a particular date. This is performance.

Price

The UCC will fill a non-existent price term in a contract if the parties' actions indicate there is a contract. However, it is recommended that you understand the price term of your agreement before you start performance. Your contract should also establish how many units you are to deliver, at what price, and whether it is in U.S., Canadian, or Belizian dollars.

Quality Control

Does your contract require an international standards (ISO) certification or total quality management (TQM) reporting? Do you need to deliver a sample prior to the contract becoming effective? Are you building the product according to the buyer's specifications? Are there any tolerances allowed? Does "class A goods" mean the same thing to the buyer and the seller? Have you done business with this party before so that your prior performance can establish these standards?

Bailout

Does the agreement allow for an escape? Are you bound to deliver goods in the future, or is this a single delivery agreement so that once you have performed this stage you can bail out of the remainder?

Time to Perform

If the parties do not identify the time of performance, the UCC implies a "reasonable time." But what is reasonable to you and what is reasonable to the other party may be different, so you should identify specifically when performance is due, both from the delivery and payment sides of the transaction.

Non-Conforming Goods

Under the common law, the party must deliver exactly what the contract calls for or the buyer does not have to accept the goods. Under the UCC, however, if a party ships goods reasonably believed to be acceptable by the other party, even though they do not match exactly with the terms of the agreement, and if the buyer doesn't reject those goods within a reasonable amount of time, then the UCC recognizes the deal.

Place of Delivery

Where are the goods or services to be delivered? Who pays for shipment? Who bears the risk of loss while the goods are in transit? Does the training on how to use the product take place in your office or theirs? Are your travel time and expenses covered? Failure to review the delivery terms of the agreement carefully can result in all of your profit being utilized to pay for these costs. Along with this you should consider when payment is due and what, if any, are the carrying charges.

Warranty

A warranty is a promise or representation about the goods which is part of the deal and creates an expectation that the goods will conform to the promise. A warranty can be created by a description of the goods, a sample or model, or a verbal or written statement. It is not necessary to use formal terms, such as a "warrant" or "guaranty," but a warranty must be more than an opinion that the quality is "good" or some other unspecified term. Obviously, it is best to deal with warranties in writing so that there is no confusion as to what is intended. Take note that you may have made a warranty by sending a sample unless you disclaim any implied warranties on the sample.

Under the UCC and under most state warranty legislation, there are implied warranties of "fitness for particular purpose" and **merchantability**. The shorthand definition of merchantability is that the goods should be fit for the normal use of these products and are of the same quality of similar items manufactured by others. The other implied warranty, "fitness for particular purpose," is where the seller at the time the deal is made has reason to know of a particular purpose for which the goods are required and that the buyer is relying on the seller's skill or judgment in selecting or furnishing suitable goods. Both of these implied warranties can be avoided if in your written contract you expressly disclaim them in bold print and refer specifically to them by name. It is highly recommended that you consult with your lawyer before offering any warranty, and before attempting to disclaim the UCC implied warranties.

Remedies

Liquidated damages: the accurate forecast of cost to obtain goods or services elsewhere

Liquidated Damages

Sometimes the parties to a contract will provide for specific consequences if one party breaches the agreement. This is generally referred to as "liquidated damages." The courts do not allow the recovery of liquidated damages if they are really a penalty rather than an accurate forecast of the reasonable cost of obtaining the goods or services elsewhere. Nevertheless, you should review these provisions very carefully because if they are enforceable they can often be quite severe.

Arbitration

The concepts of arbitration and mediation were discussed earlier. Many contracts provide for mediation or arbitration, in place of a party's rights to bring a lawsuit to enforce the agreement. You should consider whether that is beneficial to you before you enter that term into the agreement. Many small businesses prefer to use arbitration or mediation because of the high cost of trying to pursue a lawsuit in court.

Professional Fees and Expenses

Most well-drafted contracts will provide for the winning party to recover their attorney and other expert's fees, such as appraisers, accountants, etc., and all court costs against the losing party. You should make sure that this term also covers arbitration, defense of your position if the other party goes bankrupt, and other such fees and costs in any appeals.

Specific Performance

Specific performance is a remedy which is rarely allowed by the courts outside of real estate transactions or transactions involving unique and irreplaceable property. The "specific performance" decree requires the party to actually perform instead of granting the injured party money damages.

For example: Friendly's Auto agreed to sell Dana Buckle a standard model American car and then failed to deliver. Dana had to buy a replacement at Honest John's and it cost $500 more than the car at Friendly's. More than likely the court would find that Dana could be "made whole" by having Friendly's paying damages. These damages would be calculated as the difference between the price at which Friendly's had agreed to sell the car and the price Dana had to pay Honest John's for the same car, namely, $500. However, if Friendly's had agreed to sell Mr. Buckle the one-of-a-kind customized motorcycle that Dennis Hopper rode in Easy Rider, *then the court could find that motorcycle is so unique that damages are not adequate compensation. Buckle could not just replace that bike in the marketplace somewhere else. Under those circumstances, specific performance might be required by the court, and Friendly's would have to locate the specific motorcycle he requested.*

Venue

Many contracts will provide that they are to be judged under the laws of a certain state and that any law suit or arbitration must be brought within that state. You must be extremely cautious when using these provisions. The laws of each state can be quite different and what is commonly accepted practice in your state may be unenforceable in another. In addition, your lawyer may not mind handing the arbitration in Hawaii, but you may not be able to afford that if you reside in Colorado.

Notice

Arc you required to provide notice under the agreement when you have reached a certain production level, or even prior to beginning your performance? Whom do you notify and how often, and where? You should not ignore these provisions.

Parties

With whom are you dealing? Is it the parent corporation or a shell with no assets? You may wish to consider the requirement of a "personal guaranty" if the party turns out to be Blue's, Inc., rather than the financially secure Ms. Blue. A guarantee by Ms. Blue places her in the position of responsibility if her corporation breaches the deal. Look at our discussion of guarantees in an earlier chapter for more information on this.

Clarity

Is the agreement written so that a third person (a judge) who is not in your industry could understand what it requires? If you have to submit this contract to arbitration or litigation, it is most helpful if the judge is able to understand it.

Merger

Does the contract require that any modifications be in writing, and does it exclude all other prior agreements? These terms can have very serious consequences to a party who may be relying on verbal change orders. There is a rule, both in the common law and the UCC, that says where the parties intend the written contract to be their final agreement, then it cannot be contradicted by oral terms. This is known as the "Parol Evidence Rule." There are many exceptions to this rule and it is different in each state. However, the courts are much more likely to enforce the parol evidence rule where the contract contains a clause requiring all changes to be in writing.

Estoppel

Generally, a party to a contract may not deny the existence of a contract or a change to the performance under the contract when the other party has begun performing under the agreement and the first party knowingly allows the other party to continue its performance. Therefore, even if the other party's performance is not identical to the terms of the original contract, the doctrine of "estoppel" can modify the written contract.

Let's say your greeting card design business contracts with a large greeting card supplier, Sentimental Thoughts, Inc., to deliver fifteen birthday card designs to Sentimental Thoughts on a monthly basis. For the first three months, you deliver exactly 15 birthday card designs to Sentimental Thoughts per month. Suddenly, you get writer's block and start to deliver anniversary and bon voyage card designs in addition to only 7 birthday card designs to Sentimental Thoughts each month for the next year. Because Sentimental Thoughts has never complained about your delivering only 7 birthday designs per month, rather than the original 15 designs, through the doctrine of estoppel, you have effectively changed the term of your agreement with Sentimental Thoughts that deals with the specific number of birthday designs you are to provide on a monthly basis. In order to make certain that you protect yourself, you should still document any changes by way of letters or other written memoranda.

Good Faith

Many states have adopted the requirement of "good faith" and "fair dealing" in consumer contracts. The UCC specifically provides that every contract, including those between businesses, has an implied obligation of good faith in its performance or enforcement. Many courts are now enforcing these good faith requirements. That does not mean, however, that the court will allow you to escape a bad deal just because it was one entered into foolishly. The courts are still reluctant to interfere much in transactions between businesses. The UCC also provides that if the court finds any clause of a contract to have been "unconscionable" at the time it was made, the court may refuse to enforce the contract or may enforce the remainder of the contract without the unconscionable clause. The courts have been reluctant to apply unconscionability where two merchants or parties of equal bargaining power are involved. The Code does not define the term "unconscionable," but rather, it looks to the prevention of oppression and unfair surprise. It is not intended to disturb the allocation of risk because of superior bargaining power, so again, don't think this rule will allow you to get out of a bad agreement.

When drawing up a contract, always:

- consider your role
- seek legal advice
- read the fine print

Drawing Up a Contract

Your Role

You have just seen that contracts can be very simple or quite complex. You should always determine whether the proposed agreement fits into the way you do business. For instance, if the agreement requires "ISO certification" and you thought that term had something to do with the speed of the film in your 35mm camera, then you should question that proposed term until you understand what it means. Prior to signing any agreement, you should always review the contract's provisions as if the contract was in default and then test your comfort level. Are you prepared for the consequences, positive or negative? It does you no good to enter into an agreement to manufacture 1,000 specially designed highly technical parts when your company has never manufactured even one part to such exacting standards. Can you, and do you want to, perform this agreement under these terms and circumstances?

Legal Counsel

It's highly recommended that you review any complex contract with your lawyer. To save time and expense, you should be thoroughly organized before you visit your lawyer. Outline the key elements of your understanding and any terms which are different than the contract provided to you. By helping your lawyer understand the common practices in your industry you can help your lawyer protect your best interests.

If you are asking your lawyer to draft a contract for you, then you will be dollars ahead if you can outline the basic terms. Look at other agreements which people in your industry have used in the past. The local Chamber of Commerce may be able to put you into contact with someone who has been in that business or you may find information at the library to assist you. You may want your lawyer to prepare a form of contract which you can use again and again just by filling in the blanks. There are even forms of contract available on computer software. However, always remember that every contract is special to its circumstances, and your lawyer should review the agreement before you finalize it.

Boilerplate

Understand the boilerplate before your sign the contract

It should be apparent to you by now that the **boilerplate**, **fine print**, or **standard clauses** found in most business agreements are important. In the event of a dispute, every term in that contract will be reviewed and utilized by one party or the other. Likewise, you should never assume that a printed form is "standard" and cannot be modified. As we discussed in earlier chapters, you should always attempt to modify the form in order to meet the specific deal points. If a contract provides for some "boilerplate" that is unacceptable to you, then do not accept it. You can always cross out or change a term, initial the change, and have the other party do so. Never assume that just because the print is small that the consequences of that provision are also small.

For example, let's assume you are a writer and you have just been selected by a large publishing company to publish your poetry. Just because you have received the publisher's boilerplate contract in the mail, this doesn't mean that you cannot change the terms. Read all the provisions thoroughly and determine which are most important to you. Negotiate with your publisher to change those until you are comfortable signing the agreement!

Leases

A lease is an agreement giving one party possession of another party's land or personal property like equipment for a period of time. Leases are addressed in this chapter because they are one of the more important contracts your business may sign. They involve long-term, on-going relationships between the parties and they often represent one of your largest fixed costs. Here are some things to think about when leasing your business premises.

Area

Do you know what space you actually are renting? If you are in a shopping center or office complex, a suite map is helpful. This map should also indicate common areas described below.

Rent Escalators

How does the rent change over time? Is it based on a consumer price index adjustment, appraisal, or whim of the landlord?

Triple Net

This is a shorthand expression for requiring the tenant to pay the insurance, maintenance, and taxes on the property. These payments are in addition to your regular lease payments. There are many variations to these provisions and you must review them very carefully to understand the full cost of the lease.

Common Area

Are you sharing any space with other tenants, and if so, how are the costs for those spaces allocated between you? Who takes care of it? Who pays for insurance on those areas? Examples of common areas would include parking lots and lawns.

Parking

Is there enough? Is it conveniently located? Are any spaces specifically reserved for you or your customers? Can the landlord later develop an additional building in what was your parking area and leave you with inadequate parking?

Renewal

Is your right to renew the lease clearly set out and is the mechanism for arriving at the rental for the renewal period clearly defined?

Purchase Rights

Do you have an option to purchase the property, and if so, under what terms? Do you have a first right of refusal to buy the property under the terms offered to a third party by your landlord?

Exclusivity

Does your lease provide that you are the only paint store in the complex, or can other paint stores come in and compete against you? Do you want the landlord to be able to lease the parking lot to a Christmas tree vendor, or how about a circus?

Permitted Uses

Do you want your Christian bookstore to be located next to a teenage record store? Is your assembly facility sensitive to vibrations from a warehousing operation? These are the kinds of issues you need to consider if the space you are leasing is in a business park, shopping center, or other multi-use complex.

Conclusion

Contracts are the engines in the world of business. All transactions take place in the form of a contract in one way or another. They can be simple or complex, written or verbal, performed or breached, but no matter what, if you do a deal there will be a contract. Be sure you know both what you intend to do and what the desires of the other party are. The best practice is to put it in writing and don't sign an agreement until you are completely comfortable with it.

PART V
MANAGING YOUR BUSINESS

Chapter 28
MANAGEMENT OVERVIEW

About This Chapter:
- *What is management*
- *Entrepreneurs vs. managers*
- *Creating management that fits*
- *Allocating responsibility and authority*

Ultimately, managers should know enough about all business tasks to direct and measure performance

Introduction

Just because you have sales, orders, expenses and employees doesn't mean you are managing a business. A well-managed business is a viable, organized venture in which people know where the business is going, how it will get there and what their role is. Your goal as a manager is to ensure these things occur. You set the strategies that will make your employees productive and the business profitable. First you need to understand the environment in which you operate and identify your business goals. Second, you need to create the structures and policies necessary to achieve your vision.

This chapter offers a broad introduction to the mind-set of an effective manager. It is a realistic guide to the tasks that lie ahead. Whether yours is a small or large, local or national, service or manufacturing business, the essential management fundamentals remain the same.

Remember, you're not a superhero. You needn't perform all management tasks yourself. In fact, your challenge is to manage your time and limit yourself to performing only those duties that only you can do effectively. At a minimum this includes assigning duties, setting goals and assessing performance.

This is the first step in creating the kind of company that people want to work for, buy from and partner with.

Can You Be a Manager and an Entrepreneur?

The unique qualities that make a successful entrepreneur may not necessarily make a good manager. Think about it. What traits do you associate with an entrepreneur? An exuberant sense of confidence, independence, strong passion and internal drive. The ability to thrive in the face of uncertainty and chaos.

Decide what you do best and delegate the rest

Now think of the qualities you associate with the traditional business manager: strong group orientation, masterful at working and directing others, deliberate at planning, analyzing, and ensuring consistent, quality performance. Making the transition from an entrepreneur to that of an entrepreneurial manager is truly a feat worthy of an Olympic medal!

To do this you must be aware of these differences and identify your own skill set and comfort range. This is not to say that you shouldn't challenge yourself to develop new skills. You must. You must also pay attention to your natural gifts. Decide what you do best and delegate the rest.

Smashed Bagels Come to Hoboken

Angela Minghella loved baking. She really loved bagels. Big, chewy bagels like her grandmother used to make every Saturday morning. She always knew that some day she would open her own bakery. In 1994 she made that dream a reality when she opened The Bagel Smash! in her hometown of Hoboken, New Jersey.

The Bagel Smash! offered 12 different flavors of bagels that could be toasted and smeared with a variety of toppings. But the store's real specialty was "Bagel Smashes"—bagels topped with a choice of butter, peanut butter, fruit preserves, bananas, ham, eggs, or cheese (or any combination thereof), then put into a special hot plate, toasted until brown, and smashed to perfection. They were a big hit!

Angela opened The Bagel Smash! with the help of Eloise Stein. Eloise was the previous renter of the bakery space The Bagel Smash! now leased. The partnership was fortuitous yet completely unexpected. The two had met and hit it off as one was preparing to close her business and the other interviewing to lease the space for her new business. Eloise's small, gourmet pastry shop was closing, in part, because the business was simply wrong for the location. Eloise had operated her business for two years, selling baked goods for special events. Few of the local professionals purchased from her shop during the week as they waited for the bus in front of her shop or made their way to the subway station one block away.

Eloise loved baking and when she and Angela hit it off—she found a way to stay in the business.

Management Planning is Contingency Planning

Good management structures help businesses to grow and meet challenges. Regardless of the obstacles you encounter your business will thrive if you build a structure that fits with your needs and contains the potential for learning and innovation.

Don't think for a second that just because your business is currently small and agile that it will necessarily stay that way. As you grow, neither well-timed ideas nor unique product and services will be enough to sustain success. Don't wait until you have a crisis. Make a deliberate effort now to create the structures which will support consistent performance.

Be prepared: your business will take on a life of its own!

Structures that are intelligently created allow the business to endure by being uniquely responsive to its customers. As a manager of your new business you should assume that your product or service will find uses in markets neither you nor your competitors have envisioned.

In the beginning, IBM marketed machines capable of complex mathematical calculations to scientific users. Blue jeans were created to be durable work clothing for ranchers and miners.

These are both examples of businesses that started out in one area and migrated to another. They succeeded because they had a commitment to evolving their business strategies and upgrading their management structures as circumstances demanded.

You are in the midst of creating the kind of business that people will want to work for, buy from and partner with

Remember that a manager who leads effectively is very different than a "boss." Managers build teams of people to meet business goals and objectives. They give team members the responsibility and authority to perform their duties. They measure and reward their performance, and they create the structures and policies necessary to support the business.

Structure Isn't a Dirty Word!

So you're used to working alone, shooting from the hip, running and gunning—good for you! You ask, isn't installing structures and policies going to stifle creativity and entrepreneurial zeal? The answer is a resounding no.

Structure refers to the manner in which the responsibility for different tasks is divided among the people in a business. **Processes** define the manner in which different people within a business talk to each other and get the job done.

Your task is to create durable structures and efficient processes, not stifle naturally creative fun. Contrary to some people's fears, structures allow businesses to succeed on more than the start-up energy and drive of the entrepreneur. By being greater than the sum of its parts, your business can tackle the challenges that confront it with unrivaled excellence, reliability, and innovation.

A Smashing Partnership

So in the spring of 1994, Eloise and Angela began building a new business together. They knew their biggest challenge was earning the loyalty of repeat customers. Their target? The hundreds of professional commuters who passed within 100 yards of their shop, twice a day, on their way into and out of Manhattan. The Bagel Smash! had stiff competition from the Starbuck's coffee down the street and a large national bagel chain two blocks away. If they were to succeed, The Bagel Smash! would have to be managed impeccably.

Eloise and Angela evaluated the business and the market, then identified the following key managerial objectives:

- *Absolute cleanliness and sanitary conditions*
- *Top of the line individual customer service*
- *The best, freshest, most authentic bagels available*
- *The most delicious and original toppings and combinations for bagel smashes*
- *A speedy, efficient, minimal wait service environment*
- *Well trained, highly motivated, happy counter staff*

Neither Angela or Eloise had a problem with working long hours. They knew it came with the territory, and looked forward to the challenge. But, together they wanted to build a business that would operate smoothly and reliably, even in their absence. Angela was the mother of a two year old, and Eloise still enjoyed preparing specialty cakes for custom orders. Neither wanted to run a business that caused them undue stress because things didn't work and jobs weren't done effectively.

Most importantly, they knew they simply couldn't afford a second chance to earn their local customers' loyalty.

They knew the secret lay in a well-conceived management structure and operational processes.

Creating the Right Management Fit

Smart entrepreneurs design their businesses and decide how tasks will be performed with an eye on their own working style. Since you will be the leader of the business, the place to begin is with you. What type of environment do you thrive in? What kind of people do you most enjoy working with? Reflect on the 'feeling' you want your business and office to have. What sort of behavior do you want to encourage and reward?

Business "fit" is important

Think about the following:

- My dream job is...
- My dream office looks like...
- My dream co-worker acts like...
- I work best when I can...
- I communicate best with people by...
- To achieve unrivaled excellence I require...

Hey, you're the boss! That means that you can create any kind of environment that you want. Open your heart and your mind, and remember the only one limiting your choices is you.

Next, to create a good fit, review your business goals. What values spring to mind as you review your **mission statement**? Discuss these with your friends, family and advisors. Focus on your business's main objectives.

Good managers design their companies to maximize their business's unique strengths. Today corporate managers define these as **core competencies**. This is just a fancy way of describing the things that your business does better than any competitor. They must also be key activities that your customers value. In the course of managing your business you should repeatedly renew focus on your core competencies. Your goal is to leverage these strengths for maximum competitive advantage.

Lastly, business management must fit with the industry and the markets in which it competes. Most good managers examine who their customers and competitors are, industry trends, and the strengths of competing products and services. These elements impact how businesses design and perform internal functions such as marketing, finance, accounting and sales.

Structures support performance and growth

Smashing and Other Activities...

Before Angela and Eloise hired anyone or sold a single bagel (though Angela was testing recipes and baking test batches every night into the wee hours...) they decided to sit down and list the key activities that needed to be performed at the Bagel Smash! They decided to describe how critical each one was to the business's success. This way they could begin to see a picture of where they needed to concentrate the most time, energy and resources. They ordered their list from most critical to least critical:

Most Critical Activities	*Critical Activities*	*Least Critical Activities*
1. Baking bagels	*1. Cleaning the store*	*1. Ordering supplies*
2. Serving customers	*2. Organizing the store*	*2. Managing supplies*
3. Training	*3. Pricing and promotion*	*3. General maintenance*
4. Managing cash	*4. Coffee making*	*4. New product decisions*
5. Cleaning the store	*5. Financial planning*	*5. New locations*
6. Employee management	*6. Budgeting*	*6. Community activities*
7. Payroll and accounting	*7. Long range planning*	*7. New technology review*

With this list in hand, Eloise and Angela began to form a picture of their successful business. They realized that, the activities that were most critical to the store's success, were activities that they both enjoyed doing the most. This reconfirmed their beliefs that they had chosen the right business to open!

Angela took responsibility for all bagel baking. She would work from 4 a.m. until 10 a.m., baking bagels then helping to serve the morning rush of customers. She knew it was essential that the store's bagels be consistently fresh and delicious. She would be the bagel "chief," baking all bagels for the first 3-6 months. Then, as business warranted, she would hire and train an experienced baker or two to help. Angela would also order and manage all supplies.

Eloise took responsibility for managing the store. She would ring up all sales, price the bagels, prepare all toasted bagels and smashes, train all non-baking employees, and maintain the store's impeccable organization and cleanliness. In short, she would do what she loved: creating a welcoming and smooth running environment where customers came first. It would be a special type of neighborhood bakery, with fast service, friendly faces, and yummy food that she had always wanted to run.

The First Step: Identify Activities

The first step in designing management structures is to identify the key activities of the business. Which are key to your continual survival and success? Which are less critical on a daily basis but important for on-going performance? Some of these activities may be specific to your business, and may not fit neatly into traditional functional categories. Listed below are the functions that most businesses must perform.

Many these are discussed in greater detail in other areas of this book. For now, you should use this list as a starting point for your own brainstorming.

- Accounting
- Inventory
- Human Resources
- Marketing & Sales
- Logistics Management
- Quality Control
- Financial Planning & Budgeting
- Research & Development
- Manufacturing
- Engineering
- Customer service
- Purchasing

Think of these traditional functions as processes that your business goes through everyday. While you're at it, consider how you can improve performance. Try the following exercise as you define these functions to fit your business.

Invent the structures today to support your vision tomorrow

Identifying, Simplifying and Allocating Tasks

Task	Explanation
Identify	Look at your past and future performance. Review the different ways you get various tasks completed. Define a "good" or "successful" process. Pool insights of your team.
Set the boundaries of these tasks	Identify context in which you perform individual tasks. Separate one task from another. These are discrete service jobs that your business performs.
Identify ways to simplify your tasks	Pare down individual tasks to the most basic elements. How can you make them more efficient? This focus allows you to avoid redundancies.
Allocate the necessary resources	Identify what your business requires to perform highest quality work. This is the starting point for creating a system of budgetary forecasts and controls.

The three processes

Now is a good time to consider the different categories of tasks businesses perform. **Operational processes** directly create value for your customers, employees, owners and stakeholders. **Strategic planning** and **controlling processes** create the context and resources for operational processes. They provide short and medium term guidance to steer operations. Some of these processes include developing performance measures, setting policies regarding rewards and recognition, and allocating resources. Lastly, **navigational processes** create the purpose and character of a business. These envision the future of the business, decide how decisions are made, how people interact, and define overall organizational objectives.

3 key processes:

- operations
- planning
- controlling

Step Two: Allocate Tasks

The next step businesses take is to allocate responsibility for various tasks. Since you might be the only employee your business has, begin by asking yourself which tasks you do particularly well. Which tasks are you less comfortable with? Where are you cutting corners because you lack the time, interest, or expertise?

Based on this, identify the key activities you will perform and those you will delegate.

If you have a team assembled, which individuals, personalities, and qualifications fit with which tasks? Chances are you or your employees are or will be performing several tasks at once. What are these? Do the individual tasks you are performing logically fit together? Would it be more efficient to separate tasks and reassign them among your team?

When we use the word "team," we are not necessarily referring to a group of full-time employees hired by your business. It can be a **virtual team** composed of you and a collection of part-time or outside service providers. This concept of a virtual team, or the management team that works together via phone, fax and computer modem, is an important one for many businesses today. It allows you to benefit from the skills of many different people without actually having them inside your business.

Outsourcing at the Bagel Smash!

Once the "most critical" duties were sorted out, Eloise and Angela began to look at less critical items. Who would manage payroll? Clean the store? Price the menu?

The partners decided that they simply didn't have the time or energy to do all of the duties themselves. They would have to allocate some tasks to full or part-time employees, or even outside contractors.

The financial management of the business concerned them. Neither knew very much about accounting (and neither had much interest, for that matter). So they decided they would use the accountant that had helped Eloise manage her business. Art Donner was a long-time accountant and financial manager, who worked part-time with many small business clients. They met with him and worked out a contract whereby he would keep all of their books, manage payroll and pay bills. He would meet with Eloise and Angela every two weeks to review the business's financial health. If and when they needed additional financing for equipment or an upgrade of their store, he could help them do that too.

The remaining duties of cleaning and organizing the store, making coffee and ringing up sales during peak business hours, would be handled by 3-4 part-time counter employees that would be hired and trained by Eloise.

Outsourcing

Outsourcing refers to the practice of hiring people outside of your business to perform tasks. These can include but are not limited to accounting, marketing and sales, purchasing, inventory management, and market research. Today large companies do this to reduce their overhead, "remove" costs from their income statement, and focus their resources on their core strengths.

This strategy can offer start-up businesses many benefits. You have limited resources and time, and you must carefully choose the battles you will wage. If others can do something better than you, why not benefit from their expertise? Allow them to make your business more competitive by contracting with them to do what they do best.

Focus!

Having identified which tasks you can do best and allocated responsibility for the rest, you must discipline yourself to focus on your activities. One of the biggest challenges for entrepreneurs is to contain their impulse to try to do everything. The key to being a successful entrepreneur is knowing enough about all of the elements of managing a business to be able to identify quality performers when you see them, and let them do their jobs.

Step Three: Set Expectations

The next step in creating management systems is to set goals and objectives for people performing tasks in your business. What can the business expect of each person? Who should be held accountable for specific tasks? What is the time frame for task completion and assessment?

The dedication, vision, and ethics of a manager determines whether a business is managed or mismanaged

Building a great organizational structure takes time. It also takes a real commitment to thinking critically and creatively about your business. Give your team plenty of time to learn how to work together and share ideas. And, most importantly, try to identify what each person needs to do to help others perform best.

Other Issues

We have listed some other issues for you to consider as you go about making your management systems responsive to the market, your customers, your suppliers, and your employees.

Good Communication

One of the biggest obstacles for businesses is poor communication. How do different people, separated by space, time and different operating styles communicate and work together? Imagine an army in which privates set their own marching orders without ever hearing from the general. Obviously, things would not run well. For businesses, failure to design effective communication practices can lead to marketers selling at the wrong price, financial planners creating wrong budgets and operations producing the wrong products. Failure to communicate can also lead to:

- A lack of cooperation
- Poor coordination between different functions
- Inefficient use of time and resources
- Missed opportunities for creative problem solving
- Diminished "team spirit" and morale

- A resistance to change
- A lack of discipline
- Failure to meet long-term goals

How do start-up businesses ensure that effective communication is built into their businesses? They begin by establishing formal practices like scheduling daily or weekly staff meetings. In these, members can be updated on goals and performance, raise questions and gather feedback. The following are a few additional suggestions to ensure a reliable flow of information within your business:

The biggest obstacle in business is communication

- Regularly compile and circulate a 1 page operating report of problems and proposed solutions
- Schedule a 'war room' meeting for all core members of the team
- Schedule regular company sessions to address issues, problems and opportunities
- Pursue suggestions for process, product and structural improvements in your business
- Manage by walking around; don't stay in your office
- Rotate the responsibility to present a profile of one of your business's key customers or key competitors
- Don't be afraid to open your "books" to employees

Job Descriptions at The Bagel Smash!

Together, Angela and Eloise described what their employees would have to do, how they would be evaluated, and how each job would fit within the overall business. They focused on the counter employees, who would be the "face" and personality of the store for customers:

"All counter employees of The Bagel Smash! should think of working at the store as an opportunity to meet the entire neighborhood and become friends with the people who come in. Customers are neighbors to us. You will be responsible for treating customers are they would a very special guest in your home. You will "take ownership" of a customer as soon as they enter the door. Smile. Greet them, take their order, make their Smash and cash out their sale. Thank them for their business! Most customers are in a rush, particularly in the morning, so speed is of the essence. All counter employees will know how to work and "trouble-shoot" all equipment including the cash register. The customer experience will be a seamless one: in the door, ordering, paying, and out the door with their bagel in under 5 minutes."

Angela saved the "less fun" duties of the job for last:

"At the end of each shift, employees will sweep the store, (mopping only for closing shifts), thoroughly clean counters, wipe down smashing machine, cash register, all table tops, display counter, coffee area, and clean the bathroom. You will restock any supplies and list any inventory that needs to be reordered."

Map Out Your Business

Businesses often create an **organizational chart** to represent the way different functions of the business fit together. Think of this as a strategic map or a visual record of the relationships among people. How will your group function and how will your people report and communicate with one another?

Most businesses link their people on the basis of function, products, or the geographic regions they serve. Consider any configuration that is appropriate to your needs, but remember to keep it simple.

The most common structure for businesses is **functional**. Functional structures are created on the basis of the different major tasks performed by the business. In its simplest form, the functional organization chart begins with the President or CEO and moves down to include sales and marketing,

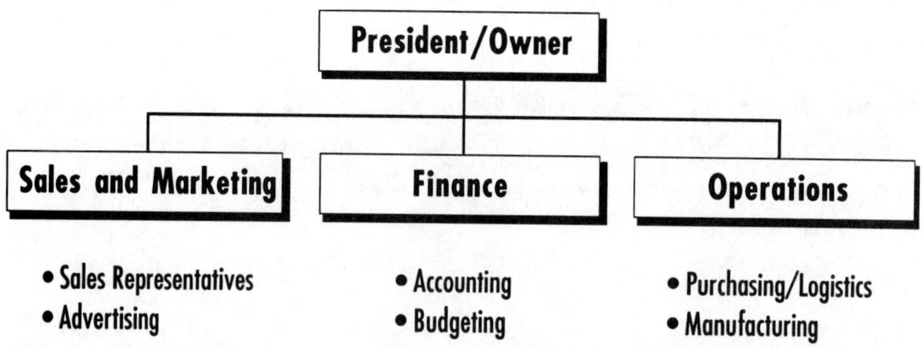

Functionalization allows businesses to easily group people who share responsibilities and basic skill sets. They are best for performing hiring, firing, training, and coaching of people within individual functions. Functional managers can also best determine the specific resources they require to get their job done. This can include personnel, equipment, time, information, and budgets. Functional managers play a key role in cost and quality control since they understand their specific tasks better than anyone else.

An example of a business structured along functional lines would be a metal foundry that supplies small parts to tractor manufacturers. It has a finance department to manage financial resources, an accounting department to allocate costs, a marketing and sales department to identify the product, pricing, promotional and distribution strategies, and a manufacturing department that produces the goods. Each functional area works together to achieve overall organizational goal of manufacturing and marketing high quality tractor parts.

Some of the downsides of this type of structure is diminished customer orientation, less employee flexibility and a tendency to focus on narrow tasks rather than overall business goals.

Testing Structural Integrity

Buildings and bridges aren't the only things that need to be checked and re-checked for structural flaws and weaknesses. Develop the habit of looking back on structures you've created and decisions you've made in the past. In addition, review the assumptions on which you've based these. Using the following criteria, test the appropriateness of each of your business practices:

- Does it provide a means for getting into business more quickly?
- Does it lower the risk of market entry?
- Does it enhance flexibility?
- Does it build on your personal strengths?
- Does it maximize your business's resources?
- Does it allow you to evolve and redirect resources easily?
- Does it make your business attractive to investors/lenders?
- Is it appropriate for your kind of industry?
- Is it consistent with the kind of life you want to lead?
- Can it result in the kind of company you're proud to call your own?

A good fit here creates a powerful and effective management strategy. All management decisions should be guided by your short and long term goals. Likewise, the way a business is managed is impacted by internal and external factors.

Below is a chart that summarizes these factors that impact your past and future management decisions.

Short Term Goals	Long Term Goals	Internal FIT	External FIT
Sales targets	Employee growth	Your personal goals	Your customer
New orders	Sales targets	Your personality	Your market
Turn-around time	New markets	Your ideal corporate culture	Your industry
Cost control	New products	Your business goals	Your competitors
Market share	New learning	Your product	Time constraints
Hiring goals	Profitability	Your personal skills	Financing
Project goals	Market share	Your business' core competencies	Prices
Work team goals	Partnering	Your resources	Supplier mix
Cash management	Selling the business		Partners
	New products		New products
	Attracting talent		

Get Advice

One of the most important things you can do for your business is get outside advice. Ask a mentor, a colleague or professor to evaluate the way you plan to structure your start-up. If you can afford it, try a paid consultant. Today, there are more voices of experience for entrepreneurs than ever before. You should also seek out advice from friends or business acquaintances who work in larger businesses. How did their company tackle similar issues? Your motto here is to learn from the successes and mistakes of others. Then improve upon their ideas and tailor their advice to fit your business.

The Bagel Smash! Management Processes

Angela and Eloise did not want The Bagel Smash! to ever become a huge operation. It was conceived of as a neighborhood spot, where regulars could drop in, get their Smash and a coffee. Customers could hang out if they had time, or be on their way if they didn't.

The owners imagined at most they would have a team of 10 - 12 employees, including bakers and counter people. To keep the tight, family feel of the business they decided that every month all employees would meet for an afternoon tea at the store. This would be an opportunity to voice concerns, ask questions, make suggestions for product or customer service improvements, and just chat.

The Bagel Smash! would have no formal hierarchy or management structure. People would fulfill their specific job responsibilities and if they wanted to do more or help out in other areas, they could. Eloise and Angela were quite happy to evaluate employees' talents and interests, and match the job to fit them. They wanted happy, satisfied team members. They wanted a group that was guided by a shared purposed of making the customers of The Bagel Smash! happy and loyal.

How Will Your Business Look?

This is a good time to talk about physical appearances. Take some time to consider the way your working space will look.

Don't underestimate the importance of the physical layout of your work space. Remember that summer job you had at the real-estate office where there were no windows? Or the flickering track lighting that made your head pound and sapped your energy? Or the messy warehouse where you couldn't find anything?

Many extraordinarily successful businesses allow their employees to stamp their own personality on their work space. This includes but is not limited to bringing pets to work (one software company even has dog food stations), creating larger kitchens for lunch time cook-ins, selecting music to work by, and rearranging the work space to fit employee preferences.

Design your place of work to be inspiring, comfortable and encourage team work. Most of all, it should be appropriate for your needs. The space you create is a powerful tool that can help make you and your employees happy, productive and successful!

Management tip: encourage creativity and innovation

Entrepreneurial Management Tips

- Stay true to your vision
- Remain flexible
- Encourage creativity
- Do what you do best and give the rest to others
- Focus on your customer
- Control costs and conserve cash
- Respect your people
- Do things that result in the kind of company you're proud to call your own

One of the most valuable things businesses can do is ensure that they have fun and work creatively. The more people enjoy their work, the better they perform. The more creative businesses are, the more innovative they can be in solving problems and outperforming competitors. The happier your employees are the better they will serve customers.

For the entrepreneur, this is the icing on the cake. You've designed your ideal company. Consider whether or not the business you've created is one in which you want to work. If there's any doubt, you need to question how you've structured your business. Make your business fun, flexible and innovative. Here are several ideas for making your business more fun.

Top 10 Ways to Have Fun & Be Creative

- Hire curious and creative people
- Take vacations
- Encourage different interaction patterns through physical work space
- Bring in guest speakers and pursue interesting educational programs
- Measure your curiosity daily
- Make your work space wacky and colorful
- Give a party for your best clients
- Take your employees on a picnic
- Rearrange your schedule and insert random activities
- Send your employees to a ballgame

Making the Team a Reality at The Bagel Smash!

To ensure team spirit and shared purpose, Eloise suggested that employees who stayed for the entire first six months of operation (a long time for a retail operation!) would get a percentage of the profits the store earned. All employees would be trained for 3 days (7 baking days for bakers) and evaluated by the owners after their first two weeks. After that, their performance at The Bagel Smash! would be evaluated every 6 months. Angela suggested the idea that the employees also be able to evaluate the owners' performance. Eloise loved the idea! They decided that at their employee afternoon teas they would collect and discuss "Eloise and Angela Scorecards." They liked the idea of 360 degree feedback and improvement...and worked to make it a reality.

At these meetings, The Bagel Smash! employees would also get a health report for the business. At any given time, Angela wanted employees to know about daily sales, major costs, sources of revenue and profitability. She believed that employees with a big picture of the business would perform better and have greater pride in the business. This "open book" policy has worked well for them.

The management planning and brainstorming that Angela and Eloise did clearly paid off. Today the business is thriving. It has become the favorite of locals. A one-of-a-kind treasure, drawing customers on weekends from Manhattan, Newark and beyond. Angela and Eloise are contemplating a change from their original plans: opening a second store!

Conclusion

In designing your new company, you are doing nothing less than creating a model work environment. And why not? You know better than others what makes for a good, productive work place for you. Here you are concerned with creating the business that will perform all of its tasks in a uniquely competitive way.

You are creating a business structure that protects the spirit of independence and creativity. At the same time it must fit with your management style, personality and environment. Defining tasks, processes, organizations and structures that will help you manage your business is a definite priority. You should manage by design, not by default.

In addition, you are designing the kind of business where you will want to spend your time. Keep an eye on your long-term goals and don't get discouraged by the details of creating the organization. Chances are, you've already encountered most of these elements at some point in your life. So roll up your sleeves, take a deep breath, and have fun as you dive into the task of designing the way your business will be managed.

Chapter 29
FORMING AND MANAGING TEAMS

About This Chapter:
- *What is a team?*
- *A leader versus the boss*
- *Teamwork challenges*

Introduction

This section will introduce you to the basics of creating, managing, and benefiting from teams within your business. As an entrepreneur it is especially important for you to understand the process of building a team. This relates directly to your ability to be something more than a short lived, one-person success story. Team building skills will allow you to be an effective leader and organization builder—the cornerstone for growing a successful company.

What is a Team ?

A **team** is a group of people who work together to achieve shared objectives, each contributing individual strengths and sharing rewards. It may seem silly to remind you of such a simple concept, but, given the multiple challenges an organization faces both internally and externally, operating a team can become very complicated. It's important to return to this basic understanding of what teams are, and why they are created. Creating an organization in which teams can perform and flourish should be a key part of your overall strategy for growth.

Groups versus teams

It has been said that a team is the fundamental building block of an organization. Family units, groups of friends and civic organizations demonstrate that a collection of individuals will naturally divide into groups with different allegiances. A team, however, is not naturally occurring. Teams must be initiated and built. Ideally, a team is defined by **participatory leadership**, shared responsibility, open communication, joint purpose and focus on the future. A team that is performing at its highest level responds rapidly and creatively to challenges. Do you think your business is oriented towards groups or teams?

There are many types of functions that teams can perform within a business. Among those presented below, choose which you would benefit from, and which is most appropriate to the type of business you operate. The categories of teams presented below are in hierarchical order from the most detailed to the most basic.

Conquer challenges with teamwork!

- **Strategic Planning Teams:** Determine strategy, mission and policy
- **Issue Managing Teams:** Responsible for specific technology or work issues
- **Directing Teams:** On-going but part-time teams charged with managing the coordination of complex organizational tasks
- **Project Specific Teams:** Temporary teams, composed of individuals with mixed skills and backgrounds given the task of addressing a specific and timely issue or problem
- **Brain Trust Teams:** Act as catalysts and supporters of decision making and business changes
- **Task Teams:** Responsible for the core tasks of the business

Depending on the needs of your business, you may chose to create several teams to perform specific functions, or simply organize all of your core personnel into a single team which would handle a broad range of responsibilities. Your fundamental goal is the same: to create a cooperative, interdependent unit, committed to open communication, creative thinking and achieving a single vision.

The Business That Sells Fun

Red Speed, Inc. is a southern California start-up dedicated to fun. Started by Nate Miguel and his cousin Jamie, Red Speed rents out ATVs (All Terrain Vehicles), Harley Davidson motorcycles, Jet Skis and Sea-Doos. They rent to weekend fun seekers who want to explore the desert, mountains or beach on their own terms.

Most of Red Speed's customers are tourists visiting southern California from Europe. Red Speed will deliver rentals to customers' hotels, complete with trailers, helmets and other accessories. They will even arrange for and deliver rental trucks or vans to pull the trailers. Red Speed was conceived to be a full-service business, that provides no-worry, no-hassle weekend escapes for true outdoors adventure.

Aside from Nate and Jamie, Red Speed has 9 other employees: two telephone order/ sales people, six mechanics and the office manager. Once reservations are taken and processed, most of the business's time is spent maintaining and upgrading equipment. Red Speed is dedicated to staying ahead of the latest adventure-sports trends and making its rental equipment the easiest to use, most reliable and highest quality available.

Today Red Speed has earnings of over $7 million a year, and has one of the largest fleets of rental Jet Skis and Harley Davidsons in the country. Its rentals have an impressive 90% utilization rate. They are out of commission due to mechanical repairs or overhauls only one out of 10 days. The business does not have to do much advertising since it generates more business than it can accommodate from word of mouth referrals and repeat customers. For the busiest months, Red Speed has a waiting list for every type of equipment it rents. Red Speed's customers are loyal, the equipment reliable and impeccable, and the business profitable and growing.

How does Red Speed manage to do it?

Why Do You Want a Team?

At times it must seem like an impossible task: being customer focused, market driven, forward thinking, and detail oriented. You might ask yourself, "On top of all that, why do I need to create a team based organization? Isn't that for the McDonald's and Motorolas of the world to do?" Or perhaps you subscribe to the Groucho Marx school of thought: "I wouldn't want to join any club that would have me as a member!" Consider this: by virtue of being a small business you already enjoy many of the qualities which corporate America covets. You have a collaborative atmosphere, fast communication and the ability to respond rapidly to the market. Chances are, this has not occurred as a result of deliberate planning on your part. It's happened because you may only have a couple of people in your business. But with just a little foresight you can lay the foundation for a smooth running, highly effective team or group of teams that can carry you along the way as your business grows.

There are many benefits of a strong team. Teams demand performance and encourage people to give their best. **Multi-disciplinary** teams increase the variety of problems that can be solved by your organization. A variety of personality types enhances the richness of your decision making and work process. Team structures place less emphasis on the traditional business hierarchy. By leveraging a variety of skill sets and personalities, teams allow fewer people to do the tasks of many people. This can reduce management costs and communication log jams. Because they require clear goals, teams can aid in promoting your "business vision."

Teams reduce communications log jams

Your employees also benefit from being part of a team. Individuals within a team can enjoy a greater sense of identity, recognition and fulfillment in their tasks. When expectations and rewards are clearly defined, people feel a greater sense of control.

The process of building a team and creating the environment in which a team can thrive offers many benefits. This process forces you to reevaluate the kind of environment you want to work in, and the types of people you value most. As you put in place the various structures to support your team, your own communication and leadership skills will be finely tuned.

Finally, a word about "creative juices." Large corporations are forming teams in order to infuse their organizations with the excitement and sense of empowerment that entrepreneurial ventures enjoy. Businesses of all types have realized that creating teams rejuvenates people. Employees become more creative and responsive to customers.

Evolving Away from the Lone Ranger Model

Creating a team culture in your business requires a transition away from what might be called "The Lone Ranger" mentality. Whether you have 2 people or 200 in your organization, you must shift your focus from your individual capabilities (as the founder and star entrepreneur) to those of your entire staff. Your suppliers, customers, partners, and employees don't judge the quality of your products and services simply on the basis of what you are capable of as an individual. The business is judged by what it can accomplish as an organization. You are building a new organization on one key principle: **cooperation.**

You can't grow if you can't change. Changing requires that you look at your business in a new way. At some point in your efforts you will realize that you can't do everything yourself. Perhaps you'll say to yourself, "AHHH! How am I supposed to get all this done? There's no one else around me who can do it like I can!" This is one of the main reasons so many start-ups fail. The transition from being a one-person show to sharing responsibilities is difficult. But in order to grow, you must make changes.

Being a Leader vs. Being a Boss

A boss is someone who instructs and disciplines people. "The boss" sets goals and expectations, and limits ways in which people can achieve their tasks. In the absence of the boss, motivation suffers, performance falls, and focus is lost. Under this traditional model of management, the major source of motivation is the interest in avoiding penalties or in earning the favor of the boss. Given the opportunity to identify their own goals and the freedom to select the best way to achieve them, people's performance improves dramatically. People are more likely to perform because they are excited by their challenges.

The key traits of a leader are trust, excellent interpersonal skills, inspiration, motivation, and direction. Leaders are more than visionary thinkers. They are doers who initiate and complete projects. A leader generates an emotional connection with people, attracts and inspires people towards a common cause. A successful leader has learned the art of managing through influence, and understands that people prefer to do things for their own reasons. A leader will discover these reasons and motivate people to achieve positive results. Think about it: wouldn't you rather be part of a bigger and bolder effort rather than just having a job?

Are you a team leader? Do you have the necessary skills to lead? You're good at one-on-one communication, but how are you at one-to-group communication? The word "learn" has been used several times to describe the process of leading. It's true, a small percentage of people are born with the skills needed to be truly outstanding leaders. The rest of us must learn through study, trial and error.

A leader inspires:

- trust
- motivation
- direction

To begin this process, take a moment to reflect on what you already know about leadership and what it means to be a leader. What are your reasons for wanting to be a leader? What are your strengths and weaknesses?

The following is a list of questions that may help:

- When in a leadership role, how did you perform? How did you feel?
- What was the outcome?
- What are your greatest misgivings about being a leader?
- What do you think are the most important attributes of a leader?
- Who are the leaders you've most admired or responded to and why?
- What leadership traits and skills do you think you have?
- Which traits and skills are you lacking?

Having reflected on these aspects of your personality and ability to lead, consider the following skills necessary to empower teams:

Team leadership should be:

- Coherent, future-focused and consistent
- Able to commit team members to their efforts
- Able to clearly understand team roles, functions and expectations
- Skilled at leading efficient, focused meetings
- Able to sustain a positive, empowered climate
- Able to diagnose weakness in the team and correct it

How Red Speed Works: Good Leadership

The owners of Red Speed, Nate and Jamie Miguel have built their success on good leadership and teamwork. Though each member of the team has specific responsibilities, and criteria for performance review, all have the same goal in mind: maximize customer fun time. This means staying on top of ordering parts, upgrading equipment and anticipating problems before they occur.

Nate spent 6 years in the Navy, as part of a jet fighter maintenance crew aboard the aircraft carrier U.S.S. Enterprise. There he learned the skills that made Red Speed a success: utter team cooperation. Key to having a team that "thinks as one mind, works with as one body" is clear division of duties, continuous and clear communication, common goals, and shared rewards. With the help of his cousin Jamie, he made these things pay off at Red Speed.

Empowering Your Team

Empowerment is a term that has been used so widely by management consultants that it has evolved into an entire management philosophy. This simple concept has been employed to guide everything from stuffing sausages in Wisconsin to the development of supercomputers in Silicon Valley. But what does it mean exactly?

Empowerment is the process of giving employees the authority and the tools needed to self-manage. In many cases this means stripping away or "flattening out" layers of management so that functions traditionally performed by managers can be performed by line employees. These functions include setting goals and objectives, assessing performance, and restructuring work processes. Some organizations have even created teams empowered to hire and fire members and evaluate and contract with outside suppliers.

Regardless of the industry or the size of the business in which it exists, an empowered team sets its own goals and has the responsibility of selecting the best means to achieve those goals. Leadership of an empowered team comes from within. Decision making is by consensus.

How can you begin to implement this process in your business? The starting point for creating an empowered team is establishing a shared vision. **Vision** is more than a business goal. A vision uses the talents of your team, contributes to the organization and provides a sense of fulfillment to the members of the team. This vision returns to the fundamental questions guiding your business: "What business are we in? What's our true purpose?"

Consider the following differences between a vision and a goal.

Vision	Goal
Consciously chosen and clearly articulated	A specific target that is measurable
Ongoing general direction	Has a beginning, middle and end
Taps into the talents of your team	An element of the purpose
Creates a sense of fulfillment for team members	

You must play to win, not to avoid losing

Why have a vision? Because it provides a context for all decision making and a yardstick to measure progress. It provides a focus for collaboration, shared responsibility, and motivation for excellence.

Your second task is to create a climate of shared responsibility within your team. This means that in order to reap the rewards, each and every member of the team must perform specific, stated tasks. These functions are selected by the team members. Each member has a responsibility to contribute to other members' efforts. If one member does not perform effectively it is the responsibility of the entire group to assess the difficulty and remedy it.

Building Your Team

Now that you know what an empowered team can do, how can you make it a reality for your business? By breaking the team building process into a series of steps you'll find it's easier than you expect.

Identify Needs

Determine which area of your business could most benefit from the strength of a team. Identify the key issues for this team. Have an open mind. Businesses use teams to do everything from selecting suppliers to creating new marketing strategies. Use knowledge of your business and your creativity to guide you.

Identify Key People

First identify the types of skills that your team must possess in order to accomplish its goals. By mixing people with different backgrounds (like mixing a sales person with a financial planner), your team will be able to explore a wider range of solutions.

Gather, Inform and Listen

Having assembled your team, share with them the who's, where's, why's, and how's of the team's creation. Encourage and listen to your people's feedback. At this early stage, your active participation as a leader is crucial. Before the structures for decision making have been decided upon, it is important that you provide direction and decisiveness necessary to propel the group forward.

Set Your Sights!

At this point you must clarify the purpose and goals of the team. Clearly set forth the team objectives that are specific, measurable, and time bound. Without these parameters, teams tend to lose focus.

Establish a Forum

Creating an environment for open communication and constructive confrontation among all the team members is the most basic element of an effective team. To ensure that all team members are able to contribute openly and regularly, your team must:

- Identify common ground and points of disagreement
- Encourage full expression of all viewpoints
- Regularly share both positive and negative feedback
- Monitor the resolution of issues and conflicts
- Listen, listen, and listen some more!
- Support and trust one another

Training: The Beginning of Teamwork at Red Speed

For Red Speed, teamwork begins with hiring good people who have excellent skills. Nate and Jamie begin by hiring and training all of their employees carefully. Red Speed focuses the bulk of its energy on the employees who are most critical to the business's success: the equipment-care team. All mechanics hired have at least 3 years experience working on motorcycles. Nate, in particular, tries to hire former navy or army mechanics because they understand (better than others), the kind of operation he strives to run. Mechanics are then trained at Red Speed by spending two weeks repairing each type of equipment the company rents out. New mechanics work as buddies with experienced employees, so, by the end of their 8 week training period, they have begun to develop an equipment expertise and a solid working relationship with their new team mates.

Set Your Ground Rules and Procedures

You've assembled your team, identified your mission, and now you've got to make your first team decision. How do you set up the procedures that will ensure all members will participate? How do you deal with the nitty gritty of making decisions?

The team should decide how it will function as a decision making body on a day-to-day basis. Logically, this is dictated by the size of the team and the types of challenges. Will its decision making be formal or informal? If you are a member of the team, will you remain the leader? Will leadership become a collective function or migrate to another member? What are the time constraints?

At this stage, your team must ensure that it has regular access to relevant information. Here are some additional procedural issues that your team should address:

- Who holds authority and in which situations?
- How are people affected by decisions involved in the decision making process?
- Is information collected quickly enough?
- Are authority and responsibility matched when tasks are assigned?
- Are decisions effectively communicated?

- Is the team coordinating its resources effectively?
- Does the team set aside time to learn from experience?

Your team must create a pattern of identifying issues, exploring problems, gathering information, infusing new perspectives, challenging alternatives, eliminating choices, and selecting the best possible course of action. This process should become second nature to the team. Visualize this as the **critical cycle** through which your team is perpetually moving.

The purpose is to keep your team moving forward despite internal and external challenges. Maintaining the ability to be focused yet open to new ideas requires dedicated attention to the group dynamics. Setting up these procedures and enabling your team to hit its stride within this critical cycle will go a long way in making your team effective.

As you continue to build your team, remember that Rome wasn't built in a day. Progress occurs incrementally. Taking baby steps can make your team building process smoother and a lot more fun.

Responsibility and Authority at Red Speed

It is the responsibility of every mechanic at Red Speed to meet the company's goal of 90% equipment utilization. This means, that on average, a broken motorcycle, Jet Ski or Sea-Doo must be repaired and out the door within 1 day. Routine maintenance checks between rentals must average no more than 30 minutes.

How does Red Speed ensure quality with such a short turn around time? By clearly allocating responsibility, giving team members authority for making key decisions, and encouraging initiative.

Empowerment equals authority plus responsibility

Nate and Jamie feel that it is impossible to expect people to exercise responsibility and initiative if they have no authority. Therefore, they spend more time helping their employees to see what they can do, rather than telling them what they can't do. Every mechanic at Red Speed has the authority to order new parts and allocate their time as they see fit. They work in pairs, with every member of the team qualified to repair any type of equipment.

Rentals are generally returned in the late afternoon, and rented out again in the morning. Therefore, the busiest time of day is between 3 - 7 p.m. This is known as the "Jam Time," when mechanics must be "on deck." During this time it is critical for new parts to be easily accessible, the floor organized and uncluttered, and the team working at its best. When Jam Time ends it is the responsibility of each mechanic to organize and clean their workspace. They also quickly complete an equipment status report and update their supplies need list. This takes only a few minutes on any one of three computer terminals in the repair area.

With that they head home with a clean work area and a clear picture of what needs to be done the next day.

Attack!

Your team knows more about their challenge than anyone else in your business. A course of action is recommended. The team must clearly map out who is responsible for each action. Deadlines should be set. Your team's number one goal is to improve or remedy something, and to do this they must roll up their sleeves and get dirty. Now is the time to set them loose!

Evolving and Adapting

Continual improvement is one area of critical importance to teamwork. Teams can only improve by assessing performance to determine how successful the outcomes of its actions have been. Your team must consider how individual members have contributed, and how effectively the team works together. Use the following as a guide in post-project team review:

- Consider a project your team tackled. Did you use the procedures set up by the team? What were the biggest challenges and successes? Solicit feedback from all members.
- Are members individually and collectively pleased with their performance? What would they most like to change for the next time?
- Which member(s) of the team tend to communicate more freely? Why aren't others doing so? How can you create ways to involve these people?
- What is the quality of the team's output compared to others?

Nate Miguel: Traffic Controller

The most important thing for smooth operation at Red Speed is team coordination. This responsibility belongs to Nate. Every evening, after "Jam Time" Nate reviews computer reports to determine what supplies are needed. Before the mechanics head home for the day, Nate quickly "debriefs" them to uncover any problems they encountered and special challenges they anticipate.

It is Nate's job to restock the repair area, estimate the "time to completion" for repairs, and allocate team responsibility for specific jobs based on rental demands. Several of the mechanics specialize in Harley Davidson repairs, so, he makes sure that if bikes are being returned in the morning, these mechanics are ready to jump on the maintenance job. If not, he allocates them to other in-coming repairs.

Because most of its business comes from Europeans on vacation, Red Speed often has reservations for equipment 6 months ahead of time. Therefore, Red Speed usually knows well in advance what its equipment needs will be. Nate maps out a flow of specific equipment through the shop, and allocates a percentage of extra time for larger repair jobs that will inevitably crop up.

Mechanics arrive at Red Speed in the morning knowing what pieces of equipment they will be doing quick maintenance on and which larger repair jobs are pending. They plan their time with their work buddy accordingly, knowing that the supplies and support they need is waiting for them.

Reaping the Rewards and Having Fun!

Everyone who has ever played a team sport has experienced that brief moment of ecstasy when all team members do the right thing at the right time, and it all works. It's this moment of feeling part of a truly collective mission which is one of the most rewarding aspects of being a member of team. When your team has one of those euphoric "CLICK!" moments, take time out to fully recognize and savor it! Remember what it feels like. Take a team photo. Have a team dinner. Do something to celebrate.

Are there other rewards that can propel and motivate your team? How do you reward your team for a job well done? Let the goals that the team itself has set out be your benchmark. Set key deadlines for the team to review performance, and judge if its goals have been met. If they have, then the pay out for your business is money well spent indeed: you've bought creative thinking, cooperation and fun for your business!

Reward successful teams

Here are some suggestions:

- Peg performance to financial rewards
- Offer nonmonetary rewards such as time off, a better office, etc.
- Hand out props, trophies or other small incentives
- Offer promotions and new responsibilities to effective team members

Remember to stop and smell the roses! Take notice of the uniqueness of your business and the special people who surround you. Give yourself and your team the time to relax and enjoy the exciting experience of creating a truly successful business. You are in the process of inventing your own corporate culture; make it fun, take it easy once in while, and enjoy the moment.

Pie Time at Red Speed

During peak business months, Nate and Jamie meet at the end of every week with the Red Speed team of mechanics. During these 30 minute gatherings (time is of the essence) the team reviews its performance for the past week. What was the average utilization rate for equipment? What special repair challenges came up? What team coordination or cooperation issues came up? This is the time for members to speak up, ask questions and resolve conflict. Nate has found that it is during these informal meetings over coffee and pie (his mother makes a wicked strawberry rhubarb) that some of the shop's best process improvements have come about. The best to date? The idea to install an easy to use software system for managing inventory and tracking project completions.

He figures that upgrade alone helped the business jump from 70% utilization to the now famous 90% equipment utilization rate.

Team Challenges: Manage, Learn & Overcome

The biggest challenge to creating and maintaining a team is managing group dynamics. Personality conflicts, peer pressures, conflicting loyalties, and old habits can cause a team to work at cross purposes. Collaboration takes patience and skill to develop. Building trusting relationships takes time. Your daily task as team leader is to keep communication open, and address issues and solve conflicts. This communication need not focus on specific problems. Create an atmosphere within the team where people can freely express positive and negative views. In this way, you can vent frustrations and overcome negative feelings, thus helping people to focus their energy on the mission rather than on the inter-team dynamics. Consider these communication enhancements:

- **Description**: "I see it this way, how do you see it?"
- **Equality**: "We are in this together"
- **Openness**: "What do you see as the key issue here? Let's hear your ideas"
- **Problem-Orientation**: "How do you feel this could be a problem? Let's work together to find a solution"
- **Positive Intent**: "Can we step back and focus on our common objective? Here are my motives in this case"
- **Empathy**: "I appreciate your concern, I understand how you feel"

Constructive conflict is a tremendous source of team energy

Even in the most openly communicative environments, conflict emerges. In teams, positive conflict can be a tremendous source of energy and spirited debate. Use it to improve team performance. In the following context, constructive conflict can bring creativity and realism to a team:

- When there is a flexibility in thinking among group members
- When divergent thoughts are clearly presented and fully expressed
- When team members feel free to give their honest opinions
- When techniques for conflict resolution are understood and used.

One of the most common problems encountered by teams is the tendency towards **Groupthink**. Here the team develops a distinct personality which limits its ability to search out and consider new perspectives. Groupthink teams reject minority views in place of majority views. Often in the rush to make decisions and see decisive progress, teams can fail to investigate issues completely and to create a full range of robust alternatives.

Keeping clear lines of responsibility and accountability within the team is also a major challenge. However, this difficulty can be overcome by assisting your team in returning to the basics: talk, listen, and focus on the mission. Teams must update their missions, renew their cooperation and openly solve both internal and external problems.

Rewarding the Red Speed Team

The final ingredient to the Red Speed recipe for success is a unique team compensation strategy.

For every month that the company achieves its equipment performance targets and other customer service goals (number of complaints, refunds, and referrals, to name a few) each employee earns a percentage of the business's profits. When the business falls short of its goals, this percentage of profit sharing drops. If, in slow months the business earns no profits (this has happened only twice in 4 years) no bonuses are paid out. Employee performance is reviewed by Nate and Jaime every 3 months, and employees anonymously review each others' performance every 6 months. Red Speed routinely pays for employee training seminars, assisting its mechanics in honing their skills and upgrading their expertise.

Other employee benefits such as the Spring and Fall team adventure weekends, Christmas parties, 75% discounts for employee friends and family, and all the strawberry rhubarb pie you can eat, make Red Speed a fun place to work. Red Speed has truly created a team that is trained, managed, and rewarded for success...and they truly do deliver—fun!

Conclusion

Team work can be one of your business's most enduring competitive advantages. The discipline of creating and leading a team will commit your company to a course of continually challenging your processes and assumptions and open the door to steady growth. As many management consultants have pointed out, teamwork is not a destination, it is a journey. Happy trails!

Chapter 30
MANAGING HUMAN RESOURCES

About This Chapter:
- *Begin with your business plan*
- *Interviewing and hiring people*
- *Compensation and motivation*
- *Creating the company handbook*

Introduction

The most important asset any business has is its people. For this reason, one of the most important jobs you do will be to hire, train, and motivate your employees. If you do these things well, you have a good chance of building a stable, sustainable business.

If you are like most entrepreneurs, one of the most difficult challenges you face is allowing people to help you. That's right! Most entrepreneurs succeed because they are a "jack-of-all-trades": multi-talented, highly motivated and full of ideas. While these traits are valuable, they can also represent a major stumbling block as you try to build a business composed of more people than just yourself.

If you want your business to grow and perform consistently in your absence, (you need a day off too!) you must empower your people to perform. These need not be full-time employees or even working "for you" in the traditional sense of the word. Your employees might be a combination of full-time employees, temporary staff, independent contractors, and part-time helpers. Regardless, your task is the same: to prepare what is alternately known as human resources, personnel, or employee relations management. This is the process of developing a system of rewards, policies, guidelines and practices that relate to all employees of your business. Writing job descriptions and performance evaluations, setting salary levels, and creating a competitive mix of compensation are also elements of this task.

This chapter offers some valuable insights to help you select people who share your vision, train them to perform, and reward and motivate them to grow personally and professionally.

Begin with Your Business Plan

Your business plan will aid you in defining the tasks that must be done in your business and reviewing the types of skills and personalities needed to do them. Revisit the goals you've set out for your business and reaffirm the core competencies that will make your business uniquely competitive in the marketplace. Your business plan is your guide as you build your business, one person at a time.

Tool Kit for Managing People

The basic skills that allow you to manage your people to inspire loyalty and excellence are discussed below. Just because you've seen certain human resource practices used elsewhere, that doesn't mean that you should necessarily emulate them in your own business. Think how differently the employee handbook at a computer company with 20,000 employees would look compared to the handbook used in a bicycle repair company with 20 employees! The industry in which you operate, the products you produce and your core competencies will all govern how you manage your employees. Begin with the basics (policies for hiring, training, rewarding and motivating) and build on them to fit them to your own personality, vision, and regulatory environment.

Job Descriptions

Before hiring even one employee, the first thing a good manager does is clarify work roles by writing clear, concise job descriptions for each task that must be performed in the business. The job description specifies the details of the work to be done, including:

- Tasks to be performed
- Performance criteria
- Skills or qualifications
- Importance of each duty
- Supervision
- Future projects
- Training
- Growth and advancement

Having a job description in hand will be essential as you begin your search for that perfect person to add to your business. A carefully written job description will also establish the performance criteria by which the employee's work will be judged. Consider the following sample job description for a marketing manager.

Rosann's Rockin' Rollin' Tires

Job Title: *Marketing Manager*

Department: *Sales and Marketing*

Reports to: *President*

Responsible for creating the market development strategy and processes for our line of environmentally friendly, recycled tires. Focus on new product introductions and work closely with sales force to ensure they have the tools necessary to launch product and meet schedule commitments. Manage communications between the president and the sales staff and act as an advocate for the different product and customer segments. Monitor and track progress against plans and communicate changes to plan. Must be willing to work on accelerated schedules, manage many tasks simultaneously, be flexible and communicate effectively with external and internal partners.

Minimum Qualifications: *BA/BS in Marketing/Communications or equivalent, 3 years product management experience, creative ability, marketing skills and independent judgment. PC Skills: word processing, spreadsheet, and presentation software skills.*

The ideal candidate will flourish in a fast paced, entrepreneurial setting and know how to have fun. Knowledge of tire or automobile markets is essential.

A sample job description

Hiring Smart People

Hiring smart people is the second step in creating a strong, capable management team that will grow your business. It will be important early on for you to have a layer of talented people to whom you can delegate responsibility and authority. Your team will be performing the primary functional tasks of your business: marketing, accounting, selling, producing, financial management, and servicing the customer.

Consider your first hires as key people who will be an integral part of your evolving business. Your standards for these people should be high but realistic. Expecting too much and rewarding too little is one of the major mistakes made by entrepreneurs. Beware! This creates resentment which ultimately will result in poor performance and high employee turnover.

A Note From The World of Sony Entertainment

Consider this example of a hiring policy: The former president of Sony, the multinational electronics company, instituted a formal company-wide policy whereby managers were required to seek and hire employees that were ***smarter*** *than they were. In the aggressive, fast paced and technically innovative industry of home electronics and entertainment, this policy was key to Sony's very survival: it ensured that the company cultivated the industry leaders for tomorrow.*

There are two major criteria that guide the hiring process. The first is real world qualifications in a functional or technical area. The second criteria has to do with style, attitude, and personality. No doubt you're under time pressures, but investing time in selecting good people now will pay off later. Here are the basics:

Learn good interview techniques

Have face-to-face interviews

You should like the people you work with, and they should be personable. It is important to cut through the fluff and "talk turkey" as soon as possible. What has this person specifically achieved in the past 5 years? Let the applicant's resume be your guide, but not your limit. Some of the most revealing questions and "meaty" interviews result from interviewers following their instincts. Get the person to talk about their achievements, goals, and values. Try to pinpoint specific projects they've started and finished. When finished, you should clearly understand their past performance record. Don't forget to take notes!

Use "what-if?" questioning

Presenting potential employees with a selection of possible business and interpersonal scenarios can offer you insight into their personality and work style. Ask them how they would react to a specific "crisis" in your business, to an ambiguous or uncertain situation, or their approach to a given challenge. How would they better market your product? Control for costs or control your inventory? This type of questioning can help you to separate the "doers" from the talkers, and the substance from the fluff.

Check references
Reference checks allow you to cross check details and verify the highlights of a particular candidate's qualifications. These checks also can offer you valuable additional insight into the candidate. How do they work under pressure? Are they detail-oriented and able to follow through on tasks? How disciplined are they and how much supervision do they require to be productive? Use your interview notes and their resume as a guide as you dig for more information.

ZAP your weak spots by hiring people with different skills sets, experience levels, and personalities

A warning: characters to avoid
Let's take a moment to draw a few composite sketches of people your business should stay away from. These people can be drains on your resources and thorns in your side! They will almost certainly present themselves at some point in your business's life.

The Master of The Universe: This is the expert you hired to deal with a specific problem who sees themselves as the savior of the business. This person maneuvers for attention and status from you and your staff, and appoints themselves to identify, quantify and correct all ills of the organization.

The Ambitious Policeman: This person works to "police" standards and procedures within your business, and to be the "detail person" extraordinaire! They may patronize other employees, waste precious time on small projects to make themselves uniquely indispensable to you. These perfectionists lose sight of the forest through the trees.

The Sales Vulture: This person may have come highly recommended as a "rake in the sales" kind of person, but to you they are just downright abrasive and cold! They may earn the highest salary by virtue of commissions and incentives, and constantly remind you of their "fair market value" at competing firms.

The Troublesome Techie: This person is the theoretical genius who was hired to add some muscle to your operations. They seldom miss an opportunity to demonstrate their technical superiority and are notoriously bad at sharing their knowledge and helping others to learn. This person can be stubborn and limited in their thinking and unwilling to adapt to new design or product specifications.

The Business Stiff: When business is not doing well, this person may be recruited by investors or your partners to inject some "good old fashioned business sense" into the organization. Chances are they have a lot of education but little actual experience in your industry. Their focus will be on trimming the "fat" from the organization (this usually means firing people) and setting strict guidelines for "turning the business around."

Compensating Your People

The rewards that businesses offer their people can be divided into two categories: regular compensation and benefits, and additional rewards and incentives. Basic benefits describe those things which all employees receive, regardless of their level of performance. Rewards and incentives are given above and beyond base compensation to motivate employees to exceed performance targets, and enhance the level of innovation within a business.

Compensation packages are your employees' meat and potatoes; rewards and incentives, their dessert!

Capable people who understand what they are to accomplish and are truly motivated to assist the "cause" of the business are difficult to find. The special people you find who can invest their spirit in your business, are treasures indeed and should be cherished. Challenge, compensate and reward them well.

Salary

This is the annual or monthly dollar amount you offer your employees for the job they do. The guiding principle here is: Know what your people are worth, and create competitive compensation packages to pay them accordingly. Many small businesses lack the cash flow to pay out big salaries. You can still attract the best. Use creativity to compensate and reward your people in other ways: stock options, flexible work hours, and vacation time. An employee who is only concerned with earning a large salary is not the kind of person who should be working for a start-up anyway! Pay the salary you can afford, then use other intangibles to motivate them. Search and outplacement firms can provide valuable information as you seek to identify appropriate salary levels.

Vacation time

Vacation leave practices are often dictated by the geographic area and industry in which a business operates. Your key decision is whether to have staggered vacation times or to plan for a two-week operation shut down once a year.

Holidays
Although some holidays are considered standard paid time off for many businesses (Christmas, Thanksgiving, New Year's Day, President's Day etc.), it is entirely at your discretion which holidays you choose.

Sick leave
Sick leave practices are usually dictated by the region and industry in which a business operates. You can decide to manage your policies any way you choose: you can decide how many sick days you will pay, and how many you will tolerate before disciplinary action is taken.

Health and medical coverage
This is one of the fundamental benefits that many employers offer to their employees. However, in earliest stages of a business's life providing this benefit simply may not be financially possible. Just as soon as your business is able and can qualify, you should consider getting some form of group medical coverage for your company. It is far better to have modest plan that has high deductibles and simple benefits than to have no insurance at all. Your business can begin by paying a small fraction of the cost of coverage, then grow into increasing its contribution. Many medical coverage packages also include some form of life insurance and dental care coverage. Shop around and ask a lot of questions in order to find your best deal!

Motivating and Rewarding Your People

What does it mean to motivate someone? It means to inspire and stimulate them to realize their performance potential, and help them to have fun in the process! In business, some might assume that salary is the most important motivator for employees. This isn't always the case. Often, new challenges and learning are at the top of the list of what employees consider important. Creating this type of motivation is of critical importance for a small, growing, business.

Employee Motivation:

- $
- Learning
- New challenges
- New opportunities

You should develop year-long motivational training strategies for your business. For example, these may include a schedule of programs that your sales people can look forward to throughout the year: in February they will attend a tactical sales seminar, in August they will be trained in international selling techniques, and to ring in the New Year in January, they will participate in a class on fun and selling. You may also want to create an agenda of internal sales, productivity, or quality contests. Each month gains will be measured, winners selected, and fun prizes awarded.

The lean and mean (but generous) Travel Agent Machine

In the notoriously low-profit margin world of travel, where agents earn little besides commissions, travel businesses have had to use creative tools to attract and compensate their employees. One particularly clever executive allows her agents to purchase mileage points for their own use at rock-bottom prices, take several vacations annually (for field research!) and work out of their homes on their own terminals. Her best achievement: creating the legendary tradition of the ***office party****. These events are infamous: the turnout is huge, people have fun, and most importantly, the expectation before the parties is a powerful employee motivator. The most popular part of these parties? Creatively thought-up and enthusiastically received contests with exceptional prizes for* ***everyone****: around the world airline tickets for agents and their spouses, hotel vouchers, and free rental cars! Now that's an incentive!*

This schedule provides markers throughout the year that will keep your people motivated and forward looking. You should also post your business's performance goals prominently around your work space. If for example, a t-shirt printing business is shooting to hit an all-time production high of 1,000 t-shirts per week, the number 1,000 might be posted at key spots on walls, or printed on t-shirts to be worn by employees.

Good people managers build motivational elements into their management processes that continually refresh people's awareness of the business's goals and rekindle their enthusiasm. One way to do this is to build into your system incentives for exceeding targeted levels of performance. Most businesses do this by rewarding employees who exceed their sales quotas or complete projects ahead of schedule. How much employees are rewarded depends upon how much they have exceeded their targets. Your incentives can be as creative and wacky as you like! Consider creating incentives for:

- Reaching or exceeding quality standards
- Lowering customer complaints
- Exceeding order turnaround time standards
- Acquiring new skills or expertise outside of one's functional area
- Exceeding targeted inventory turnover
- Exceeding accounts receivable collection period targets
- Exceeding sales quotas

Incentives allow the business to pay for performance once it has been delivered. The best example of this is an incentive-based compensation system for a salesperson. Two of the most common ways to reward employees are:

Stock purchase plan

The stock purchase plan (or the opportunity to buy shares in the ownership of the business) is one of the most widely used system of rewards in entrepreneurial ventures. Where start-ups are concerned, everyone wants a piece of the action! This is particularly true in high-growth, high-tech industries like those in California's Silicon Valley. If work in this type of industry, the issue of stock options will invariably come up in the first interview with prospective employees. The stock purchase plan gives employees added incentive to help the business succeed, and allows the business to partially compensate its employees with earnings it has not yet produced. As your company grows, this plan should be tailored to fit your business. Always engage your attorney to help you review your choices and the tax and business benefits of each.

Profit sharing

In the early stages of your business, stay away from promises to share profits. It will be a while before your business is generating profits (at least until you hit your break-even point,) and it will be even longer before you've generated enough to cash to pay out on a formal plan. When and if you chose not to reinvest profits into your business, consult your attorney and bankers for guidance on this type of plan.

Mentoring

On a final note: an integral part of your job as the leader is to help other people succeed in your business. As your business grows, your time should increasingly be spent mentoring or "coaching" as opposed to "doing". This means relinquishing your role as the "shining star" of the team and helping others to bask in the spotlight of success. The key to this method is delegating responsibility and authority for functional tasks, and focusing your energy on creating the strategies that will allow your business and its people to succeed.

Help others to bask in the spotlight of success!

Use these examples to inspire your thinking, but remember; you need to create a strategic plan to motivate your team just as you would any other key element of your business's management. With this in place set them loose, cheer them on and watch them excel!

Firing People

You've selected your employee carefully, checked their references, written a clear job description and set attainable goals. But somehow, the employee just isn't performing. One of the least pleasant things you will have to do as a manager is make the difficult decision to ask someone to leave your company. There are several reasons why you might arrive at this difficult decision:

- The employee has stolen from the company
- The employee has not performed as expected
- The employee has a personality conflict with other members of the team
- The company can no longer afford to pay the employee

When you do act, it should be quick and clean. There is a standard process used to terminate an employee:

- Have a private conference with the employee in a private area
- Describe the problem, and performance you expect from them and date by which it must be delivered
- Schedule a follow-up review
- Meet again to share your assessment of the employee's performance
- At each stage, document the issues in writing and problems the business has with the employee, and their improvement or failure to perform
- Make decision to keep, terminate, or move the employee to a different part of your business

At the time you terminate an employee, it is important to tell them why they're being fired; and, if possible, to share with them your insight as to how they might improve in their areas of weakness.

The company handbook sells the company from the inside out

The Personnel and Company Handbook

Early in your business's life, you should develop an employee and company handbook. You need not hire an expensive copywriter and graphic designer to do this. Your business's handbook can look any way you want it to, but it should contain the following:

- A letter from you, the founder, team leader, and coach
- The company mission statement
- Your employee relations policy
- Your employee benefits package
- A "principles of doing business" statement, including its purpose and author, who should use it, an explanation of its terms, and the time frame it covers
- Your employee performance appraisal and problem resolution procedures
- Vacation policy and holidays
- Organizational reporting structure and functions

Consider the following two examples of a company mission statement and statement of business principles:

Couch Potato, Inc. Mission Statement

Couch Potato, Inc. is a homegrown company that was founded on the principle that a comfortable couch makes for a comfortable home. We are committed to selling and servicing the most comfortable, long-lasting couches in California. We strive to maintain the highest standards of customer service and product quality. Our goal is to educate our customers about the benefits of buying durable, high-quality, well-designed and ergonomically correct couches for their families. We are committed to staying on the forefront of couch technology and continually earning our title as the couch experts. Lastly, we will always, and without exception, do things the Couch Potato Way!

Couch Potato, Inc. Principles of Doing Business

- *We source, sell, and service the highest quality couches*
- *We except all returns, no questions asked*
- *Whatever is best for our customers is best for us*
- *We deliver our couches on time, intact, and with a smile*
- *We hire creative, committed, fun, and honest people*
- *We help our employees develop personally, professionally and to exceed their own expectations*
- *We laugh at ourselves when we need to*

The 'open-door' policy—easy access for problem resolution

The purpose of the handbook is to provide information that will be needed by managers and employees regarding all issues, practices, and procedures related to employee relations. The key elements are:

Employee Relations Policy

This is a clear statement that speaks to your business's commitments to its employees. What qualities and skills does your business value in its people? Consistency? Humor and wit? Creativity? Speed? Accuracy? Loyalty? Pick and choose and write it down! This statement also broadly outlines the structures and policies that the business utilizes to nurture and manage its people. This can include a brief summary of health, educational and training benefits, and promotional policy.

Problem Resolution Policy

This statement indicates who, where, and when your business resolves problems. This is the management's concrete tool for resolving failures to perform, personal conflicts, and employee complaints. More importantly, it provides employees with a clear indication of how and with whom they can present their issues and problems. Consider some of the situations you might want to include:

- Drug or alcohol abuse
- Excessive absenteeism
- Interpersonal conflict
- Poor performance
- Theft

Corrective action should include:

- Verbal warnings
- Written warnings
- Counseling
- Termination

Employee Development and Performance Appraisal Policy

Outlining this policy is vital to the professional development of your employees. This statement should emphasize the on-going, joint responsibility of both the business and the employees to develop and demand the highest standards of quality. Here again you will lay out in broad terms the core objectives of the business. This statement may offer an explanation of your business's policy regarding employee development and training. It can also outline how frequently and by which measures employees' performance is judged.

The Worker Bill of Rights and Responsibilities

1. To understand the entire process of which they are a part
2. To initiate inquiries & problem solving activities beyond their scope of responsibility
3. To continually share the process they are engaged in with other employees
4. To think creatively and innovatively
5. To sustain their curiosity and learning
6. To enjoy themselves

Employee Benefits Policy

This statement identifies who is eligible for which benefits, and when. It clearly describes the benefits that your business offers to its employees.

Employee Compensation Policy

This statement describes how your business compensates its employees. It should address full-time, part-time, contractual, and temporary employees, and the various job classifications that exist within your business. It should also address:

- How and when salary is paid
- The hours of work
- Overtime compensation
- Holiday pay

As with all employee-related issues, you must make sure you are in compliance with Federal, State, and Local regulations. It is very important that you have your trusted legal advisor review your company handbook and any other policies and practices

Outsourcing

At some point in your business' life, you may want to explore the possibility of hiring people outside your firm to perform a few business tasks. This may include accounting, selling, public relations, or product design to name a few. These are referred to as "independent" contractors because your business does not provide the normal package of benefits to them. In effect they are their own independent businesses. There are generally three categories of outsourced employees:

Focus on your core competencies and leave the rest to contracted experts

- "Trial" employees
- Long-term project employees
- Short-term employees
- Part-time employees

Corporate Culture

Several times in this text the concept of the "culture" of your business has been mentioned. There is a growing discussion about this phenomena and it bears further discussion here. A business's culture is usually a function of its values. These values may range from how employees dress, to the "lingo" they use, to how they deal with each other and their customers. Values govern both the spoken and unspoken "rules" of behavior in a business. These can be very difficult to change once they are in place. And they vary from company to company. For example, the corporate culture would be very different at a skateboard manufacturer than it would be at an accounting firm. For this reason you should pay particular attention to the values you endorse and reward at the outset of your new business.

Conclusion

In the rush of day-to-day pressures to make products, fill orders, and collect payments, the important task of creating company policies is often pushed aside. A skilled manager will ensure that systems and organizational structures are in place to train and motivate employees to invest their spirit in growing the business. Creating your personnel policies is a key element in good management practice.

Create a fulfilling and enjoyable place to work, hire smart people, motivate and compensate them well and you will have a better chance of success in your business. Employees are critical to your success. Treat them well!

Chapter 31
OVERVIEW OF FINANCIAL STATEMENTS

About This Chapter:
- *Basic accounting concepts*
- *The Income Statement*
- *The Balance Sheet*
- *The Statement of Owners' Equity*
- *The Statement of Cash Flows*
- *Cost-Volume-Profit Analysis*

Introduction

Accounting is a process of measuring, recording, and communicating financial information. The most important step in this process is communication. Financial statements are the means of communicating business information.

People use financial statements to study a business's past, present, and future. Users of financial statement information generally fall into two categories: internal and external. Internal users include owners and managers. They utilize financial information to get feedback about decisions they have made, evaluate performance of the business, and identify planning opportunities and needs. External users include bankers, investors, partners, governmental agencies, and competitors. For them, the information is helpful in evaluating potential investments, determining credit worthiness, or assessing taxes.

Financial statements tell the story of what happened to the business over the past year. Comparative statements also include information from previous years. Sometimes, financial statements are prepared as a forecasting tool for the future. These are called pro forma statements and result from the budgeting process.

Basic Accounting Concepts

Accountants utilize basic principles to guide their work. It is easier to understand financial statements if you first understand a few of these principles.

Historical Cost Principle

The historical cost principle answers the question "How much?" The principle states that all amounts should be recorded at the exchange price of the transaction at the time it occurred. Amounts are not adjusted later for changes in the fair market value. When you read a financial statement, you are looking in the past. Current fair market values are not shown. For example, suppose a business purchased land in 1978 at a price of $50,000. In

1996, the land is worth $250,000. Only the historical cost of $50,000 will be included in the financial statements. Why? Accountants choose this approach because fair market value estimates are very subjective and can change frequently.

How much? Financial statements reflect historical cost not current market value

Economic Entity Concept

Let's say a sole proprietor buys a computer for personal use. That computer will not be included in the financial statements of the business, even if business funds are used for the purchase. If the computer is purchased for business use, it will appear on the statements of the business. The economic entity concept calls for the separation of accounting records and information of a business from those of all other entities, including owners.

Trying Something Different!

Louisa Egan operated a busy travel agency in Peekskill, New York. She was a shrewd and knowledgeable business woman. She traveled frequently herself and knew her clients and the destinations she recommended personally. She specialized in customized adventure travel packages.

By the fall of 1994 she began to feel as if she had reached the point of diminishing returns. She decided to close her office space and manage a small pool of her favorite clients from her home office.

Within 6 months, she was bored. Louisa knew she didn't want to go back into the travel business full time. She began to toss around other business ideas with her youngest daughter, Anne, who had just graduated from business school.

Louisa decided she wanted to start a new business. She wanted to create and sell a tangible product. She wanted to build a business that, several years down the road, she could pass on to her daughters to manage.

Accrual Versus Cash Accounting

A business decides to hire an attorney to do legal work. The attorney completes the legal work in December and the business pays the bill in January. The attorney will have a revenue and the business will incur an expense. But, will the revenue and expense be recognized in December or

January? Under the accrual basis, the transaction would be recorded in December when the work was completed. Under the cash basis, the transaction would be recorded in January when the cash was paid.

The accounting profession recommends the use of the accrual basis of accounting. However, most individuals and some small businesses use the cash basis. The two methods result from answering the question "When?" The **cash basis** of accounting is usually easier to understand and states that revenues and expenses occur when cash changes hands. The **accrual method** states that revenues and expenses occur when the action takes place, even if cash changes hands on a different date.

When?

The accrual method says to record revenues and expenses when the action takes place

Full Disclosure Principle

This principle states that full disclosure is required of events and circumstances that affect the user of the financial statements. This is done in the statements themselves or in attached footnotes. As a result of recent lawsuits, the amount of disclosure required has been steadily increasing.

Limitations of Financial Statements

Financial statements are the accepted means to communicate financial information about a business. However, there are limitations to the usefulness of financial statements.

Historical Cost Principle

The historical cost principle and the significance in determining amounts shown on the financial statements we've discussed previously. Accountants chose this method to make the accounting information more reliable. It also can make the information irrelevant. Who cares how much was paid for something 50 years ago? Isn't it more important to know how much it is worth today? Remember, you won't find that amount in the financial statements.

Off-Statement Transactions

Despite attempts to make financial statements comprehensive, there are still many transactions which are not reflected in financial reporting. This can result from complexity of the transaction, barter transactions that are not recorded in the books, or as a result of correct application of accounting principles that allow transactions to be "off-statement".

Use of Estimates

Perhaps you think accounting is cut and dried? An exact science? Most of the time it is, but accountants often use estimates. Accountants use estimates of income taxes due, bad debt losses, and many other categories. Of course, accountants must always strive for fair reporting of financial information.

Garbage In, Garbage Out

Financial statements are compiled from the company's daily record-keeping. If the record-keeping has been less than great, so will be the subsequent financial statements.

Jammin'

On June 15, 1995, Louisa's Jams turned out its first commercial-sized batch of jams for resale. Louisa and her husband had been making homemade jams every summer for the past 23 years. They used raspberries, blueberries, strawberries, and peaches from local farmers. When Louisa and Anne brainstormed for business ideas, they kept returning to the idea of Louisa's Jams.

Anne had researched the market for specialty jams and condiments and talked to several specialty food representatives. She estimated their overhead expenses and the amount of jars they would have to sell to be profitable. The numbers seemed realistic to her.

She and her mother decided to go for it.

Anne then negotiated a long-term lease of an old combined bottling and commercial kitchen facility on the outside of town. Attached to the back of the building was a warehouse space.

The facility needed a lot of work, but it did have usable kitchen and extensive bottling equipment. Anne negotiated with the owner to get the first 6 months of rent free in exchange for restoring the facility.

Anne calculate that Louisa's Jams could produce 10,000 jars of jam during its summer months of production. The busiest month would be June, when blueberries and strawberries were harvested by local farmers.

It would be a seasonal business since it would only operate its production facility during the summer. In winter months the business would only need warehouse space to hold inventory and a small office space to manage sales, finance, and marketing operations.

Anne figured that Louisa's Jams could rent out its excess kitchen capacity during its "down" months, which was in fact, most of the year. She asked around, and before long came up with 3 different local businesses that were interested. One was a small catering company called Peekskill Caterers.

Revenue from these sub-leases would cover the maintenance and overhead costs for the large facility. In fact, depending on how well she managed the facility, the sub-leases could end up providing Louisa's Jams with some serious income.

The Income Statement

The income statement is a summary of actions which took place during a given time period. Think of it as a video. It shows what happened to the business over a given span of time, but only in regard to two types of activities: the act of earning and the act of depleting resources. The income statement has a simple formula:

Revenues - Expenses = Net Income

Revenues are the earning activities, such as selling a product, charging rent, or receiving interest on a loan. **Expenses** are the cost of resources used up in the process of earning a revenue. Typical business expenses include insurance, advertising, wages, and payroll taxes.

The general formula for an income statement is expanded to provide more detail:

The income statement is a summary of actions which took place during a given time period

Revenues - expenses = net income

Your Business
Income Statement
For the Year Ended December 31, 1996

Sales		$450,000 ❶
Less: Cost of goods sold		(200,000) ❷
Gross Profit		$250,000 ❸
Less: Operating Expenses ❹		
Wages expense	$80,000	
Payroll tax expense	20,000	
Insurance expense	5,000	
Rent expense	24,000	
Advertising expense	3,000	
Utilities expense	1,400	
Depreciation expense	1,300 ❺	134,700
Net Operating Profit or Loss		$115,300
Other gains and losses:		
Interest revenue		700
Interest expense		(1,200)
Net Income Before Taxes		$114,800
Less: Income Taxes		30,000 ❻
Net Income		$84,800 ❼

ITEM 1—Sales: Revenues for retail, wholesale, and manufacturing are earned mainly through sales. In a service business, it is called Fees Earned or Services Revenue. Notice that there is a separate category, called "Other gains and losses," which includes revenue earning activities other than from your primary operations.

ITEM 2—Cost of Goods Sold: The major expense for retailers, wholesalers, and manufacturers is called cost of goods sold.

Cost of goods sold is aptly named. It is the cost of the products that the business sells. This sounds simple enough but there are many variations to consider. For example, assume that you buy some inventory for $5.70 each and later buy some more for $5.90 each. When you make a sale, how will you know which cost to put into cost of goods sold? Should it be $5.70 or $5.90? If you can specifically identify the products sold, you can answer the question easily. If not, you must use one of three assumptions: 1) the first in are the first out (FIFO), 2) the last in are the first out (LIFO), or 3) an average.

Manufacturers must consider three different costs in their cost of goods sold:

- **Direct materials**—those materials that become an integral part of the final product and can be easily traced into it. For a furniture manufacturer this would include wood and hardware.
- **Direct labor**—the cost of labor spent creating the final product. In the case of the furniture manufacturer it would be the cost of workers who actually build the furniture.
- **Overhead**—a catchall, encompassing all other manufacturing costs not already included in direct materials or direct labor.

Manufacturers have three parts to cost of goods sold: direct materials, direct labor, and overhead

ITEM 3—Gross Profit: The subtotal "Gross Profit" is the amount of every sales dollar that remains after covering the cost of the products sold. When you subtract all other expenses from the gross profit, the result is net income (or loss).

ITEM 4—Operating Expenses: Operating expenses are all expenses (other than cost of goods sold) incurred in your major line of business such as wages, rent, advertising, payroll taxes, utilities, depreciation, and many more. You can group these expenses into subcategories if you wish. For small businesses, operating expenses normally include all expenses except cost of goods sold, interest expense, and income tax expense. These expenses are separated because they are significant for financial analysis.

ITEM 5—Depreciation Expense: In common usage, depreciation represents the decrease in value of an asset. Have you heard someone exclaim, "I just bought a new car and it depreciated $1,000 when I drove it off the lot!"

Accountants use depreciation to spread the cost of equipment, buildings, and tools over the life of the asset. The cost of these items is an expense of doing business, just like wages or rent. The only difference is that the equipment has a longer useful life and should not be shown as a one-time expense. Let's say your business bought a piece of equipment for $25,000 and you expect to use it for 25 years. Is this an expense of doing business? Yes, but the expense is recorded over the 25-year useful life.

There are several methods of calculating depreciation but most small businesses will use the methods allowed under federal income tax laws: 1) the straight-line method, or 2) the Modified Accelerated Cost Recovery System (MACRS). The simplest is the straight-line method. To calculate it, simply divide the cost of a piece of equipment by its estimated useful life. In the above example, depreciation expense would be ($25,000/25 years) $1,000 per year.

ITEM 6—Income Taxes: Income taxes constitute an expense of doing business. Whether you will include this on the income statement or not depends upon the legal structure of your business. Income taxes are not considered an expense for sole proprietorships or partnerships. This is because the taxes are levied on the owners, not on the business. Income taxes are levied on a corporation, so they would appear on the corporation's income statement.

ITEM 7—Net Income: Finally—the **bottom line**. For the income statement, that means:

Revenues - Expenses = Net Income

The critical relationship to remember is: as revenues go so does net income. As expenses go up, net income goes down. The idea here is to profitably sell as much as you can and to keep your expenses as low as you can. This is fundamental to business success.

Louisa's Jams Seeks Capital

After the first year of operation, Louisa and Anne realized that they had underestimated the amount of money it would take to operate their business. Their costs for upgrading their facility and maintaining the old equipment was considerably more than they had expected. Anne sat down and calculated that if the business invested in new bottling equipment, it would save on the costs of continually repairing the old run down equipment (that she thought had been such a bargain) and it would have larger and more reliable production capacity.

The cost of the new equipment they would need was over $50,000. It was time for Louisa's Jams to look for external financing. It was time to clean up the business's financial statements and fine tune its business plan, and create what Anne called, "A really kick butt financing proposal!"

The Balance Sheet

The balance sheet is like a photograph. It shows the financial situation of a business at a particular point in time. The information presented in a balance sheet is related to that day and that day only. The formula for the balance sheet is:

Assets = Liabilities + Owners' Equity

Assets are economic resources *owned* by the business. These assets are acquired using funds supplied by creditors or owners. **Liabilities** are amounts *owed* by the business to creditors. **Owners' equity** is amounts *owed* by the business to the owners.

The balance sheet presents the total of what the business owns and who has a claim to those resources. It divides up the asset pie:

The balance sheet presents the total of what the business owns and who has a claim to those resources

The Asset Pie

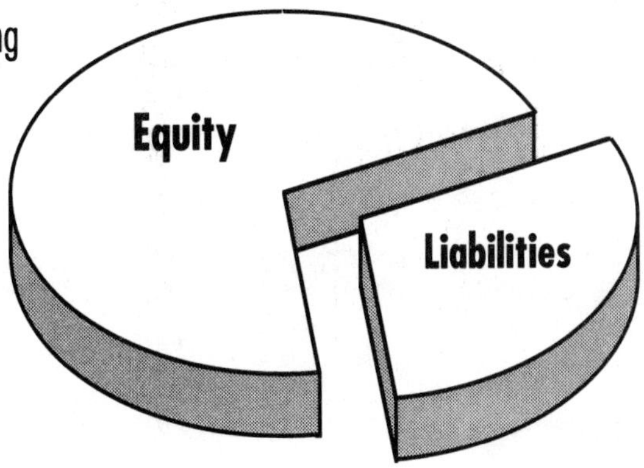

Most often, owners' equity is described as a residual amount—the amount left over after all liabilities have been subtracted from assets. This is true but perhaps not a helpful way to think about equity. Recall the discussion of the economic entity concept. If the business is thought of as separate from the owners, then, to the business, the owners are just like all other creditors. Any amounts loaned to the business by creditors must be repaid some day. Creditors generally expect to earn interest on their loan. Owners hope to get back any amounts put into the business plus some profit. Equity represents the amount the business owes to the owners for amounts invested plus profit.

Equity represents the amount the business owes to the owners for amounts invested plus profit

Number Crunching

Louisa was new to the process of gathering the data to update financial statements. While she had operated her travel agency, she left all that sort of "number crunching" to her accountant and her business manager. But this time around she was fascinated. She was curious to find the answers to some questions that had been nagging at her, like:

- *Which types of jams were most profitable? And what type of future products would be most profitable to offer?*
- *Were her costs in line with her competitors?*
- *How much debt could her business afford to carry?*
- *How attractive was her business to potential investors?*
- *Had the business broken even yet?*
- *Was her daughter doing a good job of managing cash?*
- *What portion of the business's earnings came from renting out excess kitchen capacity?*

Anne knew that updating the business's financial statements would give them the answers to these questions. It would also be a powerful reminder of why Louisa's Jams was profitable and prepare the business for seeking additional capital.

Your Business
Balance Sheet
As of December 31, 1996

ASSETS:		
Current Assets: ❶		
Cash	$ 35,000	
Accounts receivable	70,000	
Inventory	120,000	
Other	12,000	$ 237,000
Property, Plant & Equipment: ❷		
Land	$ 80,000	
Buildings	250,000	
Equipment	175,000	
Less: Accumulated Depreciation	(105,000) ❸	400,000
Intangible Assets: ❹		
Patents	$10,000	
Goodwill	60,000 ❺	70,000
TOTAL ASSETS		$ 707,000
LIABILITIES:		
Current Liabilities: ❻		
Accounts payable	$ 45,000	
Wages payable	32,000	
Other	6,000	$ 83,000
Long-term Liabilities: ❼		
Notes payable		$ 245,000
TOTAL LIABILITIES		$ 328,000
OWNER'S EQUITY:		$ 379,000 ❽
TOTAL LIABILITIES AND EQUITY		$ 707,000

Assets = Liabilities + Owners' Equity

ITEM 1—Current Assets: Current Assets are resources the business owns which it expects to convert into cash or use up within one year of the balance sheet date. Segregating assets provides information about short-term ability of the business to make payments and stay in business. In our example, your business already owns assets which it expects to convert into $237,000 cash in the next year. That is to say, in addition to the $35,000 of existing cash, accounts receivable will be collected, inventory will be sold, and other assets will be converted into cash for a total of $237,000.

ITEM 2—Property, Plant & Equipment: Property, Plant & Equipment includes assets expected to last more than one year. Remember, these assets are listed at historical cost. Our example shows buildings for $250,000. That represents the cost of the buildings when they were acquired, not their market value today.

ITEM 3—Depreciation: Depreciation has already been discussed as a means of spreading out the cost of long-term assets. How much cost has been expensed in the past is the function of the Accumulated Depreciation amount listed on the balance sheet. It indicates how much depreciation expense has been recorded in the past. In the example, accumulated depreciation is $105,000. Therefore, $105,000 of depreciation expense has already been recorded, so out of the total cost of buildings and equipment of $425,000, there remains $320,000 of depreciation expense to be recorded in the future. Land is not depreciated because the life of land is infinite.

Intangible assets are recorded at historical cost

ITEM 4—Intangible Assets: Intangible Assets have no physical presence. You can touch the piece of paper that legally evidences a patent, but you cannot touch the patent itself. The patent is merely a legal concept. The most common intangible assets are patents, copyrights, franchises, trademarks, organization costs, and goodwill.

Many valuable assets are included in this category. The brand name and logo for Louisa's Jams would fall into this category. How important to Nike is their "swoosh" or Ronald McDonald to the McDonald's Corporation? Very important! Yet, these assets might not be large amounts in the financial statements. Intangible assets are recorded at historical cost. The only cost to Nike of the "swoosh" was probably a fee to the marketing firm which designed it. Further, intangible asset costs are expensed in a manner similar to depreciation called amortization. The amount on the balance sheet is the original cost less accumulated **amortization** and may not be a very big number but may represent something very important to the company.

This creates problems for small businesses trying to obtain financing. What if the most valuable asset the business owns is a patent? The patent will only be included on the balance sheet at the amount it cost to obtain it. You could total attorney fees, filing fees, and the purchase price if you buy the patent from someone else. However, research and development costs are not included. The result is that your most valuable asset is included on your balance sheet at a fraction of its worth to the business.

ITEM 5—Goodwill: Goodwill is the intangible value of a business. Assume that you buy a company with a reputation for great customer service. Chances are you will have to pay more because of their great reputation. It is difficult to put a dollar value on an intangible asset. That excess is called goodwill. Goodwill is recorded as an intangible asset.

Goodwill is the intangible value of a business

ITEM 6—Current Liabilities: Current liabilities are debts a business expects to pay within the next year.

ITEM 7—Long-term Liabilities: Long-term liabilities are debts the business owes that are due more than one year from the balance sheet date. This often includes notes payable to the bank and investors.

ITEM 8—Owner's Equity: For a sole proprietorship, the owner's share of the business is listed as one amount, usually called **capital.** A partnership follows this same format, except that one capital amount is listed for each partner.

The owners' equity for a corporation is divided. The amount invested into the corporation by the stockholders is called **capital stock.** Profits which are owed to the owners are called **retained earnings.**

Louisa's Jams Takes a Closer Look at Profitability

Anne decided to begin with a cost/volume analysis to answer her mother's questions about how the business was generating its profits and how close she was to recouping her initial investment.

Louisa's fixed and variable costs included the following items:

Fixed Costs:	*Variable Costs:*
Lease payments, salaries, equipment maintenance, equipment depreciation, utilities, insurance, marketing, advertising	*Hourly wages, jars, labels and lids, berries, sugar, gelatin*

Anne calculated that for every $4 jar of jam they sold, their variables costs were $0.55 and fixed costs were $1.45. This meant that each jar generated $2 of profit. If the business continued at its current sales levels, it would repay its initial investment by the end of the year. Louisa was very happy to hear this.

By looking at Louisa's Jams' balance sheet, Anne calculated that the business's debt/equity ratio was a healthy 25%. This meant that for every dollar asset held by the business, only $0.25 was borrowed! Many businesses would feel that this was too little debt, and that by injecting more borrowed money into growing operations, the business could generate a better return. Anne and Louisa realized that the business could certainly afford to carry more debt.

Statement of Owners' Equity

The statement of owners' equity can be viewed as a bridge between the income statement and the balance sheet. The three statements are interrelated. The income statement details the income producing activities of the business over a specified time period and delineates net income. Net income is for the benefit of the owners. The statement of owners' equity adds the net income to amounts already owed to the owners. The adjusted owners' equity amount is then listed on the balance sheet.

The format differs somewhat depending on ownership structure. For sole proprietorships, the statement will appear as below. Partnerships will use the same format, but with a capital account listed separately for each partner.

A sole proprietorship should use the format below:

The Sole Proprietorship
Statement of Owner's Equity
For the Year Ended December 31, 1996

Beginning capital	$70,000
New investment by owner	10,000
Net income	50,000
Withdrawals	(40,000)
Ending capital	$90,000

A corporation should use the format below:

The Company, Inc. Statement of Retained Earnings For the Year Ended December 31, 1996	
Beginning retained earnings	$100,000
Net income	250,000
Less: dividends	(150,000)
Ending retained earnings	$200,000

Louisa's Jams Analyzes Its Cash Flows

As Anne and Louisa updated the business's statement of cash flows for the past years' operations, they found the following:

- *25% of the business's revenue came from leasing out its excess capacity.*
- *For any given month, the business had an average cash balance of $50,000. This was more than it needed on hand.*
- *The business generated 75% of its revenues in September, when its largest customers placed and paid for orders.*

Anne and Louisa drew several conclusions from this information. They concluded that the business should buy its new equipment in October, when the business had the largest cash receipts. They also lowered their target amount of money to borrow, deciding instead that the business could afford to reinvest a larger portion of its profits in the business. In essence, they had underestimated the business's ability to help pay for its own expansion.

This was good news.

They also realized that they were earning some sizable cash from their sub-leasing activities. If they could more aggressively manage that area of the business, they calculated they could increase overall revenues by 10%. From now on Louisa's Jams would also lease out excess warehouse space and excess bottling capacity. In the future, they would also consider offering a fuller service facility to their tenants, including commercial food production planning and budgeting assistance.

The Statement of Cash Flows

The Statement of Cash Flows presents the amounts and sources/ destinations of cash inflows and outflows

One of the tools used for cash management is the Statement of Cash Flows. When businesses use the accrual method of accounting, they provide very useful information about their past, present, and future financial situations. The accounting profession believes the accrual basis is better than the cash basis. However, it would be nice to have a simple explanation of how the business acquired and spent cash. A fourth financial statement is required.

The Statement of Cash Flows presents the amounts and sources/destinations of cash inflows and outflows. No new data is required to fill this statement. The information it contains is derived from the other financial statements. While that may sound straightforward and easy, preparing the statement of cash flows is often a very difficult task. In essence, the statement converts amounts already recorded using the accrual method of accounting to what the amounts would have been if the cash method was used. Most small businesses have their outside accountants prepare this statement!

Your Business
Statement of Cash Flows
For the Year Ended December 31, 1996

Cash flows from operations: ❶	
Net income	$90,000
Depreciation expense	50,000
Increase in accounts receivable	(80,000)
Increase in inventory	(40,000)
Decrease in accounts payable	(10,000)
Cash provided by operations	$ 10,000
Cash flows from investing activities: ❷	
Purchase of new equipment	$ (55,000)
Sale of old equipment	40,000
Cash used for investing activities	$(15,000)
Cash flows from financing activities: ❸	
Proceeds from new borrowings	$ 135,000
Principal payments on borrowings	(85,000)
Payment of dividends	(30,000)
Cash provided by financing activities	$ 20,000
Net increase in cash	$ 15,000 ❹
Cash balance 12/31/95	20,000
Cash balance, 12/31/96	$ 35,000

ITEM 1—Cash Flows from Operations: The statement of cash flows is divided into three categories. The first category details cash inflows and outflows from operations. There are two ways to present this information. The indirect method is shown in the example on the previous page. Your accountant may choose to use the direct method, but it is simply a matter of form. The final answer will be the same under either method: what net income would have been under the cash basis of accounting.

The indirect method can be very helpful in understanding the difference between net income and cash flow. Ever thought, "I have a large net income but no cash! How can that be?" Let's review the example to help explain.

The statement of cash flows: what net income would have been under the cash basis of accounting

In our example, the business had $90,000 of net income. This number is taken directly from the bottom of the income statement. Net income needs to be adjusted so that it accurately reflects the amount of cash held by the business today. First, net income includes depreciation expense, which is just a process of cost allocation and has nothing to do with cash. The cash was spent when the business bought the equipment, perhaps five years ago. Depreciation does not cause additional cash to be spent, so it is added back to net income on this statement. Three very crucial operating accounts need to be looked at now. The accounts receivable from customers has increased over what it was last year. That means many of our sales have not yet materialized into cash. Inventory is higher than it was the previous year, so some of our cash must have been used to build up our inventory. Accounts payable has decreased so we must have used cash to pay off more debts than normal. The statement of cash flows has helped us see that the business has lots of net income but not lots of cash due to slow collections, increased inventory, and fewer outstanding bills.

ITEM 2—Cash Flows from Investing: The second section shows cash inflows and outflows from investing activities. For small businesses, this primarily relates to buying and selling property, plant, and equipment.

ITEM 3—Cash Flows from Financing: The final section lists cash flows from financing activities. These include borrowing money, paying off debts, issuing more stock, and paying dividends.

ITEM 4—Net Increase in Cash: The statement concludes with the net change to cash during the year. That amount should always equal the difference between the cash balance at the beginning and the end of the period.

Cost-Volume-Profit Analysis

Cost-volume-profit analysis uses the break-even analysis to formulate "What if?" analysis. It can be a very useful tool for entrepreneurs who want to see how expenses change when sales volume changes.

To perform this analysis, divide expenses into two categories: variable and fixed. **Variable expenses** are those which change in total amount given changes in sales volume. **Fixed expenses** stay the same in total amount despite changes in sales volume. Here is a picture:

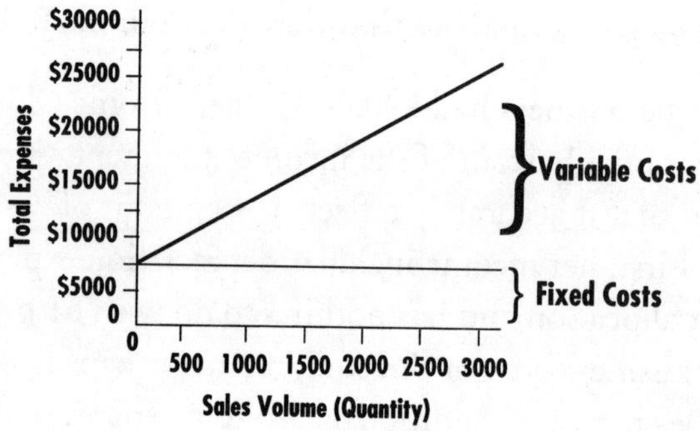

Most small businesses find their expenses are fixed, with the exception of cost of goods sold

Most small businesses find their expenses are fixed, with the exception of cost of goods sold. For example, consider a retail shoe store. The store is open 60 hours per week and the owners have determined that one worker is needed during every operating hour. The cost of paying for 60 hours of work is fixed, no matter which employee receives the pay, because an employee must be on site. The monthly rent expense is also fixed. Other major expenses, such as utilities and advertising, might change from month to month but, if the owners are working with a budget, the dollars spent probably don't vary much. So, the only variable expense is the cost of the shoes that are sold.

Now, if a line depicting total sales is added to our graph, the break-even point can be readily seen: that point at which total sales dollars and total expenses are equal.

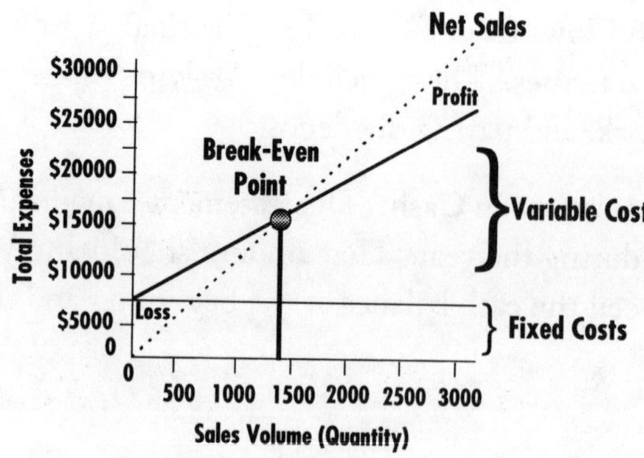

The break-even point is calculated by using the following formula:

$$\text{Break-even point} = \frac{\text{Total fixed expenses}}{\text{Contribution margin per unit}}$$

The **contribution margin** is the sales price per unit minus the variable expenses per unit. It is the portion of the total sales price per unit that goes towards paying off fixed costs. The formula can be adjusted to add a desired net income.

$$\text{Break-even point} = \frac{\text{Total fixed expenses + desired net income}}{\text{Contribution margin per unit}}$$

Assume the following for the shoe store:

Average sales price per unit	\$ 30
Variable cost per unit	\$ 10
Total fixed costs per month	\$ 3,000

The break-even point for the store is 150 pairs of shoes, calculated as follows:

$$\frac{\text{Total fixed expenses}}{\text{Contribution margin}} = \frac{\$3,000}{\$20} = 150 \text{ units}$$

If the owners hope to make \$2,000 net income per month, the store must sell 250 pairs of shoes.

$$\frac{\text{Total fixed expenses + net income}}{\text{Contribution margin}} \qquad \frac{\$3,000 + \$2,000}{\$20} = 250 \text{ units}$$

Now various questions can be asked about the business to see what changes. What if total fixed expenses increase by 20%? 280 pairs of shoes must be sold to maintain the desired \$2,000 in net income.

$$\frac{\text{Total fixed expenses + net income}}{\text{Contribution margin}} \qquad \frac{\$3,600 + \$2,000}{\$20} = 280 \text{ units}$$

What happens if the cost of shoes goes up or the store has to lower its sales price and the contribution margin decreases \$4 per unit? Now the store must sell about 313 pairs to meet its goal.

$$\frac{\text{Total fixed expenses + net income}}{\text{Contribution margin}} \qquad \frac{\$3,000 + \$2,000}{\$16} = 312.5 \text{ units}$$

As a rough measure for understanding your business, cost-volume-profit analysis is very useful

This type of analysis does have its limitations. Most businesses sell a wide variety of products, so using an average contribution margin per unit won't help you calculate needed volumes by product. Also, identifying what are variable costs and what are fixed is not always easy. However, as a rough measure for understanding your business, cost-volume-profit analysis is very useful.

Louisa's Jams Gets Its Bottling Equipment

In the end, Louisa's Jams compiled and presented a strong financing proposal to 4 local banks. In its proposal it clearly stated that it wanted to borrow $30,000 to pay for new bottling equipment, based on its projected sales (growing at 20% a year).

The business was approved for a $30,000 loan one month later. Louisa and Anne knew that the time they had put into planning their business and creating and utilizing their financial statements had paid off. They had a firm grasp on their business's profitability and cash flows and were excited to be able to bring Louisa's Jams to an ever-growing audience.

More than that, they were fast becoming the most famous mother/daughter business team on the East Coast!

Conclusion

Communicating financial information is vital to running a healthy business. Successful entrepreneurs depend upon that information to help them make decisions. Here the basic ideas behind financial statements were discussed along with the general format and some ways to analyze the data. The financial statements are the end result of the accounting process. In the next Chapter, *Keeping Books and Records*, that accounting process will be discussed, as well as organization and business record keeping.

Chapter 32
KEEPING BOOKS AND RECORDS

About This Chapter:

- *What makes a good accounting system?*
- *The paperwork*
- *Types and modules of accounting systems*
- *Tax considerations*

Introduction

Donald Peterson seemed like a nice guy and a good bookkeeper. But he is now serving a 105-month federal prison sentence for embezzling millions of dollars from small businesses. At first he wrote company checks to himself under a different name. Later, he took on a partner and gave him blank company documents used to create forgeries. If someone got wise, he simply moved on to another business with a new identity. He hid his thefts by "cooking the books," handing his employer false financial statements. Incredibly, he said the owners seldom looked at them. Even fewer ever asked to see the bank statements and none ever looked at the canceled checks. He said that perhaps the theft was a "good learning experience" and helped make his victims more careful business people.

This is a true story and, unfortunately, embezzlements from small businesses happen every year. In many cases, the theft could have been prevented if the business owner understood and paid attention to their own accounting system.

In this chapter, you will be introduced to some aspects of accounting systems. This chapter is not intended to make you an accounting expert or solve all your accounting problems. The goal is to help you understand what these systems do, how they do it, and your role in managing them.

It's a Dirty Job, But...

Individuals generally do not start a small business so they can stay up nights keeping the books. Someone has to do it but it doesn't have to be you. Fortunately, there are many good bookkeepers and accountants out there who are happy working with those numbers that drive you crazy or that you don't have time to record. However, as Donald Peterson's true story shows, it is very important that you understand your accounting system and review carefully its results.

Why do we need accounting?

- tax information
- lenders
- owners

Why do you need accounting? First, there are some legal requirements for keeping books and records. The federal government demands that you maintain records to support the figures on your tax return. Second, your banker or lender will require that records be kept. Last, the records are more important to the business owner than to anyone else. Remember, accounting is a means of gathering information to run your business. Sometimes you just need the overall picture and sometimes you need detail. Your accounting system should give you all the information you need.

A quick word about terminology. You will hear people talk about **accounting, record keeping**, and **bookkeeping**. All three terms are used in this chapter. What is the difference? Well, in common usage there probably is not much difference. All three terms refer to keeping track of business transactions. The important thing to note is that all three terms refer to systems involving accounting books and records. The records are source documents which support amounts entered in the books.

Miami: City of Sweat!

Health and fitness is big business in Miami. People are willing to pay for the best aerobic classes, latest trends in cardiovascular equipment, and most challenging instructors and personal trainers. Sally Garcia was a fitness enthusiast herself. She was a certified aerobics instructor and personal trainer who worked as an independent contractor at several of the cities highest quality gyms. After her divorce, she took 3 months off to travel with friends. During that time she reassessed her professional life and decided she was ready for a bigger challenge.

Sally had worked with enough clients to know what they thought of the existing fitness clubs in her area. Most people felt that the clubs were too loud and impersonal. All of her nearly 25 clients longed for a smaller, more personal club. They all agreed that they would be willing to pay up to 50% more for such a luxury.

She decided to make her move.

What Makes a Good Accounting System?

It Works for You

Every business is unique and a good accounting system recognizes and serves that uniqueness. The accounting system is supposed to provide you with needed information. Your decision making should not be hindered because your accounting system cannot provide you with the information you need.

Cost vs. Benefit of Information

Can you manage your business using a standard accounting system? Customizing standard systems or creating new systems to fit your needs can be very time consuming and expensive. Some important questions to consider are: How much detail do you really need? Is it worth the cost of getting it? Is it really important?

Keep it Simple!

Simplicity is the key to an accounting system which gets used and used properly. Try to eliminate duplication of effort, summarize whenever possible, and set up standard procedures to eliminate guessing and uncertainty. Make it as simple as possible. Systems that are complicated to use most often don't get used.

Keep your accounting system simple!

Owner Involvement

The best accounting systems are developed and operated under the watchful eye of the business owner. You do not have to do the work yourself, but you must understand the system and be able to interpret the output. Remember, the more involved you are, the better your accounting system will function.

Internal Controls

A good accounting system includes policies and procedures to safeguard business assets, promote the objectives of the business, and assure reliability of the financial statements and compliance with laws and regulations. These policies and procedures are called **internal controls.**

Internal controls help you safeguard your assets

Lunar Gym is Launched

Sally opened her health club, Lunar Gym, in September 1994. For her the business was a logical outgrowth of her passion for fitness. She never claimed to be a business woman. She relied on her general manager to take care of all business-related tasks, including keeping the gym's books and records.

Sally priced her gym memberships slightly higher than her competitors. She offered full club memberships as well as class-only series punch cards. When she felt she needed to increase her membership numbers, she would place an ad in the local paper and offer a discounted membership special. In this way, Sally managed all of the club's marketing efforts.

Sally knew that her management style was "seat of the pants" at best. But she loved what she did, and the business seemed to be profitable. She knew nothing about bookkeeping, but she left that to her business/front desk manager, anyway. All she knew is that the rent was getting paid, her members seemed happy, and she had the best instructors and the fullest aerobics classes in town.

That all ended one day in 1997 when the bank called to tell her they would not cover any more of her bounced checks.

The Paperwork

This chapter began with a discussion of record keeping and stressed the importance of documenting business transactions. Let's take a look at some of the typical paperwork used. You might not need all of these forms for your business or you might find that additional paperwork is required. Remember, every record keeping system is unique.

Invoice

The seller's request for payment. This is the "bill."
Information included:
Seller's name and address
Invoice date
Buyer's name and address
Description/quantity of goods sold
Dollar amount per item and in total
Credit terms
Method of shipment
Payment due date

Purchase Order

The buyer's request for goods.
Information included:
Buyer's name and address
Date

Seller's name and address
Description/quantity of goods desired
Expected price of the goods
Special shipping instructions

Receiving Report

Indicates that goods have been received.
Information included:
Date
Description/quantity of goods received
Seller's name and address
Condition of goods received
Name of person who received the goods

Checks

Authorize payment out of a bank account and serve as evidence that a bill has been paid.
Information included:
Date
Check number
Business name and address
Payee's name
Dollar amount
Description of check purpose
Authorized signature

Every record keeping system is unique

Cash Register Tapes

Give daily sales totals.
Information included:
Date
Description of item sold
Per unit price of items sold
Total sales amount
Method and amount of payment
Change required

Time Cards or Tickets

Help determine wages owed to employees.
Information included:
Employee name

Time period
Pay rate
Hours worked, by day
Total hours worked
Supervisor approval

Payroll Authorizations

Document employee status and pay information.
Information included:
Employee name and address
Date of hire
Pay rate
Job title
Authorized work hours
Benefits information
Method of payment
Who hired the employee

Types of Accounting Systems

Your accounting system helps you keep track of financial information. You will collect the data, record it, classify and summarize it, and then report it in the form of financial statements. You need some organized method of doing all this to avoid reporting incorrect or misleading information. Accounting systems can be as simple as your checkbook or so complicated that it can baffle a bunch of computer programmers. Let's take a look at some common systems, starting with those more complex.

Computerized Accounting Systems

Oh, the tedious tasks the computer can do for us!

Oh, the tedious tasks the computer can do for us! We can enter a single amount and the computer will place it in the proper journal, record a new total in the General Ledger, and provide us with up-to-date financial statements. Sounds great, but are computerized systems right for every business? What kinds of systems are available?

Computerized accounting systems can be extremely complex, relatively simple, and everything in between. In the simplest form, the computer does the mechanical tasks of adding and subtracting, while most of the "brain" work is done by the bookkeeper. More complex systems are capable of providing management with information much too difficult to accumulate by hand. Most businesses find what they need lies somewhere in the middle.

In order to use a computerized accounting system, the business must have access to computer **hardware** (equipment) and **software** (programs that make the computer work.) In general, **computerized accounting software** can belong to one of the following groups:

- **Spreadsheets:** These programs are readily available for purchase and relatively inexpensive. Popular packages are Microsoft Excel, Lotus 1-2-3, and Quattro Pro. Spreadsheet programs are like large worksheets with rows and columns which can be set up to look just like the journals and ledger accounts described above. The more complex the business, the more difficult it may be to customize a spreadsheet program to provide desired information. However, many small businesses choose to use spreadsheet programs because their accounting needs are not extensive and the programs are affordable.

- **Point-of-Sale Systems:** You know those scanners that most grocery and department stores use at the checkout stand? Those may seem like the old cash registers but they are really sophisticated computerized accounting systems. Data about merchandise is programmed into the computer when it is received and every transaction automatically updates inventory records. This provides valuable information to store management about what is moving fast or slow and what needs to be ordered. The program also automatically updates the accounting system by recording sales and cash received. These systems are expensive but they can save the business money by helping eliminate errors at the checkout stand and by constantly updating inventory for use in ordering and pricing decisions.

- **General Packages:** Several companies sell computerized accounting packages that can be adapted to most businesses. Prices vary greatly with the sophistication of the system. Leading sellers are Quicken, QuickBooks, and Peachtree. Some packages offer accounts payable, accounts receivable, and payroll modules, while others (like Quicken) are much simpler and include only a basic check register and cash receipts book. However, the simpler packages may not have good audit trails or the ability to look back and check your previous work.

Many companies and trade associations offer specialized computer accounting systems

- **Industry Specific:** Many companies and trade associations offer specialized computerized accounting systems designed to fit the needs of businesses in a particular industry. These systems often include project or inventory control modules. You can find specialized systems for restaurants, retailers, wholesale nurseries, construction companies, etc.

Whether a computerized accounting system is right for your business is often a matter of cost versus benefit. If the benefit you will receive is greater than the cost of installing and working with the system, then it is a good idea. Remember to define "cost" very broadly; take into account dollars, time, and frustration! Implementing a new computer package can try your patience. There are likely to be misunderstandings, befuddling results, and baffling error messages at first. You should continue to manually record your information for a time while testing your new system. In most cases, initial problems can be overcome and the system can function well to give you helpful information.

If you decide to use a computerized accounting system for your business, think about the following before making your selection:

Think carefully before choosing a computerized accounting system

1. What are the hardware requirements?
2. How easily can the system be modified to suit my needs?
3. Does the computer supplier have support personnel who can help me if I have problems?
4. What happens if my needs expand in the future? Does this system have additional modules that can be added?
5. How user friendly is the system?
6. What types of training are available for learning this system?
7. Does the system produce the types of reports and documents I would like to have?
8. Who will work with this system in our business? Do I need to hire someone?
9. Are other local business owners using this software?

Lunar Gym's Bookkeeping Crisis

There was a big problem. Sally realized that her general manager spent most of her time managing the front desk. She was unqualified to be keeping books and had little interest in the financial operations of the business. So who was steering the ship?

It appeared that no one was. By doing a little bit of digging, Sally found that her manager had been keeping only the most basic of records, and that the club had been regularly bouncing checks for the past 6 months.

She looked back over the three years she had been in operation and wondered,

- *Was she making any money?*
- *Where was all her cash?*
- *Could she afford the upgrades to the club's facilities she had been planning?*
- *Would she be able to get financing for the upgrades or was her credit ruined?*

Before she could grow her business, Sally badly needed to clean up her record keeping mess and take a good hard look at her business's finances.

Write-it-Once Accounting Systems

There are a number of **manual accounting systems** available that reduce repetition by allowing you to write one amount and update several books at once. This is done using special carbonized forms. For example, before you write a check to pay a supplier, you would place cards representing the cash and accounts payable accounts below the check. When you write the check amount, it will automatically transfer as a reduction to those accounts. These systems eliminate errors that occur when amounts must be written in more than one place.

Check Registers

The simplest form of accounting system, often sufficient for the needs of a small business, is a check register. These differ slightly from your personal check register in that many columns are provided to record the source of cash receipts or the reason for checks written. Monthly totals allow the business owner to easily prepare a simple income statement. However, it can be difficult to prepare a balance sheet from this information; you may need some help from your accountant!

The General Ledger includes details of all accounts

The Modules of an Accounting System

Whether computerized or not, accounting systems are often divided into several modules. A **module** is a distinct part of the accounting system that requires special paperwork and accounting tasks. The accounting system is divided into smaller parts. Larger firms will have a whole department for each of these areas. Active smaller businesses may have a different bookkeeper assigned to each module.

General Ledger

The General Ledger includes details of all the accounts. Details from the other modules will be fed into the General Ledger. You might consider it the control module.

Every account is given a unique account number. These numbers are listed in a document called the **Chart of Accounts**. You can assign numbers in any fashion desired but accountants do use a standard scheme. It is best to systematically establish account numbers like this:

Type of Account	Begin Account # with:
Assets	1
Liabilities	2
Owners' Equity	3
Revenues	4
Expenses	5

You can use account numbers to help you create special reports. For example, let's assume Wages Expense has been given the account number 520. The account number can be extended to indicate location and department. Then reports can be created by location or by department. You might record information for Wages Expense in account 520512.

520 Indicates that this is Wages Expense
05 This expense is from the Albany store
12 These wages are for employees in the auto repair department

Inventory

Accounting for inventory can be very difficult and is beyond the scope of this book. The total amount recorded for inventory is the multiplication of two numbers: the quantity of goods times the cost per unit. Hopefully, your inventory is turning over quickly, but this does make the accounting process more difficult. There are several methods used to determine the quantity and the cost of the goods. This is a good subject to discuss with your accountant!

Accounts Receivable

One accounting tool that gives valuable information about credit customers: the **Accounts Receivable Subsidiary Ledger**. Controlling accounts receivable is very important to maintaining an adequate cash position. Remember that each account is like a single sheet of paper on which information from the journals is recorded. The Accounts Receivable account includes debits for all sales made on account and credits for all the customer payments received. However, it is not separated by customer. That information would be very helpful for identifying slow-paying customers and determining if future credit sales should be made. The Accounts Receivable Subsidiary Ledger keeps credit sales and payment information by customer.

One accounting tool that gives valuable information about our credit customers: the Accounts Receivable Subsidiary Ledger

Accounts Payable

The **Accounts Payable Subsidiary Ledger** helps keep track by vendor of amounts owed. The total of all balances in the subsidiary ledger should equal the balance in the Accounts Payable controlling account in the General Ledger.

Lunar Gym Brings In the Big Guns

What Lunar Gym needed was someone whose sole responsibility was to keep the books, manage all of the business's finances, and safeguard the business's assets. This person would steer Sally's operations by providing real-life, financial guidance on what she could afford and how she could maximize her financial returns.

Up until then, Sally had simply assumed that the financial records, however sparse, were reliable and accurate. She thought they might come in handy someday when she sought additional financing to improve her facility. She was in the process of realizing (perhaps too late!) that financial records are an essential tool for day-to-day management.

Sally's first move was to hire Cindy Evangelista, a CPA and freelance financial planner to help her get her books in order and Lunar Gym back on track. Cindy also happened to be a member of the gym, so Sally negotiated a barter exchange for her time: Cindy would receive a full, lifetime club membership and would be kept on retainer for a monthly fee of $150.

Property, Plant and Equipment

A careful list of all long-lived assets must be maintained. These records allow calculation of depreciation expense and help record subsequent disposal of assets. A subsidiary ledger, tied in total to the account balances in the **General Ledger**, is often kept for these assets. The subsidiary ledger should include date purchased, name of supplier, a description of the item, check number by which paid and the amount. Separate ledgers are often kept by type of asset: equipment, vehicles, building, furniture, etc. An item should be removed from the ledger only if it is physically removed from the business: junked, sold, traded in, or destroyed.

Payroll

Accounting for payroll is complicated by all the federal, state, and local rules

Accounting for payroll is complicated by all the federal, state, and local rules you must follow. Trying to find out what information to keep and how and when to report it can be a big headache! You might consider using a bookkeeping service to help with payroll accounting, even if the rest of your accounting modules will be handled internally. There are many companies offering these services and you can have them perform all the payroll functions (updating employee records, writing payroll checks, preparing payroll tax reports) or they can help you set up procedures for doing some of the work yourself and let them handle the more complicated aspects.

Typically, the components of a payroll system include:

- **Payroll Register:** Summarizes the payroll for the period, including employee name, hours worked, pay rate, total gross pay, deductions, and net pay.
- **Employee Earnings Record:** Keeps the payroll information listed above for each employee.

The Tax Man Cometh

You know what they say: one of the things you can always count on is taxes. Businesses pay sales taxes, property taxes, income taxes, payroll taxes, excise taxes, and taxes disguised as licenses and fees. It can be pretty overwhelming for the small business owner to sort through all the requirements. It is also far too much information to present in this book. This is another area where you will need help! However, it is important that you have some general knowledge about these business taxes. Two of the bigger ones, income taxes and payroll taxes, are discussed next.

Taxes: one of life's certainties!

Income Taxes

How a business is taxed depends upon its form of ownership. Your business can be operated as a sole proprietorship, a partnership, or a corporation. There are also some variations of these forms, such as a limited partnership, an S Corporation, and the new Limited Liability Corporations (LLC's). Federal income taxes apply to these organizations like this:

How the business is taxed depends on how it is organized

- **Sole proprietorship:** Business income or loss is included in the personal income tax return of the sole proprietor. The business itself does not pay income tax. The sole proprietor includes a Schedule C in their personal income tax return, which generally is due April 15th. The sole proprietor may be required to pay quarterly estimated income taxes and self-employment taxes.

- **Partnership:** Business income or loss is included in the income tax returns of each of the partners. The business itself does not pay income tax. This applies whether it is a limited or general partnership. The partners include partnership income or loss on Schedule E in their personal income tax return. The partnership must file Form 1065 by April 15th. Partners may need to pay quarterly estimated income taxes and self-employment taxes.

- **S Corporation:** These work very much like a partnership for income tax purposes. Business income or loss "flows through" the individual tax returns of the corporate owners. Form 1120S must be filed by March 15th.

- **Corporation:** The business is taxed on its business income. The shareholders do not pay income tax on profits earned by the corporation. However, when shareholders receive a dividend from the corporation, they will pay personal income tax on that amount. The corporation files Form 1120 and pays its income tax by March 15th. Corporations may be required to pay quarterly estimated income taxes.

- **Limited Liability Corporation:** LLC's, like the S Corporation, are not taxed directly for income tax purposes. Thus, LLC's enjoy the pass-through tax benefits of Partnerships and S Corporations.

Fortunately, income taxes are based on the same general accounting concepts used to prepare your financial statements. Unfortunately, some of the specific rules are different. So, you cannot simply take your business income statement and forward it to the Internal Revenue Service with a check to pay your taxes. The differences between your income statement and your tax return fall into one of three categories:

1. Amounts included on your income statement that are not allowed on your tax return.
2. Amounts on your tax return not usually included on your income statement.
3. Amounts that will be included equally on both your income statement and your tax return, but in different years.

Our income tax system is very complicated. It is the result of a political process and sometimes changes with the political winds. Very few small businesses prepare their own income tax return. A discussion of professionals who can help with this chore, is discussed later in this chapter.

Payroll Taxes

Payroll taxes can be imposed on the employee and the employer.

The employer must withhold the taxes from the employee's paycheck and forward the amount to the government

Paid by the Employee	Paid by the Employer
Federal Income Taxes	State and Federal Unemployment
State Income Taxes	Social Security (FICA)
Social Security (FICA)	

In addition to the above, many states impose accident insurance or worker's compensation taxes on the employer. There may be county or city taxes to pay as well as taxes to support public transportation.

Our income tax and social security systems are on a "pay-as-you-go" basis. Companies and individuals do not wait until income tax returns are due to send in the entire amount of tax owed. Instead, the government collects the money as the year goes along. For employees, this is done through their employers, who act as collection agents for the government. The employer must withhold the taxes from the employee's paycheck and forward the amount to the government. This requirement must be taken very seriously. The government will prosecute violators. Do not consider money withheld from employees as available to meet other business debts. Penalties for failure to make timely tax payments are high.

The employer has several forms to prepare in regard to payroll:

Form #	Name	Description
941	Employer's Quarterly Federal Tax Return	Reports federal income and social security taxes withheld from employees and social security taxes imposed on the employer. *These forms are due one month after the end of the quarter.*
940	Employer's Annual Federal Unemployment Tax Return	Used to report federal unemployment tax for the year.
8109	Federal Tax Deposit Coupons	Used to make deposits of withheld income and both employee and employer shares of social security taxes. Also may include deposits for federal unemployment insurance.
W-2	Wage and Tax Statement	Given to each employee to detail earnings and amounts withheld. *These must be sent to employees no later than January 31st.* A copy is also forwarded to the government.
1099	Wage Statement	Given to contract employees.

There also may be forms required by state and local governments.

The timing of making deposits for payroll taxes is based on the total amount due. The requirements are subject to change and you should get current information from the Internal Revenue Service or your accountant.

How Had Things Gotten So Bad?

One of the first pieces of equipment Sally had purchased before opening her health club was a computer check-in system called an "Aerobitron." The computer hardware and software had cost her almost $7,000 and was supposed to record members' visits, membership dues and other receivables, accounts payable, and other vital business information.

Unfortunately, Lunar Gym's front desk staff rarely entered information into the system. Most worked at the check-in desk as a result of barter arrangements. Most had been inadequately trained on how to use the system. Often times Sally would pass the front desk and realize that the Aerobitron hadn't even been turned on.

Clearly, Sally liked to find clever ways to save money. However, it began to look to her like her "shortcuts" in personnel and other areas were costing her more than they were saving her.

Had she taken the time to be thoroughly trained on the system (or have her front desk manager receive proper training), the Aerobitron software would have been a valuable tool for Lunar Gym. It had many customizable options, and included in her monthly service contract was staff training and customer support. She had failed to use either.

Sally worried that the Aerobitron mess wasn't the only mistake she had made. How many others would she discover upon closer inspection?

What Records Do I Need to Keep?

Generally, businesses keep records either to meet laws and regulations or to have data to review when trying to make business decisions. You will need some past records during your business planning process and when you analyze trends. The records are very important for documenting the financial history of a business when it is being sold. Income tax regulations require that records be kept during the three-year period that your tax return is subject to IRS audit. There may be times when some of your records from seven years past will be useful for tax purposes. There isn't a complete, standard list of records and retention times that everyone follows, but here is one idea. Your accountant should be able to help you modify this list to fit your business needs.

Type of Record	Retention Period
Bank Statements	7 years
Business Licenses	Until Expired
Check Register Tapes	3 years
Check Registers	Keep Permanently
Cancelled Checks	3 years
Financial Statements	Keep Permanently
General Ledger	Keep Permanently
General Journal	Keep Permanently
Inventory Records	7 years
Invoices (Accounts Payable, A/P)	3 years
Invoices (Accounts Receivable, A/R)	3 years
Property, Plant & Equipment Records	Keep Permanently
Purchase Orders	3 years
Receiving Reports	3 years
Tax Returns	Keep Permanently
Time Cards or Tickets	3 years
Travel Expense Records	7 years

We keep records either to meet laws and regulations or so we have data to review when trying to make business decisions

How to Choose a Bookkeeper

As a small business owner, you probably don't want to handle all the bookkeeping tasks yourself. You will need assistance. How do you find a good bookkeeper?

Of course, you will want to follow the general procedures and think of the considerations discussed in regard to hiring any employee. But there are some specific considerations when hiring a bookkeeper.

1. **Write a job description** which states which modules in your accounting system, and which specific functions in those modules, will be the responsibility of the new bookkeeper. Some bookkeeping positions are "full-charge," which means the person works with every accounting module.

It can be difficult to learn anything that will help you discover a dishonest bookkeeper, but you certainly won't know anything if you don't ask questions

2. **Consider carefully if applicants have the right type of experience** to do the job. You do not need to hire the most experienced applicant but you should judge if the applicant will be able to handle the level of responsibility in the job. Do you have other bookkeepers on staff who will supervise and train the new employee? Or will this bookkeeper be in charge? Do you need someone to come in and start everything from scratch, or are your systems in good working order?

3. **Check applicants' accounting knowledge** with tests or interview questions. Your CPA can help you design questions appropriate for the job description you have written.

4. **Consider the requirements of your current computerized accounting program.** Is it important that the new bookkeeper be familiar with that program? Or, perhaps you want someone who can help you select a computerized accounting program and design your internal controls.

5. **Check references!** Be sure previous employers were happy with the person's performance. You can also talk to them about what tasks the employee did and relate them to the job description you have written, looking for a match. It can be difficult to learn anything that will help you discover a dishonest bookkeeper in advance, but you certainly won't know anything if you don't ask questions.

Using an Accountant

Very few small businesses can get by without some professional accounting help. There are a wide variety of services to choose from.

Accounting Services

- **Bookkeeping:** You can hire a bookkeeping service to do any or all of the tasks required in your system. Often, outside services are used for accounts receivable, accounts payable, and payroll.

- **System Design:** You may need help designing your accounting system and internal controls.

- **Income Taxes:** Almost certainly you will need help planning for and preparing your income tax returns!

- **Write-up:** You may be able to maintain the books yourself but need help putting together the financial statements and other reports. Some firms will help you design your accounting system based on software they use. You give the firm your accounting information in the form of input sheets and it is entered into the computer by the accounting firm personnel.
- **Auditing:** As your business grows and prospers, you may need an independent audit. Sometimes an audit is required by loan agreements or when a business is to be sold.
- **Temporary Services:** Perhaps all you need is some help getting through the year-end closing of your books or preparing your annual budget. Maybe you have a busy season when extra help with accounts receivable or inventory would be great. Consider using one of the temporary service agencies in your area.

Very few small businesses can get by without some professional accounting help

Worse News for Lunar Gym

The next day was not a good one for Sally. She and Cindy, the CPA, met before the club opened to review the business's records. She felt a mixture of relief and fear. Relief that she would soon get to the bottom of her business's difficulties. She had confidence in Cindy, who she knew was bright and honest. But Sally was afraid of the other "land mines" waiting for her in her business. How bad was the situation?

It was bad. They quickly realized that Sally's front desk manager had been throwing away bills, incorrectly recording expenses and revenues, and failing to collect membership dues in a timely manner. They pored through all the files and receipts they could find. Most were crammed into in the two large drawers in the bottom of the front desk. How could Sally have been oblivious to such a disaster, right under her nose?

One of their most disturbing discoveries was that Lunar Gym had more than $10,000 in outstanding accounts payable, and for each day she didn't pay, she was being charged for late fees. Her desk manager had prepared an accounts payable ledger, but most of the bills were not recorded in it. Sally dug a little deeper and found a pouch full of checks for membership dues that had never been deposited. No wonder she was bouncing checks!

She felt completely responsible for not having taken a larger role in the day-to-day operations of her business. Sally resolved that things would change that very day.

Who Can Do This Work?

There are several types of accounting professionals. The services they offer and the rates they charge varies according to their qualifications or how many tests they had to pass to get their license!

Certified Public Accountants (CPA's) are the only accounting professionals who can perform an independent audit. They are highly-skilled, highly-trained accountants and offer auditing, income tax planning and preparation, estate planning, financial planning, and write-up services. Although their rates may seem high, they can often save you money by refining your accounting system or helping you reduce income taxes.

If you remember that most accountants charge you by the hour, you will be diligent about giving them organized, complete information

Some states have other professional accountants who are not CPA's. These may include **Public Accountants** and **Licensed Tax Consultants**. These individuals have also passed rigorous examinations and been licensed by the state. They may not perform an independent audit and, while most are glad to help you with tax return preparation, not all offer income tax planning services. As the name implies, Licensed Tax Consultants specialize in income tax return preparation. Public Accountants can be very helpful in designing your accounting system, performing weekly or monthly bookkeeping chores, or doing payroll.

There are also many bookkeeping firms with very well-trained staff ready to perform bookkeeping functions for you.

The Next Day...

By early the next afternoon, Cindy reported back that there were more big problems. She had discovered a total of $8,000 in uncashed checks for membership dues. Cindy worried that as a result, the business might have been underreporting its profits and might have a sizable tax bill for the next quarter.

Together Sally and Cindy made some quick calculations, and were pleasantly surprised by what they found. They calculated that if they collected all the gym's past due accounts, deposited all of the "lost" membership dues, and negotiated for more time with some of their largest creditors, the gym could pay its taxes and begin to operate in the black by year's end.

They both agreed that the next step was finding a new qualified, motivated, and trustworthy front desk manager to replace the existing manager... and quickly!

How to Work with Your Accountant

If you remember that most accountants charge you by the hour, you will be diligent about giving them organized, complete information to reduce their time on your project! Many small business owners bring their data to the accountant without any preliminary preparation at all, sometimes literally in a shoe box. This will cost extra. Now, perhaps you have considered that and have decided that your time is valuable and you are willing to pay the accountant to organize your records. Just remember that you still need to be involved with the final outcome and monitor the system to see that all is functioning correctly. Review the financial statements carefully.

Your accountant will be able to help you better if they have a good understanding of your business. Some accountants specialize in clients from particular industries. This helps them understand the accounting issues you face. They still need to know particulars about your business and you. They cannot devise tax-saving plans without knowing your goals and the financial situation for you and your company. You will need to be very candid with your accountant, so find someone you can trust. Professional accountants keep strict confidence regarding client information.

Your accounting system should provide management information first and address tax requirements second

If you hire an accountant to help you design your accounting system, be very clear about the information you need. Sometimes accountants can be too focused on income tax requirements and design a system that responds to those laws but does not give the business owner all the useful information desired. Your accounting system should provide management information first and address tax requirements second.

Lunar Gym Takes Aggressive, Corrective Action

In their final analysis, Sally and Cindy also realized that Lunar Gym was undercharging for its club memberships. Not only could her market bear a higher price, but, at her existing rates, she was not generating enough revenue to reach target profit level.

They also decided that the club shouldn't expand until it was fully utilizing the space it had. This meant utilizing under-used space to generate extra revenue for the club. A good example was converting the childcare room during off-peak hours into a massage therapy space. This would even out the club's revenue stream throughout the day, and offer clients a fuller service club.

Within a month Sally had hired a new front desk manager. This manager was responsible for maintaining all club membership records, paying all bills, depositing all membership dues, and working closely with Cindy to input the data to maintain the business's general ledger and financial statements. Before starting full-time at the Lunar Gym, the manager attended a one-and-a-half-day training seminar on the Aerobitron and a two week intensive refresher course on bookkeeping. Three weeks later all of the front desk staff were trained and using the Aerobitron like champs.

Conclusion

This chapter is not intended to turn you into an accountant overnight. Accounting is complicated, time-consuming, and detailed, but extremely important for your business. In addition to providing information to bankers and other third parties, your accounting system is the basis on which you will supply your tax information. The business owner must be involved in the accounting process. Don't let a Donald Peterson happen to you. Use your accounting information to organize, manage and grow your business.

Chapter 33
BUDGETING

About This Chapter:
- *Why should you have a budgeting system?*
- *What makes a good budgeting system?*
- *Preparation of an annual budget*
- *Feedback from your budget*

Introduction

Remember Alice in Wonderland? She didn't know which way to go. Poor Alice. She didn't know where she was going. So, how would she know when she arrived? She needed a plan and a map. A plan would help her decide where she was going and a map would show her where she was, where she had been, and how to get where she was going.

Previously, the importance of business planning and all the benefits it can provide was discussed. Like Alice, a business needs a map, something to help judge how far it has come and how much further it has to go. Businesses need budgets.

What is a Budgeting System?

The budgeting system is the process of converting into numbers the strategic and operating decisions you make in your business plan. The budgeting process is a subset of your planning process. Strategies, goals, and objectives are determined and then future sales, expenses, and cash flows are forecast.

Notice the process is emphasized rather than the outcome. Budgets are the outcome of the budgeting process and are very important. They are a tool within the process. Budgets are used for feedback and evaluation of business results. But the process itself can prove very valuable.

Budgeting is an important part of your planning process

Why Should You Have a Budgeting System?

An effective budgeting system has many benefits for the business.

Get to Know Your Business

When you prepare budgets, you look at every aspect of the business. You get to know the business very well. That familiarity is handy when opportunities present themselves or changes occur.

The Best Little Caterers in Peekskill, New York

Peekskill Caterers was owned and operated by Sarah Erhenberg and her business partner, Jason Spears. They operated their business out of space leased from another local business, Louisa's Jams. Louisa's Jams operated out of a large, converted commercial kitchen space, with lots of extra workspace and an attached warehouse. They paid a monthly fee for rent and for use of the commercial cooking equipment.

The only restriction on them was that during the month of June, the peak summer jam making month for Louisa's, they had to relinquish use of the facilities. That was fine for Sarah and Jason who both enjoyed having a full month to take off each summer.

Sarah and Jason were both enthusiastic about catering, and completely dedicated to making Peekskill Caterers the best catering service in the Hudson River Valley area.

Their specialty was preparing what they called "epicurean adventures," meals prepared in a variety of ethnic styles, using only the freshest ingredients and most authentic herbs and spices. Their best-selling dishes were East Asian Feasts, combining plates of curries, barbecued satays, vegetarian maasalas, and dumplings. All were prepared with their own unique Pan-Asia flair, incorporating their favorite influences from French and Cajun cuisine.

Always Be Prepared

Be prepared: Unexpected situations can cause you to be reactive rather than proactive

Unexpected situations can cause you to be reactive rather than proactive. You certainly cannot anticipate every challenge your business will face, but the more knowledgeable you are, the easier it is to understand how changes affect the business and what actions should be taken.

Fuel Creative Ideas

By examining the business closely, opportunities to reduce costs, improve products, or increase efficiency can be found. The budgeting process draws attention away from the daily routine of doing the work and focuses your attention on how the work is done.

Provide Benchmarks

Alice could go anywhere in Wonderland and think it was fine because she didn't know where she was going. A business without budgets has no means of determining success or failure. Benchmarks, or markers along the route, aid in charting progress.

Uncover Potential Bottlenecks

If getting raw materials is a significant problem in manufacturing your product, the budget process is likely to reveal that. Then you can plan purchases to avoid such problems.

Coordinate the Parts of the Business

The budgeting process focuses on goals and objectives of the business as a whole and helps assure that all functions of the business are moving in the same direction. Many small business owners have difficulty expressing their business goals to their employees. The employees act according to what they believe the owner wants but they might have the wrong idea. When preparing budgets, goals and objectives are expressed, in writing.

A business without budgets has no means of determining success or failure

Involve Employees in the Business

People do a better job when they care about their work. Involving employees in the budgeting process links them emotionally to the business.

Why Don't All Businesses Use a Budgeting System?

If budgeting is such a good idea, why don't all businesses go through the process? Consider this conversation between a small business owner and her SBDC counselor:

Business Owner: We are just too busy to take time out for budgeting.

SBDC Counselor: Why are you so busy?

Business Owner: I don't know. It just seems like we never have the right materials or the right workers here. So, I am always trying to put things together at the last moment.

SBDC Counselor: Well, maybe you would have a better idea of what to expect if you prepared budgets. Then you could be sure the right materials and people are here when you need them.

Business Owner: Yeah, maybe. But, it just isn't as easy as you say. Our business is very unique and very complex.

SBDC Counselor:	Sometimes the best way to work with something so complex is to break it down into its simplest parts.
Business Owner:	True, but it will be too hard to know some of the information. Then what?
SBDC Counselor:	You're right. You can't get it perfect every time. But you can still come up with very valuable forecasts. And the process will help you identify issues about the business that demand your attention.
Business Owner:	Well, I know my business. There aren't any issues hiding from me, so I don't need this budgeting system to point anything out.
SBDC Counselor:	You may be surprised. Forcing ourselves to look closely at all aspects of the business often unveils some very interesting decisions to be made.
Business Owner:	But I don't want to face those things right now.

It is difficult to jump into a new process, so owners and managers who have never tried budgeting are likely to shy away from it. If you have suffered through an ineffective budget process, you are probably not inclined to go through it again.

The Budget Cycle

The budget process is never ending. Don't think of it as an activity you do for a few days and then ignore. Recall the planning process:

The planning process never ends!

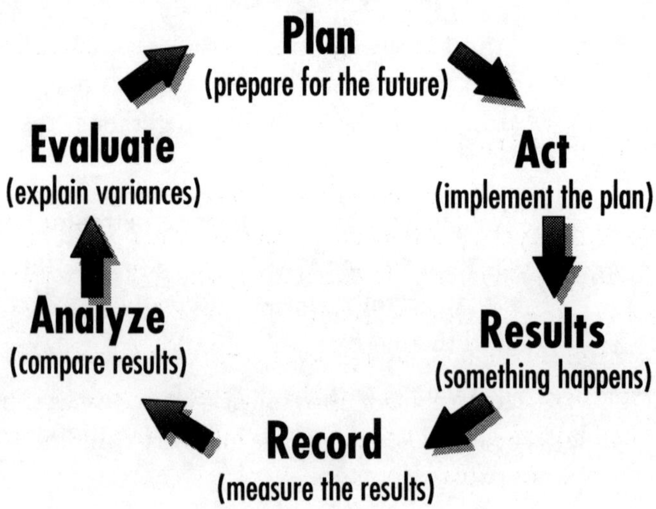

The cycle never stops. First comes planning, then those plans are put into operation. Next feedback and evaluation occurs, which leads to more planning, which starts the cycle all over again.

Budgeting is part of the planning, analyzing, and evaluation functions within this process.

Are There Profits to be Made at Peekskill Caterers?

Sarah and Jason thought that they were doing a good job of keeping their budgets. Yes, they were busy and often created their budgets "on the fly," but they were both very financially responsible and had confidence in their ability to estimate their costs.

They were wrong. When they sat down after completing a major Thanksgiving dinner project to calculate their profit (and decide if they could afford a holiday ski trip) they found that they had not only not earned their target 30% profit, they lost money!

They were shocked, and decided that however they were budgeting and projecting expenses, it was not working. They decided to ask Louisa's daughter Anne if she could give them some help. She had recently graduated from business school and kept all the books and budgets in order for Louisa's Jams. They were already good friends, and she agreed to help them create realistic and usable budgets in exchange for them catering a dinner party for her 30th birthday that April.

They sealed the agreement with a handshake, and made an appointment to meet at Anne's house the next afternoon.

How are Budgets Used?

Budgets are the outcome of the budgeting process. They result from the planning stage of the cycle, but they are needed for the operating and evaluation activities. Budgets guide purchasing, scheduling, marketing, personnel, and financing activities. Notice the operative word is "guide" rather than "control." The budgeted process is educated guesswork and not always absolutely accurate. That is why the continuous budget cycle is so important. The budgets guide our work but when deviations occur, the results are evaluated, more planning is done and forecasts are adjusted.

The evaluation of budgets is done by comparing budgeted to actual amounts. Variances are noted and questions asked. It is said that financial statement analysis doesn't give answers, it only creates questions. The same is true when evaluating budget versus actual costs. If budgeted labor costs were $140,000 and the actual amount was $152,000, a variance of $12,000 is shown. This comparison has identified the variance but it does not tell why this happened. So, the obvious question is "Why did labor costs go over budget?" Perhaps a special sales order came in and workers were added to get the order out on time. Maybe labor hours were underestimated and labor costs were higher than anticipated. Whatever is found out gives feedback for the continuing planning process.

Budgets are also useful for communicating plans. As you will remember, budgets can help keep employees on the same track as the business owner. Budgets are also an integral part of your business plan and financing proposals. A banker isn't likely to approve a loan without reviewing and understanding your budgets.

A banker isn't likely to approve a loan without reviewing and understanding your budgets

Budgets vs. actual results can help to judge employee performance. This is called **responsibility accounting**. Try to associate business activities and costs with the individual controlling those costs. This assumes that costs can be attributed to various functions within the business and that someone can control them. If this is true, budget reports can be generated by function or by person and used for performance evaluation.

What Makes a Good Budgeting System?

If you have participated in a poor budgeting system, you probably can easily tell what made it so bad! But what makes a good budgeting system?

A "good" budgeting system is one that is effective and efficient. An effective system achieves the many benefits discussed earlier in the chapter. The effective system fuels creative ideas, provides benchmarks, coordinates the functions of the business, etc. An efficient system accomplishes these things with the least turmoil and the most communication. The efficient system allows us to move smoothly through the budget cycle in a timely manner.

So, an effective and efficient budgeting system has the following attributes.

Involvement

Budgets coming "from the top," with little input from employees, are likely to meet resistance. You might hear things such as "He doesn't know what I have to go through here." "They don't understand." "How can this budget be approved?" Or, "Let's see her come down here and do this." A participatory process increases acceptance. The person performing a task is in the best position to evaluate the task and help set budgeted amounts.

When you use a **participatory budgeting process**, don't forget to keep owners and top management involved. No one will believe the process is for real if the owners don't seem to care.

The One That Gets Used

It is very frustrating to put lots of time and energy into a budgeting process, prepare some great-looking budgets, and then see them sit on a shelf and gather dust. If that happens, it will be very difficult to get participation in the future. Also, if the budgets aren't used, the feedback and evaluation portion of the budget cycle is not occurring. Valuable information for future planning is lost.

The best budgeting system? The one that gets used!

Performance Evaluation

It is very important to do performance evaluation in a positive, rather than a negative, manner. You have the choice between the carrot and the stick. Punishment might motivate your employees but the possibility of a reward often does a better job.

Remember, variances between budgeted and actual amounts cause questions to be asked. Variances can be used to identify unproductive behavior and help employees make corrections. Be sure to explore variances thoroughly rather than immediately using them to fix blame.

Create Desired Behavior

When budgeting, try to take a realistic viewpoint. Consider that budgets can cause certain behaviors. Assume your salespersons receive a bonus if their sales exceed their budgeted amount. If you set the budget too low, the sales staff will believe they can easily meet the target and have little incentive to work hard. But if the target is too high, they may think it is impossible to meet and give up without trying. Either way, you have caused behavior which has an effect opposite of what you desired.

Making realistic **budget assumptions** is very difficult. You may not get it right the first time but that is the benefit of the continuous budget cycle. The feedback you get about the targets you have chosen will help you evaluate your policies and come closer to hitting those targets the next time around.

Allow Creativity and Flexibility

Budgets should bend but not break. If the system is too rigid, the participants won't think creatively. That is what you find when the budget is prepared by simply taking last year's numbers and increasing them by some percentage. Of course, past figures shouldn't be ignored. Comparisons of budget versus actual in previous years is very valuable information. However, your budget system should encourage new ideas and not be overly dependent on past assumptions.

Document Assumptions

Budgets should bend but not break

Budgeting involves forecasting the future, which cannot be done without making lots of assumptions. Those assumptions should be written down. It is not possible to remember them months later. You will need that information when evaluating variances and to explain your budgets to your banker.

Use What You Have

Try not to create extra work for yourself. Make use of computerized spreadsheet programs to ease the clerical drudgery of preparing budgets. Many computerized accounting systems have the capacity to accept budget amounts and produce reports comparing budget to actual figures. You should design your budgets to reflect your accounting system, or make changes in your accounting system if it will result in more useful information. Remember to let your planning process guide what you do.

A Closer Look at Peekskill Caterers

Sarah and Jason had been inundated with catering jobs for the holiday season, yet they were not generating enough profit. In fact, when they looked over their statement of income and cash flow records with Anne, they found that they had lost $500 last month and nearly $900 the month before that. What was going wrong?

They reviewed their pricing and budgeting procedures with Anne.

When Peekskill Caterers bid for a job, they would estimate the number of hours of the actual job and the number of hours needed for prep time. Usually, Sarah would just add a few extra hours on to the total party time to arrive at a total number of billable hours. Sarah would also calculate the total cost of the food they would need to buy, and combine these amounts to create a flat fee for the job.

Peekskill Caterers purchased most of their high-quality ingredients from local farmers or butchers, and were often able to negotiate bulk rates. For special cuts of meats or seafood, they would have to order in advance and pay more. Likewise, in a pinch, she or Jason, or one of their helpers, would run out to the local gourmet specialty food boutique to get supplies they had forgotten or run out of.

In the rush of preparing job bids, Sarah rarely incorporated these costs into her total cost estimates.

Anne asked the partners how they incorporated overhead into their bids.

"Overhead? Oh, you mean like rent and stuff?"

"Yeah, how do you allocate those costs in your bids?"

"Well, we figure that just comes out of our hourly fee. We don't make any special provisions to cover rent and stuff. It seems too complicated and messy."

Anne thought to herself, "Oh boy we're in for a long morning..." She rubbed her head and poured herself another cup of tea.

Preparation of an Annual Budget

Take a look at the first-quarter master budget for Walt's Machine Shop. Start with the sales forecast.

Months	Jan	Feb	Mar	Total
Product/Service #1				
Units Sold	30	40	50	120
Price per Unit	$300	$300	$300	$300
Total Sales	$9,000	$12,000	$15,000	$36,000
Product/Service #2				
Units Sold	70	70	80	220
Price per Unit	$500	$500	$500	$500
Total Sales	$35,000	$35,000	$40,000	$110,000
Product/Service #3				
Units Sold	2	2	2	6
Price per Unit	$3,000	$3,000	$3,000	$3,000
Total Sales	$6,000	$6,000	$6,000	$18,000
Total-All Product/ Service Sales	$50,000	$53,000	$61,000	$164,000

In other chapters, many key points were discussed about marketing products and services. Product mix, pricing, competition, and advertising was discussed. Now it is time to project sales. This is a critical component of the master budget because all other budgets are driven by forecasted sales. The projected number of sales units tells how many to make or buy, which tells how many workers are needed, which tells labor costs and other expenses that must be paid. Then, cash inflows and outflows can be forecasted. You see, it all hinges on the sales forecast.

One word of caution: Be realistic! Resist the temptation to inflate sales estimates just to make the business look good. If the business isn't profitable, perhaps it should be abandoned. On the other hand, sales forecasts that are overly conservative may cause you to undercapitalize and be unable to support future sales growth. Insufficient inventory may be ordered or not enough people hired.

Basing all other budgets on the sales forecast can lead you back to the beginning again. For example, if your projected sales leads to a negative cash position, you may wish to come back to sales and see if you have been too conservative. Changing forecasted sales units will affect all your other budgets and perhaps lead to a positive cash balance. However, please avoid the temptation to determine the cash balance you want and juggle the sales forecasts until you get that amount.

Remember, budgeting is a continuous cycle. When you examined your marketing strategies, you probably made some initial sales projections. Now you can refine those. Later on, after you have compared actual results to your budgets, you may need to revise the figures for future months.

The sales budget shown above uses a very simple format. You can add more detail if desired. In your business plan, you already identified your products and services and determined a pricing strategy. Now you need to add quantity. Often, history is used as a base and projections are made from there. Gathering sales history may be a simple task of reviewing your records, but it can be complicated if you are trying to look at data by product or product line. Many small businesses do not keep this detail. If you have not, and find that it would be useful, you can change your record keeping system to give you this information in the future. An alternative method is to multiply total sales by your product mix ratio. For example, assume you have estimated that 65 percent of your sales normally come from a particular product line and 20 percent from a second line, etc. These percentages can give a rough estimate of sales history by product. You should use percentages of sales dollars to do this.

One word of caution: Be realistic!

Another tool you can use is an industry average. We talked about sources of these averages previously.

When you are forecasting sales, pay particular attention to past trends in the industry and your business. Trends often repeat themselves, that's why they are called trends. You may relate a past trend to what was happening in your marketplace and learn something very valuable for the future. Or, you may find a trend that you do not expect to be repeated. Then you should not use it when forecasting sales.

Previously, the product life cycle was discussed. Knowing your product's position in its life cycle is very helpful when forecasting sales. Also, if your product is seasonal, that should be reflected in your forecasts.

Now that Walt's has completed the sales forecasts, a cost of goods sold budget can be prepared.

The sales forecast is the place to start

Cost of Goods Sold Budget

Months	Jan	Feb	Mar	Total
Product/Service #1				
Units Sold	30	40	50	120
Cost per Unit	$45	$45	$45	$45
Total Cost	$1,350	$1,800	$2,250	$5,400
Product/Service #2				
Units Sold	70	70	80	220
Cost per Unit	$150	$150	$150	$150
Total Cost	$10,500	$10,500	$12,000	$33,000
Product/Service #3				
Units Sold	2	2	2	6
Cost per Unit	$300	$300	$300	$300
Total Cost	$600	$600	$600	$1,800
All Products/Service Total Cost	$12,450	$12,900	$14,850	$40,200

Recall that cost of goods sold should reflect the cost to the business of the product it is selling. Service businesses will not have this expense. For retailers and wholesalers, you can refer to manufacturer and distributor catalogs or recent invoices for cost information. Then you can make a few refinements. The cost per unit you use to forecast cost of goods sold should be reduced by expected cash or quantity discounts and increased by freight charges. In other words, use the net amount you expect to pay.

Manufacturers usually prepare a production budget which shows how they expect to produce the projected sales units. Manufacturers incur three different costs for the units they produce: direct materials, direct labor, and overhead. There are many ways to incorporate these costs into the cost of goods sold projection. You may wish to add more detail to your schedule. In the example shown, the projections are in the simplest form. Walt's Machine Shop has included only direct materials in its cost of goods sold budget. Labor and overhead costs have been forecast separately and included in the operating expenses budget. This simple presentation doesn't follow the accounting technique known as "full absorption costing," which calls for all three manufacturing costs to be included in the cost per unit. However, Walt's is using these budgets internally and to show their banker and CPA, and the simpler version is good enough.

Manufacturers might also consider that they have three types of inventory: raw materials, work in process, and finished goods. Walt's has chosen to ignore this because their jobs are relatively short and work in process is never very much. If the manufacturing process is lengthy and costs are tied up in work in process for a long time, the cost of goods sold budget should reflect that. This will affect the cash flow projections as well.

The next step for Walt's is to budget operating expenses.

The Sorry State of Budgeting at Peekskill Caterers

Anna realized that Peekskill Caterers had no formal budgeting process. She knew that they had plenty of business, and with proper budgeting and pricing, they could easily operate in the black.

Anne began by gathering a little more information about Sarah and Jason's catering business. She found that:

- *Theirs was a very seasonal business. They generated 65% of their total revenue during the peak holiday season between November and December and during July and August when many people entertained at their summer houses in the historic Hudson Valley area.*
- *For events for 6 or more people they hired an additional person to serve and help clean up, at $12 an hour.*
- *30% of their total food supply costs came from "last minute" trips to the local gourmet specialty food shop.*
- *For the past three peak seasons they had underestimated projected sales by at least 40%. This explained their "last minute" shopping for supplies and their general feeling of never having enough time to plan for personnel needs or for supplies.*
- *Over the same period of time they had overestimated their projected sales for slow winter months by at least 30%. Likewise, they failed to account for the higher cost of produce and supplies during these months or for the higher utility costs for heating their space.*
- *In total, Peekskill Caterers underestimated their catering costs by as much as 15%.*

Operating Expenses Budget

	Jan	Feb	Mar	Total
Labor				
Salaries and Wages	$30,000	$30,000	$30,000	$90,000
Payroll Taxes & Benefits	$8,695	$8,695	$8,695	$26,085
Total Labor Expense	**$38,695**	**$38,695**	**$38,695**	**$116,085**
Non-Labor				
Occupancy Expenses	$3,355	$3,480	$3,355	$10,190
Outside Services	$650	$650	$650	$1,950
Insurance	$200			$200
Advertising	$300	$1,050	$300	$1,650
Miscellaneous	$100	$100	$100	$300
Total Non-Labor	**$4,605**	**$5,280**	**$4,405**	**$14,290**

You can have as much detail as you wish for your operating expenses. Walt's has divided their costs into labor and non-labor, but you can use any categories that make sense for your business. Often, it is helpful to have additional schedules which support the amounts listed in your operating expenses budget. For example, Walt's may have a schedule giving the details of occupancy costs.

Often, it is helpful to have additional schedules which support the amounts listed in your operating expenses budget

The distinction between fixed and variable expenses must be considered when preparing operating expense forecasts. Remember, fixed costs will remain the same in total no matter what you forecast for sales. Variable costs will change in total with changes in sales volumes.

Cash Flow Projections

The sales forecast, cost of goods sold budget, and operating expenses budget lead to the cash flow projections. We cannot overemphasize the importance of managing your cash. This is so important that the entire next chapter, *Cash Flow Management*, is devoted to this topic.

Projected Income Statement, Balance Sheet, and Statement of Cash Flows

The projected income statement, balance sheet and statement of cash flows are prepared in the same formats as previously discussed, and are not included as examples here.

Feedback from Your Budgets

Budgets are used to get feedback about business operations. This is done by preparing performance reports. These reports compare actual results to budgeted amounts and show variances. Variances can then be investigated and corrective actions taken, if needed.

For many small businesses, performance reports for the business as a whole are sufficient. However, if your business is organized into functional departments (sales, production, shipping, etc.) or according to product line, or if you have more than one location, you should prepare your reports according to that organizational structure. Remember, the idea is to use these reports to learn about the business and assist in further planning. The more detail you have, the more feedback you get. The danger is that you can get buried in too much detail.

When performance reports are prepared for more complex organizations, they usually start at the bottom and work up. Each report "rolls into" another report until you get to the report showing the business as a whole. For example, let's assume that Walt's has organized the sales staff into regional offices. The salespersons in each region report to a regional director who, in turn, reports to the marketing manager at the main office. Walt's prepares monthly performance reports by region and in total. The reports for January included the following:

Sales Performance Report for January

Total Sales	Budget	Actual	Variance Over (Under)
Region 1	$10,000	$12,000	$2,000
Region 2	$25,000	$24,000	($1,000)
Region 3	$15,000	$16,500	$1,500
Total Sales	**$50,000**	**$52,500**	**$2,500**

Sales Performance Report for January

Region 2	Budget	Actual	Variance Over (Under)
Salesperson 1	$15,000	$12,000	($3,000)
Salesperson 2	$10,000	$12,000	$2,000
Total Sales	**$25,000**	**$24,000**	**($1,000)**

Notice how the report for Region 2 feeds the report above it. The total budgeted and actual amounts in the Region 2 report match the figures listed in the report for all sales. Remember, the important thing is to break down the data in order to get feedback about the business. In doing so, you can design these reports in any appropriate manner.

Difficulties are often encountered with allocation of costs common to all levels of the business. For example, if *Walt's* prepares performance reports by functional area (sales department, production, administration, etc.), what should they do with the cost of the copy machine or receptionist or all the other things that the departments share? All these common costs could be placed in a single performance report. Or, techniques can be used to allocate these costs to various departments. If you don't allocate and the costs are excluded from all performance reports, then no one will be looking at those costs to see if they are in line with the budget.

A basic axiom is used when designing budgeting and performance reporting systems—keep it simple! This is a good time to consult your CPA!

A Thanksgiving Dinner Run Amok

A perfect example of Peekskill Catering's difficulties was a Thanksgiving dinner they catered for a party of 12. When Sarah wrote up the invoice for the event, she estimated that her costs broke down as follows:

- *10 hours of work time @$20 an hour*
- *$250 in food costs*
- *$350 for wine and champagne*

When Anna worked with her, reviewing receipts and overhead expenses, they found that her actual costs were:

- *20 hours of work time, including 3 hours of research, menu planning, and client management, 10 hours of prep and shopping time, and 7 hours for cooking and clean-up time*
- *$350 in food costs, including special orders and last minute runs to the gourmet food store*
- *$350 for wine and champagne*
- *$40 in overhead expenses, calculated as a percentage of total overhead of number of hours used in the kitchen. Overhead expenses include rent, kitchen supplies, utilities, gas, insurance, and taxes.*

In total, Sarah had undercharged her client by 30%.

By working through her exact expenses in this way rather than approximating them as she usually did, Sarah recognized what a big difference a budgeting system could make. She also realized that with Anne's help, she and Jason could create a simple and easy-to-use system that would allow them to better price their services and generate greater profits.

It is important to investigate the cause of variances before jumping to conclusions. Sometimes, a variance that looks bad at first actually results from something that is good, or vice versa. Walt's performance report for January:

Performance reports compare budgeted to actual amounts

Region 2	January Budget	January Actual	Variance Over (Under)
COST OF GOODS SOLD			
Product/Service #1			
Units Sold	30	42	
Cost per Unit	$45	$40	
Total Cost	**$1,350**	**$1,680**	**$330**
Product/Service #2			
Units Sold	70	65	
Cost per Unit	$150	$157	
Total Cost	**$10,500**	**$10,205**	**($295)**
Operating Expenses			
Labor			
Salaries & Wages	**$30,000**	**$32,000**	**$2,000**

Analyzing variances: 'Good' or 'bad' can only be determined while considering the goals and objectives of the business

It is easy to assume that all expenses which run over budget are bad and all savings versus budget are good. But remember, "bad" and "good" should be determined by how well you are meeting your goals and objectives. For example, if you take the above performance report for Walt's at face value, you might think that something is wrong regarding Product 1. January expenses were higher than budget. However, notice that the detail indicates this excess occurred because more units were sold than expected. In fact, the company managed to decrease costs per unit. So, that is good, right? Doesn't every business strive to cut costs? Sure, but how this gets done is important too. What if the unit cost decreased because the purchasing manager bought cheaper, lower quality goods? How does that fit with the company's objectives? If Walt's has identified its market niche as producing high-quality, long-lasting products, these purchases are contradictory to success in that niche. Or, maybe it fits very nicely if Walt's goals include becoming the discount machine shop in the area. "Good" or "bad" can only be determined while considering the goals and objectives of the business.

Peekskill Caterers Begin Budgeting

After several meetings with Anne, Sarah and Jason adjusted their sales forecasts for the coming season, taking into account what their sales had been for the preceding 3 seasons.

They calculated their total overhead expenses and budgeted them for each month of operations for the next year. Their overhead increased during peak winter months when they had higher heating costs and electric and gas costs for operating their kitchen equipment for longer hours.

They decided they would allocate these overhead expense to catering jobs based on a 5-month year of operations. The reason was that they had so few jobs during the remaining 7 months that the business had to be able to generate its total income during peak months.

With better sales projections for the coming season, Peekskill Caterers would be able to order the correct amount of supplies in bulk ahead of time. They could buy more supplies at lower bulk rates and make fewer last minute trips to the higher priced gourmet specialty food shop.

Recognizing that certain last minute purchases were inevitable, they built an additional percentage to cover this into their total supply costs.

Peekskill Caterers also budgeted for hourly kitchen and serving personnel, annual kitchen supply needs like bowls, knives, and aprons. Sarah also budgeted for health coverage, gas for their truck, and insurance.

The group finished their meeting with Anne by creating a simple computer spreadsheet template for their budgets. This way they could easily track overhead costs and supply costs, to make sure they were meeting their projected budgets.

Sarah and Jason left the meeting feeling more in control of their business than they ever had. The were organized and confident that they would be able to easily maintain their budgets and return to profitability.

Often, variances are interconnected. For example, the report for Walt's shows that salaries and wages in January cost $2,000 more than budgeted. Why did this occur? Perhaps it resulted from the actions taken by the purchasing manager.

If inferior materials were used, there may have been difficulties creating the final product. Perhaps laborers had to work overtime to fix problems that occurred. Overtime pay was not anticipated in the budget. Or, maybe the extra labor cost had nothing to do with the materials used. Walt's sold more units in January than expected. This might have resulted from a special order that could only be produced after hours, and overtime pay was necessary.

Which variances are chosen to explore in detail? This is a difficult question. It usually isn't possible to spend the time necessary to evaluate every variance. Some businesses will investigate all variances above a certain dollar amount. Other companies look at the relative size of the variance rather than absolute dollar amount. A variance more than 5% from budgeted dollars might be investigated, while a variance only 0.5% different than budget might not. The problem is that some variances are actually created by more than one phenomenon. A small variance might be masking several larger variances that balance each other out. There might be something important to learn from these factors.

Some variances are actually created by more than one phenomenon

The tendency is to focus our efforts only on expenses with actual amounts higher than budgeted. You also can learn a great deal when costs are under the budgeted amount. You can determine which are beneficial actions and use this information to continually improve your processes and your products.

As you can see, preparing the performance reports is the easy part! Deciding what the reports are telling you is much more difficult. However, if you take the time and make the effort to understand the meaning behind the numbers, you will find some very valuable information about your employees and your company.

Conclusion

The budget process might seem difficult and time consuming, but the benefits far outweigh the costs. Without this process, you don't have any benchmarks, no way to see if you are doing better or worse than expected. You might wander like Alice through Wonderland, never sure where you are or where you are going. And, unfortunately, going down the rabbit hole for a business usually means going out of business.

The budgeting process was discussed and examples of some budgets presented. One of the most important budgets for small business is the cash flow projections. Cash is the lifeblood of business. It is discussed in the next chapter.

Chapter 34
CASH FLOW MANAGEMENT

About This Chapter:
- *Managing the cash flow cycle*
- *Preparing cash flow projections*

Introduction

Small businesses fail every day. They share one common problem: they are out of money! There may be lots of reasons why they are out of money, but the fact remains that a business cannot operate without cash. Cash will flow in and cash will flow out of your business. Managing that flow is one of the most important things you do.

Importance of Cash Flow Management

Cash is the lifeblood of business

Cash is the lifeblood of business. Without cash the business will cease to exist. You must pay careful attention to the health of your business as measured by your cash position. This is particularly true for many small businesses as they tend to be undercapitalized. This means the business is operated on a very tight budget, without a great investment of funds: equivalent to living "from pay check to pay check." Careful cash management keeps the business from becoming delinquent on its debts and protects its credit rating.

It is equally important to manage your cash position carefully in good times when the business is flush with cash. Idle cash doesn't help profitability. Planning for growth? This presents cash flow management challenges. You might encounter a cash drain in the beginning as you establish new markets or open new stores. Good times or bad, careful **cash flow management** is an essential part of every business's success.

Reasons for Holding Cash

Why do businesses hold cash? In general, there are three reasons:

1. To meet current and upcoming planned expenditures
2. As a precaution against unexpected expenditures or a drop in revenues
3. To meet contract or regulatory requirements, such as compensating balances mandated by a loan agreement

The amount of cash you hold, your "cash cushion," depends on why you are holding it and your attitude about risk. How much chance are you willing to take that you will not have enough cash to meet your obligations? What amount of safety margin makes you comfortable? Remember, there is a trade off between risk and reward. If you keep an extra $10,000 in your checking account "just in case" you might be missing opportunities to put that cash to use and earn a greater profit.

Of course, some businesses would love to have an extra $10,000 but never do! Perhaps the checking account balance never gets above $500. Deposits are made just in time to write checks. As you might suspect, these businesses have a greater risk of cash shortages.

Baked Alaska

The scenario experienced by Baked Alaska, Inc. is a common one: a small business with big customers who can all but set their own payment terms. Like many small manufacturers, this backpack and purse design company buys its supplies frequently, in small quantities. It cannot afford to buy 1,000 yards of canvas, even though it would lower its per unit costs significantly. Instead, Baked Alaska buys fabric and trim every several weeks, sews its backpacks, and replenishes its supplies as production warrants. The business survives by making its products in comparatively small batches, so that it doesn't carry inventory, and it can quickly change its designs to stay on top of the latest fashion trends.

While Baked Alaska makes frequent purchases, it doesn't have frequent inflows of revenue. The problem comes from Baked Alaska's largest clients, like Macy's and Clothestime. These businesses often pay their accounts in 90, 120, or even 180 days. That's a six month loan that Baked Alaska is making to a giant, national retailer!

Baked Alaska is in line for some serious cash flow problems.

Cash Management Keys

Whether you take high or low risk with your cash balance, careful cash management is the key. There are several cash management techniques which can help you, including:

1. Managing the cash flow cycle
2. Establishing good internal controls for cash

3. Preparing cash flow projections
4. Managing excess cash

Let's take a look at each of these management tools.

The Cash Flow Cycle

The cash flow cycle (also known as the cash-to-cash cycle) represents the length of time that cash is tied up in business operations. If the cycle can be shortened, cash will be freed to begin the cycle again or to invest in other projects. The cycle looks like this:

Manage your cash flow cycle!

Therefore, how long cash is tied up in business operations is a function of 1) how long inventory remains before being sold, 2) how long it takes your customers to pay, and 3) how long before suppliers are paid. Managing cash flow is managing these activities. To shorten the cycle, you can speed up sales, speed up collections from credit customers, or slow down payments to suppliers.

Managing Inventory

Total inventory cost is a function of two variables: the quantity of goods in inventory and cost per unit. Both these variables are considered when managing inventory. You can reduce your investment in inventory by decreasing the quantity held or its cost. Reducing the per unit cost of inventory calls for careful attention to the purchasing function. A manufacturer also must monitor labor and overhead costs.

Why are you holding inventory? Businesses hold inventory to meet actual and potential customer orders, to guard against supplier shortages, to "corner the market," or because they have taken advantage of **quantity discounts** offered by suppliers. A bad reason for holding inventory, but a very common one, is that the business just has not taken the time to properly manage it.

How often does your inventory turn over?

Ratio analysis is a means of evaluating how effectively the cash flow cycle is being managed. Inventory turnover ratio:

$$\text{Inventory Turnover} = \frac{\text{Cost of Goods Sold}}{\text{Average Inventory}}$$

This ratio tells the average number of times inventory turns (is sold) during the year. We can convert this into days by dividing the inventory turnover ratio into 365 days:

$$\text{Average Days in Inventory} = \frac{\text{365 Days}}{\text{Inventory Turnover Ratio}}$$

For example, assume the following for Blodgett Brass Company:

$$\text{Inventory Turnover} = \frac{\$\,3{,}900{,}000}{\$\,300{,}000} = 13 \text{ times per year}$$

$$\text{Average Days in Inventory} = \frac{365}{13} = 28 \text{ days}$$

On the average, Blodgett's inventory is in stock for 28 days before it is sold. Whether this is high or low depends on the environment in which Blodgett operates. They should consider industry averages, their geographical location, their financial history, and any other special circumstances. However, if they wish to decrease the cash-to-cash cycle, Blodgett may try to turn their inventory more often than every 28 days.

How can they do that? The obvious answer is to increase sales. Another way is to reduce inventory. The first step is to eliminate obsolete and slow-moving products. Careful evaluation of what sells and what doesn't is vital.

Good buying decisions have a substantial impact on inventory levels. For each item in your inventory, you must consider how many and where to buy and how much should be paid. Experience really helps! Also, there are several mathematical models you can use to help determine the optimum level of inventory to hold and how much and when to order. One is the **Economic Order Quantity** (EOQ) model. You can find out more about EOQ in many business math books. The EOQ formula attempts to calculate the optimal quantity of inventory that should be ordered, considering costs of ordering and storing the goods, anticipated sales, and cost of the units. There are also many computer programs which could help you determine ordering strategies.

Some businesses have turned to **Just-In-Time systems** to reduce inventory levels. These systems attempt to get inventory to your operation just in time to be used or sold. In that way, you have significantly decreased inventory levels and reduced the cash flow cycle. This may be easier said than done. The process requires special cooperation between you and your suppliers and generally is very difficult for businesses with wide swings in sales volumes or start-up firms with new or poorly developed supplier relationships. Many firms have installed only some of the Just-In-Time concepts and modified the process to suit their needs. You can find many books and articles about JIT systems.

Good buying decisions have a substantial impact on inventory levels

Average Collection Period

Delinquent bills was not Baked Alaska's problem. Nor was it the choice of the accounts it sold to. Baked Alaska's problem was that it was not being adequately compensated for the time its money was tied up in accounts receivable. Baked Alaska was essentially giving its customers money for free. Therefore, the solution was to be found in a better accounts receivable strategy.

Baked Alaska's owner, Alice Deloix, sat down with her accountant and looked closely at her prices, the size her largest customers' orders (in \$), and the average collection period. They found that Baked Alaska's average collection period was 103 days! They were concerned, but not shocked: long payment terms, that extended into the next season, were not at all uncommon in the industry. Alice realized she couldn't change the way the industry operated, but she could change what she charged her customers. This way, she could bank the difference, and use it to create a working capital "cushion" to fund her daily operations.

Managing Accounts Receivable

Businesses sell on credit in order to make the sale in the first place. Making the sale is the reward but extending credit creates financial risk. When managing accounts receivables, businesses are always trying to balance financial and marketing goals, and their associated risks and rewards. Taking on new credit customers may help achieve sales goals, but if they prove to be slow-paying customers, the cash flow cycle may be lengthened and your financial position weakened. On the other hand, if you don't offer good credit terms, are you losing sales?

Ratios can also be used to help evaluate effectiveness of credit policies. Receivables Turnover Ratio:

$$\text{Receivables Turnover} = \frac{\text{Net Credit Sales}}{\text{Average Net Receivables}}$$

This ratio indicates the average number of times receivables turn (are collected) during the year.

This can be converted into days by dividing the ratio into 365 days:

$$\text{Average Collection Period} = \frac{\text{365 Days}}{\text{Receivables Turnover Ratio}}$$

What is your average collection period?

Here's another example for Blodgett Brass Company:

$$\text{Receivables Turnover} = \frac{\$\ 7{,}200{,}000}{\$\ 650{,}000} = \text{about 11 times per year}$$

$$\text{Average Collection Period} = \frac{365}{11} = \text{approximately 33 days}$$

On the average, Blodgett's customers take 33 days to pay. Just like with the Average Days in Inventory, Blodgett must consider their environment before evaluating whether this ratio is high or low. If they wish to decrease the cash-to-cash cycle, Blodgett should try to reduce the average collection period for their receivables. To do this, Blodgett should review their:

1. Criteria for extending credit
2. Credit terms offered
3. Collection activities

If your business sells to customers on account, you need policies to monitor who gets credit and how much. You are evaluating credit risk. The same factors bankers use when evaluating a loan can be used by you when considering credit for your customers. Here is a brief summary:

- **Credit History:** Credit history for new and repeat customers should be reviewed. Don't assume that all circumstances remain constant for your customers. Special attention should be given if a customer wishes to increase their credit balance or asks for special terms or extended credit. There are many agencies which can supply credit histories and ratings.

- **Character:** This refers to your evaluation of the customer's intention to pay. Consider their reputation and look at business references.
- **Capacity:** Capacity is the customer's ability to pay the debt. You need to look at past and present financial reports and observe their current operations.
- **Collateral:** Usually, there is no collateral for an accounts receivable transaction. You may be able to retrieve the merchandise but that is not always possible.
- **Conditions:** You should consider general and local economic trends.
- **Capital:** Customers with a solid financial position are less likely to default.

It isn't likely that your credit evaluation will eliminate all bad debts. It is difficult to judge the likelihood that a potential customer will be a collection problem and even good customers can fall on hard times. So, businesses try to reduce the risk of loss by performing the credit evaluation diligently.

Your business should have clear, written procedures about what customer data is required and which employees have authority to grant customer credit.

The credit terms you offer customers include the credit period and cash discounts. If you extend the time before customers must pay, you will lengthen your cash flow cycle and may cause a cash crunch. Your bills may be due before expected receipts from your customers. Remember that there is a cost to having funds tied up in receivables. The money can't work for you until you get it. If you shorten the credit period, your customers might have a cash crunch of their own and either become delinquent on their account or buy elsewhere. Determining the optimum credit period may take some experimentation. Also, review what your competitors are doing.

Cash discounts are given for early payment of invoices. For example, you might offer your customers terms of **2/10, net 30**. This means that customers paying within 10 days of the invoice date will receive a 2% discount. Otherwise, the normal payment period is 30 days. Businesses offer cash discounts to attract customers and to reduce the average collection period of receivables. The discount given is the price the business pays for these benefits. Two percent may not sound like much but remember that it is causing the customer to pay 20 days sooner than they would without the discount.

The part of credit sales that business owners like least is trying to collect from delinquent customers

The part of credit sales that business owners like least is trying to collect from delinquent customers. There are collection agencies who will do this for you, but they charge a high fee and most businesses resort to this only after other efforts have failed. How much effort you put into collecting receivables is a trade off between the time and money you spend to do it versus the cash lost.

Consignment Sales?

Alice and her accountant also discovered that Baked Alaska had a substantial amount of inventory, without even knowing it was holding it. Several of its oldest customers were high-end specialty boutiques that only sold merchandise on consignment. They would display backpacks in their store, and write a check to Baked Alaska for a percentage of their sale price when they sold one to a customer.

This meant that Baked Alaska's backpacks were sitting in stores without Baked Alaska generating any revenue from them. Alice's accountant totaled the merchandise value in these accounts. It came to over $1,000 worth of inventory. Alice and her accountant quickly decided that it was crazy for them to have backpacks sitting on consignment when they were unable to fill all of the straight sale orders that were coming in. They made an executive decision on the spot to discontinue all consignment sales.

The best strategy is to not let accounts become delinquent in the first place. Careful review before extending credit will help. Also, an effective accounts receivable billing system will assure that customers receive timely, accurate invoices. If customers believe you will notice if they are delinquent, they are more likely to pay on time. Errors on invoices can cause disputes and delays, so every effort should be made to avoid them.

An effective management tool for keeping in touch with collections is to age your accounts receivable. An **aging report** lists all receivable amounts by how long they have been outstanding. Here's an example.

Bullfrog, Inc.
Accounts Receivable Aging Report
January 30, 1996

Customer	Total Due	Under 30 Days	30-60 Days	61-90 Days	Over 90 Days
Acme, Inc.	$1,400	$1,200	$200		
BitCo	$3,570	$2,070	$850	$650	
Cox Corporation	$2,090				$2,090

Use an aging report to identify slow-paying customers

The aging report allows you to identify slow-paying customers, follow up on collections and evaluate credit and collection policies.

Many retailers shift the credit risk and collection burdens away from themselves by becoming a **revolving credit merchant**. National credit cards, such as VISA and MasterCard, offer revolving credit financing to consumers. The retailer, after making the sale to the consumer, turns in the credit card charge slip and receives 95 to 98 percent of the total credit charge. Risk of nonpayment is born by the bank or other financial institution which issued the credit card to the individual. To become a credit card merchant, you need to fill out an application and sign an agreement with a bank or other financial institution offering the service. There are many such institutions offering different services and terms for their merchants, so you should check around before signing an agreement. Talk to your banker, other merchants, and your business counselor for some ideas. Or, if you have a newly-registered business, look in your mailbox. The financial institutions will find you!

Some businesses speed up collections, and thus reduce the cash flow cycle, by using a **lockbox plan**. Customers send their payments to a local post office box which is opened daily by local bank personnel. The amounts will clear the bank quickly and be available sooner in the business's bank account. The bank may charge a fee or require a compensating balance for this service. This type of arrangement is normally used by businesses with a large volume of payments from customers.

You can also shorten the cash-to-cash cycle by assigning or **factoring your accounts receivable**.

You can assign your accounts receivable and use them as collateral for a short-term loan. This is also known as pledging your receivables. The lender will review the collectibility of your receivables and lend you some percentage of the total. You repay the loan, plus interest, as you receive payments from your customers.

To factor your receivables means to sell them to a financial institution. The factoring agreement may be on a "with recourse" or "without recourse" basis. Who has the collection risk? If factored with recourse, the financial institution may seek funds from you should receivable collections be less than anticipated. You still have collection risk. If factored without recourse, the financial institution cannot seek additional funds from you. As you can imagine, the financial institution will be very careful before entering into this type of transaction and will charge you more, if they determine your receivables are "high risk." Factoring does not result in a loan and no interest is paid. The factor's fee will be the difference between the accounts receivable sold and the cash the factor gives you. One advantage of factoring is that the factor typically will assume all administrative responsibility for collection. Customers send payments directly to the factor. Some businesses see this as a way to reduce overhead costs by eliminating accounting tasks.

Both assigning and factoring your receivables are effective ways of speeding up cash inflows. However, these methods can be very expensive. Interest rates charged on short-term loans for which receivables are assigned usually will be several points above the prime rate. Factoring can be even more expensive than accounts receivable lending. Depending on the quality of the receivables, the factorer may offer as little as 80% of the face value. Factoring is not generally recommended for small businesses unless the receivables are of very high quality, with little collection risk, and the business owner needs cash quickly.

Payment Terms

Alice had researched her competitor's payment terms, and her accountant knew what their money could be earning were they to put it back into operations or into other market investments. Within minutes, Alice and her accountant worked out Baked Alaska's new payment terms. They were as follows:

- *Prices for all Baked Alaska backpacks would increase by 10%*
- *Cash discounts would be given for early payment of invoices as follows: 5/10 (that is, a 5% discount for accounts paid within 10 days)*

Customers paying in more than 30 days would be charged interest on their orders. Baked Alaska decided to factor these terms into the initial order price for its largest customers, who routinely paid in over 30 days. This way, the company would earn interest on its outstanding receivables.

Alice and her accountant decided to see how the new terms worked for 6 months. At that point, they would meet to reevaluate Baked Alaska's receivables and cash flow and fine tune the strategy if they needed to.

Managing Accounts Payable

The final component of the cash flow cycle is how long it takes to pay your bills. Within reason, this is the one piece of the cycle businesses should try to extend. Certainly, you do not want to become delinquent on your bills, but you do not need to pay too quickly either.

Using a ratio to monitor this process is more difficult than with inventory or receivables because our suppliers are likely to offer a wide variety of credit terms. However, you may find it helpful to compute the average time to pay for purchases.

$$\text{Average Time to Pay for Purchases} = 365 \text{ divided by } \frac{\text{Total Purchases}}{\text{Average Accounts Payable}}$$

Blodgett Brass has the following ratio:

$$\text{Average Time to Pay for Purchases} = 365 \text{ divided by } \frac{\$5{,}100{,}000}{\$490{,}000} = \text{about 35 days}$$

Do your suppliers offer cash discounts for early payment? Should you pay early enough to take the discount? These points were discussed in relation to accounts receivable. Everything said there is now true for you, but from the customer's perspective! What you have to balance is the benefit of taking the discount versus the disadvantage of giving up the money sooner.

A tickler system is very helpful in controlling payments to creditors. Ideally, bills are paid just as they are due or, if cash discounts are taken, just at the end of the discount period. A tickler system can help you do this. Bills to be paid are sorted by when they are due. This allows you to know what funds will be needed when, and be sure that those funds are available.

Historical patterns are often used to forecast cash collections

Accounts Payable

Next on Baked Alaska's cash flow health check was its accounts payable. Alice asked her accountant to calculate the company's average time to pay for purchases. She found that it was only 15 days. This meant that Baked Alaska regularly dipped dangerously close to insolvency during the 103 days in which it was waiting to collect revenue. In fact, Baked Alaska had averaged 1 bounced check a month for the past year. Alice was shocked. She knew her business was profitable, so why was she bouncing checks? Again, she and her accountant found that it was because of the way the business managed its cash.

They decided to make some more changes.

Preparing Cash Flow Projections

There are many different types of budgets such as budgets for sales, cost of goods sold, and operating expenses. These budgets serve as the basis for creating a budgeted income statement and balance sheet and, perhaps most important of all, the cash budget. The cash budget is also known as a **cash flow projection.**

Months	January	February	March	Qtr Subtotal
(A) Beginning Cash Balance	$25,000	$12,840	$2,469	$25,000
Cash Receipts				
Cash Sales	$30,000	$31,800	$36,600	$98,400
Collect Accounts Receivable				
Within discount period	$12,740	$13,504	$15,543	$41,787
After discount period	$5,000	$5,300	$6,100	$16,400
Collected in following month	$1,550	$1,600	$1,696	$4,846
Sales of Fixed Assets				
Miscellaneous Income				
(B) Total Cash Receipts	**$49,290**	**$52,204**	**$59,939**	**$161,433**
Cash Disbursements				
Cash Purchases (Merchandise)	$12,450	$12,900	$14,850	$40,200
Pay Accounts Payable				
Labor Expenses	$38,695	$38,695	$38,695	$116,085
Owner Withdrawals	$1,500	$1,500	$1,500	$4,500
Non-Labor Expenses	$4,605	$5,280	$$4,405	$14,290
Purchase of Fixed Assets	$250,000			$250,000
Debt Payment - old				
(C) Total Cash Disbursements	**$307,250**	**$58,375**	**$59,450**	**$425,075**
Net Cash Flow (B - C)	**($257,960)**	**($6,171)**	**$489**	**($263,642)**
Adjustments to Net Cash Flow				
(+) New Debt	$200,000			$200,000
(+) New Owner Investment	$50,000			$50,000
(-) New Debt-Interest Paymts	($1,500)	($1,500)	($1,500)	($4,500)
(-) New Debt-Principal Paymts	($2,700)	($2,700)	($2,700)	($8,100)
(-) New Owner Withdrawals				
(D) Adjusted Net Cash Flow	**($12,160)**	**($10,371)**	**($3,711)**	**($26,242)**
Ending Cash Balance (A + D)	**$12,840**	**$2,469**	**($1,242)**	**($1,242)**

The cash budget is also known as a cash flow projection

An example of cash flow budgeting can be presented for *Walt's Machine Shop*. The format used is the same as that in the business plan workbook that accompanies this text.

The information comes from the other budgets but is organized so that cash is highlighted. Preparing a cash budget can help you anticipate cash shortages or plan for using excess cash.

The cash flow projections worksheet is often confused with the income statement. Remember that your income statement may reflect the accrual basis of accounting. The cash flow projections only concern cash coming in and going out.

It is important to realize the difference between the statement of cash flows (an accounting statement) and your cash flow budget. The statement of cash flows and the cash flow projections differ in that 1) the format used for presentation is different, 2) the statement of cash flows generally shows what happened in the past and the cash flow projections is concerned with the future, and 3) the statement of cash flows is a summary of totals for the year and cash flow projections is for the next 12 months.

Timing of Collections and Payments

The worksheet for Walt's Machine Shop breaks sales into two parts: sales made for cash and sales made on account. This is necessary to reflect the delay between making a sale on account and finally collecting the cash. To do this, Walt's estimated how customer payments will flow into the business. In addition, Walt's offers credit customers terms of 2/10, n/30. If customers pay invoice amounts within 10 days, they receive a 2 percent discount off the invoice amount. Otherwise, the entire invoice amount is due within 30 days and no discount is allowed. Amounts still owed after 30 days are past due. In this case, it is necessary to estimate what percentage of customers will pay in time to earn the discount. The discounts allowed are subtracted from the estimated collections on accounts receivable.

Walt's has estimated that 60% of sales are for cash with the remaining 40% on account. The historical collection pattern for credit sales is as follows:

Customers paying within 10 days	65%
Customers paying after 10 days but within 30 days	25%
Customers paying after 30 days but before 60 days	8%
Customers not paying at all	2%

Historical patterns are often used to forecast cash collections. Any discounts allowed are subtracted from projected sales dollars as are expected bad debts. By doing this, the amount of expected cash collections is determined.

Historical patterns are often used to forecast cash collections

Another need is to consider potential discounts in relation to accounts payable. Walt's has a place in their budget for cash purchases and purchases on account. However, in this example, they make all purchases for cash and need to use only one line in the cash flow projections. If it is significant, you should consider the timing of how you usually pay for your purchases and any discounts you expect to receive.

Buying Inventory

The answer was clear: Baked Alaska needed to more closely match the timing of its expenditures with its revenue collection. Altering its pricing and accounts receivable strategy was just half of the equation. How could it improve its management of accounts payable?

Alice realized that she or one of her two production managers was authorizing the purchase of supplies several times a season. There didn't appear to be any real reason for this. Why should the business buy supplies more than once a season, if the products it produced during that season stayed the same and it knew what its orders were ahead of time?

Baked Alaska divided its year into 5 seasons, each with a different collection of backpacks and purses. This was a lot, but it gave the company a distinct competitive advantage in a field of other small designers that offered only 3 collections a year. Baked Alaska pieces were always cutting edge. Baked Alaska had a fresh look that commanded attention from sales representatives and buyers alike.

Alice decided that the company had to start projecting for sales levels and planning for the inventory of canvas and other supplies it would need ahead of time. This way, she and her partners could make less frequent, larger volume purchases, and negotiate better prices from suppliers. She also decided to negotiate 30-60 day payment terms from all of her suppliers. She figured the increased cost of carrying accounts payable would be more than offset by the money the business saved in bank fees and bad credit.

Her accountant agreed. One year later they again reassessed the business's cash flows. They were pleasantly surprised by what they found. Average accounts receivables were down to 72 days, the business's profits were up 8%, and Baked Alaska hadn't bounced a single check in the past 12 months.

Operating Expenses

In general, your cash flow projections will include the same operating expenses as shown on your operating expenses budget and your budgeted income statement. Depreciation expense is an exception. This expense is included on the budgeted income statement because you want to allocate over time the cost of long-lasting assets. However, depreciation expense has nothing to do with cash, so you will not find this expense in the cash flow projections.

Owner Withdrawals

One area of cash flow projections often missed by small businesses is owner withdrawals from a sole proprietorship or partnership. If the family has other sources of support, it may be an acceptable budget assumption that the owner will not withdraw cash from the business. However, if the family will need cash withdrawals to survive, these should be included in the cash flow projections worksheet. Many small businesses fail, in part, because the owner did not anticipate or under-anticipated personal cash requirements. Budgets have a way of coming true. If you don't budget any compensation for yourself, you might not get any!

Borrowings and Cash Balances

The cash flow projections worksheet has a place to record anticipated new borrowings and payments on debt. Notice that in January Walt's plans to buy some new equipment. The purchase is shown as a cash outflow and the money borrowed from the bank as an inflow. This format makes it easy to see if the business will generate enough cash to repay its loans. Don't forget to budget interest and principal payments.

Walt's has a negative cash balance projected at the end of March. What valuable information! Now the owner knows that something will have to be done to prevent this. Perhaps he will have to forego his withdrawal. Maybe some purchases can be postponed or the business could borrow on its line of credit at the bank.

You may need to consider **minimum cash balance requirements.** Some businesses have a policy of not letting their bank account dip below a specified dollar amount. You may have balance requirements established in a loan agreement. Look carefully at the ending cash balance for each month of the cash projections and consider if minimum cash balances will be maintained. If not, you should look for ways to bring additional cash into your business.

Cash flow projections can be very useful when evaluating alternatives for your business

Assumptions

Remember that these are estimations only. It is easy to get caught up in trying to be very precise and spend tremendous effort on your budgets. Simplifying assumptions is acceptable! If your business experiences very few bad debts, you might wish to ignore those in your forecasts. If you do make assumptions about your projections, be sure they are reasonable and document them in writing. This is helpful when explaining your projections to outsiders, like your banker, and allows you to remember why you used a particular number! Later, you should compare your assumptions against what actually happened to see if assumptions for future cash budgets should be altered.

Playing the 'What-if' Game

Cash flow projections can be very useful when evaluating alternatives for your business. This is especially true if the projections have been made using a computer spreadsheet program. You can play the "what-if" game. You might say, "What if we were able to increase our sales by 15% next year?" Adjust your sales and expenses and put the new estimates in your cash flow projections worksheet to see the effect on your cash position.

Conclusion

If cash is the lifeblood of business, then consider yourself the doctor. Do an examination of your business cash position (do cash flow projections) and prescribe ways to make the business healthy (manage the cash flow cycle). The importance of these procedures cannot be overemphasized. If you do not pay attention to cash flow, if the doctor is out, the long-term prognosis of the business is doubtful.

PART VI
MARKETING YOUR BUSINESS

Chapter 35
INTRODUCTION TO MARKETING AND SELLING

About This Chapter:
- *The difference between marketing and selling*
- *The importance of marketing for the entrepreneur*
- *Who markets?*
- *The start-up marketing plan*

Introduction

Imagine, for a moment, a world without marketing. There are no displays of glossy new cars in a showroom. No friends-fly-free airline tickets. No speedy drive-through oil change service. No hamburger just the way you like it. No telephone calls with easy-to-use calling cards. No ATM card purchases at the grocery store.

Chances are you have been among the customers who have bought these products and services. People buy from these businesses because they give us what we want in the most convenient and cost-effective way. We give them our business because they earn it.

These are businesses who have successfully used marketing. They have spotted new trends and created products and services that customers want. They put offerings on the market with the right message, in the right place, at the right price, and customers bought the product. They have turned new opportunities into new businesses.

Marketing describes everything your business does to come to the marketplace and exchange your goods or services for money. Researching and deciding who your customers are is part of marketing. Creating your product is part of marketing. Deciding where and at what price you will sell is part of marketing. It's not hard to see that marketing makes business possible.

The challenge: to get the right product, with the right message, in the right place, at the right price

Businesses that fail to recognize the importance of marketing invariably stumble as they try to sell the wrong product, at the wrong time, place, and price, to the wrong people. Need proof? Market failures by major corporations disappear so quickly and quietly that you rarely even hear about them. But here are a few to consider: Federal Express's ill-fated *Zap Mail*, Coca Cola's New Coke, the DeLorean sports car, and the Edsel.

Now look at the huge successes enjoyed by the Swatch watch, the GM Saturn, the Big Mac, Teva sandals, and Starbuck's coffee. These businesses and their products succeed in part because their strategies are marketing driven. They use world-class marketing techniques that every business can and should use. They understand their customers, their competitors, and create a marketing strategy to match their strengths.

Selling is the tail end of all of your marketing efforts

Where does selling fit into all this? Selling is part of marketing. **Selling** is the moment when you agree on a price and quantity of a purchase with your customer. It is the culmination of the research, positioning, pricing, and distribution strategies that marketing has created. If you have done a good job preparing these marketing elements, selling your product or service becomes much easier.

Good Marketing Makes Selling Easier

Succeed in business with careful, clever marketing

If selling is just another part of marketing, why have we included it in the title of this chapter? Because selling is the moment of truth for all businesses. It is the instant in which you match your product to your customer, and find out if all of your market planning and research efforts have paid off. The selling effort really begins with valuable insights that your market research has produced, such as who your customers are and why they buy what they buy.

Buyer behavior tells you how to go about selling to your customer. What motivates your customers to buy? Who and what influences their purchase decisions? The answers to these questions tell you what you can do to enhance the way you sell your products or services. Why would you want to do this? To maximize individual sales and create loyal repeat customers. After all, your business can't survive if it only has "one-hit" customers who don't come back.

Marketing Beginnings

Marketing was first recognized as a key business function among traders of farm goods and basic manufactured goods at the turn of the century. Marketing was the means of exchanging goods and bringing them, literally, to the marketplace. As time went on and industrialization took hold, marketing became more focused on production: increasing output and efficiency. Before the 1950's comparatively little importance was placed on the actual selling of goods. It was thought that high-quality products would sell themselves. In the mid-1950's, with falling consumer demand and supply levels bouncing back from World War II shortages, businesses found they needed to update their product and sales-oriented approach. Some businesses began to shift strategy towards **customer orientation**: researching and listening to their customers and developing their products and services accordingly. In the increasingly competitive economic conditions of the late 1970's and 1980's, businesses began shifting their marketing strategies again towards **competitor orientation**. This was a focus on customers and competitors, with an eye towards long-term profitability. With the recessions of the early '80's and '90's, businesses were under pressure to reduce costs, yet find new ways to differentiate their products in a crowded field of domestic and foreign competitors. Businesses began taking a more proactive marketing stance by returning to their **core competencies** and targeting niche markets.

What will the next century bring in business marketing strategy? What role will your business play?

The chapters in this section of the book will help you understand and leverage the power of marketing for your business. This is your key to creating your product or service, finding your customer, and making profitable sales. This chapter will explain the relationship between marketing and other business functions such as finance, accounting, and operations. It also describes your start-up marketing plan.

Customers vote with their dollars

After working through this chapter, you will understand why careful and clever marketing management should be the cornerstone of your business.

A Marketing Case Study: The Boot Doctor

Mary and her brother Sam grew up outside of Denver on a farm wearing sturdy leather cowboy boots when they worked the cattle on horseback. Over the years Mary became an expert at resoling and stitching her favorite boots to extend their life and improve their appearance. She and Sam revived old cowboy boots as a hobby. They repaired their own, their parents', and eventually their friends' and neighbors' boots. They even created a unique mixture of glue and rubber cement which they called "Boot brand X" that could be formed to fit onto the old sole and extend the life of the boot.

After working for a local bank for several years, Mary became inspired to start her own business. What could she do? What did she know well and what were her hobbies? Why, boots of course! She remembered how important well-maintained boots were to her, and how great it felt to revive a favorite pair of boots. She also had difficulty finding a place to have her boots repaired in her part of Colorado. Inspired, she decided to look more closely at the market for boot repairs.

Customers and markets are the reasons that businesses exist

What Is a Market?

A market is composed of actual or potential buyers of a product or service, and the sellers who offer goods to meet buyers' needs. Businesses can target **mass markets** composed of many people with broadly similar needs (as do Wal-Mart, Nike, or AT&T) or **niche markets** composed of fewer customers with specific, very similar needs (like accounting software for legal practices, dog training services for owners of Rotweilers).

Markets are impacted by economic conditions, the quantity and quality of competitors, consumer trends, governmental regulations, trade barriers and agreements (like NAFTA), and cultural and demographic shifts. How well you understand your customer and your market conditions will determine how effectively you are able to navigate your business around obstacles and take advantage of new opportunities.

Effective marketing is essential to survival and growth

How Marketing Fits with Other Business Activities

If you think about it, marketing is linked to all of the major functions that you perform in your business.

Finance is essential to quantifying and evaluating marketing performance. Finance is key for developing marketing budgets, controls, forecasts, and estimating profitability. It tells you how to allocate resources: Will you keep selling a product or replace it with another? Will you shift your distribution strategy to a lower cost or more effective alternative? Can you afford to develop a new product for a different customer segment? What is the most cost-effective way to finance additional production capacity to meet rising customer demand? Financial analysis quantifies your market strategy.

Accounting allocates marketing costs and is key for computing profits. Activities that serve several product lines like research, development, and production overhead must be allocated to individual products in order to calculate their net profitability. Accounting separates these costs and precisely tells you how much it costs to promote, produce, and distribute a particular product or service. This allows a business to set its prices accordingly.

The marketing function directs **operations** and **production** and informs them what and when to produce based on market conditions. Marketing creates the forecasts and schedules that allow a business to produce new products on a timely basis. How big is a given market and how many units will be demanded in a given month? Should you have a seasonal production schedule which follows peak consumer spending periods? How much capacity should you have, at what locations, during what time period? This sort of forecast information is generated by marketers who pass it along and coordinate with production and distribution functions.

The entrepreneur's competitive strategy:

- small size
- speed
- customer orientation

Marketing also communicates to production who the customers are and what they need. Marketing research guides product development to precisely fit customer needs. Likewise, production communicates back to marketing the specifics of the product performance.

You may have a partner or two with whom you divide up these functions, or you might be lucky enough to do them all yourself. Big or small, every business performs these functions. Marketing, finance, accounting, operations, and production all work together to make a business successful. It's important to see how all functions are closely linked by the long-term vision for the business and marketing strategy. These guide decision making and make all functions within the business pull together for common goals.

For small entrepreneurs it is essential to save time and resources by coordinating activities. Your advantage over your competitors is your small size, speed, and ability to focus all your efforts on the goal of delivering the most value to your customer.

Building a Better Mousetrap: Customer vs. Product Orientation

What ever happened to the business that believed the world needed a better mousetrap simply because they could build one? They pumped time and money into creating the snazziest mousetrap complete with bells and whistles. At the end of all their efforts, customers didn't buy the mousetrap. Why? Because the old one worked just as well and cost a lot less. In short, the world didn't need what they thought was a "better" mousetrap! The moral of the story? Businesses that set their goals without first looking to their customers' needs are doomed to failure.

Businesses that focus solely on improving productivity and designing new products around new technology suffer from a **product orientation**. These businesses sell what they produce rather than make what they can sell to satisfy customer needs.

When businesses focus on their internal operations at the expense of their customers, they risk developing a product their customers don't need and won't buy. Inward focus can allow your market and customers to move right out from under you.

Most successful businesses have a **customer orientation** and design all of their marketing strategies around the needs of their customers. Customer orientation impacts nearly everything a business does and guides all of its strategic decision making. Typical strategies used by customer-oriented businesses include carefully researching and segmenting individual customer markets. Then they customize pricing, product placement, and promotional strategies to fit these segments. Finally, they tailor personal selling techniques to fit the buying styles of their customers. This practice is so important that we've dedicated two chapters to it, Chapter 4 *A Customer-Driven Philosophy* and Chapter 39 *The Art of Selling*.

Marketers continually challenge and revise their goals and strategies

The Boot Doctor Researches Her Market

Before Mary could sit down and prepare her marketing plan, she needed more information. She began her market research by gathering census data from her local chamber of commerce. She checked demographic patterns for her community and estimated how many cowboy boot wearers there were based on the number of farmers and ranchers in her area. Next she counted the number and types of cowboy boot sellers within 100 miles. She estimated how often people needed and wanted their boots repaired by interviewing friends, neighbors, and family. She also created a simple one-page survey which she implemented at the local mall. Using open-ended questions, she asked where and how often existing needs were being met, what were the most common boot problems, and what people wanted most from a boot repairer. She also asked which businesses provided similar services, how often people repaired their boots, and how much people were willing to pay. At the end of her efforts, Mary was able to confirm her hunch that there was indeed a market for a full-service, custom boot repair business in her area.

She identified her market: loyal cowboy boot wearers of all ages, located within 100 miles of her town, having spent $100–300 on their boots and willing to spend at least $60 on annual boot repairs. These people would repair at least one pair of boots in the fall and the springtime, depending on how often and where they wore their boots. Ranchers and city professionals alike fit into her target market. The only qualifying criteria was they loved their boots and were willing to pay for their upkeep.

Successful marketing objectives and strategies also requires that you understand the **operating environment** in which your business exists. This environment includes the external trends and influences that impact a business as it tries to meet customer needs. These include competition, the economy, technology trends, government regulations, demographic and lifestyle shifts. Marketers evaluate changes in customer needs and market conditions and adjust their strategy accordingly.

By understanding and anticipating external influences, marketers create objectives that give broad direction to the business. By identifying outside trends and internal competencies, they work to answer the questions "What business should we be in? Which direction should we head in the next 1, 3, and 5 years? Are we serving the original customer base we planned to serve?" These decisions impact the business's choice of industry and its long-term investment decisions.

The Marketing Process

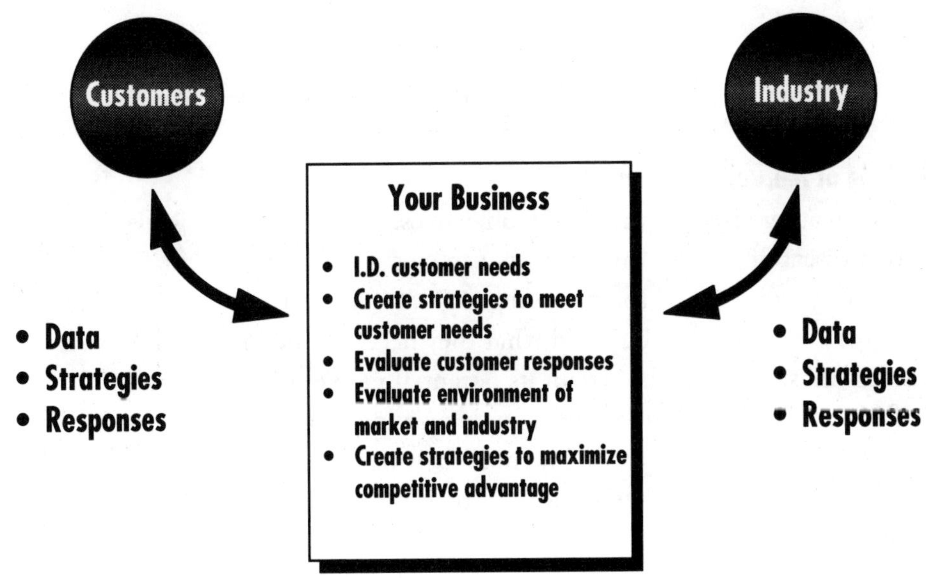

The Boot Doctor Identifies Her Mission

Mary knew her product, knew her market (she'd been living there for all her 29 years), and knew there was a need for her service. It fit her lifestyle and her area of expertise. She could initially work out of a small room in her house. As the business grew, she could rent a more centrally located spot in town. She would promote her business in three ways: through word-of-mouth and referrals, classified ads in her local newspapers, and a snappy colorful display with fliers that she would place in the major western supply stores in her area.

But what was Mary's positioning strategy for her service? She would return worn out boots to top form with the best tools, materials, and boot expertise around. Her competitive advantage? In-depth knowledge of cowboy boots and unique tricks for extending their life and reviving their original luster. She was a true boot expert, and a likeable, neighborly one to boot! Mary had successfully begun her marketing efforts long before she invested $1 in actually starting her business: she had preliminary knowledge of her customer, her service, her price range, and where and how she would deliver her service. Now that's aggressive, smart marketing.

The Role of Marketing Research

Key to creating effective marketing objectives, is careful and well-planned **market research**. Before any business can create a winning product positioning strategy and the marketing mix to match, it must identify who its customers are, how they buy, and what they need. More importantly, a business must research the size of its potential market to know if it is profitable to proceed. Are there enough customers out there to support this type of business? Can I profitably meet their needs? Where are my customers and what do they value? Market research answers all these questions.

The basic low-cost market research process is presented in the next chapter.

Who Markets?

When most people think of marketing, they think of highly visible **consumer products marketing** which focuses on marketing products for final consumption by individuals. Designing the colorful labels for candy bars that will catch a hungry shopper's glance, choosing just the right radio station to air a snazzy new Coca-Cola jingle, or fighting to get space in the grocery store for a "New and Improved" laundry detergent are all well-known elements of consumer products marketing.

Mary Meets Her Goals

With her market research done, her positioning strategy in place, Mary created her marketing plan. The most important part of her plan? Her goals. She aimed to be the name of the game in boot repairs within 100 miles of her town. She would average 60 pairs of boots a month during her first year. After introductory discounts, she would settle on her preliminary price of $60.00 per pair. After 6 months she would investigate extending her service offerings to include delivery service, custom foot pads, re-dying, and repairs by mail. Mary thrived on looking ahead to bigger challenges, but she knew she first had to meet her goals.

Eighteen months later Mary had met her goals! Things had been slow going at first. She'd needed to perfect her technique, find reliable, cost-effective sources of supplies, and develop her routine for repairing boots. Her biggest challenge? Scheduling her time and sticking to her budget. She beat these challenges by hiring a local accountant to keep her books for a small monthly fee. She also sought out owners of other service businesses and studied how they managed their time and money. She attended her first western wear trade show and shared a booth with 2 other entrepreneurs at 3 local rodeos. After eighteen months Mary was the name of the game in boot repairs in her 100-mile area. Word was spreading about the expert Boot Doctor who could revive any boot!

Every business in every industry must market its products and services. **Business-to-business marketing** represents a larger annual sales volume than does consumer products marketing. This is the sale of industrial components as inputs to other businesses that then manufacture intermediate or finished products. Business-to-business marketing can also involve the sale of support services to manufacturers of industrial products.

One of the fastest growing sectors of the U.S. economy is in the marketing of services. **Service marketing** involves the sale of intangible services, offered by people to both individual consumers as well as businesses. Airlines, banks, accountants, automobile mechanics, and babysitters all market their services. Marketing services is different from marketing tangible products for several reasons. Services tend to be more variable in quality (services are "produced" usually at the moment of delivery) and services cannot be stored for later sale.

Successful Entrepreneurs Use Marketing Aggressively

Why do we keep trumpeting the virtues of marketing? Because most small business owners do not use it effectively. Unfortunately, marketing is not one single task you can do to succeed. It is a collection of strategies and tactics that aid small businesses in succeeding. You may not be able to build a huge factory and churn out 100,000 widgets a day or use the latest, most expensive technology, but you can find your niche in the marketplace and deliver superior value. You can succeed by creating a marketing strategy that plays upon your unique strengths, small size, and flexibility to serve your customers well. Aggressive entrepreneurial marketing will allow you to:

- Maximize your profits
- Attract the attention of the right customers
- Keep focused on customer needs thereby providing superior service
- Create a niche market in the face of larger competitors
- Identify new opportunities quickly, and respond creatively
- Maximize resources and control costs

The most important part of marketing for the entrepreneur? Stick-to-itive-ness. Consistency. Commit to a well-researched strategy that will continually guide your business.

The Start-up Marketing Plan

The centerpiece of all your marketing efforts is your marketing plan

Would you consider taking a long trip in your car without knowing where you wanted to go, what route you would take, and which specific turns and stops you would make along the way? Of course not! What we've just described is the process of creating a plan for your trip. For a business's marketing efforts this is called a marketing plan.

Your business's **start-up marketing plan** tells what you want to accomplish, how you plan to go about doing it, and what specific tools you will use in the process. These three important elements governing marketing efforts are known as objectives, strategies, and tactics.

Objectives describe what the business plans to accomplish in chosen markets. This may include such things as controlling 20% of the market, increasing sales by 50% in the next six months, or having 100 new customers by year end. Using the driving example, the objective might be "to drive from San Francisco to Denver in a 5-day period."

A good marketing plan will help you get in and stay in business

Strategies describe the business's general plan for achieving its objectives. These may include targeting customers who are between 24-40 years old, targeting a niche market for customized bridal gowns, or positioning your business to be the premium-priced, high-service leader. In marketing, strategies show how customers will be segmented into target groups. They show how products will be positioned in the market to maximize the business's competitive advantages.

Strategies and tactics are also used to guide each element of the marketing mix. **The marketing mix** is composed of product, price, promotions, and placement. The goal of marketing strategy is to align these four elements to complement each other in achieving the same marketing objectives.

Businesses use strategies and tactics to achieve their objectives

For the driver with the objective to go from San Francisco to Denver, a strategy might be "to drive via Bakersfield to see relatives before crossing the Rockies."

Tactics are specific actions used to support strategies and achieve objectives. Businesses use marketing strategies with specific tactics for each of the major elements of the marketing mix. By designing complementary strategies with specific strategies, businesses work to achieve their marketing objectives. Some marketing tactics might include repackaging heavy products in smaller, easy-to-lift containers, offering a two-for-one promotion to customers, creating a classified ad emphasizing your customized services, or distributing your products only through specialty boutiques.

Once again, for the Denver bound driver with the plan to stop in Bakersfield, a tactic might be "to take highway 580 to Route 5, then head south to Bakersfield."

The objectives, strategies, and tactics that compose the marketing plan focus a business's efforts and guide its decision making. When the plan is written down it becomes a base-line that can be referred to, challenged, and fine-tuned.

Your marketing mix is only as strong as its weakest link

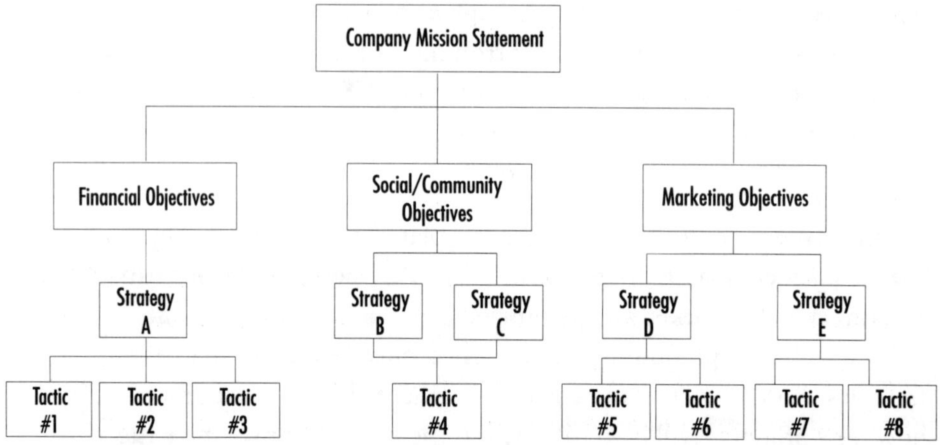

Why Every Small Business Needs a Marketing Plan

You may be thinking "What does this have to do with me? I only have one part-time employee!" By virtue of being a small business owner, you have limited time and money to achieve your marketing goals. You need to be clear on your goals, committed to your strategies, and in control of your tactics. Your margin of error is smaller than for large businesses. You may have loan payments due, another job to hold down, and a family to support. This is no time to spin your wheels. A carefully thought-out marketing plan will organize your thoughts. It prevents duplication of your efforts. It will keep you from spending your business's precious capital on the wrong things. It will help you get in and stay in business. The portion of time you set aside to research and design your marketing plan in the beginning will more than pay off in the end.

Be Quick! Be Original!

For most entrepreneurs, the goal of marketing strategy is to gain control of a tiny slice of a much larger market. Few resources require that entrepreneurs choose their battles carefully. Your strategy must reflect this. As a small business you have the flexibility and speed to use unconventional tools and strategies. There are no set rules or precedents to follow as you create your strategy—you are your business. Be creative, innovative, even outrageous, as you prepare your marketing plan.

A small business is not a little big business. It is a unique and highly creative entity

Tina's Custom Coffee Stand

The concept was new in Denver, but not in Seattle: an espresso coffee stand that offered coffee made from the highest quality, freshest beans, mixed any way you can imagine. Simple espresso? No problem. Double no-foam latte with almond flavor? Sure. Double decaf mocha with non-fat milk? Right away! In Tina's words, her ***core concept*** *was "To provide high-quality coffee the way people want it."*

Tina decided to locate her full-service coffee stand on the ground floor of a high-rise office building in downtown Denver. Her target ***customer profile?*** *The busy business person who likes to network and schmooze. Her customers would come from her building and others nearby. She envisioned her coffee stand as the perfect venue for "clients" to quickly get the espresso drink they wanted while being able to get out of their office and be "visible." Tina's goal was to operate the highest quality, most customer-friendly, classy espresso stand within her downtown area.*

Starbuck's coffee was 2 1/2 blocks away and always had a waiting line. She knew her service had to be faster and more personal than theirs. There was also a larger espresso cafe right around the corner, but their beans were not fresh. She knew that her coffee had to be fresher than theirs.

Tina's customers wanted fast, excellent service. They wanted hot, fresh, high-quality espresso drinks. They wanted their espresso made exactly their way and none other. She knew that she was the closest espresso source for all 1,600 people who worked in her building and the three adjacent buildings. She knew she had to earn these people's loyalty quickly and completely.

Tina's ***marketing objective*** *was to have 60 percent of the market for espresso drinks within her building and the three neighboring buildings within 6 months. In all three buildings she estimated that there was a total of 250 espresso drinkers, who drank at least one espresso drink a day. Sixty percent of that market meant that within 6 months her objective was to have 150 regular customers.*

Tina knew from gathering her research (talking with others in the business, reading beverage industry journals, and attending a gourmet food and beverage exposition) that within the espresso drinking population there were many different types of customers. Based on this information she segmented her customers into the following:

- *"The high-caffeine, high-calorie Herberts:" preferred traditional espresso drinks and sweet snacks in the a.m. = 50% of her market*

- *"The high-caffeine, low/no calorie Susans:" preferred espresso drinks with low or non-fat milk and healthy fruit or non-fat snacks in the a.m. = 40% of her market*
- *"The decaf, low/no calorie 'healthy' Heathers:" preferred decaf coffee drinks with low or non-fat milk, healthy fruit or non-fat snacks in the a.m. = 10% of her market*

These segments and percentages guided Tina in stocking and promoting her coffee stand. After a month in business it became clear that her information was on target. The vast majority of her coffee drinkers drank espresso with low-fat milk but enjoyed doughnuts and cinnamon rolls. In other words: they drank low-cal, but ate high-cal.

Tina and her espresso cart had a powerful ***competitive advantage****. She was conveniently located and offered truly personalized service. Both of her nearest competitors positioned themselves differently. Starbuck's aimed to serve many customers very quickly. The espresso cafe around the corner was a neighborhood "hangout" joint. Tina's cart was different. She* ***positioned*** *her business to be the source of the highest quality, most personalized coffee service around. What* ***tactics*** *did she use to achieve this? She knew all her customers by name: she kept a Rolodex file for each customer. On each card she noted their favorite drink and their birth-day. She also held their "frequent sipper" punch cards. Each time they bought an espresso they got a point. At ten points they got a free espresso drink. Thus, she created built-in customer loyalty. Aside from being a very charming, espresso-expert hostess, Tina gave her customers a very real reason to keep coming back: every tenth coffee was free!*

Contents of the Start-up Marketing Plan

Your finished marketing plan might be 10-15 pages long. But first try containing the key elements in a single paragraph. The truly condensed entrepreneurial marketing plan contains the following information:

- What your business wants to accomplish in its markets, expressed as specific objectives
- Who is your target market?
- What is your marketing niche?
- What is your product positioning? What is your competitive advantage?

As you write your marketing plan, think creatively

- How does your business plan to accomplish its objectives? Which marketing tactics will you use?
- What resources will you require to implement the plan? What is your budget?
- How will you implement specific marketing mix strategies?
- When and how often will you review your plan and make changes?

A world-class marketing plan takes a lot of work and several revisions. Give it careful thought, make it brief, to the point, and focused. Never lose sight of your prime purpose: to maximize profits. Maximizing profits requires being true to your customers' needs, clearly setting goals, and accurately forecasting and budgeting.

Eventually, you will want to create a more detailed marketing plan that includes projections for the long, medium and short term. You may even want to include in your expanded marketing plan several "what if" scenarios and contingency plans. Customers and markets are dynamic and invariably require you to tweak or fine-tune your marketing plan from time to time. Prepare for this by building change directly into your plan.

The most important part of any marketing plan is committing yourself to it and using it. This should be a living, working document that you refer to regularly and re-examine at least every 3 months.

Continually review customer needs: your business depends on it

Marketing Objectives
The most fundamental part of your marketing plan is setting your objectives. These are choices about where your business is headed in the long and medium term. Consider your customers before you set your marketing objectives. Then set specific boundaries and controls to give sharp focus to your objectives. Those steps are listed here:

Step 1: Clarify Customer Needs
- In your market research you collect the raw information about who your customers are, where they live, what they spend, and why they buy. Condense this information into short, clear statements. If you haven't done so already, consider drawing up a customer profile. A **customer profile** is a clear statement describing, in as much detail as possible, who your customer is.

- No one has endless resources to experiment with different concepts and marketing mixes. So make sure that your customer profile fits perfectly with your core marketing concept the first time. A **core concept** describes the pre-set direction for all marketing efforts. It spells out in 10 words or less the business's basic premise. Remember, for Tina and her coffee cart business the core concept was: "To provide high-quality espresso the way people want it."

Step 2: Set Your Objectives

- Marketing objectives arise out of market research and market analysis. In your findings, you might have estimated your market to be worth $200,000 in sales each year. You could decide that a realistic marketing objective for you is to control 15% of that market or have $30,000 in sales in the next 12 months. Or, because of fierce competition, you could set your marketing objectives simply at having a certain number of customers in the first 6 months. Other marketing objectives for businesses are to:
    - Achieve a percentage growth rate in sales
    - Add more variations of existing products
    - Enter a new market with an existing product
    - Introduce a new product to a new market
    - Diversify into different areas of business

A major difference between business success and failure is market strategy

Step 3: Use Market Controls to Give Focus to Objectives

- Lest your efforts become scattered, use the concept of **market control**. Businesses set boundaries around their objectives in order to sharpen their focus. Boundaries might include specific sales targets in units or dollars or percentages of markets. They refer to periods of time and specific products or services. Marketing controls might include:

- Creating a time table for your promotional, pricing, product, and distribution strategies: What will each strategy have achieved in 3, 6, or 12 months? At what specific points in time will you measure and re-evaluate your strategy?

- Establishing performance goals and standards for each marketing strategy: How many sales will it generate? How much time or money will it save? How many new customers will it attract? How many new distributors will it produce?

- Creating budgets for your promotional, pricing, product, and distribution strategies: How much will be spent on each marketing tool over a specific period of time? How will expenses be tallied and tracked? How will money be re-allocated if the need arises?

- Evaluating your marketing strategies: How successful has each element of the marketing mix been? Is your product satisfying customer needs? Are you effectively using service to enhance your product? Is your pricing method on target for delivering profits? Is your distribution network cost effective? Are your distribution partners performing as you planned they would? Are your promotional messages hitting your intended targets? Are they generating sales while staying within your budget?

Marketing Strategy

Marketing strategies are the approaches that businesses take to achieve their objectives. Just as there are different routes the driver can take to get from San Francisco to Denver, there are many different ways for businesses to achieve their marketing objectives. Several of the most useful for entrepreneurs are listed below.

Segmenting your market: Businesses commonly divide their market into segments, then target specific segments with specific product offerings. **Market segments** are groups of customers with similar needs and characteristics. Market segmentation is the opposite of mass marketing, which aims to sell a single product to as wide a market as possible.

Segmentation strategy: a football team doesn't try to tackle all players on the opposite team, just the quarterback, running back, or receiver

The advantage of market segmentation is the ability to create products to better meet customer needs. Businesses large and small segment markets in order to maximize their marketing dollars and better tailor their offerings to customers. McDonald's, although it is a mass retailer, creates products to appeal to specific market segments: lunch salads for dieters, kiddie value meal packs for young families, Big Mac combo meals for big appetites, and Arch Deluxe hamburgers for adult tastes.

The purpose of market segmentation is to identify a target market. **Target market** refers to the group of customers (market segment) whose needs a business tries to anticipate and satisfy most with its products or services. You'll recognize your prime target market if it:

- Is large enough to generate profits
- Has unique characteristics and is measurable and definable
- Has growth potential
- Is accessible
- Has un-met needs

To segment markets, most businesses group all of their potential customers by needs, desired benefits, behavior, and lifestyle characteristics. Using these criteria, try to segment your entire base of potential customers into 3 or 4 different segments. Which is the most attractive? Can you identify a viable target segment? Try prioritizing three such segments based on which one you would like to focus on first. Second. Third.

Entrepreneurs usually target niche markets. A **niche market** is a small slice of a larger market that has unique characteristics and un-met needs. Generally it is too small to support large, well-established businesses. For this reason, niche markets provide unique opportunities for entrepreneurs. It is much easier for businesses to target niches than it is to try to enter larger, mass markets. Niche markets have very specific characteristics (size, location, tastes) that clearly separate them from larger markets.

Positioning Your Product or Service

Through **product positioning** the marketer communicates the benefits and features of the product or service to customers. Positioning infuses a product or service with personality. It determines which niche your product is designed to fill and separates your product from competitors' offerings. The positioning statement tells your target customers exactly why they should buy your product.

Positioning statements summarize why customers should buy your product

As you create your positioning statement, ask yourself if your offering and its positioning in the market:

- Offers a benefit to your target audience that really matters?
- Delivers a benefit that is real?
- Truly separates you from your competitors?
- Is unique and difficult to copy?

Clever entrepreneurs don't settle on the first or even the second positioning statement they come up with. They keep searching for the perfect positioning statement until they are completely satisfied with their findings. Excellent positioning doesn't come easily. It demands that you look at a lot of information and think clearly. Don't despair. The better you understand your market and your customers, the closer and closer you'll come to that "gem" positioning statement.

A crystal clear positioning statement is key to good marketing efforts

Identifying Your Competitive Advantage
The ideal positioning strategy is one that gives a business the greatest advantage over its competitors. It creates a competitive advantage. Your business's **competitive advantage** comes from offering more value to your customers than your competitors. Value can come from, among other things, a higher quality product, lower prices, better service, or more convenient distribution.

If you are able to provide more innovative and personalized customer service, you have a competitive advantage over your larger competitors. Therefore, you might position your business as the "personal service, we-take-care-of-you-boutique." You would only position yourself in this way if your customers value service. A competitive advantage has two key criteria:

- It must be something your customers value
- It must be something you do better than your competitors

In some cases, a business may decide not to enter a given market because it cannot find a position that gives it a competitive advantage. The purpose of your marketing strategy and tactics for your marketing mix is to enhance your business's competitive advantage. Some additional examples of competitive advantage are:

- Developing a new technology
- Serving a specialized customer niche
- Establishing unique distribution channels
- Obtaining production cost advantages due to better sourcing, location, or processes
- Developing a stronger base of financial resources (i.e., through cheaper debt or additional equity)
- Building a unique brand identity

Competitive advantage comes from something customers value

Introduction to Choosing Tactics
When businesses know who their customers are, what they want, and how they will position themselves, their next task is to select their marketing tactics. **Marketing tactics** are the specific action steps that detail how each

marketing strategy will be achieved. Tactics are used to achieve overall marketing strategies and individual strategies for each of the four elements of the marketing mix.

Tina Creates Her Promotional Tactics

Just as Tina needed a strategy to guide her selection of product offerings, her pricing, and her placement, she knew she needed a well-thought-out promotional strategy. Her promotional strategy had to help achieve her objective of controlling 60% of her local coffee market. It also needed to communicate her positioning as the highest quality, more personalized provider of service to her customers. To do this she designed her first promotional tactic.

With the help of a graphic designer friend, Tina created the "Espresso Update." This short, easy-to-read page contained information on the "bean of the week" and a coupon for a discounted espresso drink. Tina updated it frequently and faxed it to customers late in the afternoon so they could redeem the coupon first thing in the morning. Later, when her goal was to increase her afternoon sales, she began faxing coupons directly to her customers' desks at two o'clock in the afternoon.

Let's return to our road-trip metaphor for a moment. Once the driver has set his objective to drive from San Francisco to Denver, and his strategy to drive via Bakersfield to visit relatives, he next needs to decide which specific roads he will take. His might choose to take Route 5 or Highway 280 South. Maybe he'll stop for a night in Gilroy to buy some garlic. Maybe he'll wait to fill up at his favorite gas station in Coalinga. These are the specific actions or tactics he will use to achieve his objective of reaching Denver.

It is very important to measure the effectiveness of your marketing tactics. By doing so you can double the effectiveness of your marketing budget. Measurement allows you to improve and revise your marketing calendar and separate the tactics and strategies that are winners from the losers.

How can small businesses do this? Easy. Ask your customers where they heard of you. You can ask them in person, in a brief questionnaire, or train sales people to inquire as they take orders.

Commonly Encountered Strategy Traps

- Not sticking with the strategy long enough
- Not testing the strategy before implementation
- Not challenging the assumptions and data on which the strategy is based
- Not focusing the strategy enough on specific goals
- Not adequately controlling the budget for strategy implementation

See Chapter 38 *The Marketing Mix: The Four P's* for a more detailed explanation. This chapter also outlines specific marketing tactics for entrepreneurs.

The Importance of Consistency

When implementing your market strategies and tactics, consistency is of utmost importance. You may be lucky enough to witness instant results from your clever tactics. But chances are it may take considerable time and effort before you see concrete results.

You may find that those flyers you distributed last week haven't yielded any new customers this week. Or perhaps that promotional package you sent to all of your distributors hasn't increased your orders as much as you had forecasted. Remember, one of the most important things you can do is give your marketing tools a chance to work. It's hard for impassioned entrepreneurs to be patient, but, in many situations, be patient you must. While some marketing tactics will deliver instant gratification in the form of more sales, others might take six months or a year to yield their bounty. Unless you give them the time to work you'll never know if they can work.

The lesson? Be consistent in your marketing efforts and your message. Keep up your strategy.

Anita's Paddock Horseboarding Services

Objective:

1 year to control 20% of the market in the 3 surrounding counties for horseboarding.

Strategy:

To position horseboarding services as the most expert, personalized service available; to target English-style riders and their jumping and dressage horses.

Tactics:
Yellow Page ads, under 3 different headings: veterinary services, horseboarding, and riding lessons; newspaper ads, once a week in two local newspapers; price services at slightly higher than other competitors to differentiate and communicate "premium" service message.

Conclusion

Why do you need marketing? Because without it your business won't know what and where to sell, who to sell to, or what price to charge. Researching markets, identifying the target customer, creating appropriate strategies, budgeting, and controlling marketing efforts are all key to marketing success. Having done these things, selling your product becomes much easier. Selling is the completion of one marketing cycle and the beginning of the next. When marketing research pays off and the product truly fits the customer, businesses create repeat sales to loyal customers.

By understanding and utilizing basic marketing principles, you can create the kind of smart strategy that will allow your business to take on the competition and win.

Chapter 36
MARKETING RESEARCH TOOLS

About This Chapter:
- *What is marketing research?*
- *The market research process*
- *Using your data wisely*
- *Free and low-cost sources of market information*

Introduction

Market research provides businesses with essential information that allows them to identify opportunities and develop the right marketing mix to profit from them. Solid market knowledge allows businesses to test alternate strategies and evaluate marketing performance. Most importantly, market research tells businesses if their product or service can be the foundation of a profitable business.

Market research is a fancy way of describing the activity of gathering information to make informed, intelligent, strategic decisions. Which stores should be targeted to sell a product? Where should you locate your retail shop? What product should you produce and in what quantity? What should you charge for services?

Market research provides the answers to all of these questions that relate to marketing strategy. Your marketing strategy is the road map for your business, so you must make sure that the information on which it is based is sound. If not, you could miss your market altogether by steering your business in the wrong direction.

Market research also helps businesses find and eliminate "weak links" in their marketing mix. Analysis of a competitor's pricing strategies can tell you if your pricing strategy is on target. Analysis of various distribution options can tell if the product is where the customers are and when they want to buy it.

It is an essential on-going process of maintaining an understanding of the changing external environment in which businesses operate. Market research is periodically used to update knowledge about target customers. And it will help a business predict future changes in its market. It also gives businesses feedback so they can challenge their assumptions and fine-tune their marketing mix.

Market research helps you find out if your hunches are correct

What Is Market Research?

Market research is the process of evaluating all aspects of your potential market. It encompasses planning, collecting, and analyzing data about your customers, industry, and competitors to help steer all marketing strategy. Market research is about getting the facts that support or negate your assumptions. The golden rule for marketers? In order to be useful, market research must be valid, reliable, and representative of target customers.

How Do Small Businesses Gather Market Research?

While large corporations have the budgets to create entire market research departments or hire research consultants to test their ideas, smaller businesses have to be more creative. Limited budgets mean most entrepreneurs depend on their sales people, distributors, and themselves to conduct and gather market research. Make no mistake: quality market research can be gathered for little or no money. But it does take effort.

Gathering market research can be expensive or low cost, depending on the sources a business uses and the scope of the research. For the inspired and dedicated entrepreneur, there are many valuable, low-cost, or free market research sources available. All research should be guided by an initial set of research objectives; these help to guide research budgeting and keep the research effort well within preset budgetary constraints.

Demographic vs. Psychographic Data

Businesses gather demographic data in order to discover who and where their customers are. **Demographic data** describes specific characteristics of an individual such as age, level of education, occupation, income, marital status, and address.

Psychographic/lifestyle data describes an individual's activities, interests, opinions, and beliefs. This data gives marketers insight into such things as how their potential customers live, make buying decisions, or plan for the future.

Good demographic and pyschographic data is particularly key for small businesses. Their success is most often built upon knowing their customers better and satisfying their needs with more personal service than larger competitors. To do this, businesses need to have the right answers for these questions: Where are my customers? Why do they buy and how much are they willing to spend on my kind of product? What are the product or service features that are most important to them?

To illustrate the magnitude of demographic and pyschographic trends, consider the following three major demographic trends that have directly impacted marketing strategy in the '90's. These are the types of trends that entrepreneurs utilize to build business opportunities. Keep in mind that trends like these manifest themselves at local, state, national, and international levels. Even the smallest and most rural communities are touched by trends like these and thus have business opportunities to match. So don't count your community out: If you don't see these trends around you yet, get ready, before long you will.

Surf the tide of changing trends

Three Major Demographic Trends

Shifts in the age make-up of the American market

- In the U.S., 77 million baby boomers (people born between 1946 and 1964) make up 1/3 of the total population and represent more than 1/4 of the economy's purchasing power. In the last decade of this century, baby boomers' income is expected to double. The size of the youth market (people aged 12-19) is expected to continue decreasing, but their spending is increasing. The mature market (individuals 50 years old and over) commands half of the discretionary income in the U.S. and holds 77% of its assets. Within 30 years, 1/3 of all Americans will fit into this group.

Changes in family composition

- Increases in the divorce rate and the percentage of working women, and a decrease in the birthrate after 1960, have all caused major changes in the make-up of the typical American family. In fact, it seems no one can agree on whether or not there exists a typical American family anymore. Single-parent homes, smaller families in married households, and a decline in the proportion of teenagers are also key trends.

Increasing proportion of working women

- In 1990, 58% of women worked, as compared to 33% of women in 1950. Women are entering the work force at younger ages and changing the face of American business in nearly every industry. The time crunch that many working women feel has helped to fuel the boom in catalog and telephone shopping and other time-saving services.

"You have to see the future to deal with the present."
—Pop-culture tracker, corporate consultant, Faith Popcorn

3 Major Psychographic/Lifestyle Trends

Shifting male-female purchasing roles

- Because more women are working in addition to having a family, men are playing a larger role in child care and household duties than ever before. Because women are earning more money and achieving more professional independence, they are spending more money on travel, dining out, entertainment, and luxury products.

Increased interest in "healthy" lifestyles

- In 1990, half of all American grocery shoppers read the labels on the food they bought. Americans are quitting smoking, drinking fewer alcoholic beverages and eating less red meat. Fat-free, low-fat, low-salt, sugar-free, and "natural" products are more popular than ever. Americans are more interested in fitness: they are jogging, climbing, hiking, biking, and swimming more than ever before.

More conservative lifestyles

- In the 1980's, the youth market began to become more concerned with career, personal style, and lifestyle choices. As a result, today they are spending more on clothing, personal grooming products, and automobiles. Young adults and teenagers are more involved with household and food purchases than ever before. The increase in the number of divorced households and the frequency with which young adults are transplanting themselves to pursue jobs and education means more are setting up their own households at younger ages.

Trends Spell Opportunity for Small Business

New trends like these may be years in the making, but when they are recognized they spell tremendous opportunity for new businesses. And not just for businesses in large cities. Small town or rural entrepreneurs can investigate how these trends spin-off into micro trends that mean business opportunity in their areas.

For example, you may think that the increase in working women in America has no importance for you. But when you look closer you just might find that in the past 2 years traffic on your local highway has increased by 20 percent, and that 30 percent of that traffic is women commuting to work. Seeing an opportunity, you might investigate opening an express dry cleaner/coffee stop that caters to professional women. Where? Why somewhere along the highway, of course!

Get the picture? Look around, ask questions, and use market research to put your business in the right place at the right time. This way you can detect micro trends within your community and move swiftly to take advantage of the entrepreneurial opportunities they present.

The Market Research Process

While research consulting firms and consumer products manufacturers undertake large research projects, small firms can do truly effective market research as well. Gathering market research needn't be a confusing task. Even though small businesses can't shell out big dollars for market research, they can approach market research like world-class corporations do. How? By using clever, time-tested techniques like breaking the research process into small parts. This organizes your efforts, and, incidentally, makes it a lot less intimidating.

Market research is basic exploration that tells you the who, what, where, why, and how of your business

Look at your market research as bringing you closer to creating just the right product or service for your market and adding another brick to the solid foundation of a profitable business. So, just like the big players, let's start at the beginning.

Understanding Your Customers' Buying Behavior

If your goal is to create a profitable business, you must identify and satisfy your customers' needs. One of their most important needs is the ability to buy in the manner, time frame, and place that they choose. Market research helps identify customers' needs and perceptions of product offerings. It also uncovers their attitudes that influence what and how they buy. This dynamic is known as **buyer behavior.**

Before you begin your market research process, it is important to understand how and why different types of customers make purchases differently.

How do individual consumers make purchase decisions?

Final consumers who buy products through retail outlets make their decisions in many different ways depending on the products they buy. Just think how differently you go about buying a car, a candy bar, or aspirin. In general, consumers' purchase behavior involves identifying their need, gathering information, evaluating alternatives, and evaluating their purchase to determine how satisfied they are.

Consumer purchases vary according to the following:

- **Their level of involvement in the purchase**: How important is the product to customers? What percentage of their income does its price represent? How often do they buy the item? How complex or unique is the product? How risky or visible is the product?
- **Their degree of brand loyalty**: How important is a particular brand to customers? Do they have a positive or negative feeling towards one brand because of past purchases? Do they associate the brand with particular events, memories, related products, or people? Or do they fail to distinguish between different brands altogether?
- **Their habit and learning**: How complex is the decision process for a given product? How much must customers learn before being able to make an informed purchase? Is the product purchased habitually? Or must customers learn something new or change old buying behavior before buying? Do customers make an active decision to purchase?
- **Consumer motivation**: Why is the customer making the purchase? Is it satisfying physiological (food, shelter), safety (protection, security), social (acceptance, friendship), ego (prestige, success), or self-actualization needs?
- **Consumer perceptions**: How do consumers perceive different brands and product offerings? What are their attitudes and means for evaluating different products? Do consumers have a positive or negative image of a product based on past experiences?

It is dizzying when you realize how many social, economic, cultural, and geographic influences affect consumer purchases. However, as a small business you can understand the basics and seek out as much information as your business warrants. The more you understand about how and why your customers buy, the better your marketing strategy will be.

How do organizations make purchase decisions?

Businesses that sell to other businesses count among their customers industrial buyers, institutions like hospitals and hotels, government agencies, and intermediaries like distributors, wholesalers, and retailers. These buyers all use goods in their own production of goods or resell them.

In some ways these buyers make their purchase decisions in the same way consumers do. They identify their need, seek information, and evaluate choices. Their purchases are also guided by how important the purchase is to them, the level of complexity of the product, and their motivation.

For the most part, organizations buy very differently than do consumers. The products they are buying tend to be complex and very important to their own operations. For these reasons, organizational purchases require more planning and involvement. Their purchases have more risk because if the components they are purchasing fail, so will their finished products. In these situations, buyers and sellers tend to form longer-lasting and more intimate business relationships. Because there is generally more negotiation and on-going business between buyers and sellers, personal selling tends to be more important in organizational markets than in consumer markets.

For important or high-cost purchases, businesses tend to use teams to make purchase decisions, and define product specifications. **Product specifications** are requirements set by potential users that dictate product performance and type. Within the buying team individuals tend to fall into the following roles:

- **The Gatekeeper** regulates the flow of information to the buying team and finds alternative products and vendors.
- **The Influencer** has some leverage from experience, position, or technical expertise to influence the other members of the buying team.
- **The Buyer** makes the final selection of which product or service to purchase. He or she helps to evaluate different product choices although he or she often defers to others on the team who have more technical expertise.
- **The User** is the person who ultimately uses the product. This person helps to identify key product specifications and evaluate the product after it is purchased.

Note that these roles may all be filled by the same or different people. What is their importance for the small business owner? For example, you wouldn't want to spend all your time selling to John who is the gatekeeper when Susan and Peter are really the important influencer and buyer. By knowing how your customers make decisions and who fills each one of these roles, you can focus your efforts, maximize your resources, and effectively sell your product. For more information on this see Chapter 44 *Dealing with Large Organizations*.

Now let's move on to the process of gathering your market research.

Define Your Research Objectives

In market research, starting at the beginning means identifying what you do and don't know about your market. It also requires that you recognize your business's primary marketing problem or opportunity. Are customers spending less on your type of product? Is there a viable distribution channel for your product? Are production costs prohibitively high? These are typical marketing problems that invite more market research.

If you are considering a foray into an industry that is new to you, there probably will be a great deal of information you don't have. Like many businesses, your research objectives might be to describe events, trends, or cause-and-effect relationships in your marketplace or to define a specific problem to guide additional research.

Afraid of getting off track? As you are trying to figure out which market data is relevant to your business, look to where your sales come from: your customers. Ask yourself the following four questions to keep research on track:

- Who are my customers?
- What's on their minds?
- Where can they be reached?
- What do they buy?

Keep your research objectives simple, specific, and clear

This initial phase of your market research process should include writing down, as precisely as you are able, the information you feel you need to solve your marketing "problem" or fill in the most important gaps in your knowledge about your market.

As you begin to define your research objectives, consider doing the following:

- Ask why you need given information and if it is readily obtainable
- Rephrase questions about your market to get a new perspective
- Prioritize your questions
- Test your objectives by creating sample data about your market. Does it help answer questions and set strategy?

Twila's Wedding Dresses

Twila Robinson was in 7 different weddings in one year and was left with 7 different bridesmaids' dresses that she felt were ugly, ill-fitting, and of poor quality. She was fed up. When she was helping a girlfriend plan for yet another wedding, her friend suggested that they work together to design and sew her wedding dress and bridesmaids' dresses. The project went so well that the seed of a new business idea was planted in Twila's head.

She loved to sew and make clothing for herself and her friends. Twila had also helped design and sew two wedding dresses for some very tough customers—her two sisters-in-law.

Twila worked in sales for a local department store and was interested in generating some extra income for herself. She also wanted to explore opportunities to use her creativity and work more flexible hours. She decided to look around and investigate what the opportunities were for designers and seamstresses of wedding and bridesmaids' dresses in her community. She needed information. Her research objectives were:

- *To define the market size for wedding gowns and bridesmaids' dresses in her region by tracking marriage rates, population size with age breakdowns, and income levels*
- *To estimate the geographic area of her market*
- *To gauge potential sales volume for the first year*
- *To find out how much brides were willing to pay for dresses*

Twila's major marketing problem: Could she count on the current wave of weddings to continue and support her in a full-time business? Or would she have to operate part-time and continue her sales job? How could she compete with the high- and medium-end bridal sections in local department stores?

Conduct a Situation Analysis

A **situation analysis** is a preliminary look at the information that is already available about your market. It tells you whether it is necessary to spend time and money gathering your own, original market research. The goal of a situation analysis is to identify what secondary information is available to you and what primary data you will need to generate yourself. A good situation analysis delivers a lot of information, yet takes little time.

Secondary data is information that has already been gathered and published. This information might come from academic research studies or published articles in magazines, trade journals, or newsletters. It might come from talking with or reading census reports or reports compiled by distributors, middlemen, customers, competitors, or other knowledgeable people in the industry. Many research questions can be answered through readily available (and free) secondary data.

Primary data is collected by a business for the purpose of answering its own, specific questions about its customers or markets. Gathering primary data may involve observing customer behavior or designing questionnaires or surveys to learn more about a representative customer population.

Identify Primary Research Required and Plan Research Design

If after completing a situation analysis, you find that there is insufficient secondary data available about your market, then you will need to gather your own primary data.

The market research test: Imagine you have answered all of your most pressing marketing questions. Can you set your market strategy with confidence? Do you know exactly what your customers want and will pay for?

When businesses gather primary data they are generally gathering **qualitative data.** Qualitative data is data that cannot be quantified or counted. It reveals the quality of a subject's experience or beliefs. Qualitative research is gathered by allowing customers to answer questions in an unstructured manner. A person's preferences for chocolate or vanilla, political beliefs, or interest in backpacking are examples of qualitative data.

Quantitative data describes things in quantities that can be measured and analyzed with statistical analysis. What do your customers earn each month? How old are they? How much do they spend each month on groceries? Rent? Gas? How many kids do they have?

There are two major methods that businesses use for gathering this type of primary data:

Surveys

The most important and widely used method of collecting primary data is through surveys. Surveys can be used to gather both qualitative and quantitative information from respondents, including facts, opinions, and attitudes. The first step in creating a survey is to decide to whom it will be given. This group, chosen from the target population, is known as a sample. A **sample** is a subset of the larger population that you are targeting. The **population** is the group that includes all the people whose opinions, behavior, preferences, and attitudes will influence your marketing strategy.

Selecting the sample can be done randomly, thus ensuring that each member of the population has an equal chance of being included in the sample. Samples that are selected randomly have a greater validity. Using statistical analysis, they represent within a certain margin of error the larger population one is seeking to get insight into. Non-random sampling can be comparatively time-consuming, expensive, and more complex to design and execute.

Sample groups can also be selected in a non-random manner. Non-random sampling is usually done to save time, money, or simply because it is more convenient. On the other hand, it is harder for a researcher to calculate the degree to which the non-random sample represents the larger population.

Businesses who use non-random samples try to choose respondents who are representative of their target customer base. Respondents might be selected because they live in a specific geographic region or fall into an age, income, or lifestyle category.

Twila Creates Her Research Plan

Twila decided to give herself one month to gather her market research data. She began by going to her local book store and buying every magazine she could find on brides and wedding planning. What sort of dresses were women buying? What styles were popular? Who were the major manufacturers, fabric suppliers, boutiques, and designers? Where were women buying dresses?

Next she went to her local library and gathered the census data for her city and county, and scouted out the Yellow Pages for all bridal gown shops and tailors she could find. She telephoned and visited each one, to find out all of the things a prospective customer would want to know: what products and services they offered, what they charged for dress design and sewing, how many fittings they required, and how long it took them to deliver a finished product. She even asked them for the names of past clients with whom she could speak.

This information was helpful, but Twila needed more specific information about the needs and tastes of prospective clients in her area. She decided to organize several focus groups. She used non-random sampling to select her participants. For participants, she chose two girlfriends and eight other women who had been referred to her. She divided them into two separate focus groups which she held at her house on two different evenings. Twila was careful to use open-ended questions and encourage all of the women to participate. She also made sure that the discussion stayed roughly on-track and covered the following topics:

- *How satisfied were they with their wedding and bridesmaid dresses (price, service, style, quality, selection)?*
- *What was the most important criteria to them in selecting a bridal boutique and wedding dress?*
- *What would they change about their dress buying and alteration experience, if anything?*
- *What was their preferred environment for trying on, purchasing, and having fittings for a dress?*
- *How important were friend's recommendations in their selection of boutiques and dresses?*
- *How far would they be willing to travel for a good seamstress and designer?*
- *How much would they be willing to pay for a good seamstress and designer?*
- *How would they describe their ideal wedding dress buying experience?*

Twila decided to round out her research by checking what information was available on the Internet. She went to her local chamber of commerce where there was free access to the World Wide Web. Using the search engine Yahoo! and AltaVista she punched in several of her subject words: bridal, fashion, and weddings. From there she was pleasantly surprised to find a whole selection of Internet sites. These in turn led her to other Web pages that gave her information on the latest wedding trends, buying patterns, and colors for dresses.

With this information in hand, Twila felt she had a solid level of knowledge on which to base the beginnings of a marketing strategy.

The method of sampling that you choose will depend on the amount of time and money you have budgeted and the type of research you are conducting. Chances are because your new business is small, you will opt for some form of convenient, non-random sampling. This may include a list of current customers, people who you believe fit your customer profile, members of your church, or people who shop at your grocery store. However, as you gather your list of respondents, make sure they represent a reasonable mix of your potential customer base. Too many of any single type of respondent will skew your findings.

Below is a brief summary of random and non-random sampling techniques:

Random Sampling Techniques	Non-Random Sampling Techniques
Computer programs can select random samples from electronic lists of names (telephone books or customer lists)	Select targets to question on the basis of convenience
Using a list of people (i.e., telephone list), assign a number to each name, select numbers from a table of random numbers, and choose the numbered entries on the list that correspond to those random numbers	Use your judgment to determine who is best to include in the sample on the basis of how well the person represents your targeted population
Decide on a "skip interval" and select names that are every *n*th on the list	Use a quota system that designates how many respondents of each gender, income bracket, geographic location, educational level, or other criteria that you will sample
	Gather respondents on the basis of referrals from other respondents

Remember: As you research your market, you are not seeking to confirm your opinions...you are seeking the truth

The most common types of survey research include:

Personal interviews: These can either be with **focus groups** or **individuals.** Focus group interviews are the most widely used questioning technique for gathering market research because they can yield very in-depth information. Individual interviews are used to gather qualitative data about a target group. They can be conducted door to door, in a mall "intercepting" people as they shop, or at a booth or trailer set up by the business conducting the research.

Careful: if you ask the wrong questions, you'll get the wrong answers

Recipe for the Perfect Focus Group

- Assemble 6-10 people who represent your target customer
- Gather in an informal, relaxed setting
- Add one interviewer/moderator with good listening skills
- Initiate "open-ended" questions
- Listen as participants share ideas, respond to one another, and stimulate one another's thinking
- Guide discussion gently for no more than one hour
- Consider videotaping the session for later review

Telephone interviews: These are best used for shorter interviews (5-10 minutes). They can be more economical and time effective than personal interviews. However, with the increasing frequency with which businesses of all types are calling people at home, it is getting harder and harder to find people who are willing to interrupt their at-home family time to speak with a stranger over the phone. For this reason, it is necessary to develop a telephone questionnaire that is short and concise.

Mail surveys: These can be inexpensive for the researcher and convenient for respondents to complete. The response rates for mail surveys can be lower than other types of surveys and they can take a lot longer to compile. Offering a prize or benefit to mail survey respondents can help increase your response rate.

Remember, with surveys of all types your goal is to gather reliable, relevant, and accurate information. It does your business no good at all (in fact, it does a great deal of harm) to base your marketing strategy on faulty research findings. To avoid this, be sure not to taint your respondents' answers with leading questions or feedback from you. Always ask open-ended questions with an open mind. The most valuable answers you will get will be ones that are spontaneous, unprompted, and free-form.

Creating a Survey? Try These Tips:

- Keep questions short, simple, and to the point
- Make it very easy for the respondent to complete
- Use a rating scale of 1-5, 1 = strongly disagree 5 = strongly agree
- Surveys should take no longer than 5-10 minutes to complete
- Be careful not to bias the answers with your question construction
- Offer respondents some reward for completing the survey (money, discounts, simple gift, lottery ticket, prize)
- Say, "thank you"

Observation

With observation, businesses try to record what their customers do naturally. Through observation, marketers try to determine how consumers behave as they buy and use a product, or how they are influenced by some marketing strategy being used by the business. The only pitfall of observation techniques is that the presence and/or bias of the observer can influence the behavior of the subject.

Museums, department stores, and even professional sports venues use observation to better understand visitors movements and needs. Most retail stores utilize check-out scanners or other simple computer software to observe what and how much customers buy at different times and at different price levels. Many businesses have found that simply tracking past behavior of their customers helps to predict their future behavior.

Conduct Secondary Research

After conducting a situation analysis, many small and start-up businesses find that the majority of the information they need to make intelligent marketing decisions can be found through secondary research. However, it is not uncommon for entrepreneurs to use a combination of secondary and primary research. Secondary research can lead to the use of primary research to gather limited, specific information about customers.

Typical information sought through secondary research is market size, location, and growth patterns. Businesses also use secondary information to get a better quantitative understanding of their customers: where they live, how numerous they are, their income brackets, educational level, and buying patterns.

Ask questions and seek answers!

Finding secondary research is simply a matter of investing the time to seek it out at public sources and talking to people. Below is a condensed resource list for collecting secondary data. Several books offer valuable listings of secondary data of all kinds. The best of these is *Find It Fast* by Robert I. Berkman. Additionally, an extensive resource guide is contained in the Start-up Student Workbook.

Using the Internet for Market Research

The sources of quality secondary data are almost limitless. A number of the most current sources of information can be found on the Internet. If you do not have a PC computer and an Internet account (via a local access provider or CompuServe or America Online), do not despair. Many public libraries, chambers of commerce, and community colleges offer free Internet access. Seek these venues out and use them. At this stage of your research use your creativity and enthusiasm to guide you: ask questions and seek answers!

Major Sources of Secondary Data:

- Public libraries
- University libraries
- Government (federal, state, local) departments and agencies
- Departments of Commerce
- Trade associations
- Industry associations
- Chambers of commerce
- Local newspapers
- Business periodicals: *Business Week, Wall St. Journal, Journal of Commerce, Inc.*
- *American Marketing Association Bibliography Series* (Chicago)
- *Communications Abstracts* (Beverly Hills, CA: Sage Publications, Inc.)
- *Journal of Marketing* (Chicago)

Analyze Data and Prepare Final Summary

After your data has been collected, the next step in your research process is data analysis. The purpose of analysis is to interpret and draw conclusions from the data that has been collected.

A business that wants to thoroughly understand its market or survey findings will be more rigorous in its research design and data analysis. The most comprehensive form of data analysis uses statistical models to test the validity and representativeness of the findings. Inexpensive statistical computer software packages can be purchased to perform many of these types of analysis.

However, for most small businesses it will suffice to gather the data, review its completeness, and work to draw reasonable conclusions from it. It is a good practice to:

- Challenge the validity of your research findings
- Check for completeness and timeliness of data
- Recheck to ensure the findings are representative of the larger population
- Assign value and weight to the findings
- Review your findings and conclusions with a mentor or industry expert

Note that the last recommendation made for concluding your market research process is **to review your findings with your mentor**. It is important throughout your entrepreneurial venture to seek insight and feedback from some experienced business person. This person can become your entrepreneurial mentor. Now is a particularly critical time to get assistance from an experienced business person. Before you create a marketing strategy, you want to make every effort to get an outside perspective through a mentor and other knowledgeable people to test the soundness and validity of your market data.

Lastly, you should summarize your findings. This brief summary contains your conclusions and your action plan. It need not be a formal document. This is simply a way for you to consolidate your findings and focus your efforts. Revisit this summary frequently and compare it to new conditions in your market. It will remind you that your market is a dynamic, changing place. Successful marketers know this and revise and update their marketing strategies as needed.

At the end of the market research process, your business should be able to incorporate all of your findings into a market strategy. Your target market and marketing mix should flow logically out of your market research process.

Drawing Conclusions: How Big Is Your Market?

After finishing gathering your primary and secondary research, you should be able to answer the following questions:

- Who is your target customer?
- Where do they live?
- How much do they earn?
- What is their educational level?
- What do they spend annually/monthly on your proposed product or service?
- What time of year do they buy most/which types of products?
- What are their saving patterns?
- What are their spending patterns?
- What are their leisure activities?
- What is their occupation?
- What is their family structure?
- What are their numbers: by city, county, and state?
- What is the amount of your product/service they buy annually/each visit?
- What motivates your customers to buy?
- Who are your best prospects?
- Should you emphasize yourself, your quality offerings, your selection, your price, or merely the existence of your business?
- What do they read or watch or listen to in the way of media?

Old, New, Cheap, and Sneaky Market Research Methods

- Enclose pre-stamped envelopes with mail surveys
- Tap into the knowledge of the reference librarian at your local library
- If you are already in business, prepare a questionnaire for your existing customers
- Talk with other business people in your area, benefit from their expertise
- Get on-line and use browsers such as Yahoo! to research your key words
- Create snappy, brief surveys for people who use the kinds of products or services that you will provide: look for them in parks, malls, ball games, the beach, downtown, at hardware stores...wherever they may be.
- Be honest and friendly: most people like to help "the little guy"
- Read advertising and marketing industry periodicals as they often contain valuable research findings
- Cheap, fast research on-line. Some entrepreneurs and big businesses are now posting market research questionnaires on the World Wide Web. For as little as $500 you can put a questionnaire on the Web, and get answers to your questions in a few days (rather than the 4-6 weeks traditional questionnaires can take). Quick response time is critical to getting to markets more quickly than your competition. Check out the M/S database marketing site at http://www.msdbm.com.

Conclusion

The role of marketing research is to provide businesses with the information necessary to identify marketing opportunities and problems, understand buyer behavior, and develop marketing strategies. This aids you in evaluating your customers' reactions to your proposed strategies.

As the creator of a new business, you may never feel that you have all the information that you need to answer all of your questions about your market, but, you don't have to rely solely on your intuition or spend thousands of dollars for expensive market research. There is some middle ground: there is a great deal of free and valuable market information available to the entrepreneur. Your task is to define what you need to know and set out in an organized and creative manner as you seek your answers. With determination and follow-through market research will guide the creation of a truly successful and original marketing strategy.

Chapter 37
MARKET ANALYSIS

About This Chapter:
- *The situation analysis*
- *Understanding your industry*
- *Performing a competitive analysis*
- *SWOT analysis: positioning in your industry*

Introduction

You wouldn't go for a drive with a blindfold on would you? Then why would you want to embark on an entrepreneurial venture without first knowing what the terrain looks like? Competitors, economic trends, and industry standards are the major factors that compose a business' external environment. Unfortunately, these elements are out of most businesses' control. But, businesses can understand these external factors and navigate their way intelligently around obstacles and towards opportunity. How do they do this? Businesses tailor their marketing strategy to fit the changing demands of their environment.

Before a business can create a winning marketing strategy, it must understand its own strengths and weaknesses, or its core competencies. **Core competencies** are things that a business does better than any of its competitors, whether it's product design, distribution, customer service, production, or promotion.

The more you understand the environment in which your business operates, the better your chances of success. Your marketing strategy will be more intelligent and better tailored to the realities of your market. And you will be able to competently assess whether or not to enter into that business environment in the first place or redirect your entrepreneurial talents to greener pastures.

Insights gained through market analysis help set the business's course

Looking only at the external environment for a business, however, is only half the picture. In order to create a truly successful venture, businesses need to also look at their internal capabilities. What are their unique areas of expertise? What is their unique passion, drive, or angle on a product or service? What can they do better than any of their competitors?

Many small businesses never look at themselves in this way and go on to succeed in spite of themselves. For the rest of us, why not use every tool available to enhance our chances of success? If you can understand what you do well and create a strategy that maximizes your strengths and minimizes your weaknesses, you will be far ahead of the game.

A business's experience, knowledge, skills, financial resources, and technical excellence define its internal capabilities. Analyze your internal and external environment. Fit them together into a unique and complementary strategy. This is a true recipe for business success.

How Is Market Analysis Different from Market Research?

Market research tells you who, where, and how large your potential market is

While market research produces qualitative and quantitative data about customers and their lifestyle, demographics, and buying behavior, market analysis helps businesses to better understand the external environment in which they compete. Market research will tell you what the size of your market is, who your customers are, what they like and dislike, and whether or not they need or want the service or product you are offering.

Market analysis, on the other hand, tells you how attractive the business environment is for you in your chosen industry. Who are your competitors? How fierce are they? On what basis do businesses compete?

Market analysis tells you how that market operates and if you want to start a business in that environment

Market analysis also guides your decision whether or not to even enter a market. If your analysis leads you to a "no-go" decision, it may be the most valuable information you could ask for. It will save you time and money to find out ahead of time that this target industry is not for you. Perhaps while investigating one industry you may identify an even better opportunity in another industry, in which case you can keep looking for a business concept in a more hospitable environment.

The goal of this chapter is to help you better understand your environment, determine the level of attractiveness of a given market or industry, identify competitors' strengths or weaknesses, and identify your business's strengths and weaknesses.

Turnstile Advertising

While waiting to enter an Orlando Magic basketball game, Martin Hering, an advertising professional, saw an amazing opportunity. He noticed that as fans walked through the entrance turnstiles, they always looked down before passing through. He realized immediately that he'd discovered a unique place to put advertising messages.

On that fateful day in Orlando, the idea for the Turnstile AdSleeve was born.

Martin Hering had the benefit of a professional background in advertising and media. While considering new business opportunities, he had wisely focused his efforts in his area of expertise: promotions and advertising. But, before leaping forward with this novel idea, he would rely on market research to tell him who he would sell his ideas to and how large his potential market of advertisers and sports venues would be. He would rely on a market analysis to tell him who his competitors would be, what his core competencies were, and how attractive the professional sports mass advertising industry was for his business.

With some advice from an entrepreneur and the help of an engineer, Martin developed the Turnstile AdSleeve into an innovative and highly lucrative advertising medium, and inaugurated his company, Entry Media, Inc.

Competitive Analysis

You may think that competition exists only to make your life difficult, but the truth of the matter is that competition is the very reason there are any business opportunities at all! When market needs go un-met, new opportunities arise for businesses who are able to identify these needs and create unique ways to satisfy them. Capitalizing on such needs is one way to gain a competitive advantage. **Competitive advantage** is an edge over competitors when you offer greater value to customers. Value can come from offering more or new benefits or the same benefits offered for lower prices.

To identify opportunities to gain competitive advantage, businesses usually perform some form of a **competitive analysis.** This involves assessing your potential market's overall attractiveness. A competitive analysis usually has three components, which yield the following information for decision making:

- Industry analysis—whether or not you want to be in this market or not
- Competitor analysis—who your competitors are and what their strengths are
- SWOT analysis—what are your business's strengths, weaknesses, opportunities, and threats

On what basis will you compete in your market? The goal of your business is to find and exploit its competitive advantage

Industry Analysis

The goal of the industry analysis is to identify how attractive your industry is to operate and compete within. Use this analysis as a tool to help you better understand how you can compete in your industry.

Using a scale of 1 to 5 (1 being the least and 5 being the highest) rate the degree to which each criteria listed below applies to your industry.

The factors that help determine an industry's attractiveness are:

- **Easy entry**: This describes how many barriers there are for new businesses trying to enter the market. These can be a plus if a business is already established in the market. High production costs, long set-up times, complex technical knowledge requirements, and logistical challenges are all examples of barriers to entry. The greatest barrier to entry is a competitor with a large marketing or cost advantage. A low score here means that your industry is very difficult for new competitors to enter.

- **Level of competition**: This describes the number of competitors in the market and the nature of their competition for customers' dollars. When competition is intense, the opportunities for gaining an edge (or even entry into a market) are few. When a market is mature and sales are leveling off or decreasing, competition is the most intense. Revenues might be falling, technological breakthroughs are few, and businesses begin to compete on the basis of price alone.

- **Availability of substitutes**: This describes how easily customers can use substitute products from other industries to satisfy their needs. An example of this would be for customers of rental car companies who fly low-cost, short-hop airlines rather than driving.

- **Buyer leverage**: This describes the bargaining power that buyers have over businesses in the market. If buyers have many choices of products and spend comparatively little on products in the industry, then their bargaining power is high. They can drive down the price and heavily influence the content of the product and the service that is delivered.

- **Supplier leverage:** This describes the amount of bargaining power that suppliers have over businesses in the industry. A business that relies on a limited number of large suppliers is vulnerable to price increases and suppliers dictating the terms of the sale of inputs. This can make a market less attractive to businesses by raising their costs and reducing their ability to control their markets.

Using the rating scale described above, calculate the total of the points you gave your industry for each of the above criteria. Look below for an explanation of your score.

- **17-25 points:** Your industry is very competitive! You best rally your troops and be prepared for an uphill struggle. Chances are the cost of competing in this industry is high, as are the risks. You may want to consider other related, more "user-friendly" industries where there is less extreme competition (remember the phrase: move on to greener pastures?). This industry might be experiencing market maturity or a slow down. Ask yourself: Are the rewards high enough to offset the risks and costs of market entry?

- **10-17 points:** This score places your industry in the middle of the pack in terms of attractiveness. Entering this industry won't be a walk in the park, but it certainly won't be as risky or as costly as entering some other industries. There may be real challenges in several areas, but these are offset by opportunities in other areas. Look before you leap!

- **5-10 points:** Can it be true? Do industries like this exist? Yes, they do, but not for long! Therefore, if you're lucky and clever enough to have identified an industry like this that has low competition, is moderately easy to enter, and is in its most immature stage, you best move, and move fast! Chances are other businesses big and small will soon get wise to what you've stumbled on to: a market, just begging to be exploited. Put on your seat belt and full speed ahead!

Now you're beginning to think like an entrepreneur. You're developing a critical eye that can identify problems and opportunities in your industry. The next step is to turn your attention to your business.

SWOT Analysis: How Does Your Business Rate Within Your Industry?

Know your strengths and your competitors' weaknesses, and hit them where they aren't!

This tool is particularly important for entrepreneurs who are considering entering a market for the first time. SWOT is just a snazzy way of saying that you are examining your business's Strengths, Weaknesses, Opportunities, and Threats. It is an important part of your competitive analysis because it gives you a baseline reading of your business's core competencies which you can compare to those of your competitors. The result of this analysis is an aggressive strategy that allows you to focus on areas where you are the strongest and your competition is the weakest. Unless you are looking for a long, expensive, frustrating struggle, you will want to avoid challenging your competitors head-on by competing in areas in which you share core competencies.

Now wrap up your SWOT analysis by examining the opportunities and threats that your industry and specific product market contain. A word to the eager, strategically minded entrepreneur: don't skimp here since this can be the most entertaining part of the whole exercise. What other opportunities or threats can you detect in your market?

For Martin Hering and his start-up business, Entry Media, Inc., a competitive analysis would show just where Entry Media's strengths lie and where the business could compete most effectively (and profitably!) in the already crowded and highly competitive sporting venue promotions industry. A basic SWOT analysis for Entry Media might look something like this:

<u>Entry Media, Inc.</u>

Strengths:	*Expertise in promotions and advertising.*
Weaknesses:	*The sports advertising industry is huge and highly competitive.*
Opportunities:	*Currently no advertising placement on entrance turnstiles. A unique place for advertising.*
Threats:	*Once the idea catches on, Entry Media will have to move even faster to shore up contracts with advertisers and sports venues.*

Through SWOT analysis, Martin determined that the market was ripe for his idea and that if he didn't move on it now, his window of opportunity would soon close.

The Competitor Analysis

This analysis is basically a SWOT analysis of your individual competitors, both actual and potential. You can gather information about your competitors in many ways. Call them up and ask all the questions a potential customer would ask. Talk to other businesses who have dealt with your potential competitors. Ask what they are known for in the industry, what their strengths are, how long they've been in business, new product or service offerings they will be announcing in the future (if they'll share this info with you, you're lucky!). Regardless of how you gather your information, try to get it from as wide an array of sources as possible to ensure it is accurate and up to date.

Use your powers of observation to evaluate each of the elements of your competitors' marketing strategy. What products and services do they offer? What are their prices? What is their distribution network? How are they positioning and promoting themselves?

Answering these questions will allow you to form a picture of who your competitors are targeting and why.

Your competitive analysis should include the following:

- **Placement**: Where do your competitors locate their businesses and why? Where do your competitors sell their products or service? How do they distribute their goods?
- **Promotion**: How do your competitors promote their products or services? What is their advertising message?
- **Pricing**: What is the price structure your competitors use? How are they positioned?
- **Product**: What are your competitors' products? How large is their line? How is their product unique? What need does it fill for customers? What type of packaging do they use?

Analyzing your competitors also can yield valuable information on marketing practices your business can emulate or improve upon. It can also help you predict their future plans as well as their response to your business's entry into the market.

Look before you leap:

- challenge assumptions
- re-check data
- review conclusions
- fine-tune with mentors

Drawing Conclusions: Do You Want To Compete in This Industry?

You've just completed your first competitive analysis. Each of the three elements, your industry analysis, your competitor analysis, and the SWOT analysis for your own business, has hopefully given you new insight into where your core competencies lie. Now you should complete the process by drawing some conclusions about how and where you will compete in your industry. This is the first step in creating your marketing strategy.

Now you are setting the direction that will guide all of your strategic marketing. Be clear and condense it down to a singular concept that is expressed in 4 or 5 sentences. You might even try to condense it once more down to **10 words**. Most business concepts that cannot be stated in 10 words are not worth pursuing. The simpler the better. If you can't do this, chances are you need to beef up your knowledge of your market and your customers, and fine-tune the purpose of your business.

The core concept for Martin Hering's Entry Media, Inc.? It might sound something like this: "To provide unique, effective sporting venue promotion to clients."

Conclusion

It is especially important for entrepreneurs to create a unique competitive advantage over their established competitors. Understanding your competitors, your industry, and your own business is key to developing this competitive advantage.

The more competitive your industry, the better you will have to be in identifying unique ways to create value for your customers and exploit the weaknesses of your competitors. Remember that market analysis is an on-going process. Your competitors, your industry, and your business's strengths are continually changing.

Think of the time you spend analyzing your markets as an investment in your business that will save you time and money in the future. These are powerful tools for focusing your business's goals and increasing your odds of success.

Chapter 38
THE MARKETING MIX: THE FOUR P'S

About This Chapter:
- *Managing your product & creating a product image*
- *Pricing strategies for small businesses*
- *Aggressive promotional strategies*
- *Placement of your product: distribution strategies*

Introduction

People buy things because they meet their basic survival needs like eating, safety, or shelter. Products are bought because they make our lives easier, they make us look or feel better, or they project an image we like. People buy to influence other people, and to feel differently about themselves.

Entrepreneurs who realize the many facets of people's buying decisions see opportunity at every turn. They improve existing products to meet needs in new ways, or create innovative products to satisfy entirely new, unmet customer needs. A business that understands the many ways to deliver value to the customer is in the strongest position to succeed. For example, a ski hat might be the warmest on the market, but how does it look and feel? How durable is it? What image does its label communicate? Does the manufacturer back up the hat with a 100% return policy?

Those businesses that think creatively and expansively about what their products represent to their customers are the most successful marketers.

What Is a Product? What Is a Service?

Technically speaking, a product is defined as a bundle of attributes and benefits, designed to satisfy customer needs. A product can be service, too. A service delivers benefits like time savings, convenience, expertise, labor, or comfort. Benefits are specific things that help customers to solve a problem or satisfy a need or a desire. A product can even be a combination of a tangible item and intangible services.

Products and services often do far more for us than what they were specifically designed for. Sure, laptop computers make doing word-processing out of the office possible, but they also make us feel up to date, "plugged in," and more in control of our work schedule. The personalized prescription service at your local pharmacy allows you to quickly and painlessly receive exactly the medicine you need, when you need it. It also gives you the feeling that you are safe and cared for. It may even remind you of a simpler time when everyone knew all their neighbors and looked out for one another.

Select a product or service you are interested in or in your area of expertise

The Product Basics

The first thing that businesses have to decide is what products and services to offer. For the entrepreneur, this idea usually comes from a hobby, an area of expertise, or professional experiences. A product should always be based on the needs of a customer. The best product ideas are those that meet existing or new customer needs in innovative ways, or improve upon an existing product by producing a higher-quality product cheaper and faster, or improve its packaging or promotion.

The purpose of this section is to familiarize the small business owner with the steps that go into creating a product strategy. It describes how you can create a plan for what you will offer, how you will package it, and what services will enhance it.

Your Product Line

A **product line** is a group of products offered by a single company. Usually these are similar products that build on the same strengths of the business and create a wider customer audience. Kellogg's various breakfast cereals, Boeing's line of jets, and the garden supply store that offers gravel, seedlings, soil, and shovels are all examples of product lines. The auto mechanic that repairs used Nissans and Toyotas is an example of a line of services.

All businesses must decide how many products to offer, whether to add new products, and how to position the entire product line. These are decisions regarding **product strategy**. They set the medium- and long-term direction for a business's products.

Another strategic decision is the **depth of the product line**. This describes the number of different sizes, models, or flavors within the product line. When a bakery decides to offer different types of doughnuts (chocolate, glazed, or cinnamon) it is determining the depth of its product line.

The **breadth of the product line** describes the diversity of products a business offers. If a bakery decides to branch out and offer french bread, frozen pizza crusts, sour dough bread, and bread sticks, it is extending the breadth of its product line. Particularly for new businesses, adding new products can be highly risky. New products may require marketing and operational skills outside of the business's core competencies. That is why, before making any product line extensions, it is important to revisit your business's strengths and your long-term market objectives.

The Real Estate Developer Who Didn't Know Malts from Schmalts

In 1994 Catharine Paine managed several real estate properties outside of Portland, Oregon. She managed them very well. She knew how to deal with clients and was familiar with legal restrictions, tax issues, environmental, and safety codes. In the spring of 1996 she had the opportunity to join a partner in developing a chain of 1950's style hamburger and malt shops. Her partner also came from the commercial real estate industry. They figured that between the two of them they could find prime locations, build cost-effective and attractive structures, and manage their properties with a unique expertise. So they moved quickly! Two months later their first restaurant was open in time for the spring season. Ten months later they were out of business.

What happened? Some months after opening the restaurant Catharine and her partner realized that they knew everything about real estate but nothing about restaurant management. They knew nothing about dealing with vendors, food preparation, selling, staff training, and customer service. They completely relied on the manager they hired to run the restaurant. They spent all of their time dealing with property management issues and scouting out their new locations. Were they spending their time in the wrong place? Yes!

Their failure? Expanding their product line too far outside of their area of expertise. Once they realized this, it was too late. They were entering the fall season, sales were slowing, and their projected revenues for their first summer were simply not enough to carry the business through the winter.

The lesson: know your area of expertise and your capabilities. Perfect what you are doing first. Then expand incrementally and slowly while building upon your core strengths. You can learn many new things, but not all at once. Pace yourself!

Where do new product ideas come from?

For the new business, competitors can be a valuable source of inspiration for new products. Skillful adaptation means learning from the mistakes and successes of others. Who better than your competitors? In many cases in the past, it has been the second, third, or even fourth imitator who realized full-scale success from a product idea initiated by someone else. The fourth imitator succeeded because he or she was able to learn from the mistakes of others. Investigate products that your competitors have introduced and then abandoned. Why did they abandon them? What were the product's strengths and weaknesses? What can you "borrow" from those ideas?

The "Basics"	Hot Products and Markets	Hot Markets
Nesting	Rain-Forest Goods	Outdoors/Sporty Professionals
Plain and Simple	Portable Phones	Early Retirees
Healthy and Sensible	Sport Utility Vehicles and Mini-Vans	Vegetarians
Political Correctness	Rollerblades, Surfing Products	Surfing
Environmental Responsibility	Convenience Products	Beach Volleyball
Mid-Priced Goods	Sports Snacks and Drinks	Catalogue Buyers
Coziness or "Snug"	Multi-Use Products/Space Savers	Latchkey Kids

What Do These Trends Mean to Small Businesses?

The things listed above may not represent opportunities for everyone, but they do represent powerful trends that all entrepreneurs should know about. If you haven't seen them in your community yet, chances are it's only a matter of time. In other areas, they are already evolving or being supplanted by new trends. The point of including these lists is to get you thinking like an entrepreneurial marketer. There are big changes occurring in many markets today. The more you can keep a sharp eye and an open mind, the more opportunities you can tap into.

Recipe for the Perfect Product Mix

Clever, on-the-ball businesses are constantly looking at the tangible and intangible benefits their products deliver. Why? So that they can insure that they are hitting their target audience with the right product. If not, they work quickly to revise their product offerings. How do they do this? By using market research to keep track of who and where their customers are and what their life-styles are like.

The next section identifies the major elements of the product mix. These variables are just as important for a small business as they are for a large business.

Packaging

A key element of your product is its packaging. Packaging helps to communicate and promote your product's image. Distinctive package design can attract target customers' attention and boost sales. Businesses that offer a line of products often design similar packaging (shape, color, size) in order to tie the line together in the minds of customers. Packaging also serves a very basic function of protecting products and providing information to customers about use, ingredients, quantity, and expiration date.

Clever design of your packaging can lead to increased sale of your products. Many businesses, old and new, have achieved success by cleverly identifying new ways to package existing products. By changing the packaging, they were able to entirely reposition the product in the minds of customers, hit new customer segments, and, in some cases, open new channels of distribution.

Consider these examples as inspiration:

- Coffee offered in single-serving tea-like pouches
- Business computers made more user-friendly and "repackaged" as personal computers
- Mixed wildflower seeds in a can sold as "Garden In a Can"
- Shower gel in a tube with a hook on the end
- Soap on a rope
- Toothpaste in a stand-up container
- Dijon mustard in a squeezable container
- Juice in a box
- Sunblock on a string to go around your neck
- Popcorn in a pouch—for microwave cooking

Service Enhancements

Even manufacturers of the simplest, lowest priced goods can find unique ways to enhance their offerings with good customer service. Service is one of the least expensive and most sure-fire ways for small businesses to compete with larger businesses. Why? Because customers would rather be treated like a valued friend rather than a number! And, most are willing to pay a little extra for the pleasure. Yes, they **need** the product or service they are buying from your business, but they **want** the time savings of free delivery, peace of mind of having their regular orders on file, and the "warm-fuzzy" feeling of being greeted by name.

By virtue of small size and mobility, small businesses can enjoy much closer customer contact than larger competitors. Consider the product enhancing service ideas listed below and think creatively to come up with some of your own.

Customers demand higher standards for service and customization than ever before

Customer Service Tricks

- If you don't know your customers by name, you should!
- Start a basic customer data base with (at least) their name, birthdate, special requests, and usual purchases
- Offer free or low-priced delivery
- Set up a fax and phone help/information number
- Create your own "frequent customer" program—with rewards for repeat purchases
- Create a colorful, brief, informative customer newsletter
- Attach helpful tips and tailored promotional messages to invoice statements
- Have convenient, flexible hours that fit your customers' schedules
- Offer free, convenient parking
- Give away free samples
- Send birthday greetings and offer birthday discounts
- Offer free demonstrations and installations

Making Profits with Mini-Marketing

Among many businesses there is a shift away from mass markets towards mini-markets that demand customization and direct interaction with customers. Mini-marketers know their customers individually by name, address, telephone numbers, income, lifestyle, and brand preferences.

Mini-marketing is the product of the new information economy. This new phenomena holds a great deal of opportunity for entrepreneurs. Because of computers, fax machines, and the Internet, businesses now can know their customers as never before, and take the guess work out of creating marketing strategy.

Just how do entrepreneurs go about using mini-marketing? By keeping track of customers by name in a basic data base. This can be a simple Rolodex of names or a computer data base (there are many inexpensive and easy-to-use data base software programs available). Simply keeping track of who your customers are and what they buy, allows you to deliver the type of service they need. You can target them with information, promotions, and recommendations that fit them to a "T."

The Web's Most Successful Music Store

A perfect example of mini-marketing comes from brothers, Jason and Matthew Olim, founders of an Internet based start-up that sells compact disks. Their products are the latest CD releases but also something traditional music retailers aren't offering: more information about nearly any recorded music or musician, and truly customized service. Using their own software they "follow" customers as they browse through the Internet site's pages of artists and information. Simultaneously they provide promotional and informational messages that are tailored to fit individual customers.

The CD guys group their customers based on their purchases and interests. Post-purchase they follow-up with their customers via e-mail to share information about new releases and sales promotions. Aggressive, highly targeted marketing is what they owe their success to. In their first 5 months they registered 70,000 customers and average almost 13,000 visitors to their Internet site each day.

Branding Your Product or Service

A **brand** is a name or symbol that represents a product. Evian water, the Saturn car, the Bic pen, and STP motor oil are all brands. A well-established brand associated with a quality product is a very valuable asset. Small businesses can create a unique brand image or "vibe" for their product which will differentiate it from other products. This might convey an easy, good-time feeling; it might be a professional, reliable image; it might be colorful and quirky. This is your real chance to be creative. Think about what your customers' values and styles are and combine that with your own flare.

"Coca Cola is the most valuable brand in the world."

—Fortune Magazine

A **brand image** is communicated through the product's benefits, its packaging, advertising, and the service delivered along with it.

Tips for Creating Your Brand

- Create a plan: how will the product be conceptualized, packaged, distributed, and promoted
- Design your product with care: use shape, color, design, and varied consumer uses to differentiate your product
- Name your product with power: buzz words are key to consumer recognition and recall
- Package your product creatively: use the package as a message platform
- Look at the big picture: everything that has to do with your business should have the same consistent, clear look and identity
- Use merchandising: pay attention to product presentation on the shelf
- Expand your offerings: use product array to create a theme

Although lacking the resources of their larger competitors, small businesses can create powerful brand images for themselves to differentiate their offerings. How? By learning from brand powerhouses like Procter and Gamble, Kraft, and Coca Cola. These corporations have succeeded in part by creating categories of products that have distinct "personalities" or brands. These can become as important to customer's opinions about the product as the content itself.

"It is not beneath the dignity of any business person to imitate, adapt, and improve upon the innovations of other companies." —Gordon A. Baty, author and entrepreneur

What makes a good name?

- It should suggest product benefits: Sunkist, Mr. Clean, or Beautyrest mattresses
- It should fit the brand image: Nissan Pathfinder (adventure), Round Table Pizza (cozy food for friends and families), Ding Dongs (silly, playful food for kids)
- It should be easy to pronounce and recognize
- It should not be previously registered with another company

Product Entry Strategies for Start-ups

Entrepreneurs often have the slimmest of budgets with which to introduce their products or services to the market. That's why it's all the more important that they use their wiles, energy, and creativity at this early phase of their business. Every new product, whether it be it an innovative offering or a simple revamp of an existing product requires a well-thought-out entry strategy to insure its success.

Customers are attracted to a new product because is has a price, quality, or service advantage over other products. When businesses establish a new product in the market, they must use each element of the marketing mix to communicate the same message and support their efforts. This ensures a consistent, more memorable message for customers.

Recipe for successful product introduction:

- Overall marketing objective: introduce the product, encourage trial, establish distribution
- Product strategy: differentiation from competitors, highlight unique advantages and benefits
- Promotional strategy: build brand awareness and differentiate product "personality"
- Distribution strategy: build distribution network to make product easily available
- Pricing strategy: start at lower prices to encourage trial, then slowly increase prices

Think of your entry strategy as an introduction to new friends... your customers

A wonderful moment occurs when a new product enters its growth period and sales increase and are sustained. This is the point at which the product becomes profitable. This is a time for champagne and a hearty pat on the back. Enjoy! But not for too long. If yours is an entirely new product innovation, no doubt competitors will begin to take notice and move in to offer similar products. Even if it is not an innovation, this is the time to consolidate your product gains and reinforce your product position. This means that all of your marketing efforts should be focused on getting repeat purchases and continuing to attract first-time users. Some successful product maintenance strategies include:

- Thank you notes to customers
- Follow-up customer calls and visits to gauge satisfaction
- Customer newsletters with company and new product information
- Fliers to past customers offering discounts tailored to their purchasing track record
- Frequent buyer programs with discounts

It costs more to get new customers than to maintain existing customers

These strategies remind your customers of why they bought from you in the first place. They also encourage your customers to buy from you again. Remember: it is five times cheaper to sell to existing customers than to go out and find new ones. Once you have a customer, your product strategy should be focused on keeping their business.

Product Strategy Summary

Product strategy for start-ups begins when they decide what products or services to offer. This decision is based on what your market research has shown you about your customers' needs and tastes. How will your packaging, warranties, brand image, and service enhance your product? This too is part of your product strategy. Once you identify this mix and the unique "personality" of your product, stick with it. After you test your customer and market with periodical market research, your commitments to a sound strategy is one of the your best tickets to success.

Price: the key to profitability

Your Price

For businesses of all types pricing strategy of products and services is the ultimate measure of marketing skill. Why? Successful pricing maximizes profits while providing the greatest possible value to customers. It requires marketers to perform a virtual juggling act by taking into account their costs of doing business, the price sensitivity of target customers, and the impact of their prices on competitors.

Product pricing can spell business success or failure. Price must coincide with the level of quality customers perceive they are receiving from the product. The relationship between price and perceived value is truly unique: the higher the price, the higher the perceived value by customers—but only up to a point. Set too high, a price can flag customers that they have paid too much for the value they are receiving. If it is set too low, customers question the quality of the product. Skilled marketers can set their price at the level where it fits with their positioning strategy and allows them to earn a good profit.

It might seem too basic to point out, but price is key to your product's profitability. **Profit** is total revenue minus your total costs. **Total revenue** is your price times the number of units you sell. Therefore, price directly affects profits.

The goal of this section is to introduce you to the major calculations you will have to perform in order to profitably price your products. It also reviews several of the pricing strategies most applicable to an entrepreneurial venture.

Different industries price their products and services differently. You will discover the specific pricing practices used in your industry while you perform your market analysis. You should also review trade journals, trade association documents, and talk with businesses in your industry. First-time entrepreneurs need to thoroughly understand pricing issues in their industries before they begin to price their products and services.

Determining Your Costs

No matter how good you believe your intuitions are, before you make a single decision about what you will charge your customers, you need to first measure what it costs you to produce and deliver your product or service. This is especially important for sole proprietors who at some point will hire additional people to work for them.

Basic Cost Concepts

Variable costs are costs that vary directly in relation to the amount of products produced. These costs include the cost of labor and raw materials used to make the product, plus the cost of sales and distribution.

Typical Variable Costs

- Inputs and supplies
- Depreciation on equipment
- Overtime wages
- Sales commissions

Fixed costs are expenses that a business has regardless of the quantity of units it produces. For example, the cost of installing a commercial oven is constant regardless of the number of loaves of bread baked over the lifetime of the oven.

Typical Fixed Costs

- Salaries and wages
- Payroll taxes
- Vehicle leases and maintenance
- Office supplies
- Office equipment
- Machinery and equipment
- Marketing expenses
- Land
- Rent
- Insurance
- Utilities

Total costs are the total expenses of producing and marketing a product. Total costs are the sum of total fixed costs and total variable costs.

Break-even analysis pinpoints the level at which total revenue equals total cost and profits are zero. As the volume of units sold increases beyond this **break-even point**, a business begins to earn profits. Calculating your break-even point requires you to plug in your price, various levels of units sold, and total costs.

Identifying your break-even point requires that you first calculate your costs and your revenue. Below are the basics of price calculations:

Total Revenue = Price x Quantity

Total Cost = Total Fixed Costs + Average Variable Cost Per Unit x Quantity

The break-even point occurs when:

Price x Quantity = Total Fixed Costs + (Average Variable Costs x Quantity)

Or, looking at the same equation a different way, the quantity needed to achieve break-even is:

Break-even Quantity = Total Fixed Costs ÷ (Price - Average Variable Costs)

Sam Granville knew a business opportunity when he saw one. One hot day in July 1993 he passed a newly constructed house on the eastern shore of Maryland. The lot was large and the house stood out starkly on the newly cleared, nearly barren lot.

Dotted around the house were small maple and pine saplings. Their small size only accentuated how new and empty the land looked. What this lot needed was a mature shade tree to give the property a sense of hominess and history.

His idea: expand his small landscaping business into a tree relocating business. The target customer: owners of new houses and developers of subdivisions. His product? Beautiful, healthy, mature trees that deliver badly needed charm to new construction sites.

Once he had completed his preliminary market research and analysis of his customers and competitors, Sam began work on his marketing plan, and calculating his costs and prices for his services. He knew what the market would bear in terms of price, but what would it really cost him to relocate 1/2-ton trees to his customers' lots?

Sam began by calculating his costs of moving a single tree. Sam estimated that on average, it would take him 2-4 hours to move a single tree. He also estimated that in his first 6 months, he would be able to move 30 trees a month. His costs broke down as follows:

Variable Costs (per tree moved):	
Labor (1 helper, 4 hours per tree @ $15.00/hour)	$ 60.00
1 tree spade and tractor operator (3 hours @ $30.00/hour)	90.00
Diesel fuel for crane & tractor (15 gallons per job @ $1.90/gallon)	28.50
Fertilizer & burlap	250.00
Tree	250.00
Miscellaneous office expenses (phone, fax, supplies)	20.00
Total Variable Costs	**$ 698.50**
Fixed Costs (per month):	
Miscellaneous landscaping equipment (shovels, mini-tractor, winches)	$ 2,000.00
Office equipment (computer, desk, chair, etc.)	3,000.00
Rent	300.00
Tree spade lease payments	250.00
Tractor lease payments	200.00
Total Fixed Costs	**$ 5,750.00**
Total cost of relocating 30 trees a month ($5,750.00 + 30 trees x $698.50) =	$ 26,705.00
Total revenue for relocating 30 trees ($1,500.00 x 30)	$ 45,000.00
Net Profit	**$ 18,295.00**

Sam's fixed costs remain the same regardless of how many trees he moves. He has already leased his mechanized tree spade and bought his computer and his landscaping equipment. However, Sam's total costs rise over time because his total variable costs (labor, gas, and trees) go up as he moves more trees.

Sam calculated his total revenue for a given price level. If he charged on average $1,500 per tree, and he moved 30 trees a month, his total revenue would be $45,000 per month. At 20 trees a month his monthly revenue would be $30,000. For Sam, the break-even point in his business occurs when he relocates between 5 and 6 trees. At this point he has covered all of his fixed costs and variable costs. From that point on, he begins to earn profit.

Sam's calculation for break-even quantity is below:

Break-even Quantity = Total Fixed Cost ÷ (Price - Average Variable Cost)

Break-even Quantity = $5,750.00 ÷ ($1,500.00 - $698.50)
= 7.17 trees per month

Setting Your Prices

Setting the price for your product or service begins with your pricing objectives. Are you primarily interested in your own cost issues, undercutting your competitors or matching their prices, or in building customer demand and loyalty? Or are you aiming to achieve a particular return on your investment?

By carefully researching the effect of your prices and manipulating your strategy, your price level is capable of helping you achieve any of the objectives listed above.

Three of the most common pricing strategies are described below. Entrepreneurs often need to be aware of each of these strategies and the impact that their prices will have on their customers and their competitors. Pricing is not an exact science, often businesses experiment with several different price levels before settling on a single pricing strategy. They also may adjust their prices frequently (though not so often as to frustrate customers). Many entrepreneurs combine their knowledge of different approaches to achieve the optimal price for their marketing strategy.

Cost-Based Pricing

Cost-based pricing is the most widely used pricing method. It is simple and low-risk because it is based on known factors, costs. Cost-based pricing requires that businesses total all of their costs and add a **percent margin** or **target return** on top to determine the sale price. A target return is usually expressed as a percentage of total costs.

Cost-based pricing also has its pitfalls: it ignores the consumer demand impact on prices. Hence you might end up setting a price that is out of sync with what the market will pay. Cost-based pricing tends to work well in industries in which consumer demand and competition are stable, and therefore, reasonably predictable.

Sam Granville calculates his price based on his target profit margin.

No doubt about it, Sam had a leg up on the competition. He had grown up on a fruit farm, and knew just about everything there was to know about caring for trees. But he wanted to be exact when he embarked on setting price, which is an area in which he had little knowledge. He knew, based on his market research, that he could charge on average $1,500 per tree. But he wanted to calculate his price based on his costs and his target profit margin (40%).

Once he finished calculating his costs he decided to use cost-plus pricing for his services. This was the simplest method he knew and he figured if he needed to change his strategy later, he could. Below are his calculations based on moving 30 trees in one month, with a target profit margin of 40%. Sam used the following equation for his calculations:

$$\frac{(\text{Units} \times \text{variable cost per unit}) + \text{Fixed Costs}}{\text{Units}} \times \text{Profit \% Desired} = \text{Per unit price}$$

$$\frac{(30 \text{ trees} \times \$698.50) + \$5{,}750.00}{30 \text{ trees}} \times 1.40 \text{ Profit Margin} = \mathbf{\$1{,}246.00} \text{ (Price per tree)}$$

Competition Based Pricing

Although cost-based pricing is the simplest way to price products, many businesses alter their prices based on the prices of their competitors. This is particularly common in large, highly competitive industries like airline travel, soda pop, and crude oil. The risk in this type of strategy is that the cost structure of competitors might be significantly different from your own.

Follow-the-leader pricing sets prices at the level of an industry's price leader. This is used particularly in industries that sell highly standardized products such as farm commodities, industrial raw materials, or computer floppy disks. These industries tend to be dominated by several large companies.

The method of **pegged pricing** establishes a business's prices in line with industry-wide norms. Pegged pricing tends to occur in industries in which there is no clear price leader. Businesses using this method might use the industry norm as a starting point, then offer a slightly higher (**premium**) or lower (**economy**) price to establish a niche within the industry. Once they've done this, the business will work backwards to calculate if they can make an acceptable profit at that price level.

Pricing based on **projected responses by competitors** is just that. Businesses take into account the response of their competitors prior to taking action. Businesses may set very low prices to discourage new competitors from entering the market, or they may set their prices at mid-range levels in order to discourage their competitors from starting a price war.

You may want to develop some "what if" pricing scenarios based on anticipated competitor responses. These might sound like this: "If my competitor responds by lowering their prices, then I can afford to lower prices to ___ level".

Experimenting with different price levels can be very difficult for a new business; it can take time and resources that the business just cannot afford. What is the entrepreneur to do without disturbing their entire sales effort? You do have a few options.

You might try setting slightly different prices in different geographic areas or creating intermediate "models" of your products to test the price sensitivity of your customers and competitor reactions. You can also offer short-term discounts to see how the price affects demand for your products.

The pricing strategy you chose will depend on your positioning strategy and core competencies

Retail Price

Retail price is generally established by taking the wholesale price and multiplying it by a given percentage. A retailer who uses a 25% mark-up would buy Sam's trees at $1,246.00 and sell them at $1,246.00 + $311.50 = $1,557.50. Many retailers double or triple the wholesale price. Retailers are in the business of selling goods rather than producing them. But they have labor costs and overhead associated with selling. Retailers' selling price must include these costs and still offer an acceptable level of profit.

Consignment Selling

Consignment is the business of placing your product in the custody of a retailer who will sell it. A retailer does not buy the product from you, but pays you only after the product is sold. The producer retains ownership of the products and is responsible for them until their sale. Commissions for sales and payment terms are negotiated between the producer and the retailer. The average commission for consignment sales is between 25 and 40 percent of the wholesale price.

Distributor Price

A distributor is an intermediary who does not sell directly to the end-user. Distributors buy products in large volume at wholesale prices and resell them to retailers. Because distributors buy in large quantities, they expect to receive a "volume discount." The products are then marked up from 25 to 40 percent (depending on the industry) and sold to retailers.

Price Adjustments

List price is the "official" price that businesses charge, from which they subtract any discounts. Sometimes the list price is the same as the final selling price, but not usually. Adjustments are usually made to both the **trade**, or distribution channel partners, and the final customer.

Businesses offer discounts of all types to buyers who satisfy some criteria that reduces their selling costs. For entrepreneurs, strategic discounting can be a powerful tool to increase sales or even out seasonal demand.

Quantity discounts are a powerful way for businesses to increase the amount of units they sell. Generally, businesses offer lower prices to customers who buy in bulk.

Trade discounts are given to channel members like distributors or representatives when they perform some of the marketing functions ordinarily performed by the manufacturer. These may include creating advertising, promotions, or technical support to customers. Trade discounts are also often used as a leveraging tool for new products in distribution channels or retail outlets.

Seasonal discounts can be used to encourage customers to make their purchases during off-peak selling times. This can help to lower inventory levels when demand is down.

Businesses will also offer **cash discounts** to customers when they pay for their purchases in cash, rather than on credit. This is usually used by manufacturers and their distribution channel partners to encourage speedy payment of bills to minimize their accounts receivable.

Coordinating Price with Other Elements of Your Marketing Mix

No matter which pricing strategy you use for your products or services, it is essential that it be consistent with the other elements of your marketing mix. Summarized below are issues to consider as you link your price to the other three elements of your marketing mix:

- **Product Strategy**: Is your price in line with your customer's perceptions of quality? If not, then you should consider lowering your prices, improving your quality, or increasing your efforts to educate your customers about your product's quality.

- **Distribution Strategy**: Is your product's price level consistent with the distribution outlets you are using? High-priced, premium products should be distributed selectively. Likewise, lower priced, economy products should be distributed on an intensive basis to maximize their availability to the larger, price-sensitive market. Your prices and the image of your distribution channels must match. Even more important, is your price "distributor friendly"? Are you using distributor discounts effectively to maximize the chances that your product will be among the first that your distributors recommend and sell?

- **Promotional Strategy**: Is your advertising message consistent with your product's price level? If yours is a premium-priced product, is your advertising image one of quality and service? If yours is a lower priced product, is your advertising image one of value? Are your sales promotions undercutting your own pricing strategy and profitability? Are coupons or price discounts being used more often than not and encouraging only short-term business by fickle customers?

Common Pricing Errors

Listed below are some common pricing problems:

- Basing price on current, artificially low overhead costs vs. projecting into the future to anticipate how overhead might rise over time.
- Assuming that because you are the newest competitor on the block, you must have the lowest prices.
- Trying to compete head-to-head on price with larger, resource-rich competitors. Try instead to offer higher quality or more individualized, attentive service.
- Basing prices on manufacturing costs vs. on the value of product to customers. Costs may be far lower than the value of product to customers.
- Failing to include in the price an allowance for warranty costs, future service, research and development costs, cost of capital, dealer discounts, sales commissions.
- Ignoring the way customer demand for the product will change at different price levels. Estimate how much sales volume might increase if prices are lowered 10 or 20 percent. At what price do you earn the maximum profit given how much customers demand at different price levels?

- Failing to use some form of **market skimming** in which you enter a market with a high price until you have satisfied demand or competitors move in, then gradually lowering price over time.

Pricing Summary

Pricing is the most telling measure of a business's marketing skills because it requires an in-depth understanding of the customer, total costs, and competition. The impact of pricing on a business is profound: it can determine the success or failure of a product.

Given this, it is no wonder that businesses spend so much time measuring their costs and tracking their customers' reactions to different price levels.

For the entrepreneur, the most critical element of pricing is understanding costs. Once you know exactly what your fixed and variable costs are to produce your product or service, you can select the pricing method that is best for you. Different industries demand different pricing strategies. Try to understand the most common and effective practices in your industry, then tailor your strategy to fit your business. Pricing your product or service need not be confusing or intimidating. Learn the basics and build your skills as you go. Ask questions, do your calculations, and watch as you reap profits!

Promoting Your Product or Service

What is Promotion

Promotion is everything you do to communicate with your target customer and encourage the sale of your product or service. What do you communicate to your customer? The uniqueness of your product or business, of course! A special, memorable, positive reminder of your business. A creative reason to buy from you. Or, a simple message to raise people's awareness about your product or service.

A business's promotional mix is the box of tools that it uses to achieve promotional objectives. The **promotional mix** is composed of advertising, sales promotions, and publicity.

If you are starting a small business and want to get off the ground, you must use promotion. Even the best product or service won't sell if people don't know it exists. This can be the most creative part of your entire marketing effort. The greater your imagination the more memorable your impact will be. The whole goal of promotion is to catch and hold people's attention, and get them to buy your product. The reality of small budgets means that entrepreneurs must be even more creative and aggressive than their larger competitors.

Your promotional message is the beginning of your dialogue with your customer

The more aware you become of how effective a good promotion can be, the more attention you will pay to it. Paying more attention and analyzing your promotions means that each of your efforts will be more and more effective. Most small business owners never fully utilize all of the different promotional tools that are available to them.

The goal of this section is to help you to think like an experienced promoter. It seeks to give you the basic information that you will need as you embark on promoting your business's product or service and equip you to ask the right questions as you go along.

The Basics of Promotional Strategy

As with every other element of the marketing mix, successful promotional efforts require the creation of a strategy. How do you go about creating a promotional strategy? By selecting the mix of promotional tools you will use to communicate your message.

First, you need to set your promotional objectives. If you are introducing an original product your promotion objectives will be quite different than if you are simply adding another product to your line or releasing a product to compete in a well-established product category.

Most entrepreneurial ventures introduce new products or create a new spin on an existing product. Your first objective is to establish an awareness of your product among your target customers. Your goal? To create a solid base of loyal customers who buy from you and will spread the word about you to friends and neighbors.

When creating promotions, the sky's the limit!

New Product Promotional Objectives

- **Raise awareness**—by focusing on advertising
- **Create positive attitude**—through public relations, networking, advertising
- **Encourage product trial**—through sales promotions, coupons, free samples
- **Influence existing buyers to buy and buy again**—through powerful personal selling, advertising, consistent follow-up

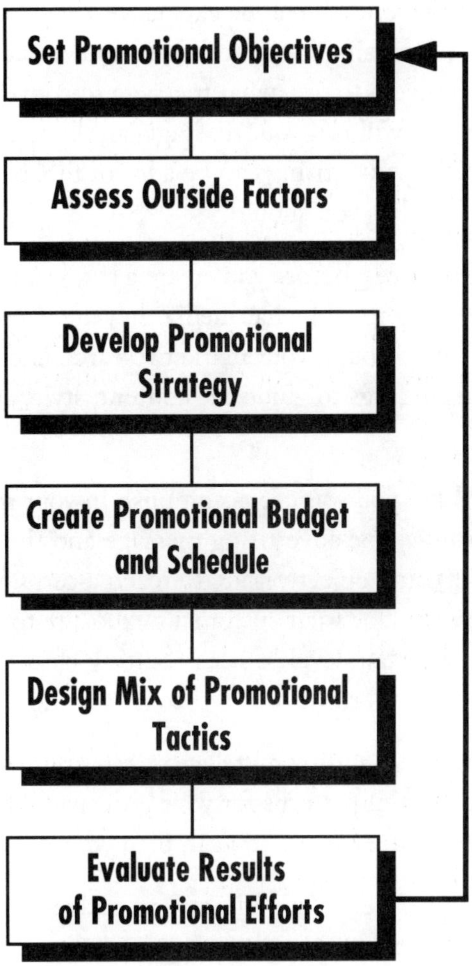

Advertising

It's hard to imagine anyone who's lived in the United States in the past 30 years and doesn't appreciate the huge role that advertising has had on American popular and consumer culture. Advertising is the most well-known, expensive, and flashy method of communicating with consumers.

Advertising delivers paid, promotional messages through mass communication channels such as television, radio, magazines, and the Internet. Its goal is to communicate messages about a product, service, or company. Advertising messages may serve to raise awareness, influence customers to buy, or increase a product's visibility.

Businesses may use advertising to promote their individual products or their business's overall image.

The Advertising Planning Process

Advertising is not for everyone. It can be expensive and time consuming to create a truly effective advertising message. Once you've decided to advertise, you must decide which media to use, what message to convey, what feeling to create, how frequently you will run your message, and how much you are willing to spend. Creating advertising can be a lot of fun, but to get the most out of your advertising dollars you should:

Identify your target audience. Before you create a single ad, you first must know who you are speaking to and what media they are exposed to. Your target audience is defined through your market research and your market analysis. Review these findings to guide the content, style, and placement of your advertising.

Set your objectives. What you want to accomplish in your market through your advertising determines the advertising message and the medium you settle on. Typical advertising objectives are to reach a certain percentage of the target market, increase the target customer's exposure to your product/ business, or to achieve a certain level of sales. Setting clear goals lets you gauge after-the-fact whether or not you've gotten your money's worth.

Industry sources, newspapers, radio and television stations can offer good estimates of the monthly sales patterns for your industry. They know what their viewer demographics are so that you can plan your objectives realistically.

Create your advertising budget. Your advertising budget is one part of your overall promotional budget. How much you allocate depends on your objectives and your resources. It also depends on how widely and how frequently you want your message to be heard. How much will you spend on each ad message per month? How much on developing and producing an ad piece?

Design your advertising strategy. This is the most strategic and creative part of the entire advertising management process. It relates directly to your positioning strategy. How will you encourage your customers to buy? What will your message and your medium be? Will you use humorous short radio spots to highlight how speedy your service is? Or will you use a simple and classy color image to convey your premium quality? How about a spokesperson or a competitor comparison?

Select Your Media Menu

The types of platforms that you can choose to carry your message are varied. For small businesses, the selection usually is based on which provides the most "bang for the buck." This means that cost, speed, and effectiveness will be your major criteria for selection.

- **Television** ads can communicate information about product usage and benefits using sound, color, and motion. Cable TV can be a great, lower cost, highly targeted medium since they target viewers with very specific interests. Home shopping channels are also a great way to promote and sell products with very little risk or expense.

- **Radio** can provide constant, flexible coverage to reach a wide range of audiences. You can choose the time, day, and exact station to hit your target audience with multiple ads. Local radio advertising can be a very cost-effective way to spread a message. The cost of radio advertising has risen much more slowly than any other major advertising medium. Radio stations have staff and equipment to help produce ad spots. Be sure to write your own message. You don't want your ad to sound just like everyone else's.

- **Newspapers:** Newspapers are great for running short-term price promotions and coupon offers to very specific audiences. Newspapers reach a comparatively "upscale" audience and are useful for targeting specific geographic regions. By placing different coupon ads in various local papers, you can measure which is most effective for spreading your message. Newspaper ad salespeople can advise you on the best placement, day, size, and length of run for your ad.

- **Magazines:** Magazines are a very targeted way to communicate a message to an audience. There are magazines for just about every special interest you can think of. They are often saved and read more than once by more than one person, so businesses get more "bang-for their-buck" with magazine ads. Advertisers can use colorful ads placed next to relevant articles to maximize their visibility. Small businesses can often negotiate to use lower cost "remnant" space in magazines when it is available.

- **Direct mail:** The fastest growing and most flexible media for advertisers, direct mail allows businesses to send segment-specific promotional information to its customers and tailor its message to the audience. It can provide a great deal of detailed information on product usage and benefits.

- **Signage:** Billboards, buses, parking meters, gas pumps, and even turnstiles at sporting arenas are spots that are available to post advertising messages. These are among the lowest cost mediums. Messages must be clear, short, and quickly noticeable to be effective. Carefully placed signs near where target customers live, shop, and commute is a highly effective way to hit a target market.

- **The Yellow Pages:** Yellow Page listings can be an essential way to promote your product or service if customers typically use the Yellow Pages to get information about your type of businesses. People who use the Yellow Pages are the hottest prospects of all because they are in a buying mood. Businesses may locate their listing in several different sections. One advantage of this medium is that small businesses can appear as big as their larger competitors.

- **Classified ads:** Many small businesses use only classified ads to promote themselves. Magazines, newspapers, and classified-ad newspapers all sell space for classified ads. These ads are less expensive than traditional ads and can contain more information. Classified ads are often offered at a discount to advertisers who use frequent listings. Chances are, if you see classified ads in your local paper or favorite magazine for your type of business, you could profit from placing ads there too.

Sam's Specialty Trees—Sample Print Ad

Would you like a beautiful mature oak tree in your yard? You will have it made in the shade! A blossoming cherry? A magnificent magnolia? Let Sam's Trees and Landscaping help. We provide expert service to relocate, landscape, and care for trees of all kinds. Call us at 628-6720 to get information on tree varieties and landscaping designs to improve the appearance and value of your property. We are sensibly priced and guarantee all of our work.

Selecting your advertising media. Media are the outlets that carry advertising messages, such as television, radio, magazines, newspaper, billboards, direct-mail or the Internet. Today businesses have more choices of media than ever before. They also have the choice to invent their own by creating their own home page on the Internet or publishing their own "mini-magazine." It's easier and lower cost than you might think to communicate advertising messages.

How do you select the media that is right for your message and your budget? You should judge all media by the exposure they offer to your target customer. **Reach** describes the percent of your target market that see your message. **Frequency** describes the number of times individuals in your target market see your message.

Impact and cost are also two major criteria for selecting an advertising medium. Different advertising mediums have different impact, based on their reputation, audience, and other advertising content. Based on reach and frequency information you can estimate how much it costs you to advertise per customer you hit. This way you can create a standard by which to compare your advertising choices.

For businesses who are introducing a new product, the frequency with which an advertising message is heard is more important than the reach. It takes several exposures to a message before people are even aware of it and absorb it, much less take action on it! For entrepreneurs who are trying to fill a market niche, the objective is to reach targeted people frequently.

Reach the most people the most times for the least cost

Schedule your media messages. Once you've selected your advertising tools, you need to decide when you will use each one. If yours is a seasonal product, you will want to coordinate your message with your customers' purchase cycles. Advertising messages can be aired in a few large "bursts" at scheduled intervals. They can also be spread evenly over a period of time to maintain customer awareness. When new products are being introduced, businesses often use a "burst" strategy with a cluster of advertising to create an early and intense impact to build customer awareness. Seasonal businesses and businesses offering short-term sales promotions also use this strategy.

Sales Promotions

Different businesses promote their products and services in different ways. Businesses who sell consumer products offer **consumer promotions** that are generally short-term incentives to encourage buying. Businesses print coupons, organize sweepstakes or contests, and offer free samples or rebates for cash back on purchases to encourage new use of their product or service. The sky is the limit for the clever entrepreneur designing a consumer promotion.

Vance's Vans and Trucks bought and sold used vehicles in Cheyenne, Wyoming. In early summer, business was particularly slow but they were expecting a big influx of used trucks for the fall. Vance decided to create a new customer sales promotion. They decided to invite potential customers to trade in tractors, trailers, and even snow plows towards the purchase of a truck. His only restriction? The vehicles had to be less than 5 years old and in good working condition. Vance had a cousin in the tractor business and knew that he could more easily resell the equipment than could his customers. Why not help them out?

Vance's promotion would last 3 days, on the weekend following the Fourth of July holiday. His target audience? Men between the ages of 21 and 50. His choice of advertising medium to get the message out fast and frequently? The local country western radio station. At $300 each, three times a day, he felt sure that in the week preceding his sale he would get the message out to at least 50% of his target market. He was right. By the end of the sale he had nearly cleared his lot of trucks, and made a handy deal to resell to his cousin 20 snow plows, 13 trailers, and one lawn mower.

Trade promotions are incentives that businesses offer to retailers and wholesalers for stocking their product. These can include cash allowances for promotional efforts or discounts for volume or seasonal purchases. Some businesses even create sales contests or sweepstakes to encourage channel members to put in their best efforts to sell a product.

Importance of Different Promotional Elements in Different Industries

	Consumer Goods	Services	Industrial Products
Advertising	Med/High	Med	Med
Sales Promotions	High	Med	Med
Personal Selling	Low	High	High
Publicity	Low/Med	Low/Med	Low

Direct Marketing

Direct marketing is among the least expensive (per sale generated) and fastest growing marketing methods today. It includes mail-order catalogues, door-to-door sales, telephone marketing, and even on-line marketing on the Internet. What do all of these efforts have in common? They work to make a sale on the spot, without a middleman between the seller and the buyer. Because these methods are so direct, businesses can better measure their effectiveness, target their audience, personalize their marketing efforts, earn higher response rates, generate repeat sales, and compete with even the largest competitors.

For any direct-mail strategy, businesses must begin with the right list of recipients. These can be bought from brokers or generated in-house. The goal of direct marketing is to make it as easy as possible for customers to buy. Direct marketing efforts should always ask for an order, tell the person what to do next, contain high-quality graphics, and use repeat mailings. Some other tips for creating a powerful direct mailing include:

- Use brightly colored envelopes
- Write your recipient's name in LARGE print
- Do several repeat mailings
- Ask for the order in the headline
- Make your offer very hard to refuse
- Print important information in a second color
- Include an easy-to-use response form
- The best months for direct mail are January, February, and October
- Offer free gifts; emphasize your warranty or no-questions-asked return policy
- Project your response rate and plan for supplies

Red and black are the best direct mail colors!

Mail order catalogues are another story altogether. Beginning a full-scale catalogue operation is best for businesses that have a large enough base of actual or potential customers (in the range of 25,000) to pay for a quality catalogue design, production, and a large mailing. Smaller businesses can create a simpler, shorter catalogue, but the commitment is nearly as large. Printing prices go down the more catalogues you print, so this project is not for the unprepared or uncommitted. Some key information about creating catalogues is below:

- Black and white printing is the least expensive
- 25,000 copies of a 100-item, black and white plus one color catalogue cost (including postage) approximately $20,000, or 80 cents each
- Compile or purchase your mailing lists carefully

- Keep your writing simple and to the point
- In your text, compel your reader to action…to buy
- Include an order form inside
- Make it easy to read, convenient, and full of variety
- First try a smaller test run, then increase volume as you smooth out problems

Public Relations

Public relations are organized efforts businesses undertake to present themselves in a positive way to the broadest public audience: potential customers, government officials, stockholders, lenders, and other businesses.

The goal of public relations is to generate good publicity about a business. **Publicity** is unpaid communication about a business or its product or service in the mass media. Because it is unpaid, publicity is the most credible of promotional sources. Good publicity is a great promotional tool for small businesses.

How does an entrepreneur generate publicity? By preparing press releases for radio, newspapers, magazines, or local television stations. A **press release** is written by a company to announce a new product or news about the company. Join several of your local trade associations, chamber of commerce, community clubs and take or make opportunities to speak in public or write articles for newsletters. Some great ways that entrepreneurs can generate publicity for their businesses are:

Publicity can be the most credible promotional message of all!

- Co-sponsoring local sporting or charity events
- Participating in local fund-raisers by donating prizes or time
- Hiring local students to be interns
- Giving lectures to local trade organizations or chambers of commerce
- Sending your small business story to your local newspaper or trade association

Trade Shows

One of the most targeted and effective ways to promote your offerings to the customers most likely to need them is at trade shows, exhibits, or industry fairs. The people who attend these events aren't just potential customers. They are serious prospects! They have come to do some serious pre-purchase information gathering. For some businesses this is the primary promotional method they use. Consider the following trade show tips:

- Visit shows before you display at one: gather information on your competitors, selling techniques, new products, display tricks, and network, network, network!
- Research and categorize your prospects before you attend: know by name which companies or buyers are your best prospects, drop them a note ahead of time telling them where you'll be (enclose a map or a picture of your booth) and invite them for a sample or gift.
- Create brochures or fliers to circulate.
- Create catchy displays that fit your marketing image: use video, film, slides, music, lights.
- Visit trade show display companies ahead of time to get ideas.
- Attract passersby with merchandise, selling abilities, and your charm.
- Set up your own booth or share a booth with a seller of compatible products.
- Staff your booth with enough people to give quality attention to prospects.
- Staff your booth with friendly, charismatic, and knowledgeable people: these are your "charm patrol."
- Throw a party for hot prospects in your hotel suite.
- Create a trade show budget and track all expenses.
- Follow up with all prospects you met within 10 days, otherwise you're wasting your time.

Everything you do at trade shows should be geared towards generating SALES!

Word of Mouth

Like a nice set of waves that originated half a world away, word of mouth is the happy result of promotional momentum created over time. A positive reputation spread from person to person is also the result of excellent service genuinely and creatively delivered. Creating stellar products that perfectly satisfy your customers' needs will make a lasting impression that they will gladly pass on to others.

Word-of-mouth advertising can grow out of messages that originated in other media like radio, direct mail, or magazines. Distributing brochures to every customer and creating a unique catalogue also reinforces your relationship with customers and increases the likelihood that they will mention you to others. The best way of all to get recommendations? Ask for them!

Networking

Chances are, if you've got the gumption to start your own business, you also have the charisma and ability to interact with a wide variety people. Use it!

By networking and increasing your circle of professional and personal contacts, you are using one of the most time-tested, inexpensive marketing tools. Continually widen your circle of contacts to include possible investors, customers, consultants, bankers, employees, vendors, distributors, and other entrepreneurs. Take every opportunity to speak publicly and when you do, bring lots of business cards and collect lots of business cards. Always follow-up on new contacts with a brief note then a phone call. You can even create a networking schedule for yourself that includes lunch dates (for example, at least 3 times a week), follow-up notes and calls, lectures, charity events, trade shows, and classes and seminars. Set aside some time to work on these things every week.

Newsletters

Small businesses who create newsletters are able to keep up a much coveted "dialogue" with their customers. In order to be effective, newsletters should be published regularly and consistently, contain valuable information and up-to-the-minute news, be easy to read and enjoyable to look at, communicate your marketing image, and focus on solutions for customers' problems. Even businesses on small budgets can hire a professional to help create an inexpensive but well-designed newsletter.

Brochures

Brochures allow businesses to go into greater detail about their business and their products or services than almost any other promotional medium. People expect detailed information in brochures, so be sure to deliver it to them in a compelling way. You should also:

- Include photos of your products or jobs you've completed.
- Use color photos or images if you can: it increases your customers' retention.
- Use the same logo or company headline on the cover as you use elsewhere.
- Include your experience, skills, and training.
- On the back cover include your telephone and fax number, address, hours.
- Create a pocket for the back page where you can tuck additional information and price sheets.
- Consider creating a video brochure, a 2-5 minute video presentation of your business.

Managing Your Promotions

Managing promotional efforts involves setting budgets, creating a promotional calendar, and measuring the effectiveness of each strategy. Because small businesses have less money to spend on promotions, they must make sure that what they do spend is as effective as it can be. Therefore, the more carefully you manage your efforts, the better you will be able to stay within your budget and fine tune your methods as you learn which work best for you.

The purpose of the brochure is to attract and inform

The following are the steps involved in managing the promotional effort:

Set your promotional budget

Creating a promotional budget entails allocating funding to each of the elements of your promotional strategy. Businesses do this in one of two ways. Either they decide on their total budget then divide it among each of their promotional tools or they set the spending levels for each element then total that to arrive at their overall promotional budget.

Before you can do this, however, you need to prioritize each of the elements you intend to use. This way you can allocate funding first to the most important and distribute the rest among the less important elements. Perhaps the best way for the new business owner to approach budgeting is somewhere in between. Try sitting down and creating your promotional "wish list" of what you would like to achieve with each element, and what each item will cost. Tally up the total. This will give you your "ideal" high-end promotional budget. Obviously, you will not have the resources to realize your wish list, that is why it's called a wish list! But it does give you a starting point.

Next, using the total amount of money you have available to introduce your product, estimate how much you can afford to allocate to your promotional efforts. Don't despair. Businesses promote themselves every day for free, and you can too. Chances are you can make your promotional dollars go a lot further than you think you can.

Your promotional efforts require careful management to reach the right people with the right message at the right price

Create your promotional calendar

By creating a time-line for the use of your different promotional tools you can better plan your budget, focus your efforts, and prevent "gaps" in your promotional efforts. The promotional calendar usually outlines which promotions and events are planned for different weeks of the year and the total budget for each event. It tells how long each will last and what its main message and purpose will be.

The Boot Doctor: Marketing Schedule & Budget

Marketing Tactic	Monthly Cost	Time Frame	Comments
Networking	$40	6 months	Attend trade shows, rodeos, community events
Classified Ads	$50	3 months	2 newspapers, once a week; evaluate after 3 months
Fliers	$70	3 months	Designed and printed by sister, distributed by self and teenaged neighbor

A well-defined promotional calendar keeps you on track

Measure the Effectiveness of Your Methods

Your promotional budget is not worth the paper it is written on if you don't stick to it and measure the effectiveness of your methods after the fact. Why? Because entrepreneurs must focus their limited time and money where they will be the most effective. And the only way to know what worked and what didn't is to measure. One sure way to get information is to ask customers when and where they heard of you.

You can also count coupons, measure the number of participants in contests or sweepstakes, and measure sales levels during short-term promotions.

Free/Low Cost Promotion Methods

Barter allows you to trade your products or services for ad space. Even if your local newspaper doesn't need your product, they might need something. Trade with the person who has what they need and you've got yourself some ad space for less than you'd pay ordinarily. Why? Because you're "paying" for space with your product valued at its full retail price (which includes your profit margin). Keep in mind that radio and television advertising space is always negotiable. There's even a magazine called *Barter News* dedicated to informing people about barter.

Businesses that use **cooperative advertising** receive cash fees from larger companies for mentioning their brand names in their promotional efforts. An example of this would be the painting contractor who includes the name Dutch Boy or Sherwin Williams in their brochure.

Personal letters are a great way to introduce yourself to carefully researched prospects. You can create completely customized letters that include specific information about your prospect's need for your product or service. A personal letter can build a relationship with a new customer and shows what you can do for them and tells them you will be following up. Do so with another letter and a telephone call or visit.

Fliers that you create and distribute in your area can be a very economical way to spread the word about your new business. People who see the flier may not act on it immediately, but if properly designed, it will catch their eye and raise their awareness. This is the first step of turning them into a customer. The goal of a flier is to sell. Use your unique style or humor to present the facts and inform your customer why they should buy your product. Choose your basic idea, combine it with a fitting picture or image, then explain more fully what you are offering.

Promotional Tricks Worthy of the Entrepreneur

You must select the most cost- and time-effective ways to promote your products or services, and as you do, look for short cuts. Don't forget to choose methods that are consistent with your positioning strategy. Be careful to choose tools that communicate the same message as the rest of your marketing mix.

Consider the following promotional tips for entrepreneurs:

- Create advertising specialties: imprinted pens, t-shirts, bumper stickers
- Really use your business cards: use the front and back to give information on your business and products
- Make wacky colored or unusually shaped business cards
- Send humorous promotional postcards
- Offer samples, seminars, demonstrations
- Think community involvement: help organize 10k runs, fund-raising activities, network and get your business's logo and name out there
- Sponsor off-beat, memorable events
- Attend trade association functions, chair committees, speak at community events
- Offer gift certificates

A rule of small business promotions: "Rely on brain power, not dollar power!"

- Use trial sizes to encourage sampling
- Contact past customers: invite them in when you have new products
- Have a "leads" breakfast: sponsor a breakfast with local entrepreneurs who aren't direct competitors and get a high-profile local speaker
- Fax: choose your targets carefully, and deliver speedy service, product updates, and promotional info to customers via fax
- On-line computer bulletin boards spread the word to exactly whom you want, when you want
- Toll-free telephone numbers are becoming less expensive; use one to increase your response rate
- Catalogues, newsletters, and brochures are easy to produce using desktop publishing software
- Look for cut-rate advertising in regional editions of national magazines; look for newspapers' "zone" editions that offer cut-rate prices and give you top-rate exposure
- Home shopping networks spread your product's virtues far and wide with little direct cost
- Use telephone hold time to air snappy easy-to-listen-to prerecorded marketing messages

Summary of Start-up Promotions

For entrepreneurs, textbook promotional techniques are just the jumping off point to more unconventional, lower cost techniques. The only things that should constrain your creativity are your own preset budget and time. Even the best promotional strategies won't sell a business that offers poor quality, bad service, or worse yet, unneeded products. Start with a good understanding of your customer, the highest quality product, and let your own passion for your business fuel a truly inspired promotional campaign.

Placing Your Product or Service: Distribution Strategies

If you can't get your product where your customers are, when they want it, even the best product at the best price, won't sell. If this doesn't catch your attention, think of it this way: distribution represents between 15% and 50% of the final price of a product. If you choose the wrong distribution channels, you risk placing and pricing yourself right out of your market.

All businesses rely on some form of distribution network to sell and deliver their products or services to their customers. They might do this entirely themselves, they might work with intermediaries, or they might use some combination of the two. This is the final element of the marketing mix, the fourth "P" which refers to the placement or the distribution of the product.

Distribution describes all activities that are involved in moving goods from producer to customer. In the broadest sense, a business's physical distribution system is composed of taking orders, packaging, inventory management, storage, transportation, and follow-up service. The goals of a distribution system are to be on time, dependable, accurate, safe, and able to satisfy customer needs.

Distribution strategy is about choosing the most cost-effective method to deliver the product to your customer. The strategy must fit with the rest of the marketing mix (the product, price, and promotion). Imagine a premium jeweler trying to sell their goods at Target. Or a manufacturer of bargain clothing trying to sell their goods through industrial selling agents. Or a gasoline company selling door to door. Each of these businesses will not only miss selling opportunities, but will spend uselessly in the process.

Businesses that use too many intermediaries and have too many people taking mark-ups, end up setting their final selling price above what their customers are willing to pay.

Service businesses also must distribute their offerings. Where will your clients come to get their taxes prepared? Will they contract with you directly? Will you set up an office? Will you use fax, e-mail, and the telephone to deliver services?

The type of product or service and how it is positioned and priced all determine how it is distributed.

Distribution and Small Businesses

Few businesses have the time, money, or expertise to deliver their products themselves directly to their customers. This is certainly true for start-up businesses. Small businesses should let other businesses do what they can't do, and focus limited resources on what they can do well. For small businesses one of the toughest things to do is get noticed by customers. By hiring professional distributors, or **outsourcing** certain distribution tasks, they can more easily enter new markets. They may even outsource others to package, store, and deliver their goods, while they focus on other things like customer service, product design, or promotion.

Another major challenge for small businesses is gaining entrance into traditional distribution channels. A good example of this is the prohibitively high "slotting fees" that many grocery chains charge to producers in order to put their products on the shelf. Luckily, there are more ways for small businesses to bypass these obstacles and distribute their products more quickly than ever. Door-to-door, home shopping networks, classified ads, mail order, the Internet, and fax-on-demand are some examples.

In the distribution game, if you miss the mark, you miss your market

This section will introduce you to the basics of distribution strategy and highlight some of the most effective ways for entrepreneurs to distribute products and services.

Distribution Basics

Businesses in every industry rely on distribution partners. **Intermediaries** help businesses move their products through the **distribution channel**, the avenue by which the product travels from manufacturer to final customer. This channel is composed of a group of independent businesses including manufacturers, wholesalers, and retailers who deliver products to final customers.

Channel partners are all of the businesses who act as intermediaries to help buy and sell, assemble, store, display, and promote products. These are called "partners" because they act together to serve the customer. Ideally they cooperate and coordinate their efforts to maximize their effectiveness and reach pre-set goals. These partners are specialists at getting the right product at the time at the right price to the right place.

Types of Channel Intermediaries

There are several types of intermediaries that businesses work with to distribute their products:

- **Retailers** do not produce anything but are specialists at selling directly to final customers. They buy their products from manufacturers, distributors, and wholesalers, then **markup** the price to cover their costs and make a profit.

- **Wholesalers** buy and sell bulk merchandise to other wholesalers or retailers. Wholesalers never sell directly to the public. Their expertise might lie in repackaging, storing, and reselling particular categories of goods. An example of this would be the wholesaler who represents all types of dried fruits and nuts, buys them in bulk and repackages them into smaller bags to resell to Safeway, Albertson's, and other grocery chains.

- **Distributors** buy merchandise from manufacturers and resell it to wholesalers, retailers, or sometimes directly to the final customer. A good example of a distributor is a Northern California coffee company, Peets Coffees. They buy coffee beans direct from growers and roast the beans themselves. Peets then sells to wholesalers who repackage and re-label the coffee to sell to other retailers. Peets also packages their beans themselves and sells them directly to customers in their own coffee shops.

- **Agents** charge a commission to facilitate sales between manufacturers and their final customers. Agents do not take title to the products they deal with; they simply represent businesses and their products. **Manufacturers' agents** sell a business's product in a specific geographic region, usually on an exclusive basis. **Sales agents** are different in that they often have more control over setting prices and terms of sale. It is not uncommon for them to take over all or part of the marketing effort for a product, including promotion and distribution strategy.

- **Brokers** unite buyers with sellers, and have only short-term relationships with each. Like agents, they do not take title of the products they broker.

Basic channels of distribution

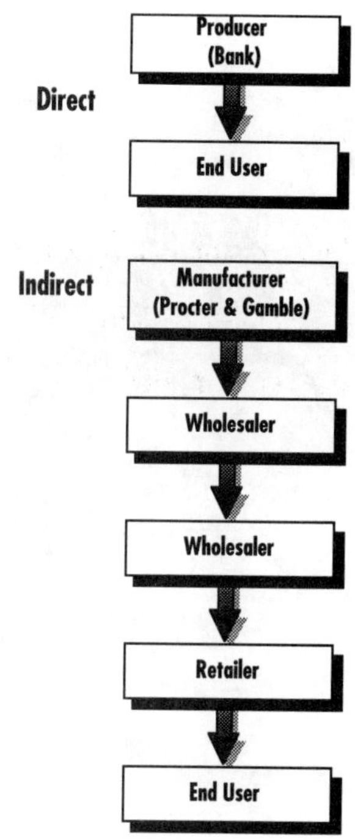

Selecting Your Distribution Strategy

Like setting any strategy for your business, a distribution strategy requires that you know your objectives, time and budgetary constraints, and the strengths and weaknesses of each of your alternatives. Distribution objectives might include achieving targeted service goals, increasing speed to market, safety and reliability, or reducing costs. Do your customers value speedy delivery? Is your product such that it requires technical support before a customer can use it? For cost or service reasons, do you need to retain complete control over the handling and delivery of your product?

Most industries have well-established distribution practices that include knowledgeable and capable intermediaries. However, your task is to identify which distribution option is best for your product, set your own strategy, and measure your own results. In some cases, traditional distribution channels might be inaccessible or not cost effective for your products. In this case, you will have to exploit other more "entrepreneurial" methods to distribute your products or services.

The Macatawa Pickle Company

Mort Fabrikant started making his spicy sweet pickles at his summer cottage in western Michigan in 1975. With the help of his daughters he made them every season and gave them to friends for Christmas, birthdays, and house-warming gifts. In July 1995, after eating a pickle with her burger, his daughter Katrina said, "This is the best pickle I've ever had. Dad, it's time to go into business!" Mort had to agree. In his 20 years of casual summer pickle making, he had sure come up with one winning pickle recipe. All his friends and neighbors agreed! Hence the idea for the Macatawa Pickle Company was born.

But how was he to sell his pickles without giving up his day job?

With a few phone calls and several trips to the library, Mort had the production problem licked. He learned about a small food-processing company that would prepare, package, and label his pickles. The real problem would be distribution!

He called all the major grocery chains in western Michigan and the Chicago area and kept getting the same story: No room for more pickles, no space for The Macatawa Pickle Company. Mort would have to come up with a plan of his own if he wanted to share his pickles with the world. So, he began to think.

Mort Fabrikant knew he had a great product but needed the chance to test how well it would sell to the public. Because grocery stores wouldn't stock his pickles, he was locked out of traditional distribution channels. Then one day, while thumbing through one of his favorite catalogues, The J. Peterman Clothing Company, he had a flash of inspiration. He would begin as J. Peterman did. He would bypass grocery stores altogether and sell pickles with a small classified ad in a magazine. He decided on Gourmet *magazine. If orders came in, he could package them and send them himself with very little overhead. If they didn't, well, then he knew that he'd have to look for another distribution strategy. After several days, he finally settled on this classified ad:*

> *The World's Best Pickle Discovered in Macatawa, Michigan!*
>
> *After 20 years the secret is out. From the fertile green gardens and sunny lake shore of Macatawa, Michigan, comes the ultimate gourmet snack and condiment: The Macatawa Pickle. Pickled and jarred once a year in the sunshine of July, but enjoyed all year long. For your first jar and recipe, call 1-800-Macataw, and ask for Mort.*

Below are some general guidelines for deciding if your business needs distributors. Chances are you will want to use distributors if:

- Customers are scattered geographically and often require speedy, small quantity deliveries
- Products require little or no technical selling
- Basic repackaging or customization of products is required to fit local customer needs
- Distributors are traditionally used in your industry

Businesses' distribution strategies vary according to whether they produce consumer goods, industrial goods, or services. The next section reviews the basics of distributing in each industry.

Distributing Consumer Goods

Consumer goods are those products that are produced and sold to the final consumer. These products include everything we buy in the supermarket as well as bicycles, running shoes, and over-the-counter allergy pills. Below are several of the methods that are used to distribute goods in consumer-product industries.

- **Direct marketing**: Some businesses avoid intermediaries altogether by directly marketing their products to their customers. They may use door-to-door sales, their own retail stores, and telephone or catalogue orders. By selling directly to the end customers, your business is able to completely control how your products are sold and serviced. You can remain on top of changes in your market and quickly respond to customer needs. Directly selling to consumers can also be faster and lower in cost (in the case of telephone and catalogue sales) than any other distribution method.

For start-up businesses, one of the most important elements of direct selling is keeping a data base of past, present, and potential customers.

- **Manufacturer to retailer**: Most producers of consumer products rely on intermediaries to sell their products. In the case of large manufacturers selling to large retailers like KMart, Macy's, or Sears, businesses may bypass wholesalers entirely and sell directly to retailers who in turn sell to consumers. Businesses choose this strategy because retailers might be able to provide storage and logistical support more cheaply and effectively than wholesalers. On the other side, this gives the retailers more control over the terms of their transaction with the manufacturer.

Other businesses choose to distribute their goods to retailers via wholesalers or other intermediaries. This strategy is used by larger manufacturers who are selling to many small retailers. Wholesalers can be particularly helpful to businesses introducing new products. They can use their leverage and expertise in the industry to push the product into retailer outlets. Businesses can also use agents and brokers to sell to wholesalers or to retailers. These intermediaries operate on commission only and can be a handy replacement for a small business's in-house sales team. They can present a line of products professionally, coordinate in-store promotions, and share their in-depth knowledge of markets and customers.

Distributing Industrial Goods

Industrial goods are products that are manufactured and sold as inputs to other businesses who make them into finished products.

Direct marketing to other businesses: This type of distribution is much more common in industrial markets than in consumer markets. Many industrial manufacturers have only a few, very large customers who can cost effectively be sold to directly. Many industrial products are higher cost and more complex than consumer products. They also figure prominently in the production of other products, must meet certain quality standards, and be delivered on time. In short, buyers and sellers in industrial markets are tied together closely in a partnership. In-house sales forces, telemarketing, and catalogues are the major ways that industrial manufacturers market directly to their customers.

Manufacturer to intermediary: For industrial products, wholesalers and agents can provide a more cost-effective way for selling many small products to smaller customers. Intermediaries can also be very helpful for getting a new product established among industrial customers. They can also provide technical and promotional support, depending on the terms of their contract.

How to Evaluate Your Intermediaries

Once you've decided that you do need to use intermediaries and have decided on which types to use, your next task is to evaluate them. You should consider their:

- Selling ability
- Record for paying bills on time
- Promptness and accuracy in handling orders
- Cooperativeness and compatibility with your business's operating style
- Willingness and ability to offer marketing feedback
- Dun & Bradstreet credit rating

Managing Your Intermediaries

Begin with a clear, simple contract that covers the following:

- Sales staff and quotas
- Pricing policy - flexibility in offering discounts, etc.
- Minimum reorder and inventory quantities
- Geographical territory to be covered
- Handling of house accounts
- Training and technical support for the distributor
- Terms of payment
- Management of service and repairs
- Return policy
- Reports and feedback from distributors on sales and market conditions

The Benefits of Sales Representatives

A high-quality, professional representative can be the best friend a small business has. They are easy on a business's cash flow since they add no fixed costs to the business. They are usually paid on commission or when they make a sale. Or they pay outright for products in advance. They are specialists in the product category and geographic region in which they operate. Chances are they know the industry and prospective customers far better than you do. Outside reps may have special technical knowledge of products and be able to more effectively offer technical support or service than you can. They can also help shoulder the responsibility of promotions and advertising.

The Downside of Sales Representatives

It all sounds so perfect, but there must be some downside to using sales reps. And there is! Your product might be just one of many product lines that the rep carries, and lacking the right incentives, you might get lost in the shuffle. Some representatives may require a great deal of support to sell effectively. Lastly, sales representatives can be difficult to train, monitor, and motivate, and may require a concerted effort to get your money's worth.

Finding and Recruiting Excellent Reps

The first step in building a first-rate sales team is finding the right people to staff it. Trade journals, directories, and magazines can provide information about who the major representatives are, what lines they carry, and what types of customers they serve. There are also national and local representative and dealer associations and lists of representatives maintained by local and state chambers of commerce. You can also inquire with businesses that deal in similar products as yours, and ask if they can recommend a good representative for a given territory.

Things to Consider When Selecting Sales Representatives

- Evaluate their selling technique, contact base, and technical know-how
- Gauge their personality to see if it's compatible with your business
- Review their track record
- Take them on a sales call and watch them in action
- Clearly define your sales expectations
- Get reliable references and follow up
- Put them on a 3-month trial basis to assess the "fit," then reassess the contract

Careful selection of intermediaries can make your business more profitable

Managing a Sales Representative Team

Managing representatives effectively is like managing any other group of people. It can be painless and pleasurable or it can be time consuming and hard work. The best way to ensure that it is the former is to look at the task as a manager would. Anticipate problems you may have and try to create safeguards against them. Create contingencies for when and (God forbid) if they do happen.

How does a manager approach managing representatives? By doing the following:

What You Should Do for Your Sales Reps

- Contact your representatives at least once a week. Check on their progress, resolve questions, or just chat to keep each other "in the loop."
- Give each representative a good sales manual. It doesn't need to be anything expensive or snazzy. It should, however, be a collection of the best "sales ammunition" you can think of. It should contain the basics such as product specifications, current prices, competitive comparisons, and good product photos. You may also want to include selling angles with arguments and counter-arguments, excellent satisfied customer references, and reprints of articles, endorsements, and samples.
- Create an informal representative newsletter. The point? To keep them up to date, attentive, and motivated. In it you can announce winners of sales contests, new product developments, commonly asked technical questions, and territory sales volumes. Get their attention and hold it!
- Give regular and immediate support to representatives. If they have questions or problems, do not delay in giving them immediate, personal attention. Be prepared to attend initial and major sales calls.
- Maintain your own record of sales leads. Do this so you have an on-going understanding of who your prospects are and can evaluate how they are being sold.
- Always pay your commissions on time. Be reliable, accurate, and speedy!
- Give your sales representatives lots of quality sales leads. The more qualified prospects the sales representatives have, the more product they can sell.
- Follow through with product promises. If you promise on-time delivery and top quality, deliver. Give your sales reps the goods to back up their efforts. If they truly believe in the product and know it lives up to its promises, they will sell more confidently.

What Your Sales Representatives Should Do for You

- Give weekly updates on prospects and sales efforts
- Prepare regular expense reports and receipts
- Call for product or technical expertise when needed
- Stay current on industry and market trends
- Communicate any customer problems or complaints
- Offer regular feedback on the sales territory
- Be honest and positively represent the business

Licensing

Licensing is an arrangement whereby businesses sell to other businesses the rights to produce or market their brand name or product. This allows manufacturers to reap the benefits of their product's established reputation and brand without the risk of investing in new products. It effectively transfers the responsibility of marketing and production to the licensee.

Joe Boxer Goes Home

The goofy and prank-prone Joe Boxer Company of San Francisco made its name by making, you guessed it, boxer shorts. From the mid-1980's onward, Joe Boxer sold boxer shorts and pajamas sewn out of truly unique fabric prints: chile peppers, glow-in-the-dark light bulbs, fish, food, and fruit. They grew and grew and began distributing their shorts in Joe Boxer theme mini-stores nestled in the men's departments of department stores.

Then they got the idea: why not take our fabric out of people's drawers (ha ha!) and into their beds? But Joe Boxer knew that their strength was designing silly fabrics, not manufacturing and distributing linens for beds. So they contacted one of the biggest names in the bedding game, Martex. Over 2 months they sold the idea and negotiated a licensing agreement. Martex would buy the rights to use the Joe Boxer name on sheets of Joe Boxer designs that it manufactured. Martex would also use its existing distribution network to place the sheets in department stores across the U.S. Joe Boxer really learned the lesson of good licensing: focus on what you do best and expand product offerings and increase revenues without increasing costs or exposure to risk.

Placement Strategies for Entrepreneurs

Now for the good news: aside from all the traditional distribution methods, entrepreneurs have another entire collection of distribution tools available to them. These require a little more creativity and energy to use, but the rewards will speak for themselves. Unconventional distribution methods can be among the most effective and least expensive for small businesses. Consider those below as a starting point for your own ideas. Your only goal is not to let yourself be constrained by precedent and to find the most cost-effective and unique way to deliver value to your target customer. Many small businesses have successfully differentiated themselves by choosing unique distribution channels.

- Consignment selling
- Mail-order catalogues
- Classified ads
- Fax-an-order
- Telephone orders/voice-mail orders
- Overnight delivery
- Home shopping networks
- The Internet
- "Bundle" your products with other related products and "piggy back" on their distribution

Distribution Conclusion

Distribution strategy impacts how products are perceived by customers, the level of service that is delivered, and the selling price of the product. Creating a distribution strategy that fits with your overall product positioning and the rest of the marketing mix will bring you one step closer to realizing the success of your business.

H_2O Repairs of Glendale, Arizona

For farmers in Arizona, the only thing better than an efficient irrigation system is a skilled person to ensure it runs reliably and smoothly. Without a reliable source of water, it doesn't take long for crops to wither in the hot Arizona sun.

James Rodriguez is their man. He began H_2O Repairs after working for a larger irrigation management company in Glendale, Arizona, for 10 years. He had worked with nearly every type of irrigation system used. He knew all of the major customers in his western area of Arizona. With his lean business (just he and 2 partners also from another company) James was able to offer faster service and lower prices. Furthermore, his was a very specialized business: his only service was repairing and rebuilding of the actual pump that feeds water into the rest of the irrigation equipment.

The first year marketing objectives for H_2O Repairs were to repair or upgrade on average 10 irrigation systems a month, or have at least 500 billable hours a month between James and his two partners. The marketing strategy for the company was to focus on small and medium-sized farms. James wanted to position H_2O Repairs to be the lower cost, most reliable, and "local" source of irrigation pump expertise.

The paired down marketing plan for H_2O contained the following marketing mix strategies and tactics:

H_2O—The 4 P's

Marketing Mix Element	Strategy	Tactics
Product	Specialize in offering the most reliable and expert repair of pumps for farm irrigation systems	Set free estimates; guarantee all work on pumps for 30 days or free repair
Price	Offer lower prices and more flexible payment to customers	Charge $25.00/hour plus parts, undercutting largest competitor by 15%
Promotion	Raise awareness of H_2O Repairs' specialized expertise, lower priced yet speedy and reliable service	List business in the Yellow Pages in three places: under Farm Equipment, Irrigation Systems, and Repair Services; create an H_2O Repairs' brochure to fax to 300 potential customers, include a "bio" page on James Rodriquez and his partners with details of past projects and testimonials by loyal customers
Placement	Deliver services directly and quickly, taking no more than two hours to respond to emergency repairs	Locate office and equipment in southwestern Glendale, Arizona, within 40 miles of the target cutomers; utilize three trucks (privately owned by each member of H_2O Repairs) fully equipped to repair or upgrade five major types of irrigation pumps

James Rodriguez created this list of his marketing strategies and tactics within the first 2 months of beginning H_2O Repairs. He used it to make sure that the elements of his marketing mix worked in unison to achieve his marketing objectives. Within his first year he reviewed these strategies and tactics 4 times. Was his pricing on target? Was his promotional brochure the right medium and with the right message? Was his location correct to best serve his customers?

H_2O Repairs used its marketing plan as a working document. As his base of customers grew, James expanded the plan to include details of projected sales, revenues, and expenses. He knew there might soon come a time when he would need outside financing for additional equipment. He also knew that before long he would need to expand his team of service experts. For H_2O Repairs, the marketing plan was truly a launching pad for growth and success.

Conclusion

Product. Price. Promotion. Placement. Recognize what many start-ups don't: by using these four elements, you have the power to design your business's success. From start-up to growth and expansion, businesses create strategies for these elements that work in unison to achieve market objectives. When start-ups take the time and energy to create just the right mix of strategies and tactics, they save time and money. They serve the right target customers. They succeed in positioning their product in exactly the right place at the right time. They differentiate themselves from competitors. What more can a business ask for?

The lesson of this chapter is this: take the time to understand and utilize the power of the marketing mix. Your efforts will separate you from your competitors and put you one step closer to achieving business success.

Chapter 39
THE ART OF SELLING

About This Chapter:
- *The history of selling*
- *Solving your customers' problems*
- *Six steps to success*
- *Closing the sale and asking for business*

Introduction

Sales is considered by many to be the heart of a business. Why? Because a product or service must get into the hands of a customer before a profit can be made. Every entrepreneur is a salesperson. Whether selling a product or service or selling themselves to obtain financing, entrepreneurs need effective sales skills.

The thought of selling can be overwhelming to some. But in truth, selling is really only about building a one-on-one relationship and solving problems. You have the opportunity to develop your own style and techniques that will distinguish you from your competitors. Your approach should fit your personality, highlight your expertise, and be as comfortable to you as a well-worn glove. As a start-up business owner, you must also develop a structure within the business to manage sales and effectively maintain customer satisfaction.

This chapter presents some of the most effective selling strategies and tactics for entrepreneurs. Our goal is to lift the veil of mystery that surrounds truly successful selling, and put start-up business owners on the right track for selling themselves and their products or services. The lesson of this chapter is that, regardless of your background, you can learn to be a confident and effective salesperson.

To become successful, you will need to develop and hone your own selling style

The Evolution of Sales Techniques

During the twentieth century sales techniques have changed a great deal. Perceptions of salespeople have shifted dramatically from a sneaky huckster to a trusted consultant and problem-solver. In the 1930's and '40's hard-sell methods were employed by the order taker using a hard-close technique. This changed during the war years when demand for goods was greater than supply and salesmanship was not valued by companies. Enter the '60's and '70's—relationship selling was the preferred and accepted method of selling. Many sales were made over long, expensive martini lunches. The reason many people think of sales disdainfully is because of these images:

back-slapping, glad-handing, and the hard sell. To many people, sales was considered a last resort profession for shifty people who used deceit and manipulation to make the sale. Many sales techniques ("tricks of the trade") were used to get the order even if the customer didn't want or need the product. The description of a good salesperson was one who could "sell ice cubes to an Eskimo."

Fortunately, selling has changed dramatically in the 1980s and 1990s. Today, salespeople focus their efforts on listening, understanding customers' needs, and providing solutions. They have become technical experts in their fields and can easily understand how to adapt their product to their customers' needs.

Salespeople emphasize quality products and superior customer service. A **value added** approach involves providing a service or an association with a customer that is valued as much or more than the product itself. There is superior value in a quality product guaranteed to perform and backed up by quick customer service.

Selling today is 100% customer driven

Enlightened salespeople understand that long-term success means keeping customers satisfied after the sale. Satisfied customers who place repeat orders are critical to long-term success. Smart businesses know that it costs more to get a new customer or to get an old customer back after you have lost them than it does to sell more to an existing customer. To keep customers happy you must talk with them to understand their needs. What would help them do their job better? What will solve their problems? Finding these answers requires developing and practicing excellent listening skills. Listen to your customers to become their trusted problem-solver and expert consultant.

Professional Sales People

There are many rewards derived from selling. Being a salesperson offers fun, excitement, financial rewards, and fulfilling, long-term relationships. Many people want to be involved in sales and most people can be taught to sell. The primary characteristics that businesses look for in people as they build their sales organization are:

- High energy
- Self-motivation
- Ability to understand the big picture

- Persistence and perseverance
- Technical knowledge
- Good communication skills
- Good listening skills
- Ability to use product knowledge to solve customer needs

Selling and Channels of Distribution

No matter how good a product or service, unless a business has an effective distribution network, it will not generate sales and profits. Therefore, it is necessary to understand the relationship between sales and channels of distribution.

Retail and service companies sell directly to end-users more often than manufacturing companies. However, the choice of which distribution methods you utilize will depend upon how your target market traditionally has purchased similar products or services. Do customers buy direct or from distributors? Sales agents? Retailers? Do they buy in bulk? Do customers require technical support? After-sales service? It is incumbent upon you to analyze buying behavior and business practices in your industry. This will aid you in a selection process to determine the best channels for you:

- In-house sales team
- Wholesalers or distributors
- Agents or brokers
- Retailers

The chapter entitled "The Marketing Mix: The 4 P's" presents a more detailed discussion of distribution and sales management.

Copiers West is Born

Robert Chavez turned fifty-five years old last February and decided on that very day to make some changes in his life. Robert worked in the service department of a large Japanese office equipment manufacturer for the past twelve years. Based in Tempe, Arizona, Robert was responsible for all the follow-up service activities in the Phoenix area. He knew that the biggest customer complaint involved service response time, equipment reliability, and price. Robert and his office manager, Anna Gambera, felt they could "do it better" than their employer could.

Their plan: to become the independent sales representative for a competitor and sell and manage their own service contracts. At several office equipment trade shows Anna and Robert had been impressed with the people they met from one large American copier manufacturer. They knew the product was high quality, and that the company was aggressively expanding into the Western states. To solidify Robert's skills, he enrolled in a 5-week copier repair course. Anna drew up a proposal to the company and locked up the territory and the service contract for customers. They inaugurated their new business: "Copiers West."

Optimizing Sales Opportunities: Six Steps to Sales Success

Whether you plan to perform selling functions yourself or work through an intermediary, it is necessary to understand the principles of good selling and the steps necessary to make successful sales calls. This information can be applied to your own personal selling and also give you guidelines to determine the capability of the sales organization through which you choose to sell your products.

Step 1: Prospecting and Prioritizing Accounts

Before you make your first sales call or begin building your sales organization… STOP! Get organized. Prior to proceeding you should determine:

Prospecting is an everyday job

- Your target customer profile: size, location, needs, problems, goals
- What unique value your product or service has for target customers
- How your offerings are better than those of competitors
- What resources do you have to encourage consumers to buy your product

Try brainstorming all the possibilities with close associates familiar with you and your business. Think about sales possibilities locally, in the U.S., in the world. Go ahead, think small and think big. This is a "blue sky" session where everything and anything is a possibility. Have some fun! Then step back and sort out your list of potential sales prospects. Sort your lists into the following categories:

- **Short-term/Long-term Prospects:** The short-term list includes prospects that can be developed and sold to immediately. Long-term prospects are larger organizations that require more time to build relationships with. Salespeople often create a time-line for these prospects that outlines each step of the selling process. This helps to keep the selling process on track.

- **Most Profitable/Least Profitable:** Analyze the potential profitability of all the accounts listed. You may be able to see a pattern emerge that will point you in the direction of the most profitable accounts. Or, you may find that the larger accounts provide less profit per unit of sale, but overall provide more total dollar profit. The small accounts could provide more unit profit but require greater effort and time.
- **Prestige Accounts:** You may determine there are some high-profile accounts that would provide great exposure for your business. However, everyone else wants these accounts because of their prestigious nature. You may decide to make less profit on some of these accounts or even make them a loss leader just to get your name associated with them.

After developing these lists of accounts, begin to develop your sales targeting strategy. It may be helpful to develop a matrix. Which accounts should be targets first? Which are critical to your overall success that you must have? Which are the bread and butter accounts?

The Value of Networking

Networking often has a negative connotation because we all have been the target of someone's networking scheme. However, **networking** is critical to a business owner's success. There are positive, non-intrusive ways to network. A well-thought-out plan should involve quick, concise conversation and can be mutually beneficial. Networking has become accepted as a way of life today because everyone knows the value of good contacts. Most people can identify with job changes, starting a new position, new company, or making that first sale. The key is to network in a positive, professional, and genuine manner.

You should consider joining organizations or clubs that are in your field. This is an excellent way to meet new people and potential prospects. If you are a sole proprietor, these organizations allow you to be with other like-minded people and give you an opportunity to keep up with new developments in your field.

The Value of the Computer

Computerizing sales information saves money and streamlines selling activities. Start-up businesses can better prepare for selling by developing their own prospecting and account information on computer software. In

Prepare and be on target

computerized sales files, businesses keep records of sales targets that can be updated as priorities change. Keeping good account information also makes your efforts more professional and organized.

There are many inexpensive software packages available today that are specifically designed for small businesses. These are designed to be user-friendly for people who may not have a great deal of computer experience. Software can be utilized to help manage multiple business functions such as purchasing, accounting, payroll, and financial planning. If you have limited knowledge of computers, there are many training seminars, books, and computer consultants who can help you.

Copiers West Sells and Sells

By June, Robert Chavez and his partner Anna Gambera were in business. The aggressive battle for customers was in full swing. Most businesses in the Phoenix area already had copiers and service contracts with larger competitors. Robert and Anna knew that if they could get in their customers' offices, they could get their customers to switch copier providers to Copiers West. They could provide high-quality copiers and better, lower cost service than any of their competitors. The key was getting in the door.

The success of Copiers West depended on how well it knew its customers' needs. It also depended on Robert and Anna's expertise in their product and its unique benefits versus the competition. They began by targeting small and medium-sized businesses in the Phoenix area with less than 100 employees. Then they began cold calling in person.

Step 2: Planning and Preparing for Sales Calls

Successful sales calls begin with well-thought-out and researched **selling plans** before you ever approach a target customer. Consumers and buyers are too well educated and savvy to fall for slick sales techniques. Whether it is a simple sale, a call on one person who is capable of making the buying decision, or a complex sale where multiple buying influencers take part in the decision, proper sales call planning helps ensure success. In fact, planning the call is the biggest part of the selling process. Face-to-face selling time is actually very short. Proper planning allows salespeople to maximize time with buyers by asking the right questions and presenting valuable, relevant information. It allows them to sell their products by solving problems.

Analyzing Buyers

Before you can sell, it is important to have an understanding of the way different people participate in the buying process. A few examples are listed below:

- **Decision maker:** This buyer will be able to say "yes" or "no" to your proposal. In a simple sale, the buyer is generally the decision maker. In a complex sale, the decision maker is not always readily available or identifiable. The decision maker is often swayed by several other buying influencers.
- **Gate-keeper:** Gate-keepers don't make the final decision even though they may want you to believe they do. Their purpose is to screen potential suppliers and gather information. This role is often played by purchasing agents and attorneys.
- **Guide:** This buying influencer wants your product or service and will guide you through the sale. This buyer will not be the decision maker, but will be a strong coach or ally. He or she can be an inside "mole" who can provide information about the buying process. If there isn't a guide immediately available, develop one!
- **User:** These people actually use the product or service you are selling. They do not make the final purchase decision but they do have strong influence over purchase decisions. They often have the most knowledge of the product and substitute offerings.

Sales strategies are critical to your success

Understanding these buyer roles helps you to develop a strong sales strategy. Each of these buying influences are interconnected. You may have a great relationship with the decision maker, but the user will kill the sale if she or he doesn't like the way your product performs. You may not be able to get through the gate-keeper to the decision maker initially. However, with consistent promotional efforts you can target the user who has the power to activate the whole purchasing process.

Talk about the features; sell the benefit

Buyer Orientation
People make purchase decisions in many different ways. However, there are some general "types" that salespeople can be prepared for:

- **Security:** This buyer has a desire to keep things steady and does not want any risky propositions—a "don't rock the boat" kind of person.
- **Power:** Demonstrated authority and capability are important for these buyers. They may not be fun to call on, but they do make decisions and get things done. These are "Attila the Hun" types.
- **Relationship:** This buyer has strong affiliations to people and tends to be open and friendly. This is great if he can make a decision, but not so great if he wastes your time. This buyer is warm and cuddly, just like a "teddy bear."
- **Enlightened:** These buyers will make good informed decisions. They tend to gather facts, weigh strengths and weaknesses, and make decisions they feel will make their business grow. These are the "professor" types.

It is important to identify the buyer's orientation because your selling strategy will change depending upon the buyer's characteristics. If you are calling on a security buyer, you will want to minimize his exposure to risk and make him feel comfortable. Power buyers will want answers, now. They will want to be recognized for their position and influence. The relationship buyer will expect you to socialize a bit prior to getting down to business. Being well informed and knowledgeable about your product will serve you well when calling on an enlightened buyer.

Determining purchasing roles and orientation helps salespeople to understand buyers' mind set. What would make your customers' job or task easier? What would save their time? Why would they buy? Why won't they buy? Selling products from the customers' point of view always produces a more successful sales call.

Step 3: First Contact
The objective of the first contact with potential customers is twofold:

1. To make a positive first impression and peak their interest
2. To ask questions, listen, and glean information to help you to satisfy their needs and make a sale.

In order to get the most valuable information during the first encounter, salespeople should prepare open-ended, targeted questions. The effective planning and presentation of questions is directly related to the quality of information you receive. Here are some suggestions:

- **New Information:** Use new information questions to find out about customers' business issues, discrepancies between their current and desired state, and to uncover missing information. "Describe to me, show me, explain to me..."
- **Feelings and Attitudes:** Try to uncover desires and better understand values. Asking feeling questions will help you discover any hot buttons or intense feelings about things related to your product or service. "What is your opinion, reaction… How do your feel about...?"
- **Confirming:** Use confirming questions to verify if you are on the right track, have made the proper assumptions, or drawn the correct conclusions. "Are you still? Do you continue to...?"
- **Agreement:** Use this type of question to obtain agreement on an action that will close the sale. "Do you intend, agree, plan...?"

Copiers West's First Visit

In their initial visit, Robert and Anna of Copiers West focused on gathering the following information about prospective customers:

- *The type of business*
- *How the prospects' copier needs were currently being met*
- *How satisfied they were with the copier and the service arrangement*
- *The key purchase decision maker*

At the cold call Copier West would demonstrate the following:

- *The prospect's copier needs, problems and costs, and key business issues*
- *Knowledge of their competitors' offerings*
- *Expertise of their product and its cost savings*
- *Ability to deliver service excellence*

For Robert Chavez and Copiers West, the key selling point was his expertise in copiers, lower cost, and better maintenance service.

Sell from the customer's point of view

Step 4: Make the Presentation

Isaac Stern, the famous concert pianist, was once asked how he played so effortlessly. His reply… "practice, practice, PRACTICE!!" And so it is with most things in life, the more we work at it, the better we are. This includes making sales presentations.

After listening to understand their customers' needs and problems, salespeople share information about their product offerings. They often begin by framing the concept of their product or service. Buyers buy **concepts** of what the product will do for them, not the product itself. A man buying a hot new red Ferrari is not buying a car. He's buying power and prestige. If he wanted a car for transportation, he would buy a Ford or Honda like thousands of other car shoppers. He's buying what driving the red Ferrari will do for the way he looks and feels.

Think about your last significant purchase. What were you really buying? Were you buying the product or what the product would do for you? Understanding this concept will help you plan and frame your sales presentations.

Salespeople also give information about their product's features and benefits. **Features** describe how the product looks and performs. **Benefits** describe how the product meets a need or solves a problem.

Develop your own feature and benefit statements for your business. Remember to sell benefits, not only features.

What would a professional presentation look and sound like? The following ideas should start you on your way:

- **Your appearance counts:** Wear clothing appropriate to your industry. If you are in the golf business, a polo shirt and casual pants will do nicely. If your clients are bankers, a suit would be in order.
- **Your attitude counts:** A professional, sincere, honest, and energetic approach is best for most situations.
- **Your first comment counts:** Begin with a key question or strong statement based on your research and/or the first call. A comment that shows your client how your product or service solves their problems or provides tremendous benefits is best.
- **Your presentation of benefits counts:** Sell benefits by showing your clients what is in it for them.

- **Your creativity counts:** Canned sales pitches don't go far with today's sophisticated clients. Use your own creative ideas to develop a presentation that is your own.
- **Rehearsal counts:** Don't go in cold; practice several times ahead of time.

Step 5: Objections

If life were perfect, your job would be easy and every client would immediately purchase everything you pitched. Unfortunately, it rarely works this way. Your clients will undoubtedly have some objections or some reason why they don't wish to buy. A good salesperson anticipates customer objections and is prepared to respond to them.

Below is a four-step process to overcome objections.

1. **Listen carefully.** This is nonverbal encouragement designed so that you can gather information on the actual problem.
2. **Acknowledge the problem.** Verbalize your understanding of customer issues.
3. **Explore problem areas** in depth by asking questions and to clarify meaning.
4. **Respond to the objection** by recommending a solution to the problem.

Some typical objections are:

Persistence, perseverance, and practice!

- Your price is too high
- I need to talk this one over with my team
- I don't think your program will solve my problem
- I am satisfied with my current supplier and don't want to change
- Your competition has better delivery times
- I have heard your company is new
- I have heard you have financial problems
- I had a bad experience with your company last time

You may have to repeat this process many times in the course of a sales call. You should also keep in mind that the first few objections may be "minor resistance" and may not be the real issue at all. Persistence does pay off when matched with civility and an honest desire to solve your clients' problems.

Welcome objections as you would opportunities

Copiers West Solves Their Customers' Problems By Saving Them Money

Robert and Anna would follow up each cold call with a telephone call to set up a meeting with the office manager. By now they had gathered specific information about the prospect's business and copier needs. Now was their chance to demonstrate their expertise and grab the interest of the decision maker. They demonstrated a unique understanding of their prospect's copier needs and interest in cost savings. Robert and Anna had a great success rate. Four times out of ten when they followed up over the phone, they were able to get appointments with the office manager, their prime target.

With their preliminary information in hand, Robert and Anna would approach the appointment with the confident attitude that the customer was ready to be sold. In every meeting the rule of thumb was to ask questions and listen far more than they spoke. They used high-quality pictures of their copiers and a simple table to present the comparative cost savings of their service contracts over their competitors. They also made it a point to know what their prospect's potential objections might be ahead of time. They listed these and prepared for them with solutions:

Column A: Customer Objection	***Column B: Copier West's Solution***
• *The hassle of switching equipment*	• *Free installation and training, first month free*
• *Lost time for copier upgrade*	• *Same day installation and training*
• *Need to see copier before committing*	• *Nearby showroom with all models and equipment*
• *Difficulty of getting out of existing service contract*	• *Free paper work prep, explain ease of getting out of no-obligation copier lease agreements*
• *Fear of using more complicated equipment*	• *Copiers West equipment is easier to use, more ergonomic*
• *Concern about service delays from smaller provider*	• *Demonstrate track-record for personal service, money back guarantee if longer than 1 hour repair response time*

Robert and Anna found that by presenting their information and confidently stressing benefits which solved their prospect's problems, they could earn the respect of office managers. Once they had this, they could become their prospect's partner and valued consultant. Then they would listen as the prospect asked questions and raised objections. They always probed for more information when met by an objection. Their goal was to better understand the prospect's concerns and needs, and eventually let the prospect arrive at the realization that Copiers West was the obvious choice for cost savings and better service.

With their personal style and expert approach Robert and Anna were able to get their foot in the door. They asked the right questions, listened carefully, and presented solutions. Their business grew and grew. They had become truly successful salespeople.

Step 6: The Close

The biggest reason for lost sales is the failure of sales people to ask their clients for the order. Why is this? What is the problem with asking someone for their business? Your product is great, your service unsurpassed, so go ahead and ask "Can we do business today?" The two major reasons most people won't ask for the order are fear of failure and fear of rejection. Nobody likes to think of themselves as a failure or to be rejected by other people. In most instances your client isn't rejecting you personally, nor have you failed personally. There are many reasons why clients don't buy, especially during the first try. They may not have the authority to sign a purchase order. They may have purchased this month's allotment the day before. They may want to get to know you better before they do business with you. There are almost as many reasons as there are customers.

Don't be discouraged; persistence pays off. Remember, if you have a quality product or service that is fairly priced, you have no reason to fear the reactions of the buyer!

Uncover the underlying problem preventing the sale...and solve it

There are many methods salespeople use to close the sale. Some of the major ones are listed below.

- **Basic close using an application form:** Begin by asking the customer a question from the application. Write in the answer. Proceed to the next item. As long as the customer does not stop you, she or he has bought.
- **Close by offering alternate choices:** Offer alternatives: "Do you like green or blue?"

- **Close by constructing a balance sheet:** For indecisive prospects, remark that a tally of the reasons for and against the concept will make the decision for them. Take a sheet of paper, draw a line down the center and help the prospect to list the reasons for buying your product/service.
- **Close by asking questions:** For a procrastinating prospect who is reluctant to make a commitment but won't tell you why, ask questions: "Is there something you don't understand about my company or our product?" "Is there anything I didn't make clear?" Summarize the presentation one question at a time.
- **Close by citing examples:** People will listen to stories. Tell about experiences of those who did buy your product or service.
- **Close with a secondary question:** "Do you prefer two of these or three?" When a prospect makes the minor decision, the major decision is close.
- **Close by isolating the objection:** Change a prospect's "I'll think it over," to a specific objection. Respond that the prospect obviously wouldn't spend time thinking it over unless he was seriously interested. When that is confirmed, say "Just to clarify my thinking, what phase of this program is it that you want to think over?" Then probe until the objection is isolated.
- **Close using prospect's objection:** Hear your prospect out. Listen to their objection. Give them a chance to explain. Sell them on their own objection. Expand it. Next, get the prospect to agree that this one objection is the only thing standing in the way of a sale. Then overcome the objection with fact.
- **Close with a closing question:** When a prospect asks a question like whether they could get what you're selling in such and such a way, don't answer with a "yes." Instead, ask the prospect if that's the way they want it. If the prospect answers "yes," the prospect has bought.

As you can see, there are many ways to ask for the order. Remember what they say at Nike: JUST DO IT!

Hey, It's Me Again!

Well, you have really worked hard. You made eight personal sales calls on the prospect, you have sent twelve faxes answering technical questions, you met seven people on the purchasing team and the vice president in charge of the project, you revised your formal offer three times and the last one was finally, finally accepted. You got the order. Congratulations!

Now it's time to get back with your customer and sincerely thank them for their business. Of course you will need to make sure delivery happens as scheduled, and they get exactly what they ordered. If there are any problems they deserve your immediate attention. A satisfied customer is the best source for new business. In fact, your new customer is a hot prospect immediately after making a purchase. This is an excellent time to sell something to go along with the previous sale. These so-called **add-ons** could be additional colors, sizes, or complementing products. Remember it takes a lot less energy to get a reorder or an add-on than it does to get a new customer who has never dealt with you before.

A satisfied customer is the best source of new business

Conclusion

Personal selling is on the critical path of your roadway to success. Nothing happens in business until somebody sells something. No longer the glad-hander, today's salesperson is a relationship-oriented, consultative problem solver. Very few people are born salespeople; very few people can't learn to be good company representatives. Selling should be fun, challenging, exciting, and financially rewarding. By learning some selling skills, doing your homework, and developing your own style through practice, there is no reason why you can't be successful at asking for the order… and getting it.

PART VII
FINANCING YOUR BUSINESS

Chapter 40
FINANCING YOUR BUSINESS

About This Chapter:
- *Why do you need financing?*
- *Choosing debt or equity*
- *Financing proposal*
- *Determining how much you need*
- *Tips for developing a successful banking relationship*

Introduction

Every day thousands of businesses are forced to close their doors. The most common reason given for the high failure rate of small businesses is lack of adequate **capital**. Capital is any asset that a business utilizes to create value and generate profits. Capital can include financial resources, equipment or even human capital. **Working capital** describes a business's most liquid asset, cash. This is the type of capital that growing businesses usually lack. A business can't survive without the cash to invest in people, equipment and supplies. It cannot survive without the cash to pay its expenses. Business owners, regardless of their size, need to know how to obtain capital necessary to grow their business. It is rare indeed where a business does not need additional capital to grow.

This chapter explores just what financial capital requirements are for growing companies.

Financing Needs

The first step towards success when dealing with the various sources of capital is to understand why your business needs financing. At what stage of development is your business? Are you planning a new venture, just getting started, expanding a successful venture, or managing a business that has matured? This section describes typical reasons why a business would seek financing.

The first step: understand capital requirements

Research & Development Money

Small business is the source of many innovative products and services. But to investigate and realize innovations, an entrepreneur needs **seed capital** or **pre-venture financing**. This type of capital may be used to fund market research, technical research, strategic planning, and product development. All this must be accomplished before a business can even offer a new product or service to its customers.

This type of early stage funding is usually provided by the owners of the business or investors. These businesses are usually too risky for lending institutions.

Start-up and New Growth Financing

Start-up costs include professional fees, inventory, equipment, deposits, marketing materials, and working capital. The list of costs is different for an existing business. New growth related costs might include the cost of upgrading equipment to expand capacity, compensation for additional employees, research and development costs for new products, bulk purchases of supplies or inputs, or additional working capital to support larger orders with longer payment terms. Regardless, businesses new and old, cannot grow without an injection of capital.

Purchase a Business

Some entrepreneurs elect to purchase an existing business or a franchise. In addition to start-up costs, other items such as **goodwill** must be financed. Goodwill describes a business's **intangible assets**. These might include an established brand name, patents, trade marks, copyrights or a favorable location. It may also include expertise or knowledge possessed by the people within the business. When an entrepreneur purchases an existing business they can usually only finance the portion of the purchase price that is linked to **tangible assets** like equipment, inventory or buildings. Goodwill is usually financed by the owner carrying a separate financing contract or by the purchaser in cash

Seasonal Working Capital

As we introduced above, working capital is money that is used in day-to-day operations to pay for things like supplies, payroll and utility expenses. Working capital is used to cover regularly occurring expenses that do not fit into any asset category.

Seasonal working capital is capital that is used to cover seasonal fluctuations in a business's expenses and operations. Often times the demand for a business's products and services varies from month to month, and season to season. A good example of this are ski resorts who rely on the winter months to generate all of their revenue for the year. At the same time, during the summer, ski companies overhaul their equipment and undertake major projects to groom ski slopes. During this time they have many expenses but little revenue. Businesses like this often require additional seasonal financing to supplement their working capital.

Permanent Working Capital

Permanent working capital is funding that a business requires on a regular, on-going basis to cover such expenses as payroll, debt repayment, utilities, marketing campaigns and rent. It is rare that any business is able to fund its expansion solely from its own profits. It is almost always necessary to increase its working capital with outside financing of some sort. Before a business can do this, however, it must clearly distinguish between seasonal and permanent working capital requirements. Loans for seasonal capital are usually paid back within one year. Permanent capital loans are financed as a **term loan** and repaid over several **terms** or years.

Your business may need both. Take a look at your sales records for the past year or more. Do you see any fluctuations in revenues that appear to be caused by seasonal demand for your products or services? Do you have a different levels of expenses at different times of the year? By differentiating between your permanent and seasonal working capital needs, you will better be able anticipate the money your business needs.

A final note about working capital: One of the most common reasons small businesses fail is their inability to properly anticipate working capital requirements. Often small business suffer from a disproportionate level of cash versus fixed assets. Fixed assets cannot be quickly converted into cash to pay bills. If a business depends too heavily upon its daily receipts to meet operating expenses, when income from sales slows, creditors may force the business into bankruptcy.

Relying on more flexible forms of assets, like renting property and equipment versus purchasing it, allows a small business to keep more of its capital liquid.

Equipment Acquisition

A business can serve a limited number of customers with its existing equipment. Expansion for business owners often requires the purchase of additional equipment. Commercial banks usually provide loans for this type of financing.

Real Estate Acquisition

A well-established restaurant is located in a building it has leased for 15 years. The owner of the building decides to sell and the restaurant owner wishes to purchase the building to ensure long-term use of the business site. This is an example of real estate acquisition.

The Fireman, the Idea, and the Collar

In 1990, at age 18, Michael Quinn became one of the youngest firemen in San Francisco fire department history. An ambitious fellow, he soon signed on for additional training, and earned a seat as the Emergency Medical Technician (EMT) on his engine team. Mike was often the first at the scene of an accident to evaluate injuries, administer first aid and secure all those injured.

Mike routinely stabilized injured people so that (once the ambulance arrived) they could be transported to the nearest hospital. In his first year alone, he stabilized over 150 people for spinal cord and neck related injuries.

Mike was utilizing a temporary stabilizing neck brace called a C-collar. However, he was frustrated by the poor quality and design of the collars. They came in only three sizes, and in the hustle and bustle of many accident scenes, he and other EMTs would make mistakes in visually estimating the size of the injured person's neck. Frequently, they would have to fit and refit collars until they found the proper size. Mike knew that each time a person's neck was shifted to remove and refit a collar, the potential for additional injury increased.

He knew there had to be a better way.

Debt or Equity?

Business assets are financed by either debt or equity financing. A description of these two important types of financing follows:

Debt

Debt is a direct obligation to pay an asset, usually cash, to a creditor in exchange for having supplied your business with an asset, usually money. The creditor expects to be paid **interest** on the money as well as having the **principal** repaid. The amount of individual debt payments depend on the amount borrowed, the length of the loan, and the interest rate.

Short term loans are for less than one year. These are almost always seasonal working capital loans. The most flexible form is called **a line of credit** and allows the entrepreneur to borrow the money as needed up to an approved limit. This is like having a credit card that expires in a year, but with a much lower interest rate! As funds are repaid, the line of credit is replenished and the funds can be borrowed again.

You can use debt or equity financing

Intermediate term loans are for three to seven years. These loans are for permanent expansion of working capital or to acquire equipment. The loans are generally at a fixed interest rate and may have a penalty for early repayment of the principal.

Long term loans are for ten or more years and are usually for real estate transactions or equipment purchases. These loans are generally at a **fixed interest rate** although **variable rate loans** may be available.

Virtually every small business loan through a bank is **a secured loan.** This means the business, or the business owner, has pledged assets as collateral for the loan in case the business is unable to repay its debt. An unsecured loan simply means that no collateral has been pledged. Your business must be a very low risk to obtain an unsecured loan from a bank. Very often, people will obtain unsecured loans from family or friends.

The Quinn Collar is Born

By September 1996, Mike and a friend, an engineering student, made a sample of what they called The Quinn Collar. The changes they made to the basic design of the emergency C-collar were few, but critical. Instead of coming in three different sizes, the Quinn Collar came in one size that could easily be adjusted to fit different neck sizes. This way EMTs could avoid the risk of applying and removing different collars until they found the one that fit best.

Mike tested the idea on ten other EMTs he knew in various engine companies throughout the city. He spoke with the father of a friend who was a neck and spinal cord specialist and incorporated his feedback. Once again, a few minor adjustments were made and everyone felt that the collar was a remarkable breakthrough in C-collar design.

Mike's engineer friend was able to create test models of the new collar, but needed more time and expert assistance to create a design for mass production. In the next several months they borrowed $2,000 from family members to pay for attorney fees to apply for patent protection. At the same time, they enlisted the help of Mike's girlfriend, a recent graduate of business school, to help them write a business plan.

Within 3 months their idea began to fall into place. They had developed a vision for the way they could produce, market and sell their new collar. They began work on determining the amount of capital they would need to launch the business.

What was the best source of funds? Mike and his friend knew little about financing, or business management for that matter. They had a bankable idea, but they needed help and money. They decided to form a partnership between the three of them.

Equity

Equity involves no obligation on the part of the business to repay money. However, equity does involve selling a portion of the ownership of your business. The individual supplying the money becomes an owner, or an investor in your business.

If your business is a **partnership,** then the person or group who has invested in your business becomes a partner and will have rights as defined in your partnership agreement. An investor may become either a **general** or **limited partner.** This is generally negotiated and clearly outlined in the partnership agreement.

If your business is a corporation, the investor becomes a stockholder in the business and has rights to exercise the powers of a stockholder as defined in your bylaws. The investor may become a holder of either **common** or **preferred stock.**

The major difference between the two is that preferred stockholders receive any dividends (a percentage of profits) that are paid out by the business before common stockholders.

4 Tips for Financing Your Business

1. The more assets your business requires the more financing it will need. Likewise, the more rapidly sales grow the greater will be the business's asset requirements.

2. You should always finance your business's growth so that you maintain an appropriate level of cash, cash equivalent assets, or financial liquidity. You can measure the level of your liquidity using **the current ratio** (current assets divided by current liabilities). Set a target ratio which your business must maintain. A current ratio of 2 means that your business has twice as much current assets like cash as current liabilities.

3. There is a limit to how much debt you can use to finance your growing business. The total amount of debt your business can carry is limited by the total amount of equity you have invested in the business. Banks and other sources of financing expect that any outside financing be matched by owner's equity.

4. Internal and external sources of equity are available to your business. Equity initially comes from the owner's investment in the business. This is known as **external equity** because it does not derive from business operations. **Internal equity** arises from the business's own profits from operations being reinvested in the business.

Choosing Debt or Equity

There are advantages and disadvantages to both debt and equity financing. Let's look at some of them.

Ownership

A business owner using equity to finance a business is granting the investor a share of future profits. The investor is also acquiring the ability to exercise some control over operation of the business. The loss of control is permanent unless you have negotiated a **buy-out** clause that allows you to buy the shares back from the investor at an agreed upon price. In the best cases, the right investor can provide the business with additional management expertise.

How do you decide between debt and equity financing?

An owner may lose control under debt financing if the loan agreement contains restrictive covenants. Examples are limitations on dividends and salaries that can be paid out, mandatory compensating savings account balance, and requirements to maintain a minimum level of inventory.

Obligation to Repay

Using debt financing places pressure on the business to make scheduled loan payments to repay **principal** and **interest**. During start-up and early growth phases, an expanding company may have difficulty meeting these obligations.

Tax Considerations

The interest portion of a loan payment is tax deductible and the principal portion is not. Dividends paid to any owners, including passive investors, are not tax deductible.

Capital Structure

The capital structure of a business is the mix of debt and equity financing it uses to fund its base of assets. Each type of financing has a different impact on your business's financial position and cash flow.

Equity is a permanent source of funds for your business while debt is always temporary. Acquiring equity financing also increases the asset portion of your business's balance sheet. It need not be paid back, because it is not a debt.

The higher the percentage of debt financing a business uses, the greater the monthly payments it must make to repay that debt. This increases the risk that the business's cash flow will not be adequate to meet debt payments.

Carefully managed debt can also carry many benefits, most notably, **financial leverage.** Leverage exists as a result of the fact that interest payments, or **interest expense** of debt financing is a **fixed cost.** It is agreed upon at the outset of the debt contract, and is held steady overtime, while the business's operating income may rise. This means that the business has the borrowed funds at its disposal, to aggressively invest in its business, thus producing a greater return than what it must pay on its debt. It has effectively combined borrowed money with the owner's own money invested in the business, to achieve leverage and earn a greater return than otherwise would have been possible. In this positive scenario, the business benefits.

Unfortunately, if the business operations are not as profitable as forecasted, the business will earn a lower return and have difficulty meeting its debt obligations.

Industry

Every industry defines a given mix of debt and equity or a **debt to equity ratio (D/E)** as standard or acceptable. Creditors are reluctant to provide debt to businesses with D/E ratios that are outside of this standard range. Talk to your banker, accountant, or local Small Business Development Center representative to determine the norm for your industry. Both creditors and investors will have their own ideas about how much risk is associated with your business. Risks specific to your business would also include industry, geographic and technological considerations.

How Much $$ to Launch The Quinn Collar?

Mike and his two partners laid out their business objectives: to market a unique, patented C-collar for the temporary stabilization of victims of neck and spinal cord trauma. They would contract the actual manufacture of the collars to a medical supplies manufacturer, and would negotiate to have their C-collar distributed by an existing network of medical supplies distributors. This way they could operate a "lean and mean" operation that leveraged its most valuable asset: the patent on the Quinn Collar. Eventually if things went well, they would hope to attract a larger medical supplies company to purchase the rights to the Quinn Collar patent.

They began by using common sense, educated guesswork and industry research to calculate how much financial capital it would take to launch their new venture. They took into account their projections for sales for their first 3 years, their operating expenses for years one through three and any start-up costs for equipment, research and development, attorney's fees and marketing costs. They also took a look at the average asset to sales ratio of other small medical supply businesses. With this work complete, they settled on the sum of $150,000 for their first two years of operations, assuming they achieved their target sales level of $200,000 in that period of time. They decided that they would pursue a bank loan for $60,000 of their total required $150,000. Their calculations for their asset requirements broke down as follows:

Cash	*$50,000*
Accounts Receivable	*35,000*
Inventory	*45,000*
Total Current assets	*130,000*
Total Fixed Assets (Computer, office equipment etc.)	*20,000*
Total Assets	***$150,000***

Timing

When seeking a source of equity capital, the length of time before a business gets a response or even receives capital varies widely. It almost always is a much longer wait when a business is seeking debt.

Cost of Proposal

Any business that is seeking financing of any kind (including financing from friends and family) must prepare a **financing proposal.** No matter how great your business, how obvious the potential success of your idea, no business speaks for itself. You must communicate its strengths, weaknesses, and needs to others. A financing proposal presents a business's financial position, the quality of its management and the degree of risk it offers potential lenders and investors.

You should consider obtaining assistance with the preparation of financial statements and projections, preparation and review of legal documents, and research for marketing and technical information. The cost for these services varies a great deal depending upon the amount of assistance you need and the area of the country you live in. Seek out assistance from your lawyer, CPA, SBDC representative or business consultant.

When obtaining debt capital you may not require legal services until it is time to sign the loan agreement. Before starting your search for potential investors you should meet with your attorney to verify that you are in compliance with state and federal securities regulations.

Owner Preferences

A business owner with a desire to retain absolute control will have a difficult time working with an investor. On the other hand, an owner that feels there are advantages to having another voice in management decisions may welcome the right investor.

Raising equity capital requires good sales and communication skills. You are selling both your business's promise of profitability and yourself as a qualified manager of your business. The ability to utilize networks of business and personal contacts is also useful.

Before pitching your business you should take stock of yourself. How will growth in your business affect your personal goals, your family, your employees and your current customers, are you prepared for the added responsibilities of a larger business? Change, both good and bad, is inevitable during periods of high growth. Are you aware of what the changes will be?

Lending Community

Can your business realistically service the additional debt? If the lending community is reticent, equity financing may be the best alternative.

Potential Investors

Can you offer an attractive rate of return to an investor? If equity seems like an attractive option then you should test the reaction of some potential investors.

Using a Business Plan as a Financing Proposal

A comprehensive business plan is a the essential starting point for preparing a financing proposal. Some portions of a business plan are not included in a financing proposal and a financing proposal requires some information that is not in your business plan. Businesses should update their business plans on an annual basis. It is a great management tool and will aid in the development of a financing proposal.

The essential starting point: The Start-up Business Plan

Develop Your Business Plan

The preparation of a complete business plan enables businesses to accurately predict their financing needs. Rather than approach your banker each time a financing need presents itself, it is advantageous to identify all anticipated financing needs and present them as a package.

Unconventional Financing Techniques

- Barter financing: share space with similar businesses, set up mini-business space within an existing business.
- Landlord financing: negotiate to have your landlord pay for some needed upgrades, add that to the rent, and amortize it over the life of your business's lease, or negotiate free rent for a piece of the business.
- Use other people's credit: have the business of an acquaintance buy the inventory or supplies that you cannot get credit to cover; then pay them back according to their supplier's terms.
- Contract financing: if yours is a service business, negotiate to have customers prepay for services through one-year all inclusive contracts.
- Concession sales: if you are a retailer, sublease part of your retail space to other vendors whose products complement your own.
- Staged financing: look for financing for your business in stages, starting with enough financing to help you get your business up and running so that you can prove you can be profitable.
- Trade credit: negotiate aggressive payment terms and credit from your suppliers.
- Leverage future commitments of business (as documented in letters from customers) to increase your business's credibility and likelihood of receiving financing from a bank.
- Buy a business instead of starting one from scratch: there are many ways to finance the purchase of an existing business. It is not uncommon to be able to negotiate financing from the seller for as much as 80% of the purchase price, or to incrementally repay the purchase price from future cash flows from operations. It is also easier to get bank financing for an existing business than for a start-up.
- Set up a home office: save on office space rent and get home business related tax deductions by creating a usable and productive workspace in your home.
- Participate in a small business incubator: these have been set up in many cities to provide workspace and support services for a collection of small businesses. Many state and local governments sponsor incubators by providing below-market rent and other low cost services to start-ups.

Identify Possible Sources of Financing

Once you have determined all of the financing your business needs, you should begin shopping for sources. Don't approach these sources until you know the exact needs of your business. How much money will you need? When? When will you need additional money? How quickly will you be able to repay it? Acceptance guidelines vary from one financial institution to the next. Spend some time learning about the person and organization that you are going to approach. Find out what information they specifically require. Some of the things you should know about any funding source before you even approach them for money, are:

1) To whom should I submit my proposal?
2) How are decisions made regarding financing?
3) When will the decisions be made?
4) What types of businesses/industries have they lent to or invested in before?
5) If they don't supply the funds, can they help you find other financing?

Here are some additional questions for bankers:

1) What other services can you offer my business?
2) Does your bank make SBA-guaranteed loans?
3) Do they participate in other government loan programs?
4) What is the handling charge on credit card receipts?
5) Can you supply my business with a line of credit?

The answers to these questions will provide valuable information. It is important to sell decision-makers on you as well as your business. Trust and confidence are key to approval of your financing proposal.

Prepare a Financing Proposal

The financing proposal is a document you prepare for the purpose of obtaining capital for your business. It is a sales document! Your customers will not buy from your business unless you satisfy a need. The banker is no different, the banker has a need to make sound, low-risk loans. The banker does not require all of the details in your business plan but at the same time, needs some information not in your business plan.

Your financing proposal is a sales document!

Your financing proposal demonstrates that you thoroughly understand the factors that determine your business's success, and have carefully reflected on your business objectives and the requirements needed to achieve them. This document also demonstrates your proactivity in achieving your goals and avoiding pitfalls before they occur. The next section of this chapter discusses the specific contents of a financing proposal. Remember, the goal of any financing proposal is to educate the lender and make the lending decision an easy one.

Customize Each Financing Proposal

Think of your financing proposal like any marketing effort. Your job is to know the customer and satisfy the needs of the customer. Carefully research your audience first, keeping in mind the questions we listed above. Then tailor your proposal so that it speaks directly to the interests, concerns and needs of your target funder. You should also personalize your proposal with the name of the person receiving it, the name of the financing source, and specific references to financing programs offered. It is true that you are the bank's customer but you will increase your chances of obtaining financing if you realize that you are selling the promise of your business to the bank. In this case, the bank is your customer!

Outline of a Financing Proposal

Cover Letter

A short, one page, letter on business stationery addressed to the person who will be reviewing your financing proposal. You may wish to thank the person for previous conversations and confirm future appointments.

Sample Financing Proposal Cover Letter

November 20, 1996

Ms. Nancy Pelozza, Loan Officer
Westside Bank
San Francisco, CA

Dear Ms. Pelozza:

As agreed in our recent conversation, I am presenting on behalf of my firm, Quinn Collar, a formal loan proposal for your consideration. As discussed in the body of this document, the loan request is in the amount of $60,000. The following repayment schedule of this amount is proposed:

(Insert proposed repayment schedule here)

The proceeds of the loan will be used for the following applications:

(Insert Intended Application(s) here)

In support of this request, the following documents and exhibits are enclosed:

(Insert List of Enclosures here)

It is my understanding that a variable interest rate equivalent to X percentage points above the prime rate would apply to the approved loan.

Thank you for your consideration. I eagerly await your reply.

Sincerely,

Michael S. Quinn, Partner
The Quinn Collar
San Francisco, California

Summary of Financing Request

This is the first page and it should summarize the major points of your entire proposal. Specifically, it should quickly and clearly cover the purpose of the financing, the amount, the terms being requested, source of funds for repayment, and the collateral being offered. The reader now knows what to expect in the pages to follow.

Use of Proceeds

Your financing source wants to know the details of how you will use the money. This is also an opportunity to highlight the amount of capital being invested by existing owners and use of business funds.

Collateral Offered

You can skip this page if you are seeking equity financing or an unsecured loan. If you are seeking debt that will be secured, then list the assets that will be used and their current market values. Collateral for your loan is negotiable, so don't begin by offering every asset you own! Remember that the financing proposal is a marketing document, but the values listed for your assets must be based on sound reasoning.

Investor Return

You can skip this page if you are seeking debt financing. This is your opportunity to present to the investors the financial return they can expect on their investment. You should state if you will have an option to "buy-out" their investment at a future date for a predetermined amount.

Table of Contents

A list of the pages that you are taking from your business plan.

Business Plan

Select only the pages needed to support the financing being requested. Submitting your entire business plan is not recommended. We suggest that at minimum you include the following pages from your business plan:

- Executive Summary
- Business Concept
- Cash Flow Projections
- Projected Income Statement
- Balance Sheet
- Break-even Analysis
- Projected Cash Flow Statement

- Tax Returns (last 3 years)
- Management information
  - Resumes for all key personnel
  - Personal Financial Statements for all owners
- Market research studies

Determining How Much You Need

Small business owners are often unsure about how much financing to ask for. The amount is based on future projections and we are all rather uneasy about predicting the future. It is critical to determine the amount before beginning your search for a suitable source of financing. It is fine to ask a loan officer, "What is your reaction to the amount I am seeking" but not acceptable to ask "How much can I borrow?" This section discusses the two most important considerations when you are determining how much funding you will request.

Depends on Type of Financing

How your business will use the funds and the type of collateral you will offer will both determine the amount you request.

The amount available for financing the purchase of a piece of equipment may be determined by a bank rule limiting such loans to 75% of the purchase price. The financing of real estate and fixed assets is usually limited by clearly defined maximum percentages of the transaction that is to be financed.

Determining the amount of financing needed for **permanent working capital** or **seasonal working capital** is more difficult since the amount needed depends on the accuracy of the financial forecasts.

Cash Flow Projection Is Always the Key

Cash flow is key

The key item in any financing proposal is the business's **cash flow forecast**. It defines the amount of money you need to borrow, particularly for working capital, and demonstrates the monthly payments that the business can afford. The number of years required to repay a loan depends on the length of financing being sought. A one-year cash flow projection may be sufficient for a seasonal working capital loan but a five-year loan to permanently expand working capital requires a three to five-year forecast.

C's of Credit

How are lending decisions made by creditors? Here are six factors that lenders consider when evaluating your financing proposal.

Do you know what a credit check will reveal about you and your business?

Credit & Financial History

The financial history presented in your financing proposal should include a summary of your personal credit history as well as a summary of your business's financial performance to date.

Your business's financial history should include clear financial data tables and text summarizing your business's performance. You should include sales, cash flow and profits as well as key financial ratios like the Current ratio (described above), the Inventory Turnover ratio, and the Receivables Turnover ratio. These and other measures of financial performance are presented in more detail in Chapter 34 *Cash Flow Management.*

Do you know what a credit check will reveal about you and your business? If not, and you are concerned, it is wise to have a credit company perform the check so you will know what to expect. Banks and other lending institutions routinely check the credit history of potential borrowers. As a small business owner, you should expect to have the credit check cover you and your business. You can order a copy of your personal credit history by contacting organizations like TCI Credit Bureau or EQUIFAX. Both will send you a copy of your credit report for a small fee.

Character

The soundness of a small business loan is often more dependent on the trustworthiness of the owner than the track record of the business. Your reputation in your local area is important and you should be able to give some good local business references.

Capacity

Bankers make a loan with the expectation that a business will be able to make loan payments from its profits. Capacity refers to the ability of the business to repay the loan with cash generated from operations. Your financial projections address this concern but bankers also will be influenced by past financial history of your business. As previously mentioned, if your business has been marginally profitable but you have optimistic projections for the future, you will have to make a compelling case to convince potential lenders that yours will be a profitable business in the future. Your personal and business's track records are the major criteria by which your financing proposal will be judged.

Collateral

What happens if the business can't make its loan payments because of poor sales or lower than predicted profits? The bank will look to satisfy the debt by taking title to the **collateral**. Collateral are those assets that you are willing to pledge and that the lending institution will accept as security for a loan. Collateral is necessary to obtain a loan, but collateral without **capacity** or secure value usually will result in a negative answer to a financing proposal.

Conditions

How will expected economic trends impact your business? You addressed this question and others about risk in your business plan. Now you need to share your assessment of risk with your banker.

Capital

Are you committed to your business? Small business owners often act insulted when asked this question. The banker wants to see your commitment in terms of both time and money. You are asking the banker to supply debt financing for your business. The banker is watching your debt to equity ratio. How will you or your business provide the equity portion of the project you are seeking to finance?

Be prepared before seeking financing!

Quinn Collar Financing Strategy

After several months of juggling research and business planning meetings with each of their other professional and personal obligations, Mike and his partners settled on the following:

- *They projected $60,000 in sales the first year, $140,000 in year two.*
- *They estimated their net profits would be 15% of sales, or $9,000 in year one and $21,000 in year two.*
- *They negotiated with a manufacturing contractor to extend credit on production, resulting in estimated accounts payable of approximately 10% of sales.*
- *Each of the three partners would invest $15,000 each of their own money in the business, in exchange for 5,000 shares of common stock each.*
- *They would approach their local bank for a short-term line of credit of $30,000.*
- *They would apply for a mid-term loan from the bank for $60,000.*

- *In exchange for the loan, Quinn Collar would agree to the bank's two loan requirements: 1) The business's current ratio (current assets divided by current liabilities) not fall below 1.80; 2) No more than 60% of the business's financing come from debt, or stated another way, the business's total debt versus total assets should not be greater than 60%. Failing to meet these two requirements would mean that the bank loan would have to be repaid immediately.*

The Quinn Collar Projected Balance Sheet
(at end of year one)

	Assets	
Cash	$50,000	
Accounts Receivable	35,000	
Inventory	45,000	
Total Current Assets	130,000	
Fixed Assets	20,000	
Total Assets	150,000	
	Debt and Equity	
Accounts Payable	6,000	(10% of $60,000 sales)
Credit Line	30,000	
Total Current Liabilities	36,000	
Long Term Debt	60,000	
Total Debt	96,000	
	Equity	
Common Stock	45,000	($15,000 x 3 partners)
Retained Earnings	9,000	(15% of sales)
Total Debt and Equity	$150,000	

Tips for Developing a Successful Banking Relationship

Deal with Banks Located Close To Your Business

You will be more inclined to visit your banker, and the reverse will be true, if your banker is local. Only choose a more distant banker if no local bankers understand your business needs. Local banks generally have a stronger commitment to supporting local businesses; therefore, are more receptive to local loan requests.

Make an Appointment, with the Right Person

First you need to identify the right person to talk with at the bank. Then make an appointment, whether your goal is to obtain some preliminary information or to present your financing proposal.

Select a Banker That You feel Is Comfortable with You

Naturally this works both ways. You should feel like you can tell the banker your concerns and he will listen. Likewise, you want a banker who tells you his concerns. It is extremely frustrating to be told "no" to a financing proposal but receive no explanation.

Select a Banker that Has an Interest In Your Type of Business

Find a banker who either has existing clients in your industry or expresses interest in learning more about your industry. A banker who is knowledgeable will be able to offer you advice and advocate for approval of your financing proposal.

At the end of the day, the decision to lend you money depends on the financier's confidence in your management ability

Ask the Banker for Advice About Your Situation, Not Money

During any meeting with your banker, ask for advice. Bankers meet with many business owners and see how various owners deal with problems. Your banker is also knowledgeable about local attorneys, accountants, and business consultants.

Present a Complete Financing Proposal

Want to leave a good impression with your banker? Make sure your financing proposal is complete the first time and you will leave a positive impression. The majority of entrepreneurs approach bankers with poorly thought out proposals, so this is your chance to shine.

Determine the amount you need before approaching possible financing sources

Tell the Truth

The financing proposal is a marketing document. This means presenting your business situation in a positive light based on fact. If you approach the transaction trying to hide facts about your business, you are probably going to be unsuccessful. As hard as it may be, disclose problem areas at the beginning and then work to overcome them. If you hide them and then the banker uncovers the problems, he will think you are either not trustworthy or dishonest. In either case, you won't obtain the loan.

Uses and Benefits of Loan

The banker is looking for the capacity of your business to repay the loan. Show the banker how the proceeds of the loan will be used to improve capacity to repay.

Be Flexible

If your banker offers a suggestion about how your proposal might be modified, listen before you reject their advice. The suggestion might not work for your needs but the banker would not make a suggestion if it wasn't important to the process.

Be Patient

Entrepreneurs think bankers take way too long to make decisions and bankers think business owners are always in a hurry. Find out before submitting your proposal how long the process will take and then provide the information needed by your banker. Finally, realize that the process may take longer than anticipated. The lesson to learn here is to start the process well in advance of when the financing will be needed

Do All of Your Banking at the Same Bank

Some entrepreneurs are always shopping banks in hopes of saving some service fees and getting a better interest rate. It always pays to shop around but, having done so, choose one bank to supply all the services you need.

Recommend Business Associates to Your Banker

Once you have developed a good relationship with your banker, support them by introducing other business owners to them. They need to make good loans and helping them find good business owners will be appreciated.

Conclusion

Begin immediately to implement some of the concepts covered in this chapter. Start by developing a good relationship with your banker. At the same time, start "working" your personal and professional networks and make sure that you have a well thought out business plan. These actions will make your request for financing more fruitful.

Approach your next search for financing by taking the following steps:

- Determine why you need financing
- Select debt or equity. If debt, determine what type
- Develop a well-researched, to the point financing proposal
- Present a customized version to each potential source of financing
- Be persistent!
- Be professional
- Demonstrate confidence and integrity
- Know your financing target
- Maintain close relationships with financing sources

Chapter 41
MONEY SOURCES

About This Chapter:
- *Conventional sources of funding*
- *Financial institutions*
- *Federal loan programs*
- *Alternative sources of financing*

Introduction

Small business owners often think only of banks when they look to finance their businesses. There is, however, a wide variety of other ways to finance a small business. This chapter provides information about the many alternative money sources available to small, growing businesses. This should be viewed as a starting point as your individual circumstances, location, and goals will all influence your selection of money sources.

Conventional Sources of Money

Personal Funds

National studies show that four out of every five new businesses are launched with the **personal funds** of the owner. The exact percentage varies from year to year but the fact remains that personal funds are the number one source of funding for a new business. Here is a review of sources of personal funds:

- **Savings:** This category includes money in a savings account, a money-market account, a certificate of deposit or even money in a shoe box under the bed.
- **Investments:** Besides stocks and bonds, this includes stamps, coins, jewelry, and precious metals.
- **Life insurance:** Many life insurance policies, typically whole life, allow you to borrow against the cash surrender value of the policy.
- **Second mortgage:** You may be able to borrow a percentage of the equity you have in your home. This includes refinancing your house or taking a second mortgage loan.
- **Personal loans:** You may be able to obtain a personal "signature loan" at your bank or credit union.
- **Spouse income:** Determine how much is available on a monthly basis to help finance your business needs. You may want to invest this monthly amount in your business or use it as the basis for obtaining a loan.

Four out of five new businesses are started with the owner's personal funds

- **Family and friends:** While not really a source of personal funds, your family and friends may provide capital because of your personal relationship with them.
- **Credit cards:** Credit cards are presented last because they should be considered only as a last resort.

The School Teacher Turned Coppersmith

For 29 years Ryan Mikus was a high school teacher in Kalamazoo, Michigan. When he wasn't correcting tests or coaching soccer, he was indulging his passion for coppersmithing. He created a work studio in the old barn on the back of his property where he made lamps and candle holders. He particularly admired the styles of the copper masters active during the Arts and Crafts movement—popular during the late 19th and early 20th centuries. When he retired in 1997 he decided to try to turn his hobby into a business.

After several months of perfecting his designs and production techniques (each lamp was made by hand), Ryan was ready to spring into business. On the advice of several friends and family members he took his 3 best lamps to several well known home design stores in Kalamazoo, Holland and Detroit. He was surprised and inspired by the overwhelmingly positive feedback from the store buyers. "How much for 10 like this?" one asked. "How many can I have by Christmas?" another inquired. Ryan knew now was the time to begin building his business.

Ryan decided to sell his lamps under his own name, inscribing each one individually with the words: "Hand-crafted in the studio of Ryan Mikus, Kalamazoo, Michigan." The mission of his business: to create an array of elegant original hand-crafted copper lamps, vases and candleholders.

First he would need financing to buy materials, upgrade equipment, buy a computer to help him manage his business and hire an assistant coppersmith.

Financial Institutions

This section examines financial institutions that provide **debt capital** or debt financing needed by small businesses.

Debt Financing means that an individual is incurring some form of obligation to pay back money that has been lent to their business. Sources of debt financing often require some form of **asset** as **collateral** to ensure that the debt will be repaid.

Banks
Savings banks generally specialize in home mortgages and automobile loans. This doesn't mean you can't approach them for a business loan but it is not their major business line.

Commercial banks are interested in business loans

Commercial banks are interested in business loans. Their loan officers are accustomed to processing business loan applications and are familiar with other financing options if you don't qualify for a loan from their bank.

There are many different banks that serve different markets. Small community banks are very focused on serving local businesses. A large commercial bank with hundreds of branches operates quite differently.

It is important to understand that banks usually don't make loans to businesses in the start-up phase. They prefer to make a government guaranteed loan. Government guaranteed loan programs are discussed in detail later in this chapter.

Credit unions
Credit unions are started and managed by employees of a company, members of a labor union, or other groups. If you or a family member belongs to a credit union, you may be able to borrow some of your needed capital from it.

Consumer finance companies
Consumer finance companies make small personal loans 100% secured by collateral. They charge higher interest rates and processing fees than banks and credit unions but are more flexible about approving financing requests.

Commercial finance companies
Commercial finance companies focus on business loans and operate similar to a consumer finance company.

Commercial finance companies also make SBA guaranteed loans. Examples of these institutions are AT&T Capital, GE Capital Credit, and The Money Store.

Leasing companies
Leasing companies rent fixed assets to businesses and individuals. A lease is merely a long-term agreement to rent. There are three kinds of leases:

- Financing leases are the most common. The lessee maintains the equipment and may have the right to purchase the equipment at the end of the lease.
- Operating leases are also called maintenance leases. The lessor is responsible for the maintenance of the equipment.
- Sale and leaseback is similar to a financing lease. The owner of a fixed asset sells it to another party who then leases it back to the original owner.

Ryan Mikus knew that a computer was essential in order for him to successfully operate his business. He needed a powerful enough computer to maintain his sales files, surf the net for supplier and design ideas, and manage his financial records.

Given his current level of sales (he had already begun selling a few lamps a month) Ryan knew he did not have the revenue he needed to buy a computer and printer.

*After talking with several computer resellers he discovered that he had two options for financing the computer equipment he needed. He could use traditional equipment financing or he could lease the equipment. If he took a loan out and bought the equipment he would have a new **asset** (the computer) as well as a new **liability** (the loan to pay for the computer) on his **balance sheet**. He would own the computer, maintain it and **depreciate** the value of the computer on his balance sheet over time.*

*If Ryan signed a lease for the computer equipment, he would not take ownership of the equipment, and it would not appear as an asset on his business' balance sheet. Nor would he have the corresponding liability of the loan to pay for it. Instead, he would pay a monthly lease payment, which would be recorded on his books as an **expense.***

Ryan was new to the whole business of financing and leasing, and so enlisted the help of his accountant (his brother-in-law, Bob). After reviewing his credit worthiness, cash flow projections and the type of equipment he needed, Bob recommended he go with the lease. His had several reasons for this recommendation:

- *Ryan could record the cost of the computer equipment immediately as expenses, thus lowering his business's net taxable income*

- *His lease payments would conveniently include all down payments, taxes installation, insurance, and maintenance*

- *The computer supplier would provide all service and technical assistance, allowing Ryan to focus on creating his lamps*
- *The lease would allow Ryan to update his computer when better technology comes on the market or replace his equipment if it no longer fit his needs*

After Ryan and Bob researched different kinds of leases, they decided he would negotiate a ***closed-end operating lease*** *with a company located in Kalamazoo. This lease would include all maintenance, equipment substitutions and a cancellation clause. At the end of the lease period Ryan would not own the computer, and would be free to upgrade to newer equipment or, cash flow permitting, buy different equipment elsewhere.*

The lease that he negotiated for his computer equipment was as follows:

- *Power PC with laser printer, 28.8 modem, 24 MG RAM, 2 Gigabyte hard drive, CD ROM, keyboard and 15" monitor*
- *2 year term*
- *Monthly payments of $350.00*

Here are some of the advantages and disadvantages of leasing:

Advantages of a lease

- A lease often requires no down payment.
- Your business will not have a liability on its balance sheet.
- You may be able to make payments over a longer term than with a loan.
- You can update high tech equipment by ending one lease and starting a new one with new equipment.

Disadvantages of a lease

- A lease almost always costs more than a loan.
- You probably won't own the asset at the end of the lease.
- Business does not have an asset on its balance sheet.

There are three kinds of leases: financing, operating, and sales/leaseback

Checklist for Leasing Agreements

- Cost of the lease: How much is each payment and when are payments due? What is the real amount of rental fees or interest? Is there a "grace period" before you are assessed charges? What is the total amount you will have to pay over the lifetime of the lease?
- Extra Costs: Must you pay security deposits? Installation charges? License fees? Taxes? Penalties for early cancellation of the lease?
- Lease flexibility: What are the provisions for skipped or late payments?
- Service: What maintenance and service will be provided and by whom? Is there a guarantee for the equipment? Must you pay for service? Will you receive a refund for downtime if the equipment fails?
- Insurance: What level of insurance coverage is included in the lease? Will you be assessed an insurance fee or be billed separately by the insurance provider?
- Equipment Upgrades: What are the provisions for upgrading or replacing equipment during the term of the lease? How much will it cost you?
- Residual Value: What will the equipment be worth at the end of the lease period? (This directly impacts your lease payments.)

Small Business Administration
The U.S. Small Business Administration (SBA) was created in 1953 to assist small businesses. The SBA has both direct and guaranteed loans.

The term **direct loan** simply means that the SBA makes the loan directly to the small business. A **guaranteed loan** is where a financial institution makes the loan to the small business and a portion is guaranteed by the SBA. The following information is taken from SBA materials. It briefly discusses the average number of employees or annual sales volume required to be considered a small business by the SBA.

- **Manufacturing:** Maximum number of employees may range from 500 to 1,500, depending on the type of product manufactured.
- **Wholesaling:** Maximum number of employees may not exceed 100.

- **Service:** Annual receipts may not exceed $5 to $14.5 million, depending on the industry.
- **Retailing:** Annual receipts may not exceed $5 to $13.5 million, depending on the industry.
- **Construction:** General construction annual receipts may not exceed $7 to $17 million, depending on the industry.
- **Special trade contractors:** Annual receipts may not exceed $7 million
- **Agriculture:** Annual receipts may not exceed $0.5 to $3.5 million, depending on the industry.
- **CDC loans:** An optional size standard applies: net worth of $6 million or less and average annual net earnings of less than $2 million.
- **LowDoc:** Under $5 million in sales and less than 100 employees.

Certified Development Companies
A Certified Development Company (CDC) is a non-profit organization sponsored by state or local governments or by private interests. The purpose of a CDC is to contribute to economic development and job creation by making government loans. The exact nature of these loans varies. Contact your local Small Business Development Center (SBDC) or Chamber of Commerce to find the CDC that serves your area.

Community Development Loan Funds
The most famous of the financial institutions involved in this type of lending is South Shore Bank in Chicago. To find out who makes community development loans in your area call the National Association of CDLF at (215) 923-4754.

Rural Economic & Community Development
The Rural Economic & Community Development (RECD) a federal agency, offers loan programs for small businesses in rural areas.

Federal Loan Programs

SBA 7(a) Loan Guaranty Program
This is the largest of the SBA loan programs with over $10,000,000,000 in loans in federal fiscal year 1995. That's right—$10 billion! The loan is made by a private lender to a small business and the SBA guarantees a percentage of the loan. Historically, this percentage has been about 90% but recent budget problems in Washington may cause some changes. The 7(a) loan program was designed to help small businesses obtain long-term financing for needs such as working capital, machinery, equipment, fixtures, leasehold improvements, building acquisition and construction. On January 1, 1995, the maximum amount guaranteed by the SBA was reduced to $500,000.

The LowDoc Program is for loans of $100,000 or less

Special variations of the SBA 7(a) program include:

- **LowDoc:** A variation of the 7(a) loan program for loans of $100,000 or less. The program will finance either new or existing businesses and places less emphasis on collateral. It features a rapid approval process, usually two or three days. The following is taken from a current SBA brochure:
    - LowDoc is for small business loans of $100,000 or less.
    - The applicant completes the front of a one-page SBA application; the lender completes the back.
    - Lenders will require additional information from the applicant.
    - For loans over $50,000, the applicant includes a copy of U.S. Income Tax Schedule C or the front page of the corporate or partnership returns for the past three years.
    - Personal financial statements are required for all guarantors.

- **GreenLine:** Another variation of the 7(a) loan program. This loan program provides a term commitment, of up to five years, for a revolving line-of-credit loan to finance the cash cycle of your business. SBA will guarantee a maximum of 75% of your bank loan with a dollar limit of $750,000. Your business must meet the same eligibility criteria as for a 7(a) loan and the following collateral requirement. A GreenLine must be secured by a first lien on the assets being financed (i.e., inventory, receivables, contracts, etc.). Personal guarantees will be required. Secondary liens on machinery and equipment, real estate, and personal assets may be required where necessary.

- **Women's Pre-qualification:** Another part of the 7(a) loan program. As the name implies, this program is only for women-owned small businesses and is intended to provide greater access to capital. The maximum loan request is $250,000.

- **CAPlines:** The program where the SBA helps small businesses meet their short-term and cyclical working capital needs. The SBA guarantees 75% of the line of credit up to a maximum of $750,000 with a maximum maturity of five years.

Guaranteed loans
Both of the loan programs described in this section are available through commercial banks. The small business must be "export-ready."

- **Export Working Capital Program:** The SBA will guarantee up to 90% of a loan with a maximum of $750,000. Loans are for twelve months with two annual renewal options. The loan may be used as described below:

    - Pre-shipment working capital (To finance the labor and materials for manufacturing or purchasing goods for export)
    - Post-shipment exposure coverage (To finance foreign accounts receivable generated from export sales)
    - Combination of pre- and post-shipment financing

- **International Trade Loan:** This is a long-term loan program for small businesses engaged or preparing to engage in international trade. The SBA can guarantee a maximum of $1 million for facilities and equipment and $250,000 in working capital.

Export programs for small business

Direct loans

As the name implies, these are loans that are made by the SBA directly to the small business owner. The maximum amount of an SBA Direct Loan is $150,000 and such loans are only available to applicants unable to secure a bank loan or a 7(a) loan. Direct loans are available only to businesses in high unemployment areas, Vietnam-era or disabled veterans, handicapped persons, low-income individuals and businesses located in low income neighborhoods. Direct loan funds are very limited and applicants are generally placed on a waiting list.

SBA 7(m) MicroLoan Program

These direct loans are made through intermediary lenders, generally nonprofit organizations with experience in lending and technical assistance, such as a CDC. This short-term loan has a maximum of $25,000 and preference is usually given to small businesses owned by women, low income individuals, or minorities. Some intermediary lenders may require that borrowers complete a training program or receive business counseling. Loan proceeds may be used to purchase furniture and fixtures, machinery and equipment, inventory, supplies and working capital.

SBA 8(a) Participant Loan Program

Eligible small businesses must be 8(a)-certified firms. These loans are either direct loans or through lending institutions with the SBA guaranteeing the loan. Loan proceeds may be used for fixed assets or working capital.

CDC Programs

- **502 Loan Program:** This loan programs focuses on providing long-term, fixed-asset financing to small businesses in rural areas. Contact your local CDC to determine if your business is eligible. Eligibility criteria include type of business and the population of the community where your business is located. The loan is processed by a CDC.
- **504 Loan Program:** This loan program supplies long-term (10 to 20 year), fixed-asset financing through a CDC. Typically, 504 loan proceeds are provided as follows:
    - 50% by an unguaranteed bank loan
    - 40% by an SBA guaranteed loan
    - 10% by the small business borrower

Contact your local CDC to obtain more information and begin the application process.

Certified Development Companies (CDC) are sponsored by state or local organizations

RECD Programs

- **RECD Intermediary Relending Program:** The Intermediary Relending Program (IRP) makes loans to small businesses and other legal entities in cities having a population of less than 25,000. The loans are made by intermediaries such as CDCs or other public or private nonprofit organizations. The loan can finance up to 75% of a project with a maximum of $150,000. Loan recipients must document their inability to finance the project through commercial credit or other government programs. This program often appears locally under the name Rural Development Fund.
- **Business & Industry Program:** The Business & Industry (B&I) Loan Guarantee Program has a goal of encouraging the commercial financing of rural business. The business owner applies through a commercial financial institution and together they submit an application to RECD. Most types of businesses in cities having a population of less than 50,000 are eligible. There is no official minimum loan but typically loans begin at the SBA 7(a) maximum and can be as high as $10 million.

Other Government Loan Programs

State, county and city

The loan programs offered by state and local government vary greatly from state to state. Many counties and cities have established **small loan funds.** Check for such programs in your local area. The local government may operate the program themselves or contract with another agency, such as a CDC, who has experience managing loan programs.

Revolving loan fund

Local and regional revolving loan funds were originally capitalized with grants from the Economic Development Administration, the HUD Community Development Block Grant Program and/or other sources. These loans take a subordinated security position to a loan from a private lender. Loans are limited to eligible borrowers in particular counties or cities. Specific standards and rules vary from region to region.

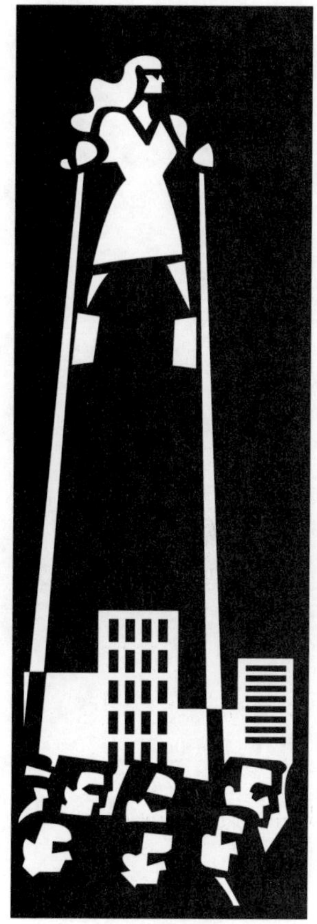

Other Sources of Money

The previous section discussed a wide variety of sources of debt capital that are frequently used by small businesses. This section covers some less common sources of debt capital as well as sources of equity capital. All sources described here are available to and used by small business owners but are not as common as those in the previous discussion.

Equity

Preliminaries

If you decide to seek **equity capital** it is important to remember that you are selling a portion of the ownership of your business. If your business is presently a sole proprietorship, (owned by one person), it will have to become either a partnership or corporation. How you structure your partnership or corporation is a complex issue and you should seek legal counsel. Let's take a brief look at some important issues.

With equity capital, you sell a portion of your business

If your business is a partnership, then the provider of equity capital will become a partner. How much of your business the investor will own is a matter of negotiation. You should have a written Partnership Agreement that carefully details the rights and obligations of each partner. Most partnerships are general partnerships. Limited partnerships have specific accountability and tax considerations. If you are intending on forming a Limited Partnership, you will want to consult an attorney well versed in these legal and tax considerations.

If your business is a corporation, the source of equity capital becomes a stockholder in the corporation. A corporation may issue preferred stock in addition to common stock. Preferred stockholders do not vote at stockholder meetings. It is also possible to issue more than one class of common stock and that not all classes of common stock have voting rights. It is also possible to sell the investor either warrants or rights for shares of stock in your business.

Limited Liability Companies are a new and increasingly popular form of business ownership. If you are interested in obtaining equity capital in conjunction with this new form of business structure, consult an attorney who is up-to-date in this new area.

Be aware that obtaining equity capital is a long and time consuming process when compared to debt capital. Sources of equity capital will demand more information, take longer to review it, and you will need to utilize attorneys and accountants to complete the process.

Venture capitalists

Venture capital is capital that is invested in an unproven business concept. These are high-risk investments in very young companies. In return for taking this level of risk they are looking for investments that can provide them with very high rates of return on their investment.

Seed Ventures Capital Club

Seed Ventures Capital Club began when 4 successful entrepreneurs got together for dinner one spring evening in 1992. They met to discuss ways they could help other businesses get started in their communities. Each of the original four members were successful, retired entrepreneurs. They had money to invest and each was enthusiastic about investing in ventures that were too risky for banks. The members contributed equally to their venture capital fund, which was then invested in start-up businesses they all agreed had the most potential. Their goal was to help 'the small guy' with a good idea, and a business plan good enough to transform a concept into a company.

They knew that venture capital clubs are increasingly important sources of seed funding for small businesses. So they banded together to select and fund businesses they felt have potential. In exchange they would often help steer a company by sitting on a board of directors.

It was the mission of Seed Ventures to "recycle" their capital into the next generation of emerging companies. They preferred to invest in several moderate sized projects, rather than a few big projects. Their preferred parameters for investment are:

- *$20,000-100,000 per project*
- *Businesses willing to accept and act on their managerial and strategic consulting*
- *Service or manufacturing businesses with a strong management team*
- *Businesses that emphasize high quality, "old-world" service or products*
- *Businesses that are based in their communities that draw on the skills and expertise of local talent*

Seed Ventures looks for projects to invest in that complement their existing portfolio of investments. They enjoy facilitating networking among their businesses, creating a coalition in which the "sum is greater than the parts." When Ryan Mikus' business plan and funding proposal came before them at one of their dinner meetings, Seed Ventures liked what they saw, and decided to take a closer look.

Investment clubs

In some communities a group of local business people will pool their money to make investments in both new and established businesses. This allows smaller investors to participate and allows larger investors to spread their risk.

Finding investment or venture capital clubs is simply a matter of keeping your eyes open and asking everyone you know if he or she knows whom to contact. Local Chambers of Commerce are a good source of information. There is no official listing of these groups and they range in size, investment strategies and targeted industries. Some are high profile and easy to locate, while others are much harder to identify and contact—and aren't listed in any phone book.

Ryan Mikus stumbled onto Seed Ventures after researching investment clubs on various small business related sites on the Internet and speaking with his local Chamber of Commerce. He prepared an executive summary of his business plan, and a cover letter in which he clearly outlined how much funding his business needed. After working closely with his brother-in-law, Bob and an advisor at the SBDC in Kalamazoo, he calculated that he would need $30,000 for the first year of operations. If sales followed as he planned, he estimated that he would need only $10,000 in year two.

Ryan Mikus sent his package of materials to 10 different investment clubs and individual investors.

His coverletter and business plan summary was one of nearly 30 that the Seed Ventures received in December of 1996. They liked his punchy, to the point writing style, and moreover, they liked his business idea. His high-quality, hand-crafted copper lamps made in his own barn fit with their investment strategy. They decided to meet with him.

Investment bankers are in the business of providing capital to start up and young businesses

Investment bankers
The term Investment Banker is often confusing because of the word banker. Investment Bankers are in the business of providing equity capital (not loans) to new and young businesses. They do this by selling shares of stock in your business to their customers. They rarely deal in amounts less than $1 million and are only interested in businesses that will offer attractive rates of return to their customers. They are interested in the same types of businesses as Venture Capitalists but take less risk.

Private investors, wealthy individuals
Every area has some local entrepreneurs who have been very successful. These people, sometimes referred to as "**angels**", are often a source of both debt and equity capital for local small businesses. Your attorney, accountant, or banker can often put you in touch with these types of individuals.

Professionally managed pools
Large institutions often pool their money into a partnership that invests funds in small businesses.

Strategic partnerships
Large corporations often invest in small businesses that will help the corporation enter new markets and provide a return on investment. It is important to understand that their motive is more than profit. They are looking for small businesses that fit into their strategic mission or long-range plan. For this reason these relationships are most commonly referred to as strategic partnerships. There are three common forms for such investments:

- **Stock purchase:** The large corporation buys some of your stock and becomes a stockholder in your company.
- **Joint venture:** The corporation and your business form a partnership. The corporation provides capital.

- **Licensing agreement:** You retain total control of your business but sell the corporation specified rights to use/sell products or services that are developed and owned by your business.

Employee Stock Ownership Plans

Employee Stock Ownership Plans (ESOPs) are similar to other methods of selling equity in your business. The difference is that you are selling the shares of stock to your employees only and not to outside investors. This provides your business with equity capital to use for expansion and gives your employees a vested interest in the success of your business. This is not an option for a start-up company unless you are well-financed upon starting.

Small Business Investment Company (SBIC)

The SBIC Program is the only venture capital program that is sponsored by the federal government. The SBA licenses private venture capital firms and these SBIC's have a portion of their financing guaranteed by the SBA. They provide equity capital and long-term debt to small businesses with significant growth potential.

Specialized Small Business Investment Company (SSBIC)

SSBIC's operate the same as SBIC's but have additional financial leverage provided by the SBA. This is done in return for agreeing to invest in, or loan to, small businesses whose owners are socially or economically disadvantaged.

Initial Public Offerings

IPOs: hot new stock issues

The term Initial Public Offerings (IPOs) refers to the first time a corporation offers its shares of stock for sale on a publicly traded stock exchange.

Government regulation of IPOs

The federal government passed the Securities Act of 1933 which began government regulation of publicly traded securities. The Securities and Exchange Commission (SEC) was formed and is the agency that enforces federal statutes relating to securities. Any agreement that obligates your business to pay another party a portion of your profits or to make interest payments is a security. The 1933 act was passed to fulfill two objectives:

1) To provide full and fair disclosure to prospective investors of the character of new securities.
2) To prevent fraud and misrepresentation in the sale of securities.

Thus, the federal government closely regulates the issuance of publicly traded stocks. However, several cost effective options are available to the entrepreneur seeking equity capital. Consult a securities lawyer before you begin to issue any shares of stock.

Small Corporate Offering Registration (SCOR)
Forty-two states allow SCOR offerings which enable small businesses to originate and sell their own stock offering to investors with a minimum of cost and regulation. Most small businesses can raise up to $1 million per year provided they have equity equal to at least 10% of the amount of capital being raised. Form U-7 is the registration form for corporations registering under state securities laws that are exempt from SEC registration under Rule 504 of Regulation D. Average costs to prepare a SCOR offering are under $25,000.

Intrastate Offering
An intrastate offering is a security offered and sold only to residents of one state. Such an offering is exempt from SEC regulation but is still subject to the securities laws of the state where the security is being offered. Such state laws are often called **blue sky securities laws**. In order to qualify for the intrastate offering exemption your business must:

1) Be incorporated in the state where it is making the offering;
2) Carry out a significant amount of its business in that state; and
3) Make offers and sales only to residents of that state.

There is no fixed limit on the size of the offering or the number of investors that may purchase your stock.

After several meetings and a visit to the coppersmith shop, Seed Ventures settled down to look closely at Ryan Mikus' business plan and decide whether or not to invest. They evaluated his business proposal, considering the following:

- *Is there a potential for consistent growth and profits?*
- *Does the business offer a target return on investment?*
- *How strong is the management? Can it be easily improved?*
- *What are members' gut-feel about the business concept and the principal owner(s)?*

Seed Ventures had made many successful investments in new businesses based on the success formula outlined above. For them, their gut-feel was perhaps the most important criteria. They had a good gut-feel about Ryan Mikus. In addition, they were most impressed with his business plan. They felt his lamps were truly of the highest quality, his cost and revenue projections on target, and his market potential solid. Their only concern was that Ryan was a sole proprietor. Seed Ventures had learned in their own businesses and other investments, that partnerships had a higher rate of success and were generally more stable businesses. They decided that they would invest in Ryan's business, but would require that he find a partner who had stronger management skills. They would help Ryan to identify and recruit this partner.

Pending this, they would invest $30,000 in Ryan's business in the first year and $10,000 in the second year. They would then reevaluate his operations and profitability and make a judgment about whether to invest additional funds.

In exchange Ryan agreed to meet with members of Seed Ventures as frequently as needed to make sure his business was on target. Seed Ventures usually met with their businesses once or twice a month at first, then asked for status reports each month thereafter. They reserved the right to suggest management and/or strategy changes in the business. In most cases this advice was much appreciated and put to good use.

Other Innovative Sources of Financing

Suppliers

A supplier can be a source of capital in two ways. First, a major supplier may be interested in providing you with equity or debt capital. A strong motivation for the supplier is often a desire to work with a proven wholesaler or retailer in your geographic area.

Suppliers: sources of capital or favorable terms

Second, you may be able to negotiate favorable terms for your business if the supplier is motivated by having your business present in your area. These favorable terms can include discounts, extended payment periods, increased cooperative advertising, or any other concession that can help your business conserve its capital and succeed. Your success will put money in the pocket of your supplier.

Find a Loan Guarantor

Small business owners often find that they cannot support the collateral and capacity requirements of their loan application. As a result, they are turned down for the loan or are offered a smaller loan. It is possible to overcome this problem by finding a third party that will guarantee your loan payments. This third party is someone with assets that can be used as collateral for your loan.

The banker is thus able to satisfy collateral requirements and you get the loan. The third party is assuming the risk of making the loan payments if you default. The cost of such a guarantee varies greatly.

Use a Loan Broker

Loan brokers are in the business of finding financing for business owners and other individuals. They often charge an up-front flat fee although it may be a percentage of the loan amount being sought. You usually pay a fee for their services whether or not you are successful in obtaining financing. Some brokers will charge a smaller up-front fee and then take a percentage of the loan upon approval. In any case, you should select a loan broker very carefully. Ask for references of businesses that they have helped finance.

Venture Capital Tips

- "Yes" to investment requests comes fast–usually within 21 days. If you don't get an answer within this time, save your energy and focus on other investors and funding sources.
- Use easy math. Investment analysts are continually approached and hear many pitches for funding. They respond better to easy equations and simple math. Make your calculations simple, clear and to the point.
- Demonstrate that you are at risk. Investors are more likely to seriously consider funding your business if they know that you have a very high incentive to succeed: your own personal money is tied up, you are trying to repay personal debt or recover a former lifestyle.
- Don't pay yourself too much money. Make sure your uses of funding are clearly described, and the important money goes towards essential expenses of establishing and growing your business. No golf club dues, expensive lunches or exorbitant salaries!
- Have a plan for getting to market. Venture capitalists want to see concrete, aggressive plans for generating sales and earning profits. They want to know the exact timing for getting a product or service to market and how long it will take to become profitable.
- Toot your own horn! Highlight any awards, media coverage and partnerships, major clients, including larger, well-established organizations with whom you have done business or partnered.

Franchising

It is possible to purchase some franchises with little money down and obtain the start-up financing directly from the franchiser. When a direct loan is not possible, the franchiser might guarantee your loan with a lender familiar with the franchiser.

Owner Contract, When Buying a Business

When selling their business most entrepreneurs want the buyer to obtain financing so that they can be "cashed out." This is often not possible and the seller must carry a contract for a portion of the selling price. The term of such a contract, interest rate, and collateral are all negotiable between the buyer and seller.

With Seed Venture's help, Ryan Mikus met Betsy Dykstra, a 29 year old business development manager for a major lamp company in Holland, Michigan. She was in operations for 2 years and had managed sales for the last 3 years. She also had an MBA from Michigan State. Ryan Mikus' business was exactly the kind she had been wanting to work with and she and Ryan personally hit it off well. They made good partners.

The partnership between Ryan Mikus' Coppersmithed Works and Seed Ventures also worked well. In the first 6 months he met with members of Seed Ventures more than 10 times, getting guidance on establishing wider distribution, investing in additional equipment, and evaluating a possible move to a better equipped workspace. By the end of his first year of operations, the business was breaking even and Ryan's lamps were being sold in fine furniture stores and "gallery" stores in Michigan, Illinois, Indiana, New York, California, and Colorado. By doing his homework, writing a good business plan and searching for funding Ryan gained a new partner who filled in his weak spots, investor "angels" who funded his venture, and a promising young business.

Grants

There are a few grant programs for small business owners. This section describes two programs of the federal government that are operated through the SBA.

Small Business Innovation Research (SBIR) Program

The SBIR Program began in 1982 and is designed to stimulate technological innovation and give small businesses the opportunity to propose concepts to meet the research and development needs of the federal government. There are 11 federal agencies participating in the program and the SBA publishes Solicitation Announcements on a quarterly basis. There are three phases to the program.

- Under Phase I a small business can receive a grant up to $100,000 to develop a prototype or otherwise prove a concept.
- Under Phase II a small business that successfully completed Phase I can receive as much as $500,000 to further develop the prototype for production.
- These is no government funding for Phase III where the product is actually placed into production.

Small Business Technology Transfer (STTR) Program

This program started in 1992 and is similar to the SBIR program. The small business submitting an application must collaborate with a nonprofit research institution.

Conclusion

There are many ways to finance a new business. Creative combinations of leasing equipment, public or private loans, angel investors, and supplier agreements, can become a patch-work of seed money to grow your businesses. However, entrepreneurs must first know exactly how much money their business will need and what its projected revenues and expenses are. With a well researched business plan and carefully written funding proposal, entrepreneurs can use their innovation, drive, and sense of purpose to find just the right source of funds. As an entrepreneur, your perseverance, persistence and confidence in your idea you will inspire potential lenders and investors to become as enthusiastic about the promise of your business as you are.

PART VIII
TURNING IDEAS INTO ACTION

Chapter 42
OVERCOMING BARRIERS AND PITFALLS

About This Chapter:
- *What to expect in your start-up*
- *Identifying common challenges*
- *Overcoming barriers and pitfalls*

Introduction

Aligning your personal and business goals, testing the feasibility of your business concept, and estimating your business's financial requirements are all part of the initial planning process for start-up entrepreneurs. As a new entrepreneur, it is particularly important that you are willing to look at both the positive and potentially challenging aspects of your new business venture. This chapter will highlight some of the barriers and pitfalls your venture may face, not as a means of discouraging your entrepreneurial enthusiasm, but as a means to help you anticipate, analyze and remove obstacles as you encounter them. Searching for ways to effectively overcome or minimize barriers will enhance your entrepreneurial success.

"No greater enterprise will ever begin if all obstacles must first be overcome."
—Napoleon Hill

What to Expect

Today there are more opportunities than ever for small businesses. But there is also a growing collection of hazards, a universe of detail; a plethora of downright confusing issues to deal with. Entrepreneurs have more to gain, more to keep track of, and more to lose than ever before. So how can you stay on top of it all?

Luckily, there is no shortage of tools at your disposal with which to overcome obstacles. Computer technology, mentors, temporary and contracted workers, and the Internet are all tools that can help your business grow faster, and better than you thought possible.

Anticipating Murphy's Law, "Anything that can go wrong will go wrong" may be one of the healthiest attitudes a start-up entrepreneur can adopt. Educating yourself as to the most common problems, challenges and mistakes made in your particular type of business is one of the greatest things you can do to ensure your success.

To resist change is to resist progress

Change is Constant

Today's fast-paced business environment presents many challenges to start-up and existing entrepreneurs. You should expect to be in a continuous cycle of learning, asking questions and finding innovative ways to solve problems. The question is: how?

As in any new endeavor, the hours in the day don't seem to allow for all the demands of your time. Studying, however, is not one of the activities that can or should be eliminated. Study your industry, the competition, the *Wall Street Journal*. Read everything you can, from philosophical approaches to business to the *Harvard Business Review*. The more your read, the more you will recognize the need to try to incorporate change in your business. To resist change is to resist progress.

Who Has the Answers?

The sharp entrepreneur doesn't attempt to "go it alone." Using a team of informed experts eases the burden of trying to learn everything at once. Recognize your own abilities and use good judgment in choosing other people to fill in your knowledge and experience gaps. As an entrepreneur, you have already made the decision to enter a world filled with ambiguity. Learn to actively involve needed experts who can help you shorten your learning curve. Delegate responsibility. Seek out advisors and mentors for additional insight and support. Above all, try to remember that you don't have to have all the answers, but you must be willing to ask all the questions.

Stay focused!

All Things to All People

One of the greatest temptations for start-up entrepreneurs is to try to be everything to everybody at the same time. Staying focused, maximizing resources, and targeting product or services to the market keeps your business focused on planned goals and objectives. Resist the reaction to move outside of your initial focus and beyond your core strengths.

Alignment of Personal and Business Life is Rare

While undercapitalization heads the list of common causes of small business failure, spousal or partner relationship issues ranks a close second. Your investment of time, energy, and financial resources in your business requires family support. Perfect alignment of personal and business worlds is difficult to achieve, particularly in the start-up or growth phase. Involving your family members in critical decisions, keeping communications intact, and having fun are keys to personal and business success.

Common Barriers and Pitfalls

The following section reviews the most common challenges to start-up businesses, and offers some suggestions for overcoming the following challenges.

Cash Flow Crisis!

Cash flow—life line of a successful business

Cash flow problems occur when entrepreneurs underestimate their start-up costs and overestimate their cash flow. By preparing a sample cash flow projection, you'll become aware of how it can help to monitor your current **cash position** and project your future cash needs.

Suggestions

- Plan, plan, and plan again. Your cash flow projection, like all other parts of your business plan, should be a living, breathing, up-to-date document. Continually review your progress, comparing your estimated to actual cash flow. Revise your projections monthly.

- Identify other available resources. Recognizing that neglecting cash flow analysis can bankrupt your business is the first step. Identifying a back-up plan if projections fall short will prevent the "reactive panic" at the front end of your project. Build a rapport with your banker well in advance of anticipated needs, and keep your banker informed of your positive progress and your potential challenges.

- Keep an eye on overhead. The keys to longevity for entrepreneurs are to keep your overhead down, to jump on opportunities and to develop banking relationships early on in your business.

- Look at all of the "what if's," not just the good ones! You have prepared a sample cash flow projection based on what you thought were realistic expectations. Now project a "worst case" cash flow scenario, and ask the tough questions: What if the sales aren't made? What if collections are twice as slow as anticipated? What if my material costs are double what I expected? Studying the results of a worst case scenario will aid in the preparation of a back-up plan.

Credit Issues

New businesses face the challenge of establishing **lines of credit** with suppliers. A start-up business, having no credit history is limited in its ability to establish open lines of credit with suppliers or service providers. The result is additional strain on your cash flow.

Suggestions

- Recognize that you may have to start out on a **cash on delivery** (C.O.D.) basis with suppliers, and plan appropriately in your cash flow projections. Establish a positive payment history from the start by agreeing to the C.O.D. terms, or by asking for small open lines of credit with short payment terms. Pay promptly to build a positive credit history, thus increasing the term and amount of your credit line.

- Keep in contact with your suppliers. Let them know via newsletter, memo or phone call how your new business is doing. Establishing a personal relationship will go along way towards establishing a credit line.

Growing Too Fast

A common problem among start-ups who have latched onto a significant technological breakthrough (like laser technology in surveying equipment) or tapped into a fast-paced trend (Internet service providers) is that there may be a much greater demand for the product or service than anticipated. While this problem may seem like one you would want to have, growing too fast can destroy the business that does not have access to the **capital** required to grow.

Suggestions

- Take time to anticipate **ramp-up costs** if your business falls in the category of "rapid growth." If you have limited personal access to additional financing, you should create a cash flow model that highlights how much additional funding would be needed to keep pace with exploding market demand. While it may not be possible to include all of the anticipated ramp-up costs in initial start-up financing, knowing the range of additional funds required is essential to determining the ongoing needs of your company's high growth stage.

- Consider the approach for the next level of financing early. Bank negotiations for second level funding can take time, particularly if the time between the first round of funding and required expansion funding is short. Initial Public Offerings (IPO) are very time consuming to prepare and coordinate. Planning and projecting are the keys.

Being in a Hurry

Enthusiasm for your new business is certainly admirable. Being in a hurry, however, may result in poor decision-making which causes more problems in the long run. Prior planning allows you to act more quickly and solve problems before they reach the crisis stage.

A common philosophical trap of start-up entrepreneurs is the "I'll give it a year" attitude. This is reflective of the desire to be an instant success. Similarly, the anxiety surrounding your first sale or contract can lead you into poor decision-making. Reactions like cutting the price before market acceptance for your product takes hold, changing products mid-stream, or deciding to "just do everything myself", are a few examples of potentially bad decisions caused by hurrying.

Suggestions

- Slow down long enough to analyze the long range consequences of a decision. Further, review decisions before you implement them, particularly in the early stages of your business development. Develop a method that works for you.
- A common reaction to time pressures is to throw money at a problem. Entrepreneurs regularly fall into the trap of plowing all of their life savings into the project to save the time of having to go through the bank lending process or face other time-consuming issues. More money will not cure all the problems you face.

Government Regulations

In the everyday shuffle of managing a business, small businesses often overlook smaller, yet essential details. One of the most important areas (and the difference between being in and out of business, in some industries) is governmental regulations.

Suggestions

- Allocate responsibility to someone in your business to stay on top of Occupational Safety and Health Administration, Environmental Protection, tax and other relevant legal guidelines. What documents must be prepared? What expert assistance do you need? Are there new ways you can minimize the business's tax burden? Is your business complying with the latest product labeling and safety regulations?

- Create a schedule for all filing, inspection and reporting dates and clear, well-organized files containing all relevant materials.

Ignoring Employee Management Issues

As businesses grow, their character inevitably changes as the solo entrepreneur transforms into a team of people. The business team may include full or part-time employees, independent contractors, suppliers, advisors and assistants. Small businesses often focus on sales and meeting orders at the expense of the people who make those sales possible: employees. This often results in poor communication, loss of efficiency and low morale.

Suggestions

- Clearly allocate responsibility and authority by creating and updating an organizational chart for your business, including written job descriptions. Who reports to whom? For what tasks is each person responsible? By when? How frequently will their performance be evaluated?

- Reassess and update your employee compensation and incentive plans as needed.

- Set clear goals and targets for each person's performance, and update them frequently with a formal, written job performance system.

A Lack of Innovation

It's not unusual for successful, growing businesses to settle into comfortable patterns of behavior, missing out on excellent opportunities to stay innovative and competitive. Businesses can become infatuated with their own excellence, and ignore technological developments, changes in customer demand or competition. Before they know it, their rocketing growth has slowed and fizzled, and they are left to wonder why.

Suggestions

- Never stop learning. Stay abreast of new practices and technology available in your industry, attend trade shows, Chamber of Commerce functions and read trade journals.
- Always ask yourself and your team, "Can we do this better?" "Are we letting ourselves be as creative and efficient as we can be?"
- Stay close to your customer. Has the market for your products or services changed? Are customers' needs and preferences changing? Have their habits changed?

Tips for Fast Growing Businesses

- Maintain a diversified base of customers.
- Review the activities of your employees and independent contractors.
- Always evaluate customers' ability to pay.
- Make sure that your insurance coverage grows along with your business.
- Plan leadership and employee succession.
- Stay on top of cash management and financing needs.
- Have contingency plans for slack in market demand and economic down turns.
- Stay on top of tax and other governmental regulations.
- Maintain a balance in how you spend your time.
- Enjoy the ride—have FUN!

Conclusion

Small companies that are well managed can run circles around average large ones. How? By staying on course with a clear focus on a market niche and letting your business's core strengths guide your growth. It is also important to anticipate challenges and create contingencies before you actually need them, and, before you get buried.

These suggestions are as valuable for fast growing businesses as they are for small business simply hoping to maintain their market position. It's a lot to think about, but if you allocate responsibility, enlist the help of mentors, partners and experts, you can stay on top of your business as it grows, and better yet, overcome obstacles. Remember, the only thing stopping your business from being completely successful is you: Your ability to plan, learn, innovate...and act.

Chapter 43
MANAGING GROWTH

About This Chapter:
- *Small vs. big*
- *Profitability before growth*
- *Monitor and control of a growing business*
- *Financial considerations*

Introduction

Businesses grow everyday without deliberate effort on the part of their managers. Simply by virtue of taking orders, delivering products and collecting payment from an expanding base of customers, a business can grow. Businesses also grow because their management has made the strategic decision to grow. Frequently they do this by attracting and utilizing additional financing to expand their product offerings, extend their geographic reach, or tap into new markets.

The biggest challenge confronting entrepreneurs is how to intelligently and deliberately grow their businesses. All too often entrepreneurs leave the future of their businesses to fate: they surf market trends and congratulate themselves for being in the right place at the right time. They let the market determine how fast the business grows. Unfortunately, they have it all backwards!

This chapter will aid you in mastering the forces that affect your ability to manage growth. After exploring why you would want to grow, the tools and strategies necessary to grow your business will be discussed. Many are financial in nature and have been discussed at greater length in other parts of this book.

Why Grow?

Why would you want to grow your business? You've figured out the best way to operate, you've mastered the pricing of your products or services, and feel you are serving your customer better than anyone else. Your business fits you like a glove, why would you want to change by growing?

Businesses, for a whole range of reasons, choose to face higher risk and increase their debt load in order to grow. Most do it to enhance their earnings and profits. Consider the major reasons that you would want to grow your business:

- To dominate the competition
- To enhance profits

- To master new challenges
- To hit your break-even point sooner
- To achieve economies of scale
- To acquire volume discounts on inputs and materials
- To enhance your company's status and prestige
- To acquire a broader, more diversified customer base
- To reach more attractive customer segments
- To better serve your customer by being more accessible, having more resources, and offering lower prices

The benefits of growing your company are not just limited to your market presence or bottom line. Well-managed, smart growth can mean exciting, exhilarating, and fulfilling times for your entire business team.

Grow only if it delivers additional and proportionate competitive advantages and opportunity for profitability

Yes, But Should I Grow?

So you know what the benefits of growth are and why you want to grow your business, but should you? Can your business honestly perform better or achieve more by being larger than it is now? What will the cost of that growth be?

Today there are two major schools of thought on this subject. One says "bigger is better": in order to be a player, you must dominate your market and spread your company's business over the widest base of customers possible. This fuels **globalization**, a strategy popular with many of the largest businesses in America today. The other school of thought promotes the idea that "small is beautiful": being small and specialized allows businesses to target niche markets, and tailor their products to customers better than any of their larger competitors. This approach seems to be supported by the development of the fastest growing segment of the American economy: small businesses. By virtue of being small and agile, these businesses target their customers' needs with precision.

Think carefully before you leap into the task of growing your business. Growth simply for the sake of growth serves no other purpose than to dilute your precious resources and energies. As your business evolves your primary goal should be to grow only in as much as it allows you to increase your profitability.

Likewise, the strategic choices you make regarding your business should be motivated by goals to increase competitiveness and customer loyalty. To achieve this, you need not necessarily be larger than you are now. Companies in all segments of the economy are trying to mimic small businesses by downsizing, reorganizing, re-engineering, and creating employee teams. Learn from them: if you can better serve your customer and your market by being small, then by all means, stay small.

Grow to increase profits

What Is Managed Growth?

If you decide to grow, your task is to learn how to grow successfully. Entrepreneurs who are successful in the long term distinguish themselves not just by a keen understanding of their market and the forces that drive it, but also by their ability to plan their own growth. They do this by identifying trends before these impact their business. They plan for their financial needs and begin laying the groundwork for additional financing long before they need it. They create management controls to sustain their performance and utilize budgets to safeguard their cash. Lastly, these keen managers create a confident, professionally managed business that can attract the best investors, employees, and customers.

Many businesses do enjoy great success simply by going with the tide. However, the success they enjoy is rarely sustainable, and is usually based on circumstantial factors. The results of failing to manage and plan for your business's growth can spill over to affect nearly all areas of your business's performance. The pitfalls of failing in this type of planning include:

- Experiencing only limited, short-term growth
- Inability to maintain consistent standards of performance
- Unprofessional behavior
- Poor employee morale
- High employee turnover
- Loss of profitability
- Inefficient use of resources
- Loss of customer loyalty
- Diminished quality of products
- Inability to focus on core strengths
- Paralyzed or overworked leadership
- Cash crunch and bankruptcy

It's sad but true: many start-up businesses give entrepreneurs a bad name. Owners are unprofessional, overworked, unfocused, and unable to provide a consistent, quality environment for employees to serve customers. Why?

Because they fail to take precautions and plan for their future. Don't let your business be so intoxicated by the "quick hit" of big orders and exploding demand that you fail to equip your business for long-term survival!

No Pain, No Gain

Human nature seems to dictate that most people simply don't like change. Change leads one into unknown territory and that uncertainty can be downright scary. On the other hand, the most exciting and positive events seem to happen in times of change. During times of transition, your employees develop new skills, challenge themselves, and discover their potential. As many successful entrepreneurs have proven, growth without uncertainty and crisis is simply not possible. This doesn't mean that your business must be subject to disaster or a near melt down: a crisis simply defines that place where the next move is frightening and requires that you let go of old ideas and begin anew with forward momentum.

Sustained growth: equipped for long-term survival

Warning: Slow Down!

Before you dive into an aggressive growth strategy, let's take a moment to discuss too much growth. Are you missing any warning signs that you are growing too fast? You might ask if there's such a thing as too much growth. Unfortunately, experience proves there is. All too often, businesses go from booming sales to bankruptcy because they fail to notice the warning signs of out-of-control growth. Some of the problems associated with too-rapid growth are:

- It obscures weak management, poor planning, and inefficient use of resources
- It causes employee well-being, training, and loyalty to be overlooked
- It dilutes good leadership
- It causes undue stress and burnout
- It causes the business to stray from its original goals and objectives
- It causes leaders to retain all control and fail to delegate
- It complicates communications among team players
- It causes quality of products and services to diminish

If this sounds familiar, you may want to consider putting limits on your business's growth. This is not as crazy as it may sound! Since well-managed, measured growth is the easiest to sustain, why not create a safeguard to keep your business on track? You could limit your business to a set level of customers, a specific geographic region, or a particular order size.

These limits need not be permanent; they will contain your growth to a manageable level for a specific period of time. The goal is to keep the business operating within its "maximum performance" range.

Here are some specific problems that signal trouble for growing companies:

- You have cash flow problems and difficulty paying bills
- You have high employee turnover
- You overlook the details of running your business
- Your customers are complaining
- You've lost focus on your business's core competencies

In a growth company profit is a requirement <u>not</u> a luxury

Updating Your Business Plan

Let's say that after careful review and consideration, you decide that now is the time to grow your business. The next step is to review and revise your business plan. Even the most well-researched and ingeniously written business plan can become out of date when conditions change. Your customer's profile or market segment can shift, economic conditions can change, your competitors can introduce ground-breaking products, or a new technology can emerge. All of these can make your original business plan obsolete.

In order to ensure that this doesn't happen, you must periodically update your business plan. And you must certainly update it before you set out to court additional financing for your young business. To do this, ask yourself the following questions. The answers will guide the evolution of your new and improved business plan.

- Are the original goals for the business still reasonable?
- What are the potential threats and opportunities for my business?
- Are my assumptions still valid?
- What are the business's strengths and weaknesses?
- Can I measure my progress according to my original standards?
- Is the business able to provide the highest quality product or service it can?
- Does my business plan reflect my business today?
- What resources does the business require to perform and achieve its goals?
- Are my customers' needs being expertly and uniquely served?
- Can my business operate more efficiently that it is currently?

Remember, your business plan will be used by current and potential investors, customers, suppliers, partners, consultants, and lenders to gauge the profit potential of your budding enterprise. Think of the growth phase you are entering as beginning an entirely new business. Look at your challenges and opportunities with fresh eyes, and set new goals for yourself. By updating your business plan you are creating the document that will guide this exciting phase of your business. Coincidentally, this will also be the tool that may very well allow you to attract additional financing to grow!

Tools for Growth: Management Reporting and Controls

Growth provides:

- Opportunities
- Motivation
- Choices

Before we discuss how to put your investment capital to work in a given growth strategy, let's review the key tools your business will use to manage its growth. What are these tools? They are trained management, smart employees, and control systems, to name a few.

Cash Management

Why is cash so important in growing your business? Aside from enabling you to pay your bills, cash on hand signals to many investors the health of your business. Well-devised cash management strategies show potential investors that you know how to run a profitable business and will be able to service your debt. For this reason, the time to cultivate relationships with potential sources of financing for your business is while you are doing well: meeting your plan, managing your cash, and feeling confident.

Your ability to skillfully manage cash determines your business's ability to grow. On the other hand, poorly managed cash can drain a business's vitality in the blink of an eye. Take a moment to look at several of the biggest drains on cash that a business can have:

- Interest payments on debt
- Cash tied up in excess inventory
- Uncollected accounts receivable

Unfortunately, projecting, monitoring, and conserving cash is not one of the more exciting parts of managing a business. But it can be the most important! A cash flow projection and a budget can be your best survival tool. If you're not good at tracking spending and calculating your cash balances, make sure you enlist the help of someone who is.

Cash Management Tips:

- Work out a format with your accountant that fits your business's needs
- Schedule your accounts receivable by major accounts
- Pinpoint collection problems one by one
- Schedule major cash payments by supplier
- Plan at least 6 months in advance
- Review and update your plan weekly
- Deal with cash shortages before they occur
- Use your banker as a partner

Banks judge businesses on the basis of profits not sales

Good Management Skills

The manager's essential task is to ensure the internal health of the organization. This means creating a system of internal "checks and balances" which allow the business to perform consistently, professionally, and profitably.

So you're great at schmoozing with investors, charming bankers, and crunching numbers with venture capitalists, but can you run day-to-day operations? When we talk about the management of a new business we're talking first and foremost about its leader, YOU. The success or failure of a business hinges on the ability of the entrepreneur to shift gears and effectively:

- Delegate
- Think strategically
- Manage resources
- Manage people
- Manage time
- Closely manage complex issues

Good Team Building

The key to being a good leader is creating a good team. This means gathering committed and inspired people who can work together toward common goals. As discussed in Chapter 29 *Forming and Managing Teams*, these people need not all be full-time employees, but they do need to be aligned on a common purpose and in close communication with one another.

Your role as the leader of your business is to delegate the responsibility and authority necessary to perform key tasks. If you hope to grow your business, you cannot do it alone. So start building a **high-performance team** now.

Good Time Management

Given the time demands on your business and limited resources, effective **time management** is more important than ever. Why do you need to develop and practice good time-management skills? People can only be in one place at a time, and only do one task at a time. Understanding how to maximize your time will improve productivity, improve the quality of performance, lower your stress level, and enhance relationships with employees, suppliers, and customers. Your family might even appreciate the benefits of a calmer, more organized you.

Here are some of the basics of time management:

- Identify how you spend your time: How much time do you spend on each task?
- Identify wasted time
- Identify your "high-performance clock," those times of day when you are most productive; use this time for your most demanding tasks
- List your personal priorities

Then:

- Work with a team
- Rank your tasks by importance
- Delegate
- Complete your tasks in a single session, if possible
- Set aside an appropriate amount of time to finish your tasks
- Set aside regular time for family, exercise, hobbies, etc.

Strategies for Growth

So, your business is profitable. You are on course with your personal and business goals. You're up to date on the dynamics of your market and you know the direction in which you want to go. You are inspired and your team is excited. Excellent! You want to take your business to the next level, either by increasing your customer base, tapping into a new market, or offering additional products or services. You need a strategy to accomplish this. What businesses need most at this stage is additional financing. Chances are this is what you will need as well. Below are the factors that differentiate various growth strategies:

- Level of risk
- Speed with which growth is allowed
- Cost of growth
- Implications for the future of the business
- Degree of management control allowed

Financial Considerations

If you are going to grow, you probably will need more money than your business can generate internally. Operating a growing business requires careful management to cultivate external financial resources before they are needed.

What does this sort of planning entail? It requires making intelligent, forward-thinking decisions about your business's financial needs. It means getting access to crucial external **seed capital** when you need it.

Using your knowledge about your business as a guide allows you to select the method of financing that is right for you. The remainder of the chapter will describe the broadest selection of choices for financing. Financing for your business can come from:

- Individual investors (the public)
- Private investors (wealthy individuals)
- Professional investment funds (venture capitalists)
- Foundations (grants for special causes)
- Corporations (joint ventures and equity investments)
- Commercial banks
- Investment banks

Additional internal financing for your business can come from:

- Reinvestment of profits from sales
- Sale of assets
- Credit from suppliers (extended payment terms)
- Customers (payments in advance)
- Employees (stock purchase plans, wage/salary concessions)

Begin to cultivate external financial resources before they are needed

Your job in seeking additional sources of financing for your growing company is to choose two or three of these and focus on them. You may choose a source of financing based on the length of time the funds are available, the costs involved in acquiring them, or the amount of control over your company you are able to retain.

Securing capital will require selling investors on your track record, business plan, quality employees, personal vision, professionalism, and future growth.

Capital Acquisition Checklist

- Update your business plan
- Document your business's track record
- Identify new opportunities, problems, and challenges
- Show your business plan to potential investors to get feedback
- Identify how much money you need over what period of time
- Review your financial statement and know it like the back of your hand
- Update your targeted sources of financing often
- Be straightforward, direct, and honest
- Be confident, optimistic but realistic
- Show conviction and demonstrate passion

You may ask, "How am I supposed to be confident and direct when this entire business seems so new and uncertain?" It's a fact that there are far fewer successful entrepreneurs out there than there are sources of financing. Also, there are more eager venture capitalists and investors than there are profitable ventures to invest in. For this reason, if you've demonstrated your ability to manage a profitable and growing business, you have every reason to be confident.

Utilizing Capital for Growth

Once you've decided whether or not to pursue additional internal or external financing, or debt or equity financing for your business, you will need to decide which strategy you will employ in putting the new funding to work for you. So now you have the cash, what will you do with it? Consider these brief summaries of the costs and benefits of some additional growth strategies for your business:

Acquisition

Acquiring an additional business is a fast method to grow your business. An acquisition can take many forms depending on:

- Tax considerations
- The business goals of the participants
- The industry/type of companies involved
- The regulatory environment
- The amount of assets involved

The successful acquisition of a business entails negotiating the structure and favorable price of the deal. This depends on your strategy for growth. The starting point for growth by acquisition is an evaluation of your potential acquisitions':

- Cash flow
- Assets
- Sales, cash, profitability, and break-even projections
- Market position
- Management team
- Organizational "culture"
- Advantages of merging or "synergy" with your business
- Legal considerations
- Management of the new business entity

Joint Venture/Partnership

Growing your business by entering into a partnership with another business is an increasingly common growth strategy used by both big and small businesses. This entails choosing a partner with complementary skills, technologies, customers, or products, to achieve things neither business could do alone. Today, joint ventures are very popular ways to:

- Minimize risk
- Achieve economies of scale
- Create "synergies"
- Gain technical know-how
- Expand geographic reach
- Acquire patented products, technology, or processes
- Expand the customer base
- Lower costs, pool expenses
- Increase product offerings

Just because you manage a small business, doesn't mean that a joint venture or partnership doesn't offer you the same benefits it offers bigger companies. This strategy is widely used and written about today. All of the benefits listed above apply to your business just as much as they apply to the Microsofts and GE's of the world. Despite all the fancy terminology and complexity of structuring such an agreement, these partnerships are tools like any other: they help you to better serve your customer, be profitable, and increase your competitiveness in the market.

There are other methods to expand growth. Some to consider:

- Going international
- Franchising (with you offering the franchises)
- Enlarging your product or geographic area

Conclusion

The biggest challenge confronting businesses that grow is maintaining professional, consistent performance. All too often the demands on a growing business's time and resources prove too much; they fail to serve the customers, move away from their core competencies, and experience cash management problems. In the worst cases, they lose control over their profitability, resulting in a crisis where the business's very survival is on the line. Failing to follow a cohesive plan, businesses can fall in the trap of reacting rather than acting. These threats to your growing business can be avoided by careful, well-thought-out planning.

This chapter has presented a basic mix of the tools and strategies that aid in planning, growth strategies, and sources of financing to fuel your growth. Only by reaffirming your vision for your business can you tap into the essential motivation and inspiration that will fuel continued growth. With these insights in hand, you are prepared to expertly guide a thriving business to long-term success. So what are you waiting for? Go for it!

Chapter 44
DEALING WITH LARGE ORGANIZATIONS

About This Chapter:
- *The government*
- *Big business*

Introduction

Imagine your little company just received an invitation to bid from the U.S. Forestry Service. They need 25,000 Forester Hats delivered over the next six months. It would double your business! You feel excited, ecstatic, and frightened. What do I need to do to win the bid? Aren't there a lot of rules when you deal with the government? Can I produce that many hats in six months? Will they pay me on time? Although dealing with large businesses and the government as a client can be both enticing and daunting, many small businesses do so today. The U.S. government learned during World War II that it needed to rely on the quick response of small businesses to get needed war materials. Today's changing economic environment fosters small businesses who are able to supply larger companies with products and services faster than larger competitors can. Small businesses can reap many rewards through their alliances with large businesses and government alliances. Perhaps you can too!

Having a large organization as your client does entail some risks and changes in the way you normally do business. You may have to put up more resources on the front-end in your marketing efforts, pre-qualification procedures, and budgeting. Your administrative costs may be higher due to increased record keeping and procedural requirements of the larger organization. Also, some big businesses and the government are slow to pay your invoices, so this may put a strain on essential cash flow. However, with careful planning you can learn to successfully navigate the requirements of doing business with larger organizations.

Doing Business with the Government

As a small business owner, why would you want to complicate your life by doing business with the government, a confusing bureaucratic organization? There are actually very good reasons why you might want to:

- There are 1,200 U.S. government buying offices all over the country. There is probably one fairly close to you.

- The U.S. government is the largest purchaser of products and services in the world. Getting a government contract could dramatically improve your business. Of the $200 billion the government procures every year, nearly 20% of the business is given to small businesses.
- Many government contracts are long term, generally awarded for five years. Winning these contracts can provide steady cash flow.
- The U.S. government buys everything. It's likely they buy what you make.
- Doing business with the U.S. government may help you diversify your markets.
- There are U.S. government programs set up to help small businesses compete with larger business.

Government Small Business Programs

During and after World War II it became very evident that the government needed many suppliers of all types of goods and services in the event of another emergency. As a result, the Small Business Act of 1958 was enacted to require that more contracts are awarded to small business owners. The government recognizes three types of small businesses:

- **Small Business:** Every industry has a small business size established by the Small Business Administration. Each industry has a Standard Industrial Classification (SIC) code which indicates a size standard. It is categorized by the number of employees, or a maximum amount of annual revenues.

Small is beautiful

- **Small Disadvantaged Business:** This classification requires that you first meet the standards in the SIC code above. At least 51% of your business must be owned and managed by people who are socially and economically disadvantaged. This group includes Black, Hispanic, Asian and Native American minorities.

- **Women-Owned Small Business:** To qualify you must meet the SIC code standards and must be 51% owned, managed and controlled by women.

As a small-business owner, you can be at a real advantage in dealing with the U.S. government versus the playing field operating in other business arenas. The U.S. government has set goals stated as a percentage of procurement dollars to be spent with small business. Some bids are specifically set aside for small business which means these are the only bids that will be accepted. There is also the Small Business Administration's 8(a) Program in which only small disadvantaged business firms can apply and be accepted.

Jane Hayward and Karen Summers, both former office managers, started their company after they coordinated several office moves for their respective employers. Their company, Interlink, Etc., manufactures lightweight office furniture on wheels. Hayward and Summers decided to bid for a government contract to supply office furniture after finding out about the government's program for women-owned businesses. Their successful bid to provide office furniture for the regional Social Security Administration offices in Texas and Oklahoma has netted them over $100,000 in sales for their first year of business!

Government Market Study

Now that you know how helpful obtaining government business can be to your business, how do you go about attacking this market?

First, define your geographic government opportunities and determine what government offices are located in the area near your business. Be careful not to stretch your boundaries too far and thus fail to perform. This will endanger future government business opportunities. As you look at your geographic opportunities, consider the following guidelines:

Look at geography first

- **Size:** Consider your size and what geographic area you really can handle. If you are a very small business, you may want to select a small area with an option to grow into a larger area over time. If you are already a larger business, you may want to go for an entire state.

- **Location:** Where are you located in relation to government facilities? If you are in a populated area, you will discover more government opportunities than in a smaller, rural area.

- **Experience:** How much experience do you have and how good are you at what you do? If you are new and still learning, you may want to stay close to your core competencies. However, if you have been in business a long time and enjoy good market share, you may want to expand your customer base.

- **Type of Business:** Does your business require you to be on-site or can you manage the business from a distance? If you can manage from afar, your selling area can be much larger.

Where are Government Buying Offices?

After assessing how large a geographic range you can handle, identify the **government buying offices** within the geographic area you have defined. There are ten regions grouped by the Small Business Administration. Identify your region and go to your local Small Business Administration Office and ask for a listing of the buying offices in your region.

Government and Personal Selling Techniques

Now is the time to meet with the appropriate people in the buying offices and begin to employ the sales process you learned in Chapter 39 *The Art of Selling.*

- Call the buying office closest to you and ask for a Standard Form 129—Solicitation Mailing List Application. Fill out the form in detail. Remember, insufficient and incorrect information may keep you from getting the opportunity to bid.
- Next, call the buying office and speak with the small business specialist (SBS). They are responsible for recruiting new small business to ensure government standards are met and small business procurements are managed effectively by that office.
- Verify that this office does buy what you have to sell. Schedule a meeting with the SBS and the buyers who purchase the product or service you sell.
- Make the sales call and remember some of the basics of personal selling:
    - Be on time
    - Dress appropriately
    - Be prepared—bring several copies of your Form 12g so you can distribute to each buying influence and well as business cards and company brochures.

- Keep it short—The meeting probably won't take more than 30 minutes, so be prepared to make your points succinctly.
- Follow-up—This is as important as the meeting itself. You need to work with your SBS to ensure you have been added to the automated bidders list. Keep following up to determine if there are additional business opportunities.

- Contact the requisitioner—The buyer doesn't necessarily buy what will be bought; the **requisitioner** does. It is the buyer's responsibility to ensure the products and services meet the requisitioner's needs. If you have a new product, you may need to meet with the requisitioner. This can be arranged through your SBS.

Sell, sell, sell

Submitting an Offer

After you have successfully completed the steps above, it will take the buying office a couple of weeks to get your company loaded into its automated bidders list. Once in the data base, you will have to wait until a requisition comes in for the items or services you sell. There is a rotating system on the automatic bidder list which rotates offers among the different bidders. That way, the same bidders are not always selected.

There are three types of Solicitation:

1. Small purchase procedures. This is for procurements of $25,000 or less. The procedure is called a **Request for Quotation**. Your response is called a quote.

2. Sealed bidding procedures. This procedure calls for an **Invitation for Bids.** Your response is to offer a bid. The government will use a sealed bid in the following situations:

   - There is sufficient time for the sealed bid process
   - No additional information or discussion needs to take place
   - More than one sealed bid will be received
   - The bid is made based on price or other price-related decision criteria. A firm price contract will be awarded if your sealed bid is accepted.

3. Negotiated procurement procedures. This procedure is used when procurement is expected to be over $25,000. You will receive a **Request for Proposal** and your response is called a proposal. You will be expected to submit both a **technical proposal** and a **price proposal.**

How to prepare an Offer

Although you may have prepared hundreds of commercial offers during your career, doing business with the government can be both different and difficult. There are certain issues that you must be aware of such as:

- **Always respond**—that includes a "no bid." This way you will remain on the bidders list, as "no response" names are deleted.
- **Be on time** with your bid as the government will not accept late submittals.
- **Complete all the paperwork.** If you are unable to answer any of the multitude of questions, contact the appropriate official for assistance.
- **Be careful not to overlook any items** that might affect your price.

If you follow these simple guidelines and are patient, thorough, and professional, you are in a position to be considered for the contract award.

How to win a Government Contract

Winning contracts isn't easy, and you must work hard to be successful. Here are some keys to winning governmental contracts:

- **Be responsible.** Have your financial affairs in order, be prepared to submit references for similar work, be able to meet delivery schedules, and have the necessary technical skills and equipment necessary to do the work.
- **Have the most advantageous price.** All other things being equal, you should have the lowest price.
- **Be responsive.** Submit on time and comply with all the terms and conditions, warranties and specifications in the bid request.
- **Follow-up.** Contact the SBS to make sure you have done all that is required to be considered for the award.

Let's face it. You can't win them all—but you can try. By following these tips, you stand a much better chance of being successful than if you do not adhere to governmental "good business practices."

When Ken Dyer decided to grow his computer reselling business from commercial clients to the government, he knew that he would have to vary his approach to selling. He consulted with a friend who had prior experience as a state agency buyer.

Ken contacted his local government buying office and scheduled a brief, 15 minute presentation. Dyer emphasized the cost advantage to the buyer of dealing with a local reseller. He made sure that he followed up with the buyer and submitted a sealed bid well in advance of the due date. After waiting three months, Ken was elated to find out that his bid had been accepted. He won the bid to provide computers to the state's Division of Motor Vehicles while the division phased out its outdated equipment.

Types of Contracts

There are many types of governmental contracts. The major ones are listed below:

Firm-fixed-price contract

This is probably the government's most commonly used contract. It represents an agreement by the contractor to supply a particular product or service at a fixed price that won't change during performance.

Sharpen your pencil!

The Fixed-price contract with economic price adjustment

This contract allows the price to be revised upward or downward in case of a specific economic contingency. Usually there is a ceiling on upward adjustment but no floor on downward adjustment.

The Cost-plus-fixed-fee contract

In this type of contact, all of the contractor's costs of performing the work are paid by the government, plus a fixed fee. The amount of the fee is negotiated prior to award and doesn't change during the contract regardless of any changes in the cost of performance. This arrangement gives the contractor very little incentive to control costs since the fee remains the same whether actual performance costs are high or low. It can only be renegotiated if there is an increase or decrease in the scope of the work.

The Cost-plus-award-fee contract

This contract provides for reimbursement of all allowable costs incurred during performance and for both a base fee (profit) and an award fee (more profit).

The Time and Materials/Labor-hour contract

This type of contact is used by the government to buy labor at a fixed price (including all overhead, general and administrative expenses, and profit) and materials at cost.

The Indefinite-Delivery contract

These contacts are generally used to procure common supplies, commodities, or repair services. The three classifications are:

1. **Definite quantity contracts** are those which provide for delivery of a known quantity of a supply or service over a known period of time.

2. **Requirements contracts** provide for the filling of all requirements for a specific supply or service during a specified contract period. The quantity to be bought during the contract period is unknown at the time of award. This type of contract guarantees the contractor that all requirements for the supply or service contracted will be purchased from him or her and specifies a maximum amount to be procured. Deliveries are scheduled on the basis of orders placed with the contractor.

3. **Indefinite quantity contracts** provide for a contractor to furnish an indefinite or unknown quantity or a supply or service during a fixed period of time. They specify a minimum quantity the government will purchase and a maximum quantity the contractor will be required to deliver during the contract performance.

Of course there are an infinite variety of contracts, most of which are based on the above mentioned types. It is paramount that you understand the terms and conditions of each bid request prior to submitting your bid. Why? Because you will be bound to the terms and conditions as stated in your submittal. Failure to understand the type of contact can cost you dearly!

Post Award Activities

You won one! Congratulations! Now what? Actually, beyond following the definitive instructions in the purchase order issued by the government, there is very little difference than with any other contract.

The key is to put the customer first. You must do everything in your power to ensure that customer satisfaction is "job one." Here are a few pointers:

- Complete all paperwork exactly as requested
- Immediately report any problems that occur always citing "cause and cure" or what happened and how and when you will fix it
- Deliver exactly what was purchased on time
- Keep the lines of communication open—talk to your client
- Thank them for their business

The Mentor Program

The Department of Defense's "Mentor-Protege Pilot Program," established by Section 831 of Public Law 101-510, has a threefold purpose. First it gives major contractors an incentive to help small disadvantaged businesses enhance their capabilities in performing contracts. Second, it establishes business relationships between major contractors and small disadvantaged businesses. Third it increases the participation of small disadvantaged businesses. The major advantages for you are:

- Aid from the mentor in management or technical matters
- Loans
- Cash purchases
- Advance payment

In other words, you have access to the resources of a larger firm. If this type of close arrangement appeals to you, pursue it.

How To Work With Prime Contractors

Who are **prime contractors** anyway? Well, they are all those "Big Business" companies that are awarded huge contracts we all read about. Companies like IBM, Bechtel, Lockheed and the like. Why would this be of interest to the small business owner? Because when these giants are awarded major contracts, they are required by law to subcontract a portion of the work to small and small, disadvantaged businesses. Therefore, it may be in your best interest to solicit their business.

All of the marketing and sales techniques mentioned previously come into play here. As these prime contractors operate under the government's "Rule Book for Procurement" much of the same principles apply:

- **Do your paperwork.** Paperwork is very important to government contractors, a fact borne out by the mass quantities of paperwork government contracts require: certified payrolls, written change proposals, materials submittals, quality control plans, and much, much more. Most contractors dislike paperwork for two reasons: First, many don't know how to do it, and second, it costs them money. If you work with contractors, be prepared to do your share correctly.

- **Talk to them just as you would any other client.** Keep the lines of communication open. The subcontracts manager wants to know what is going on so they can keep their supervisors and the government advised.

- **Do the work on time and on schedule.**

There are a few differences between the government procurement and prime contractor procurement systems. Here are some of the most important:

- **Bid openings.** Contractors are generally not required to hold public bid openings or disclose bid opening results. Some do have public openings; some don't.

- **Solicitation publication.** Contractors are not required to publish their solicitations exceeding $25,000 in the Commerce Business Daily.

- **Determinations of Non-responsibility.** Prime contractors aren't required to refer determinations of non-responsibility to the Small Business Administration for review.

- **8(a) Program.** Prime contractors don't use the Small Business Administration's 8(a) Program to make awards to small disadvantaged businesses. They do, however, use other means such as set-asides.

- **Full and Open Competition.** The Competition in Contracting Act requires the government to provide for full and open competition. This means it must allow all responsible sources that request a solicitation package to submit a bid. This requirement doesn't apply to prime contractors. They must achieve effective price competition, which means they only need enough bids to ensure a fair and reasonable price.

Dealing with Big Business

Just as government agencies have certain requirement, procedures, policies and professionalism, so will large private companies. So it helps if you enter this arena with the right attitudes. It helps to remember the following:

- No matter what business you are in, your business is service. Determine what your big business partners want and deliver it.
- As a smaller company, you are able to exhibit many of the qualities large companies are attempting to emulate. Some qualities, such as speed, focus, and teamwork make up some of the core competencies of your company. Use them to your advantage when dealing with big business.
- As a niche or specialized company, do what you do best. Be honest about your capabilities and stick to your specialty.

Big business—big sales?

Competition is very, very keen when you attempt to sell your product or service to companies in the Fortune 1000. Unless you have a one-of-a-kind product, or a very unique service, the Fortune 1000 may not be where you want to market your goods.

Know Thy Self

If you have thoroughly and honestly assessed your human, financial, and physical (plant and equipment) strengths, and think you are ready to tackle the bigger clients, go to it! Remember, this determination should cover not only today's situation, but it should also assess your ability to expand while keeping the quality level high and the price competitive. If you can do all this without disrupting relationships with current clients, you might be ready to move into the "big time."

Service is the name of the game

Doing Business with Big Business

By dealing with big companies your company greatly benefits in the following ways:

- Big business purchases tremendous amounts of goods and services and probably buys what you sell.
- Doing business with larger companies may help diversify your markets.
- By selling directly to big business, you indirectly enter new markets.
- By doing business with large professional companies, your company can become "smarter" by learning from your association with them.

- Large companies often enter into long term contracts which can stabilize your cash flow.

These are only some of the many benefits for the smaller company.

Marketing and Selling

There are no miracle ways to approach these giants. All of the approaches to marketing and personal selling that have been mentioned elsewhere in this book apply to big business. The key is to commit to a marketing plan and stick to it. In other words, be patient and persistent.

Let's take a moment to review the key elements of marketing strategy, and focus in particular on some issues that are specific to a strategy that targets larger companies.

The first step of creating any marketing strategy is understanding your customer. How did you arrive at your decision to target big business? Perhaps they offer a unique opportunity to access larger markets, they are geographically close, or they offer you a longer-term, more stable source of revenue. Whatever the reason, you want them. As you would with any customer, you need to take some time and research your target. Start by answering these key questions:

- What is the nature of my customer's business?
- What is the single most important competitive factor for them??
- What is their core competency?
- Who are their competitors and where is their industry headed?
- What do they look for in partners?
- What is their "culture"?
- What is their buying process? Who are the key decision makers, users, gate keepers, and influencers? (For detailed discussion of this, see Chapter 39 *The Art of Selling*.)

These questions are designed to get you thinking about all the ways to understand your customer. Look at their business from every possible angle and imagine that their issues are your issues (since they will be if you win their business). With these insights, turn your attention to tailoring the four "Ps" of your marketing mix to match the needs of the large corporation.

- Product
- Price
- Promotion
- Placement

Ramona Davies regularly tackles big corporate clients with her skill set and industry knowledge. She is one of only a few "trend gurus" who regularly provide their clients in the consumer products industry with up-to-date market information and reliable predictions for what the next best trend will be. Ramona started her career at an international consulting firm doing marketing studies focused on the food products industry. By gaining an expertise in the coffee segment, and building a rapport with several major clients, she was able to start up a marketing forecasting firm that focuses on the coffee industry. Because she proved her worth to her clients while she was still working for the consulting firm, the large businesses felt comfortable continuing their business relationship with her when she started her own consulting business. By leveraging her market intelligence, Ramona is able to do business with major corporations in several countries.

Partnering with Big Businesses

Many factors in the current business environment have merged to create a climate in which businesses are partnering. Increased risks of doing business, global competition, new technology, and the demand for faster business cycle times are some of the new realities of business. However, joint ventures and partnerships have been used for a long time by entrepreneurs eager to expand their businesses or enter new markets. Some other reasons small businesses may partner include:

- Access to new technology or expertise
- Broaden their geographic scope
- Achieve economies of scale
- Build synergy with complementary skills, products or processes
- Increase sales
- Side-step or comply with trade regulations
- Pool costs and perform innovative joint research
- Learn new things from larger partners

A joint venture involves the creation of a separate business entity composed of two or more active business partners. These are also called strategic alliances or partnering agreements and can involve a wide selection of business, nonprofit or governmental organizations.

When considering entering a partnering agreement with a larger business, the first stop should be your attorney's office. Partnerships come in many different shapes and sizes and are tailored to meet the particular needs of the parties involved. The key to a successful agreement of any kind is understanding what each side wants, needs and brings to the partnership. Know what your choices are, the costs and benefits of each (financial as well as strategic, and competitive risks and benefits) before you enter any agreement. Also crucial for a successful partnership is a good fit between the different parties' personalities and business cultures.

If you have the product and service that big business wants, they may come to you. Big business wants quality, professionalism and reliable relationships with their partners. The major difference with big business is that their standards are often higher than other businesses. The key is to know who they are and what they want, and then set your strategy to meet their needs. This is how to successfully compete for the contracts with big businesses.

Conclusion

Should you decide it is time to go after the government and big business, prepare to do things differently. Yes, there will be more paperwork and bigger challenges. These large organizations each have their own way of doing things. The key to a successful business relationship is to lead with those characteristics that give you a competitive advantage, clear focus, speed and teamwork. Customer service is also critical to your success. Sharpen your pencil, deliver on time and remember, "small is beautiful!"

PART IX
CONCLUSION

Chapter 45
CONGRATULATIONS AND BON VOYAGE!

Entrepreneurs are the folk heroes of business today. You create jobs, launch innovative solutions, and spark economic growth in your communities. You turn risk into opportunity, fueling a more productive economy. You offer customers the products and services they want most, at prices and places customers want them. You combine opportunity with innovation.

Entrepreneurs fill gaps left by large corporations and government, providing viable opportunities and rewarding livelihoods for thousands of people. Every year entrepreneurs provide the dynamic leadership that leads to economic growth and community vitality.

"There is only one success—to be able to spend your life in your own way."
—Christopher Morley

As a NxLeveL graduate you are poised to join thousands of new entrepreneurs in energizing the economy by creating your own livelihood, your own way. You have begun the exciting process of transforming your idea from concept to a profitable business. You have invested the time and energy required to develop your skills and knowledge by completing the NxLeveL for Business Start-Ups program. Before you start on your new venture, we want to share some final thoughts with you.

The Nature of Profit

Businesses serve many purposes. They satisfy demand, fill needs, provide employment, facilitate the flow of goods and services, and spark innovation. However, as a business works to achieve these results, it must also work to generate profits.

The nature of profit dictates that a business entity must generate more money than it spends in the course of doing business. Any money left over after all expenses have been paid is profit that can then be paid out to the owners and investors. Or it can be reinvested to help grow the business.

Entrepreneurs are free from the traditional limits of standard pay for standard work. You can invent your work, your product, and the way you do business. But entrepreneurs are still bound by the laws of profitability.

The profits that result from the operation of a business must compensate owners for their time and investment in the business. Entrepreneurs also must be rewarded for the risks they have taken and the energy they have spent in the course of growing their business.

Such compensation is not the only reward entrepreneurs enjoy. Independence, creative freedom, and the fun of launching and managing a business all offset the long hours, risk, and uncertainties entrepreneurs face.

Customer Orientation

Where do profits come from? Customers. The genesis of any profit generated by your business is the satisfaction of customers' needs. People will pay for a quality product or service that meets their needs. How much will they pay? That depends on the type of need, reliability, level of innovation, and amount of convenience the product or service delivers.

In order to satisfy market needs, you must thoroughly understand your customer. Who are they? What are their most pressing concerns? What problems do they encounter on a daily basis? Where do they go to work? Play? Eat? Sleep? The answers to these and other marketing questions will guide you as you develop your product and your overall marketing strategy. In short, your business must fit your customer like a glove.

Remember, every effort you make and every dollar you earn is directly linked to satisfying someone's need. We think this customer orientation is critical to your success.

Opportunity Comes in Every Shape, Size, and Color

People who start up businesses, people who buy existing businesses, franchisees, people who invest in fast-growth ventures, artisans and craftspeople, consultants and contractors, all lay claim to the mantle "entrepreneur." Indeed there are as many different entrepreneurial opportunities out there as there are people thinking about them. What is your hobby? Best talent? Life goal? Biggest challenge? Innovative idea? What is the fuel that has launched the entrepreneur inside you?

"One's passion is whatever he is most interested in, and yours is success."
—St. James M. Barrie

Being a successful entrepreneur begins with finding your unique strengths and interests. Once you've done this, you must use them to your best advantage in order to build your business around these strengths. When you love what you do, you work harder, with more creativity and greater efficiency. When this synergy occurs, you have a powerful advantage over your competitors.

Learning and Entrepreneurship Go Hand in Hand

The power to succeed doesn't just come from knowing what your personal strengths are. It also comes from identifying your weaknesses and building your skills to compensate for them. Entrepreneurship is a continuous cycle of questioning, analyzing and learning. This is an atmosphere in which the truly curious-minded succeed.

Recognizing what you don't know and being willing to work to "beef up" your skills are critical elements of entrepreneurship. Remember, you needn't become an expert in every area of business management. However, you do need to understand enough about every element of your business so that you can ask the right questions and ensure that your business tasks are being done well.

You should never ignore areas of your business that intimidate or confuse you. Every aspect of business can be easily managed when it is broken down into smaller parts. Taking the time to ask questions and seek help makes every problem solvable. Once you've done this, you can make choices about allocating responsibility, resources, and, if need be, engaging the services of experts for certain aspects of your business. At the end of the day, no area of your business should be declared "off limits."

In the course of launching your new business, you must continually upgrade your knowledge and strengthen your skills. Can you imagine anything better than meeting challenges, learning, and increasing the profitability of your business?

Find a Partner, Create a Team

Committing yourself to a cycle of acquiring new skills doesn't mean that you must personally do everything. One of the most important things first-time entrepreneurs can do is to collaborate with a partner or a team. Collaboration is an essential ingredient in promoting creativity and efficiency, since one person can't possibly do or know everything.

The benefits gained from partners or teams are varied. Among other things, they can assist you in answering questions such as: Are your assumptions valid? Are you considering every option? Are you still on track? Keep in mind that being an entrepreneur does not mean you should or must work in a vacuum. When you feel overwhelmed by the challenges of your new venture, the insight and support of others will fuel you to continue. When you surround yourself with people who have complementary skills and alternative points of view, you save time, spread the burden of responsibilities, increase the credibility of your start-up, and improve the decisions you make. In short, by creating a pool of talent your business can draw on you increase the likelihood that your business will succeed.

The Impact of Technology

Few would deny the positive impact technology has had on business in recent years. Fewer still can ignore the positively explosive future of the information superhighway. If you haven't already climbed aboard this high-tech trend, perhaps the time has come to avail yourself of these powerful business tools.

Data management and communication tools are becoming more friendly and affordable for millions of users. Hardware prices are falling. Many software applications for communications, word-processing, database management, graphics, presentation and networking are pre-packaged to aid you in solving your business problems. Training to learn how to use these systems and improve your bottom line is readily available in most communities. We strongly encourage you to take a ride on the high-tech highway.

Ethical Issues

Moral leadership is not just an issue we face in our family life. Entrepreneurs face tough choices every business day. Business ethics are principles of right and wrong that often go far beyond mere legality.

Entrepreneurs realize a personal freedom few business people experience. Fair-minded entrepreneurs take great care in exercising their obligations to others in the community such as customers, employers, suppliers and investors. Emerging business leaders can demonstrate this sense of integrity and honesty in the day to day operation of their enterprises. After all, small businesses should reflect the higher ethical standards of the entrepreneurs who run them.

Community Involvement

No business operates in a vacuum. Everyone is a part of the communities in which they work. Your current and future customers, suppliers, employers and investors are also part of your community. Most businesses are tied to their community through investment or through markets. Self interest provides ample motivation for most entrepreneurs to be involved in their community life. In addition to arguments of dollars and cents, when businesspeople work for the betterment of their community significant contributions to the quality of life follow.

Communities need the leadership, innovation and persistence that most entrepreneurs possess in abundance. By "giving back" to your community you can experience both the economic and personal benefits such actions produce and your community will reap the benefits that only entrepreneurs can bring to the table.

The Rewards of the Business Plan

At the risk of repeating ourselves, we must reiterate that researching and writing a business plan is simply the most valuable thing you can do.

A business plan not only tests the viability of your idea, it provides you with a detailed and documented path to follow.

The business plan and all of its individual components: financial statements, marketing plan, organization and structure of the business, the description of the products and services the business will provide, etc. is not a static document. As your business changes, so must your business plan change. Revising and refining your plan on an ongoing basis are the heart and soul of "continuous improvement" and are critical to your success.

"If you don't know where you are going, you probably will end up somewhere else."
—Laurence J. Peter

A business plan should be compelling, easy to read, and informative. The answers to the questions anyone interested in financing, supplying, or working with your business should be outlined in the business plan. The best business plan consists of equal parts: inspirational narrative and architectural blueprint.

By this time, you probably have realized that one of the most valuable results of developing your business plan was the actual experience of constructing it. You have researched and fine tuned your business idea and developed an understanding of what it will take to make it a reality. Your have challenged your assumptions and become an expert on your idea. You are now in position to seek funding, attract partners, customers, workers, and suppliers.

There Are Many Paths To Follow

In the process of preparing your business plan, you have gleaned answers to your most pressing questions. Will you launch your original business idea, or, have you found some weaknesses in your idea? Will you seek a partner before you begin? Do you need to step back and reassess the time and energy commitment and the sacrifice your business might require? Will you dash out and discuss a loan application with your local banker?

As you can see, there are many paths you may take from here. We hope that by participating in this NxLeveL program you have gained significant knowledge about the basics of marketing, financing, producing, and planning a new business, and that you have a much broader view of the route that lies ahead in your own exciting, unique entrepreneurial journey.

We also realize that it is possible that you may have decided that entrepreneurship is simply not for you. Perhaps the risks and time commitments required for a long-term project do not mesh with your personal goals and interests. If this is the case, you will have saved yourself time, money and heartache. The introspection and self-analysis you have gone through will serve you well as you move on to redirect your efforts and find another business idea or another career better suited for you.

Welcome To the Entrepreneurial Network

Are you ready to take the plunge? If so, by participating in this NxLeveL program, you have joined a broad, national network of kindred spirits and fellow innovators. To date, thousands of people have emerged from NxLeveL programs. Many of these inspired entrepreneurs, with completed business plans in hand, are taking the steps necessary to make their business idea a reality.

We encourage you to take advantage of this rapidly expanding network of people and resources. The most valuable asset NxLeveL gives its participants is access to other people who have participated in and taught programs. The depth and breadth of their combined business and life experiences are golden resources. By sharing ideas and supporting one another, these entrepreneurs learn from each others' mistakes and explore new ways to achieve their goals. They also enjoy the comfort of knowing that others have experienced similar challenges, risks and rewards.

One way to participate in this network is to visit the Web site maintained by the Western Entrepreneurial Network. Another is to build on the relationships you formed with your fellow class participants. In addition, local trade associations, chambers of commerce, and Small Business Development Centers sponsor many events for small businesses. Attend, contribute, and benefit from them!

We are proud to welcome you into the NxLeveL network of entrepreneurs, and look forward to your rich contributions and future success stories.

The Journey Ahead

You have embarked on a journey into the world of entrepreneurship where the number of opportunities for reward are as numerous as the risks and the challenges you'll encounter. On this journey, initiative, creativity, and ingenuity triumph.

You have begun by arming yourself well. As one of the many people who have taken the time and expended the energy to study the basics of entrepreneurship, you now have tools with which to build your business and enhance the chances of its success and profitability.

The entrepreneurial vision is truly one of the most powerful and magical forces a person can possess. It can transform the quality of your life, enable you to achieve your goals, and provide you with the means to leave a legacy for your family and community. This vision is always a unique one that emerges from your own experiences, passions, and perspectives. When you combine your vision with your expanding knowledge of business, we hope your entrepreneurial journey will become fulfilling, profitable, and fun. Remember: the core principles of entrepreneurship are passion, persistence, and doing what you love.

Bon voyage and good luck, friend!

Part X
Appendix

GLOSSARY OF TERMS

The business world is filled with specialized terms. Understanding the business vocabulary will enhance your ability to understand entrepreneurial concepts and allow you to feel less threatened by the language in business discussions.

This section is designed for easy "look up" of common business terminology and defines acronyms frequently used in business.

8(a) Program: A program authorized under the Small Business Act, that directs federal contracts to small businesses owned and operated by socially and economically disadvantaged individuals.

ABELS (Automated Business Enterprise Locator System): An electronic database, sponsored by the Minority Business Development Agency, which provides information about purchasing goods or services from minority businesses.

Accounts Payable (A/P): An unpaid balance of money owed by your business, generally referring to amounts owed for inventory, supplies, and other such ongoing expenses.

Accounts Receivable (A/R): An unpaid balance of money owed to your business by customer accounts.

Accrual Method of Accounting: An accounting system in which revenues are recorded when earned and expenses are recorded when incurred, no matter when cash changes hands.

ACE (Active Corps of Executives): An SBA management assistance program matching volunteer business executives with business owners seeking advice on how to operate their businesses more effectively (also see SCORE.)

Acid Test Ratio: The relationship of "quick assets" (cash and other assets immediately convertible to cash) to current liabilities. This ratio is used by lenders to measure the ability of a business to meet its current debt obligations (quick assets divided by current liabilities).

Action Plan: A detailed plan, used internally, which includes objectives, actions, and a budget for the next year.

ADA (Americans with Disabilities Act [of 1990]): A set of federal laws that prohibits discrimination on the basis of disability; areas of compliance include job accommodations, hiring, access to public buildings.

Advertising: Paid, on-going mass communication from a business to customers. It communicates messages about a product, service, company in mass media like television, radio, magazines, or newspapers.

AEO (Association for Enterprise Opportunity): A national trade organization for microenterprise development programs throughout the United States. Members provide business training, peer support, and credit opportunities to owners of very small businesses.

Aging of Accounts Receivable: The listing of accounts receivable according to the length of time the unpaid balance has been owed. Analysis is a management tool used to focus on accounts that are not being paid in a timely manner, uncollectible accounts, and potential cash flow problems.

Amortization: The process of liquidating a cost over a long period of time (i.e., a home mortgage) which is amortized by periodically making a payment which is applied to reduce the principal amount of the mortgage.

Annual Work Plan: A detailed document which is the result of operational planning. Highlights from this plan are included in the business plan.

Arbitration: A system administered by the court system to resolve disputes and is increasingly used in lieu of litigation.

Articles of Incorporation: A document filed by a corporation with a state's department of commerce which states, among other items, why the corporation is being formed, what type of business it will be, and serves to register the corporate name.

Assets: Any items of value owned; items on the balance sheet that reflect value owned including cash, accounts receivable, notes receivable, property, and property rights.

Assumed Business Name: The name a business operates under. Most states provide for the registration of assumed business names which allow a way to protect the name from misuse by others.

Assumptions: Management's reasons or justifications for projected income or expense items on cash flow or other financial projections; assumptions should be documented and included as part of the financial information report to which it pertains.

Average Revenue: The average amount of money earned from selling one product or service.

Balance Sheet: An itemized report which lists assets, liabilities, and owners' equity at a given point in time. The standard balance sheet formula is: Assets = Liabilities + Owners' Equity

Bankruptcy: Condition in which a business cannot meet its debt obligations and petitions a federal district court for either reorganization of its debts or liquidation of its assets.

Barriers to Entry: Any factors that inhibit a business's ability to enter a market.

BBB (Better Business Bureau): A non-profit association that attempts to provide consumer information about businesses and attempts to control unethical business practices.

Bid Pricing: Pricing used by organizational buyers in which requests for proposals invite interested sellers to bid on a set of specifications developed by the buyer.

Bill of Lading: A shipping contract which outlines the terms of the shipping agreement and the means by which goods will be shipped.

Blue Sky: A law regulating the sale of securities, real estate, etc., especially designed to prevent the promotion of fraudulent stocks.

Board of Directors: The group of individuals elected by stockholders or appointed by management of a corporation who are responsible for directing the policies and overall affairs of the corporation.

Boilerplate: The detailed standard wording of a contract.

Bottom Line: The last line of a financial statement used to show net profit or loss.

Brand Image: Represents the overall impression of a brand by customers. This is formed by new information and past experiences.

Brand Introduction Strategy: Establishing market position for a new brand by building a distribution network and creating awareness and first-trial among consumers.

Brand: A name or symbol that represents a product.

Break-Even Analysis: Identifies the point at which total revenue equals total cost and profits are zero.

Break-Even Point: The sales level at which neither a profit is earned nor a loss is incurred. The basic Break-Even Formula is: S (break-even level of sales $'s) = FC (fixed cost $'s) + VC (variable cost $'s). Analyzing the break-even point will help to predict the effects of changing costs or sales levels on the income of a business.

Bridge Loan: A temporary, short-term loan used until more permanent financing is secured.

Brokers: Professional intermediaries who bring buyers and sellers together. Brokers do not have formal or lasting relationships with either party. They are primarily used by businesses that do not need to maintain their own full-time sales force.

Business Concept: A brief, but compelling, description of why a business exists.

Business Dissolution: For enumeration purposes, the absence from any current record of a business that was present in the prior time period.

Business Ethics: The principles that guide interaction with customers, employees, suppliers, partners, lenders, and investors.

Business Failure: The closure of a business causing a loss to at least one creditor.

Business Plan: A document presenting information about the past, present, and future of a proposed or existing business venture. Sections include: summary and overview, detailed information sections on management and organization, the product or service of the business, the marketing plan, financial condition and projections, the operating and control system, growth plan, and any pertinent attachments.

Business System: The dynamics and expectations that pertain to members of the business, including family members and non-family members, exclusively as occupants of business roles whether in senior management or at lower levels.

Business-to-Business Marketing: The sale of products or services to business for use in manufacturing and processing other products.

Business Trust: An unincorporated association organized to conduct business for profit. It is operated by a board of trustees for the benefit of certificate holders.

Buy-Sell Agreement: A contract which sets forth the terms and conditions by which associates in a business can buy out other associates.

Buying Center: A group of business managers who work together to select products and vendors and make final buying decisions; usually composed of individuals with different skills, backgrounds, and interests.

Bylaws: An agreement among shareholders of a corporation for the structure of the business. They typically include provisions for the annual meeting, size and manner of election of the board of directors, number and duties of the officers, voting requirements for merger, and similar matters.

Capital Expenditure: The spending of money on equipment, plant purchase, or expansion.

Capital Expenditures: Business spending on additional plant, equipment, and inventory.

Capital: Cash and/or material assets, tools, property, or equipment owned or used in a business.

Capital Stock: The total stock authorized or issued by a corporation.

Carrying Costs: The cost of tying up money by holding inventory, plus additional costs like taxes and insurance on inventory.

Cash and Carry Wholesalers: Wholesalers that sell from warehouse facilities. Buyers pay cash and transport their own merchandise.

Cash Basis: A method of recording income and expenses in which each item is entered as received or paid.

Cash Discount: A discount offered to buyers who pay bills within a specified period of time.

Cash Flow Projection: A financial planning document used to analyze, forecast, and understand when and how cash flows into and out of a business. This forecasting tool is useful in determining when and how much money a business needs to borrow during an annual cycle and/or to service debt.

Cash Flow: The movement, or flow, of cash in and cash out of a business.

Cash Method of Accounting: An accounting system in which revenues are recorded when cash is received and expenses are recorded when paid.

Cash Receipts: Cash generated from sales, accounts receivable, and loans.

CDC (Certified Development Company): A nonprofit organization that contributes to the economic development of an area by making government loans to businesses.

Certified Public Accountant (CPA): An accountant certified by a state examining board as having fulfilled the requirements of state law to be a public accountant.

Channels of Distribution: The network through which businesses move their products to their customers.

Chart of Accounts: A document for listing the unique account numbers given to every account.

Civil Law: The body of laws regulating ordinary private matters as distinct from laws regulating criminal, political, or military matters.

Closely Held Business: A business owned by a small number of persons (usually under 25) and whose interests in the business (shares, stock, partnership certificate, LLC memberships) are not publicly traded.

Code of Federal Regulations: Codification of the general and permanent rules of the federal government published in the Federal Register.

Collateral: The assets pledged to a lender to secure or support a loan.

Common Law: Creation of law through judicial application of precedent, much of which was inherited from England.

Competitive Advantage: Established when a business performs some marketing activity better than competitors: producing a better product, selling it for a lower price, distributing it more effectively, providing better service, or offering a wider variety of product or service configuration.

Competitive Analysis: Measuring a competitor's strengths and weaknesses.

Compound Interest: Interest earned on the principal and on previously accumulated interest.

Consideration: Something that suffices to make an informal promise legally binding, usually some value given in exchange for the promise.

Consumer Data Bases: Demographic or financial information about individual consumers gathered from applications for credit, drivers' licenses, or telephone service records.

Consumer Promotions: Short-term sales promotions to consumers.

Consumer: The final user of a product or service.

Continuous Budget: A budgeting technique in which twelve months are always shown, with a new month added constantly.

Contract: A formal agreement or a promise or set of promises between two or more parties that is legally enforceable.

Convenience Goods: Products that consumers buy frequently and without much reflection.

Cooperative Advertising: Advertising in which manufacturers and retailers pool their resources to promote both the product and the store. Manufacturers offer retailers allowances to advertise the manufacturer's product, allowing retailers to also include the name of their store.

Copyright: The exclusive right to reproduce, sell, publish, or distribute literary or artistic work, i.e., works of authors, composers, etc.

Core Competencies: A way of describing the things a business does better than any of its competitors.

Corporate Mission: A broad statement of what business or businesses the company should be in.

Corporate Refugees: People who have lost a high paying job in a large corporation and begun a new career based in their home.

Corporation: A group of persons authorized (by the state) to function as a separate legal entity having privileges and liabilities distinct from those of its individual members.

Cost Advantage: One type of competitive advantage in which a business can reduce production or marketing costs below those of competitors and is able to lower prices or channel savings into other areas.

Cost of Goods Sold (COGS): Costs associated with the sale of a product or service, which may include materials, freight, direct labor, and overhead.

Cost-Plus Pricing: A basic pricing method in which a business determines its costs then adds a desired profit margin.

Cost-Type Contract: A contract that provides for payment to the contractor of allowable and reasonable cost plus a profit.

CRA: Community Reinvestment Act (of 1977) - A federal statute enacted to ensure closer ties between financial institutions and their communities, and to foster greater access to and more information about small business loans.

Counter Offer: An offer or proposal made to offset or substitute for an earlier offer made by another.

Criminal Law: Concerns the rights of society as a whole versus the actions of one person.

Culture: The implied beliefs, norms, values, and customs that define a society. Culture leads to common patterns of behavior. Like countries, businesses can have cultures also.

Current Assets: Cash or other items convertible to cash within one year or items that will be used up by the business within one year; generally cash, inventory, short-term notes receivable, and accounts receivable.

Current Liabilities: Monetary obligations that are due to be paid within one year; generally accounts payable, wages payable, taxes payable, current portion of long-term debt, interest, and dividends payable.

Current Population Survey (CPS): Monthly survey conducted by the Bureau of the Census that provides estimates of the number of persons working, the number unemployed, and related employment data.

Current Ratio: Current assets divided by current liabilities, generally indicative of whether or not a business has sufficient current assets to meet the payment schedule of its current debts. The higher the ratio, the more likely a business is able to meet its current obligations.

Customer Orientation: When a business creates all of its product or service strategies around the needs of its customers.

Cyberspace: A linking up through a modem to access the World Wide Web which is often referred to as cyberspace.

D&B (Dun & Bradstreet): A firm that gathers and sells financial/credit information about businesses for other businesses or individuals.

Dealer: A distribution channel intermediary who is granted the right to exclusively sell a company's products in a franchise agreement.

Debt Capital: Business financing that normally requires periodic interest payments and repayment of the principal within a specified time.

Debt-To-Equity Ratio: The relationship of creditors' money to owners' money in a business, indicating the extent to which a business is dependent upon borrowed funds for its operation.

Decision Maker: The individual in a family or business who is ultimately responsible for the final selection of a product or service.

Demand Deposit: Money that is on deposit with a financial institution and that must be available to the depositor "on demand," such as a checking or savings account.

Demographics: The statistical study of population characteristics. Also, objective characteristics about consumers like age, income, occupation, marital status, education, or location.

Depreciation: The portion of the cost of tangible operating assets (such as buildings or equipment) recorded as expense for the accounting period; results from spreading out the cost of long-lived assets over several years.

Direct Labor: For a manufacturer, factory labor costs that can be directly traced to the products.

Direct Loans: Loans made by the Small Business Administration directly to a small business.

Direct Mail: Presenting a product or services to the customer via mail without the use of middlemen.

Direct Marketing: The sale of products or services by a producer directly to the final customer. Also, presenting promotional information directly to potential consumers via direct door-to-door selling, telemarketing, direct mail, catalogue, direct response TV advertising; any presentation of a product or service directly to the consumer without the use of a middleman.

Direct Materials: For a manufacturer, those materials which become an integral part of a finished product and can be conveniently traced to it.

Direct Response: Marketing that allows the consumer to consummate the sale without outside interaction; asks for an order, aims for instant results, provides easily measurable results.

Direct Writer: A type of insurance agent who represents only one company.

Discretionary Income: Amount of spendable or savable income available after providing for the basic necessities such as shelter, food, clothes.

Distribution System: A group of independent businesses composed of manufacturers, wholesalers, and retailers created to deliver what the customer wants, when and where they want it. Also known as a channel system.

Distributors: Usually wholesalers of industrial products.

Dividend: A share of profits paid to stockholders of a corporation.

Double Taxation: Occurs when corporate net income is taxed, then dividends are paid to stockholders and taxed again as income to the stockholders.

Down-Sizing: The elimination of employees, often in large numbers, as a cost-cutting measure; also known as "right-sizing."

Drop-Shippers (desk jobbers): Wholesalers who provide limited services, take title to the merchandise but do not take physical possession. They obtain orders from wholesalers and retailers and forward these orders to the manufacturer who sends the goods directly to the wholesaler or retailer. Commonly used for bulky commodities like lumber, iron ore, or gravel.

Durable Goods: Products that are used over time (computers, CD players, dishwashers)

Economies of Scale: A concept for mass production which means the more that is produced with the same machinery and overhead, the lower the per unit costs.

Employer Identification Number (EIN): An identifying number of a business entity obtained from the IRS by filing application form SS-4; a "social security number" for a business entity.

Enterprise: Aggregation of all establishments owned by a parent company. An enterprise may consist of a single, independent establishment, or it can include subsidiaries or other branch establishments under the same ownership and control.

Entrepreneur: One who creates or launches new business ventures, often assuming the risk and management of the business.

Equity: The amount of the owners' investment in the business; what remains after total liabilities are subtracted from total assets; also called "net worth."

Equity Capital: An investment in exchange for partial business ownership. The investor's financial return comes from dividend payments and from growth in the net worth of a business.

ESOP (Employee Stock Ownership Plans): A plan in which shares of stock are sold to a trust for the benefit of the corporation's employees.

Establishment: A single location business unit, which may be independent, called a single-establishment enterprise, or owned by a parent enterprise.

Estoppel: A rule of law which requires a party to perform where they led the other party into believing there was a contract.

Expenses: The outflow or other using up of assets by an entity in order to sell goods or services; expenses are subtracted from revenues to determine net income.

Export Management Company (EMC): A firm which buys and then repackages goods for export.

Factoring: A method of financing in which the business sells its accounts receivables at a discount for cash.

Family Business: A business in which two or more family members have a significant ownership interest and/or participate in the senior management, and where the ownership may be passed on to a the next generation.

Feasibility Study: A study to determine if a business opportunity is worth pursuing.

FICA (Federal Insurance Contributions Act): Legislation under which taxes are levied for the support of Social Security.

Financial Intermediary: A financial institution that acts as the intermediary between borrowers and lenders. Banks, savings and loan associations, finance companies, and venture capital companies are major financial intermediaries in the United States.

Financial Statements: Accounting reports that generally include a Balance Sheet, an Income Statement (also called a Profit & Loss Statement), a Statement of Owners' Equity, and a Statement of Cash Flows.

Financing Lease: A lease that usually does not provide for maintenance service, is non-cancelable, and lasts the expected economic life of the asset.

Fixed Costs: Costs that do not vary significantly with the volume of out-put or sales, i.e., utilities, rent, depreciation, interest, administrative salaries. Also, costs that are constant regardless of quantity of products or services sold.

Fixed Rate: An interest rate that does not change during the life of the loan.

Fixed-Price Contract: A contract that provides for a specified price (or, in some cases, an adjustable price) for the supplies or services being procured, usually within a stipulated contract period. Under this type of agreement, maximum risk and responsibility are placed upon the contractor.

Flexible Budget: A budget which includes a range of activity levels, used to compare actual results to a budget which reflects actual sales volume.

Focus Group: A group of 6-12 people interviewed for the purpose of gathering general qualitative data about their preferences, opinions, beliefs, and experiences. Moderated by a trained professional who provides open-ended questions. Also, a selected group of potential consumers (or other defined category of participants) who participate in a structured discussion for the purpose of providing their unbiased reactions to a product or service.

Franchising: The linking of a parent company (franchiser) to independent "offspring" companies via a contract that allows the independent company owner (franchisee) to buy the license (franchise) to own and operate the business according to the parent company's comprehensive conditions and stipulations.

Freight Forwarder: A person or firm that arranges to pick up or deliver goods on instructions from a shipper or consignee from or to a point by various necessary conveyances.

FTC: Federal Trade Commission

Full-Time Workers: Generally, workers who work a regular schedule or more than 35 hours per week.

FUTA: The Federal Unemployment Tax Act.

Gatekeeper: The person in the purchasing process who controls the information flow to the buying center; may also recommend and approve potential vendors.

General Ledgers: A business record which includes details of all accounts.

General Merchandise Wholesalers: Full-service wholesalers that offer a broad assortment of merchandise. They often lack depth in individual product lines, but perform several services like storing and controlling inventory, processing orders, and transporting goods.

General Partnership: Two or more persons who jointly own a business; general partners participate fully in management of the business, and liabilities are personal and unlimited.

Goodwill: Non-tangible value of a business, generally referring to the difference between the business's market value and the market value of its net tangible (appraisable) assets.

Gross Domestic Product (GDP): The most comprehensive single measure of aggregate economic output. Represents the market value of the total output of goods and services produced by a nation's economy.

Gross Profit: Net sales (gross sales less returned merchandise, discounts, or other allowances) minus cost of goods sold; also referred to as "Gross Margin."

Groupthink: The practice of approaching problems or issues as matters that are best dealt with by consensus of a group rather than by individuals acting independently.

Guaranteed Loans: A loan made by a financial institution to a small business with a partial guarantee given by the Small Business Association.

High-Involvement Purchases: Purchases that are more important to consumers because they are related to their self-identity and involve some risk. Consumers generally spend more time and energy making these purchases.

Home-Based Business: A business where the primary activity of business or primary operating office is in one's own home.

IBDC (Indian Business Development Centers): Established to increase the number of minority owned businesses, help existing firms expand, and minimize business failures for Native Americans.

Income Statement: A financial report showing revenues earned, expenses incurred in earning the revenues, and the resulting net income or net loss; also referred to as a Profit and Loss Statement.

Incorporate: To legally form a corporation by filing a certificate of incorporation with a state's secretary of state.

Independent Agent: A type of insurance agent who offers products and services from a variety of companies.

Independent Contractor: A self-employed individual, not an employee of your business, who has his or her own business, has many occasions to work for others as a freelancer, and is responsible for their own acts, contracts, and withholdings.

Industrial Buyers: Buyers of products and services used in the process of creating other products.

Industry Profile: A compilation of pertinent information about a specific industry, such as its size, trends, growth potential, and history.

Informal Capital: Financing from an informal, unorganized source; includes informal debt capital such as trade credit or loans from friends and relatives and informal equity capital from informal investors.

Infrastructure: In business management terminology, the managerial support structure that surrounds the direct management team, referring to advisors, consultants, lawyers, accountants, bankers, and insurance agents.

Infringement: A breach of a law, right, or obligation.

Initial Public Offering (IPO): A public offering of securities by a first-time issuer.

Innovation: Introduction of a new idea into the marketplace in the form of a new product or service or an improvement in organization or process.

Innovations: Products or services that are new to both customers and to the business.

Institutional Advertising: Advertising that is "non-promotional," meaning it stresses identity and features and benefits related to the identity of the business rather than promoting specific merchandise or services.

Intangible Assets: Those assets which, literally, cannot be touched; these include a business's good will, customer lists, and patents.

Intellectual Property: Ownership or exclusive rights to processes or other products resulting from intelligent thought, such as trade secrets, copyrights, patents, or trademarks.

Intensive Distribution: Distributing a product through many retail outlets. Usually used for low-cost, frequently purchased "convenience" products.

Internal Controls: The policies and procedures a business establishes to assure reliability of its accounting records, to safeguard its assets, and to promote its goals and objectives.

Internet: It literally means a network of networks. The Internet is comprised of thousands of smaller regional computer networks scattered throughout the globe.

Inventory: The supply of materials owned and held by a business, including new raw materials, intermediate products/parts, work-in-process, finished goods (including merchandise purchased for resale), intended for internal consumption or for sale; an asset listed on a business balance sheet.

Investment Bankers: A financial institution that arranges long-term financial transactions for its clients, often guaranteeing the sale of securities within a certain amount of time and at a specified price.

Invoice: An itemized listing of goods or services sold; given to the buyer for payment purposes, usually detailing costs, discounts, payment terms, freight charges, shipping dates, and any other information pertinent to the sale.

IPO (Initial Public Offering): The first "offering for sale" of stock to the general public.

IRA (Individual Retirement Account): A savings plan that allows individuals and/or employees to set aside funds for retirement and defer paying taxes on those funds until withdrawn.

IRS (Internal Revenue Service): A federal agency created over 125 years ago to interpret and enforce the U.S. tax laws which provide for the assessment and collection of revenue used for operating government.

Joint Liability: Where one joint debtor has the right to insist that a co-debtor be joined in the liability. The liability is required to be apportioned among the debtors.

JTPA (Job Training Partnership Act): Initiated in 1982, this statute focuses on the management of programs to train people entering the work force.

Just-In-Time (JIT): The practice of producing only the exact amount of products needed by customers and delivering them at the exact time they are needed. Businesses who buy from JIT suppliers minimize inventory holding costs and expedite their turn-around time.

K-1: The tax form given to partners and members of LLC's showing their share of business profits or loss.

Keyman Insurance: Life insurance taken out by a business on an essential or very important employee with the company as beneficiary.

Keystone: A retailing term referring to doubling the cost of an item of merchandise to determine its retail selling price.

Large-Business-Dominated Industry: Industry in which a minimum of 60 percent of employment or sales is in firms with more than 500 workers.

Lead Blocker: In marketing terminology, someone who can provide entrance into a targeted market, such as an influential/reputable citizen within the market, celebrity endorsement, or someone with an established customer base.

Leasehold Improvement: Any improvement made to leased property; such improvements become the property of the lessor at the end of the lease and are categorized as an intangible asset to the lessee.

Letter of Credit (L/C): A document issued by a bank that guarantees the availability of funds or guarantees a loan up to a specified amount that can be drawn on by a business's creditor (or supplier) only under specific terms and conditions.

Liabilities: Short-term and long-term debts owed.

Liability Insurance: Insurance covering the insured against loses arising from injury or damage to another person or property.

Licensing Agreement: A legal contract in which the licenser grants to the licensee rights to use specific property rights in return for which royalties will be paid.

Limited Liability Company: This is a new form of business entity which is a hybrid between a partnership and a corporation. They are highly flexible, provide limited liability to their members, and avoid double taxation.

Limited Partnership: A partnership (two or more individuals jointly owning a business) which allows for general partners and limited partners; limited partners are usually financially liable for debts only to the extent of their investment, and have limited or no control over management of the company.

Line Extensions: Additions to a business's product or service offerings that deepen the existing product line (offering more varieties of the same products or services) rather than broadening it (offering more varieties of different products or services).

Line of Credit: A predetermined amount of short-term financing (generally from a bank) available for a business to borrow against on an "as needed" basis and repay during the specified life of the line.

Liquidated Damages: Specific consequences set out in a contract for one party breaching a deal.

Liquidity: The readiness and ease with which assets can be converted to cash without a loss, generally describing the degree of solvency of a business.

Licensing Agreements: Documents that formalize an arrangement by which one business sells to another business the right to use their brand name or market their product or service.

List Price: The stated price that would appear on a product line sheet or a catalog or be quoted by a salesperson. This is a business's official price before any discounts. This is also known as the final selling price.

Lone Eagles: Individuals who live and work away from the markets they serve.

Long-Term Debt: Loans scheduled to be paid back over a period longer than one year.

Long-Term Liabilities: Debt which will not mature within the next year.

Loss Leader: Merchandise or services purposely sold at a loss to increase customers, sales of related items, or promote awareness of services.

MACRS (Modified Accelerated Cost Recovery System): The system of calculating depreciation used for income tax reporting.

Manufacturers' Agents: Agents that sell a company's product in a particular geographic area, usually on an exclusive basis. They do not take title to the goods they sell and earn their money through commissions. These agents also carry the product lines of other manufacturers and sell only to wholesalers, retailers, and industrial buyers.

Mark-Up: The percentage by which a product's base price is increased to realize a desired profit margin. This is used with cost-plus pricing and is expressed as a percentage of the price of the product.

Market Price: The price at which goods or services could reasonably be expected to sell to bona-fide buyers.

Market Segment: A uniquely identifiable sub-market of a larger market that is homogeneous in nature.

Market Share: The percentage of a market's total sales (in units or dollars) that a business receives.

Market: A segment of a population considered actual or potential buyers; or, a gathering place for selling and buying.

Marketing Mix: The four marketing variables that a business can control to achieve a competitive advantage and sell to their target customer. These are product, price, placement and promotion, also known as the four P's of marketing.

Marketing Plan: The document that describes how a business will go about marketing its products or services. Contains information on target markets, product positioning, competitive advantage, and the marketing mix.

Marketing: The sum of all activities that influence commercial movement (sale) of goods and services from the provider to the consumer.

Mass Merchandisers: Stores that sell at lower prices than department stores and specialty boutiques, and offer a very broad assortment of products.

MBC (Management by Communication): The practice of effective two-way communication.

MBDC (Minority Business Development Centers): Established to increase the number of minority-owned businesses, help existing firms expand, and minimize business failures.

Mediation: A less formal and non-binding process than arbitration.

Medicaid: Federally aided, state-operated and administered program that provides medical benefits for certain low-income persons in need of health and medical care.

Medicare: Nationwide health insurance program for disabled and aged persons.

Merchantability: An implied warranty meaning that the goods are fit for normal use and are of the same quality as similar items produced by others.

Merchandising: The planning and promotion of sales by presenting a product to the right market at the right time.

Merger: A combination of two or more businesses into one.

MESBIC (Minority Small Business Investment Companies): Privately owned venture capital firms whose private capital is supplemented (leveraged) by debt or preferred equity which is provided through open-market financing guaranteed by SBA.

Metropolitan Statistical Area (MSA): A geographic area defined by the Office of Management and Budget as a large population nucleus with at least 50,000 persons, together with adjacent communities that have a high degree of economic and social integration with that nucleus.

Mini-Marketing: The practice of marketing strategies on individual customers.

Minority-Owned Business: For the purposes of the Bureau of the Census' 1987 Characteristics of Business Owners (CBO) survey, businesses owned by members of the following minority groups: Black, Hispanic, and other minorities (primarily Asian, American Indian, and Alaska native).

Mission Statement: A written statement, in the broadest terms, describing what the business hopes to do and be.

Moonlighters: People who keep their full-time job and develop a business on the side. When the business takes off, they usually go full-time into the business.

Net Income/Loss: The result after subtracting all expenses and taxes from total revenue.

Net Present Value: A calculation used to show what future dollars are worth today.

Net Profit: Sales minus variable costs and fixed costs. Net profit is used as a starting point to measure return on investment for specific products or businesses.

Networking: Making contact with a variety of people in related fields to foster communication with additional contacts or provide information which goes beyond the reason for the initial contact.

Net Worth: The total assets of a business minus its total liabilities.

Niche Market: A special segment of a market, often defined in terms of particular buyer characteristics, for which a business feels particularly well-suited to target.

NMBC (National Minority Business Council): A membership organization which offers assistance with procurement and international trade.

NMSDC (National Minority Supplier Development Council): A business membership organization which works to increase procurement and business opportunities for minority businesses.

Non-Competition Agreement: A contract entered into to restrict an employee or owner from competing against their former business or employer. These contracts are permitted if they are narrow in time and geographical area.

Non-Disclosure Agreement: A contract where a person or company agrees not to disclose your trade secrets.

Non-Durable Goods: Products that are consumed in few sessions (i.e., food, cleaning products).

Operating Agreement: This is the agreement among the members of a limited liability company or parties to a partnership and serves in much the same way as a corporation's bylaws.

Operating Lease: A lease that usually provides for maintenance service, is cancelable, and lasts less than the expected economic life of the asset.

Operational Planning: The planning process which focuses on actions needed in the short term (usually one year).

Order Processing: The tasks required to receive and process customer orders, including transmitting orders to warehouses, filling orders from inventory, preparing invoices, and shipping instructions.

Organizational Chart : A chart diagramming the managerial structure of a business, designating specific areas of responsibility.

Outsourcing: The buying of parts of a product to be assembled elsewhere or the hiring of independent contractors to assist with business operations.

OSDBU (Office of Small and Disadvantaged Business Utilization): Located within nearly every federal department to assist minority businesses with selling to the government.

OSHA (Occupation Safety and Health Administration): A federal agency under the Department of Labor that issues standards and rules for safe and healthful working conditions, tools, equipment facilities and processes, and conducts compliance inspections.

Owner's Equity: The amount owed by the business to the owner.

Overhead: The regular ongoing operating expenses of a business, including rent, utilities, upkeep, taxes, administrative salaries; costs not directly associated with the product/service.

Part-Time Workers: Employees working fewer than 35 hours per week.

Partnership: A legal relationship created by two or more individuals voluntarily associating to carry on as co-owners of a business for profit.

Patent: Governmental granting of exclusive rights for a specified period of time to the inventor for his/her invention or process.

Pay-Back Period: The period of time required to recoup an initial investment.

Performance Bond: An indemnity agreement to protect against loss due to breach of contract; also called a contract bond.

Performance Reports: Reports to management that compare actual results to budgeted amounts and indicate variances.

Perk: A supplemental, non-monetary benefit or privilege received in addition to regular salary or wage.

Personal Financial Statements: Financial documents of an individual, often requested by financial institutions of the borrower or guarantor of a loan; generally includes a balance sheet and tax returns from prior three years.

Personal Guaranty: A contract where the individual acts as a surety or guarantees the obligations of another. Most often used by lenders dealing with a closely held corporation, where the principal shareholders are required to sign personally.

Personal Selling: One element of the promotional and sales mix which involves one-on-one communication between a sales representative and a customer.

Point-of-Purchase Displays: Promotional displays in stores; for example, window displays, end-of-aisle display racks, hang-tags, and banners.

Population: The largest possible market for a product. The broadest starting point for segmentation strategy.

Preferred Stock: A special class of stock, often non-voting, which is given priority over common stock as to dividends.

Price Promotions: Short-term discounts offered by manufacturers or retailers to encourage customers to try a product.

Primary Data: Original data collected by a business to answer specific, well-defined questions about the market. Primary data collection methods include focus group interviews, surveys, and questionnaires.

Prime Contract: Contract awarded directly by the federal government.

Principal: The dollar amount originally borrowed or financed on which interest is paid; also referred to as the "face amount" of a loan.

Private Offering: Solicitation of sale of a security to aid a few persons and at a low enough dollar threshold so that it does not trigger federal or state registration.

Pro Forma: An estimate or projection of future results from a present set of assumptions. Pro forma financial statements reflect what a business is projected to financially look like in the future based on a current set of assumptions.

Product Category: The general class of product types to which a product belongs.

Product Extensions: New variations of existing products. Extensions can be revised or repositioned products.

Product Life Cycle: The phases a product or service goes through from innovation to decline as a result of changes in consumer demand and competition. Phases include introduction, growth, maturity, and decline. These impact the marketing strategy a business uses to sell its goods or services.

Product Line: The collection of products or services that a business offers.

Product Orientation: When businesses focus on their product or production methods in lieu of focusing on their customer needs. This can lead to producing products that customers do not want or need.

Product Positioning: The way a product is priced, promoted, and placed in the market to uniquely appeal to customers. Businesses use positioning strategies to maximize their competitive advantage and differentiate their offerings from competitors' offerings. Products are frequently "re-positioned" to communicate a new feature or target a new niche in the market.

Product: All of the tangible and intangible features and benefits offered by a business. This can be a physical product or a service offering.

Profit and Loss Statement: (P & L Statement): A document that outlines a business's performance in the present, or in the case of a projected P & L statement, in the future. Details revenues and expenses to arrive at net profits.

Profit Margin: The amount of each sales dollar that represents net income, usually stated as a percentage; net income divided by sales.

Profit: The financial gain resulting from revenues after all business expenses have been paid.

Promotional Allowance: Price discounts offered by manufacturers to retailers in exchange for advertising the manufacturer's products. Allowances of this type are part of cooperative advertising agreements.

Promotional Mix: All of the strategies and tactics used by a company to communicate the benefits of its products or services to potential customers. These include advertising, personal selling, public relations, networking, sales promotions, and direct mail.

Property and Liability Insurance: A property policy provides insurance on your building and other physical assets; liability protects you against claims of injury or property loss.

Proprietorship: The most common legal form of business ownership; about 85% of all small businesses are proprietorships. The liability of the owner is unlimited in this form of ownership.

Prospecting: A key selling task in which a sales person identifies potential customers.

Prospectus: The official document that is used to advertise and sell new securities.

Psychographics: The study of psychological characteristics of a targeted population; in marketing, the analysis of targeted consumers' patterns of living and reasons for decision making based on activities, interests, and opinions.

Public Equity Markets: Organized markets for trading in equity shares such as common stocks, preferred stocks, and warrants. Includes markets for both regularly traded and non-regularly traded securities.

Public Offering: A general solicitation for participation in an investment opportunity. Interstate public offerings are supervised by the Securities and Exchange Commission.

Public Relations: Methods by which a business seeks to promote a favorable relationship with the public; marketing examples: positive publicity (news story), community event participation, customer service, civic organization membership.

Publicity: A free promotional tool which communicates product or company information to mass audiences through the media. Publicity media include newspapers, press magazines, or radio. Publicity often begins with a press release by a business.

Publicly Held Corporation: A corporation whose stock is traded publicly, and is therefore registered with the Securities and Exchange Commission.

Quantity Discounts: Discounts given to customers for volume purchases.

Quick Ratio: See "acid test" ratio.

RECD (Rural Economic & Community Development): A federal agency specializing in loan programs for small rural businesses.

Resellers: Wholesalers and retailers who buy products to resell to customers. These intermediaries do not process or repackage goods.

Retained Earnings: The accumulated, undistributed earnings of a corporation.

Return on Investment: A measure of a business's performance. Calculated by dividing net profits by total investment.

Revenues: The earning activities of a business; usually the act of performing a service or selling a product; revenues result in something of value being received by the business.

S Corporation (Sub-Chapter S Corporation): A business legally organized as a corporation that has elected the Sub-Chapter S status under the IRS Tax Code, meaning that the corporation will be taxed as a partnership whereby shareholders pay tax on corporate income or deduct corporate net operating loss on their individual tax returns.

Sale and Leaseback: An arrangement in which a business sells an asset while simultaneously leasing the asset back from the purchaser.

Sales Agents: Extensions of manufacturer's sales force. These intermediaries have more authority to set prices and terms of sale than manufacturer's agents, and may even take over a manufacturer's entire marketing effort. Sales agents specialize in specific types of products and operate primarily in industrial goods markets.

Sales Quota: An anticipated level of sales in a given selling territory.

SBA (Small Business Administration): A federal agency established to provide new and existing small businesses with advocacy, financial assistance, management counseling, and training.

SBDC (Small Business Development Centers): Established by Congress in 1980 to cooperatively join federal, state, and local governments, the educational community, and the private sector to make management assistance and counseling widely available to existing and prospective small business owners.

SBIC (Small Business Investment Company): A federally sponsored venture capital program which uses private venture capital firms and financing guaranteed by the Small Business Administration.

SBIR (Small Business Innovation Research Program): A grant program for small businesses working to meet research and development needs of the federal government.

SCOR (Small Corporate Offering Registration): A program in which security offerings exempt from registration with the Securities Exchange Commission can meet state registration requirements with a minimum of cost and regulation.

SCORE (Service Corps of Retired Executives): An SBA volunteer management assistance program, providing one-on-one counseling, workshops, and seminars for small business (also see ACE).

SEC (Securities and Exchange Commission): Established by Congress to protect investors and ensure that capital markets operate in an orderly and fair manner under existing securities laws.

Selective Distribution: The practice of distributing goods or services through a limited number of intermediaries and outlets. This enables manufacturers to have greater control over the way their products are sold.

Several Liability: Even though there may be two or more debtors, the entire debt can be collected from one of them without apportionment.

Shelf Life: The term or period during which a stored product remains effective, useful, or suitable for consumption.

Short-Term Debt: Loans that are due within one year.

Short-Term Interest Rates: Interest rates for short-term borrowing, usually for a term of one year or less.

Simple Interest: Interest paid on the principal of a loan only, not on the principal plus accrued interest.

Size Standard: Standard based on the amount of a business's annual gross receipts used to determine eligibility for small business set-aside programs in government procurement.

Slotting Fees: A required fee by a retailer for stocking an item.

Small Business Innovation Development Act of 1982: Federal statute requiring federal agencies with large extramural R&D budgets to allocate a certain percentage of these funds to small R&D firms.

Small Business Innovation Research (SBIR) Program: A program mandated by the Small Business Innovation Development Act of 1982, requiring federal agencies with $100 million or more of extramural R&D obligations to set aside 1.25% of these funds for small business.

Small Business Investment Company (SBIC): Privately owned company licensed and funded through the U.S. Small Business Administration and private-sector sources to provide equity or debt capital to small business.

Small Business: A business smaller than a given size as measured by its employment, business receipts, or business assets. The SBA's Office of Advocacy generally uses employment data as a basis for size comparisons, with firms having fewer than 100 or fewer than 500 employees defined as small.

Sole Proprietorship: Unincorporated, one-owner business, farm, or professional practice.

Squeeze Out: Techniques employed by one or more owners of a business to remove another owner.

SSBIC (Specialized Small Business Investment Companies): Privately owned venture capital firms whose private capital is supplemented (leveraged) by debt or preferred equity which is provided through open market financing guaranteed by SBA.

Standard Industrial Classification Code (SIC Code): A numerical code which identifies a business based on the type of business or trade activity.

Stewardship Principle: The expectation that members of the family must conform to higher standards of conduct and be held to higher expectations for performance in the business system compared with non-family employees.

Stockturn: The number of times the average inventory turns over (i.e., is sold) in a given period.

Strategic Planning: The systematic process of evaluating the long-term impact of the business environment; includes developing a mission statement, identifying goals, and designing strategies to achieve those goals.

Subcontract: A contract between a prime contractor and a subcontractor or between subcontractors to furnish supplies or services for performance of a prime contract or a subcontract.

Succession Plan: A plan, preferably formal, whereby the controlling owners arrange to pass on authority and assets in the family business to the next generation or to non-family buyers of the business.

Succession: The passing of control, that is legal authority, over operations to new leadership, usually but not in every case to family members in the next generation, along with the transfer of ownership (equity) interest in the business.

Surety Bond: These provide security from claims filed against a business.

Survey of Income and Program Participation (SIPP): A longitudinal survey conducted by the Bureau of the Census, designed to collect information about cash and non-cash income, assets and liabilities, and taxes paid, and a variety of labor market data.

SWOT Analysis: An analysis of the strengths, weaknesses, opportunities, and threats facing a business.

Tangible Assets: those assets which, literally, can be touched; e.g., equipment, buildings, inventory.

Target Market: The specific group of individuals who are chosen as most likely potential customers for the goods/services of a business and to whom the business wishes to appeal.

Target Return on Investment: An established level of financial return on an investment. This guides price setting.

Telecommuters: Work for a company by using a computer terminal set up in an employee's home. This terminal is linked by means of a computer modem to the company's central computer.

Telemarketing: The selling method whereby businesses use the telephone to contact and sell to potential customers.

Term Loan: A loan having a payoff due date of longer than one year; most commonly used for equipment, real estate, or other fixed asset purchases.

Terms: The conditions or provisions specified for repaying loans or paying invoices; usually includes the time limits, amounts to be paid, discounts.

Test Marketing: A way to experiment with a new product or service or marketing strategy. Businesses measure the effectiveness of the test before they initiate the strategy on a larger scale. Test marketing is used for specific, short periods of time.

Torts: A wrongful act causing injury to a person for which a civil action may be brought to recover damages.

Total Revenue: The total amount of money generated through the sale of a product or service.

Trade Discounts: Discounts offered to wholesalers or retailers who perform some marketing functions on behalf of the manufacturer.

Trade Name: The name of your business, registered with the secretary of state's office, also referred to in some states as "fictitious" or "assumed" name.

Trade Secrets: Confidential methods, processes, customer lists, and similar business information which are not of common knowledge.

Trade Shows: Large events at which different manufacturers, product and service providers set up booths to share information and promote their offerings to potential buyers.

Trademark: A symbol, letter, device, or word that identifies a product; it is officially registered, generally in a secretary of state's office, and by law grants exclusive use to the owner or manufacturer.

Turnover: The rate at which items are sold.

UCC (The Uniform Commercial Code): A uniform business law and finance code.

Undercapitalization: Having too little capital (money or other resources easily converted to money) to carry a new venture through early development stages.

Unsecured Loan: A loan backed only by the strength of the borrower's signature and, therefore, is uncollateralized.

Variable Costs: Costs that do change significantly and in direct proportion to the volume of output or sales.

Variable Rate: An interest rate that changes during the term of the loan.

Venture Capital: Money used to finance new or unusual undertakings.

Vertical Integration: The business strategy of controlling many or all of the sourcing, manufacturing, and distribution tasks required by the business. Vertically integrated businesses may grow or manufacture their own inputs, and process, package or assemble inputs, and store, distribute, market, and sell finished products directly to their final customers.

Warranty: A promise or representation about goods which is part of the deal and which creates an expectation that the goods will conform to that promise.

Work Done for Hire: A doctrine which states that ideas created while employed or commissioned by someone else are owned by the employer or commissioner.

Working Capital: Resources available in a business to cover short-term expenses determined by subtracting current liabilities from current assets.

World Wide Web: A wide area hyper media information retrieval system which provides computer access to a large universe of documents. The Web provides users with a consistent means to access a variety of information.

Zoning: The division of an area into zones, as to restrict the number and types of buildings and their uses.

INDEX

Q

R

S

T

U

V

W

X, Y, Z